ANTHROPOLOGY IN THE MEANTIME

Technological Lives, Scientific Arts, Anthropological Voices
A series edited by Michael M. J. Fischer and Joseph Dumit

ANTHROPOLOGY IN THE MEANTIME

EXPERIMENTAL ETHNOGRAPHY, THEORY, AND METHOD FOR THE TWENTY-FIRST CENTURY

MICHAEL M. J. FISCHER

Duke University Press Durham and London 2018

Printed in the United States of America on acid-free paper ∞
Designed by Courtney Baker
Typeset in Minion Pro by Westchester Publishing Services

Library of Congress Cataloging-in-Publication Data
Names: Fischer, Michael M. J., [date] author.
Title: Anthropology in the meantime : experimental ethnography, theory, and method for the twenty-first century / Michael M. J. Fischer.
Description: Durham : Duke University Press, 2018. |
Series: Experimental futures : technological lives, scientific arts, anthropological voices | Includes bibliographical references and index.
Identifiers: LCCN 2018005826 (print) | LCCN 2018009816 (ebook)
ISBN 9781478002222 (ebook)
ISBN 9781478000402 (hardcover : alk. paper)
ISBN 9781478000556 (pbk. : alk. paper)
Subjects: LCSH: Ethnology. | Anthropology.
Classification: LCC GN316 (ebook) | LCC GN316 .F57 2018 (print) |
DDC 305.8—dc23
LC record available at https://lccn.loc.gov/2018005826

COVER ART: General Akashi Gidayu writes his *jisei* or death poem (seen in the upper right) as he prepares to commit *seppuku*. *Akashi Gidayu*, in the series *One Hundred Aspects of the Moon*, Tuskioka Yoshitoshi (aka Taiso Yoshitoshi), 1890. Wood block print. Courtesy of the author. Photo by Thorsten Trimpop. The *jisei* genre originates in Zen Buddhism and the three marks of existence (*sanbōin*): the material world is impermanent, attachment to it causes suffering, and all is emptiness. Such poems were written by poets, warriors, nobles, and monks, expressing an enlightened way of looking at death and reality without affect or attachment (*satori* in Japanese, *wu* in Chinese).

To my fellow journeywomen and men, colleagues and interlocutors, of the MIT Laboratory for New Ethnographic Methods, Contemporary Social Theory, and Emergent Forms of Life (ETL: Ethnography, Theory, Life) who have worked up and down the scales of multilocale ethnography from eagle-eye views to anaconda meanders, naga floodings of the fertile earth, desert oases, urban galactic polities, archipelago seas, and the habitats in-between.

The different places have been enriching, the people inspiring, the diverse cultures exhilarating. But it was at the margins of all these individually brilliant experiences that I found the most enlightening of spaces and moments. They were so singularly beautiful that one had to invent vocabularies to describe them, these uncharted territories, unexperienced happenings, unfathomed depths, these images at the margins. —KUO PAO KUN (Chinese and English language playwright of Singapore), *Images at the Margin*

CONTENTS

PROLOGUE. CHANGING MODES OF ETHNOGRAPHIC AUTHORITY

> Along with Galileo, the *malin* [the evil in the world[1]] sweeps away the revolutionary illusion, the humanist hope. Descartes takes note of all this, accepting the setback but refusing to abandon hope. One must live. Once the revolution is over, the war of position begins. —ANTONIO NEGRI, *Political Descartes*

No doubt, as will become clear in a few decades, we live in another time warp like that of 1633, when, with Galileo's condemnation and the burning of his books, the humanist crisis came to the fore, shocking such figures as Descartes into recognizing that humanist freedom had lost out against a flow of history that was no longer in favor of bourgeois, civil, and humanist ideals and would need an absolutist state as defense against both the nobles and revolts from below (Negri 1970/2006). According to Antonio Negri's compelling reading, Descartes came to represent the world after the burning of Galileo's books "as *malin*, as inverted truth, as a *fable* of a power that does not want truth to live in the world" (Negri 1970/2006, 147; emphasis in source). The arrow of history and conceptions of time do not move in one direction but move with variable speeds (accelerations, differential speeds), backward and forward (*à la* Karl Marx in *The Eighteenth Brumaire of Louis Napoleon*[2]), in ouroborus eternal returns (of the seasons, of cycles of life-death-life, of repressions-returns), spiral fashion picking up once abandoned elements into new formations, with multiple competing streams, eddies, and currents, only retrospectively seemingly linear.

New social structures and new "forms of life" (both biological and social, sometimes quite intertwined) are emergent in ways we cannot quite foresee, despite confident predictions. If floods of populations flee rising seas, poverty, environmental toxicities, and tyrannies, and if receiving societies are destabilized, health care systems collapse, and infrastructures are overwhelmed, in such circumstances, new forms of organization, good and bad, will form in the con-fusions, chemical like reactions, and sub-version circulations—not necessarily as centralized totalitarian forms, or charismatic cults, as past imaginaries would have it, but perhaps in decentralized weavings of new stronger textures of social life, post the hackable Internet of Things on which our critical infrastructures for living (water, electricity, information) seem now to depend more fragilely than we thought only a few years ago. By then perhaps we will have renewable clean energy. By then perhaps we will have understood what it takes to live again in the oceans and in space, and to find biological repair mechanisms for what has been destroyed.

Certainly, at the very least, *in the meantime, the time of anthropology*, will be one of *constant experimentation*. This is *the space for ethnography*, a *third space* of the "reality principles" and "anthropology from a pragmatic point of view,"[3] between the fantasies of nostalgia and apocalypse, between horizons of the Holocene and the Anthropocene. Here in this third space the actually existing worlds of anthropology from a pragmatic point of view can flourish: ask not what the human being or the world is but what we may expect of them—and of them in the plural. These worlds can flourish not merely by observation and participation but also by helping relay experiences in one place to other places, reflecting upon the experiences, and articulating what is going on beyond, inside, and around the formal structures of nation-states, transnational organizations, and NGOs, helping to rebuild newer, more flexible and robust structures from local municipalities and intentional communities on up, using tools being developed, such as participatory budgeting, also in huge Asian cities.[4] They can flourish by ground-truthing statistical patterns, algorithmic simulations, and governance metrics; by finding and propagating modes of flourishing, well-being, and new paths of conflict management, new multiscale synergies and mutualities.

This book stakes out a claim, a twenty-first-century extension of the still canonical "grounded theory" of Barney Glaser and Anslem Strauss or the still valid advice of Robert K. Merton, that work at the mesolevel of theory is the most productive, what this book will call "anthropology in the meantime." Retooling for the twenty-first century is required, and is developing, in a context of more layered media (as research tools, as means of emotional persuasion in the public arena, and as habituated modes of communication) and where small networks and local cultural niches can be leveraged and become as important as standardization across such networks and worlds.

"Anthropology in the meantime" is a methodological injunction to not get carried away by either dystopian or utopian extrapolations that govern so much of contemporary "theory" but to do the ethnography of how the pieces of the world interact, fit together or clash, generating complex unforeseen consequences, reinforcing cultural resonances, and causing social ruptures.

Anthropology and Ethnography in the Meantime

Anthropology in the meantime is the (im)practical, life-affirming use of ethnographic methods in the gaps between the *financial* or *design experimental* (computational, prototyping, and "demonstrations-as-products" to be continually replaced) and the *experiential experimental* (slowing down, affect savoring, lifeworlds of playful artistry). The *gaps* between surprise-producing scientific experiments, pleasure-producing aesthetic experiments, and code-producing test-bed experiments are interactively productive ones. These gaps are where anthropology reflectively and critically weaves its magic of understanding.[5] These are the gaps between, on the one hand, the explosive energy of "now time" (*Jetztzeit*) that in sudden collisions of past and present arrests or interrupts the flow of naturalistic time,[6] and thus, on the other hand, dialectically, allows for the *recursive* reconstructions of, or reconfigurations of the conditions of possibility for, the afterlives of now time, and thus of the work required to bring about livable, meaningful, emergent futures. This is *anthropology in the wake of the future.*[7]

Anthropology *in the meantime* is precisely *not the suturing* of these gaps, rushing to judgment, but the reflective play with the gaps as opportunistic heterotopias for realizing worlds differently, constructing alternative futures. As recursive, restless, continuous social reanalysis, anthropology operates in these gaps or *third spaces*—the spaces of analytic, comparative, or juxtapositional cultural critique; spaces of questioning and interpretative work that themselves are spaces of value added (even if often incommensurable, or nonreducible to metrics). These gaps and third spaces are the lining of technology that needs to be pulled out and examined lest the technologies we build around us turn deadly, as they often do. Anthropology provides the smartness, sensitivities, or sensibilities[8] that sensors and algorithms fail to provide despite their advertising and public relations. It requires patience, taking time, *slow time*, for *figuring out how* peopled things intersect, interact, interfere, inter-refer. It requires the time for *locating* con-texts, for *listening*, for *attending to* the telling detail, for *sounding out* moods, anger, passion, nonverbal communication. It requires the time for *looking* under the hood of memes and slogans, beyond the framings of photographs and films, for how stories are being coded for which targeted audiences, how jokes are mobilized (offensively, defensively, or as phatic filler), and how futures are preempted and rerouted. It is a form of ground-truthing, of showing when aggregate statistics, models, and maps produce errors that do not match what is happening "on the ground," in reality, among actual people.

Anthropology *in the meantime* attends to the *peopling of technologies*, without which technologies do not exist, do not get built, maintained, repaired, upgraded, reconfigured, or replaced. Anthropology in the meantime attends to the gaps between visions and implementations, to the differential gears of accelerations and decelerations of contesting and layered social movements (changes in the directions of history), to the politics of the rise and fall of branded communities of expertise or practice. It attends to the messiness of the interplay of theory and practice, justice and law, regulatory science and experimental science, speculation and artistry (imaginaries, Disney-like imagineering or marketing, loosening up frozen ideologies, allowing sub-versions).

Anthropology *in the meantime* is the study of what Henri Lefebvre resonantly called *l'homme totale* (the fully human person) who dwells in a lived space of the imagination, sustained and made accessible by the arts, literature, and human creativity.[9] It thus also resonates with what Marcel Mauss called *total social facts* or what British social anthropology and later ecological approaches articulated as the rule or law that "you cannot change only one thing." Interconnections and interventions make for ramifying, and often unpredictable, implications, consequences, and cascading effects. Ethnography in the meantime is an anthropology emergent out from the chrysalis of the twentieth century. Ethnography in the meantime is *slow time*: it is the mapping, tracking, or inquiry into cascades, changes, and implications.

A Colloquy of Essays

This book also makes a claim (following both Theodor Adorno and Clifford Geertz) for the value of the essay form as *one* way of doing precisely anthropology in the meantime with grounded theory, not instead of monographs, group projects, and other forms, but as a supplementary form or parergon (the more that is at work) to direct attention to the spaces for which traditional frames and theories no longer suffice. The essays are essays in conversation, not just a collection, that hopefully add up to more than the sum of their parts. While each essay can be read independently, they are intended to gain depth and force as they speak to one another. They are conversations with two of the leading edges of anthropology: with the humanities, and with the sciences and technological developments. Among the key matters of concern in every essay is the epistemological and ethnographic value of thinking through local and multiple cultural genres, rhetorics, and logics, open to other languages and other cultural tools; through visual media as well as writing; with literature as well as ethnographic monographs and articles. The short opening essay, "Experimental Ethnography in Ink, Light, and Sound and Performance" (chapter 1), is both a model to show that one can write in plain prose and flag a series of experimental moves that have shifted the fields of anthropology, cultural studies, comparative studies in history and society, intellectual history, philosophy, and others over the decades; and that this applies to ethnographic film or cinewriting, and perhaps to the social and cultural landscapes of sound, and ethnographic performance for civil activation, as well as ethnographic writing. Chapters 2 and 3 continue the discussion by directing attention to the issue of cultural genres, away from more parochial European philosophical ones on ontology and metaphysics, or scholastic ones on logical distinctions. The ethnography at issue in chapter 2 (largely the northwestern Amazon) is followed out further in chapter 5, while that in chapter 3 (on Germany and Iran) is picked up again in chapter 9. Ethnography in the meantime, I argue, is required in all these spaces rather than jumping to quick conclusions, criticisms, or glib evaluations. Critique and ground-truth are required iteratively to explore the gaps and topologies of third spaces between actors' imaginaries and practical realities, between the promissory motivations (for capital and psychological investments) and the adjustments and redirections along the way.

The second matter of concern thus, "ground-truthing," pursued more explicitly in chapters 4 through 8, is that of dialogue, listening, and friendship across cultures and through the hieroglyphic longitudinal work across the corpus of individual anthropologists. This involves reading, probing, looking for their competence and skills (linguistic, elicitatory, attention to inequalities, etc.) to do the *ground-truthing*, the field science, the living with and engaging with the people being written about and for whom, anthropologists hope, the ethnographies are also being written, as well as for students and audiences in general. The listening involves listening across conflict boundaries, not just dyadic conversations. This is a matter of hospitality (chapter 8), which, like the gift of which Marcel Mauss (1925) wrote, can contain aggression and hostility as well as generosity and social bonding, and applies also to ecology and our biological place in our planetary or Gaian nexus.

The tone and tuning of the writing of ethnography, thus, is not merely a matter of ground-truthing or empirical data collection but also one of address, tact, and tone. And tonality means also resonance with other modalities of discourse. In chapters 7 through 9, attention shifts to actors' philosophical registers, not only academic philosophy but also vernacular philosophies and attention to the contexts out of which those philosophies arise. In all three chapters, but particularly chapter 9, I argue that juxtaposition can be a helpful mode of conversation across cultures, genres, forms of speech, and traditions, so as not to tear things out of context, to compare and contrast without doing violence to nuance, multiple registers of meaning, and potentials for new meaning formation, in the original sites of locution.

A fourth matter of concern, fundamental to all the above is thus that of the materiality, temporality, and recursivity, as well as conceptual development, in ethnographic works over the past century and especially the past three decades with the arrival of the Internet, the web, the interconnected Internet of Things, and smart city and smart nation initiatives. These matters of material change in modes of writing, information availability, and sequestration (chapter 10), are intertwined with those of temporalities and historical horizons, and conceptual recursivity of reworking old ideas and cultural resources (chapter 11), with new and differently targeted ones in the development of anthropological approaches for new circumstances (chapter 12). The notion of "zen exercises" in chapter 12 is intended to allude to what used to be debated as matters of objectivity (evaluating situated knowledges or differential points of view informed by class, gender, religious, worldview, etc., positions within contentious social worlds). For this, ethnography and anthropological perspectives are both urgent and indifferent (indifference here not in the sense of lack of concern but in the sense of critical understanding about placing in context particular interests, perspectives, and understandings, a critical understanding that can be mobilized for debating and intervening in the service of the social good, and preserving or creating new cultural and social commons on which flourishing of "the human condition in its plurality" [après Hannah Arendt; see chapter 9] can exist).

In the epilogue, I attempt to draw together the arguments and thematics of the volume, while simultaneously incorporating the imaginaries that inhabit our worlds and direct our anticipations toward the future. Much of the future imaginary even in Western writing is located in Asia (e.g., from William Gibson's *Neuromancer* [1984] on immersive cyberworlds to Ramiz Naam's *Nexus* [2012] thriller on psychotropic expansions and national security state global war). I've become particularly interested in such writing from Asian points of view by technoscientifically literate authors. But while broadening the purview of ethnographic registers in Asian hard science fiction literatures, where much of the contemporary imaginary is sited—and that explore current disasters from avian influenza and other emerging pandemic threats to intensifying threats from earthquakes, tsunamis, volcanoes, and industrial disasters such as the Fukushima Daiishi nuclear plant meltdown, and rising sea levels—I remain dedicated to the hard work of actual ethnography and juxtapose the work of my fellow ethnographers with those of the science fiction writers working the same terrain (and often themselves scientists and physicians with strong empirical bents).

Perfect Pitch in Ethnography

Ethnographies as literary forms are like novels, except they have to stick to reality. They work best when you can lose yourself as a reader in their worlds. Recognition, understanding, connecting the dots, and theory emerge like the ambrosia of immortality in the Hindu story of churning the ocean. They arise from the work of interpretive value added by both writer and reader. Statistics, charts, crime scene maps, photographs, articles in scientific journals with their temporality of emergence rather than settled fact, and all those sorts of supports are aids and heuristics along the way. It is like the challenge in hard science fiction: as author, you have to stick to actually existing scientific knowledge and technologies we currently have or at least have the knowledge to build; yet like hard science fiction, ethnographies too have speculative edges. The speculation works through comparison, juxtaposition, and contestation with other ways of organizing social life. The speculative work, as in comparative zoology or genomics, is to be found in variation and difference, teasing out the particularities, the unique qualities, linkages, genealogies, precursors, genitors, biomechanics and biochemistries, and families of resemblance. Rising above all in ethnography are the acoustics: the nuances and accents need to be right, lest it sound wrong. Nothing worse than a period film about Vienna where the actors speak with Berlin or Hannover accents and idioms—hard to take it seriously. Similarly, ethnographies of other cultures and other language settings challenge the writer for translations (glosses, literal translations, and cultural expansions).

Traduttore, traditore: Translator, traitor. Hence the need for local critical apparatuses, the aids across language divides, to explain, to draw into the delicate webs of meaning so easily torn by rough handling. Not much different if those other cultures are scientific or occupational specialties with their own argots and practices, good hands and intuitions based on deep experience that are quite different across even collaborating fields. Synthetic biology, for instance, is riven by opposing intuitions and practices between engineers and biologists, and challenged by the requirements of safety and security, and legitimating requirements of "human practices" taking knowledge and instruments beyond laboratory walls.

A good ethnography has perfect pitch and cadence or at least allows you to understand what perfect pitch and cadence would be. Matters of tone and tuning are also matters of ethics, of tact, and of address.

Ethnography for Whom, with Whom? Ethics of Ethnography?

Ethnographies used to be *of and among* peoples *in physical environments* and shaping ecologies: deserts, mountains, cities, ports, islands, villages. Increasingly they are done *with* people *for* their own utilities, whether helping departments in hospitals learn what each other do in order to ease workflow hang-ups; helping communities map and document illnesses around toxic waste or show environmental justice inequalities; planning with boomers for active "aging in place communities"; or redesigning urban spaces to make them more livable. The *shift in prepositions* "of" and "in" to those of "for" and "with" make an important difference, as does the *pluralization* of grandiose nouns and *points of view* (History, Reason, Progress; histories, reasons and cultural logics, enlightenments and corrections; hegemonic "naturalizing" rhetorics, class or gender positions, ethnic and religious histories and sensibilities, traumas inscribed in nervous systems and muscle memories).

Ethnographies used to be of and among peoples in places for the use of *philosophizing* and *comparative criteria:* What is rationality? Is rationality universal? (E. E. Evans-Pritchard's *Witchcraft, Oracles, and Magic among the Azande* [1937] remains a touchpoint text.) How is risk differently structured in different settings? What is the difference between ritual purity and hygiene? (Mary Douglas's *Purity and Danger* [1966], drawing on fieldwork among the Lele, remains key.) Is gambling irrational or meaningful? (Clifford Geertz's *Daedalus* essay "Deep Play: Notes on the Balinese Cockfight" [1972] is still a model text.) Ethnographies might be for the use of, or in contestation with, *administration*: do not withdraw male labor from agriculture, with its mutual aid reciprocity, to use as labor in copper mines and then pay them bare nutritional wages, if you don't want agrarian collapse and famine. (Thus the warning of Audrey Richards's *Land, Labor, and Diet in Northern Rhodesia: An Economic Study of the Bemba* [1939].)

Today ethnographies are often *multilocale* mappings across sites of strategic access to *multiscale* distributed industries and processes. Such methods are required to understand diasporic feedback in the weaving of national cultural, political, and affective textures (Mehdi Abedi's and my *Debating Muslims: Cultural Dialogues in Tradition and Postmodernity* [1990]; Orkideh Behrouzan's *Prozak Diaries: Psychiatry and Generational Memory in Iran* [2016] and its diaspora). Such methods are also needed to understand industrial accidents and "natural" disasters of transcontinental chemical industries (Kim Fortun's *Advocacy after Bhopal: Environmentalism, Disaster, New Global Orders* [1991]); different vernacular understandings of climate change and overcoming resistance to public discussion (Candis Callison's *How Climate Change Comes to Matter: The Communal Life of Facts* [2014]). They are required for understanding the recursive building of software infrastructures and on- and offline communities (Chris Kelty's *Two Bits: The Cultural Significance of Free Software* [2008]); or the transnational trade in changing notions of death, interchangeable human parts, psychosis of transplantation, and socialist versus free market access to care (Aslihan Sanal's *New Organs within Us: Transplants and the Moral Economy* [2011]). Many of these are exemplary forms of the work of the Laboratory of New Approaches to Ethnography, Contemporary Social Theory and Emergent Forms of Life at MIT.

One reason multilocale ethnography is so important is that socialities tend to be linked overlapping small worlds. Experts in a field tend to know one another, and their networks lead to other small worlds. In this, and many other ways, mentoring lineages, network analyses, and snowball interviewing techniques are important tools for unpacking larger questions of global processes such as those listed above, whether or not they strictly match the various mathematical and algorithmic models of small-world experiments.[10] What is ethnographically important are the knowledges and lines of exchange, competitions and collaborations, that are built up within these small worlds, and how they articulate with other circles, networks, and chains of distribution. Ethnography is less concerned with the formal correctness and linearity of communication, and more with the social worlds so connected, their intensities, modes of attributing credibility, trust, hierarchies, linguistic and behavioral codes of recognition and shibboleths of exclusion, and ways of viewing the world in relation to other ways of viewing the world.[11]

Ethnographic fieldwork used to be focused on oral face-to-face interactions and performativity in situ. Two generations of ethnographers (from 1920 to 1960) looked askance at too much reliance on written texts as abstracted from context, and likely to mislead. This was a form of Plato's argument in the *Phaedrus*, made famous again by Jacques Derrida (1972/1981), but also by anthropologist Jack Goody (*The Domestication of the Savage Mind*, 1977), by Jesuit language historian Walter Ong (*Orality and Literacy*, 1982), and by classicist Eric Havelock (*The Muse Learns to Write*, 1986), that writing changed the situational understanding of communicative acts, abstracting them, making them seem impersonal and wrongly definitive, much as models and simulations today explicitly simplify. When detached from their original contexts, they can mislead, and are better deployed dialectically with ground-truthing, with ethnography. Anthropologists were like Socrates in relying on the dialogic face-to-face contexts where possible, and like Socrates (or Harold Garfinkle [*Studies in Ethnomethodology*, 1967] or Erving Goffman [*Presentation of Self in Everyday Life*, 1956]) in often upsetting the taken-for-granted naturalness or truth of particular social norms. These aesthetics of ethnographic authority (being there, knowing who was saying to whom in what speech genre of sociolinguistic register, seeing how what was being done did not accord with what was being said, looking for the unsaid and the unsayable,[12] what was indicated through allusion, posture, gesture, or tone) had their time and place, and they continue to be invaluable under changed conditions of time and place. The dialectic is ever more important between written archives that provide documentation but often leave much out or falsify, and fieldwork that provides situated perspectives for parallax correction, questioning, and reframing but that cannot encompass everything, and can also be subject to people not cooperating, withholding, misdirecting, making of the tapestries of fieldwork engagements each themselves puzzle fields of social action.

In more recent ethnographic work, as explanatory demands for wider contexts increased, archives and other writings, including earlier fieldwork studies, became important tools to account for the varieties of discourses and opinions and socially grounded arguments *within societies* and across different accounts and by different anthropologists (Robert Redfield 1930 versus Oscar Lewis 1951, on the Mexican village of Tepotzlan is a classic teaching pair). Reported beliefs by individuals of themselves or by third-party observers (anthropologists) are constructions and interpretations built out from disputations, disagreements, politics, fights, experiences, not so much the search for unique authority, origin, or philosophical deduction. This anthropological understanding has its predecessors (and objects of study) in the stories deployed in the scholastic debate traditions of Islam and Judaism, Catholic casuistic logics, Buddhist and Jain parables, and epics whose narrators adjust the meanings according to their audiences, and stress the limited understanding of any particular actor, including the narrator. Internal arguments and attention to genre forms and to local critical apparatuses of evaluation became crucial elements of valid ethnographies. The world has become too well known (through film and television, the Internet and cell phones, but also tourism, expatriate living, and business travel in development and humanitarian industries as well as education and commercial ones) for claims through single perspectives or summaries to carry weight.

In earlier ethnographic work, there was purification of reality by actively ignoring novels, films, and other aesthetic works that could not be reduced to symbols of beliefs. In more recent ethnographies, attention to imaginaries, fictionalized forms of self-presentation, writing, film, arts, speech, and performance genres of both everyday life and of social memory have become increasingly important to the work of tapping into and exploring "immanent critiques," differences and struggles within interpretive traditions and within conflicted modernities.

In earlier ethnographies of the 1940s and 1950s, there were often formats of presentation presumed to set up accounts of particular social assemblages for comparison with others often continuous with human geography formats: ecology, kinship, politics, economics, law, religion, and so on were chapter titles or serial volume titles. Key institutions, symbol constellations, and rituals were used to unlock cultural logics, ethnosemantics and classification systems, values and worldviews. In recent ethnographies such topics are often folded into quite different formats organized around compelling matters of concern that overflow localities and typologies. Instead of traditional kinship studies (interesting in their own right and for certain places and contexts), it is today often more important to explore the social "kinship" relationships developed through lineages of scientific mentoring, or linkages among scientists whose work coalesces in advances for reproductive assisted technologies or transgender technologies [Najmabadi, *Possessing Selves*, 2014], or legal precedents and legal reasoning to give recognition in court for new forms of family. Religions no longer command but share and dispute territories, and often have conflicted relations to their own pasts. Money, diseases, and legal battles overflow what once were thought of as boundaries. Aporia, ambiguity, risk, trauma, asylum, refugee status, and uncertainty have become new epistemological objects requiring ethical choreographies, settling into, at best, temporary ethical plateaus of decision making.[13]

Ethnographic "writing"—print, film, digital, sonic, performance—has become increasingly inventive and aesthetic in the sense of modes for seeing or apperceiving, for understanding anew, for following over time, across space, up and down scales or granularities of organization.

The uses, formats, and goals of ethnography have changed in both subtle and explicit ways over the past few decades. It has a renewed role in ground-truthing models and theories not just in academia but also in corporate life, and in policy making (Adams, ed. 2016; Cefkin, ed. 2009); in claims for new technologies (e.g., production of anime [Condry 2013]); in clinical trial labor (Cooper and Waldby 2014); and in allying with grassroots resistance and criticisms of hegemonic technocracy (Wiley 2018), or mainstream discourses that are tuned out by much of the public (Callison 2014).

Ethnography's primary modes of dissemination continue to be in long-form print media (the ethnographic monograph, the ethnographically informed essay), but with important shifts into online forums (*Somatosphere*; *Savage Mind*), sometimes with secondary print forms (*Limm*), and into film and video formats (Chris Boebel and Chris Walley's film *Exit Zero* [2015], on family and class in postindustrial Chicago; Robert Lemelson's film *Forty Years of Silence: An Indonesian Tragedy* [2009] and Joshua Oppenheimer's *The Act of Killing* [2013] on the aftermaths of the enormous massacre of alleged communists in 1965); and Sulfikar Amir's *Healing Fukushima* [2017] on the network of local doctors responding to the triple or six fold compound disaster there in 2011. There is also a growing tradition of ethnography in corporations (with its own association, EPIC, Ethnographic Praxis in Industry Community), a legacy of pioneering work in XeroxParc, IRL (Institute for Research on Learning), and various anthropological consultancies (Suchman 2006; Cefkin, ed. 2009).[14]

"Ethnography in the way of theory" (Fischer 2009a) is also a transformed mode of theory building from within rather than as outside observers, both challenging theories and models, and providing the tools for making them otherwise: here exemplary cases are provided by work on synthetic biology (putting the presuppositions of biology, engineering, safety, and privacy into conversation), the ethics of clinical trials (attending to class, gender, and access to care inequalities), the organizational innovations for directing research patents, dollars, and expertise by patient groups.

Ethnography can also provide modes of moral philosophy and self-cultivation, in analogous ways to novels and theater, for both writer and reader, particularly by rich evocations of the challenges staged in social arenas of varied locations, scales, and intersections of multiple technological changes (chapters 7, 9, and 12). The discussion about emergent forms of life poses ethical decision making at the center of some ethnographic accounts, not simply as individuals making decisions but also the affordances and constraints of technologies and discursive regimes, and the trade-offs of decision making, where none is entirely satisfactory. I have previously reworked Gilles Deleuze and Felix Guattari's term "plateaus" into *ethical plateaus* as momentary stabilizations of contradictory forces or intersections of new technologies that require decision making where the morality is unclear, contested, having no perfect way to resolve but only temporarily coming to a degree of stability, until all is again destabilized and has to find a new plateau (Fischer 2004). Didier Fassin and Richard Rechtman (2009) provide an example in their account of the shifting historical sociology of trauma.

Increasingly, ethnography also informs and corrects guild histories by returning to sites of long-term fieldwork over longitudinal time (chapters 4, 5, 6, 7, 12). Johannes Fabian's *Time and the Other* (1983) and *Out of Our Minds* (2000) remain cautionary and vivid about the nineteenth century—using grammatical forms that place the described in a time distant from that of the writer; erasing, sometimes through drink and drugs, the local affordances, long-distance trading, and explanations in order to claim egoistic and heroic "discovery"—but these are less the case today except in short-stay genres. Instead there are other blindnesses that are more pervasive and subjects of ethnographic analysis, as well as occasionally imposing constraints on ethnographic work itself: project time, short-term contracting, industrialization of aid, and almost obscene increasing inequalities between rich and poor (making hypocritical much so-called ethical theory or ethical review), not just among classes or groups but also in the extractive debt systems among countries.

The anthropologist remains a figure of speech, a token of comparative humanistic social science, of cosmopolitical theory of unsocial sociabilities informed by actually existing societies, and a parallax perspective, an interlocutor crisscrossing and revisiting presuppositions and assumptions and ways of doing things.

Ethnography is a way of slowing down rapid assessments, of asking the provenance of judgments and statistical claims, of weighing layered causalities, and, of course, of representing (in both the sense of political conveying and of translating into visualizable text).

Anthropological Parergons for the Humanities

Cultural forms, lively languages, and works of art are important trading zones, crucibles for emergent transnational idiolects and dialects, in anthropological analysis.

Cultural forms and emergent forms of life are dynamic and dialectical. Cultural forms may be "traditional" (with or without traceable histories and variant uses), but increasingly they are not just "hybrid" or "transnational" but entirely new syntheses, culturally, technologically, and epistemologically. We live in worlds of fusions, borrowings, and montage, and yet not in worlds of mere shreds and fragments, nor just in Fredric Jameson's (1990) superficial worlds of pastiche without histories or depth, but indeed where histories constantly return in deep and powerful ways, sometimes interfering with one another, sometimes referencing one another, but all "working through" into unanticipated *emergent forms of life* full of, first, surprise, and then sometimes retrospective recognition, as deeper patterns manifest. For the anthropologist, cultural forms are often scaffolds or skeletons, legacy structures, to which commentary and interpretation from within or comparison from without can attach similar/different, new/old empirical objects, events, conjunctures, and intersections into generative arrays, matrices, classificatory positions, and reconfigurations. The structural possibilities of stories, theater, praise songs, rituals, and forms of debate can take on quite transformed affordances in new settings, while preserving or reanimating older understandings.

We are used to this in problems of translation across languages, but with increasing pressures on quick takes and instrumentalized understandings, we often forget these resources when working in development, health care, planning, and other practical fields. Countering such forgetting is an important anthropological contribution, and theoretically is crucial to serious comparative/contrastive work all too easily left by most social sciences at high-level generalities, easy to criticize in endless series of mindless "contributions," avoiding the detail work. But the ethnographic details are pebbles that destabilize pretty theories and explain why the best-laid plans often fail.

Lively languages. Languages are littered with prepositions, metaphors, complex rhetorical figures, simple tropes, pluralizations, phonemic binaries and distinctive features, grammatical presuppositions, and etymologies generating disparate, even sometimes contradictory, meanings. Like land mines found after the fact, they are recognized through their effects. Systematic study of this semantic and social liveliness lies in the skills learned in the anthropological disciplines of linguistics, sociolinguistics, pragmatics and metapragmatics, poetics, rhetoric, and other such domains. Deconstruction may have rediscovered some of this and has shown how to deploy it to unhinge and probe conventionalized readings and understandings, and thus to uncover alternative and more open possibilities, not only in old texts but also in advertising, popular discourses, and everyday life.

The *work of art*,[15] as a probe analogous to the work of anthropologists, explores imaginaries that animate and anticipate practical action. Art has become an economic engine and a development goal in many parts of the world. Biennales and art shows are big business in the same way as trade shows that often accompany scientific (not merely engineering) meetings. Cities across China have designated special zones as creative and design (not just innovation) spaces, and the Chinese premier, Xi Jinping, in February 2015 called for "maker spaces" in every high school in China. Globally the ideology of teaching has increasingly been infused not just with the buzzwords of innovation and value creation but also design, project-based learning, rapid prototyping, and above all that elusive value of "creativity." Like anthropologists, artists often have feet in several worlds, not merely that many have day jobs (including commercial art and advertising) while they do their "real" art on their own time or in separate spaces, but, more importantly, that art operates in tension between finding the patronage, grant funding, or business model and pursuing the three C's (commentary, criticism, critique) within the world that artists inhabit or try to speak to.

Tone and Tuning of Ethnography

Don Brenneis, casually walking with me along the streets of Chicago during recent anthropology meetings, dubbed the original versions of chapters 9 and 10 with the lovely epithet "tone poems." I don't know if he was being polite or slyly critical, but I admit to a certain aspiration to get the tone and the catacoustics (the sonic refrains) of ethnographic writing to accurately register time, place, and theoretical interlocutors. It is like the satisfaction or dissatisfaction with a film about Vienna (my prelife) or Iran (some of my formative graduate student years) in which the accents are not quite right: it can ruin the pleasure, the ability to watch, and the ability to take the aesthetic or conceptual effort seriously. This of course varies, and it means more vigilance to these issues than an impossible demand for ethnographers themselves to always be virtuoso sociolinguistic mimics.[16] Where sensitivity to ethnographic or historical accuracy crosses over into the pleasure of watching a play by Euripides, Shakespeare, or Ibsen reset in a different place and time, dress and context may be a fine line, one often dependent upon political resonance, another kind of music.

Thus while many were powerfully moved by Peter Sellars's American Repertory Theater production of Euripedes's *Children of Herakles* in 2003, with an international cast (a Kazakh epic singer, for instance, replacing the odes of the Greek chorus) during the post-9/11 war on Iraq (the Second Gulf War), the classicist-quibbling reviewer for the *New York Review of Books* was inexplicably and pedantically put off.[17] For most reviewers and the local audience, however, the 430 BCE play was returned to its powerful public debate function, complete with ritual and raging passions, set as if in a Congressional hearing or a war crimes trial. The play pits Athenian proclamations of democracy and defense of refugee children against both external threats from Argos, which wants the children returned for execution, on pain of war, and the bloody sacrifices and possible internal self-destruction of Athenian principles that the children's asylum entails. The Argive envoy-lawyer, played by Elaine Tse, in business suit with briefcase, is icily legalistic in laying out her side's claims, the options open to her opponents, and enforcement threats, reminding several in the audience of then secretary of state Condoleezza Rice asserting American imperial power under President George W. Bush. The public debate function was supported by preshow panels with refugees from Bosnia, Guinea, Cambodia, and elsewhere, and with human rights lawyers, immigration service lawyers, trauma therapists, and others; and postshow screenings of films from places producing large numbers of refugees, including Werner Herzog's *Lessons in Darkness* (1992), shot in Kuwait in the aftermath of the First Gulf War, showing massive oil fires burning out of control, Texas firefighters attempting to quell them, scenes of devastation in Kuwaiti hospitals, and Saddam Hussein's former torture chambers.

One could say the difference in reception was one of discipline or of prestructuralist yearning for authenticity and historical accuracy versus a poststructuralist recognition, understood by all epic storytellers, that a Euripidean, Shakespearean, or Ibsen play is defined not by an original version or interpretation but by a structural set of potentials that constitute its corpus and its resonances. When a potent play, or ethnography, sets off reverberations, parallels, and contrasts, it creates new ways of seeing and understanding. It functions as cultural commentary, criticism, and critique (all three quite different things) in the best senses. Ibsen's plays, restaged in India to highlight struggles over caste and gender rather than only class and patriarchy (*Doll House*), or restaged in Singapore to highlight struggles over planning versus whistle-blowing (*Public Enemy*), have a power that is often not achieved in productions true to nineteenth-century Scandinavia.[18] Similarly, Ong Keng Sen's versions of *King Lear* explore contemporary issues of Asian haunted and unsettled intercultural ghosts, using the stylized dramatic resources of Asia, while remaining true to Shakespeare's themes of internalized parental figures and parental projections about children betraying them. These are, Ong says, "very close to Chinese melodrama where parents always debate whether their children are 'filial' or 'unfilial'" (K. S. Ong 2013, 244). His production in 1997, he says, "aimed to be a morality tale for young generations who kill their fathers, but then realize that it is almost impossible to break free from their heritage" (244). The allusion is to a variety of political strong men, including Singapore's Lee Kuan Yew and his promotion of a distinctive Asian form of democracy or neo-Confucianism. Despite Japanese feminist playwright Rio Kishida's scripting, Ong wrote, "Japanese critics felt threatened by the fact that Goneril was interpreted by a Chinese opera singer, while the Father was performed by a Japanese Noh actor" (245).[19] In the version of the play performed in 1999, *Lear Dreaming*, Ong Keng Sen notes, "There are still ways in which this new production can resonate politically, and I am now aware that I cannot stop people from making those readings. For instance, people could ask why the Mother, a Korean court singer, kills the Japanese king. One possible interpretation has to do with the issue of Korean comfort women, and I subscribe to that reading to an extent. However, I am more interested in the human aspect of the story," and in the exploration of dramatic forms, such as those of a matrilineal Sumatran community storytellers (245).

The notion of "tone poems" provides a kind of tuning fork. Both Kant and Derrida wrote essays titled "Raising the Tone" of debate, and ethnographers should be doing that as well. Tone poems can be used dismissively in music as "program music" that provides the signature lines one hears when a character or a plotline is introduced, that makes the music subordinate to the text or story or other extramusical form. But I have always thought of Paul Celan's poetry or Donald Barthelme's short stories as tone poems that depend as much on the sound for meaning as the text itself. I never could quite figure out Barthelme's stories until I heard him read and realized how his distinctive cadence and inflections made them perfectly obvious, and they became among my favorites. Celan's poetry, of course, like Joyce's *Finnegans Wake* in a slightly different way, is more complex, depending on layerings of allusions as well as sounds.

Chapters 4 through 6 use the life work of particular anthropologists over the longitudinal course of their careers as vehicles for surveying regional archives of ethnography and longitudinal appreciations of social change. A certain pleasure, and I hope honesty, comes from having written them for presentation face to face to their subjects while they could receive, respond to, and correct my accounts. Clifford Geertz was a first-rate stylist and wordsmith, the author of five classic monographs on Indonesia, a comparative volume on Indonesian and Moroccan Islam, and a volume with Hildred Geertz and Lawrence Rosen on Morocco. His essays, collected in *The Interpretation of Culture* (1973) and subsequent volumes, walked the line between ethnography and philosophy. Many of these essays became as famous as those of Émile Durkheim's students were to an earlier generation: Marcel Mauss's *The Gift* and *On Prayer*; Robert Hertz's *Death and the Right Hand*; Henri Hubert and Mauss's *Sacrifice*; Franz Steiner's *Taboo*; and many others, foundational for British social anthropology as well as French thought.[20] Geertz's monographs on eastern Java and Bali remain touchstones for all subsequent ethnography in Indonesia and Southeast Asia. Stanley J. Tambiah similarly produced a series of monographs on Buddhism in Thailand, a master work on the world-conqueror, world-renouncer pattern of South and Southeast Asian polities, and two important volumes on militant Buddhist politics in Sri Lanka, and one on ethnic violence in South Asia. Jean Jackson, apart from her classic ethnography of a nearly unique situation of marriage rules requiring one to marry someone of a different language along the Vaupes River in Colombia, like others teaching in MIT's anthropology program (Martin Diskin and James Howe), has been engaged in defense of Native American rights with full interest in tracking historical changes in the struggles over those rights. I try to take a reading of what is state of the art in ethnographic and historical accounts of indigenous groups of the Amazon today. But this essay is also another response to the empirically thinning discourses that are the subject of chapter 2, as well as an extension of an earlier essay, "In the Science Zone: The Yanomami and the Fight for Representation" (2001).

In chapter 7, Veena Das's long-term fieldwork on health care among the poor in New Delhi illustrates the power of ethnography to analyze three cultural registers (advocacy, ethics, and contradictions and ambi-valences) through seven "scenes of instruction" built around nine characters or case studies. The seven scenes of instruction involve seven narrative motifs that are also at play across Hindu, Greek, Jewish, and Islamic myths in families of resemblance: (1) visibility-invisibility; (2) control over desire/passion; (3) direct seeing/witnessing versus delegated narrating/reporting; (4) female counterpower to male hierarchy; (5) humiliation by disrobing and power through restraint and asceticism (*tapas*); (6) "human beings propose, but destiny proposes otherwise"; and (7) paired ritual/epic tales. In order not to allow cultural forms to be essentialized, temporally distanced, or separated from our own lives, I frame the essay in both a contemporary case of health care for a professional friend and in my explorations of the biomedical and bioscientific research in India.

Chapter 12 builds on the analysis of chapter 7 by reviewing a series of recent ethnographic works as parables or allegorical forms of writing culture or cultural commentary, or what I call seven kinds of "elementary" zen exercises: (1) ethnographic practices of camaraderies and trajectories (à la the discussion of the friendship topos discussed above and explored in chapters 5 through 9); (2) the exercise of picking case studies with a certain detachment from the world, not a detachment of indifference but a meta-stable standpoint from which critique and politics can emerge; (3) calligraphies of human lives in settings of extreme social violence that incorporate hope, self-organizing defense, and paths forward; (4) the aporia of forced incorporation of alien cosmologies and ideologies; (5) the containment of poisoned histories and divided cities through contemporary forensics of massacres and through rebuilding and disciplining of pilgrimage sites; (6) horizoning by climate change modelers as practice rather than as jeremiad; and (7) unfinished exercises and lifelines.

Chapters 9 and 12 return to the notion of hospitality and the relationship between philosophy and anthropology. In particular, I am concerned that this relationship not be one of subordination, ethnography as illustration of philosophical formulations, but that ethnography be itself a source for philosophy, as it often has been in the past, and that philosophy be historicized and made ethnographic. The relationship then becomes one of illumination back and forth, a relation of juxtaposition, that provides points of attachment for creative and productive dialogue beyond mere comparison, beyond the dialectic of seeing (*theoria*) and conceptualizing (theory), attentive as well to the affective body of interpersonal emotions, the tropes of vulnerability and calls for social justice, and the ear, face, and critical apparatuses of the other as places for ethical ethnographic exchange.

Temporality and Recursivity in Ethnography

Chapters 11 and 12 recall *Writing Culture* and *Anthropology as Cultural Critique*, and chart the material and conceptual differences since then, focusing attention on the material platforms that have changed. Chapter 11, in part, updates "Before Going Digital/Double Digit/Y2000: A Retrospective of Late Editions" (Fischer 2000a), as well as "Worlding Cyberspace: Towards an Ethnography in Time, Space and Theory" (Fischer, 1991), and "Raising Questions about Rouch" (Fischer 1999). "A Polyphonic Nine-Canto *Singspiel*" (chapter 11) originally was a response to an invitation from Andrew Lyons as editor of *Anthropologia*, the journal of the Canadian Anthropological Association, who wanted something short to mark the quarter century since *Writing Culture*. Given the interest in writing tactics probed in the original volume and many of its successors, I wanted to play a little with genre, do something celebratory but also fun. Polyphony and dialogue, collaboration between anthropologist and interlocutors, was a hot topic in the 1980s, and so I thought to try to re-create the polyphony and debate or dialogue among the anthropologists as they were locked up together for a week at the wonderful School for American Research in Santa Fe. I try very hard to remain true to the original essays, channeling voice and concerns, while reminding the next generation that these are not icons to be toppled or superseded; instead I attempt to make them come alive again in the round as interlocutors, as in a theater in the round. I use initials rather than names, not to obscure anything but to make clear that these ventriloquies are my invention. Part of the discussions in those days was the ethics of, in the end, the anthropologist always being the one who holds the pen (as I do here). For Steven Tyler at the time this was in a sense unethical. He called for a therapeutic modality of ethnography, reducing the ideal ethical anthropology to only unwritten, face-to-face dialogue. I wanted a more pragmatic middle way to preserve writing, the encounters, and the anthropological analysis of the social context.

At the same time I was interested, along with my cohort, in making such writing more open. I experimented with making cofieldwork explicit. I cowrote *Debating Muslims* with Mehdi Abedi, experimenting with a variety of genres of writing: drawing upon oral autobiography processed by the anthropologist; scholastic traditions of debate and their critical apparatuses for evaluating validity, as well as their use in political debate; poetics and political debates pursued through poster art, stamps, and other visual culture; and a master novel of psychological adjustments of migration filtered through vernacular jumbles of Bollywood-style stories and distorted memories of childhood religious instruction, based upon classical Islamic hadith (the subject as well of a key example in chapter 3). I cowrote an essay with Stella Gregorian, based on interviews that we did in Armenia after the Leninakan earthquake (magnitude 6.9) on December 7, 1988, and during the fighting with Azerbaijan over Nagorno-Karabakh (majority ethnic Armenian highlanders in an enclave within Azerbaijan), using a Pirandello-like form of "Six to Eight Characters in Search of Armenian Civil Society amidst the Carnivalization of History" (1993). I experimented with Leszek Koczanowicz to textually represent counterarguments through sidebars in a lightly edited transcript on the modern cultural and political history of Poland ("One Hand Clapping: Dialogue, Silences, and the Mourning of Polish Romanticism" [1993]). And in my essay in *Writing Culture* itself, I tried to present voices and writing tactics of five groups of hybrid American ethnic autobiographical writing, both male and female voices.

Repatriation and the Work of Art in Biosensible and Maker-Space Worlds

Repatriation was the call of *Anthropology as Cultural Critique* in the 1980s. It was a call to turn the lens back on ourselves, not as implicit comparison (as in Geertz's commentary on Washington, DC, in *Negara* [1980]) but as detailed ethnography, multiscalar, up close, across multiple contexts at different strategic points of access.

Today the call of repatriation is different. It is environmental, often bioremedial, looking to regeneration where possible, mitigation and adaptation where not, or even exploratory into new environments (the warming Arctic, outer space, the oceans) requiring yet new forms of life. It is a call for attention to the multiscalar and global, up close and in context, in place across multiple contexts; to the East and West, North and South; and transversally to China and the West, the Third World and the First, indigenous and migrant, rooted and spreading rhizome-like, viral and in lines of flight, forceful and stringy.

Environmental degradation, climate change, late industrialism's toxicities and health damage, species loss, and the Anthropocene have become widespread concerns in many ethnographies, both as topics themselves but also as sine qua non settings for what might once have been screened out in the search for salvage of historical culture, ways of living, mythologies, alternative modernities, and "before modernity."

One of the interesting venues for thinking about these concerns—both conceptually and as practice—is in the work of art, an experimental space parallel to that of ethnography, often itself an ethnographic register of contemporary matters of concerns, and often exploring, reimagining, or remixing and retargeting their cultural genres or forms of expression. These latter are variable across the globe in their geographical and historical groundings, providing translation bridges or double-horned contact points between local concerns and universal ones, giving them interpretive power for understanding the way people act in differing circumstances. Theater practice (a topic on which I am currently working in Singapore) and visual artworks (printmaking, painting, performance art, and installations, on which I have been writing occasional essays)—like ethnographies and as ethnographic registers of contemporary matters of concern evoking different cultural genres and modes of expression—provide ways to stage or dramatize conflicts, interests, behaviors, and imaginaries that make up the human comedy of actions that produce effects beyond the ken of the actors. These are effects on social relations, on cultural discursive shifts, on habitats, and on possibilities and constraints for future actions. Donna Haraway has called on us to not smooth over these effects and complexities with easy philosophical, hortatory policy agenda, glib contestatory criticism, or other feel good discourse, but to engage and "stay with the trouble" (Haraway 2016).

The arts provide interesting devices because they move between the material and the abstract, providing reflective and diffractive heterotopias and third spaces, not unlike ethnography itself. Ethnographic readings of artworks furthermore can push back against universalist philosophies of art, insistently ground-truthing, looking for the specificities that allow artworks to reflect upon, and contest, their sites of production, and then travel to, and bring perspective to, new contexts. Such ethnographically comparative work of juxtaposition carries more depth and bite than emptying artworks of their specificities, making them, in the name of universal truths, banal, vague, generalities that might or might not apply elsewhere. Application, whether in case-based law or in scientific experiments as machines intended to generate surprising new knowledge, is a play between specifics and principles, a third space of imagination.

Take, for example, a group show in 2015 by a number of artists showcasing work done at the Singapore Tyler Print Institute (STPI), a show called *Recyclables: Art and Nature's Revenge*. STPI is one of the nodes of the art circles of Southeast Asia's network, albeit closer to the art market high end of the network than to the community-based bootstrapping lower end of the network for which Yogyakarta has become globally famous, and well as other loose networks in Myanmar, Thailand, Cambodia, Vietnam, and the Philippines that are also, if less well known, also bootstrapping regional as well as local social support systems for artists. I use the STPI show here as a triadic example of: (1) addressing matters of concern such as environmental issues, toxicities, and health; (2) drawing attention to a geographically grounded ethnographic arena of my current interest, such as the spectacular rise of loosely communicating contemporary Southeast Asian art scenes in Indonesia, the Philippines, Vietnam, Myanmar, Thailand, Laos, Cambodia, and Singapore; and (3) a material production site that itself fuses state-of-the-art innovation and recycling the old and traditional, while also recycling and reconfiguring Southeast Asian production venues and resources gained through the global exchanges and circulations of artists. This triad of interactions works to think art forms and tactics anew and otherwise.[21]

Well-known Filipino artist Ronald Ventura's artist statement for his STPI contributions, for instance, says the show "can be interpreted as *repatriating* what belongs to Mother Nature." He goes on to say, "We are constantly reminded of it. In the newspapers, on TV, and on the Internet. *The world is collapsing around our ears* sings Michael Stipe in one of REM's songs from the album Out of Time. The signs are all there. Global warming. Terrible floods. Strange Weather. Some species following the way of the dodo and becoming zoological footnotes. Diminishing resources. The only thing missing would be the signs in yellow-ochre-and-black telling us that the end of the world is nigh. Unless. We. Do. Something. About it" (Ventura 2015).[22]

Ventura continues, specifically regarding art making at STPI: "As we know STPI is concerned with 'pushing the technical and aesthetic frontiers of printmaking and papermaking.' And I see this institution as something where materials can be reused, recycled into something even better, more ecologically sound materials for making art. Working at STPI has made me re-evaluate my own artistic strategies" (Ventura 2015).

And Ventura goes on to layer his effort as "not just creating artworks that would resonate with the theme of conservation" but on a "meatier level" dealing with the psychological, philosophical, human behavior, and why "we do it all over again," presumably caught in repetitions that are, if not mindless, at least, unknowing, unaware, un-self-reflective, and destructive of our own lives and ambitions; but that could be otherwise ("Unless. We. Do. Something. About it"). I would like to understand the "it" as being the repetitions.

Before returning to Ventura's and the other artists' efforts in these matters environmental, material, and artistic (I will adduce here only three quick examples), it is worth noting the global reach of recycling in the STPI facility, and also the nexus of facilities like this one that are the workshops of contemporary art. The importance of such craft- and technology-support institutes has been largely overlooked by anthropologists (and art and cultural historians) writing about art worlds. Another such important figure and venue in the United States is Donald Saff's Graphicstudio.[23] STPI provides residencies for artists with little or no prior printmaking experience. The resident chief printer, Japan-born Eitaro Ogawa, trained by Ken Tyler, helps the artists (often major Southeast Asian and East Asian artists), some seventy to date, realize their visions, experimenting together with new processes.

The equipment is all "recycled" from Ken Tyler's workshops in the United States.[24] The largest press at STPI is a 500 ton ("elephant") press adapted originally for Frank Stella's very large *Moby Dick* series. To create relief work that large, you need a lot of weight. So Tyler went to an automobile scrapyard and "recycled" and adapted one of the machines used for crushing cars. The new STPI facility in Singapore is on the river so it could be brought in by ship, but they had to tear down a wall of the converted and recycled 1920s warehouse to get it inside. Another recyclable in STPI's "state-of-the-art" tool kit are all two hundred or so of Ken Tyler's limestones, originally from Bavaria, that have just the right viscosity and consistency to absorb ink only in the top two millimeters.[25] The stones thus can be reused by grinding them down after use, shaving off one or two millimeters, almost like geological exfoliation. In the 1800s, plays, music, advertisements, and manuals were printed with *these* lithographic stones, writing on stone in reverse or mirror image. You can still see the last layer printed on, awaiting reuse. Next to the lithography press is an etching press, and nearby the acid room for etching. Aside from recycling and adapting machines, Tyler was insistent on having a paper mill on site, saying you cannot have a state-of-the-art printmaking facility without having a state-of-the-art paper-making capacity.[26] You need this to have full control of the fibers and the quality, and also to enable people not only to use paper in a two-dimensional frame, but also three-dimensionally. There is a batter machine for the long fiber cotton imported from the United States. Long fibers allow better control of the flexibility of paper for sculpture and for longer paper that will not rip. (If artists want other kinds of noncotton paper, e.g., mulberry or rice paper, that can be brought in. Similarly, while there is a woodcutting workshop in house, metal cutting is done outside.)

One of the times I visited in 2015, an exhibit of Korean-born artist Do Ho Suh's residency work, "I Am Your Conduit," was in preparation.[27] This exhibit provided a nice example of how repatriation has exploded beyond its meaning in the 1980s in a world in which not only do lives and the processes of artwork such as Suh's become globally peripatetic but the very materials shift in ways that make us think about the material composition (as well as conceptual composition) of the world differently. Not all the works produced at STPI are large, but the ability to work in larger than usual papermaking frames and presses is an available affordance. "I Am Your Conduit."[28] Suh's work at STPI was done on the largest-size paper the STPI has been able to produce, too large in fact for any of the presses, and so a special screen was constructed, and a water press technique devised.

It was a globally distributed production process, as well as relying on a heterogeneous bricolage or assemblage of materials (US cotton, colored thread, gelatin, squeegees, tweezers, handcrafting, industrial presses, bugs). As I entered the work space, a woman was ironing one of the embroidered gelatin layers titled "I Am Your Conduit." It had come in a large roll from Korea, and the ripples needed to be ironed out. Each of the series is a one-off. Suh draws an image onto gelatin sheets, which are then shipped to Korea to a seamstress who stitches long colored threads onto it and ships it back. It is then attached to a big mesh screen with magnets, and then transferred onto a large bed of wet paper pulp. Lots of water is added, and it is hosed down. An ordinary squeegee is used to work the water into the paper pulp, embedding the colored threads into the paper, and dissolving the gelatin. (This process takes an hour.) Then the screen is peeled off, and what is left are the colored threads embedded in the paper, a "thread drawing." After an hour or two, paper is laid on top to stop the absorption of water, and the moisture is carefully vacuum-suctioned. The piece then takes about three days to dry. The limitation on size is the largest table that STPI has, which is in turn limited by the space of the building. (When Ogawa mentioned a thirty-meter-long panel, much to Ogawa's amused worry about how to do it, Do Ho's eyes lit up, and now says he wants to try a forty-meter-long piece.) Because of the water and the pressure, in the process of moving the color-thread-embedded paper, a lot of rogue threads can go off in different directions. So then up to ten workers sit with tweezers, picking out and repositioning threads. The morning of my visit, there were quite a few bugs, and we joked about where they came from: from Korea? "Hope they haven't carried along MERS [Middle East Respiratory Syndrome, which was newly in the headlines originating with camels in Saudi Arabia]" "Oh, you mean literally bugs!" "Yes, literally bugs!" "Oh!" (laughter). "Does one ever just leave the rogues threads as is? These swirls are rather nice, fun." "Yes, they do, some of them; and you will see in all of his thread drawings that they are not perfectly aligned. Do-Ho does doctor them. We do the first pick up of the bugs and everything, and then he will come and make the final decision. So it is never immaculate, there is always some movement."

Iconic of Suh's peripatetic journeys around the globe, the pieces in "I Am your Conduit" are striking fine multicolor thread images of a human head arched forward, in motion, and flowing lines forming robes or sometimes even walking legs, following underneath and behind.[29] Multiples create the motion of hair and wind streaming behind, of multiple heads of hair flowing upward in an elegant arch, of a running figure with hair afire, of trees with heads popping out of a bend in their trunks. Stairs and houses are other motifs, some done in this thread-embedded-paper technique, some as flat lithography, some as drawings, and some as the installations for which Suh is famed. These last are hanging, architecturally precise, three-dimensional constructions, in sheer nylon threads, of houses he's lived in. Most famous of these is his red hanging staircase and balcony. Another striking piece in blue is a brownstone façade with blue smoke strings coming out the doors and windows and a vaguely human shadow-like pile of multicolored threads on the ground behind the façade where the building once stood. A small human figure stands on the pile holding a cane, rust-red threads rising around him like smoke, an oriental halo, or flames.

Suh's work is not just syntheses of his Oriental painting and Western art training, but, in a way (as I've tried to describe elsewhere in a catalogue essay for a show in early 2016 by Indonesian artist Entang Wiharso and Australian artist Sally Smart) signs of postnational nomadic iconographies across Asia that retain elements of place, history, and biography (Fischer, 2017).

Returning to Ronald Ventura's *Recyclables*, he notes in his artist's statement, "There is irony here and a warning: For recyclables I have made hypothetical street signs that warn us of impending doom ("Point of No Return") . . . I have constructed burnt out trees ("Shadow Forests") something related to the phoenix rising out of the ashes. I have sculpted objects out of discarded materials ("Toxicity")—metals, boxes, paper and assorted scraps. A warning: to make art is to make objects that will make more toxins. Quite alarming. Dig the irony. . . . This is our Apocalypse and yet this is also our Eden" (Ventura 2015).

The most fascinating artwork for me in the joint show with Ventura of several former STPI artists' residency works was a series of stunning collages (lithography, screen print, acrylic, coated leaves on kozo paper) by Filipina artist Geraldine Javier that she called *Playing God in an Art Lab* and that instantly made me think first of bioartists who work in actual tissue engineering labs (viz., Oren Catts and Ionat Zurr), and then Donna Haraway. One image in particular struck me as the perfect colors and assemblage for Haraway's new collection of essays that I was just reading in manuscript. I took pictures to send her, and then helped make the connections through STPI for permissions for the cover image that now graces Haraway's latest book, *Staying with the Trouble* (2016), in our Experimental Futures series at Duke.

The image is one of a set of sixteen that Tony Godfrey in the exhibit catalogue delightfully calls "sixteen creatures in search of their species." It is "obviously" a Pelvissomniumpapilio, since it combines a pelvis, bones of symmetrical oversized skeleton hands, seven vertebrae on a spinal column rising like chakras, and a *papilio* (Lat. "butterfly") head.[30]

Somnium, Latin for "dream," is also the title of Johannes Kepler's novel (written in 1608; published posthumously in 1634), said to be the first science fiction as well as first lunar astronomy book.[31] Godfrey points out not only that Javier's interest in anatomical drawings, recombinatories of forms of botany and zoology, and cycles of death and life, come from her training as a nurse, but also that Steven Jay Gould's observations about the fossils in the Burgess Shale provides an evolutionary visionary touchstone for Javier and a number of other artists. Gould had pointed out that "the Burgess had been an amazing time of experimentation, an era of such evolutionary flexibility, such potential for juggling and recruitment of characters from the arthropod grab bag, that almost any potential arrangement might be essayed (or assayed)," and more generally that evolution was not a mechanical process but one where all sorts of (unpredictable) combinations might occur (Gould, 1989, 184–85). Godfrey writes, "Geraldine's species morph and mutate, from human to insect to arthropod, and their substance mutates too, from leaf to bone, bone to wool, leaf to paper. She chose bits of human skeleton that resemble insect's structures—four hands, ribs, pelvis, vertebrae—and imagined new beings" (Godfrey 2012).

In Javier's world, death is often depicted as part of the seasonal and life cycle, but, as Godfrey puts it, "Geraldine has inverted the trope: for rather than the skeleton, Death, coming to dance with lovers, priest, knights or barrel makers and kill them, it is Death himself who is born, who grows and dies, collapsing in a heap of bones" (Godfrey 2012). All the more material for Javier to work with. Perhaps there is a resonance with *Death's End*, the novel by Liu Cixin described in the epilogue that deals with what comes after the Anthropocene.

Future Sensing, Human Redesign, Ground-Truthing

I turn to the Anthropocene in the epilogue as a site for ethnographic work at the speculative edges of what we know today, an analogue to what Adriana Petryna calls "horizoning." The Anthropocene lies at the intersection of technology, disasters (natural and manmade), and "late industrialism" (K. Fortun 2012, 2014). It is a site of risk scenario building among planners and policy makers, as well as in speculative hard science fiction and in artworks. As with novels as teaching spaces for complex interactions, I am interested here in Asian hard science fiction and artworks as ethnographic registers of long standing as well as new imaginaries that anthropology can read for access to ways of thinking about forces beyond the individual's or local communities' control—whether because they are geological, as in earthquakes, or financial, as in the 1997 Asian financial crisis; whether matters of governance missteps at the level of the nation-state, or at the level of global capitalist coercive lending (Studwell 2014). Asia is a place where techno-optimism is widely ascendant, where new infrastructures, signature architecture, and social reorganization is moving at high speed, but also where some of the major recent disasters have occurred, such as the Indian Ocean tsunami in 2004 and the Fukushima Daichi nuclear meltdown in 2011. It is also a prominent site of contemporary imaginaries that collapse time into utopias and dystopias, precisely the kind of site that ethnography can temper by asserting the importance of working, documenting, exploring connections, finding alternatives, and social routing switches *in the meantime*, in the gaps and contradictions, and in analytic third spaces and parergon ethnographic experiments that can see the contemporary world otherwise.

Asia, of course, is not the only place where such ethnographic imaginaries are at work in emergent forms of life and third spaces. MIT—like STPI, and like the new experimental residential colleges at the National University of Singapore, or the new Singapore University of Technology and Design, established with the help of MIT—is such a triadic third space for future sensing (what's emergent), ground-truthing (what's grounded in contemporary capacities), and human redesign (the ethically contested arenas of prosthetic enhancement, genomic repair, and biological and medical regeneration).

Let me provide two final preliminary examples, one on Human 2.0 from MIT, and one on neuroscience and ethics from Tembusu College (one of the new residential colleges of the National University of Singapore).

In 2007, a conference was held by MIT's Media Lab called "Human 2.0: New Minds, New Bodies, New Identities."[32] As master of ceremony John

Hockenberry quipped from his wheel chair, I'd love to be upgraded to a Human 2.0. Hosted by Hugh Herr (who would show off his high-tech legs and ankles) and Hockenberry, the conference featured a series of primarily prosthetic enhancements to the physical human body and the built environment (smart vehicles, smart cities), many of which are no longer futuristic, ranging from artificial ankles to early Brain Gate insertions into the brain to help paraplegics direct their brainwaves to grab, lift, and sip from a cup; to smart, even driverless, electric cars that can store energy to be returned to the grid when not in use as described by MIT's William Mitchell. By then (2007) celebrity Stephen Hawking had already put into common circulation the ability to use eye movements to operate a computer. We are now accustomed to seeing war veterans (and other amputees, including athletes) with high-tech legs, often displayed modernistically as pure metal rods, sometimes encased in naturalistic or wildly painted casings. We have seen hand and arm transplants, even face transplants. The promises of brain-neural interface design to give back functionality to the impaired moves ahead slowly. The promises of individualized and comparative genomics (with all the attendant other "omics"—proteomics, iRNA regulation) and of gene and cell therapy (with not just recombinant DNA using enzymes to cut and splice at the test tube level but now also CRISPR-cas 9 to work at the level of cells) also slowly advance hopes of both medical regeneration and smoother interaction with our microbiomes, viruses, and other biological and ecological surrounds.

The space between the heady Media Lab–style demonstrations and the realities of daily life is a *third space of ethnography*, the space of exploring with the engineers the challenges of getting these prostheses to work and exploring with their users their flaws and complications in daily use. A charismatic course at MIT called "Assistive Technologies," initiated by the late MIT polymath professor Seth Teller,[33] continued by Grace Teo and William Lim, and now by others (Aidinoff 2015) works both sides by beginning with particular individuals addressing their needs both in engineering and in human interactive terms (engineering with and for whom?).[34] Leg prostheses often rub against the flesh, so the students worked with a wearer to design a soft interfacing, customized for the user, and adjustable (not a one-time solution). A blind-accessible modification to an otherwise inaccessible oven was created for an Italian American man who loves to cook for others (as well as for himself). Teaching students to learn to see, feel, and learn from someone differently embodied is as important a skill as the engineering: it is an ethnographic pedagogy. Instead of hackathons or other prototyping for imagined customers at a commercial scale (with and for whom?), one begins with individual needs and makes these particular lives better, including learning along with them how to make the constant required adjustments and repairs over time, and only thereafter seeing if some of those ideas are scalable or could be worked into a sustainable business plan for profit or for a sustainable nonprofit, a cooperative perhaps, or skill exchanges and community networks. Sociological imagination is needed as well as engineering modeling, prototyping and testing ("design-build-test-deploy").

In 2013 at Tembusu College, an indigenously designed new residential college of the National University of Singapore, I helped teach a course in biomedicine and Singapore society with two hundred first-year undergraduate students. I organized a panel on neuroscience and ethics for the students. One of the presenters, professor Nitish Thakor, the director of the new SiNAPSE (Singapore Institute for Neurotechnology: Advancing through Partnership of Scientists and Engineers), from the Johns Hopkins University, and much earlier from yet another model cultural setting (ITT Bombay), challenged the students at my request to think about how they could evaluate what is only speculatively possible versus what is realistically feasible. In addition he asked them to ask themselves how they individually as ethical beings would draw the line between what one can do and what one should do, and why. It was a wonderfully raucous exchange, probing, trying to think beyond ethical inhibitions to ask why and where norms be drawn and on what grounds, with what precedent cases, beyond local conventions, thinking outside of the box, finding where the red lines should be, and how they move and are reconfigured with new experiences and knowledges.[35]

These too are third spaces of ethnography: working out recursively as real-life challenges arise rather than as apodictic philosophy. The calling of anthropology and ethnography is not what it used to be, but it is as urgent and necessary as ever, together with its transformed sister disciplines in the arts and humanities, sciences and engineering, in a world of emergent forms of life.

Invitation

I invite you in the following chapters to follow me in my own trajectory through several generations of anthropology. I have been lucky to have been able to participate and feel the charisma (sense of calling, and of collective endeavor) of many anthropological engagements, beginning with my undergraduate days at the London School of Economics and Political Science (LSE), where I was immersed in classical British social anthropology, and a return briefly to the Johns Hopkins University, where I witnessed the extraordinary conference The Structuralist Controversy: The Languages of Criticism and the Sciences of Man (Macksey and Donato, ed. 1972). I then went to the University of Chicago in the golden days of symbolic and interpretive anthropology (where Clifford Geertz was on the faculty, and Paul Rabinow was a fellow graduate student a year or two senior to me; see chapters 3 and 4) and in the time of the upheavals of the civil rights movement, the Great Society experiments in civil society invigoration, and the anti–Vietnam War protest movement. I moved then to Harvard during the controversies over sociobiology and recombinant DNA, returning briefly to the University of Chicago to participate in a seven-country project on social change and Islam. I was then recruited by George Marcus to join the Anthropology Department at Rice University, where we built a graduate program, ran the interdisciplinary Rice Circle, the Center for Cultural Studies (that I directed for six years), the editorial collective that produced the eight volumes of *Late Editions: Cultural Studies at the End of the Century* (edited by George Marcus), ran the journal *Cultural Anthropology* (under George Marcus's editorship), and wrote *Anthropology as Cultural Critique*, as well as the SAR (School for American Research)-incubated volumes *Writing Culture* (edited by George Marcus and James Clifford) and *Critical Anthropology Now* (edited by George Marcus). During the Rice years, I also participated in the Benjamin Lee–led network based in Chicago called the Center for Psychosocial Studies and then the Center for Transnational Studies, which in turn was associated with the journal *Public Culture* (run by Carol Breckenridge and Arjun Appadurai), of which for a few years I was an associate editor. Following my six-year stint as director of the Rice Center for Cultural Study, in which the effort was to enliven the interface between anthropology and the humanities (including bringing to Rice people to teach in feminism, comparative religion, and film and media studies), I moved to MIT to explore the interface between anthropology and the sciences and technology, and served for four years as the director there of the STS (Science, Technology and Society Program), an exciting period when the program actually integrated historical and anthropological approaches on something like an equal basis (chronicled in Fischer 2003, chap. 9), with Lily Kay, Charlie Weiner, and Evelynn Hammonds among the leading lights on the collaborative history side (Lily pioneering serious historiography of contemporary science, Charlie constantly keeping alive the social justice and ethics side of STS, and Evelynn bringing race and diversity issues to the MIT agenda). I was also welcomed warmly into MIT's lively Anthropology Program (with James

Howe and Jean Jackson trading the duties of chair for many years; see chapter 5). I was also integrated into the Harvard Friday Morning Seminar on Mental Health and Medical Anthropology run by Byron Good and Mary-Jo DelVecchio Good, and into teaching with them at the Harvard Medical School and with Byron in anthropology. There I reengaged with Tambiah (see chapter 6), who had also overlapped with me at Chicago. Arthur Kleinman had helped found both the Friday Morning Seminar and the journal *Culture, Medicine, and Psychiatry*, which Byron and Mary-Jo then ran for many years, and through both Kleinman and Byron I had important interactions with Veena Das (see chapter 7 and 9). It was through Byron and Mary-Jo's NIMH training grant, which brought two postdocs a year to Harvard, that I met Joe Dumit, who became my closest colleague at MIT's STS Program and continues as coeditor of the book series Experimental Futures, and João Biehl and Adriana Petryna (see chapter 12), former students of Paul Rabinow, both of whom I once tried very hard to hire at MIT, and who have since become close and prized colleagues. Another important presence in the Cambridge, Mass., STS scene is my colleague and friend Sheila Jasanoff, whom we also tried to hire at one point and who has helped train a number of our graduate students. Also important over the years, both in visits to Cambridge and elsewhere (including at the SHOT [Society for History of Technology] meetings in Singapore in 2016), has been Bruno Latour, whose wit and always good humor is an inspiration, and whom I invited not only to speak in the MIT STS program (one of the largest turnouts for an STS public event) but also to do an amazing masters class with my social theory graduate students in which he displayed a Socratic technique of leading students though a mazeway of thoughts that constantly caught them having to rethink from new angles. In recent years I've been welcomed in Singapore (see chapter 12) by Greg Clancey (a former student at MIT), Ryan Bishop (a former student at Rice), John Philips (see chapter 8), Margaret Tan Ai Hua, Prasanjit Duara, Tan Tai Yong, Alan Chang, and Lily Kong to the National University of Singapore's initiatives in STS, and by Edison Liu, Bing Lim, and Huck Ng to the Genome Institute of Singapore.

My own fieldwork and ethnographic work in the meantime has slowly drifted eastward from once upon a time in Jamaica to Iran, India, and now Southeast Asia, and points in between and on the other side.

Please join me in my conversations with my friends (I don't always agree with them, you'll see, but they are friends nonetheless), and with the delights of anthropology, for which I can think of no better motto than the epigram from the late important Singaporean playwright Kuo Pao Kun I placed on the dedication page. At MIT most everyone is, or aspires to be, the leader of a lab or group. James Howe, in self-defense, put up a sign on his door, "The Howe Group." In that spirit, I dedicate this volume to my MIT students under the name "The Fischer Lab" or "The Lab in New Approaches to Ethnography, Contemporary Social Theory, and Emergent Forms of Life" (ETL: Ethnography, Theory, Life). This is only half-facetious, because I do recognize a distinctive anthropological STS style, tools, discourse, and conversation in exploring emergent forms of life through multiscale, multilocale ethnographies on social issues of global importance among my former (and present) graduate students, many of whose works I use as exemplars in the following pages. Join us.

Cover Image

The cover is a woodcut by Yoshitoshi that I call "Pen and Sword," that hangs in my living room alongside the samurai that I used as a cover image for *Emergent Forms of Life and the Anthropological Voice*. Both serve me as constant meditation images. "Pen and Sword" is, of course, a traditional image of a samurai committing hari-kari, removing his armor, and weapons, and taking up a pen to write his farewell. In my interpretation, it is the pen that is the stronger legacy, and one that deals with the demons of the world, imaged in the approaching tiger in the upper left corner, held at bay. It is an image of the emotional intensity of the struggle to make the writing, the ethnography, come out right.

Opening Keywords

Keyword refrains are suggested, at the beginning of each part, as guides, traces, shadows, openings and indexicals of theory building—a short-hand analytic weft to the ethnographic woof. Keywords here are not efforts to create new neologisms, but on the contrary to attend to and focalize refrains in the everyday speech, refrains, and engagements with others, across languages, across vocations, and across disciplines. Keys open up locks and puzzles, doors and windows, languages and behaviors (shiboleths, cues, codes). They are also music signatures. Read quickly as you would expressionist brush strokes or scan a score; later return, picking up the stitches, following the transversal connections. The index will provide a search engine for more detailed views of the stitching. But the idea of keywords here is to open up discourse for the twenty-first century, not to lock down definitions; to point to substantive issues, sites for new knowledge building drawing on the experiences of the multitudes, and building new worlds flourishing at many scales, pluralistically, of many forms and types, guided by visions and practicalities.

Ethnography in the meantime is a self-cultivation of attention like breathing in yoga. Attending to such breathing brings awareness of temporalities and recursivities, tonalities and tunings, time signatures, historical horizons, and changes in worldly references, articulated sometimes as past, present or future, at other times as familiars (what we have always been) and "others," transformations (what we will have become, could have, or might yet, become).

Times appear out of joint, cameras out of focus, and pens run out of ink (chapter 11); we need new keywords, new analyses, new framings, new platforms or media, as well as new observations, transferences, and hospitalities (chapter 9).

Past twentieth-century schools of thought and methodological tools also remain critical and in contemporary use, if often tweaked for unexpected new contexts—on functionalism or the rule "you cannot change only one thing"; structuralism or the language-like systematicity of how we think; critical theory or questions about how the taken for granted is shaped by political economy and socialization; interpretive anthropology or the value added to the cultural by mutual interrogation across linguistic, cultural, and vocational divides about the meanings of words, deeds, and things; and the postmodern or the postings across different formations of the modern, see Fischer 1997. On "religion," "kinship," see briefly in chapter 1. For broader historical and philosophical background and important legacy keywords such as the four *natures*, analytical approaches for *cultural analysis, personhood*, and the *body* as experimental shifter "between beastial and divine" drawing on experiments like those of Stellarc or technologies show-cased at the MIT Media Lab's conference Human 2.0, see Fischer 2009.

Here are a few key words from the prologue to illustrate, in order of the sections.

Anthropology in the meantime and spaces for experimental ethnography: third spaces, emergent forms of life, unforeseen social ruptures, experimental time, peopling of technologies, relays of experience;

Colloquy of essays: essay as *parergon*: dialogue and friendship; cultural genres, rhetorics, logics; vernacular philosophies; materiality of oral, written, filmic, and performance ethnographic practices; reverse and spiral temporalities; historical horizons as complex social formations and cultural references;

social commons, flourishing of the human condition in its plurality; future imaginaries.

Perfect pitch: theory emergent from the ambrosia of everyday churning; added value of interpretation and speculation through comparison, juxtaposition, and internal contestation; address, tact, and tone.

For and with whom: pluralization, prepositions, points of view, multilocale, multiscale, diasporic feedback and transcultural flows, psychosis of transplantation, linkage of small worlds, intensities and shibboleths, looking for the unsaid and unarchived, ethnographic aesthetics (modes of seeing, apperceiving, seeing anew, seeing for epistemological form); ethnography in corporations with new forms of deliverables; ethical plateaus; anthropologist as figure of speech indexical for cultural and social analysis; ethnography as taking the time for assessment and evaluation.

Parergon for the humanities: emergent transnational ideolects and dialects; translation; pebbles in the way of theory; lively languages; the work of art.

Tone and tuning: potency of ethnography setting off reverberations, parallels and contrasts; longitudinal and regionally comparative ethnographic work; advocacy, ethics, and contradiction; contradictions, social oscillations, paradoxes and aporia; detachment, critique, zen exercises; hospitality-hostility.

Temporality and recursivity: polyphony and dialogue in ethnographic writing; stepping into streams of representations and social actions; different effects of different material forms of communicative action; public sphere versus public culture.

Repatriation and work of art in biosensible and maker space worlds (Paregon for STS, science, technology and society studies): repatriation as biosensibilities and ecological attention (you cannot change only one thing); scaling and partially globalized processes, up close and across multiple contexts; artworks as cultural registers, as probes for sites of production, circuits and conduits of travel, with different production of meaning in different contexts; loosely linked art worlds, recyclables, breaking the hegemony of Western art theory; theory from the Global East; Asian imaginaries; bugs and affordances.

Future sensing, human redesign, ground truthing: anthropocene as site for ethnographic work at the speculative edges of what we know today; Human 2.0. East and Southeast Asian imaginaries; science fiction, painting, film, literature juxtaposed with ethnography.

PART I

Ethnography in the Meantime

KEYWORDS

1. Experimental Ethnography in Ink, Light, Sound, and Performance

KEYWORDS (IN THREE HISTORICAL HORIZONS):

1920S–1950S. *modernism, literary realism (translating the exotic, defamiliarizing the taken for granted), small worlds, montage, sonic alignments.*

1960S–1990S. *juxtaposition as comparative method, critical apparatuses, cultural accounting, internal contestation and imminent critique, productive double binds, dialogue and hospitality, the human condition as plural, everyday action as critiques of fanciful theory, policy plans, aggregate models, Third Cinema and cinema vérité (French vs. American versions).*

1990S–2000S. *digital infrastructures, indigenous media, smartphone video documenting, seeing through metrics and perverse incentives (ground-truthing), participatory design and forum drama as deliberative civic action, toxics and soundscapes as place making and as historical registers, multi-locale, multi-scalar granularities within globally distributed and differentiated processes.*

2. Ontology and Metaphysics Are False Leads

KEYWORDS

Gaia, ecology, biosensibilities; grammars of social action, emergent forms of life; ontology vs. ontologies; multi-species, companion species; capitalizing ecosystems; presuppositions, metapragmatics, renewed fables, parables, heuristic fictions, and language games; temporalities and anticipatory logics (the future-anterior, promissory legalities); pluralization.

3. Pure Logic and Typologizing Are False Leads

KEYWORDS

postal relations among modernities; coping with chaotic effects and assaults ("war cut"); situations of polemics and their social drama forms (alerts, trials); testing of self and of one's tools of perception, ethics, morals (truth, method, conduct); dealing with breaches of communal controls over public discussion; cultural politics (coalitional, class, migrant); torn religions and double-voiced biographies across historical and religious horizons; Greek tropes and affects (pathos, thumos, askesis).

1

EXPERIMENTAL ETHNOGRAPHY IN INK, LIGHT, SOUND, AND PERFORMANCE

Experimentalism, in the dual senses of rethinking form to expose content (the aesthetic meaning) and creating new ways of seeing and understanding (the science meaning) has characterized the conceptual edge of ethnography since at least the 1920s, as in turn it has addressed cultural rationalities, postcolonial transnational capitalist relations, and visual, sonic, and electronic media. It has done so in writing, in film, in sound, and in performance. This orientation chapter provides a rapid survey of developments over the past century in order to set the scene for the following chapters. Citations are largely put in footnotes so as not to clutter the text and make it unreadable. Even so, the citations could be multiplied: the coverage is not intended to be exhaustive but rather to sketch out tactics conceptually as they were introduced. Further historical contexts can be found in Fischer 2009a. I proceed through four broad historical horizons. Too often, accounts of ethnography get stuck in the first horizon's innovations, or they only begin in the 1980s without acknowledging the foundations on which those innovations were built. In footnote 23, I provide a quick account of my own involvements with some of the developments of ethnographic film, through teaching and talking with some of the filmmakers.

1910s–1960s. The first two generations of experiments using ethnography to build theory and cross-cultural conversation involved a series of modernist techniques for instilling a sense of "being there." These included linguistic transcripts, glosses, and translations;[1] "problem-focused" and development-related accounts of institutional domains labeled religion, ecology, or kinship;[2] internal social contradictions or schismogeneses;[3] serial cases studies to create a sense of structural fault lines;[4] comparative social structures;[5] forensic ethnographies of "development projects" such as mines and hydropower dams, and their devastations;[6] and the pairing of analytic monographs with personal fieldwork accounts.[7] Students were trained by reanalyzing ethnographies, using restudies[8] (a strategy that hopefully can be revived, see Morriera for a contemporary example[9]), and applying new forms of analysis to ethnographic and archival materials.[10]

At the same time, ethnographic film initially struggled with equipment, narrative form, and temporality: whether to capture skills of the hunt, artifacts, and rituals "before they disappeared," or to locate them as embedded in political and social changes. Both objectives had merit. As Lévi-Strauss has shown, there are logics and integrity to cultural forms that can be recovered from upheaval, population decimation, and changing hegemonies. Equally, just because one shows how a dance form or woodworking tradition operates does not mean that one cannot at the same time show the overlap of different historical horizons, or the conditions of the filmmaking.[11]

1970s–1980s. The renewal of the sense of experimentalism that came with *Anthropology as Cultural Critique: An Experimental Moment in the Human Sciences* (1986) and *Writing Culture* (1986) focused first of all on revisiting the tactics of *documentary realism* in text, but also in photography and film that capture elements not visible at the time of initial experience but that become inserted in memory through analytic and visual retrospection: for example, the experience of the Great Depression through the photography of the Works Progress Administration;[12] or today the effects of deindustrialization on communities, the sense of toxic contaminations, and politics.[13] Renato Rosaldo's study (1980) correlating the time lines of oral history and of army archives for the Ilongot in the Philippines similarly provided a double perspective not only on constructions of history, but on ways that hunter-gather groups manage space and time, something that gradually has become well recognized for Australian aboriginal societies through their oral-recounted "dreamings" (including references to Indonesian and other sailors arrivals long before the white colonial settlers) and now in their paintings. In Amazonia, similar attention to walking routes was supplemented spatially by rivers, and temporally by memories of epidemics, internecine wars, and resistances to colonial incursions (Ramos 1990/1995). Secondly, ethnographers began to recover and experiment with *surrealist juxtaposition and montage* that in the

1930s had animated mutual influence among artists and ethnographers.[14] These led thirdly to experiments staging multiple voices ("polyphonic texts") in dialogic, double-voiced, and triangulated forms[15] to reflect on *critical apparatuses of different cultural modes of accounting*, and on critique and conceptual *contestation within cultural traditions*.[16] The role of *fantasy*, *violence*, psychodynamics, or mental illness[17] was incorporated in ways that made readers gain a feel for distorted modes of perception, including more recently *ethnographic-documentary films* about civil conflict leaving postwar traumatic effects.[18] There were adaptations of cultural *genre forms* from cultures described, to give readers a feel for different styles and moments of communication and attention to the interplay of nonguild oral histories versus guild histories, including a growing interest in feminist counter-readings of many forms of official history-telling.[19] Ethnographic readings of narrative films explored spaces of cultural critique politically blocked from articulation in newspapers, and as registering the unfinished or undoing of modernities, especially through the "descent into the everyday."[20]

In ethnographic filmmaking, the 1950s through 1980s was also a time of fundamental experimentation, with contested and different forms of cinema vérité by Ricky Leacock, Tim Asch, John Marshall, David MacDougall, Robert Gardner, Jerry Leach, Gary Kildea, Jean Rouch, and Raul Ruiz; it was also the beginning of Third Cinema. In France, the idea of film vérité was to provoke people into authentic reactions. In the United States, by contrast, there was an idea of noninterference, and staging caused innumerable debates about authenticity. Ethnographic filmmakers also often reacted against Robert Gardner's style of aesthetic-poetic film, although tempered by anthropologist Akos Östör's work with Gardner (1986, 2001), a discussion that has recently been renewed with Barbash and Castaing-Taylor's otherwise gorgeously cinematic 2009 *Sweetgrass*, which replaces realistic sequencing in the annual cycle with a philosophical logic moving from domestication of sheep amid humans to a removal of humans from nature.[21] John and Lorna Marshall's longitudinal refilming among the Ju/'hoansi (San or !Kung Bushmen of the Kalahari) moved from romantic narration to activist defense of the Ju/'hoansi against being pushed into the desert fringes and being used as trackers and laborers by the South African Army.[22] In 1968, John Marshall and Tim Asch set up the Documentary Educational Resources (DER) nonprofit to archive and disseminate ethnographic films for the classroom, one of the first important such archives, opening up a way to pursue longitudinal changes over time, both "remakes" but also "overlays" with the same places and peoples under radically (or subtly) changed circumstances.

Meanwhile, Third Cinema, originating in Latin America, experimented with mixing documentary footage and narrative in a postcolonial critique of First World control over the flow of images, including the way documentaries were edited. Anthropologists such as myself taught courses insisting on using (often narrative) films made by people about their own countries and communities to explore cultural genres, sociopolitical positioning, and internal cultural critique (Fischer 1995b, c; 1997; 1999b; 2001; 2004).[23]

Another sensory innovation in experimental ethnography was to bring in sound, not only as ethnomusicologists had been doing but as what in the 2000s would develop into rich soundscapes in their own right as registers of place, environment, mood, and sense of space, as in the creative work of Ernst Karel at Harvard, or the new music notation work of Tim O'Dwyer (referenced in chapter 10). A pioneer in soundscape ethnography is Steven Feld, whose written ethnography *Sound and Sentiment* (1982) remains a classic example of taking seriously the critical interpretive apparatus of another culture, in this case how the sounds of the Papua New Guinea forest, and especially bird songs, signify for the Kaluli (Bosavi). He supplemented this with high-quality audio recordings of soundscapes, first for the Papua New Guinea rainforest, then, also with film and ethnographic writing, for Ghana as a site of jazz cosmopolitanism (2012) and for how bells (church, animal, and carnival) have created senses of space and time over ten centuries of European history (a still ongoing project). (See also Feld and Brenneis 2004; and for an inventive form for ethnography and sound, Wolf 2014). Historical soundscape studies, along with histories of the senses, are an emergent field stimulated by social history (Corbin 1995), German technology and philosophy studies influenced by Derrida (Kittler 1985 [1990], 1986 [1999]; Ronnel 1989), and science studies (Pinch and Bijsterveld, eds. 2011; Sterne, ed. 2012; Picker 2003; Thompson 2004; Morat, ed. 2014). Anthropologists have also been exploring the interactions of deaf cultures with their surrounding sonic worlds (Friedner 2015 in Bangalore), and sound in technoscientific spaces (Helmreich 2007).

1990s. The anxiety and anticipation of the coming digital, Internet, web-based, and YouTube forms of communication generated experiments to reinvent the ethnographic interview and print formats, especially in the eight-volume series *Late Editions: Cultural Studies for the End of the Millennium*.[24] At the same time, ethnography began to diffuse into applied fields beyond the traditional advertising (symbolic interactionism) and medical anthropology (health care seeking, doctor-patient relations, labeling, pathologizing, stigma, and medicalization), into nontext deliverables for corporations and user participation in urban and policy planning,[25] and into "interdisciplinary" genres in philosophy, literature, and history (e.g., "new historicism"),[26] ethnographically informed philosophy (Das 2007; Jackson 1996; Das, Jackson, Kleinman, and Singh, eds. 2014); and ethnographically informed novels (Ghosh 1996, 2004, 2008, 2011; Chandra 2006). New media began to be a topic requiring new modes of ethnographic work as well as reflection on how these media were changing modes of perception (Boellstorff 2008; Fischer 1999; Turkle 1984).

Toward the end of the 1990s and early 2000s attention began to shift toward indigenous media and the use of mobile digital video as forms of documentary and political activism (T. Turner 1992; Ginsburg, Abu-Lughod, and Larkin 2002; Wilson and Stewart 2008; Alia 2009; Schiwy 2009). There was also a flourishing of surveys of ethnographic film and studies of particular ethnographic filmmakers (Barbash and Taylor 1997; Connor, Asch and Asch 1999; Grimshaw 2001; Henley 2010; Lewis, ed., 2004; Loizos 1993; Morris 1994; Pearson and Knabe, eds. 2015; Rouch and Feld 2003; Stoller 1992).

2000s. Ethnography confronted social struggles over postconflict reconciliation; environmental pollution; climate change; new forms of media layering, including digital recursive publics and grammars of participation (Kelty 2008, 2017), and emergent grammars of social action and emergent forms of life more generally,[27] biomedicine, science studies, and big data informatics. The preparations of the 1980s and 1990s began to bear new fruit, particularly in figuring out how to deal with globally distributed, multiscale processes, including human rights and technology.[28] New experimental ethnographies worked both with multiple communicative modes and multiple strategic locales at different scales, from the global (e.g., harmonization of clinical trials or carbon and energy markets) to the national (e.g., state-mandated conservation against rights of locals to livelihoods and economic opportunity) to the local (e.g., dependence on clinical trials and NGOs for health care).[29] Ethnographies of dramatically different models for postconflict resolution in serial juxtaposition constitute a conceptual archive with which to configure new models of reconciliation and/or justice and prosecution seeking.[30] Aside from multilocale and multiscale ethnographic strategies, experimental ethnographies have tried to register differential temporalities and the fact that the arrow of time does not always move in the same direction. Science studies ethnographies have begun to register the access to third and fourth natures (Fischer 2009, ch. 3)—new biological and ecological knowledges of mutation and change; interactions with the alterities of companion species and the immunology of the biosphere—by interlacing the work of microorganisms, genes, prions, neurons, animal research, and disease, with science biography, ethnography, imperial and transnational programs, and competitions for credit and control over research.[31] Attention to genealogies and archaeologies of sociopolitical engagements can identify multiscalar loci and historical openings where alternative imaginaries, policies, and futures to those of expert– and economic lobby–led master narratives of progress and risk management can be envisioned, with space for thinking about the "public good."

Michael Fortun's (2008) *Promising Genomics*, for instance, provides an inventive use of chiasmus as a device to keep in mind trade-offs, contradictions, and ambiguities in the ethnographic material itself that play out politically, in cultural forms, as well as in the process of science discovery, patenting, and social access. It analytically presents an updating of Gregory Bateson's schismogenesis, as well as Stanley Tambiah's interest in social contradiction, oscillations, and paradoxes (see chapter 6), as well as contributing to a new series of investigations of *Lively Capital* involving promissory forms (Sunder Rajan ed., 2012), *Metrics* providing perverse technocratic incentives (Adams 2015; Adams ed. 2016), and always *Unfinished* explorations (Biehl and Lock ed. 2017); see also chapter 8. *Promising Genomics* integrates a high-profile science and political economy project together with the fishing economy, the tourist economy, and the cultural economy (Bjork, Kiko the whale, Halldor Laxness's novels) and thereby informs understandings of the overall nature of national investments and the more general dynamics of speculative economies.

The ability of recent experimental ethnographies to play up and down the entire scale, from ground to theory, policy to reality, and across globalized, distributed, or value chain processes, from locus to locus, is more than description or post facto identification of unintended consequences. Reality testing and grounded theory can upset echo-chamber master narratives that pass all too quickly from aggregation (abstracting, algorithmizing, modeling, simplifying from the data) to imperative policy formulation.[32] They provide a mode of juxtaposing (à la earlier surrealism) technological or other imaginaries with realities of implementation, and raise anew the relation between the powerful aesthetics of imaginaries and the materialities of building and maintaining socialities. The book series *Experimental Futures: Technological Lives, Scientific Arts, Anthropological Voices* (Duke University Press) is a venue for ethnographies in both the aesthetic and scientific sense of experiment, and a recognition that anthropology constantly needs reinvention for the challenges of the technological, scientifically informed societies in which we all increasingly live, whether in the center of such activities or in the interactively and relationally marginalized spaces.

In ethnographic filmmaking, too, new pathways have been charted: in personally grounded accounts of deindustrialization and marginalization (Chris Walley and Chris Boebel's *Exit Zero*, 2016, in conjunction with written ethnography Walley 2013; Rakhshan Bani-E'temad's *Our Times*, 2001, and *We Are Half of Iran's Population*, 2009, on electioneering women in Iran), in using local video and smartphone documentation, and tracking secondary reuses in art and activist circles (Fischer 2010; Lotfalian 2012), in contrasting styles of filmmaking on same or similar topics (on struggling fishing industries: *Fish Tail* (Joaquim Pinto, 2015) versus *Leviathan* (Lucian Taylor and Verena Paravel 2012); in finding ways to film interviews yet protect vulnerable individuals and groups (e.g., with ex-Colombian guerillas); in conjunction with more traditional ethnography (e.g., Alex Fattal's dissertation thesis film *Dreams from the Mountain of Concrete*, 2015); in the extraordinary films on mental health among survivors of the Indonesian massacres in 1965 by Robert Lemelson (*Forty Years of Silence*, 2009) and the controversial intervention films of Joshua Oppenheimer (*The Act of Killing*, 2012; *The Look of Silence*, 2014); in dramatizing migrant domestic worker struggles through a paraethnographic process of coscript writing with the workers in Singapore and the Philippines (*Remittance*, 2016, directed by Patrick Daley and Joel Fendelman); and in capturing the fraught tension of front line local doctors in Fukushima (in Sulfikar Amir's *Healing Fukushima*, 2017).[33] Some of the most exciting filmmaking continues along the lines of Third Cinema and the use of local footage in blurred genre filmmaking (such as Apichatpong Weerasethakul's *Cemetery of Splendor*, 2016; and Daniel Hui's *Snakeskin*, 2014; or even earlier in Iranian films that acknowledged and played with what in *Mute Dreams* [Fischer 2004] I called a dialogue between the figural and the discursive in order to put on display anxieties that are also culturally thematized[34]).

These are not your 1914- or even 1960s-style ethnographic filmmaking, but they are about what is happening today in the world, which, after all, is what ethnography is meant to help decipher.

Theater, and performance too, is another emerging, if underutilized, resource for ethnographic experimentation. It has credentialed anthropological roots in Victor Turner's collaborations with Richard Schechner in the 1980s (Harding and Rosenthal 2011), Stanley J. Tambiah's use of J. L. Austin's notion of performativity in his analysis of ritual forms (Tambiah 1985; Austin 1962), the earlier work of Erving Goffman (1956) and Harold Garfinkle (1967), and

Dorrine Kondo's work as a dramaturg with Anna Devere Smith in *Twilight Los Angeles, 1992*, a form of ethnographic portraiture called "verbatim theater" in the theater world (Kondo 1997).[35] Role playing and "design" workshopping have become increasingly popular in many fields to sensitize engineers, planners, and others to "user needs," or to teach social dynamics and leadership in team work and creating "learning organizations." Anthropologist George Marcus has pioneered a form he has dubbed "paraethnography" for the training of graduate student ethnographers by bringing interlocutors from the field back into the seminar room and having them stage problems in doing fieldwork. Felton James "Tony" Earles (2008) took these sorts of tools into the field, enrolling youths in Africa in a form of community theater as an intervention in the HIV/AIDS crisis, and using mobile video to identify dynamic indicators of likely violence hot spots in Chicago.[36] Cheryl Mattingly (2012) and Mary-Jo DelVecchio Good (2007) have done important analyses of the dramaturgy of therapy as a way of teaching medical personnel how to recognize the ways their communications with patients work.

Perhaps one of the most direct influences of Turner and Schechner today, however, is the remarkable thirty-year career of The Necessary Stage in Singapore (a collaboration largely of director Alvin Tan, who studied with Schechner and Turner, and playwright Haresh Sharma), as did Singapore's TheatreWorks's artistic director, Ong Keng Sen, described in the preface.

Good playwrights and actors are always doing what they call research, and what anthropologists would recognize as ethnography: interviewing people, visiting work sites, eliciting voices, watching postures, and attending to interactions in the real world in order to bring these onto the stage, sometimes just to get it "ethnographically right," for mimesis and catharsis, but more often, as in the work of Erving Goffman (1956) and Harold Garfinkle (1967) to stimulate more active explorations of boundary crossings, cultural tensions, and social crises. Drawing on 1970s anthropology's intense focus on sociolinguistics and performance in the context of intensifying intercultural encounters (and his own experiences in India, China, and New Guinea), Schechner aimed to produce new knowledge in the space between actors and audience, turning theater, or, as he increasingly insisted, "performance and performance studies," from mimesis to poiesis, from "mere" catharsis and scenes of recognition into active social events, adapting Turner's "social dramas" into unscripted social performances that explore, probe, and trouble audiences.[37] Performance and performance studies, he continues to argue, should not be for passive perception and reception by audiences (mirroring recognizable social conflicts, raising awareness) but should be experiential and transformative episodes (activating civil society, *experiencing* the world as it is otherwise, not always in politically correct or pleasant ways). Schechner and Turner are important, but only influences, in other performative settings: ethnographic discovery is always local. The intercultural and multilinguistic contexts of staging (theater, ritual process, performance) act translocally, rather than simply or smoothly globally, evoking different allegorical resonances, different emotional cues, different understandings. As times and political moments change, so do the spaces and modalities of social drama, performative testing of boundaries, and possibilities for ethnographic discovery.[38]

Haresh Sharma's play *Boxing Day* about the tsunami in 2004 is a verbatim theater (like Anna Deavere Smith's work) compiled from the transcripts of survivors in Sri Lanka, Thailand, and Aceh (Indonesia). It is just one particularly explicit ethnographic-style experiment in Sharma's ethnographic research style of preparation for his scripts. The Necessary Stage, Drama Box, Nine Years Theater, and other Singapore theater companies take this at least two steps further: cocreating scripts with actors of different language and knowledge backgrounds, and experimenting with forum theater in which audiences are invited to take up roles and show how they might try to handle situations differently to try to make the outcome work out differently (e.g., in one play, how to tell your very conservative parents you are gay), while the other characters react, showing how social situations might not be so easy to change.

In dance and art installation projects, as well, ethnography has become a vital tool not just for presentation but also for recovery of cultural forms and retooling for present cultural work. Multimedia artist Kiran Kumar (India-born, Singapore-raised, Berlin-based), for instance, has traveled through the Kaveri River basin in Tamilnadu with anthropologist, linguist, and theater studies scholar Saskia Kersenboom tracking Shiva temples in an inventive effort to do "live archeology" of dance traditions among the lower classes and to recover the meditative erotic and dialectical (and shamanic) movement forms of dance before their modern rationalization and codification by upper-caste nationalists in the twentieth century.[39] His ambitious project aims first to recover the dance forms of the three great empires (Chola, Kalinga, and Srivijaya) that form a continuum from more energetic and staccato Indian forms to ultraslow and fluid Indonesian forms, and, second, to thereby contribute to the emergent rich vocabulary of modern dance forms in South and Southeast Asia (Kumar 2017; Cherian 2016; Bharucha 1993, ch. 8). Similarly multimedia Singapore artist Zai Kuning, who represented Singapore at the 2017 Venice Biennale, has been trying to recover the pre-Islamic world of the Malay archipelago from Palembang, the capital of Srivijaya, to Thailand and the Riau Islands by traveling the worlds of the Austronesian sea peoples (*orang laut*) and tracing the ritual connections of pre-Islamic Malay opera. The cosmological orientations in the symbolism of the masked folk operas link the Riau Islands of Indonesia to Thailand, and across the Southeast Asian region (Kuning 2017; Massot 2003). These recovery processes of dance, movement, and cosmogenesis resonate in an interesting way with anthropologist Natasha Myers's work on dance movements as pedagogical modes of communicating, and modes of feeling one's way (visualizing, experimentally embodying, intuiting), to help figure out how particular proteins fold, among structural biologists (Myers 2015). In both cases there is a tactile, embodied, and symbolic mode of inquiry and physical engagement with the natural world.

Many anthropologists seem to have become frustrated by their old forms of writing (and sometimes activism) as having less and less of the social impact they imagined when they idealistically took up the discipline (and that iconic predecessors—Boas on racism, Redfield on education, Mead on child rearing, Lévi-Strauss on the transformational semiotic capacities of mythology and on the humanities generally—seemed to have). In response to their new positioning in the emergent multimedia worlds where cultures collide, mix, and morph (and are even used to re-veil forms of increasing injustices and inequalities with new ideological fears, pressures, and seductions), they might well look to collaborative theater and performance forms as ways to elicit workable alternative responses to social change, trauma, and building future worlds. These future worlds involve emerging technologies as well as increasingly toxic environments, which are themselves globally distributed battlefields of double-bind and opposed social forces and interests. Collaborative theater and performance forms are both pedagogical and civil society tools.

As with new approaches to ethnographic film, these are not your 1914- or even 1960s- or 1980s-style ethnographic methods, but they can help reimagine new ethnographic methods and pedagogies for today's quite different emergent forms of life.

2

ONTOLOGY AND METAPHYSICS ARE FALSE LEADS

How to address environmental and political issues in widely distributed places such as the Amazon, France, and globally will remain on the agenda for the foreseeable future. Orienting language and good intentions are needed but by themselves insufficient. On-the-ground knowledge needs to be mobilized: not just geographic and environmental knowledge, but also behind-the-scenes political economy maneuverings, incentive structures, and the mapping of unintended consequences. Attention needs to be paid to the critical apparatuses of linguistic and cultural modes of evaluation by people across enchained small worlds and socialities (both expert worlds with sound-bite amplifiers, and local vernacular worlds with force for everyday behavior and understanding). These different small worlds operate as transmission and operational links within larger distributed processes that set the grounds for decision making up and down the scales of social action. Within anthropology, Bruno Latour, Philippe Descola, and Eduardo Viveiros de Castro have become high-profile wordsmiths and slogan producers, and while acknowledging good intentions, I point out where their language breaks down and subverts those intentions. Latour is a consummate wordsmith and lexical renewer. He attempts to "bring the sciences into democracy" and dissect the "politics of nature" (2004). This is something that many of us attempt to do, in part by pointing to other ways of living or constructing relationships in the world, in part by diagnosing the toxic destructions and marginalization of populations that current capitalist expansions propagate, and in part by pointing to the expanding and gathering knowledge that the ecological, biogea, or Gaian sciences provide (Lovelock 1979; Margulis and Sagan 2003; Serres 2013).

At issue are the linguistic strategies of constructing ideologies or discursive regimes, of making particular ways of seeing seem natural or artificial. At issue are also the dramatic historical changes that societies undergo, reflected in their grammars of social action and emergent forms of life (Fischer 2003, chap. 2), and that "ontology" has a hard time accommodating, or does so only as pluralized ontologies, as if they were computer algorithms that can be changed merely by new command lines. The so-called ontological turn, propagated as a fad of lexical renewal, became a hot topic at the American Anthropological Association meetings in 2013. There were three major sessions: a panel with Viveiros de Castro and a dozen supporters and one dissenter (Elizabeth Povinelli), a distinguished lecture by Latour,[1] and a plenary at which Kim Fortun, Marshall Sahlins, and I were asked to respond to the new books by Latour and Descola, touted as flag bearers of this "ontological turn" that had just appeared in English earlier that summer. The plenary event had originally been intended to be somewhat different. Proposed by Emiko Ohnuki-Tierney as an effort to engage French and American anthropological traditions, the plenary panel, generously convened by John Kelley, instead got overtaken by the "ontological turn." Four years earlier, Viveiros de Castro had been in Paris for a debate with Descola that Latour had written up as a neutral *rapporteur* in a humorous fashion in a piece called "Perspectivism: 'Type' or 'Bomb'?" (Latour 2009). Latour was delighted by, if skeptical of, the theatrics of Viveiros de Castro "blowing up" Western thought. Perspectivism was touted as the "ontology" of Amazonian indigenous peoples, and was said to contrast sharply with the "ontology" of Europeans.

In addition to discursive structures (ideologies) and soio-historical change (emergent forms of life), a third intersecting strand, "multispecies anthropology," further muddied the field. Multispecies anthropology ranges from, at one pole, taking seriously human interactions with other species (e.g., Donna Haraway's essays from 2003 and 2007 on dog species trained and evolved for different functions in the human division of labor or bred as pedigrees shaped and sized for pleasure) to, at the other pole, mythic and metaphoric play with *human-human interactions*. These human-human interactions might, in turn, at one discursive pole, be mediated by bacteria, as in Latour's *Les Microbes: Guerrre et paix* (1984), sanitized in English as *The Pasteurization of France* (1988). In this book, Latour reflects upon the victory and consolidation of bacteriology as a new field of expertise over the hygiene movement, and while bacteria may have their own lives, at issue in that book are their effects on human interactions and diseases (farmers and microbiologists; transmission of syphilis, rabies, and anthrax), the theatrics of public demonstrations in leveraging scientific authority (among humans), and the debates in scientific journals (inscriptions by humans). Bacteriology became an "obligatory point of passage" for questions of infectious causation, displacing the more generalist hygiene movement that had sanitized an earlier stinking Paris full of miasma (Barnes 2006; Corbin 1986). Or "multispecies" can also refer to a biosecurity interest in preparations for new and globally emergent infectious disease pandemics, requiring a knowledge of the reorganization of ecologies, animal and insect control, and transportation (Spinage 2012; Fearnley 2013). At the other discursive pole, as is the case with many philosophers, are simply symbolic figurations with little concern for actual animals' or other species' lives, organizations, or ecological niches. Although Claude Lévi-Strauss shows that one can do both—attend to myth and ritual symbolic operators, and also attend to the ecological knowledge that mythic armatures can carry—most philosophical discussions are not actually so multispecies attuned.

The confusions generated among these different "brands" or "genders" of attention had the unfortunate effect, at the American Anthropological Association meetings in 2013, of overshadowing and preventing any real discussion between French and American anthropological traditions. Latour's longtime promotion of "human-non-human networks," for instance, easily melded with the ontological perspectivalism of Viveiros de Castro. Indeed, one commentator has since written, "Viveiros de Castro's multinatural perspectivism [is] a concept currently much celebrated by Bruno Latour" (Sullivan 2014, 231, citing Latour 2004, 2010b). Indeed, Descola, Viveiros de Castro, and Latour all lend themselves easily to projections of multiplying ontologies that operate like hypostasized "cultures" and "typologies" of colonial times.

The following essay is an effort to flag the confusions generated and the genres conflated. I take pains to distinguish Viveiros de Castro's ethnographic and linguistic work from his speculative ontology as different genres, signaled, as Latour might say, by different pre-positions or prepositions. Viveiros de Castro has invoked the speculative philosophy of Quentin Meillassoux as a kind of support for his own speculative work. This brings in yet another genre. Meillassoux tries to think beyond the "actually existing" world (before our world existed, after our world will have ceased to exist). While this is said to help critique the *sensus communis* (common sense) of ordinary life, the form of the critique is quite different from that pursued by ethnographic juxtapositions. The latter take us outside any single point of view, perspective, or cultural frame, precisely in order to see internal and external power relations, and semiotic processes among them, within the actually existing world. The former does not.

Discussions of the Anthropocene (to which I return in the final chapter) are another much-discussed contemporary rhetorical site where such speculative philosophy diverges sharply from ethnographic juxtapositions that provide the actual data for generalization. At best, such speculative philosophy might be grouped with the romanticisms that followed the 1968 Apollo 8 ("Earthrise") and 1972 Apollo 17 ("Blue Marble") pictures of Earth, generating discourses of planetary wholeness—the hope that suddenly people worldwide would cooperate in protection and stewardship of spaceship Earth. In contrast, ethnography (and its trackings of continued competitions, indifferences, other priorities, differential access to knowledge, mistranslations, and disinformation) might be grouped with the scientific explorations of the feedback and interactive processes that make up Gaia. Both are ongoing subjects of empirical hard work in continual updated data collection, modeling, correction, and fitting together of different scaled knowledges and experiential frames for understanding.

And so, channeling my earlier life in Houston near NASA's Johnson Space Center, as well as my present one at MIT, I began, at the plenary, with the call, "Houston, we have language problems more than a philosophy, metaphysics, ontology, incommensurability or bifurcation problem." I titled the talk "Double Click: The Fables and Language Games of Latour and Descola, or From Humanity as Technological Detour to the Peopling of Technologies" (Fischer 2013a). "Fables and language games" are terms that Latour uses of both science and his own work, but I pushed back against the playful, joking casting of humanity as *merely* a reflex or detour of technological networks.

Chapter 4 serves as an empirical and ethnographic buttress for the argument in this chapter by providing examples from Amazonia, the terrain to which Viveiros de Castro's claim about perspectivalism and ontology of predation is said to apply. Chapter 4 shows the fascinating and very lively ethnographic explorations of interactions of cosmological and sociological changes, power relations and subversions, among groups over the past four centuries and longer. That is, we need not engage in merely slogan terms (Fleck 1935) but have the ethnographic ability to be more targeted and systematic at many levels of granularity, together with the transductive linkages among granularities.

One way to redeem both Latour's linguistic and rhetorical work in *An Inquiry into Modes of Existence* (2013) and the strong desire of native rights defenders to embrace alterity-constructing "ontologies" might be to reattach it to venerable lines of French thought such as Guy Debord's *Society of the Spectacle* (1967). Along with Kim Fortun's response to Latour urging him to think about the landscapes of late industrialism (Fortun 2013), a recent set of essays under the title *Nature™ Inc.* (Büscher, Dressler, and Fletcher 2014) may also point a way to bring intentions and genre work together. *Nature™ Inc.*, invoking Debord, argues that "nature" has become capitalized through ecosystem services, carbon markets, and other financialization tactics of affixing tradable monetary amounts to ecological accounts. These capitalizations are guided by international treaty mechanisms (the Convention on Biodiversity) that channel money and capital instruments in directions that serve accumulation, are made to seem "natural" by commodity marketing of images and safaris into "pure nature" (spectacles), and absorbing some locals into the ranks of these industries. For a fascinating account of what such national reorganization looks like in one country through attempting to institute CBD rules, see Tamminen (2014) on Finland.

What is anthropologically disappointing, despite the good intentions, are the romantic accounts of animism that stress only the ecological sustainability potential and the absolute alterity of precapitalist forms of life as if they existed in prehistoric or ahistoric time. Sian Sullivan, for instance, admits that "animism is both 'a knowledge construct of the West' . . . and a universalizing term acknowledging a 'primacy of relationality'" (Sullivan 2014, 228). Sullivan acknowledges putting pigs and pests on trial in eleventh through fifteenth-century Europe (i.e., the pre-West or pre-Modern), but makes no mention of Gaia, a fully scientific effort involving many fields to encompass growing knowledges about the cycles of life on and of the earth. Efforts to live with what she calls "eco-ethical affects that enchance(d) ecocultural diversity and poetic meaning" (228) can be reinforced by our growing knowledge of the Gaia variety. We are unlikely to stop out-of-control capitalism by simply valorizing animism and attributing "affective relations" to it. Poetry alone could do just as well, without the need to invoke ethnography of knowledge systems of tribal societies. However, it is true that the charisma of being Native American adds affective weight, for instance, to the efforts in 2016 by the Standing Rock Sioux to block the Dakota Access oil pipeline from running across their land with the potential to foul their water, and to similar blockades across the Americas (see again chapter 4), with both successes and failures that are worth paying attention to. But this is due less to animism than to the modern negotiations over assertions of difference and identity, land and cultural rights, that Povinelli (2002, 2016) has written about with respect to Australian aboriginal land rights legal cases, and others have written about for First Nations treaty struggles in Canada (e.g., T. Özden-Schilling 2016).

A little more ground-truthing is in order if anthropologists are to be listened to.

Genres, Intentions and Joke Work

> *riverrun, past Eve and Adams* [even atoms], *from swerve* [Lucretian *clianamen*, Epicurean swerve of atoms, swerve as tropes, and Heraclitan "you can't step into the same river twice"] *of shore to bend of bay, brings us by a commodius vicus of recirculation back to Howth Castle and Environs.* —JAMES JOYCE, *Finnegans Wake*

Latour's *An Inquiry into Modes of Existence* (2013) is a meditation on language games. Without citing them, it is a meditation on the grammar of language games as described by Ludwig Wittgenstein (1953) and Jean-François Lyotard ([1983] 1988); and on performativity as described by William James (1890), Kenneth Burke (1946, 1950), J. L. Austin (1953); Richard Schechner (1985); and Victor Turner (1988). It is a meditation on "dreamabulatory theories of truth," as Latour delightfully does quote William James (Latour 2013a, 78). And it is a meditation on deixis and metapragmatics (Silverstein, 2003, 2017) as formal means of distinguishing modern European discursive categories and institutions, each defined by three criteria: the right pre-position, discontinuity from other language games, and felicity conditions. Latour's meditation comes with some surprising co-responses or correspondences located in rhythmic reprises or repetitions and constants across language games: these are his struggles against disenchantment (a reductive reading of Max Weber, e.g. 1922 [1968]) and toward a peculiar (even parochial) European feeling of discrimination: it is fair game, he repeatedly laments, to criticize Christianity but not other language games. We need thus, he suggests, an anthropology of Whites like him, of Moderns like him, who purify and purify their language games only to find themselves disenchanted, nostalgic for (Freud might say gently) childhood church melodies, or catacoustics, as Philippe Lacoue-Labarthe (1998) calls the tunes in one's head that keep coming back. In 2017, with the election of president Donald Trump and similar populist movements in Europe, the call for an anthropology of white supremacist and militant fundamentalist, often nonchurch, Christian ideologies that are still virulent in the body politic takes on a quite different valence and urgency than the seemingly genteel and good humored *ressentiment* of Latour in 2013.[2]

Philippe Descola's book *Beyond Nature* (2013 [2006]) provides an interesting counterpoint. He tries to think again with the "pre-Moderns," whatever that means, for here Latour, Wittgenstein, Lyotard, Austin, and James warn us to be careful about our pre-positions, our prepositions, marks of perspective and positioning. In particular, since Descola's ethnographic fieldwork was with the Achuar in the western Amazon (on the Peru-Ecuador border), his efforts at comparison in this new book invite further comparison with a number of breakthrough new ethnographies of Amazonia. I think here particularly of Lucas Bessire's work with the Paraguayan Ayoreo People-from-the-Place-Where-the-Collared-Peccaries-Ate-Our-Gardnes (Bessire 2012, 2013, 2014); of Eduardo Kohn's work with the Runa of Ecuador (Kohn 2013), and that brilliant Yanomami text by Davi Kopenawa, translated and annotated by Bruce Albert (Kopenawa and Albert 2013), which begins with a very contemporary ecological call wrapped in an ancient anaconda or harpy eagle's skin: "The forest is alive. The white people [the ghosts, those who speak strange languages] persist in destroying it. We are dying one after another, and so will they. In the end, all of the shamans will perish and the sky will collapse. . . . You must hear me—time is short" (vii).

Descola plays one of the language games of the Latourian Moderns, typologizing, looking for essential schemas composed of identifications and relations that are at best heuristics, and at worst impositions of a fourfold logic box, cross-sectioned with multiplicities of relationship typologies. Some of these crossings are unconvincing gestures to contemporary sciences—cognitive science, neuroscience, evolutionary psychology, and sociobiology—as if they could provide some confirmation, but Descola's primary effort is to assert that four particular ways of thinking are dominant, one each in four "archipelagoes" of contrasting types: animists in the Amazon, totemists in Australia, analogists in Siberia and in Foucault's renaissance Europe (Foucault [1966] 1971), and naturalists in his own asserted "common sense" and in Latour's parable Europe of the Moderns. I say "parable" or even "fictive" Europe (parables and fictions, Latour himself insists, are important sine qua nons of contemporary science), because all the Moderns named—Descartes, for instance—were not in fact Moderns by Latour's definition but are only a construction of a pedagogical or logic language game, straw men, reductio absurdum. Descartes, of all people, an experimentalist vivisectionist and anatomist who was prouder of those experiments than of his speculative philosophy, composed his notions of the pineal gland, of res extensa, and so on, post facto, to heuristically knit together plausible and temporary explanations and metaphors of what he was finding—conjectures and refutations (not ontologies).[3]

Descola reminds us of Lévi-Strauss's distinction between hot and cold societies (e.g., Levi-Strauss [1962] 1966), saying that naturalist ontologies are machines for multiplying hybrids, while animisms and totemisms are machines for preventing hybrids from further multiplying. They are cold societies assimilating all that is new into traditional categories and analogies, while we are constantly searching out new combinations.

It is logically odd, if sociologically touching, that the two Frenchmen, Latour and Descola, quote and praise each other, build a French gift-exchange social bond, even as their projects seem quite different, almost chiastic: with a *philosophe-theologian* (Latour) at one end and an *ethnographer-ethnologist* (Descola) at the other. The philosophe styles himself as a female ethnographer (an unconvincing gesture toward feminist demands for recognition, without otherwise engaging in gender analysis) of a mythical form of life called the Moderns or, sometimes, the Modernization Front (like the Popular Front) but is mostly an *eth*ologist and engineer determined to clear his networks of people, subjects, and individual actors, as well as, less controversially, of nouns that become hypostasized metaphysical Leviathans, such as God, Reason, and Society, but with a return in the end to religious feeling, to that which escapes words, or that uses words that are incommensurable and untranslatable. Meanwhile the ethnographer of the Amazon styles himself as an *ethn*ologist (grand comparativist), philosophe, and cosmologist.

Their meeting ground is their method, their common hypostatization of a limited number of modes of existence—four in Descola's case, twelve to fifteen in Latour's—that they can tabulate on charts just like other engineers (in the AIME Project, the acronymized and hypostasized "an inquiry into the modes of existence" and a webpage-based project with 175 crossings or hyperlinks[4]). But while Latour insists on a Principle of Irreduction and Free Association, Descola insists on binary axes and two-by-two logic boxes that are at best Geimasian (i.e., open to transformational development) in analogical, animistic, totemic, and naturalist directions.

Metaphysics and Ontology

As long as we are playing language games, and how can we not, I wonder what we would lose if we dispensed with the words "metaphysics" and "ontology," à la George Perec's ([1969]1994) lipogram novel, *A Void*, without an "e." Try it. Not to ban words, but their uses can be more discriminating, less black-boxed, as perhaps in the tactical use of "political ontology" for protection of Andean forms of life by Escobar (2018) and de la Cadena (2015).

"Metaphysics" is what—usually (but not only) in language—is errant, escapes closure or definition. "Ontology" similarly—at least for Heidegger and Sartre—is that which is split and dialectical, for instance, between what is ontic or phenomenological and what is ontological or beyond experience, located elsewhere: in the play or gaps among terms of reference; in the gestural, the self-reflexive, the deixical, and the pronominal (as Latour stresses); or in the cascades and the *khora* of the physical world (the Heraclitan swerves and spacings of atoms). Thus in Heidegger ([1929] 1962) and Sartre ([1943] 1956) we get the splittings between Being and Time (*Sein und Zeit*), and Being and Nothingness (*l'être et le néant*), while in the human geographer Friedrich Ratzel (1869) we get that between Being and Becoming (*Sein und Werden*). Derrida (1993) elegantly points out that hauntology and ontology in French are homonyms, and that the search for an ontology is always fully of hauntings or traces of alternative meanings, associations and histories which can upset the ontology framing and structuring.

This of course leads to questions of method, and that moment in Western philosophy of Friedrich Hegel's writings on logic, which Fredric Jameson (2013) points out was in its time a mathematical innovation preceding modern Boolean symbolic logic (1847; Hegel died in 1831) and was presented by Hegel in terms of a triad, *Sein, Wesen, Begriff*, badly translated in English, as if they were substantives, as Being, Essence, and Concept. But, for instance, Begriff, the last, is composed only as a kind of culmination and thus *future-anterior of itself*, while Sein and Wesen play out in ever-expanding series on their various Moments (punning in German on *der Moment*, a temporal notion, and *das Moment*, an aspectival or perspectival notion). Sein and Wesen, then, are a play, back and forth, *fort-da*, between everyday life and the categories and relations that inform it. "The onto-logical," Jacques Derrida says thus, "can always be reread or rewritten as a logic of loss or as one of unchecked expense [*dépens sans reserve*]" (Derrida [1967] 1978, 188).

So, what would it mean for an anthropologist, whose daily work is among the experiential, linguistic, structural, and institutional play of actually existing human beings and their interactions with their human and nonhuman companion species, ecologies, embodiments, and cultural semioses to not just inquire into the local metaphysics and cosmologies—fragmented, implicit, or located in the future-anteriors and relationalities of terms and concepts of local worlds and languages—but to also attempt to fix these in global or universal categories as constructions of the anthropologists' own metaphysics?

In these two recent books by Descola and Latour, we have before us two versions of this quixotic effort: the one, Descola's *Beyond Nature and Culture* ([2006] 2013), attempts to recapture schemas of fourfold cosmological differences that existed before the Moderns came into disciplinary being (à la Foucault) in the seventeenth century, but with roots back to (who else?) the Greeks, thus collapsing the West and the Modern into a common naturalism, which when all and said and done Descola himself claims as inescapably his own. The other version, Latour's *An Inquiry into Modes of Existence*, contemplates on the one hand multiplicities of twelve to fifteen language games, and on the other insists that at least two of these are beyond linguistic worlds, even though including words incommensurable and untranslatable beyond themselves: "love" and "religious speech." Empedocles, of course, long ago, in his poem "Purifications," versified about love and strife as the two forces that bring together or separate the four elements into the things of our empirical worlds.[5]

Love and Strife: White Mythology and Graceland

Latour's parable of the Moderns, the Whites, the Europeans, and the Evil Genius or serpent Double-Click is a Möbius strip–like variant on Jacques Derrida's essay "White Mythology" ([1972] 1982). The Whites are a coin whose inscription is worn away by use until what once was a vibrant living metaphor becomes just a dead unattended-to token, whited out, white inscription on white coin. Or, as Derrida says, "Metaphysics has erased within itself the fabulous scene that has produced it, the scene that nevertheless remains active and stirring, inscribed in white ink, an invisible design, covered over in the palimpsest" ([1972] 1982, 213). Latour's vibrant use of metaphor tries to undo the deadening of the Whites and the whitening out. The book *An Inquiry into Modes of Existence* (AIME) is formatted as a monologue or monograph, a myth, an Alice in Wonderland (Carroll [1865] 1903) picaresque tale, full of the markers of the genre, such as calling everything "astonishing" or alternatively expressing exaggerated surprise at the obtuseness of the Moderns and the Whites. The book, Latour says, is "*a charitable fiction*" (2013a, 15; emphasis in source). It is a how-to manual of instruction for an anthropology without human actors. "*Humanity is above all*," he says, "*the recoil of the technological detour*" (230; emphasis in source). The project calls for collaboration through a website—you too can be enrolled in the website's categories—a contribution Latour suggests to the digital humanities. The landscape today is of course littered with such calls for breathing life into websites gasping for traffic.

Latour takes his terms, he warns at one point, from information sciences, project management, and international legal negotiations, not exactly the most humanistic of libraries, but important language games. The project, moreover, he proclaims, must be finished by August 2014, a century after the Guns of August[6] of World War I. Game over, start again.

The project is formulated as about prepositions (or pre-positions, linguistic deixic markers of position), and in that sense follows in the footsteps of Wittgenstein and Lyotard's language games, John Austin's felicity conditions, and William James's prepositional pragmatism. Key to the modes of existence are their activities: verbs such as *vibrate* or *dispatch* [Latour, 250], adverbs, gerunds, prepositions, and two forms of deixis (*apo-* and *ep-i—apodeixis* for science or demonstration, and *epidexis*, or rhetorical flourish, for politics). Latour changes nouns into verbal forms, except to create an enemy. Society is one of these straw man enemies. He never tries to use the gerund "socializing," which generates multiple trajectories, including enunciatory communities that are more or less transient/permanent (K. Fortun 2001). Behind the scenes are cheap points still to be scored in favor of Gabriel Tarde against Émile Durkheim (Latour 2007), but mainly against social constructivism the advocates of which Latour once again demolishes delightfully, along with Heidegger and the philosophers of being-as-being (Latour 2013a, 220). Both Society and Individual are phantoms, he quips, created like children with glow lights at night drawing circles in the air that disappear as soon as the glow lights are put down. The metaphor comes in very useful again in Latour's wonderful chapter on politics.

These little tricks, prepositions, adverbs, and the like, are *an origami ontology*: the ability to create out of folds, lines, and angles quite elaborate structures, reversing the sensibility that structures are the frameworks giving coherence and form to parts. Origami was one of the devices used by Lévi-Strauss to model for himself the multidimensional complexities of the transformational topologies of South and North American mythologies. We are indebted to Philippe Descola for having this origami restored and preserved at the Musée de l'Homme. One of Latour's bon mots is that the whole is not greater than its parts but, on the contrary, the parts are greater than the whole (Latour 2012; 2013a, 420). In an origami sense that may be true.[7] The backstage ruse-target here again is Durkheim, the front stage target remains social constructivism.

Actor network theory in this book has now lost, for better or worse, its actors, and is now purely networks, at times with "padding" (Latour's term), but mainly made active through holes, gaps, and leaps (perhaps even nowadays synapses, though I don't think that word appears in the book's 488 pages). It is a double idea of passages and constants: networks are composed of heterogeneous elements, and something circulates through them, thus they are discontinuous (hiatuses between heterogeneous elements) and yet have trajectories and direction, continuous passes or passages through alternations and differences. To say something is to say something differently, to translate, to metamorphose, to metaphorize; but there are constants too: the angles of origami, or the immutable mobiles across maps, photos, surveying lines, satellite images, and the ground—these are constants.

Despite the book's attention to prepositions (Michael Silverstein might say "pragmatics" and "metapragmatics"; e.g., 2003, 2017) and to the tagging of modes of existence by three-letter codes (DNA anyone?) that Latour calls object-oriented languages (from computer science), what the book claims finally to want to be about is morality and, evasively but importantly, ecology in the Anthropocene and the sensitive Gaia—trembling with extreme weather, climate change, pollution, earthquakes, and volcanism—planet Earth on which we (for the moment) live. Latour seems convinced (by Sloterdijk [Latour, 2008]) that we have only one Earth to work with, and doesn't contemplate, as many space scientists and undersea explorers do, that we may both have to colonize beyond our current habitats and perhaps even evolve our bodies. One thinks of the anthropologist Valerie Olson's work (2011) on NASA's exploratory preparation for space exploration in extreme environments. But at Sciences Po, Latour has actors staging ways to face the emotional and cognitive challenges of an apocalyptic collapse of Gaia, not unlike the apocalyptic futurism of the Paraguayan Ayereo.

If we consider Latour's book a kind of encyclopedic novel, that is, a text that attempts to register the European world of knowledge at the moment (like *Finnegans Wake* [Joyce 1939], or *Gravity's Rainbow* [Pynchon 1973]), we can understand why there are few references but many well-known phrasings, and, more importantly, it gives us a rationale for why some corrections might be of little consequence, while others might be more consequential. When Latour asserts that, "strangely enough, in the history of anthropology there haven't been any 'first contacts' with the Whites" (2013a, 478), one wants to say, "But what about the many volumes in White Studies (Dwyer 1997; Lipsitz, 2006; Saldanha 2007). But perhaps that's just additional bibliography. Similarly there is the odd suggestion (173) that we need a museum for the Whites, when surely we have a surfeit of those. When Latour writes that we know the moral only "when we feel tormented by a moral scruple. Nothing changes, and yet everything changes" (459), we feel ourselves immediately in a Durkheimian world (Durkheim 2015) and Latour elsewhere insists like Durkheim or George Herbert Mead (1934), on the self as being through others; but here he wants to take the thought in the direction of starting over, the *reprise*, did I do the right thing, can we run it again? That's the moral struggle.

Although I might go along with much of Latour's sensibility about morality and religion, that is, the importance of the activity of reprise, of always starting over, reevaluating, I do not recognize this as dominant in the historical record. The historical record accords rather a fragile thread to tolerant metaphorical and interpretive play. Indeed, the lack of topics such as warfare[8] and the integration of former enemies, mental illness, poisonous knowledge, widening inequalities, and the now shifting transnational forces of hegemony make this a text one of benign neglect, although in one pithy sentence Latour does point out gleefully, "Anyone who accepts the Moderns' claim to have had at least the immense merit of having done away with the taste for human sacrifice must not follow the news very closely, and must know very little about twentieth-century history" (2013a, 169). "Gotcha." One wonders if Latour has in mind Stephen Pinker's improbable *The Better Angels of Our Nature: Why Violence Has Declined* (2011), defining violence so as to exclude most forms.

Like all multidimensional and tabular systems (one thinks of Talcott Parsons [e.g., 1951] or Niklas Luhmann [e.g., [1984] 1995), everything can be accommodated. "Ecology" and "Gaia" are words that come up as ways of the future, but only in the Gifford Lectures (Latour 2013c) do they receive focal attention. In one brilliant ethnographic detail, Latour does note, in passing, that European vultures have learned to eat fresh meat ever since the European Commission passed a degree forbidding sheepherders from leaving dead sheep in the fields for them.

Gaia and the Anthropocene, R.U. Sirius? I joke, but Latour points out that the term in French for "the view from nowhere" is *le point de vue de Sirius*, a view he and anthropologists in general have argued we cannot afford. He puts on the table two important projects that many of us in anthropology are already trying to join together: the first is what I have called (2003, 2009), after Wittgenstein (1953), *nurturing emergent forms of life involving biological and ecological sensibilities*; and what Latour (2013a) calls after Étienne Souriau (1943) "modes of existence." The second has to do with a kind of *diplomacy* (Latour's term): can comparative anthropology provide us with credible tools for planetary negotiations among the vernaculars and forms of life that matter (a question taken up empirically for climate change by Candis Callison [2014], and for living with toxicity by Kim Fortun [2001])? In the *AIME* book, he is still unable to say more than that we experience a double displacement from economy to ecology: "The first is uninhabitable, the second not yet ready for us" (Latour 2013a, 23).

Yet what Latour has to say about the modes of existence of the law, science, politics, religion, and economics is worth attention; as are his general rhetorical strategies of inversion, paradox, and analogical ruses to make a point. Each of the modes of existence are defined by three criteria: (1) the right pre-position, (2) a discontinuity from other language games, and (3) felicity conditions. These constitute each language game's own form of "veridication." One can tell one is speaking in the wrong language game when there is a category mistake bearing on one of the felicity conditions.

Of the twelve to fifteen language games Latour sketches, I want to draw attention to the five or six I think most delightful and instructive, and the most worked out: economics, law, politics, science, and religion (and ecology, which is not in the *AIME* book but elsewhere). For me this is the core of Latour's project, and is what will be useful for the classroom when discussing the ideas of Wittgenstein, Austin, Lyotard, William James, Walter Lippman (1925), or John Dewey (1927).

Economics

Latour repeats the Maussian and Polanyian themes (Mauss [1925] 1967; Polanyi 1944) that the disembedding of the economy is never complete, and what is at stake in the economy is never objective knowledge but instead "attachment, organization, distribution and morality" (2013a, 464). He says had economics started with these anthropological questions, "it would have become a great science of passions and interests . . . coextensive with anthropology or the history of exchange" (464). But that *is precisely* where Adam Smith (1759) started, with passions and moral sentiments. Thomas Malthus (1803), Mauss ([1925] 1967), and Polanyi (1944) followed suit, and then in the 1970s Gary Becker, as Foucault ([1979] 2008) reminds, followed with *human capital* calculations of American neoliberals that reshaped the passions of the individual into commodified, educationally calculated, and self-entrepreneurialized forms. Following on many anthropological accounts, Latour summarizes, "Everything here is hot, violent, active, rhythmic, contradictory, rapid, discontinuous, pounded out—but these immense boiling cauldrons are described to you [in economics and management speak] as the icy-cold, rational, coherent, and continuous manifestation of the calculation of interests" (2013a, 376); and "the public square appears emptied of protagonists; only the incontrovertible result of unchallengable deductions made elsewhere" (376). In addition, "organizational consultants, coaches, managers, downsizers, earn small fortunes by tracking down the multitude of 'contradictory injunctions' that pull the participants in contradictory directions" (396). "Arrangements of calculation never had the goal of knowing objectively, but made it possible to express preferences, to establish quittances, trace ends, settle accounts, set limits to what would otherwise be limitless and endless, offer instruments to those who must distribute means and ends" (464).

The Law

It is with the law that Latour is most clear about the constitution of a mode of existence that is self-contained and where he is able to identify quasi-subjects and quasi-objects most sharply. When lawyers are asked to define what they do, "they string together long sentences in which they unfailingly use the adjective 'legal' to qualify everything they say" (Latour, 359); "is there a legal *means*? . . . this *means* won't get us anywhere" (38; emphasis in source). Like Max Weber on rationalities, Latour notes, "One can complain about the law that it is formal, arbitrary, constructed but not that it is irrational" (59). He quotes H. L. A. Hart (who sounds like he stepped out of one of Annelise Riles's books (1996, 2011) or, indeed, like secretary of state John Kerry arriving in Geneva for negotiations over Iran's nuclear programs on November 10, 2013, saying he had crafted texts all prepared ahead of time with "bracketed language," that is, the spaces between brackets, open to adjustment: "Rules of law provide individuals [or representatives of countries] with *the means to* fulfill their intentions, by endowing them with the *legal power* to create, through *determined procedures* and in *certain conditions*, structures *of rights* and duties." The law, religion, and politics all produce what Latour calls quasisubjects, or what Foucault or Althusser would call positions of subjectivation and interpolation. It is an admirable feature, Latour argues, that these "allow us *never to begin with acting, thinking, speaking* human beings, capable of creating technologies, imaging works, or producing objective knowledge" (2013a, 372; emphasis in source). "Humanoids become humans by *dint of association* with the beings of technology, fiction, and reference; they become skillful, imaginative, capable of objective knowledge by grappling with these modes of existence [or language games, or Ernst Cassirer's 'symbolic forms' (1923)] which externalize and articulate thought" (372). Hence they are quasi-objects that provide offers of subjectivity to quasi-subjects which come to fill the still empty form of the implicit enunciator (372).

Politics

Latour's method provides the most insight here. For many years Latour has been metaphorizing the Icelandic *Thing*, or parliament, into the trope of the "parliament of things," nonhuman objects and human-nonhuman assemblages that require repeated discussions (parliaments) about how they matter: "matters of concern" rather than "matters of fact." At one time, he suggested that the United States was too wrapped up in its imperial entanglements to be able to think straight about democracy, and that Old Europe would provide a more seasoned and pragmatic path toward democratic development in the technological age. "But it does not appear," he pronounces, "that members of other cultures wish to become citizens of a free government—at least as long as they have not redefined the words 'citizen,' 'freedom,' and 'government' in a thoroughgoing way in their own terms" (Latour, *Inquiry*, 332). One wonders with whom in China or Iran or Brazil he's been conversing. Indeed, "democracy can't be parachuted in from a US Air Force plane," a trope explored in the Iranian films *Secret Ballot* by Babak Payami and *Testing Democracy* by Mohsen Makhmalbaf, but which Latour credits to one of the Whites, a Modern-who-has-never-been-modern, the European philosopher Peter Sloterdijk. Latour says, "Our ethnographer can stay home in Europe and discover many things" (332). I am less convinced that this is all that productive in our pluralistic world.

But these are quibbles: Latour's real message, brilliantly laid out, is that speaking politically is a matter of Circles, a kind of Nietzschean Eternal Recurrence (Nietzsche [1885] 1917): "Speak publically in such a way that you will be ready to run through the entire circle, coming and going, and to obtain nothing without starting over again; and never to start again without seeking to extend the circle" (Latour 2013a, 348). Unlike economics, which empties the agora, political speech refills it. Unlike economics, which turns down the heat of action to the coldness of calculation in order to effect distribution and call arguments to quits, political speech and the activity of moral-bearing beings engage in the violence and chaos of the agora over and over. It is in this mode of existence that the public is created phantasmatically by a continual reprise, like the metaphor of the circles and shapes created by the child with the flaming stick as long as the stick keeps moving (352). It is an ephemeral achievement when the crowd of many opinions and interests and passions can unify and come to a consensus only to turn back from unity to multiplicity and have to start again.

"If Callicles set out to judge Socrates's geometric proof by the yardstick of the Circle, he will misinterpret it as surely as if Socrates claims to be teaching Callicles the art of speaking straight to an angry crowd" (Latour, 349). They are different logoi, appropriate to different language games, different modes of existence, different forms of life. Politics is always "object-oriented" (Latour nods toward the vocabulary of what he calls the information sciences but is more specifically a term from programming languages such as Java). But politics escapes that "aberration called political science," a field Latour skewers as an effort "to replace the overheated blood of the body politics with one of those frozen liquids that quickly change into solids and allow the plastination of corpses offered to the admiration of the gawkers according to the modus operandi of the sinister doctor Gunther von Hagens" (335).[9] He comments, "Monster metaphors are mixed in here on purpose because one cannot do political anthropology without confronting questions of teratology," or abnormalities (335), and he even slams the Foucaultian term "governance" as sanitized.

Science

Science is another mode of existence whose conditions of felicity Latour has long been teasing out. Its "proofs," like "means" in the law, or the *predications* of religion, depend upon "all that is required to *maintain* scientific facts." *Maintain* is the key word here. All that is required depends upon networks of heterogeneity. "*Scientific results do not depend on the humans who nevertheless produced these results*" (Latour 71; emphasis added). They depend on chains of reference, populated with fictive beings (galaxies, particles, upheavals of mountains, valleys, viruses, DNA) that are paper and words that "have to be launched through the world like so many carrier pigeons" (250). "No science is possible, especially no abstract science, unless the world is populated by these little beings capable of going everywhere, of seeing and submitting to the most terrible trials *in place of* the researcher trapped in her body and immobilized in her laboratory. It is these *delegates* that we have trusted since the seventeenth century, to go off and travel everywhere . . . and bring back references . . . across the . . . cascade of **INSCRIPTIONS**, ideographs" (251; emphasis in source; capitals and bold in source as crossing points of the modes of existence). This aphoristic inversion—arguing that it is fictions (not scientists) that travel on scientific expeditions—is delightful and amusing but not much of an improvement upon models, hypotheses, measurements, and the other paraphernalia of ordinary science talk, and, incidentally, shortchanges field scientists who are not "immobilized in [their] laboratory," such as anthropologists. Of course, they are "characters," and they are "made." You and I are characters, too. We make up ourselves and each other as we go along. The device here is to shift the verb of action to devices and stories, away from people.

Religion

Religion becomes central to Latour's project of looking for morality-bearing quasi-subjects and quasi-objects. He searches for the enchantments that he, like so many Moderns, claim are in danger of being lost. He began, he says, as a militant Catholic student of theology, did a PhD in theology, and today is embarrassed to talk, even to his family, about why he likes to go to church. I certainly can identify with his vision for tolerant forms of speaking religiously, his stress on the power of a loving word, on going to Lourdes not for a cure but for *conversion to* a spirit of *caring for others*. Speaking religiously, paradoxically, must express both *fidelity* to the past and *innovation* to stay relevant. Latour condemns literalism, fundamentalism, and claims of religion to be both inerrant and clear in meaning. "Etymologically, religion is the relationship among, or better, the *relativism of interpretations*" (Latour 2013a, 311; emphasis in source). One wishes the Church had recognized this during the Inquisition.

Some of Latour's grammatical felicity conditions here work well: "Speaking *morally* engages one in an entirely different way from speaking *about* moral problems; again the adverb leads to a different proposition from one associated with the corresponding domain" (Latour 459). Infelicity in this mode is suspension of the reprise. Thus to say what's the point in being moral if I am saved "betrays religion and morality" (459). "What happens to us when we feel tormented by a moral scruple: nothing changes, and yet everything changes" (458).

And yet there are problems. Latour has written several essays exploring this mode of existence. "In Thou Shall Not Freeze Frame," Latour expertly picks apart three Catholic paintings to demonstrate that they do not naively depict miracles, divine messages, or resurrection but are allegories of the hide and seek of presence and salvation. They are intended to instill a transformation in the listener and speaker, bringing the good news of agape, turning away from the distant objects of the world to the presence of salvation in the world. Religious speech acts are like "I love you," a heart-stopping tiny time shift that changes a relationship when judged true (Latour 2011, 102) and can as easily be reversed by a false move, word, or gesture (104).

Oddly, however, this leads Latour to claim that "there is no point of view from which one could compare different religions and still be talking in religious fashion" (Latour, 101). So much for the many parables exchanged across religions along the Silk Road among Muslim Sufi, Christian monk, Hindu pandit, Buddhist and Jain monk, and Confucian sage; so much for the borrowings across scholastic traditions of just the kinds of deconstruction and redirection of attention to rhetoric, poetics, grammar, dialogues of love, metaphors, and pragmatics, and attention to paintings, chants, ritual, and passion plays that Latour rediscovers. Above all, Latour's claims for the self-enclosedness of religious speech is unduly pessimistic about precisely the pluralist worlds that we inhabit. I have no difficulty, myself, engaging in mourning processions for Imam Hussain, beating my chest rhythmically to the chanting; or, indeed, getting into the cadences and imagery of the call and response of a good Southern Baptist–style sermon—even though I do not accept the *doxa* that often accompany either, and indeed worry about the negative crowd effects and other negative political consequences they often generate, just as I worry about the often fanatical religious lives in which Latour's Catholic paintings participated.

More generally, I worry about the seeming tendency of both Latour and Descola (in their different ways) to interpret Christian beliefs and practices generously but to ascribe to others an inability to deploy metaphor and allegory as philosophically and with equal self-awareness. (We speak religiously, they have ontologies.)

Latour's lyrical book *Rejoicing: Or the Torments of Religious Speech* ([2002] 2013), for instance, is grounded in Catholicism, with a Protestant lament about aloneness in the world and anxiety about the reduction of the sensuality of the Church rituals to the instabilities of the Word. At times there is even a Jewish Talmudic renewal of the word, although Latour rejects "the high price of exegesis . . . the constraints of erudition" (56)—precisely that in which the weekly Jewish services revel, the *drashas* and debates, the search always for more and more of the infinite meanings of the layered and allusive and deconstructible text, meanings that make sense here and now, for those who read and interpret it as if it is, as it is, addressed to them, for they make it so, not always and every time, but often enough to come back for more as well as for the sensuous community of the rhythmic chanting and swaying, the ritual wine, the food, the family, and the honors of performing a portion.

Latour's text begins with the discomforts of doxa, as if unaware of the many religions that do not ground themselves in doxa but in varying degrees and fidelity to orthopraxis (hold the theology). Latour models his account of religious speech on that of lovers coming through a quarrel and rediscovering their love. Love needs to be directly addressed, no good telling her that you already told her last year you loved her; and certainly no good to go into the etymology of the words for love. There are at least four of these felicity conditions, and five infelicity conditions of false religious speech. Religion has to do with conversion of distance into closeness, with a hoisting of the sling of love (a kind of bootstrapping) from lovers "alone in the world" and aggregates of strangers into something like a holy people. "In religion," Latour says (ignoring the Qur'an), punning, "you don't find any directly addressed speech—any more than, in the sciences, you find clear utterances that aren't heavily rigged" (Latour [2002] 2013, 83). (Rigging can be the supports of the ship's sails, or the setups that ensure an outcome rather than surprises: scaffolding or corruption.) In a lovely passage, Latour revels in Saint Mark's Gospel, but pays no attention to its parables, rather suggesting a kind of structural analysis in columns (like Lévi-Strauss's [1967] "The Story of Asdiwal"): tags, ruptures, violent reactions, incomprehension, cautions, and refocusing. Thus the text provides models of and models for the stutterings (a Mosaic trope) of religious understanding and speech. In a Levinasian mode Latour remarks, "Let's try again. 'God is nobody' sounds strange to our ears," but it would not be "shocking . . . either for the faithful or for the unfaithful . . . to say: 'The thing that turns us into individuals who are close and present might well, in certain places and certain times, have been called God, but we could also, today, just as easily call it by another vocable, such as 'The thing that begets neighbors'" ([2002] 2013, 135)—what Levinas might call the trace of the divine present in the face of the other ([1972] 2003; [1974] 1978).

Ecology, Gaia, and the Anthropocene

The terms "ecology," "Gaia," "Anthropocene" get only passing mention in the book *An Inquiry into Modes of Existence* but are the focus of Latour's recent Gifford Lectures, "Facing Gaia: Six Lectures on the Political Theology of Nature." Latour has claimed that "the central aim of the [AIME] project is to save the planet" (2013b). Gaia is the immunological reaction of the earth forcing us to move from viewing "nature as implicit conditions of existence to *fully explicitated* [*sic*] conditions of existence." Recalling Michel Serres's ([1990] 1995) notion of natural contracts, like legal contracts, contracting limiting and expanding relationships and networks, Latour (2013b) speaks of reworking social contracts with Gaia. Gaia is now a summoning entity, as the gods used to be, requiring new rituals and a "new political body yet to emerge." The earth has been placed into a "state of exception" (Schmitt [1922] 2005), or a radicalized "risk society" (Beck [1986] 1992), "obliging everyone to make decisions because of the extremes of life and death." With his eye for rhetorical inversion, Latour says "primary qualities" (nature, objective reality, Gaia) are being now marked by sensitivity, agency, reaction, and uncertainty, while the secondary qualities of human interpretive capacities and emotions are marked by indifference, insensibility, and numbness. Although Gaia is in a "feverish form of palsy, falling catastrophically from tipping point to tipping point in a rhythm that frightens climatologists even more with the publication of each new data set" (Latour 2013c, 80), our human emotions are not matched. Unlike the urgency and speed with which the arms race in the Cold War was able to be drummed up, the politics of climate change is languid (113).

Here Latour turns dramatically Durkheimian, calling on apocalyptic prophecy, playwrights, curators, and composers to create rituals for survival. The Circles of politics are enhanced where climate skeptics show how much ways of life are threatened, whose interests conflict with whose. The membrane and loops of Gaia in which humans are cocooned must be kept "traceable and publically visible or else we will be blind and helpless" (Latour, 95). Gaia is not a sphere but "is a tiny membrane, no more than a few kilometres thick . . . not made of loops in the cybernetic sense of the metaphor, but in the sense of historical events expanding," and understanding the contradictory and conflicting connections "can only be accomplished by crisscrossing their potential paths with as many instruments as possible" (95).

The lyricism is not unlike that of Davi Kopenawa's speech to us from the Amazon (Kopenawa and Albert 2013). Let us turn, then, to Descola's view from the Achuar ([1986] 1994, [1993] 1996, 2006 [2013]), and his claim

([2006] 2013) that cosmologies can be typed into four ontologies and seven-plus-seven modes (of which he chooses to elaborate on only two—although by the epilogue the two have become four modes of identification, and six modes of relation). It is much easier to keep track of the geographical instantiations. Using Latour's notion of language games and their conditions of felicity, we might ask to whom the typology is addressed, or for what purpose. It is somewhat of an anticlimax after four hundred pages to be told by Descola that his aim is merely to propose an account of diversity, and that it is a mistake to think that the Indians of Amazonia, the Australian Aborigines, or the monks of Tibet can bring us a deeper wisdom, and that he forswears both nostalgia and wishful thinking. Good grief, then, what's the point? At least we should be making friends (Fischer 2014). This aside, we can assume a point of view from the Achuar as a reference for contrasts both within the region against other so-called animist cosmologies and across regions with analogism, naturalism, and totemism.

Seeing through Achuar Eyes

Descola tries to chart Siberian and North American groups on a north-south historical gradient from animism to analogism. He tries to chart Amazonian cultural groups as transformational sets of animism. These are thought provoking but unsuccessfully selective and schematic. They feel like a regressive revival of comparativism in human geography tradition, correlating habitats and mythologies/cosmologies, regressive in losing much of the rich detail that geographers have compiled. Insofar as theses classifications tenuously connect to Latour's project, it is through the work of the wide-mesh human-nonhuman networks of cosmological modes and relations.

Latour, by contrast, explicitly eschews direct concern with non-Europeans in the AIME project (in his Karlsruhe presentation of it, 2013b) to focus on the central institutions of modernity. In the focus on central institutions of modernity, he repeats the call of *Anthropology as Cultural Critique* of 1986, but that call was inclusive of non-Europeans (Marcus and Fischer 1986). Latour also is among the many who call for exploring digital platforms as media for emerging "digital humanities."[10]

When in the late 1970s Descola wrote about the Achuar *In the Society of Nature* ([1986] 1994), he tells us he struggled to free himself of the abstractions of his teacher, Louis Althusser. He wrote instead, he says, in a structural-Marxist Godelier frame of "domestic economy" [Godelier [1966] 1973) filled with underexploited premarket forces of production, seeing the Achuar as one of the original "societies of affluence" (quoting Marshall Sahlins, [1972]). Lévi-Strauss was a savior from Althusser. References to Lévi-Strauss are mainly to ecological features in the land and mythology, and to trade and exchange relations.

In *Beyond Nature and Culture* ([2006] 2013), instead of Althusser, Descola metabolizes Eduardo Viveiros de Castro's advocacy for a special kind of perspectivist cosmology of predation, cannibalism, and reincarnation as prototypical of lowland Amazonia, one that inverts the Western or Modern model of nature and culture. Nature here is the variable, and culture the constant. Animals are people too, and have their own communities and shamans, inverting European claims that jaguars are not persons. Descola implicitly contests Viveiros de Castro's multinaturalism-monoculturalism and cosmology of predation by showing contrasts among Jivaro; Arawak-speaking Campas; Turkano—especially the eastern Turkano, who marry (rather than steal) speakers of other languages (studied by my MIT colleague Jean Jackson); and in particular the Matsiguena, who have institutionalized the elimination of dissent, including oral jousts ending in self-beating immediately imitated by one's jousting opponent. Nonetheless, Descola describes the Achuar, following the multinaturalist-monocultural doxa, as predators, and even asserts sociobiologically that predation is deeply wired into human phylogeny. The Achuar must incorporate whatever is other in order to make themselves complete. Eating your enemies, stealing women, and so on is thus not really fierce or violent but ontologically felicitous. The animals that we eat are our affines, and the plants that we grow are our children, although Achuar know the difference: women do not give literal birth to plants; they just talk to them. Insects are not persons to the Achuar; complete persons are those who have language, that is, humans. So there is a dualism, a nature-culture divide, if one must insist on this now dogmatic division,[11] albeit perhaps slightly differently drawn. The insistence along with Latour that only Europeans are dualists and that that is the original sin of the Modern seems to fall apart. Descola's adoption of the multinatural-monocultural doxa, I think, undercuts his own rich ethnography, for instance, the "topological ballet" of Jivaro headhunting, which in Victor Turner liminal ritual fashion is a fusing together of conceptual opposites [Turner 1969]. Over twelve months, Jivaro shrunken heads are given a unique face modeling the victim's features; yet ritually they must be generic Jivaro, "never called by the patronymic . . . face carefully blackened to obliterate the memory of the patterns painted on it; . . . orifices sewn up, thereby consigning the sense organs to an eternal phenomenal amnesia" (Descola [2006] 2013: 340).

In the dispute between Joanna Overling and her disciples emphasizing altruistic mutual production of exchange of persons and generous conviviality, and Viveiros de Castro and his disciples emphasizing "generalized predation" as "the prototypical modality of relationship in Amerindian cosmologies" (Descola 327), Descola notes that the Jivaro's "ceaseless wars were a source of perplexity . . . and a motive for anathema" (327) among nonaboriginal commentators. The stakes are high. The effects of assigning the Yanomami nearby the attribute of "the fierce people," and accepting "predation" as the ontological mode of animists of the Amazon basin, has had, many anthropologists argue, serious negative effects on their legal rights, health services, lives, and rights to recognition.

Grammars of the Forest of Mirrors

The generalized predation and multinaturalism-monoculturalism doxa overlooks quite a number of things. As Alicida Ramos has pointed out, "Perspectivism bypasses the political reality of interethnic conflict." She faults Viveiros de Castro's disciples as producing accounts that make all Amazonian Amerindians look the same "regardless of where they are in the Amazon, what their linguistic affiliation is, and which historical paths they have trodden" (2012, 482).[12] The Achuar, as Descola's wife, Anne Christine Taylor, has shown, expanded and then withdrew from the effects of rubber tapping, logging, and oil drilling to the relatively isolated region that Descola selected for "salvage" anthropological study (Descola's characterization). But their trade relations with the outside world include dogs, guns, salt, and other materials that kept them within history and interactive cosmologies, as perhaps did the malaria, cholera, measles, and other diseases that affected the nearby Yanomami.

Although Descola adopts much of the perspectivist insistence on predation and cannibalism as the medium of interaction between humans and nonhumans, humans and humans, and spirits and animals, he does not fall into its unifying trap, nor does Viveiros de Castro's own earlier ethnographic work on the Arawete of the Tupi-Guarani (1992), in which he sketched a contrast with Ge social organization and cosmology. Descola ([2006] 2013) does not discuss the Tupi-Guarani and Ge contrast in his survey, nor the other features of contrastive linguistics across groups bearing on their cosmologies (see footnote 5, item 3). Instead, Descola is concerned to separate off Amazonian thought from that of totemism in Australia, because he thinks Lévi-Strauss conflated Amazonian and Australian modes of identification and relation.

In "The Forest of Mirrors," Viveiros de Castro makes a lovely start both in analyzing Davi Kopenawa's rhetoric, and in the comparative linguistics among indigenous Amazonians (implicitly demonstrating that nature/culture is only one of many dynamic oppositions by which, for instance, animals that are good to eat are distinguished from those that are not[13]). I think he is mistaken to essentialize Kopenawa's mythopoetics as something entirely different from other mythopoetics, rhetorical forms, inspirational practices, and appreciations of environments. Six interesting aporia, or switching points, are constitutive to Kopenawa's poetics and are points of logical slippages in Viveiros de Castro's own.

1. *Sources of inspiration.* First, there is an aporia (for Kopenawa) and a slippage (in Viveiros de Castro) between elixirs and the phenomenology of light, luminosity, transparency, translucence, and revelations of the unseen. The elixirs in the Amazon include inhaling the hallucinogenic powder of the *yãkõanahi* tree and the cataleptic shock of ingesting massive amounts of tobacco. In Zoroastrian and Vedic traditions the elixir is called *haoma/soma*. As Viveiros de Castro (n.d.-a) notes, citing Reichel-Dolmatoff (1975), while much can be attributed to the biochemical effects of drugs, the visions themselves are formed through a visual-semiotic process that drugs alone do not explain. Visions can be induced by incantation, song, or poetry alone. The confusion lies in Viveiros de Castro's recognition of altered states of apprehension or consciousness, while claiming that these are the whole of a culture's ontology or sense of reality, as if they, unlike us, experience only one reality, or as if only one reality is the "ultimate" one.

2. *Translation effects.* Second, there is the need to analyze the relation (or translational differences) between Kopenawa's speech to the international stage and his internal shamanic mythopoesis. One is reminded of Marshall Sahlins's brilliant rereading (1972) of Elson Best's account of the old Maori man's explanation to the Whites about the spirit of the gift (*hau*) in terms the Whites would understand, namely the spirit of capital. Similarly, Kopenawa says that the images he sees are "like the images in the mirrors I saw in one of your hotels" (Viveiros de Castro, n.d.-a).

3. *Logical operators: mirrors and crystals.* Third, Viveiros de Castro tantalizingly hints at, but insufficiently explores, the interrelations of the metaphors of refractions and grammatical features. Refractions of mirrors and crystals in Kopenawa's mythopoesis are relations, capacities, and potentialities of *multiplicity* and *passage* among worlds. To follow these we need to know how the grammatical features operate—intensifier suffixes (*-ri* in Yanomami, *-kuma* in Arawak languages), and morphemic particles (*-imi*) that express

diminutive, germinal ("fathering," as in *wot-im*, "fish father"), or inspirational features (kernels, seeds, or points of origination and regeneration). Viveiros de Castro (n.d.-a) says, "The *xapiripë* shamanic images are only so many different intensive vibrations or modulations." Is this different from saying in contemporary sciences that everything is bits *and* atoms, or, in Donna Haraway's (1997) terminology, "material-semiotic"? Grammatical features too are our ancestors; they too constitute our postdeath remains for reanimation.

4. *Relational operators for interpreting environments and forms of life.* Fourth, the refracting, dividing, multiplying relations of mirrors and crystals remind us of Neoplatonic imagery, a connection Viveiros de Castro (n.d.-a) himself makes via Plotinus and Lévi-Strauss, and that I associate with Henri Corbin's (1948) effort to connect Suhravardi's *alam-e mesal*, his own Catholic Latin *mundus imaginalis*, and a recovery of the "theosophical wisdom" of Zoroastrian rhetorical imagery, the equivalent of Kopenawa's ancestral time. The difference lies in the forest-and-river fishing-hunting-garden regime of the Amazon versus the steppe-horse-cattle ecology of the Central Asian and Iranian plateaus. "The primary dialectic," says Viveiros de Castro, "is between seeing and eating."

5. *Affects and indexicals.* Fifth, shamanic spirits "index characteristic affects," says Viveiros de Castro (n.d.-a), but he actually says nothing or little about affects. Shamanic spirits, he claims, are representatives of profusion, not representations of types. Nonetheless, he admits the spirits are distinctive animals like jaguars (a type). He wants to deny them iconic or type status, a gesture that Latour (2009) skeptically analogies to the desire for "bombs" to blow up Western thought, to provide an outside to whatever is ascribed to so-called Western thought, as if the latter were one thing, or full of the collapse of representatives and representations. To rhetorically turn representations back into representatives (asking who represents what to whom) is to reanimate things into relationships and speech acts), but we perform these transforms and clarifications all the time in Western thought. In an article in 1998, Viveiros de Castro puts "*deixis*" in the title, but he does little with it. In "The Forest of Mirrors" n.d.-a), he says that "the mythic jaguar, to pick an example, is a block of human affects in the shape of a jaguar or a block of feline affects in the shape of a human; that the distinction, in any rigorous sense, is undecidable, since mythic metamorphosis is an 'event' or a heterogenic 'becoming' (an intensive superposition of states)." That last parenthetical phrase, I think, may be the important one, but one to which, as a self-proclaimed antihermeneuticist, Viveiros de Castro pays little attention.

Ironically, he claims in "Anthropocenography" that Latour is indifferent to the philosophy of language. Latour's new book (2013) on linguistic features of modes of existence should put paid to that, and perhaps that book can help Viveiros de Castro return to his earlier investigations into the grammars of Amerindian thought.

6. *Multitude of invisibles.* Sixth, can "spirits" be homogenized as precursors-and-the-already-passed-on-to-be-regenerated? Yanomami shamanic spirits (*xapi-ri-pë*) are only one (*type*?) of the invisibles (*yai thëpë*), which include specters of the dead (*porepë*) and malefic beings (*në wãripë*). The invisibles are not always beautiful, diaphanous, or transparent light; they can be monstrous. Indeed, "the imaginary of Amazonian spirits relishes constructing corporally deformed invisible species with inverted members, inexistent articulations, minuscule or gigantic appendices, atrophied sensorial interfaces, etc." (Viveiros de Castro, n.d.-a).

Instead of engaging with these six aporia in Amazonian discourses, Viveiros de Castro grafts his work onto the speculative realism, the "ontological turn," of Quentin Meillassoux ([2006] 2008). As Viveiros de Castro explains, Meillassoux engages in the logic games of trying to think "the ancestral" (reality anterior to any life on earth) and "externality" (beyond what we can know or conceive).[14] Latour will do this more trenchantly, using Gaia within human experience.

Descola, meanwhile, is not ignorant of the history of the moving frontiers of Amazonia. He gives hints, and his wife, Ann Catherine Taylor, has elegantly outlined what we know from the early sixteenth through early nineteenth centuries, pointing out that settlement patterns, cross-ethnic alliances, and multiethnic-linguistic tribal formations (as in the Vaupes studied by Jean Jackson) were all responses to colonial frontiers first of the Inca, and then of the Spanish and the Portuguese. But there seems little place in Descola's book for the contrasts that, for instance, Eduardo Kohn finds between predators with teeth (meat eaters), and predators without teeth ("aroma or life-and-breath-inhalers"), such as anteaters, armadillos, and anacondas. Kohn elaborates a language of attraction and seduction by anacondas and whiplash beetles, as well as a semen-soul economy that can turn predators into prey, including husbands of pregnant women used as bait for white-lipped peccaries, and the love charms that are used in these varied relations (2013, 119–25). Kohn, in other words, begins to elicit a poetics, not an ontology.

The problem is that these debates are pursued entirely with Western vocabulary and inferences, at a level of abstraction that rarely deals with the ethnographic material in its own language games that would provide the grounds to know how and where the Western words lead astray, as translation inevitably does.

These are old methodological issues in anthropology (not tearing things out of context, always tracing back to the linguistic forms being used in the original contexts), and it is disturbing to see them violated in the name of abstractions called "diversity."

Conclusions to recap the argument:

1. "Ontology" is probably not a useful term for the tasks it is being asked to do, and, in any case, at issue for both Latour and Descola are ontologies in the plural. Pluralization allows technologization (object-oriented tagging, pivot tables, digitalization—the terms used by Latour in AIME and *AIME* (project and book)—but also seems to empty the meaning of the term(s), making it just what Humpty Dumpty decides it should be. *Language games* have more weight, more institutionalized force, more friction, generated by social miscues, mistakes, conflicts, protests, and social mobilizations. Language games also link into a different intellectual genealogy than does ontology, one that is pragmatic and one that unclicks deadening, or no longer useful, double-clicks. In *An Inquiry into Modes of Existence* Latour turns toward Wittgensteinian or Lyotardian language games, and Silversteinian deixis and metapragmatics, as formal means of distinguishing modern European discursive categories and institutions such as law, politics, religion, economics, religion. Each of these "modes of existence" is defined by three criteria: (1) the right pre-position, (2) a discontinuity from other language games, and (3) felicity conditions.

2. Sustained antihumanism, and/or the rhetoric of inversion, can be fun as provocation—"imagination is never the source but rather the receptacle"; "humanity is the recoil of technology"—but is less what we need than a new humanistic politics, open also to the posthuman with its human components, the cyborg and networked human socialities, and companion species, that will allow us to survive, to live after whatever catastrophes lie in store—climate change, space travel, bodily evolution, farming the Arctic as it warms, the destruction of democratic forms of representative government—and that will counter the widening inequalities and devastations of our current cannibal economies, consuming the lives of some for the luxury of others. In his Gifford Lectures on Gaia, Latour turns to a politics of the Anthropocene. Presenting AIME in Karlsruhe, Latour suggested that photography can make visible how the projections of modernism elide or misrepresent the realities of their production, exposing the blinders of a universal view from nowhere (*le point de vue de Sirius*). Under the demands of Gaia, Latour's claims for

Gabriele Tarde as a better sociologist of modernity than Durkheim may be lessening. His earlier claims for Tarde are premised on the technology of profiling and identification (tools he rightly analyzes as essential to current amok capitalism), which misses the point of Durkheim's matters of concern: how moral codes and feelings of obligation materialize in rituals, politics, and symbolic forms. It is these latter that become central matters of concern in Latour's Gaia lectures. For all the talk of the nonhuman, Latour, Descola, and Viveiros de Castro remain within metaphors, icons, and even onomatopoetics of human languages and semiotic systems. In the Gifford Lectures a metaphorics of immunology reigns, nature becomes Gaia, and the human is replaced with the earth-bound (also the name of a Mexican-US company that sells organic food).

3. Descola's comparativism revives a much-needed tradition in human geography, but needs to be able to accommodate a much wider range of empirical *and dialogical* cases for his schemas to have the logical exhaustiveness he claims: for example, Jain notions of multiple souls in onions and other root crops; or Victorian animistic lenses through which scholars such as Mary Boyce interpreted the religion of others, in her case, Zoroastrianism, insisting on turning the *amshaspands* (structured metaphorical attributes of the cosmic forces of good, like the seven to ten Vedic *prajapatis*, or ten *sephirot* in Jewish mysticism, or the mistranslations of Begriff, Sein, und Wesen) into merely personified immortals. The implicit sense that comparative religion is Christian or Christian modern seems characteristic, oddly, of French philosophy these days. In his Gifford Lectures, while still full of Christian references and imagery, this cultural specificity is transcended by a politics of monogeism (no spare planet). Latour's claims about the lack of self-reflexivity of Whites ignores a large literature on Whiteness, and seems perhaps a deflection of current historical crises and topics, such as immigration to Europe and the United States, and the use of guest workers in other places, such as the United Arab Emirates or Singapore (where the category is no longer White, but the immigration fears and political tension are similar).

4. Digital humanities, as well as visual and performance arts, are on the agenda everywhere, and Latour, to his credit, has been a fearless early adopter, if not as forthcoming about the limitations of his experiments as he might be. I apparently foolishly, or at least naively, first read *An Inquiry into Modes of Existence* as a book (laboriously taking notes, looking for coherent arguments) rather than a flow, an object in motion, a deamalgamation, open to recomposition with a few selected and trained coinquirers and redesigners. I assumed that the website was supplementary to the book, rather than the reverse (see

footnote 4), that its opaque and not very exciting web presence might not require comparative evaluation with other web projects. A similar caution applies to "Actor Network Theory," which has gradually become a how-to manual of instruction for an anthropology without human actors. Latour says he has been distancing himself from it, using it only as "cover" while AIME came into focus. The world, not just Gaia, and the media of perception are morphing faster than responses can be written, faster than clarifying debate can be undertaken.

5. The language games of the Ayoreo, the Achuar, the Runa, and others can in fact teach us many things. We must not double-click on any of the identifications made in these two books without carefully inspecting all the linkages for their ruses and deviations, their poetics and indeed their call that if all the shamans perish, the sky will fall. You must hear me; time is short.

3

PURE LOGIC AND TYPOLOGIZING ARE FALSE LEADS

Anthropological readings of novels, paintings, and films (Fischer 2004) are ways to expand coverage of ethnographically contextualized epistemic objects (content), and to juxtapose ethnographies with other analytic and aesthetic forms or genres of cultural commentary (form). One can "read for the ethnography" (content), and one can also read to locate analyses within matrices of different modes of interpretation (form). Two interesting cases to pursue are paintings by the German artist Gerhard Richter and a novel by Salman Rushdie. I have written about the Rushdie novel, the surrounding Rushdie affair, and its aftermath in the Muhammad cartoon wars at length (Fischer 1990, 2009b; Fischer and Abedi 2009), and I welcome Paul Rabinow and Anthony Stavrianakis's addition of the Charlie Hebdo events to the growing archive of analyses of media circuits and sensitive redlines for different communities. The Rabinow-Stavrianakis analysis acknowledges mine in passing but dismisses it, giving me standing to hopefully move the discussion forward onto a more productive plane.

At issue is what Rabinow has been calling "concept-work" in handling what I have called "emergent forms of life" and that he suggests we call the "contemporary." At his most ambitious, he calls for a complete overhaul of the vocabulary of the social sciences to focus on the goals of flourishing (a term he takes from the ancient Greeks but that is at least as current in Buddhist traditions, both ancient and the newer versions of mindfulness applied to the self and also the social and physical worlds; see also chapter 6). At a more anthropological level, Rabinow has directed attention to such topics as the aftermath of war (the Richter example), the sociolinguistic dynamics of violence and crises (the Rushdie example), global surveillance and pandemic or disaster preparedness (with former students Andrew Lakoff and Steven Collier), and the turning of synthetic biology into what Charis Thompson (2013), punning, calls "good science," meaning both rigorous scientific protocols and also ethical attention for whom and with whom the science is being done (in her case, stem cell science in reproductive technologies).

Gerhard Richter's paintings provide visual stimuli for discussions of recovery from the destruction of civilizational norms in World War II, a challenge that is renewed in the wars in Chechnya, Afghanistan, Iraq, and Syria today. The Rushdie affair, likewise, has provided multiple occasions for discussions about ethical norms across religious, national, and regional lines. What insiders and outsiders may say about religious ideologies is part of that challenge, not only in globalized factional fighting within Islamic worlds overspilling their boundaries into wider cosmopolitan, multireligious worlds (including violence over secular rules for governance that protect all citizens and refuse making some legally second class), but also the rise of conservative Christianity in the West politely coded as "lifestyle" or social wedge issues but often having to do more fundamentally (as in the 1920s "temperance" era) with the loss of status and livelihood by groups who are feeling increasingly left behind by a changing world (Gusfield 1986).

The intention of finding new analytic terms is excellent and welcome. But as with the efforts to do something analogous with "ontology" and "metaphysics" in the last chapter, there is a slippage between the machinery of distinction making ("concept making") and attending to the ethnographic contexts out of which distinctions arise, gain purchase, and are used politically and discursively to make the world appear to conform to its formulators' projected design, colliding with the projects of others.

Rabinow has long been also a leading practitioner of the efforts to bridge the interface between philosophy and anthropology. He is best known for his early and important introductions of Michel Foucault to the English-speaking academic world, both by applying Foucault in *French Modern* (1989), and by producing interpretations, translations, and edited volumes of Foucault's essays (Rabinow and Deyfuss 1983; Rabinow, ed. 1984, 1997; Rabinow and Rose, eds. 2003). He has also attempted to bring into anthropological discussions such German philosophers as Hans Blumenberg. But above all in his recent work he has invoked ancient Greek philosophers, especially Aristotle, regularly, with a nod to his former teacher at Chicago, Richard McKeon, who trained under John Dewey but styled himself as a student of Aristotle. This is not the place to do a full comparison of McKeon and Rabinow, but it is worth recognizing that Rabinow adopts McKeon's vocabulary about the modern world (looking for a logos to make sense of techne, and relying on an expanded rhetorics—topoi and schemata—to deal with changing sciences and technologies, arts and humanities). Rabinow combines this with borrowings of French terminology, especially from Foucault, and behind his distinction between the present and the contemporary is an effort to go beyond Foucault's history of the present.

Rabinow's most successful and pathbreaking ethnographic works were three studies of molecular biology in the 1990s: *The Making of PCR* (1996), *French DNA* (1999), and *A Machine to Make a Future* (with Talia Dan-Cohen, 2004). It is interesting that the first of these was a landmark book in science studies, and that originally it was a text drawing heavily on the philosophers Gilles Deleuze and Felix Guattari, but all such vocabulary and philosophical attempts were excised from the final text, Rabinow explained at the time to me and other friends, so that it could be read by his molecular biology interlocutors, so that the people he wrote about could also read it. I have described the accomplishments of this book elsewhere (Fischer 2003, 2009) in delineating the space of start-ups in the molecular biology political economy as well as highlighting the differences between ideas, experimental systems, and commercial kits, with credit (such as Nobel Prizes) going to the first, rather than as Rabinow suggested would be more appropriate, to the second, who actually did the heavy lifting. It's a point that would be made in parallel and complementary ways by the important books of Hans-Jörg Rheinberger (on the rat-liver system for elucidating protein cascades [1997]) and Lily Kay (on the elucidation of the genetic code by microbiologists rather than cryptographers [2000]). In Rabinow's recent work to fashion tools or concepts for analyzing the contemporary, this attention to ethnographic rigor slips in favor of logical distinctions and typologies. I argue that, while well intentioned, this is insufficient, and cannot do what it claims to accomplish.

Richter's paintings and Rushdie's novel are used by Rabinow and Stavrianakis in *Designs on the Contemporary: Anthropological Tests* (2014) to think about reform of the methods and theory of anthropology and of social thought more generally, including the relations of truth, method and conduct, testing of self and of one's tools of perception, and ethics and morals—all issues that have long been central to both philosophy and anthropology. In *Designs on the Contemporary* they struggle to align these terms under the complicated conditions of what they call the "contemporary."

Rabinow and Stavrianakis make central an effort to analytically distinguish the "contemporary," the "present," and the "actual." The "contemporary," they stipulate, is a methodological horizon of indeterminations, puzzles, trade-offs, impossibilities, and challenges to do something new with leftovers from the past. The "contemporary" thus contrasts with the "actual" (what actually is the case) insofar as the contemporary remains open to alternative ways of seeing "the present" and projecting the future. The "actual" contrasts with the "present" insofar as they define the present as an immediacy that can be reanalyzed through various distancing and defamiliarizing analytics in order to perceive or construct the actual.

These are perspectival and analytic conundra known to most religions and their parable pedagogies (*re-ligio*, "tying [conduct] back" [to truths]), to anthropology (the study of human moralities and ethics in which actors are never in control of all the background causalities or intentions of others), and in the study of probabilistic systems in which actors variously game, and thereby change, projected outcomes, as in the continually changing algorithms by which Google projects the spread of influenza or buying trends, or in the similar stock market trading programs that gamble on future Federal Reserve interest rate interventions, which themselves attempt to manage expectations through pronouncements as well as actual interventions (Holmes 2013).

The authors look for help especially to classic Greek *authors and words* (rather than, say, their social contexts and deeds), providing a lexicon of Greek (and German) terms at the back of their book. In particular they wish to distinguish themselves as beyond the historical horizons of Michel Foucault's invocation of Seneca's stoicism, Immanuel Kant's pragmatic anthropology,[1] and John Dewey's pragmatism (interpreted as reconstruction and reduction). As already noted, they use two case studies as test beds for their analysis: (1) the figure of the contemporary German artist Gerhard Richter, operating in his studio under a gray photograph of the Birkenau concentration camp (gray standing in Richter's palette for absence of colors and their cultural connotations); and (2) the figure of the contemporary British Indian and American writer Salman Rushdie extracting himself from the double binds of Muslim efforts to transcend the conditions of media and lack of communal controls over public discourse.

An Artist in and of the Contemporary

One of Richter's works (not discussed by Rabinow and Stavrianakis) to which I am drawn for sociological reasons is his design for the south transept window of Cologne Cathedral (completed in 2007). It was made of many small color squares, based on his 1974 color chart painting *4096 Colors*. It was made through the financial contributions of many large and small donors, including Richter's own donation of the completed piece. Lee Rosenblaum notes, in her *CultureGrrl* blog, that her tour guide said it was "subjected to computer analysis, to insure [*sic*] that no 'unfavorable [i.e., inappropriate] imagery' could be discerned within its ostensibly abstract patterns. (Can't you make out that fuzzy Baader-Meinhof group member in the lower left? Just kidding.)"[2] The replacement of a historic window, destroyed in World War II, with the help of a large community of named and anonymous donors, with a new window made of a nonfigural assortment of color squares seems a wonderful expression of the best of contemporary social solidarities.

Rabinow and Stavrianakis are drawn to the "indetermination" of much of Richter's work. In their reading, and that of art critics they cite, Richter paints over photographs and prints, creating puzzles that draw attention to both referentiality and abstraction (109), nostalgia and the avant-garde (107), chance and systematicity (110), finished and unfinished (116), series and ruptures, denial and affirmation. This is a tactic of what is often called the poststructural or postmodern—the effort to point out the terms of variance that are selected for any artwork or conceptual formation, and the effort at postal relations among modernities, refusing the singular "modernity." Focusing on these indeterminations that provide the ground for selection, interpretation, or reading (i.e., determinations for the moment) is what Rabinow and Stavrianakis call the "mood" or "affect" of pathos. "Affect," they specify, is not emotion, not an interiority, but a structural relation, and pathos is one of four tropes they identify, along with comedy, tragedy, and irony (overlapping with the four tropes Hayden White (1973) used in his analyses of the inability of master historians to coherently align argument, ideology, and plot). The affect of pathos, they argue, is the one proper to what they call the contemporary, because it does not rest upon momentary resolutions (comedy) nor perennial failures (tragedy) nor "as if" distancing (irony, satire). Pathos works with lack of success (thus has some relation with tragedy), also with hope (thus some relation with comedy), and with a play with relationships themselves (thus some relation with irony). Kaja Silverman's reading of Richter's work in psychoanalytic terms, therefore, they specify, is not "contemporary" because it rests on determinations that they call ironic.

Richter is of interest to Rabinow and Stavrianakis, perhaps, because there are hints of alternatives to polemics and ideologies surrounding such events as the German concentration camps, the death of members of the German Red Army, and the American invasion of Iraq. Polemics and ideologies have become stupid (in the technical sense of blunt and merely emotive). Art's function instead is to put forms on the chaos of nature and events, an entirely different register, one that Richter often finds consoling in the aftermath of the remains of war. While there is a whiff of art for art's sake in this adjacency to actual politics, Rabinow and Stavrianakis want to see it, following Michel Foucault's investigations into changing historical ideologies of care of the self, as a mode of testing of the self, of art, and of a proper mood or affect for anthropology itself.

Consolation. Richter says that at the time of the American invasion of Iraq in 2003, he took a large abstract painting he had done two decades earlier, photographed and reproduced it in multiple small images, and montaged these with clips from the German press, selected as they fit the layout rather than according to their meaning. Richter says that the newspaper articles were ineffectual and impotent, but that their plain presentation of facts "consoled me." He titled the piece *War Cut*. "Form," he says, "is all we have to cope with fundamentally chaotic facts and assaults."

Rabinow and Stavrianakis suggest that the analogue of chance effects generated by Richter's distancing and defamiliarizing techniques (overpainting with lines, black splotches, squeegee moving of paint over figural images, selecting color chips arbitrarily and then arranging them) lies in nature itself, "spontaneous, arbitrary, meaningless selection" that "result nonetheless in living forms and beings."

Richter says, "It was good to paint something like this [*War Cut*]. Something story-like. Something fantastic. The absolute opposite of war" (122). Richter's landscapes are haunted by war, the woods full of darkness and concealment. His photographs of the Alps overpainted, Rabinow and Stavrianakis say, give "an affect of danger, nature's inhumanity, uncontrollability, foreignness" (115). Rabinow and Stavrianakis are fascinated by the meaningless forms made by the overpainting that seem nonetheless to provide affects of warning, of alert. They write, "Whatever Richter's techniques are for escaping more skeptical scrutiny should be marked by cultural observers as worthy of more attention" (116). Richter works with and recreates remains, like Freud's aftereffects (*Nachtraglichkeit*, or what Rabinow calls *Nachleben*, a term he takes from

Abby Warburg referring more to styles in painting than cultural or psychic content), Walter Benjamin's ruins and dialectical images (holding past aspirations of hope in tension against current banalizations), or Adorno's imminent critique (finding redemption in seeing the world as it is otherwise, often in music or aesthetics), and what George Marcus and I (1986) called "cultural critique through juxtaposition." Richter himself notes, "Even the present has moments of promise" (132).

The photo in Richter's studio, and his tinting of other concentration camp photos to keep them "present" and active (rather than fading into already too often seen images that no longer serve as alerts), as well as his Cologne Cathedral window of color chip mosaics, are perhaps moral stances of acknowledgment and weaving of past evils into healthier, less dangerous futures even as the mechanical (now electronic) means of production and reproduction destroy or transmute many of our older tools of perception—although, of course, Richter, insofar as he is "contemporary," must not assert any such thing, and as is "actually" the case, things in the future could still break bad.

A Novelist in and of the Contemporary Who Got Caught in the Actual

Such indeterminations can perhaps be clarified by the other case study, the Rushdie affair, which has arguably higher stakes in the actual world, at least by the "metric" of lives at risk. Testing is centrally at issue here: testing of Rushdie's own sense of self, testing by Islamicists of theatrical political moves, testing of the anthropological tools of interpretation. Rabinow and Stavrianakis suggest that anthropologists' usual tools of interpretation are insufficient. They either overcontextualize or perform apologetics for the native point of view (in either case, what philosopher and anthropologist Ernest Gellner in his debates with philosophers flagged as danger in the difference between explaining and explaining away).[3] They assign Jeanne Favret-Saada to the former insufficiency, and Talal Asad, Saba Mahmood, and others to the latter.

In fact, however, ignoring their own charge of contextualizing away, they use Favret-Saada's analysis of the (failed) charge of blasphemy in the Rushdie affair as working like witchcraft accusations in France, requiring: (a) a reservoir of potential theological interpretations and sanctions; (b) a denouncer; (c) an accused; and (d) an authority capable of imposing sanctions. They simplistically identify Iran's Ayatollah Khomeini as providing that authority.

It is simplistic because of the contested nature of the fatwa (by other *mujtahids*), the history of the use of the charge that they collapse into "blasphemy" (*mahdur al-dam*, death without trial for those viewed as corruptors of the earth), used to execute and murder Baha'is in Iran (just as Agamben describes *homo sacer* for the Romans), and, of course, in the long run the fact that the Iranian state dropped its support for the death sanction, and since Khomeini died its effect lapses (fatwas have force for present action only if the issuer of the fatwa is alive). The "authority" to enforce a call for death without trial then becomes simply populist and extrajurisprudential, in what Rabinow and Stavrianakis nicely call "a situation of polemics" (86, 89, passim).

The sociolinguistic or linguistic pragmatics and genre analytics Rabinow and Stavrianakis deploy from Francois Chateauraynaud and Didier Torny (1999) draw attention to what Victor Turner (1974) would have called the "social drama" or processual phases in the Rushdie affair, which Rabinow and Stavrianakis call alerts, trials, and polemical situations. First, there are *alerts* about *future possible* victims. These alerts call for preventive *administrative* action, such as banning the book on grounds of public safety without judgment on its content. Thus the Indian Ministry of Finance banned the book's importation but explicitly said it did not contest the literary or artistic merits of the novel. Second, there follows a framing of legal grounds (unsuccessfully in this case) for a *trial* in which *past actions* with "malicious intent" are named against *identified victims*. An example is violation of lapsed British blasphemy laws. Thanks to the Rushdie affair, this was rectified in the opposite manner than called for by the Islamists by repealing the law in 2008. Third, then, are *polemical situations* played out in the media and demonstrations (book burnings, assassinations; *revelation* of truth and *exhibition of victims*).

Rabinow and Stavrianakis want these sociolinguistic analyses to provide distance so that the anthropologists are not themselves entangled in the polemical situation. But there are a number of factual, evaluative, and social analytic slippages that undo their claims to be sustainably "contemporary" and outside the field of polemics. Indeed, the essay ends on a polemical ("it goes without saying") note, citing and agreeing with the polemicist, atheist, and "antitheist" Christopher Hitchens in favor of Enlightenment values.

Factual slippages. Rushdie's novel does not, as Rabinow and Stavrianakis claim, start either narratively or logically from a "historical event" in early Islam but instead begins from the double psychological adjustments of migration and of vernacular jumble of stories told by the entertainment Bollywood film industry and in memories of childhood religious instruction.

This makes a huge difference, since it puts the evaluations of the novel on an entirely different plane, not one of proper or improper invocation of the satanic verses (that no one denies exists in the Islamic traditions) but rather on how Muslims teach one another and non-Muslims about their traditions.

Nor is it the case that the novel "dispenses with a historical frame" (77, 78), since it is about the actual world when it was written, and in fact was sufficiently in the trope of pathos to diegetically anticipate some of the reactions within its own "contemporary" frame, albeit not what Rabinow and Stavrianakis nicely call the series of "amplifiers" that turn retorts and slogans of "death to" into "actual" polemical violence. It is those amplifiers, Ayatollah Sistani would charge during the subsequent Muhammad cartoon affair that not only share the blame but violate the Islamic rules against slander and stirring up trouble against neighbors. Such violations, Sistani said, rebound to tarnish the reputation of Islam and its ability to flourish.[4] While it is true that from the earliest days of Islam the debates about the status of the hadith about the satanic verses form the ostensive (though misrecognized or superficial) focus of the subsequent "Rushdie affair," not the novel (since there is little made up in the novel on this score), the primary transgression of the novel is exposing well-known stories and debates to outsiders (including unsophisticated Muslims). It is a social transgression rather than a dogmatic or theological one. Yes, one of the interpretations of the significance of the satanic verses is as a parable of testing human desire, but equally important is its role in the methodology of determining which are abrogated verses that remain in the written transcript of the oral Qur'an.

More seriously, Rabinow and Stavrianakis assert (their voice) that a headline reading "An Unequivocal Attack on Religious Fundamentalism" is the same thing as saying "an attack on Islam" (90), thereby dismissing the agency, sentiments, and convictions of millions of educated, cosmopolitan, and liberal, as well as ordinary, normally pragmatic Muslims. Similarly, to concede to Talal Asad the claim that questions of cultural politics and their inflection by faith in absolute truth "is not recognizable as a problem to 'most Muslims'" (96) would be to mischaracterize the history of fourteen hundred years of debate among Muslims over interpretation, and the important recognition that a good Muslim should have the humility not to engage in *shirk* (the heresy of assuming to know God's intent). Theology aside, even more important are the struggles within Islamic countries over the past two centuries against absolutism in both government and theology.

Cultural politics cannot be set aside. Rushdie was rightly upset at Madhu Jain, author of a prepublication review, for privileging among the various stories and threads of significance in the novel an attack on *fundamentalism* (an attack which she would support). Rushdie recognized her tactic as a polemical hammer in a context where a scalpel-like alert was needed, where a work of art, a novel, has a chance, but polemic has none. Rabinow and Stavrianakis rightly call Jain's review an "amplifier" on the road to creating a polemical situation.

Related is a misreading of Mehdi Abedi and my analysis, which Rabinow and Stavrianakis note and quote from approvingly (an appreciated change from the usual citational absence from the many articles and books on the Rushdie affair) but then dismiss, saying, "The tragic, comic and ironic moods [analyzed by Fischer and Abedi] miss the problematic ratio of breakdown and repair" (99). On the contrary, one might argue that while Rabinow and Stavrianakis's focus on the immediate sociolinguistic *tactics* of alert, trial, or polemic is salutary as far as it goes, it foreshortens and obscures the playing out of longer-term coalitional, class, and immigrant politics that Abedi and I identify as emblematic of the contemporary across distinct if overlapping political arenas. My own other writings on "torn religions" (Islam, Jainism, Judaism, etc. [Fischer 2003, chap. 6]) point to the distinctive (nonhagiographic) contemporary double-voiced biographies of religious leaders that simultaneously track testing of self, of tactics, and of social analysis of author and subject in their parallel but different modernities. An example is Louis Massignon's multivolume biography of Al-Hallaj [Massignon 1982]).

These are never-ending struggles across shifting grounds of moral commonsense. Part of Abedi and my effort is to oppose all-too-easy defenses of either the countermodern (as Rabinow and Stavrianakis say are the cases of Talal Asad, Saba Mahmoud, and others), or of the modern, and instead to expand the understandings of metaphor, rhetoric, and interpretation in multiple traditions that allow religious figures and communities, despite lack of consensus (fundamentalist, liberal; secular, religious), nonetheless to live together and to recognize one another's arguments within their own traditions, or, on the contrary, to provide the justifications for conflict. It is indexical of the continuing struggles (breakdown and repair) between fundamentalism and tolerance that the same publisher (Penguin Books, New Delhi), urged by its advisor, Kushwant Singh, not to publish Rushdie's book, is also the publisher that was intimidated by Hindu fundamentalists in 2014 into withdrawing well-known Sanskrit scholar Wendy Doniger's *The Hindus* (2009) from the market. This replay is similar to the reprise of the Rushdie affair with new circuits and amplifiers a decade later with the Muhammad cartoon wars, within the Islamic Republic of Iran, as well as across secular and Islamic lines (Fischer 2009b).

Rabinow and Stavrianakis construct (yes, constructivism) an archive of over one hundred texts and documents relating to the Rushdie affair but omit to tell us which documents. So the claim of diligence or method tells us little why these and not other texts and documents, or why they only look at some transnational circuits and amplifiers and not others. They assemble a set of five items of *visibility* in *visual media* rather than writings, in France and the United States, to ask about anti-Muslim triggers to Muslim anger (in the actual), and to ask about how these might be understood in terms of a mode of subjectivation, a mode of transmission, and anthropological judgment. It is an odd set that they admit they can manage only to put into "a common frame" (85) through these three (unanswered) questions about subjectivation, transmission, and judgment.

The five include two covers of the Paris satirical weekly *Charlie Hebdo* from 2011 and 2012; an inflammatory anti-Muslim video uploaded in California in June 2012 said by some to have contributed to causing the attack in Benghazi and the killing of US ambassador J. Christopher Stevens and others on September 11, 2012, by militants armed with military-grade weapons, and *The Untouchables*, a popular French film based on an earlier true story documentary. Three of the five present Muslims in a positive light, two in a negative one. The five items perhaps can serve anthropological judgment as "alerts," but we are given little guidance.

In the wake of the October 2011 victory in Tunisia of the moderate Islamist Ennahda party and violent protests in Sidi Bouzid over the cancellation of seats won by the Popular List, the November 3, 2011, issue of *Charlie Hebdo* joked that it was "guest-edited" by "Mohammad," who was depicted on the cover of the satire magazine as saying "100 lashes if you don't die laughing." But shortly before this, the cover of *Charlie Hebdo* on September 19, 2012, showed a Hassidic rabbi pushing an imam in a wheelchair, both saying "Don't mock us," which was presented as a movie poster for an imaginary sequel to the French film *Untouchables* (2011) about a wealthy quadriplegic who hires a young Muslim ex-con as a caregiver. The film gave a positive portrait of the Muslim caregiver, and when it was released on November 2, 2011, became the highest-grossing non-English-language film globally. It was based on a true story and on a previous TV documentary. While one might read the September 19 cover as ironic and disbelieving, it can just as easily be read as continuing the good feelings generated by the film. Autumn 2011 in

France thus provides both a positive image of Muslims (the film, the documentary) and a skeptical one (the Charlie Hebdo cover on Tunisia). The puzzle remains how these five items actually form a set.

More trenchantly, Rabinow and Stavrianakis retell the efforts of Rushdie to extract himself from a polemical situation by writing as a form of *askesis* (training of the self to avoid folly). The effort reaches a nadir when Rushdie gives in to the suggestion of a group of Egyptian clerics that all he need do is to submit to a public declaration of Islamic faith. Not only is it "a spectacular failure," convincing no one, it feels terrible for Rushdie, a self-betrayal, a betrayal of his supporters, as well as a predictable betrayal by the clerics when he sees these same clerics on television vilifying homosexuals or defending a man's right to slap his wife (Rushdie is just an excuse in an ongoing campaign).

Logic(s), Forms, Bios (Emergent Forms of Life?)

With the test beds in mind, we can return to the methodological first part of the book, *Designs on the Contemporary: Anthropological Tests*. Chapters 2 and 3, respectively, on Logic (Dewey, Seneca, Foucault) and Forms (Aristotle, Foucault), are straightforward introductions to the terminology already used above, and will appeal to those who enjoy reminders of various Greek (and a few German) terms as cross-linguistic exercises that can sometimes bring out thought-provoking alternative perspectives and reanimate dead metaphors or turns of phrase. The danger is that, as with the James Strachey "standard" English translation of Freud, one creates a stilted jargon that can become a barrier to readers and does violence to the fluidity of ordinary talk (*Ich*, *das Es*, *Über-Ich*, ordinary words in German, turned into Latinate *ego*, *id*, and *superego*, losing much of the cultural resonance of childhood development in German daily discourse). I don't think I've lost much above in my experiment of avoiding the Greek in favor of ordinary English. Still, sometimes it helps to have immobilized foreign language tags or jargon as signposts for students to use to keep themselves on message, though for professionals a fuller comparative mode across lively languages in their lability and historical contexts can be more useful.

In the chapter on logic, facts emerge during inquiry, judgments require warrants, and logics are invented as conceptual orderings of experience that are confirmed or disconfirmed as one proceeds. These are the elementary lessons of pragmatism (John Dewey, but also Karl Popper's procedures of confirmation, and logical empiricists in their variety, such as William James and C. S. Peirce in the United States; Alfred Tarski and Ludwik Fleck in Poland; Otto Neurath, Moritz Schlick, Rudolph Carnap, Paul Lazarsfeld, Marie Jahoda, and the later Ludwig Wittgenstein in Vienna (and Cambridge); Charles Morris, Percy Bridgeman, Hans Reichenbach, and Thomas Kuhn (again in the United States). Note, particularly, that Neurath, Lazarsfeld, and Jahoda were social scientists pioneering in developing ethnographic and social psychological, as well as quantitative methods, and that Neurath was a major innovator in the visual field as well (isotypes for graphic communication of information, international road signs, etc.).

Rabinow and Stavrianakis call this "pragmatic and realist," which is fine, but then undercut themselves with an unexplained antiintellectual dig by saying it "carries with it none of the constructivist or deconstructivist baggage" (32) as if there were no value of construction in, say, geometry or origami in building on the nanoscale, or in Russian constructivism or film montage, or of deconstruction in the analysis of language through disambiguation by showing how multiple meanings can be carried by words and tropes, and how the seemingly best-laid claims of philosophers (Kant) and methodologists (Descartes) can go awry.

In any case, the observation that judgments are midstream pragmatic *reductions* operating on the threshold between the actual and the contemporary (34) makes sense in the context of the essays on Richter and Rushdie. Seneca then is used to shift the discussion toward care of the self, using asceticism and daily practices of writing as ways of distancing and reflection on the moral self apart from the flux of the present. The problem for anthropological method in Seneca's stoicism, say Rabinow and Stavrianakis, is the goal of absence of inner turmoil (36). Foucault is invoked to repair this failing by stipulating that the turn to the self is not a turn away from the world but a turn to freedom in nature (see Richter above) as opposed to the obligations, even servitude, of civic duty. The idea is that living in the present or the actual induces seasickness or motion sickness, and one needs to step back.

There is, however, a problem with using Seneca in Stavrianakis and Rabinow's earnest efforts to align truth and conduct. Seneca lived in a world of such corruption that it is hard to know what to make of what he preached and wrote. We know he did not live up to the way he preached (virtue above all). He served Nero as tutor, then advisor and speechwriter, lending Nero his eloquence to cover up Nero's crimes. He himself amassed wealth, saying with Trumpian nonchalance that philosophers could handle it, but saying little about its exploitative sources. While at a certain point he distanced himself from the imperial court, he was caught up in a coup attempt. Even his forced suicide was staged as a "hubristic imitation of the death of Socrates" (Beard 2014, 31). The classics scholar Mary Beard concludes that for Tacitus, "Seneca was the 'perfect' imperial courtier—the true *imago* [image, but also illusion] for whom . . . hypocrisy and dissembling were a way of life" (33). He wrote plays full of passion, contrasting with his restrained philosophical *Letters*. He dictated his last philosophical thoughts, says Tacitus, to circulate as an image of his life (*imago vitae suae*), using the double-dealing word *imago* (illusion, image). "Philosophy was like dissembling; it turned out not to help anyone," says Beard, "and did not save Seneca from a difficult death" (33).

The chapter on forms briefly alludes to Rabinow's unhappy engagements with synthetic biologists and his unsatisfactory withdrawal into a diagnostic "haven" (his office).[5] Again there is a turn to Foucault for repair, marking out a schematic for a field of ethics: (1) reflection on an ethical object terrain, (2) a mode of subjectivation or inducement of an attitude toward that terrain, (3) goals for an ethical practice, and (4) the ascetic discipline to achieve that attitude and those goals. Again the goal here seems to be to aid a sense of a free relationship to oneself apart from one's social obligations in the actual world, in other words (à la Stavrianakis's idealistic presentation of Seneca), self-possession, a clear-eyed conception of one's own time, and a sense of the actual in which one operates, and thereby to foster a sense of flourishing (à la Aristotle's discussions of *eudaemonia*). It is, Rabinow and Stavrianakis claim, a mode of "seizing" (*lepsis*, German *Begriff*, or concept formation), of self-possession, which is *meta* or contemporary (*metalepsis*).

Or, said differently, Rabinow in particular wants to free himself from what he regards as the stultification ("*stultitia* and *stasis*") of the "already known" as well as from the "vertigo of the merely speculative" (x), which, however, he has just conceded is what logic is all about: conjecture-refutation, confirmation-disconfirmation.

This narrowing of Rabinow's bandwidth may turn out to be self-defeating. Dewey's analytic reconstruction (the relation between the breakdown of actions based on planners or experts' claims, creating crises that generate active, informed, publics) and Kant's pragmatism (the stress on what man can be, not what he is, the struggle for a republican cosmopolitics to come), not to mention Rabinow's fellow anthropologists also working the terrain of the contemporary, may have more to offer than Rabinow lets on.

"Bios," the opening chapter, is the most open to objection. Without much discussion (contextual, testing, or otherwise), Rabinow and Stavrianakis want to distinguish themselves from Giorgio Agamben (reduction of bios to *zoe*, or bare life), from Nikolas Rose (reformatting the self under neoliberalism), and from Clifford Geertz (failure to recognize power positions vis a vis an informant), and instead champion Hans Blumenberg with a few nice-sounding phrases (history of ideas as a series of occupations and reoccupations, a chess game, rather than linear progress; nature as "embodiment of the possible results of technology," in a milieu of self-assertion or existential projects, a refraction of Bruno Latour's quip that humanity is but the recoil of technology).

There is no particular payoff in objecting to the treatment of Geertz, except to note that there are quite different possible readings of the list of charges. Geertz tells a story against himself of his mismanagement of relations with a local scholar when he felt that the scholar was borrowing his typewriter too often. According to Rabinow, Geertz failed to acknowledge the asymmetrical power, debt, and credit relations, casting these as merely the breakdown of a fiction of recognition of equality in being scholars). But the question of struggles for recognition from Hegel to Charles Taylor *is* one of power relations. Again it is hard to see the difference between Geertz contrasting analytic disinterestedness with ideology as interested socialization into patterns of belief and value, and Rabinow contrasting his call for an attitude of pathos and *askesis* with "situations of polemic" that defend patterns of belief and values. These discussions of authority, legitimacy, and hegemony go back to Karl Marx, Max Weber, Antonio Gramsci, and Ernesto Laclau, among others. Rabinow and Stavrianakis seem on firmer ground when they turn to the sociolinguistics of alerts, trials, and polemics.

To argue, as Rabinow does, not only in this text, that for anthropology the "existence of many cultures required a relativism of the truth content" (21), or his claim that hermeneutics is self-enclosed, remain unlikely. Why should getting a native point of view right, as a basic step of anthropological due diligence, imply anything about its wider, dialogic, comparative, conflictive, or integrative positioning? A similar myopia causes him to claim that *Writing Culture* (Clifford and Marcus, eds. 1986) lacked any further venues for working out its initiatives. What about the eight volumes of *Late Editions* edited by George Marcus and the editorial collective he assembled (Marcus, ed. 1993–2000), *Anthropology as Cultural Critique* (Marcus and Fischer 1986), *Critical Anthropology Now* (Marcus, ed. 1999), the journal *Cultural Anthropology*, the journal *Public Culture*, and the Center for Transcultural Studies, all of which engaged considerable networks of collaboration extending and developing arguments in *Writing Culture* and *Anthropology as Cultural Critique*? (See also Starn 2015 for a twenty-fifth-anniversary retrospective.)

Designs On . . .

Design is a contemporary buzzword from architecture and engineering, often invoked in contemporary discussions on pedagogies in favor of studio-based, project-oriented, flipped-classroom, hands-on, active learning (everything is design). It also easily carries a double meaning implying imperialist appropriation (to have designs on). The plain cover of the book's (ironic?) design seems to mimic bureaucratic project folders; the blurb on the back by Marilyn Strathern, professor emerita of anthropology and provost emerita of Cambridge University, is part of an advertising come-on that one is not supposed to take literally: "a nonpareil, a configuration of thought with no equal."

Surely conversation would improve if, instead, the book were aligned with others that mine the same terrain: one thinks of Bruno Latour's very similar/different effort to construct a metaphysics, nay even an ontology, out of Wittgensteinian-Lyotardian language games, *An Inquiry into Modes of Existence: An Anthropology of the Moderns* (2013); the parallels in my *Emergent Forms of Life and the Anthropological Voice* (2003), and *Anthropological Futures* (2009), in which questions of both "moving ratios of modernity" and pragmatically changing analytics are constantly at issue; Joseph Dumit's *Drugs for Life* (2012) and *Picturing Personhood* (2004), where Kenneth Burke and Erving Goffman's forms of grammars of social action, self-fashioning, and manipulation of means of knowing are at issue; Donna Haraway's *Modest_Witness@Second_Millennium.FemaleMan©_Meets_OncoMouse™: Feminism and Technoscience* (1997), where multiple *logi* of social justice, gender, and science are at play in serious political and conceptual occupations and reoccupations; Kim Fortun's *Advocacy after Bhopal: Environmentalism, Disasters, New Global Orders* (2001), where questions of gendered communities of enunciation constituted by Deweyan breakdown, as well as Salman Rushdie–like efforts to escape Batesonian double binds and embodied actualities counter bureaucratic classifications; Michael Fortun's *Promising Genomics* (2008), where chiasmus is a structuring feature of economic, scientific, and cultural *logi* constituting the contemporary; Rabinow's own debates with George Marcus's studio-like, staged, paraethnographies alongside fieldwork in the volume with James Faubion and Tobias Rees, *Designs for an Anthropology of the Contemporary* (2008); and the volume edited by Veena Das, Michael Jackson, Arthur Kleinman, and Bhrigupati Singh, *The Ground Between: Anthropologists Engage Philosophy* (2014).

All of these pay close attention to sociolinguistic, narrative, rhetorical, and pragmatic modes of narration. They pay attention to configurations of the contemporary, the actual and the present. They deal with nature as "embodiment of the possible results of technology," in milieux of self-assertion or existential projects, and moving ratios of modernity (viz. Raymond Williams's "dominant, residual, emergent").

In this chapter, I've experimentally rigorously used Rabinow's distinctions between the present, the actual, and the contemporary. They do work. We will see if the terminology catches on, and if it can do productive work, or if it merely causes confusion because the terms in ordinary English are so interchangeable. It is, however, useful to keep various forms of temporality in mind (a project since at least Henri Bergson), and likewise to add to the Victor Turner tool kit of dramaturgical social processes, the more politically attuned alerts, trials, and polemical situations that Rabinow and Stavrianakis provide. In the meantime, the two essays on Richter and Rushdie add to the growing literatures on each.

PART II

Ground-Truthing

KEYWORDS

Anthropology: *a field science, going into the field and checking (ground-truthing) what the fit is with theories, models, ideas, and curiosities; then making theory to iteratively explain patterns emerging from further fieldwork.*

Ethnography: *ground-truthing; also the empirical basis for building new theory, making valid comparisons, recursively adjusting judgments to how things actually work in practice.*

4. Violence and Deep Play

Revisits the historical horizon of the 1960s through the 1990s to think about changes from the Cold War and modernization theories through postcolonial, neoliberal, and globalization eras into the fast capitalism, hyperspeed information flow, and ressentiment-driven political violence of the 2000s.

KEYWORDS

contextualist stance toward social theory; life outrunning the pedagogies in which we have been trained; native models as ethnographic datums and comparativist epistemology; models of and models for; cultural systems, interpretive anthropology; "assemblages of human agents and nonhuman ones bound together in intepretivist narratives," spider webs of meaning; poiesis, praxis, and gesture; second-order modernization; science accountable to multiple constituents; war again.

5. Amazonian Ethnography and the Politics of Renewal

Provides a regionally comparative ethnographic longitudinal archive and a sharp contrast between the 1960s and the 2000s in the indigenous societies of the Amazon.

KEYWORDS

evidentials; shatter zones and refuge areas; oscillation of more hierarchical and more open social forms; assimilation vs. interculturalism; organic intellectuals; hyperreal Indians; repertoires of tactics; postmodern arts of memory; abstract vs. grounded rights; emergent forms of new political life, history writing, conflict resolution, reintegration of guerillas, and reindigenization.

6. Ethnic Violence, Galactic Polities, and the Great Transformation

Provides another regionally comparative ethnographic longitudinal archive and contrast between the 1960s and the 2000s in South and Southeast Asia.

KEYWORDS

galactic politics (mandalas, negaras*); juggernaut of mass participatory politics; shatter zones of resettlement in areas of large-scale hydroelectric power dams; political economy first, then cosmology and ritual; charisma and legitimation; cross-continental trade networks; mythic structures and social charters; speech acts and ritual action; human rights and humanitarian rights.*

4

VIOLENCE AND DEEP PLAY

for CLIFFORD GEERTZ

Ground-truthing social violence is not just about particular events but also about the often torn social fabrics of the societies in which we all live. The "torn" nature of these social fabrics may be due to historical change, making people feel their rituals and beliefs to no longer "fit" their contemporary lives, and a consequent feeling of loss of purpose or meaning or anomie. It may be due to periods of accelerated inequalities, class conflicts, ethnic conflicts over resources or control, religious conflicts over shrines, or upsetting changes to conventions of public expression and behavior. It may be due to outright warfare of many kinds. It can be due to even the violent imposition of control by authoritarian forces of order, or the alienation generated by economic coercion or lack of opportunities.

The events of the 1965 massacres in Indonesia against real and alleged communists remain traumatic half a century later, their traces still reverberating, as do the effects of Dutch colonialism there, and French colonialism in Morocco.

The next chapter, chap. 5, deals with violences of postcolonial forces (including resource extraction), frontier expansions, imperial competitions, and tribal and even clan or kin competitions from the past into the present. In chapter 6 there are the ethnic riots of Sri Lanka, the military coups of Thailand, and the communal riots of India. The thread of violence is not the only one in these chapters or in the ethnographic work with which they deal, but it is one that has emerged more and more strongly after a period of post–World War II optimism in decolonizing and modernizing projects.

I used the occasion of the American Anthropological Association meeting panel in honor of Clifford Geertz to try to review my sense of the interpretive anthropology revolution that he led, where I thought it should go, and how I thought of my own work as aligning with, extending, and modifying it. Geertz was sitting in the front row, and eventually would respond in writing to all of us who made presentations (Shweder and Geertz, 2005) including the opening talk by one of the conveners, Rick Shweder, who said Geertz's message was hindered by his style of writing, a charge vigorously disputed by others, including James A. Boon's eloquent "Geertz's Style: A Moral Matter." Geertz, after all, was one of the great stylists writing in anthropology, and achieved global recognition by way of it. His language and vocabulary provided phrases that became the very prose of anthropological discourse.

My effort to put my work in conversation with one of my teachers, and to raise the theme of violence there, was partly overdetermined by the fact that my fieldwork in Iran was conducted in the immediate period preceding the Islamic revolution of 1977–79. My first book, based on my second period of fieldwork in Iran, was on that revolution; my earlier dissertation, based in a different town of Iran, included work on religious riots against minorities strategically used by the ulema against the state; and my next major fieldwork in India occurred during the year of Mrs. Gandhi's assassination, the Bhopal disaster, and the antiaffirmative action riots in Ahmedabad (where I was working).

"Deep Play" is one of my favorite teaching tools, in part because, like Marcel Mauss's *Essay sur le don* (The Gift), there is so much more to be unpeeled beyond what even a good student's first read reveals; but also because it is, like Victor Turner's work on ritual and social dramas of unfolding conflict, easy to transfer elsewhere as an analytic model. Much of Geertz's work has that quality, not just the essays, but also the monographs on Indonesia that remain touchstones for all Indonesianists even when they disagree or find fault. On the island of Sulawesi, where I paid anthropological pilgrimage in 2017 to the Bugis shipbuilding and trading community (they are important in Singapore and elsewhere throughout the Malay world) and to the uplands Toraja, the latter put a cock at the peak of their house gables over a sunburst, representing both daily renewal, and also authority and a means of conflict resolution. When there was a dispute, one way to resolve it was by holding a cockfight. It is both violence and a form of preventing larger violence. I am glad to be able to restore here the two images, which the University of

FIG. 4.1. Jean Lurçat, *La Mort et le Guerrier ou Hommage à Garcia Lorca*, 1973. Handwoven wool tapestry, 85 × 132.5 in (1976.004). Collection of the Massachusetts Institute of Technology List Visual Arts Center, Cambridge, Massachusetts. Gift of Halcon, International, New York, in Honor of its chairman, Dr. Ralph Landau, and of Guy Fino, Manufactura de TapeAnarias de Portalegre, Portugal. Jean Lurçat (1892–1966) was noted for the revival of contemporary tapestry.

Chicago Press refused to print for reasons best known to them, of the *buzkashi* games of Afghanistan and Central Asia, and of Jean Lurçat's tapestry *La Mort et le Guerrier ou Hommage à Garcia Lorca*, which used to hang in the Landau Building (chemical engineering) at MIT.

"Blurred Genres" is a well-known essay by Geertz; *Works and Lives* is a volume of essays that he called "slideshows" on the work of anthropologists. I play off all three by opening with a direct address to Geertz, to now his spirit:

For Clifford Geertz: Errant Thoughts in a Blurred Genre—errant—but hopefully not too erring. Thoughts in a blurred genre. Between the *Festschrift*—in which one offers in tribute one's own work as an extension of one's teacher's work—and the slideshow on "works and lives." Indeed, two slides can serve as frames: a slide of a fabulous large tapestry by Jean Lurçat of a fighting cock that hung (until recently, when it was removed for repair to the backing) in Building 66, the Landau, or chemical engineering, building at MIT, a locus to which I shall return; and a slide of a painting of a buzkashi game that I brought back from Central Asia and that now hangs in my house, a game to which I shall also return.

So: errant thoughts in a blurred genre—for Clifford Geertz—in three movements: where we are now, where we have been, and on the trail of an anthropology to come. One of the conundra of trying to talk about Geertz's work is that the very language of anthropology—the prose we speak—is suffused with the metaphors he has taught us to think with: turtles and metaphors all the way down.

Section 1: Where We Are Now

Emergent Forms of Life and the Anthropological Voice;
Or:
A post-Geertzian manifesto, where "post," "posts," and "postings"
are defined as a sending-receiving relation
between fathers and sons,
and between the three or four phases of self-defined Geertzian work.

I start with an ethnographic datum, a stance toward ethics and politics, and a contextualist stance toward social theory.

We live (again) in an era in which there is a pervasive claim, or native model, asserted by practitioners in many contemporary arenas of life (law, sciences, political economy, computer technologies, education, etc.) that traditional concepts and ways of doing things no longer work, that life is outrunning the pedagogies in which we were trained, that we are experiencing emergent new forms of life—in new cyborgian, hybrid, cross-species biotechnological forms of life, in databank-networked and new materials infrastructures, in environmental and ecological changes, and in the legal, economic, psychological, and social institutional innovations that these require. *Call this native model an ethnographic datum.*

We live therefore (again) in an era in which new ethical and political spaces are thrown up that require action and can often have quite serious consequences but for which the possibilities for giving grounds quickly run out. Traditional ethical and moral guides seem not always helpful, and we are often left to negotiate interests and trade-offs in legal or other tournaments of decision-making over time, and across terrains configured with multiply interacting new technologies, what I call ethical plateaus, with due deference to Gilles Deleuze, Gregory Bateson, and the Balinese. *Call this a philosophical stance toward ethics and politics,* one that Ludwig Wittgenstein formulated when he said that giving grounds comes to an end somewhere and that "the end is not an ungrounded presupposition; it is an ungrounded way of acting" or a "form of life," a sociality of action that always already contains within it ethical dilemmas, or, in the idiom of Emmanuel Levinas, "the face of the other." The "face of the other" is particularly of concern in the peopling of new technologies and technosciences.

In coming to terms with this ethnographic datum and this philosophical stance, anthropology is pushed to develop new tools of social theory. The social theory of the last quarter of the twentieth century and the beginning of the twenty-first is created out of quite different generational, social structural, communication infrastructural, and knowledge-making contexts and experiences from those out of which classical social theory was created at the end of the nineteenth century and turn of the twentieth. *Call this a contextualist stance toward social and cultural theory.* Classical social theory is hardly passé or superseded, but Marx, Weber, Dilthey, Freud, Durkheim, Fleck, Mauss, Schutz, and others did not experience or analyze the kinds of shifts that have become focal for post-Algerian independence French theory (Cixous, Deleuze and Guattari, Foucault, Derrida, Lyotard, Baudrillard, Touraine, Abeles, Latour, et al.); post–green movement theory in Germany (Ulrich Beck, Friedrich Kittler) and Italy (Agamben, Melucci); post–cost-benefit analysis of high-hazard, high-consequence industries, from anesthesiology to aeronautics to nuclear power in the United States (Perrow); postsocialist nationalisms, and, importantly for my own work, social and cultural movements in the Islamic world seeking to move beyond patriarchal patrimonialism (inspired among others by Ali Shariati, Nawal El Saadawi, and Saad Ibrahim; and the powerful films coming out of Iran). Indeed, today, November 23, 2002,—on the very day that NATO is being expanded, and that we are contemplating war in Iraq—we continue to operate under the sign of the film *Safar-e Qandahar* (*Kandahar*) by the Iranian director Mohsen Makhmalbaf, and its image of prostheses being parachuted from Red Cross helicopters to Afghan men running on crutches to catch them.

In the 1990s anthropology began to take up ethnographic challenges in a number of critical arenas: *work on the reconstruction of society* in the wake of social trauma, structural violence, and disruption on a scale not reflected upon, though it existed, by the social sciences since the early post–World War II, post–India-Pakistan partition, and postwars of the decolonization era in which Clifford Geertz got his anthropological start. In the 1990s anthropology began to take up ethnographic *work on the new communications technologies* that mediate the contemporary analogues of what Durkheim might have called the *conscience collective* in their more differentiated, telemediated, transnationally diffuse guises, and *that transform the conditions of possibility for governance, legitimacy, and democratic civil societies.*[1] And in the 1990s anthropology began to take up ethnographic *work on the infrastructures of what we make live and who we let die.*

To map and critique these technoscientific worlds and infrastructures, interferences and mediations, dislocations and reconfigurations, cultural forces and autoimmune cultural toxicities (presented via global media from CNN to Al Jazeera) requires an anthropology attentive to an expanding variety of cultural differences that go far beyond traditionally understood cultural differences. The distinctive anthropological voice—the aspiration for cross-culturally comparative, socially grounded, linguistically attentive perspectives—continues to be a valuable jewel among the social sciences amid the pressures to simply turn to statistical indices for all policies and judgments.

Thus far the inconstant son's sendings to the father; let me turn to the generative sendings of the father to the son.

Section 2: Where We Have Been

Rethinking the Anthropology of the Second Half
of the Twentieth Century with Clifford Geertz
Or:
Clifford Geertz's four phases and my threefold epistemological interpretive grid

In his most recent of three essays surveying his own "works and lives," Geertz uses a fourfold division. There is the golden age of optimistic post–World War II reconstruction; multidisciplinarity and team research; modernization and development theories grounded in Max Weber's notion of economic, political, and cultural rationalizations; and the voluntarism of Talcott Parsons's layer cake of biological, psychological, social, and cultural systems, the latter three, respectively, being dynamically integrated, functionally integrated, and logico-meaningfully integrated with cybernetic feedback among them, such that they were always already inseparable except analytically or heuristically. This was the age of Geertz's field-defining quartet of ethnographic monographs on Indonesia.

There followed the dramatic shift of the hot spots of the Cold War into Indonesia. Thus the silver age of his migration to Sefrou in Morocco, and the efforts of the Committee for the Comparative Study of New Nations at the University of Chicago to keep the modernization theories going as they splintered and decayed. Geertz's ethnography became less monographic, and justifications were found for turning to the essay form in *Local Knowledge*, and the tributes to such literary idols as Lionel Trilling. It is this turn that contains, I think, much of the ambivalence of his own corpus of work and its uneasy relation to the work of some of his progeny.

There followed the bronze and iron ages in anthropology of the 1980s and 1990s, which Geertz glosses as a florescence of different schools and isms in the social sciences, followed most recently by a return of "unclear significance" to concerns with violence, ethnic conflict, and the like. This is the period of blurred genres, Geertz being in multiple minds about the role of Islam, and so on.

This is, however, the period in my own trajectory and that of my cohort, of *Writing Culture*, *Anthropology as Cultural Critique*, *Debating Muslims* and the Islam and Social Change Project at the University of Chicago (of which it was a part), the eight-volume *Late Editions Project*, the *Public Culture Project*, the inauguration of the journal *Cultural Anthropology*, my own directing of the Center for Cultural Studies at Rice University, and then directing the Program in Science, Technology and Society at MIT. I count myself as one of Clifford Geertz's progeny, perhaps an inconstant disciple, nonetheless both a fan and, I hope, an appreciative and constructive deployer of his insights. My own work followed along behind Geertz's early interest in ecology (I was originally trained as a geographer by my father and at Johns Hopkins), his efforts to test Weberian accounts of sociologically stratified and differentiated organized religious forms (in my case in the Caribbean, Iran, and India), his interest in the philosophy of the social sciences, in genres of literary and dramatic forms, and eventually in science and technology. And I particularly want to salute Cliff's repeated efforts to appoint a science studies person at the Institute for Advanced Studies at Princeton.

I would divide Geertz's four phases into three epistemological ones. I think one of the most fascinating features of Clifford Geertz's writings is the shift from comparativist Weberian, Parsonian, and broadly positivist or positive knowledge production, intended to help with notions of development programs for the modernization of "new nations" in old cultures and civilizations (a contradiction that soon became generative both descriptively and epistemologically). It is a shift from the rich ethnographic work of *Agricultural Involution* (1963); *Religions in Java* (1960), as its author titled it (not as it was titled in the singular by its publisher (Geertz, *After the Fact* [hereafter AF], 55); *The Social History of an Indonesian Town* (1965); *Peddlers and Princes* (1963); and such essays as "Religion and Social Change," "Deep

Play," and perhaps, but maybe not, "Person, Time and Conduct in Bali,"[2] but certainly the later *Negara* (1980). By the time we get to *After the Fact* and *Available Light* (2000), we are in the presence of an *ostad*, a master, of a very different kind of epistemology, one that plays deeply described cultures off against one another in a comparative epistemology, rather than a comparative realism, where, as Geertz himself says, "One is faced with complex and contradictory fields of significative action, most of it tacit, across which assertion and denial, celebration and complaint, authority and resistance, continuously move." He is talking about comparing Indonesia and Morocco, and he continues, "When ingeniously juxtaposed, these fields can shed a certain amount of light on one another, but they are neither variants of one another nor expressions of some superfield that transcends them both" (AF, 49). I would call this *using the epistemological resources of one culture to critique and see anew into another culture.* In this example, Geertz is musing upon the lack of gender inflections in Javanese, and its minutely graded, hierarchical speech registers, in contrast to Moroccan Arabic, which "has gender inflections for just about every part of speech, but no status forms" (AF, 46). By so musing, he comes upon the insight—which he does not actually develop, though it would be fascinating to do so—that by looking at Moroccan politics with Javanese eyes (or grammars and speech modes) he is suddenly struck by the "persistent edge of seduction and resistance, flirtation and conquest . . . ranging from the understanding of sainthood to the metaphors of insult." Moroccan politics is a world of flirtation and seduction, "where rank and station are sexually charged."

Geertz in this most recent phase of his epistemological self-reflections speaks of this sort of comparative "method," or, since he eschews the term "method," the artistic, even intuitive, skill of these fields of "significative action, most of it tacit, across which assertion and denial, celebration and complaint, authority and resistance, continuously move"—as comparing incommensurables. Nonetheless, he concedes, it is "a useful enterprise, and when the stars are right, an informative one, however illogical."

Illogical? I would submit even in passing that hermeneutics and performance are not illogical, either as method or as art, and that entertaining work in the comparative critical apparatuses of local hermeneutics is both methodical and reasonable, and at least culturally logical.

Geertz's middle passage is where I suppose the contradictions of the Parsonian vision came to accumulate so many anomalies that a paradigm shift was needed and was found in the Geisteswissenschaften of Dilthey, Weber, and Schutz, the countercanon to which we were treated by Cliff in the 1960s.

(We also found our way to Hans-Georg Gadamer's *Truth and Method*; to Walter Benjamin and Theodor Adorno; and to Paul Ricoeur, Kenneth Burke, Victor Turner, and Mircea Eliade, all of whom were important presences for my cohort at Chicago—and even, very sotto voce at Chicago, to Claude Lévi-Strauss read as Talmud for reconstructing a shattered cultural past [see, e.g., chap. 5] rather than as machine, to Marx read as decipherer of symbolic hieroglyphics of social suffering and cultural and personal-centered meaning as well as a political economist and a Saul Alinsky organizer avant la lettre[3]). This middle passage was the time of the essays of the *Interpretation of Culture*, essays that we as graduate students were enthralled by, and tried without comparable success to mimic in our various term papers, mimicking the vocabulary, the bons mots, the paradoxes, and chaismuses, and elegant turns of polished phrase: models of / models for, experience near / experience far, many, as with all good poets, borrowed form, and gaining resonance from, the sedimented metaphors in the language and epistemological threads of earlier practitioners, Dilthey's *Vorbildt* und *Nachbildt*, Kohut's experience near and experience far, Gilbert Ryle's thick description and public language routing the ghosts in the machine, Paul Ricoeur's social action leaving traces in consequences that could be read as texts, Jeremy Bentham's deep play, Alfred Schutz's consociates. The middle passage was ethnographic as well as epistemological: Morocco did not yield up the monographic ethnographic treatments that Indonesia did, though *Islam Observed* and *Meaning and Order in Morocco Society* had their brilliant insights and verbal pointillisms, such as the much-quoted image of the mental compartmentalization used by the modern Muslim of undecidable piety on the airplane with Scotch in one hand and the Qur'an for safety in the other.

This is the middle passage from cultural systems, the era of the hegemony of linguistic models: structural linguistics, generative grammars, cybernetics, paradigms, structuralisms, and the efforts to reformat phenomenology into more systematic modes, whether in Sartre's effort to fuse existentialism and Marxism or the socialization of perception through cultural forms, cockfights, calendars, teknonymic kinship namings, ethnosemantics, religion as a cultural system, models of / models for, common sense as a cultural system, art as a cultural system, ideology as a cultural system. The middle passage from these recursive, self-protective symbolic systems to interpretive modes of blurred genres, incommensurable fields of significative action, reading over one another's shoulders, and like a moiré flitting back and forth between narrative local worlds and world-historical ones, across which as well "assertion and denial, celebration and complaint, authority and resistance" continuously

FIG. 4.2. Buzkashi, painting by A. Batyr, 2002. From the collection of the author.

shift figure and ground, Gestalt and paradigm, appealing to undecidables and aporias, as when Geertz muses about the place of Islam in Indonesia, noting that in his several decades of observation its role has dramatically shifted several times—itself a sociological and historical comparativist observation. His recent essay on Gus Dur Wahid shows that he remained a shrewd and incisive commentator on Indonesia. But about Islam's place he rather wishes to leave himself open to being "of many minds."

Section 3: On the Trail of an Anthropology to Come

By way of conclusion, I would return our gaze to the three challenges of 1990s anthropology as sites of deep play, each providing its own slideshow: (1) the reconstruction of society in the wake of obliviously caused social trauma and structural violence—call this, title the slide, "The Move from Cockfight to Buzkashi"; (2) the changes in science institutions from the 1960s to the 1990s—call this, title this slide, "The Move from Union Carbide in Bhopal (and Institute, West Virginia) to the Demands of ACT UP and Patient Groups for Accountability in the Technologies of What Is Made to Live and Who Is Let

Die"; and (3) the immersion in the telemedia—call this, title this slide, "War Again, 9/11, Qandahar, and the Autoimmune Cultural Toxicities of CNN and Al Jazeera."

FROM COCKFIGHT TO BUZKASHI

On September 31, 2001, general Amin Said Tariq of the Northern Alliance in Afghanistan was quoted in a *Boston Globe* headline: "It Is Time for the Americans to Join the Game," the Great Game of and for Central Asia, the game of buzkashi. US Special Forces were photographed astride Afghan steeds playing the game. Quite apart from one's political stand on just wars or the effectiveness of global interventions, one wonders how we will play the buzkashi game with smart bombs, psychopharmacological uppers for long-range flights, nanotechnologies for smart protective uniforms, smart mobile surgical rooms, and whether we have, and how good are our game plans to pick up the land mines, destroyed schools, water systems, and battered bodies and minds. Like the cockfight of an earlier era of violence, this buzkashi focuses our attention today again on violence, bare life, and states of exception.[4] Buzkashi becomes an icon for the shift from disciplinary societies to societies of control (those that depend less on territorial integrity than on statistics, flows, codes, networks, and standards, and which when attacked create new zones of indistinction.

FROM UNION CARBIDE IN BHOPAL TO THE DEMANDS OF ACT UP AND PATIENT GROUPS FOR ACCOUNTABILITY

The biopolitics of globalization are again at center stage, and at the center of these new ethnical and political vortices are battles over the technosciences and biotechnologies themselves.

Cliff challenged us a few years ago to extend interpretivist approaches to the forms of life associated with "loose assemblages of differently focused, rather self-involved, and variably overlapping research communities in both the human and the natural sciences." He wrote,

> Of all the sorts of work that go on under the general rubric of the human sciences, those that devote themselves to clarifying the forms of life lived out . . . in connection with linear accelerators, neuroendocrinological labs, the demonstration rooms of the Royal Society, astronomical observations, marine biology field stations, or the planning committees of NASA, are the least likely to conceive their task as limited to making out the inter-subjective worlds of persons. Machines,

> objects, tools, artifacts, instruments are too close at hand to be taken as external to what is going on; so much apparatus, free of meaning. These mere "things" have to be incorporated into the story, and when they are the story takes on a heteroclite form—human agents and non-human ones bound together in interpretivist narratives.

After cautiously acknowledging the "ill-formed and variable, uncertain opening probes in an . . . ill-marked enquiry"—but I would say rapidly burgeoning field of science studies (the anthropologies of Bruno Latour and Donna Haraway, Emily Martin, Rayna Rapp, Deborah Heath, Karen-Sue Taussig, Steve Shapin, Simon Shafer, Sharon Traweek, Joe Dumit, Paul Rabinow, Lawrence Cohen, Kim Fortun, Mike Fortun, Adryana Petryna, João Biehl, Byron Good, Mary-Jo DelVecchio Good, Chris Kelty, Hannah Landecker, Jennifer Mnookin, Heinrich Schwarz, Kaushik Sunder Rajan, Cory Hayden, Margaret Lock, Gary Downey, and many others, myself included)—he notes, "Sciences, physical, biological, human, or whatever, change not only in their content or their social impact (though they do, of course, do that . . .) but in their character as a form of life, a way of being in the world" (*AF*).

What I want to mark here is a set of double movements that Geertz marked ahead on the trails of an anthropology to come, the boule movement between lives and works, the coming inevitably onto the scene after the fact, after the fact in search of and after the fact belated, the world-historical narratives, such as they are (bracketed, as Lyotard would say, or ironized with Geertzian caution), nonetheless world-historical narratives (political master stories of modernization, or of anticolonialism, "those were the Bandung days," "the days of May 1968") bursting from time to time into local worlds, and at other times carrying those local worlds along with the spinning of the globe and the spinning of webs of significance and meaning, cosmic, scientific, metaphysical, and moral-ethical.

These doublings, hauntings, and phantasmagoria, tools of poiesis, praxis, and gesture, mark out an anthropology to come, a justice to come, a community to come.

But the cockfights of science are already registered in rich accounts by scientists themselves and by observers of their forms of life: François Jacob's much-admired autobiography, much cited by scientists, provides an exemplary account of two trained roosters beak to beak in, as well, a metaphysical and cosmic competition with God:

> Seminars, true rites of initiation, free-for-alls. . . . That day an American biochemist. . . . The audience interrupted incessantly. . . . Chop-

ping up his discourse with questions . . . badgering him, provoking him, nipping at his heels like excited puppies. . . . As for [Sol] Spiegelman, he was not easily confounded . . . he listened to comments and criticisms while playing with a piece of chalk in the fashion of a Hollywood gangster with a coin. . . . The deathblow came later in a cafe on the Boulevard Pasteur . . . the theory was dissected, torn apart, shredded into tiny pieces. Bit by bit, the bull weakened. A final thrust of [Jacques] Monod's descabello. The bull's final spasm. And resistance ceased. All this amidst laughter and joking. . . . *Two trained roosters beak to beak* vying with humor and sarcasm. . . . a will to power . . . a desire for intellectual domination . . . a world full of gaiety, of the unexpected, of curiosity, of imagination. A life animated as much by passion as by logic. Science meant for me the most elevating form of revolt against the coherence of the universe. Man's most powerful means of competing with God; of tirelessly rebuilding the world while taking account of reality. (Jacob, 1988, 215)

There is a richness, a jouissance, a gamble with passion, in the sport of science, and also metaphysical depth, an agon with the mysteries of the universe and life, not just an aesthetic harmony or a pleasure in technical skill. As the Polish-born physicist I. I. Rabi, from the spa town and Hassidic seat of Rymanov in Galicia, puts it,

Some of the young people I see, who are very good, take physics . . . as a system you can do things with, can calculate something with, and they miss . . . the mystery of it: how very different it is from what you can see and how profound nature is. . . . There is no good translation of a *Witz*. It's a joke or a trick. It's the use of this kind of witty trick that I have always liked about physics. . . . I have always taken physics personally. . . . It's between me and nature. (Rabi 1960)

This metaphysical depth is often folded—like a double helix—against cultural traditions, historical experiences, and community structures. Some of the productive tensions and synergistic reinterpretations between scientific rationalities (such as they are in a post–Ludwik Fleck, Tom Kuhn, Bruno Latour, and Peter Galison era) and Christian and Jewish traditions have been explored, but one wonders in today's world why more has not been done with Hindu, Buddhist, Confucian, and Islamic traditions that lie in the background of some of the world's greatest scientists: Homi Bhabha, Vikram Sarabhai, Ramanujan, Chandrasekar, Abdus Salam, Gobind Khorana, and now the Brahmin and Muslim creators of the "Hindu bomb"—Raj Ramana, the classical pianist and explorer of resonances between Buddhist logic and high-energy physics, and Avul Pakir Jainulabdeen Abdul Kalam, the current president of the Republic of India who justifies with good cockfight and game theory logic that "strength respects strength."

Above all, the search for accountability has transformed the ways in which the institutions of science and the technosciences operate. Call it the transformation from big science and the national security state to science accountable to multiple constituents lest the complexity of the infrastructure become brittle and break down. The ethics of science—and the representations of science in both the epistemological (accuracy, reference, completeness) and political or stakeholders' senses—are no longer marginal issues left up to the sensibility of the researcher or expert. Across the sciences these are becoming matters for institutional review, efforts at transparency, and negotiations between publics and researchers over the propriety of research that involves people and publics. As the world becomes more integrated and interactive, questions of how information is collected, packaged, and made available as part of social institutions of reflexive or second-order modernization (to use Ulrich Beck's terms) become more important and open to insistent questioning, and that detouring through media circuits of advertising, advocacy, and persuasion only make all the more suspect and subject to insistent questioning. Does a local population always have to benefit, or is there a place for presumed consent to collection of various sorts of human biology data (blood; feces; cheek swabs; genetic, epidemiological, and pathology samples; medical records), which only after considerable processing can be turned into statistical and "evidence-based" knowledge and pharmacological and medical products? The answers to these questions are not in, but they are today central questions publically debated and politically negotiated—from Iceland's experiment to allow deCODE Corporation to link data banks of medical records, genealogies, and DNA samples to the Harvard-Millennium Pharmaceuticals project in China to collect DNA samples from populations in Anhui Province—and are not easily swept under the carpet. The biosciences are a deep play that directly pose questions of who shall live and who shall die, and that exert pressure toward new institutions of reflexive modernization or deliberative democracy in some of the most difficult areas of human experimental trials, informed consent, privacy and surveillance, patents and ownership of biological information, and the power of huge amounts of investments of not just money and power but also ideology and fantasy.

"WAR AGAIN, 9/11, QANDAHAR" AND THE AUTOIMMUNE CULTURAL TOXICITIES OF CNN AND AL JAZEERA

No consideration of the current conditions can avoid the new fabric of interacting media that have changed the calculus of, and conditions of possibility for, governance and legitimacy, of what democracy could possibly mean, of who speaks for whom, where all must play through the media, scientists and physicians as much as anyone, with anthropologists—for better or worse—far behind (running after the fact), and where the very use of telemedia has the effect, simultaneously, of both extending and undoing the messages, propaganda, persuasions, or pedagogies intended by the sender or patron, and where the truth is less hidden than partially revealed in measured and calculated unveilings that blur truth falsity, that, as Hannah Arendt once said, hide truth in the open where it can be assumed to be false, contaminated, or doctored, and is so by its very nature, without being any less the truth.

While Geertz never devoted much attention to the telemedia, he has directed attention to the affective and cognitive, metaphorical and interpretive tactics that form its basis. Symbolic anthropology morphing into interpretive anthropology can provide tools probing both cultural philosophical meaning making and also the sociology of cultural meanings and their operation as, and in, fields of power. One of the tasks of anthropology is to do the anthropology—cultural and social analysis—of communities of social thought and social theory itself. It is not very interesting after a while to simply debunk efforts at pattern recognition, generalization, comparison, model building, formalizations-in-the-service-of-models against which complex realities can be approximated, good-enough theory for pragmatic needs, and the like, as if they were misunderstood as universal and eternal truths. It is the recognition of immanent cultural critique, the play of communities of social thought against one another (not "recriminations") that anthropology often is particularly well poised to place into the interpretive cockfight arena for us all to see the passions and irrationalities, as well as reasons and calculations, and the social structures and cultural legitimations at play.

5

AMAZONIAN ETHNOGRAPHY AND THE POLITICS OF RENEWAL

for JEAN JACKSON

> Tukanoans have an astonishing ability to turn the most unpleasant happenings into something funny, at times even when it is happening. . . . One must laugh if possible, and savor the details for future story-telling. —JEAN JACKSON, *The Fish People*

The northwestern Amazon region provides significant initiatives in recovery of histories, local genres of thinking, and modes of renewal. As Jean Jackson and other ethnographers of the region have been detailing over the last few decades, there are experimental and emergent forms of new political life, history writing, conflict resolution, reintegration of guerillas, and novel modes of reindigenization that flexibly recognize cultural rights and human rights. Such experiments and emergent forms can give us models and conceptual tools for stalemated situations elsewhere. I am fascinated with linguistic affordances such as the evidentials in Tukano discourses, or with the way that channeling dance and ritual forms into our tellings and writings (rather than reducing them to flat distanced prose) can provide platforms or more than unidimensional stages for exploring matters of concern for our varied interlocutors that might dialogically bring a responsive smile and nod that yes, we have understood something. I begin with a such a channeling of a Tukano *pudali* feast dance chant as a prelude, and again as a concluding reprise. I use the pudali as what West Africans would call a praise song, stipulating that

FIG. 5.1. Anaconda pudali song with *wa-an-apani* stomping tubes. Bark painting, Bora, Peru (2014). [Misspelled inscription should read "*malolca de los boras*" (pueblo or village of the Bora).] Bark paintings today are done upon request. This one collected by Mike Lee of Yage Art in Iquitos, Peru, in 2014. Spurlock Museum, University of Illinois, has one of the largest collections of Tukuna bark cloth paintings, collected in 1970 by then anthropology graduate student Charles E. Bolian.

praise songs are a form of oral history writing by griots, and it is used here to explore the ethnographies of the region, and as a form of cultural critique of First World all-too-quick judgmental high theory. After the prelude as a kind of sonic tuning up, I first look back into human geography and the mythic and historical record of the region (the chopping up of the anaconda), before turning to the present and future (the repairing of the anaconda).

Prelude: Channeling *Tukano Speech Forms*

We have come to this pudali (Wanano *po'a*), we have come to this ceremonial feast, a pudali (sort of like a potlatch, or a potluck) to celebrate and dance (*lirr-paka,* another name for pudali, meaning "[he] dances" or also the spawning of the fish, in playful courtship activity), doing the wheel dance (*dzu-dzu-apani*), men and women locking arms together, and with a circular fishnet stretched on a pole over the ceremonial fire, wheeling clockwise and counterclockwise. We have come with our *wa-an-apani* (or *waana*), our stomping tubes, with our coconut weevil *deetu* flutes (that make sucking sounds) and our *ku-lir-rina* catfish trumpets (that make deep bass rumbling sounds like streams filled with migrating *boachico* "cute-mouth" fish), to celebrate the career of a woman among us, a woman like Amaru, the primordial woman, a woman who writes to open and expand the world of social relations (or perhaps to defend the closed world being lost). We bring offerings of our crafts, trade goods, the cooked meat and smoked fish of our labor to reaffirm our ties, in exchange for manioc beer, Jean's writings, her world-renown gourmet cooking, her worldly and often gender-sharp humor, to reaffirm our genealogies, to tell of our common descent and our differentiation, of our marriages and different languages or patrilects and matrilects, to claim our rights, to become ethnics in a new world, a world of *inter*culturalism and cultural rights, to be different, to bring justice to the world, to lock wrongdoers in public stocks and then to reintegrate them instead of sending them away to jails to learn evil, to be different from whites, most of whom, Jean says, have Indian blood too, and who also can learn to drink *yage* (*ja-he*), inhale snuff, blow tobacco cigar smoke, save the Amazon, and become new peoples of the future to come.

Ni'ame ni'ame yii makii yii makii
So says my son, so says my son of the Wai maha
or wai masa (the fish people).

While men engage in affect-free, punctuated jackhammer greetings, the ceremonial greetings by women are wept. Their sad songs (*kaya basa*), intended to evoke weeping, gently drift self-reflectively inward, and outward to emotionally touch a sister, sister-in-law, or cousin. The death that is referenced and mourned is not that of a deceased loved one but of the singer's own living death, her social isolation and separation (so says/writes Janet Chernlea of the Wanan and Tukano). *Sin-in-abe, sininabe* (please take this drink, please take this drink). *Sin-ina, sinina* (drink, drink), I've been so sad (*buh-ci-wetiri koro*); a woman going without (*m-ciri-nni koro*), without her mother's voice (*yii pliako iisero reba*); detested (*yabiri kow*); envied and criticized (*abiari koro*); made to feel ugly (*tiyari koro*); sickly (*thipari koro*); a wandering soul (*thinari koro*), forced to mix without her mother's voice (*su'sari koro*).

Ni'ame ni'ame yii makii yii makii
So says my son, so says my son.

I weep that "in a few years almost all [Tukanoans] will be interested in giving up what is left of their culture," so writes Jean Jackson, so says the Jean of 1983, thirty years ago (*Fish People*, 225). "Tukanoans are embarked on a journey of increasing integration . . . and for many it is a long journey toward real poverty, alcoholism, disease, malnutrition, alienation, and despair," so says Jean Jackson, so says Jean (226).

Preface: The Times, They Are A'Changin'

In 2014, however, there are two indigenous senators in the Colombian parliament, indigenous governors, indigenous local heads of native territories. In Venezuela three indigenous politicians were involved in writing the Constitution in 1999. Across the border in Brazil, many indigenous young men are joining the Brazilian military in larger percentages than other groups. One of the Colombian senators, Jean tells us, Jesus Pinacue, a Nasa senator, broke a campaign promise, and requested as his punishment the revival of an old ritual, involving meditation, a six-hour walk, 4,400 meters up the mountains, to the sacred lake, Juan Tama, where ten shamans tossed him nude into the freezing water. He walked back, and visited every protected community, every *resquardo*, to renew his commitments, before being allowed to resume his Senate seat. "Under the 1991 constitution, the Colombian state [unlike Australia or the United States] does not judge the authenticity of native Colombians, preferring to authorize indigenous organizations to assume the helm (so says Joanne Rappaport 2005, 37). Others, such as Kimberly Theidon, have written of such justice systems as ways to reincorporate demobilized guerilla fighters.

So, not so quick with the assessments of the 1970s: we first look back, then ahead. The processes of ethnogenesis are more complicated both back and front.

In section 1, I try to rethink the ethnogenesis that was being brought to attention in the work of the ethnographers of the late 1960s and 1970s, of whom Jean was among the pioneers.

Today in Colombia and northwestern Brazil there are protected indigenous territories (*resquardo*) and *emergent forms of life* that come from *heterogeneity*, and that in *Writing Culture* I called "the postmodern arts of memory," or what in Colombia is called *inter-culturalism* and *ethnic pluralism*. In section 2, I consider Jean's new work reformulating her decades-long work on indigenous rights, trying to formulate, for myself, a sense not only

TABLE 5.1. Emergent Ethnographic Archive (partial list)

Ethnographer	Ethnic grouping	Country
Chernela	Nasa/Paez	Colombia
Fleming	Tukano/Arawak	Brazil border
Hill	Wakuenai	Venezuela
S. Hugh-Jones and C. Hugh-Jones	Barasana	Colombia
Jackson	Tukano	Colombia
Jamieson	Wayuu/Arawak	Venezuela, Colombia
Goldman	Cubeo	Colombia
Wright	Baniwa	Colombia

of what this looks like in South America but how it might provide pragmatic, if always troubled, aspirations elsewhere as well.

Section 1: Looking Back: *Chopping Up the Anaconda*

Into the shatter zone and refuge area—first between the sixteenth-century Inca and Spanish empires, disrupting the gold and fine metalwork trade of the Muisca (of the El Dorado legends)[1]; then in the seventeenth century between the Dutch and Carib slavers coming up the Orinoco and the Arawak and Portuguese slavers coming up the Amazon; then in the nineteenth and twentieth centuries the impressment of labor and debt-enslavement by rubber collectors, all the while harassed by epidemics (measles, tuberculosis, yellow fever, malaria), as well as by Catholic (Jesuits, Salesians, and others) and Protestant (Baptist, New Tribe, Summer Institute of Linguistics) missionaries; and more recently by gold miners, cocaine mafias, and FARC and ELM guerillas—into this shatter zone and refuge area, there formed in the Vaupes River basin at the headwaters of the Amazon and the Orinoco, in today's Colombia, Brazil, and Venezuela, a complex of Tukanoan and other sibs that into the 1970s and beyond practiced "linguistic exogamy," made famous in the anthropological literature by Jean Jackson's fieldwork. The region has some sixteen to twenty languages or patrilects, dialects of patrilines, in five language groups (Tukanoan, Arawak, Carib, Maku, and Tupi-Guarani) of which some say Carib and some say Tukano are the oldest in the area. Tukano became the indigenous lingua franca, superseding the earlier Lingua Geral, Nheengatu, a descendant of Tupi-Guarani.

According to local metaphors and ritual practice, the ancestors, the mythic primordial people, came upriver from a cosmic center, a hole under

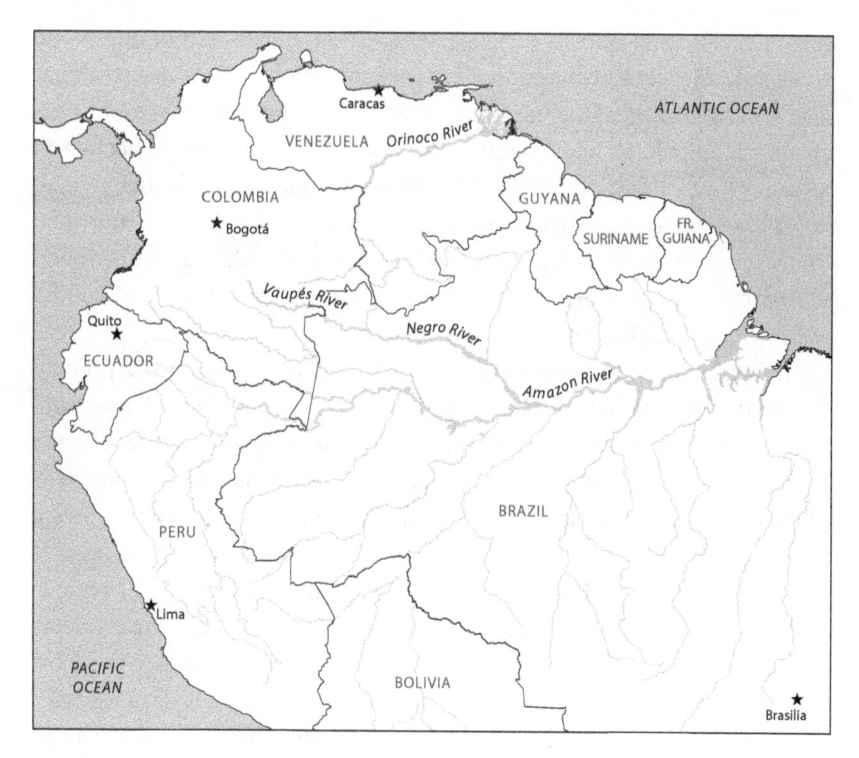

MAP 5.1. Map of Vaupes region (Vaupes River in the upper left).

rapids at Hipana on the Aiari River in Brazil (according to the Waku-enai) or perhaps from the Ewura taro swamp (according to Jean's Bara informants), where in either case a palm tree grows from earth to sky, which when felled became/becomes the wood for the sacred flutes. The ancestors were dropped off at their present living sites by large anaconda canoes or as segments of an anaconda: the jaguar or earth anaconda canoe dropping off the Barasana; the fish or water anaconda canoe dropping off the Tukano; and the sky anaconda or eagle canoe dropping off the Tatuyo. Elder brothers were dropped off first downriver, and juniors upriver further from trade connections. In female initiation rites, place naming proceeds back downriver toward the origin, mapping the region of marriage relations; in male initiation rites, naming proceeds even further downriver to Manaus, where the Rio Negro meets the Amazon, and even to the mouth of the Amazon, and then returns (in an Arapaco version in a submarine laden with trade goods) upriver, and on beyond the headwaters of the Amazon drainage basin, crossing over into the Orinoco basin and down to the Caribbean, mapping continental trade routes. In shamanic curing songs, downriver is the direction of illness and witchcraft, upriver the direction of escape into health. The Arapaco submarine is but a version of the improper sexual relations of the wife of trickster-creator, Inapirrikuli. Inapirrikuli's wife would copulate with Anaconda in return for shell money on her way back from the manioc fields. Inapirrikuli killed him with a poison dart. Anaconda rolled downriver, where Inapirrikuli found him rotting. The origin of the whites are in the white grubs he found in Anaconda's penis, which he cut off and fed, along with fish, to his unfaithful wife before banishing her.

In preparing for the new world of future people to come, that is, human beings as we know them today, Inapirrikuli (Made-from-Bone, that is, from blowing snuff in across a tray made of his dead father's finger bones), the creator-trickster figure of the Wakuenai, an Arawak-speaking group, tells of the cutting up of the anaconda, and of it being reconstituted with water, a metaphor of the devastations and reconstitutions of the low-density, widely networked set of small Indian groups from the Caribbean to Southern Brazil. These groups at times coalesced into federated alliances under ritual leaders and war chiefs to fight the Inca, Dutch, Spanish, and Portuguese. The most famous of these uprisings was in 1776, led by the Ye'kuana. It was the last in a series of uprisings, each lasting some twenty years, that ended the Spanish military and missionary effort to link the Upper and Lower Orinoco with a network of overland routes and forts. Another uprising in 1858 was led by a Baniwa man, Venancio Camico, prophesizing a world fire that would destroy the white man's economy and debt peonage, and whose teachings of resistance to the money economy was incorporated into the Baniwa male and female initiation rituals. In times of peace, these more hierarchical forms could be relaxed into open, incorporative social forms, around pudali feasting, especially in the seasonal times of abundance at the beginning of the wet season in March and April. "The Tukanoan cultural complex" as Jean writes in her new essays, is "extraordinary, unique in the world, a magnificent institution," although, if linguist Luke Fleming is correct, perhaps not quite entirely unique; he's not correcting her, he's a fan crediting her with moving the field, beyond Arthur Sorensen's effort to measure distances between languages, into the use of linguistic badges and ritual exchanges to facilitate both interethnic relations and social reproduction (Jackson, *Fish People*, 202). The trickster, Inapirrikuli, Jonathan Hill notes, "unlike the buffoon tricksters of North America . . . is omniscient, powerful, anticipates treachery and deceit of others, and *skillfully manipulates words so they cannot be interpreted literally*, his most potent weapons" (stress emphasis added).

Five interrelated themes, in these accounts, are at the center of this 1970s horizon of ethnographic work, a horizon that seems with time, to be spiraling back, returning again to pick up underappreciated or reframed bits, like a rubbing, to become clearer as more and more ethnographic, ethnohistorical, historical, archeological, and intercultural activist work is done region wide.

1970s Horizon: Five Matters of Concern

Linguistic exogamy: social structure and language forms
Political economy: impoverishment
Health and curing: epidemics, traditional medicine,
access to biomedicine
Culture Wars: anthropologists, missionaries, the state
Revitalization: shamans and rituals

"Linguistic exogamy" (having to marry a partner speaking a different patrilect), says Fleming, is an ideological mechanism, or what Jean called "ethnolinguistics badges" that allow the reproduction of the marriage exchange system, supported by the ceremonies such as the pudali or po'oa, in which a father's sister's daughter's marriage is preferential, creating a "marrying back" relationship in alternate generations.

But what I find even more fascinating (as a once student of Tarascan with Paul Friedrich) is the role of *evidentials* and pragmatics in these languages—as in "so says my son." These patrilects have varying numbers of evidentials. Evidentials will come back again in the new Guambiano history compositions that are also texts of and for intercultural politics about which Joanne Rappaport has recently written (2005).

A second theme or concern in the 1970s is that of political economy, peripheralization, and impoverishment. Offstage is the impeding invasion of the drug wars, which Jackson acknowledges but does not deal with in *Fish People*, saying she had not been back to her Bara community or the Vaupes to see it firsthand, although that violence was, in fact, in part what had kept her from visiting. She did return to the capital Mitu in 1987, 1989, and 1993. It is both remarkable and hopeful that in 2010 Rappaport could assert that the violence, which remains omnipresent, was backstaged by her Guambiano and Nasa (or Paez) activists, who insisted instead on foregrounding revitalization and building new intercultural structures. Jean seems less optimistic, at least for the Tukanoans, saying new threats "ironically are coming from Tukanoan activists trying to articulate culture and identity in a brave new world of rights-claiming initiatives." Still, Jean too writes that part of the neoliberal program to shrink the state enables opening a space for debate about how to define democratic citizenship, with demands of activists for collective land titling, bilingual education, traditional medical systems, and self-government at local and regional levels. And while she points out that CRIVA (the Regional Indigenous Council of the Vaupes) was initiated not by indigenous activists but by Catholic priests attempting to eject North American Protestant missionaries, and she denies it the appellation "grassroots," she acknowledges that the Catholic priests were unable to control CRIVA after the constitutional reforms were instituted.

A third theme or matter of concern was health and curing after waves of epidemics, obviously interconnected with the above theme. Although commented upon only in passing by Jean, this has been one of several contentious issues in the debates surrounding the efforts to advocate with and for the Yanomami in Brazil, not so far away, and about which I have written in an STS vein (Fischer 2001).

The fourth theme or matter of concern in the 1970s and continuing today is culture wars, and the role of anthropologists, missionaries, and government agencies for Indian affairs. Here the Napoleon Chagnon, sociobiology, or fierce people wars and today the new Orientalizing wars of Eduardo Viveiros de Castro are again on the agenda in Brazil (see chapter 2) but take on a very different configuration in Colombia. For every claim that the Indios are hardwired in their predatory ontology, there is the counterobservation that the real predators are the whites with their gold, rubber, and oil greed; seizures of land; and culture-destroying missionizing.

Since the 1970s a lot has changed, in particular the rise of interculturalism and social pluralism as a counterutopia to that of assimilation and homogenization. Cold War support for Christian capitalism and development has transformed even into some Guambiano intellectuals propagating Protestant churches as an escape from Catholic control over the countryside, and a stepping stone to abandonment of Christianity entirely in favor of a revitalized indigeneity. The 1980s and 1990s, Jean points out, was not just a period of liberalization and democratic transition in Latin America, but some fifteen countries instituted constitutional reforms, involving the language of diversity, intercultural or multiculturalism, and plural ethnic identities, as well as a rights discourse intended to help solve problems of the crises of representation, corruption, and lack of state legitimacy. It is a sea change, and not without turbulence.

The fifth and in some ways culturally the most important matter of concern was the role of shamans, hallucinogens, and the rituals that keep cultural worlds refreshed, flexible, and incorporative. This is quite apart from the upstaging that periodically occurs via the legal and intellectual property issues fought over *yage* (Tukanoan *jahe*) or ayahuasca (Quechua and Aymara *ayawaska*) that Jean seems to refer to with the more guarded name Banisteriopsis, the liana vine often brewed with DMT-containing plants. DMT, or N,N-dimethyltryptamine, itself is a schedule one drug, and thus illegal under the UN Narcotics Convention of 1971. But plants containing DMT are not illegal, and Banisteriopsis itself does not contain DMT. As has been pointed out with many ritual traditions, including haoma/soma in Zoroastrianism and Vedic rites, ghat in Yemeni poetry contests, or wine in Dionysian and Catholic rites, it is the inspiration and psychic processes of healing or orientation that are important. While psychotropics can be helpful, they are insufficient without the directing of cultural armatures and guides. Yage in particular is said to be unpleasant to take, and the effects are not long-lasting, so it is a poor recreational drug.

I'm suggesting a slightly reframed view of what in romantic and journalistic tropes is a Garden of Eden view of primordial Indians living in spiritual identity with the land, to a more linguistic-ethno-genetic view that prepares the ground for the rights-based ethnic identities to which Jean has devoted the second half of her career. I want to elicit, or listen for, a linguistic sensibility "in the round," rather than a flat taxonomic one, and take as resonators or tuning forks for this aspiration two comments. The first is a comment by Jean that "*Tukanoans have astonishing ability to turn the most unpleasant happenings into something funny*, at times even when it is happening; *one must laugh if possible, and savor the details for future story-telling*" (45). The second is a comment by Luke Fleming that Tukanoan women's narrative speech has a cinematic quality (2010, 104), and that women's speech in general is strikingly different in affectual quality from men's (as already illustrated in the greetings at the pudali). But also in the processual unfolding of discourse, there are switches that create moments of double reading, where an utterance may be understood first as the voicing of an opinion only to be reframed as a quotation. The verb of speaking *ni* (which also means "to be") always occurs at the right boundary of its quotative complement, meaning that it can be used to recalibrate the utterance as a report or citational mention. Double readings, recalibrations of who is speaking, and what the affective stances are being conveyed become theatrical, epistemic, and evidential-infected, shifting perspectives. Women deploy more affective speech, albeit often shifted to reported affect, while men are supposed to be more restrained and in control, particularly of anger. All this shifts dramatically in urban contexts where indigenous young men in gangs or in the Brazilian military attempt to adopt the more boisterous Brazilian masculinity codes.

"Tukanoans have an astonishing ability to turn the most unpleasant happening into something funny . . . savor the details for future story-telling," says Jackson—a thought worth hanging on to as we contemplate both their political or economic adversities *and* their mythopoetic or analogic narrations, as well as the quiet, whispered, serious ritual work of blowing tobacco or blessing speech by shamans. Incantations, acts of *be-se-se* (blessing, blowing), are often inaudible. "Even the mouth and lips are concealed as the spell is whispered directly into the substance, whether a vegetable, cigarette, or bottle of lotion that will later be used by the patient. Right mentation, a synaesthetic combination of inner speech and visualization, is understood as necessary to the effectiveness of the cure" (Fleming, chap. 2).

Section 2: Looking Ahead, the New People of the Future World, Repairing the Anaconda

By contrast with the intellectual horizon of the 1970s, the twenty-first-century horizon stresses five different themes:

Twenty-First-Century Matters of Concern
Inter-culturalism and ethnic pluralism
Rights: cultural vs. universal; abstract vs. grounded
Indigenization: strategies, control, for whom?
Language: bi- and multilingualism, literacies, masculinization/ feminization of speech, evidentials and genres of history writing.
Autonomy: penal systems; decentralized local and regional self-governance

Jean's fascinating essays on reindigenization, for me, resonate with my work in the 1980s on what I called in the language of those days "the postmodern arts of memory" and focused on "ethnicity" in the United States, articulated especially in autobiographical forms of poetry, novels, and memoirs, and focused especially on the interesting fact that spokespersons for ethnic identity were often of mixed backgrounds searching for a way to combine them into a voice that did not violate the various sources of composition, a voice that articulated the positive weaving into the fabric of the world, providing a different place than disappearance, isolation, or essentializing for ethnicity. It was a time when Alcida Ramos was also writing about the "hyper real Indian," the self-fashioning of Indians in Brazil, with the advice of NGOs to appeal beyond the authority of the Brazilian state to the international community. So too Joanne Rappaport stresses the working together of "organic intellectuals" of various sorts (going beyond Gramsci's simple two categories) in order to negotiate the internal constitutional arrangements of the state. These include the quite differently positioned indigenous people with secondary schooling or teacher training, a few with MA's in linguistic anthropology, elders and shamans, indigenous politicians working on regional and national levels, nonindigenous supporters or collaborators, and Bogota- or US-trained anthropologists.

I want to privilege the local terms of the Guambiano and others (*intercultural* as opposed to *multicultural*, for instance). I also wonder whether some variant of "the postmodern arts of memory" might not contribute to an umbrella formulation (for many different such local efforts) to get around the questions of authenticity and alterity that Jean poses as a dilemma, not unlike those that Elizabeth Povinelli posed for Australian aborigines. Rappaport repeatedly reminds us that the *indigenous linguistic anthropologists* in Colombia were *trained in structural linguistics* and that an (I think vulgar) interpretation of structuralism contributes to an output that dichotomizes (insiders/outsiders, authentic/inauthentic), whereas life is rather a (less vulgar) structuralism or poststructuralism of variations, continua, transformations, reconfigurations, and reinterpetations, using the metaphorical resources with virtuosity and as analogue operations, movements, and symphonies. The Australian aborigines, Povinelli argues, are asked to demonstrate that they are sufficiently "other" not to come under Australian law, and yet not so "other" as to be repugnant to Australian law. At stake are land rights and rights of self-governance, including penal codes. While for some of the Colombian cases (the ones in the Putumayo and Huila), as Jean points out, the situation is analogous, for others (the Muisca north of Bogota), and for many Amerindians not only in Colombia, "often living in urban areas, going for long periods of time without performing indigeneity," the goal is rather carving out spaces for "finding a better, more meaningful life" that does not necessarily interfere with their everyday work worlds. At the other end of the spectrum are groups such as the Ayoreo of Paraguay, who have incorporated or hybridized an apocalyptic Christianity as a mode of integrating their fractured worlds (Bessire 2014), perhaps analogous to the several destructions of the world and re-creation in Barasana Tukano mythology.

Jean uses the Putumayo case to establish the cat-and-mouse game between a state concerned not to recognize too many new ethnicities and communities that would have special claims on land and resources, on the one hand, and on the other land-hungry people who are using the 1993 "Law 60" to establish just such claims. It is not merely instrumental motives over land and resources but also a function of a broad institution of interculturalism, a playing out of self-determination ideologies, and a shift therefore in valorization from one of whitening to one of indigeneity. The Putumayo cases are ones where the regional and national authorities work hard to establish criteria for recognition of indigeneity that cannot be met, and communities work hard to meet each of the criteria set up as obstacles. Interculturalism thus has the effect of creating people who more and more present to outsiders as well as to themselves an Indio profile. This is accomplished through a heterogeneous set of renamings, rediscoveries of myths, and appropriation of claims to protection of the environment and sacred curing knowledge.

Jean uses the different case of the Huila Yanacoma to illustrate a repertoire of tactics to force the government to pay attention and to gain status. By cutting a road across a designated UNESCO World Heritage archeology site, the UNESCO designation is put at risk and gains the government's attention but also becomes a means for the community to enhance a tourist economy by learning to perform indigeneity, anticipating that tourists will buy crafts and watch ceremonies. Indigeneity becomes both subject position and object position, but with the indigenous subjects manipulating their objectness and hoping not to become trapped by that maneuver. Jean quotes several analysts as worrying that one can claim *Indio* status only by living as one's ancestors did in the nineteenth century or earlier. But this rings untrue, or only one of many possibilities. Since the revival of Hebrew is mentioned as a parallel to the revival of Indian languages (though the parallel is not exact, since Hebrew as a literacy was never lost, and even Rappaport and, similarly, Marisol de la Cadena for Peru, who stress recovery of colonial titles and documents, invoke Spanish rather than Guambiano or Quechua literacy), one might point out that while some Hassids may dress as their great-grandparents did in Eastern Europe (in other respects they live quite modern twenty-first-century lives of well-to-do diamond and electronics merchants), Jews adopt all kinds of subject relations with their ethnicity. So too one can imagine a series of subject positions for indigeneity to come. It is fascinating that throughout *The Fish People*, Jean should periodically refer to Jewish rituals.

At the other end of the continuum is the Muisca of Sesquile, who are recognized but who do not live on the land that is their designated territory, a steep landscape good mainly for sheep, albeit with a set of communal buildings to which the members living elsewhere can repair for communal renewal. Many of the tactics of "birth of a new nation," as Jean notes a New England Pequot phrases it regarding his community's efforts at self-recovery, are the same as in the Huila and Putumayo cases but take on a more personal and socializing cast of self-fulfillment and finding of a better way of life, an alternative mind set to that of the dominant urban modernity in which they live their nonindigenous lives. There is nothing inauthentic about this; it is how the postmodern arts of memory operate, and it is what ethnicity feels like for many in secular civil societies.

Might then the notion of postmodern arts of memory be something useful to think with, in order to create a broader frame, within which the re-indigenization efforts can be placed without getting stuck in old outworn either-or, authenticity-inauthenticity categories? The effect might be to lift the veil on some of the symbolic registers on which struggles over autonomy and land are fought. This is not disempowering if the objective is to put into alignment a series of authentic goals rather than a single encompassing status. Protection of the environment, of archeological remains, of taking up the burdens of identification with the past, of finding social strengthening rituals, of incorporating and resocializing former fighters, of strengthening self-governing commitments, and so on, and using indigeneity as a vehicle of such processes can contribute to the larger intercultural social fabric of Colombian and other societies enriching the cultural resources on which all may draw, and which can be used to disempower those factions who insist they alone are right.

Our histories are spirals, say Rappaport's Guambiano historians, unrolling and rerolling, the same as the way time unrolls and rolls back up, as does language, returning to pick up sounds or idioms for new contexts, creating dialects, like spirals, like the hand movements of the shaman during rituals, like the ancient petroglyphs (that Tukano, among others, still renew) (Rappaport 161).

Rappaport speaks of the distinction between two discourses: culturalist projects of activists in tension with discourses of sovereignty of indigenous politicians. Jean, engaging with liberal political theory, calls them cultural rights discourses and universal rights discourses. One is an inward-looking emphasis on the revitalization of cultural specificity (like the pudali that revitalizes horizontal relations among affines). The other, like the pudali that revitalizes vertical relations of patrilines, is a stress on transnational minority rights linking the local to other progressive sectors and making possible negotiation with the state (16). "Thus says," to adopt the evidential of local discourses, the Guambiano history, as it is now written by a colloquy of elders, young schooled intellectuals, indigenous linguistic anthropologists, an archeologist and even Rappaport herself in the mix.

Abstract universality may break down, and more flexible notions of grounded rights may grow. These legalities are all works in progress, and their working out is very much situation- or context-dependent. Ethical terms such as "truth" and "justice" are floating signifiers, or thin morality, empty and therefore sometimes useful in bridging contexts for international treaties or gaining some symbolic capital and recognition for particular actors. Universal human rights and cultural rights seem on the surface to be contradictions, and conflicts over their interpretation create constant needs for court adjudication, and yet there seem to be trends that make their local adjudications available for generalization and precedent making in other cases. As Jean puts it, there are "instructive examples of Indians getting it right and nonindigenous Colombians consistently getting it wrong," by which she means not the definitions of indigeneity or ethnicity but rather (if I understand) means of conflict resolution and especially reabsorption of guerillas into chances for peaceful communal life. As Jean says, "The on-going violence and a weak corrupt state has helped create an imaginary of Colombian pueblos whose values, community structure, and practices, while certainly not utopian, at times point to how much better things could be." (Note that Rappaport uses "utopia" in a different sense, as aspiration, hope, for a better future.) Jonathan Hill cites his Waku-enai informants to the effect that the shamans may yet transform white people's society (the *yarinaina*) into a giant machine based on shamanic curing practices. If not the shamans themselves, perhaps the project of interculturalism: "The ancestors have marked a path, . . . the past goes in front and the future comes behind. . . . It is as though a turn were made in the vast circular space, a new meeting with the ancestor . . . an illusion, a hope. . . . The space that is left behind and time not yet lived are a space and a time that must still unroll"—thus says the newly composed Guambiano history on pages 35–36 (Rappaport, 162). It is an imperfect history written in Spanish because some of the collaborators don't speak Nasa or Guambiano. It thus cannot be directly understood by Nasa-speaking schoolchildren. They are taught through oral translation back into Nasa and Guambiano, unfortunately still taught through old-fashioned recitation and memorization that removes the vitality of the multieyed fragments of history narrated by different authors with different evidentials, turning the history into deadly lists of names. But this too will change. It is a work in progress. It's a "text in fragments with distinct authors" (162), open to the future.

Ending Pudali

We have come to this pudali (Wanano *po'a*), we have come to this ceremonial feast, to celebrate with our *waanapani*, our stomping tubes, with our coconut weevil *deetu* flutes and our *ku-lir-rina* catfish trumpets, to celebrate the career of a woman among us, a woman like Amaru, the primordial woman, a woman who writes to open and expand the world of social relations (or perhaps to defend the closed world being lost). I have come to thank Jean for a pudali not just of intellectual and aesthetic delights but also of committed moral and ethical concerns for building a new world for the people of the future to come.

6

ETHNIC VIOLENCE, GALACTIC POLITIES, AND THE GREAT TRANSFORMATION

for TAMBI

As with the two previous chapters, this one is addressed to the ethnographer-anthropologist, whose work it discusses, at the time in person, and now in spirit. It is for me an ethical way of writing. Even when writing ethnographic accounts more generally, I try to always write as if the people I'm writing about were listening and could react. In this chapter, as in the previous two, a question of violence always hovers in the background even when not foregrounded. As chapter 5 was about ethnographies, histories, and future trajectories of the Amazon, so this chapter attempts to do something similar for South and Southeast Asia, with extensions into the maritime worlds as far as Melanesia. It also illustrates two other genre forms of which I am fond. The first is the life history as a social hieroglyph of world-historical, sociocultural changes, done with an ethnographic listening ear for the autobiographical voice (Fischer 1994), for the resonances of lived experience that give a kind of intimate body and meaning to events and how they change personhood, revealing how accretions of experiences shape character, perspective, and ethical groundings. The second is a form of histories of thought collectives, research agendas, or styles of investigation, in this case the students and colleagues of Stanley J. Tambiah.

From the teardrop-shaped island there once came a group of extraordinarily talented social anthropologists; they brought with them perspectives, questions, and empirical fieldwork that helped reshape the discipline, its calling, and its composition.[1] They traversed the temporal and social seas from Ceylon/Sri Lanka's position as the educated jewel and model democratic state of the British Commonwealth (where they were raised and educated) to its subsequent descent into a form of postcolonial violence.[2] How could they not, then, also traverse the seas from the classical social anthropology in which they trained (in England and America), becoming some of its finest practitioners, to the battered landscapes of the late twentieth century, about which they also wrote with insight and passion?[3] They attended to geographies, polities, and cultural formations well beyond those of their homeland. They attended to the larger South Asian and Southeast Asian scene, pre- and postcolonial relations, and to the work of theory in the inclusive, comparative, and transnational field science called anthropology.

In the case of Stanley Jeyaraja Tambiah (or "Tambi," as he is known to his friends and students, literally "younger brother," meaning affectionate uncle, mother's younger brother[4])—the brother and nephew of justices of Sri Lanka's Supreme Court who were trained in the transnational Anglo-colonial judiciary that sometimes rotated judges interchangeably from Asia to Africa, slowly building up a procedural system of adjudication between local conditions, traditional customary law, and codified statutes[5]—one cannot help but read an enriching projection of concern about his homeland in his work on Buddhism in Thailand, on sources of charisma and legitimation, on ritual and cosmological action, and on ethnic violence across South Asia.[6]

Tambiah's insistence that one should begin with a firm grasp of political economy and with local ethnographic grounding, rather than with cosmology and ritual, is rooted in his career trajectory. Trained originally as a sociologist at the University of Ceylon and at Cornell, Tambiah's first efforts were quantitative surveys ("The Disintegrating Village: Report of a Socio-Economic Survey," 1957); village studies of kinship, land tenure, and polyandry ("The Structure of Kinship and Its Relationship to Land Possession and Residence in Pata Dumbara, Central Ceylon," 1958; "Polyandry in Ceylon," 1966); and rural community development for a UNESCO-Thai technical assistance project in northeastern Thailand. His trajectory was redirected by engagements with the English social anthropologist Edmund R. Leach, who had originally been trained in engineering, and whom Tambiah first met in 1956 at the former University of Ceylon, renamed the University of Peradeniya. Tambiah had returned there to teach, and Leach was making a second visit to Pul Eliya, a village in central Ceylon built around an irrigation tank, where Leach had done fieldwork in 1954.[7] Leach was supportive and engaging but devastating about the quantitative survey approach, and he brought

Tambiah to Cambridge for two years (1962–64).[8] There Tambiah transformed himself into a social anthropologist, later editing with Jack Goody a classic volume in kinship studies (*Bridewealth and Dowry,* 1973), and absorbing as well Leach's incorporation of some of the then new and intellectually challenging structuralist insights of Claude Lévi-Strauss. Tambiah abandoned none of his earlier commitments; in his collection of essays from 1985 (*Culture, Thought, and Social Action*) he continued to refer to himself as a development anthropologist and to invoke Sir Edward Burnett Tylor's creed that anthropology is a reformer's science.

Much of Tambiah's stress on oscillating and pulsating models of politics and on dialectical dynamics parallels that of Leach, as evident in the latter's provocative work among the Kachin, *Political Systems of Highland Burma* (1954).[9] Tambiah remained a close friend and eventually became Leach's biographer (*Edmund Leach: An Anthropological Life,* 2002). Another of Leach's students, Nur Yalman (and Yalman's student, Dennis McGilvray), would take up structuralist analyses in Ceylon in a more strictly Lévi-Straussian fashion, but many of Tambiah's striking analyses deploy structuralist insights, particularly his brilliant handling of the cosmological and mythic reworkings of the histories of Ceylon/Sri Lanka, as well as, of course, his signature analysis of the world conqueror/world renouncer dualism in South and Southeast Asian "galactic polities." The effort to demonstrate how to integrate structuralist and historical analyses was also taken up by Marshall Sahlins in his work on Hawaii, Fiji, and classical Greece; and Tambiah's accounts should be read alongside those of Sahlins, since many of the same themes reappear, albeit handled methodologically differently. Sahlins's essay on Tambiah's work in the volume *Radical Egalitarianism: Local Realities, Global Relations* quietly acknowledges and illustrates this point, turning to the mythic dimensions of contemporary and historical ethnic violence (Sahlins 2013).

I begin with the editors' provocative title for that volume *Radical Egalitarianism* (Aulino, Goheen and Tambiah 2013), as a way of staging themes in Tambiah's work—galactic polities, charismatic circuits, collective violence, and ritual.

Radical Egalitarianism

Because of the crossings of generational time and situational space mentioned above, Tambiah's cosmopolitical analytic language is always carefully indexed to its sociopolitical origins and implications. The phrase *radical egalitarianism*[10] captures aspects of Tambiah's moral commitments to the or-

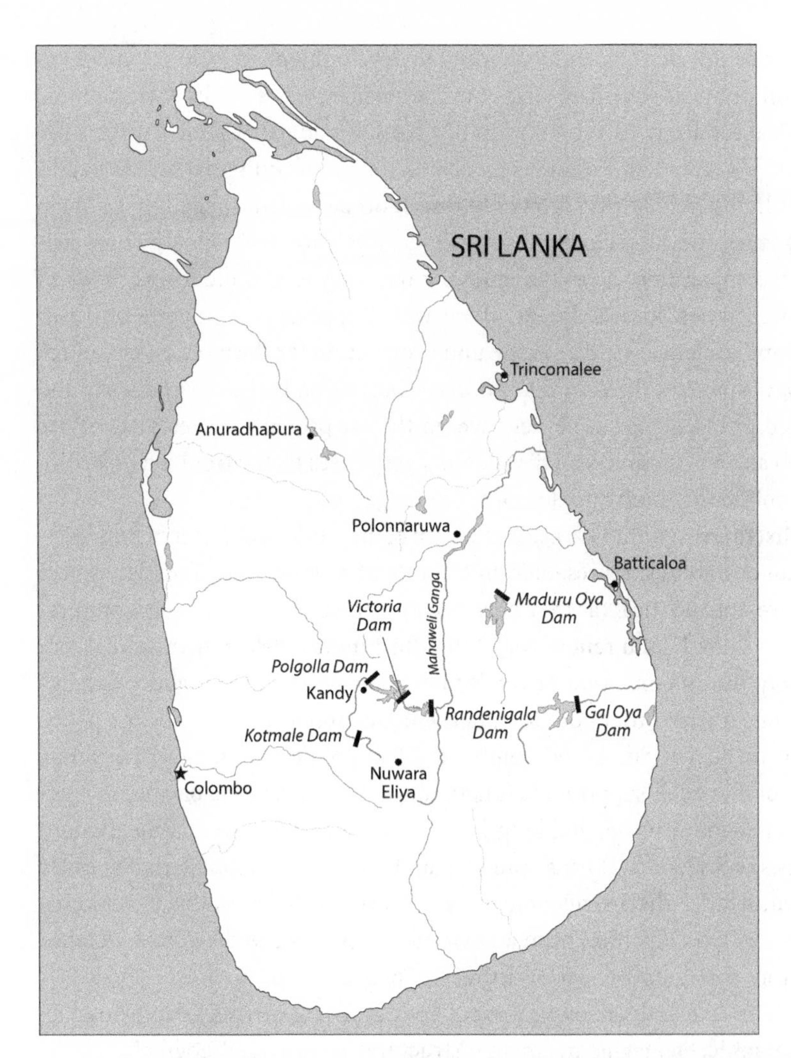

MAP 6.1. Multipurpose irrigation projects, Sri Lanka. Gal Oya Valley Multipurpose Scheme (Oya or Inginivagala irrigation dam, power plant, and resettlement project) is where the first postindependence Sinhalese-Tamil ethnic riots were incited in 1956, witnessed by Tambiah and students. During initial construction, this dam had to be re-sited when remains of an ancient dam were found. Large ancient irrigation networks, supporting rice production, existed in the dry zone surrounding the ancient capitals Anuradhapura (437 BCE–845 CE) and Polonnaruwa (846–1302 CE), after which Singhalese power moved south into Kandy. In the 1980s, six new dams were built (the Mahavelli Irrigation Project), now supplying 40% of Sri Lanka's electricity. They are on the island's longest river running from near the Kandy highlands to Trincomalee Bay, with a drainage area of a fifth of the island, now irrigating a thousand square kilometers (386 square miles).

dinary people of a society as opposed to development economists, modernization political scientists, and comprador local elites of the transnational political economy, as expressed in his "Anthropologist's Creed" (1985a). The phrase also captures Tambiah's invocation of Leach's quip that he was a radical at home in his own society but not in other societies (cited in Tambiah 2002, 261),[11] and the closely associated rationale for anthropology's repatriating, comparativist, creed of studying the "richness of the forms of life of other societies, knowledge of which will deepen and illuminate our own lives and societies" as "the reason and justification for the practice of anthropology" (1996a, 33).[12] And yet *radical egalitarianism* is also a paradoxical and loaded phrase, often quite negative, in the six primary usages that suffuse Tambiah's writings on, and his students' responses to, the troubled postcolonial politics of South and Southeast Asia.

First there is the radical egalitarianism of the world renouncer of Buddhist-Hindu cosmology, represented in the role of monks, who, Tambiah points out, are not apolitical (as they have been portrayed in some idealist interpretations of the Hindu renouncer).[13] Buddhist monks detach themselves from worldly ties in emulation of the Buddha, attempting to rise above ephemeral concerns, in order both to pursue enlightenment and to guide the polity. In the context of South and Southeast Asian polities, the sangha (corporate body of monks) is supposed to function as a ritual and moral balance to legitimate and guide power and kingship. As we have vividly seen in the modern politics of Sri Lanka, Burma, and Thailand, this can turn totalitarian as easily as democratic. The articulation of a revivalist Buddhism in the postcolonial politics of Sri Lanka has been a powerful contributor to the ethnic violence that tore that country apart in its recent long civil war.

One of Tambiah's most important contributions, carefully deploying historiographic, literary-genre, mythic-structural, as well as ethnographic methods, is to deconstruct this chauvinist ideology and show the countervailing alternative histories that have been erased by chauvinism. There is, he asserts, "no reason to foreclose on this possibility [that the framework of current Buddhist nationalism can in the future stretch and incorporate a greater amount of pluralist tolerance in the name of a Buddhist conception of righteous rule], for there are precedents that can be positively employed" (1992, 125). But, he continues, forcefully putting forth an anthropological institutional perspective against simple idealistic possibilism or wishful thinking, "new perspectives can be forged only under social and political conditions which are themselves not frozen or restrictive" (125). Much of Tambiah's brilliant analysis in *Buddhism Betrayed? Religion, Politics, and Violence in Sri Lanka* is dedicated to charting the freezing and restrictive traps into which Sri Lankan politics devolved since the 1940s, in what he argues has been a dramatic transformation from Buddhist-Hindu galactic polities to the cosmologies of unitary nation-states. The sin, of course, lies not only with Buddhist ideology or ritualized cosmology but also with the British colonial rule against which the religious revivalism arose; and in a larger sense, the sin lies with the transformations induced by nation-state identity politics, and thus with what Tambiah calls (using a transformed Indian term) the "*juggernaut* of mass participatory politics" (1992, 172).[14]

Tambiah's title *Buddhism Betrayed?* is an explicit reference to *The Betrayal of Buddhism* (with no question mark), the explosive report issued in 1956 by a Commission of Inquiry of the All Ceylon Buddhist Congress, just before the fateful 1956 elections, a "singular climactic moment" in twentieth-century politics, "when a significant number of monks temporarily organized to win an election" (Tambiah 1992, chap. 7). The report was staged not only on the eve of the election but to mark cosmologically 2,500 years since the death of the Buddha and the coming to Sri Lanka of Vijaya, coded as the first Sinhalese and a prototypical mythic hero who comes from the periphery to violently conquer and establish a new center of righteous rule. The report is one of three texts that Tambiah analyzes from the 1940s and 1950s defending the role of monks as political actors, indicting British colonialism for using Christian missionizing to weaken Buddhism, and asserting a remedy program to establish Buddhism as the dominant religion and Sinhala as the only state language.

This is not merely old politics. In 2006, on the report's fiftieth anniversary and "the 2,550's anniversary of the Buddha's death," it was reissued as a warning reminder to the United National Party government of its defeat in 1956; and Buddhist organizations once again urged the government "to implement five proposals to arrest the decline of Buddhist values and culture in Sri Lanka. The Venerable Medagama Dhammananda of the Asgiriya Chapter, Kandy, read out these proposals at a meeting held at Ananda College, Colombo on October 3" (Perera 2006).[15]

The second radical egalitarianism, one that plays into the revivalist ideology of Sri Lankan Buddhist nationalism, is the "nostalgic fiction of a simple, homogeneous, egalitarian pre-colonial Sinhala Buddhist peasant society" (Tambiah 1992, 96). It feeds into a dangerous political economy of development ideology when used as the mythic charter for the multipurpose colonization schemes to resettle peasants from overcrowded areas onto new lands: the Gal Oya Multipurpose Scheme of the 1950s (one of a number of such post–World War II Tennessee Valley Authority–styled projects, and the one where the first postindependence riots occurred, with Tambiah as a witness and reporter[16]), and the $1.5 billion Mahavali Project of the 1980s, which was to provide irrigation to 37,000 hectares of already cultivated land plus 130,000 hectares of new land and double the hydroelectric power capacity of the country. Eighteen thousand families, mostly Sinhalese, had already been resettled on these lands by the mid-1980s. Tamils saw these projects, placed in what he calls the "shatter zone" between the Tamil north and east and the Sinhalese south, as Sinhalese land grabs. When the massive riots of May 1958 broke out, it was footloose wage laborers living in labor camps, organized into a strike force by politicians to whom they were beholden, and urban thug *agents-provocateurs* disguised in monks' robes with shaved heads, rather than better-off landed peasants who rampaged to purify the land of Tamils, leading to Tamil "counterclaims of 'homelands' and Sinhalese majoritarian discrimination in settlement policy" (1992, 127). As Tambiah comments, "The elite bureaucrats of the island, the technically sophisticated economists, engineers, and architects, in collaboration with foreign experts and much foreign funding, plan highly 'industrialized' blueprints and use heavy technology for building the irrigation dams, the roads, communication facilities, and the like. But this same cosmopolitan elite, together with the leading politicians, then yokes this heavily capitalized infrastructure to a peasant form of cultivation. . . . The elite, living a different style of life and reproducing a different pattern of privileged domination in their role as planners and rulers, wish upon the vast mass of the people an indefinitely expanding network of peasant villages" (127–28).

And, he continues, "the ideologues of the society, the activist scholar-monks, the populist literary circles, the vote-seeking politicians, and the creators of rituals of national development and television dramas unite to propagate this vision of a (utopian) past that could be a prospective (utopian) future"—a vision that "hinder[s] the envisioning of a more realistic and workable regime . . . that can accommodate minorities" (Tambiah 1992, 128). Under such circumstances the provision of free education in local languages had the effect of creating vast pools of angry, unemployed literate and semiliterate youth, who had invested hope in education, but in a society without the jobs to fulfill their ambitions.

The ideology of the egalitarian, self-sufficient village, a mini-kingdom built around, as populist novelist Martin Wickramasinghe put it, *vava* (irrigation tank), *dagaba* (temple), and *yaya* (paddy field), was explicitly invoked by the politicians as they opened and dedicated the new project lands. The egalitarian nostalgia is a fascinating reworking of the hierarchies of village life. The fantasy is one in which money is rarely used, the produce of the land is divided equally between the cultivator and the treasury, there is equality of income, and poverty is nonexistent. In India, this sort of division of labor is called *jajmani* and is accounted as a division of labor among castes in an organic whole. The hierarchy is explicit in the caste system, and Buddhist ideology differentiates itself from Hinduism even in the cognate term for the moral order: Sanskrit (Hindu) *dharma,* Pali (Buddhist) *dhama.* Buddhist *dhama* is paired with equity (*sama*), in dialectical opposition to Hindu *dharma,* always signifying inequality and hierarchy (ibid, 108). But, of course, the land in the Buddhist polities of Sri Lanka belongs to the king, and is allocated, along with its manpower, with finely graded castes and tenurial rights, into monastic (*viharagam*) and temple (*devalagam*) endowments, noble estates (*nindagam*), and royal estates (*gabadagam*), with specification of duties and work owed the king.

This is an explicit caste system, and it is more like a feudal structure, or, as Tambiah acknowledges, a patrimonial structure as described by Max Weber, than it is an ideal egalitarian community. Indeed, as Weber describes, the ministerial form of government is divided into royal household duties (with the highest offices being dualistically structured—Office of the Royal Bath, Office of the Royal Wardrobe), and the whole is legitimated, as Weber argues for ancient agrarian empires, with elaborate cosmological rituals. We shall return to the cosmology and ritual below, which, as Tambiah is at pains to argue (in his critique of Geertz), is performative and constitutive, not merely reflective, mystifying, or theatrical. Tambiah argues for an understanding of this pre–nation-state patrimonial structure as flexible and inclusionary, allowing redundant and involuted bureaucracies to incorporate and assign roles to growing numbers of people, and similarly providing increasing occupational niches for immigrant groups of different origins and religious traditions and practices, which is quite different from the drive for unity and identity of the modern nation-state.

The third radical egalitarianism, of course, is the socialist one that projects backward into utopian history and forward into the utopian future the idea of an egalitarian community. Tambiah cites Henpitagedara Gnanaseeha Thero, one of the more radical Buddhist monk-scholars, as thinking of Russian socialism as being based on principles similar to those of this Buddhist conception (1992, 108). And indeed such a conception is present in much vulgar Marxist and socialist thought, and is a key component of a turn to totalitarianism in both left and right traditions.[17] Parallel to today's Muslim fundamentalists, who argue that once a unitary Islamic society has been forcibly established, democracy, equality, and social justice will reign, so too argue Buddhist revivalists. Gnanasiha condemns divisive parliamentary politics for preventing the reaching of any national consensus. By contrast, he argues, Buddhist "democracy" requires only one party so that discussion can be carried on until there is consensus (1992, 115). Further, much as under a Ministry of Islamic Guidance and Culture in Iran, "in a Buddhist-administered society, the action of man is directed to a good path not only by advice, but by closing the avenues that lead to wrong actions" (1992, 119). Pannasiha, another monk scholar, says of the issue of minorities, that to protect the hegemony of the endangered Sinhala Buddhism, "when 74% of the population is united, what can the other 26% do?" (1992, 124). He Pannasiha is complaining about the alleged favoring of Tamils in the civil service,[18] and arguing against enfranchising Tamil tea estate laborers, lest it change the electoral arithmetic.

The sangha itself, the Buddhist body of monks, is idealized as an egalitarian structure. According to the charter myth, the Buddha tells Ananada that after his death there should be no successor: only the *dhama* (doctrine) should bind the *bhikhus* (monks). The elders among the monks deserve respect, but can only teach and advise, not legislate or compel. The transactions of the sangha should be held in frequent assemblies (with procedural rules) in which all are equal and decisions are consensual. All offerings to the sangha are to be shared equally and all increase should go into a common fund (1992, 114). But again, as Tambiah will outline in great detail for Thailand, reforms of the sangha are also state centralizing mechanisms and fraught with hierarchical maneuverings.

Three more egalitarianisms appear, with strong ritual-performative characteristics, and with cosmological components: pooling-redistribution (see discussion of Ratanapruck below), social democratic welfare-politics transformed into neoliberal microeconomic discipline (Ferguson, below), and the juggernaut of mass participatory politics. This juggernaut of mass participatory politics is the most significant and will be dealt with below as a separate section parallel to the other key themes of galactic polities, charismatic circuits, and ritual action.

Galactic Polities, Revitalizing Reforms, and Theater States

Rereading Tambiah's pair of books on Sri Lanka in the context of his trilogy of better-known books on Thailand—*Buddhism and the Spirit Cults in Northeast Thailand* (1970), his masterwork *World Conqueror and World Renouncer:*

A Study of Buddhism and Polity in Thailand against a Historical Background (1976), and *Buddhist Saints of the Forest and the Cult of Amulets: A Study of Charisma, Hagiography, Sectarianism, and Millennial Buddhism* (1984)—and his essays on ritual performative action (1985b, 1990), one recognizes the same key terms throughout, as well as three overlapping dialectics and oscillations:[19] (1) between centralizing nation-states and previous fractionating mandala or "galactic" polities; (2) between actual history and charismatic ritual action that mobilizes mythic and cosmological charters; and (3) between the this-worldly royal politics of the *chakravarti* (world conquerors, universal emperors; Pali *cakkavatti,* "through whom the wheels of dharma turn") and the *dharmaraja* (righteous king) who purifies the sangha in return for the sangha's legitimating of the royal rule, becoming the "guides of the king's conscience and mentors of the people" (Wijayawardena 1956, 513, cited in Tambiah 1992, 39).

Call these three fields of oscillation or dialectic *histories, myths,* and *cross-cultural structures. Histories* have to do with kinship, marriage alliances, factions, migrations, occupational niches, conversions, wars of conquest, and the political economies of patronage, trade, production, tax and revenue generation, and redistribution. Histories of the sangha have to do also with lineages of mentorship and ordination, missions to recover or propagate meditation or textual traditions, and establishment of educational systems aligned with or dissonant to polities and states. *Myths* have to do with double narratives of heroes who from the periphery violently conquer and reaggregate a fragmenting and demonic chaotic kingdom, and are themselves transformed into benign, righteous, and virtuous rulers once they have reached and reconstituted the center. *Cross-cultural structures* have to do both with the mutual dependence of religious and political legitimacy (sangha and king), a basic Indo-European topos, with merchants and farmers as a third wheel, and with the structural binary of autochthonous versus immigrant founders ("natives of the soil" versus "sea-crossing elites") found from Fiji to Greece.[20]

The Buddha and Asoka (the third century BCE Mauryan chakravartin who ruled over most of the Indian subcontinent) are the two prototypes of the world renouncer and world conqueror. The former is a prince who, witnessing human suffering, abandoned his royal function and founded the sangha; he himself is said to have claimed that he had many times previously been born a chakravartin. The latter becomes a convert to Buddhism after witnessing the carnage created by his successful war of conquest over the Kalinga kingdom. Vijaya, the "first Sinhalese," is the Sri Lankan prototype immigrant chakravartin: the immigrant, debased prince, crossing the sea from India to establish a righteous Buddhist kingdom on the island of Lanka/Ceylon.

The Thai sangha lineages about which Tambiah writes are linked by missions from India to Sri Lanka and thence to Thailand. Buddhism radiated as well to Indonesia, Burma, China, and Japan, and as far west (we often forget) as the Mediterranean. The monastic meditative traditions and ordination lineages of Sri Lanka were renewed in the eighteenth century under the "foreign" matrilineal Nayyakar kingships of Kandy, which sent missions to Siam, returning to establish the Siyam Nikaya and to renew or build new *viharas* (temples) across the Kandyan kingdom. It was at this time that the Buddha's tooth relic was elevated to a central role in the annual *perahera* (ritual procession) in Kandy that previously had paraded only the four guardian deities of the realm. In parallel, but different, fashion, the reforms of the nineteenth-century Thai monk who succeeded to the royal throne, Mongkut, not only renewed the sangha but also deployed it as a centralizing educational institution for an incipient modernizing nation-state.

As James Taylor and Ingrid Jordt elaborate (Taylor and Jordt 2013), the reformist movements in Thailand, Sri Lanka, and Burma drew upon one another's maintenance of the old Pali texts and meditation traditions, but the reform movements in each setting developed dialectically different generative strategies. Mongkut sent two missions to Sri Lanka in the 1840s, as had his grandfather, Rama I, in the late eighteenth century, in part as legitimating dharmaraja actions. Both Mongkut and the Sri Lankan forest monk Pannananda (in the early nineteenth century) also went to Burma for training in the Mon reform tradition (dating back to a fifteenth-century sangha reform under a Mon dharmaraja). But while Mongkut would build a close-knit cadre of disciples to propagate his Thammayut sect, and would use the printing press and a simplified Ariyaka ("purity") writing system (a Romanized transcription of Pali phonetics) to propagate his version of the Buddhist doctrine domestically and to surrounding nations, in Burma a mass meditation form was propagated among the laity by the monk Mahasi Sayadaw with the support of prime minister U Nu (1948–62) as a means of revitalization after colonial rule. Mahasi Sayadaw's Vipassana (insight) meditation and Abhidhamma philosophical formulations stressed that the laity should not just give donations to the monks but should themselves meditate. Vipassana or insight meditation centers were established across Burma, Sri Lanka, Indonesia, and in the United States. Vipassana meditation was taken up in Thailand as well by the Mahanikai sect under the great abbot monk Phra Philolathma. But with the rise of Mongkut's Thammayut sect as a centralizing and nationalizing instrument, Phra Phimolathma was forcibly disrobed and imprisoned. The Thammayut monks, Jordt says, also dialectically countered the meditation emphasis of the Mahanikai sect by stressing the importance of the Thammayut forest monk meditation teachers. A charismatic dialectic ensues of devotees seeking out meditating forest monks who retreat further away from the centers of population to pursue their detachment from the world, and thereby intensify their charisma, which in turn attracts devotees further into the peripheries, thereby acting as a kind of frontier expansion and marking of the state.

The sangha-royal dialectic creates polities that are theatrical and ritually charismatic, absorbing power into their centers and weakening on their peripheries in pulsating, changing dynamics that Tambiah memorably calls the *galactic polity,* evoking both the stars (transcendence) and this-worldly leverage. It is a form that Clifford Geertz called *negara,* using the Balinese and Malay term, but that Tambiah more deeply roots in the great but snow-flaky empires of the chakravarti such as Asoka, rulers of the worlds of South and Southeast Asia. ("Snow-flaky" in the sense of being geometrically fractal and replicative or mandala-like, and in the sense of being ephemeral, loose, and disappearing, with new ones constantly forming. Tambiah says he intends *galactic* as a translation of the term *mandala.*) Tambiah's account of Thailand focuses on the nineteenth-century reforms of King Mongkut that centralized and reformed the sangha as an educational pillar of a modernizing state.

Tambiah's argument with Geertz is instructive. Geertz famously describes the symbolic politics of the Balinese negara polity, comparing it, in the margins of his text, to the symbolic and spectacle politics of Washington, DC (Geertz 1977, 1980). Geertz thereby disrupts any contrastive idea that American politics is rational and instrumental, while those of other kinds of polities are cosmological and mystified. But his account of the nineteenth-century Balinese polities is, Tambiah says, "decidedly non-annalistic," too easily splitting off a still center of expressive action at the top from instrumental action at the base and periphery. While one could do a more generous reading of Geertz's account in the context of his notion of "cultural involution" under Dutch colonial rule, the support of ever-more-refined court rituals at the expense of a politics that could disrupt the Dutch control and extraction of revenue, nonetheless Tambiah rightly insists on looking to the precolonial "periodic campaigns and changing zones of control [having] to do with the capture of booty and manpower to resettle as 'slaves' or 'serfs' near one's centers of control," which is the general pattern of Southeast Asian polities, and which can be tracked also in the chronicles and oral histories of Bali. Tambiah in fact uses Hildred and Clifford Geertz's own oral history work [1975] to demonstrate this.[21] Perennial rebellions and succession disputes, exacerbated by multiple ranked marriages and concubinages, ensure that there are few long-lived dynasties, and the cosmological state has to be continually reimaged and reincarnated. The claim to be a chakravartin is a personal achievement that cannot be inherited, although once a ruler has achieved that status he can claim to be an incarnation or avatar of archetypal heroes. Kings make multiple marriage and concubinage alliances as means of binding lesser royal families to the center, and of asserting the patrimonial role of husband to the realm, but this then complicates succession maneuvers and fights ensue.

Sri Lanka provides Tambiah with rich materials to demonstrate not only how a decidedly annalist reading can unpack the workings of mythic structures and cosmologically interpreted social action. More crucially, Sri Lanka enables him to show how one can find alternative histories critical to a political understanding of "how and why . . . incorporation and assimilation, or containment and insulation, or rejection and expulsion take[s] place with regard to outside Indian peoples and their practices, and how in due course . . . a narrative of composite yet distinctive Sinhala identity [can] be evolved" (1992, 150). This is the mythohistorical and practical work over the centuries that needs to be remembered as accommodating pluralism rather than erasing it. Invoking Lévi-Strauss, Tambiah says "Myths have their variants, . . . one should expect a corpus of related myths, especially if they are focused on themes existentially important to the cultures and societies where they circulate. . . . Such are the paradoxes and puzzles . . . that one would expect the exploration of a number of solutions [to them]" (Tambiah, *Buddhism Betrayed?*, 149).

Take, for example, the eighteenth-century kingdom of Kandy, where the royal line passed from patrilineal Sinhala to matrilineal Nayyakars, originally from Madurai in south India (Tamils). Tambiah gives us both the marriage alliances that began in the seventeenth century and two myths of the period that comment upon the incorporative mechanisms. The marriage alliances provide the way the succession passed after the death of Narendrasinghe in 1739 to a brother of a Nayyakar queen (wife of Narendrasinghe), presumably because she and her brother were of *ksatriya* status, whereas Narendrasinghe's only son by a Sinhala concubine was not of sufficient caste rank. That Nayyakar king, Sri Vijaya ("Victory"), himself took a Nayyakar queen, and his heir in turn was his sister's son. To make the succession of Vijaya work, Narendrasinghe had him educated in Sinhalese laws and customs, and both Vijaya Rajasinghe (1739–47) and his successor, Kirti Sri Rajasinghe, sponsored missions to Siam, the latter returning in 1753 to establish two important viharas of the Siyam Nikaya, elevate the role of the Buddha Tooth Relic in the annual perahera ritual, and refurbish and build new viharas across the kingdom, thus enacting their position as dharmarajas. These Tamil-origin south Indians still had some personal (Hindu) Saivite practices, and two prominent (Buddhist) monks were implicated in an assassination plot amid complaints about having a heretic, evil Tamil, as king. The dharmaraja survived and managed what probably was an expression of the chronic factionalism at court.

Tambiah reads two foundation myths as commentaries on this pattern of incorporation of Tamils into Sinhala identity. The first, recounted in the chronicles at the time of the transition from the Sinhalese king Narendrasinghe to the Nayyakar (Tamil) king Vijaya, is the defeat of Natha, one of the four guardian deities of Kandy, by Pitiye, a Chola prince disgraced because he had killed a calf and the cow had complained to the king by ringing her bell. Pitiye invades Ceylon, proceeding from the east coast toward Kandy, along the way clearing land, creating rice paddies, and initiating irrigation. Natha, losing the war of violence but winning a quest for salvation, is elevated to bodhisattva, while Pitiye is domesticated and becomes one of twelve regional deities, guardian deities of the *bandara* class. *Bandara* in turn seem to be from *pantarm*, non-Brahmin priests of the Vellala caste who came in the thirteenth century from various parts of south India with attendants, craftsmen, and mendicants of their Siva temples, and were given *radala* and *mudali* titles (the highest status rank in the Goyigama Sinhala caste of cultivators). The myth of the original Sinhala founding hero, Vijaya, is parallel: a disgraced prince, he enters the island, violently displacing the savage *yakkhas*, and with a *yakkhini* has children who are sent to settle the periphery.

These, as Tambiah points out, are widespread (cross-cultural, structural) myths of the origin of power and its creative transformation, proceeding from abroad and the periphery in acts of barbarism and violence, then domesticated and reconstituting legitimate order. They are as well more local charter myths of the domestication of the jungle for rice cultivation, often with imported Tamil labor. On an even grander cosmological register, the Buddhist genesis myth is also about the "creation of world as devolutionary differentiation," with disorder increasing through the workings of human desire, until a new order is reestablished (not unlike the differentiation of Genesis and the story of the Garden of Eden).

Tambiah works through other examples of historical incorporation and exchange, including the Chola occupation of the island in the tenth and eleventh centuries and the return raid by King Bajabahu into Chola territory, recovering twelve thousand Sinhala captives and bringing twelve thousand Chola captives back to settle and work the land in Sri Lanka; the fifteenth-century waves of Karava immigrants from south India incorporated into the lower subcastes of the Goyigama; the two rival Buddhist trading families from Kerala who controlled the coasts; and the probable arrival at that time of the cult of the goddess Pattini, originally a Buddhist and Jain deity (Obeysekere 1984). Similar caste incorporations occurred in the Hindu and Muslim-remaining Tamil speaking north (the Jaffna Peninsula).

The point here is that there is a rich tapestry of incorporation, exchange, and reworking of traditions that often gets lost in mythic charters intended to advance particular interests at particular moments of competition, and that it is the anthropologists' calling to not allow such erasures to pass unremarked. Irving Chan Johnson (in Aulino, et al. 2013) supplies another such example on the Malaysian-Thai border, where Buddhist communities under a Muslim sultan pursue their boisterous ordination parades, care for massive statues, and host pilgrims, monks, traders, smugglers, and tourists. For the past century the ritual appointment of the chief monk of the Malaysian state of Kelantan has passed through the office of the Muslim sultan, while the Buddhist king of Thailand is viewed through the television, photographs, and posters.

Indeed, *chakravartin,* Tambiah notes, might be best translated as "king of kings," in acknowledgment of the existence of lesser kings and the mandala structure of galactic polities. Shahanshah, "King of Kings," is the title of Persian rulers, divine insofar as just kings are endowed with the *farrohar,* the divine light, symbolized as well in the sacred sphere by the highest level of sacred fire composed of purified levels of many fires from the varied occupations of men, hearth fires collected into community-level ones, as well as natural fires such as lightning (Fischer 1973). Unjust kings lose their farrohar—one of the great themes of the Persian national epic, the *Shahnameh* ("Book of Kings"; Fischer 2004).

Tambiah describes the cosmic rituals of galactic polities as rites of dispersion and rites of aggregation. The former include agricultural cycle rites that begin in the royal palace, then proceed to provincial courts, and "ripple" down to the rice fields of villagers. The latter include annual oaths of allegiance as well as the royal multiple marriage arrangements, and the sequestering at court of members of lower-allied royal or provincial families to ensure their loyalty. One is tempted to rethink the structure of early Islamic polities in these terms, with Muhammad's multiple marriage alliances made explicitly for precisely these political purposes, the sequestering of members of rival clans at court, and the *bayt* (oath of allegiance).

In one of the most fascinating of the chapters in *Radical Egalitarianism*, Victor Manfredi (2013) rereads, assembles, and collates the fractious history of Nigeria as pulsating sets of galactic polities both at the national level ("adept at gerrymandering the federating units into now 37 insolvent states and over 740 unaccountable local jurisdictions," "defusing game-theoretic power blocs at the center") and at the level of the oscillations of political form in southeastern Nigeria between, on the one hand, Edo-crowned priests of tutelary divinities centered in walled market towns, and on the other, Igbo gerontocratic lineages of horticultural villages practicing the "occasional state" formation when under external threat. It is not unlike *gumsa/gumlao*, in Leach's Burmese categories.[22] (Hertzfeld [2013], suggests a similar oscillation between two styles of leadership in Bangkok politics.) The dualistic oscillation includes patrilineal symbols (Igbo *ofo* of agricultural bamboo ringed in iron bands versus Edo coral and brass regalia, representing royal monopolies of salt water wealth and sovereign authority to impose death penalties) as well as dance steps (aerobic Igbo acrobatics versus "lead-footed Edo choreography under cowrie-laden *ubuluku* smocks depicting the dry-land locomotion of Olookun, the fish-tailed ocean god"). Manfredi, like Tambiah, looks first to the political economy: the slave trade exports, raids, and middlemen in the seventeenth and eighteenth centuries, and the "vultural ecology" of today's Shell Oil economy.

Charismatic Circuits

Tambiah's essay "The Charisma of Saints and the Cult of Relics, Amulets, and Tomb Shrines," which opens *Radical Egalitarianism*, is today perhaps best read back to front for its parallel account of the enchantments of the Christian and Buddhist cults of saints and relics. Christian monks boasting of their ritual kidnappings of sacred relics—in the dark of night breaking into saints' tombs and Roman catacombs to steal bone and ash, nails, wood, and linen with which to consecrate churches in new territories—seems more exotic than Buddhist circulation of relics in today's world of cosmopolitan tasters of many religions. We tend to forget that the Second Council of Nicaea in 787 CE decreed that no church was to be consecrated without relics; that a decade and a half later two more councils would demand any altar without relics to be destroyed; that the technical definition of an *altar* in Roman Catholic canon law is a tomb containing relics of saints; or that the Vatican continues to maintain a supply room chock full of ash and bone and other relics to be used for consecrating new churches.

For those tourists who have been to Malacca in Malaysia or Goa in India, the story of Saint Francis Xavier, the Jesuit missionary who died on Shangchuan Island off the southern China coast in December 1552, and helped found a long-lasting Christian presence in Nagasaki and southern Japan, will be a vivid reminder of this circulation of relics. In February 1553, his "incorrupt body" was taken to Saint Paul's Church in Malacca, and in December of that year was shipped to Goa, where the body is entombed in the Basilica of Bom Jesus. His right forearm was ordered removed in 1614 by the fifth superior general of the Society of Jesus, Claudio Acquaviva, and was shipped to Rome to be used in the canonization of the saint (when miraculously, it is said, blood dripped from the wound) and then was put on display in a silver case in the society's church. Another arm bone was sent to Macau, intended for Japan. In front of the ruins of Malacca's Saint Paul's Church today stands a statue of Saint Xavier from 1952, dedicated to mark the four hundredth anniversary of his missionary work in Malacca (1545–52). On the day of its consecration, a casuarina tree fell and broke off the right forearm, the one that is in Rome and that he used to bless his converts. And so it remains.

Tambiah notes that, as in Buddhism, the Church changed its doctrines about the relics, originally treating remains as inviolable but then instituting the partibility, distribution, and redistribution of relics. Helen, the mother of Emperor Constantine, famously brought back pieces of the cross to be distributed by Constantine across Europe as a form of legitimating patronage for his Christianizing realm. After the tenth century, the cult of the saints was universalized through deemphasizing local saints and focusing on relics of the Virgin, Saint Peter, and the relics of Jesus, such as his cross, crown of thorns, or shroud. More recently, late-twentieth-century Pope John Paul II began a drive to canonize more saints as a way to revive the Church through the cult of saints.

Structurally, the modalities of the saint and relic cults of Buddhism and Catholicism, Tambiah argues, are very much the same. While in the opening of the essay attention is given to the way in which relics and amulets partake in the formation of communities and are a way of circulating grace (Christianity) and merit (Buddhism), and a theological gloss is provided ("the personal, interiorized, mystical illumination of the saints is seen in these religious traditions as flooding the vast spaces of the world with their cosmic love"), in fact the thrust of the essay, as in much of Tambiah's work, gradually shifts to the political legitimation that religious charisma provides.

FIG. 6.1. Buddhist monks and their charismatic amulets, pictured on a celebratory Thai stamp issue. Photo by Peter Jackson, historian of Thailand at the Australian National University, with many thanks.

The relics function as the palladia aspect of what Max Weber called the ritual legitimation techniques of the ancient empires. Patronage and exchange are the microcapillaries of this mode of legitimation; the complementary ritual functions of king and priest are the macrocirculation channels of legitimacy.

In the local traditions of northeastern Thailand, amulets are made with the image of the patron (royalty, generals, bankers) on one side and the image of the saint on the other: the Indo-European king-priest/monk and Buddhist sangha/dharmaraja complementarity. As these amulets circulate, are stolen and faked, they become saleable, stimulating further production and faking. Like the ashes and bone fragments in stupas that mark the Buddhist landscape, they are tokens for ordinary men to see and handle, yet belonging not to this transitory world but to eternity.

Michael Puett (2013) opens the door to an analogous Chinese world of religious charisma through temple networks and spirit possession associations that have formed the backbone of maritime Southeast Asia and coastal China. This is a world that is stirring once again and taking on renewed importance, but as Puett says, largely "out of sight of virtually the entire social sciences apart from anthropology." Both colonial governments in Southeast Asia and the communist government in China have tried to suppress these networks, because, and although, as Puett also says, in many areas these networks have run much of local society, including schools and infrastructure. Puett guides us through the haunted landscape of demonic ghosts produced by every death. People try to control ghosts with ancestral rites, to fulfill unfinished business in their names, and to domesticate them into gods by making sacrifices. As gods (often associated with the occupation of the deceased) they may attract more people, and temple networks propagate and become points of attachment for new migrants.

Like the Hadrami networks that come from the other direction, these Chinese networks extend across Indonesia and Southeast Asia and feed back again today to China. A new practice of women becoming spirit mediums in Southeast Asia is being imported to China, particularly in the coastal Putian (Fujian) areas from which many of these networks once originated.[23] Again there is a sea-land dialectic: as the silt filled in, creating new land, coastal boat people and fishermen established themselves on the land and claimed to have always been Chinese. In turn, then, the state attempted to incorporate or control them—in late imperial China, Puett says, by promoting the gods into its own bureaucracy, against local resistance. The entire Southeast Asian maritime world is filled with networks of sea peoples whose histories are only slowly being recovered from their invisibility to terrestrially oriented historians. The lineage system is a more flexible organizational form than anthropologists once thought, allowing people to buy in or be recruited, adopt a common name, or set up a clan house and thereby claim to be of a common lineage. In modern Singapore, many temples are small shrines in high-rise housing developments, where two days a week a medium may operate from, say, 6:00 to 8:00 in the evening. Like a nervous system with neurons and synapses, the channels of charismatic ritual and mythic structuring run everywhere.

Prista Ratanapruck (2013) takes us into yet another trading network that also uses pooling-redistributive mechanisms, both of the temple (or here, Tibetan monastery) form (as with the Chinese temple networks) and of the *cargo* (Sp. "burden") fiesta forms of agrarian Mesoamerica and the Andes highlands, the *kheirat* pooling systems of Iran (Fischer 1990c), or the Big Man redistribution systems in the Pacific, albeit with a Tibetan Buddhist inflection. The Manangis (Nepalis of Tibetan ethnic origin) were once salt and grain caravaneers between Tibet and India. In recent times, their networks, based in Katmandu, extend from India across Southeast Asia as they trade in gems, handicrafts, and other things. As in other trading networks, individual traders use local marriages to gain access to new areas. But for others, Ratanapruck describes a life on the road of communal rooming houses, sharing of knowledge, and mutual aid, and at home, in Katmandu, of pooling trade surpluses to put on elaborate rituals, including a two-week-long archery festival in which all men must bet and compete, with winnings distributed equally among the winning team—and if an exact bull's-eye is scored, the individual who wins must patronize the community at large. Money, the Manangis say, is of value only during one's lifetime, and so it is best to convert it into religious merit, including communal sharing and eighteen-day fasting retreats to count prayer beads for the accumulated merit of all.

Ratanapruck acknowledges the extractive mechanisms of pooling. She is primarily interested in the network expansion that pooling allows. But she also notes that many Manangis are monks (and some nuns), and these require support from productive members of the family. In many traditions where religious values remain strong, surpluses are often put to the support of religious institutions. In the case of Jains, a wealthier merchant community than the Manangi peddlers, surpluses often go into upgrading temples and community philanthropic organizations, as well as to conspicuous ritual processions as a sign of piety, merit making, and the power of the discipline and community. In the past, Manangis paid Tibetan monasteries, which provided loans for trade. In the present, Ratanapruck describes various forms of protection money that have to be paid, as many Manangis still move around under the bureaucratic radar in an informal, if ordered, economy. Redistributive rituals in many traditions can serve as partial safety nets, without the legitimizing moral justifications of sharing and egalitarianism erasing of income disparities that exist among the Manangis, as elsewhere. (Ratanapruck tells, for instance, of three traders who once spread their hawkers' cloths next to one another on Bangkok sidewalks, one now owning a small hotel in his home village, the other two owning three-star hotels in Katmandu, and yet another Thailand-based trader having become a millionaire; and, inversely, of monks who are forced to leave the monastery because their parents have died and they need to support their siblings.)

Donations to community rituals are public; peer pressure and status competition are explicit coercive modes. Ratanapruck likens these carefully recorded and announced monetary contributions to a potlatch (2008, 209). This is not to say that the various rituals engaged in, chanting and counting of prayer beads included, cannot concentrate the mind or build social solidarity, or that pooling does not allow the community to produce collective goods such as roads, refurbished stupas, and support for monasteries. The *meetha* (villagewide archery festival), *nandi* mechanisms of joint hosting of festivals, and the new urban Kathmandu meetha, including card games, board games, and lotteries, are fund-raisers, solidarity builders, and merit makers. Gambling is said to instill a discipline of indifference to money loss, a separation from desire, the bolstering of a "big heart," and a turning outward toward the community.

Collective Violence and Humanitarian Intervention

The way in which democracy came suddenly to masses of people in South Asia is a type case of what Émile Durkheim, in a different context, called the sociological monstrosity of the destruction of mediating institutions between the national government and the citizen. Durkheim, contemplating the oscillating swings of popular opinion in plebiscitary or referendum politics after the French Revolution destroyed parish mechanisms of intermediate levels of governance, worried that stable government policies would be hard to achieve. For Tambiah, contemplating the arrival of mass democracy after colonial rule, it was the effort to transfer constitutional power to dominant groups and the sudden production of volatile vote banks that has similarly impeded judicious governance. He turns to Durkheim particularly for his account of affect-charged crowd "effervescence," that labile surplus of affective energy that can suddenly flip from pack attack to panic flight and vice versa, and that is composed, in the case of modern ethnonationalist collective violence, of both anger and fear. In *Leveling Crowds: Ethnonationalist Conflict and Collective Violence in South Asia* (1996), Tambiah looks first to the ritualized riots of premodern moral economies described by Edward Palmer ("E.P.") Thompson, Natalie Davis, and others—my own account of riots against religious minorities in nineteenth- and early twentieth-century Iran provides another starkly defined public processional and ritual form performed before state and religious authorities inscribing public truth upon the body, analogous to Foucault's description of punishment in the opening of *Discipline and Punish* (1977; *Surveiller et punir*, 1975), and repeated in executions of Baha'is in the early days of the Islamic Revolution of 1979 (Fischer 1973, 1990b).

But, with others, Tambiah perceives a radical difference in modern mass violence, and he draws upon both the literature of modern crowd psychology (Gustave Le Bon, Georges Rudé, Sigmund Freud, and Elias Canetti) and

Durkheim. Although Tambiah suggests that most of the South Asian ethnonationalist riots are short-lived, that the heightened affect and suspension of individual reason wanes as quickly as it arises, his own account of the traps in which mass "democratic politics and ethnonationalist politics are related in South Asia" and in which "violence as mode of conducting politics has become established and institutionalized" is considerably darker. "Industrial employment, professional skills and the practice of Western medicine," he writes, have become "recategorized as entitlements and sumptuary privileges indexed as quotas assignable to preexisting ethnic or racial or indigenous groupings" (1996, 342). Collective violence orchestrated to defend or contest these entitlements creates a massive internal contradiction. "Systematically organized ethnic riots by politicians, parties, and police" destroy and then require repair by agencies of the same governance structures, particularly the health care system, hospitals, welfare agencies, refugee camps, and relief administration (330). The language of the United Nations conventions of the International Law of Human Rights—the declaration of 1948 and its two main covenants of 1966 on civil and political rights, and on economic, social, and cultural rights; along with its eight further covenants on genocide (1948), refugees (1951, 1966), racial discrimination (1965), women (1979), religion (1981), children (1989), and indigenous peoples (draft 1993)—remain important hortatory ideals but are contested and unenforceable even in signatory countries.

Time has moved on since 1996, and the debate about human rights versus humanitarian rights has intensified (Fassin and Pandolfi 2010). Mary Jo DelVecchio Good and Byron Good (2013) provide an important ethnographic case that extends both Tambiah's discussion and his more optimistic hopes. The struggle of Aceh separatists against the Indonesian central state was locked in a brutal civil war for twenty-eight years, or longer if one counts its roots in earlier broken promises. Aceh had played an important role in the struggle for Indonesian independence against the Dutch. Promises made then for provincial autonomy were broken by President Suharto, who sent Batak troops to put down resistance. Discovery of natural gas off Aceh was exploited by Indonesia with little return to the local communities, and this exacerbated Aceh's sense of betrayal. In 2004 a tsunami devastated the province's north and west coasts, and also brought the civil war to a halt. Almost miraculously, the Acenese independence movement and the Indonesian state were able to leverage the disaster into a peace accord and a new center-periphery set of relations—*almost* miraculously, because it took concerted effort on both sides, but nonetheless *miraculously* (with the help of an act of God or nature) because the tsunami also hit Sri Lanka, with no similar effect in bringing peace (which came six years later in the form of a bloody crushing of the Tamil Tigers in May 2009). Mary-Jo and Byron Good report on an extraordinary conference they convened at Harvard in 2007, bringing together leaders from all sides of the Aceh conflict, who in neutral territory could both talk and reenact some of the emotional explosiveness.

More comprehensively, the Goods report on two mental health needs-assessment surveys they conducted in the interior villages where the struggle had been fiercest, and their subsequent effort to help build mobile clinics and integrate them in a public health care system. Their work with the international NGO International Organization for Migration (IOM) and with local psychiatrists and health care workers goes to the heart of debates about the value of talk therapy and psychopharmacology, about donor metrics and timetables, about repair of torn social fabrics, and about renegotiation of center-periphery relations. The rewards of watching people return from extreme dysfunction and inability to work to social life belie extreme skeptics of medical intervention. Supporting local self-government slowly being rebuilt is equally fraught and rewarding. The "poisonous knowledge" of things done in the past, in other conflict areas of Indonesia (for example, the still-traumatic aftermath of the 1965 anticommunist massacres) as well as elsewhere in the world, has become part of everyday reality. As a Balinese anthropologist observes about his society, you have to carry on everyday life with people who killed your family. This condition of knowledge is a widespread one, from Europe in the aftermath of World War II to the brutalities of World War II in Southeast Asia, from civil war in Beirut to postcolonial and post-Soviet ethnonationalist conflicts around the world. Difficult as these situations are, life does come back, and narratives that are alternatives to those that mobilized and locked people into mutually assured destruction can and do emerge—a hope that Tambiah repeatedly expresses for South Asia.

Liisa Malkki, Marshall Sahlins, and Emiko Ohnuki-Tierney each reflect on a different facet of these issues. Malkki (2013) reflects on the double binds between humanitarianism and professionalism in the world of dealing with refugees, and for NGOs such as the Red Cross. As work by Didier Fassin and Mariella Pandolfi (2010) and others has pointed out, navigating between neutrality in the name of humanitarian emergency relief and de facto complicity in sides to a conflict is easier to accomplish verbally than in reality, as the splits between the Red Cross, Doctors Without Borders, and Doctors of the World have demonstrated.

Marshall Sahlins (2013), citing his son, Peter Sahlins, picks up the theme of the amplification of minor differences through relays up and down the transformative scale of structural conflicts. Arjun Appadurai takes from Freud the phrase "narcissism of small numbers" for the title of his meditation *Fear of Small Numbers: An Essay on the Geography of Anger* (2006). Taking cues from Georg Simmel, Tambiah says, on the same theme, "*The greater the blurrings of and ambiguities between the socially constructed categories of difference, the greater the venom of the imposed boundaries, when conflict erupts, between the self and the other, 'us' and 'them'*" (Tambiah 1996, 276; emphasis in the original). As Sahlins pithily remarks, apropos the all-too-frequent glib references to Benedict Anderson's *Imagined Communities,* "Collective subjects such as nations, 'imagined' as they may be, take on the flesh-and-blood qualities of real life subjects" under conditions of segmentary opposition, schismogenesis, or what Tambiah calls *transvaluation-focalization* and *nationalization-parochialization.* Anderson in *Imagined Communities* (1991; 1983) and, in a different way, Ernest Gellner in *Nations and Nationalism* (1983) focus attention on the materiality of print literacy in the production of nationalism, and the need for literate workers in industrial economies. Tambiah (1976) and Taylor (2013) also pay attention to the materiality of print and orthographic technologies, as Rosalind Morris (2000) does to the more recent mediations of photography and video in the transfer of spirit mediumship and political violence in Thailand.

Two things are important here: the synaptic transfer across national boundaries sparking quite different social arenas of conflict using the same symbolic resources (e.g., the transduction of the Salman Rushdie affair or the Muhammad cartoon affair [Fischer 1990b, 2009]);[24] and the vertical transductions between local and national levels of antagonisms and conflicts.

Emiko Ohnuki-Tierney (2013) turns to a current example of cross-temporal analogizing that has deformed American foreign policy: the quick assimilation of the attack on New York's World Trade Center to the attack on Pearl Harbor and (much later) kamikaze attacks during World War II (see also John Dower 2010). What makes Ohnuki-Tierney's participation in this discussion so powerful and compelling is not the reference to "inferiorization" or the way in which "liberal democracy at home in Western Europe and the United States assumes the fierce shape of authoritarian rule abroad," however true those are, but rather her own remarkable work (2002, 2006) on the roughly four thousand teenage *tokkōtai* (kamikaze) pilots drawn from a thousand university students and some two thousand other teens, newly enlisted or conscripted toward the war's end, and their desperate attempts to find meaning and rationalize the deaths to which they were being sent. As with Tambiah, Ohnuki-Tierney exemplifies an anthropologist's calling to

FIGS. 6.2–6.5. Flying canoes of the Trobriand Kula Ring. From "Papua New Guinea Kula Ring Canoes, Egum Rock (2010)." © Biosphere Foundation. https://www.youtube.com/watch?v=M_qxDIBJTik.

FIGS. 6.2–6.5. (continued)

recover the humanity of people sacrificed to the juggernauts of mass politics, and to recognize their alternative ideals, motives, and possibilities.

Flying Canoes, by Way of Conclusion

Along the trajectory of Tambiah's career he has written a series of experimental essays in the methodologies for analyzing ritual action, cosmologies, and classifications. Many of these emerge from an important, if now decaying, tradition of anthropological pedagogy: the reanalysis of ethnographies with new theories and analytical perspective, particularly of Malinowski's studies of the Trobriand Islands and Evans-Pritchard's of the Nuer and Azande. Often this was done in term-length seminars devoted to one society to allow close readings and in-depth rethinking. Tambiah's essays also take place in that liminal space-time in which British social anthropology struggled to come to terms with Lévi-Strauss's structuralism as well as to incorporate structural linguistics (particularly Roman Jakobson, but also J. R. Firth, C. K. Ogden, and I. A. Richards), symbolic and phenomenological analyses (Ernst Cassirer, Susanne Langer, Peter Berger and Thomas Luckmann, Erving Goffman, and Clifford Geertz), speech act theory (John L. Austin), and ritual dramaturgy and performative rhetoric (Kenneth Burke, Victor Turner, and Richard Schechner). Tambiah follows the lead of his mentor, Edmund Leach, and of Mary Douglas more than Lévi-Strauss, but the latter is a constant presence to react against and metabolize, as is that other student of Marcel Mauss, Georges Dumézil, whose analyses of the tripartite structures of Indo-European myth lie only slightly below the surface of Tambiah's sangha-*dhramaraja* explorations.

It is the Brazilian anthropologist Mariza Peirano (2013), another former student of Tambiah's, who draws attention to this corpus of Tambiah's work, at the same time drawing attention to yet another national tradition of anthropology that Tambiah has influenced. Even the listing of Brazilian topics for which Tambiah's work has been used, and the research agenda convened around Tambiah's work, is remarkable.

There are many golden nuggets in Tambiah's experiments with logical and formal relations that myths and rituals perform, embody, and constitute. Among my favorites are analyses of Trobriand seafaring magic to speed *kula* deep-sea canoes (flying canoes) that serve as charter myths for male-female complementary powers and name the paths of *kula* trade routes; Thai animal classifications that puzzle through the analytic methods for explicating classification and ritual proposed by Lévi-Strauss, Leach, and Douglas; Sri Lankan exorcism rites that (like Lévi-Strauss's analysis of Cuna exorcisms for the pains of blocked childbirth) act through a kind of abreaction, and utilize "maximal sensory intensity" to embody the demonic "indulgence of gross desires" that invade and are made to retreat, taking the evil with them; and the Thai royal tonsure ritual that enacts the transformation from galactic polity to nation-state through the innovations of Mongkut's reign.

King Mongkut takes the public role of the god Shiva in the tonsure rite for his designated crown prince (an innovation in the previously "notoriously ambiguous and unstable Siamese kingdom with its frequent rebellions and usurpations"). Previously a king remained secluded while his representative Brahmin priest performed the public rite. Mongkut's "innovative step (which he repeated in other cosmic rites)," Tambiah observes, had three implications: a "modernizing motive to impress the foreigners" by allowing the king to be seen in public without their having to cast their eyes down on bended knee; "the political statement" of the king's increased power and sense of security ("a king confined to his palace relies on the dubious eyes and ears of his favorites"[25]); and "a ritual motive" that heightened the efficacy of the rite. Mongkut's move consolidates, as Tambiah puts it, an "emergent meaning" that enlarges the institution of kingship (Tambiah 1985b, 160–61).

But it is the analysis of Trobriand flying witches and flying canoes that remains my favorite. The magic used by their male makers to endow the female deep-sea canoes with their flying speed is gained by younger brothers from older brothers and fathers or from mother's brothers with a *pokala* payment. The form of this magic that men retain today is but an incomplete version of the original magic that made canoes fly. So, too, I hope my token *pokala* to my older "[mother's] younger brother," Tambi, will speed the anthropological canoes of our calling.

God speed, Tambi.

PART III

Tone and Tuning

KEYWORDS

cultural genre terms for ethical, epistemological, and aesthetic reflection; relations of hospitality across cultures and disciplines, etiquettes of tact, tone, and tuning.

7. Health Care in India

KEYWORDS

urban Mahabharata; parables; women's stories and phalasutras *(scenes and ladders of instruction);* sarpa satra *(snake sacrifice) as mis en abyme; Shiva swallowing poison, poisonous knowledge; gender effects of partition, of family dynamics;* conscience morale; *behavioral economics and global health policies distancing healthcare from realities of poor communities who become "mere data points"; political economies of bioavailability, surplus health, domestic commons vs. global markets; product patent vs. process patent regimes; judicialization of access to pharmaceuticals; century-old communal hospitals to 1980s contested access to medical schools to 2000s contested distribution of care by market incentives vs. community public health; iatrogenic statistics; standardized patient methodology as paedagogy and advocacy; longitudinal moral engagement.*

8. Hospitality

KEYWORDS

hospitality-hostility; dancer-musician; immigration-xenophobia; invention-discovery; trade, hospitality, coercion; history inscribed in plants and animals.

9. Anthropology and Philosophy

KEYWORDS

stakes, skin in the game; catacoustics; hieroglyphic characters and structures of feeling; resonances among émigrés neither at home in mother or acquired languages, end of life loss of language, infant approximation and mirroring of language; Persian miniature as social form; the primitive within; passion plays, stoicism, and hal-e khosh; *ritual methodism (*rowzeh, taziyeh, khotbeh*); mute dreams (*gonge khabide*); generational analysis;* zurkhaneh *as icon of times out of joint; actual life; submerged traditions; autoimmunity; proceduralization.*

7

HEALTH CARE IN INDIA

In memoriam, N. SUNDER RAJAN, *who strove to keep the state honest and loved life (b. 1944 Pondicherry—d. 2014 Chennai)*[1]

With an intimate ethnographic ear, can we learn to listen alongside Veena Das, through her book *Affliction: Health, Disease, Poverty* (Das 2014) to ordinary ethics in challenged lives of poverty, illness, and family relations; and do so, as she does, in three often conflicting registers: advocacy, moral engagement, and acknowledgment of inherent uncertainties (in the very fabric of living these lives, including hers and ours).[2] Some ask how advocacy contributes to a larger social politics or strategic vision; whether moral engagements have action-critical alternative cultural registers; and how local tactics, enforced slow temporalities of resilience, and personal ethics can feedback back into articulate grassroots social politics, and articulate with new developments in bioscience and biotechnology.

And, second, can we productively reframe some of these questions by widening the canvas through juxtaposing and mosaicking them with other scenes of instruction from India? India provides powerful sites of poverty and production of precarity along with its expanding middle-class culture and entrepreneurial inventiveness. The unevenness of terrain provides loci of hope as well as culs-de-sac of decay and frustration. On the policy level, India provides daunting strategic questions about how to disseminate effective health care. On the theoretical level, India provides cultural-mythic registers of different traditions, as Das suggests in her paralleling of Wittgenstein's scenes of instruction, Levinas's limits on infinite responsibility, and the resources of Sanskrit stories that inhabit popular discourse and moral reason.

I proceed, thus, in three parts: I begin with the text of *Affliction*; then comment on moral engagements and sparks of references to the Mahabharata and other traditional, especially Muslim, modes and genres of ethical thought, the commentary performing what in Islamic scholarship often are called *hashiye*, marginal notes on the main text; concluding with a mosaic of coverage and gaps in the contemporary ethics of Indian health care and its anthropologies.

Reading Das's *Affliction*

Advocacy. Somewhere—in the vast practical and dramatic spaces—between the disconnects of global health models constructed with poor/flawed statistics and the piecemeal moralistic nudging of behavioral economists relying on naive individualistic psychological models rather than intimate knowledge of how lives are lived—somewhere in this vast multidimensional space of living lies the ethnographic task that for the last fourteen years Veena Das's band of researchers has pursued in the hopes of producing anthropological evidence of another kind, "of the kind that could be used for serious advocacy on sanitation, health care, or everyday violence."

Advocacy is troubled and troubling terrain. In cases of cancer clusters, citizens were often told that they were incompetent to distinguish coincidence and statistical significance, meaning, in environments of sequestered information, as are so many of our corporatized and legally defended environments, from Bhopal to Woburn, Love Canal to Fukushima, in such environments citizen science had to learn to gather epidemiological knowledge that would stand up in court and survive cross-examination. In the case of US Superfund legislation passed in 1980, citizen action panels were given money to hire independent experts. In the aftermath of Bhopal, right-to-know legislation was passed in the United States, and later in India. In terrains of proprietary knowledge, government statistics not made public, and other forms of sequestering knowledge, especially in worlds of metrics and audits that stand in for, and constitute, legally defensible knowledge, experiential knowledge of the sort anthropological tools reveal often have a hard time.

There are at least two critical and effective tools, however, that anthropology wields. The first is exposing to the light the ways in which bureaucratized statistics and models lie, hide reality, are made up, or are tissues of unrealistic extrapolations. Das treads carefully in this terrain, referring occasionally to celebrity projects such as MIT's Poverty Action Lab, proposing her team's standardized patient methodology (to which I will return) as a way, a metric even: visits to 305 practitioners (926 visits), for three common diseases, presented by twenty-two simulated standardized patients; a weekly morbidity survey of three hundred households (with 1,620 individuals participating, and a refusal rate of less than 1 percent), done weekly for seventeen to eighteen weeks, then monthly; detailed interviews with at least one and ideally all members of each household; a full day spent in each of 291 practitioners' clinics. This was done not just to expose poor-quality medicine but also positively as a *pedagogy* (teaching how to articulate disease diagnostic symptoms in vernacularly recognized ways).

The second anthropological tool is powerfully staging the living realities of life. Anthropology often operates like the theater: putting characters and plots onstage that illustrate competing interests, affects, emotions, idioms, strategic ploys, conflicts, and temporary tragedies and resolutions. Das does this skillfully, and, as she warns, not for its sentimental persuasive value, not just cultivating unmediated sympathy or empathy—she repeats this several times—but in pursuit of calling the community, politicians, policy makers, and experts alike from everyday trancelike forgetfulness into awareness. The challenge, she notes, following Emmanuel Levinas (or Stanley Cavell's reading of Levinas), is that the problem is rarely just attending to the face of the other but, in a world of competing obligations to the living, the dead and the dying, learning how to suffer separation from the other, limiting the desire for infinite responsibility, allowing a person, an attachment to life, space to breathe. At times, as in the case of Bilu, who blames himself for not being able to gather the resources for his brother's kidney transplant in time, a possibility that would have suffocated his own life and that of his new son with debts and ongoing demands for immunosuppressants and other life supports, this is a story of individuation, but at other times it is a cycling through one's contesting (almost Kantian) faculties of *the courtroom* (the accusatory voices of obligations one is unable to fulfill); *the artisanal workshop* (the cultivation and care of the self in traditionally given virtues); and *the laboratory* (the experimental innovation of new plotlines for one's own life and one's consociates).[3] Here is Ordinary Ethics, but of the most profound sort, scenes of instruction that should make the distanced policy maker see anew, differently, come out of the trance of rules, excuses, and impossibilities for helping those in need.

Ethics. Among the virtues of India amid the poverty, conflicts, and crowding is its vitality as a land of philosophy, not just in its ancient civilizational roots in conversation with the Greeks and Chinese, but in contemporary life, affording a diversity of "scenes" of profound "ordinary ethics" in engagements with illness, access, quality of care, the technological, and the psychospiritual webs of relational socialities. Das's text is structured roughly like Wittgenstein's *Philosophical Investigations*, moving through "scenes of instruction" that are arranged in pairs and triads of increasing complexity, not unlike Laura Bohannan's classic and ingeniously structured *Return to Laughter* (1954).[4]

The theaters of ordinary ethics are modern, contemporary productions, staged within the folds and social stressors of urban renewal-removal after communal riots, structural violence of rural-urban migrants living with low-income and education, unattended-to illnesses and family tensions, dispensaries that give out tetracycline no matter what your illness because that's all they have been supplied this month. The theaters of ordinary ethics are both *performative* (acting out, fusing together visceral-emotional and cognitive-moral poles of understanding) and *enchanted* with modernity's extravagant promises, for instance, of *commodities* for which one can manage only the down payment but then must sell or have one's belongings repossessed; and of *capacities* for which one struggles, only to get a beginners' incomplete schooling. Sometimes these promises are fulfilled enough to keep hopes and fantasies alive. Sometimes they are fulfilled only enough to generate dreams, visions, ghosts, jinn, *bhot*, and *pretu*, generated—as the double binds of Bilu's life dramatize—by what Das calls "the pressure on thought." These pressures on thought are "something other than rational argumentation, not simply emotion or empathy, but wakefulness," a state Bilu reaches in terms of his duty to his son.

It is a beautiful case or scene of instruction, a case of choices between *circles of obligation expanding* infinitely in Bilu's quest to make a kidney transplantation for his brother possible versus *circles of obligation narrowed* instead by saturating his immediate surroundings with care and love that make it livable. He is able to achieve this narrowed focus only with great pain and continuing "post traumatic stress," through the woman in white who comes in dreams or visions to call him first to his responsibility to care for his village (widening his circles of obligation), but then later (narrowing these) only to his newborn son. She has granted his devotional prayers for a new son after the loss of an earlier one, but on condition of his absolute devotion to that gift. The pressures of interpreting visions, dread, panic, full of dilemmas of error, misinterpretations, false leads, satanic confusions, visions expressing dark drives—these all are part of the dramatic tension of the enchanted theaters of ordinary life, of the pressures of thought, the social stressors of impossible double binds and obligations.

Contradictions and Ambi-valences. Amid the desire for "a theology of suffering," with terms such as "soul," and a troubling anticonsequentialist Bhagavad Gita maxim ("you have authority only over your action, never over the consequences," which Das reads in a comforting Levinasian mode of limiting infinite responsibilities but which sounds uncomfortably close to the warrior Krishna's self-justification in war or the urgency used in self-justification of humanitarian aid industries for pushing aside local capacity building), Das's text registers "emotional and intellectual frictions," cycling through internal voices of the accusatory other, invocations of traditional virtues, and demands for innovation attuned to present needs. Irresolvabilities structure these scenes of ordinary ethics: limiting the desire for infinite responsibility; finding *quality care*, not just access to care; and acknowledging voices this side of mental illness ("My problem is not that *I* am ill"; "But Aunty, I was not the one who was ill"). Hard to tell what is Shaytanic confusion in worlds where things are not always as they seem (*dunya nadeedani*).

Indeed, it is a truth of parables in many traditions (Fischer 1990, 110; Jain parables; and Musa-Khizr stories in Islam) that things are not always as they seem. This is a truth, as well, of psychoanalysis and counseling, of medical practitioners who attend to the corporeal demands of hope and spiritual distress (Hyun 2013), of the unseen world in its many dimensions.

Das deals with these in a series of "scenes of instruction" built around nine main figures. The opening two scenes are of failures of quality of care, each complicated by a structural aporia of imposed not knowing. The next three are further complicated by family dynamics. This is intensified in the sixth and seventh of classic family systems dynamics in which a child is designated to be the problematic figure of failure or distress, but, of course, without knowing if there is also a genetic or physiological cause. The eighth and most elaborate is of the play of forces—psychic, social, political, economic, seen and unseen causes and influences—that make interpretation dangerous and, like the philosophical *pharmakon*, potentially poisonous rather than healing.

The first scene of instruction is a story of a four-year-old child who died from a fall and head injury but was misdiagnosed in the hospital with an

X-ray, and only correctly diagnosed with a CT scan that was done too late. A technician had told the parents a CT scan was needed, but the doctor in the first hospital had responded to that, "Are you the doctor or am I?" It is a story used first to draw attention to how the poor are treated in hospitals, but also then to raise the question about the different idioms in which husbands and wives express emotion after "cumulative adverse reproductive events (miscarriages, abortions, still births, child deaths)."

In the second story, Ballo, who complains of a stomachache, weakness, lack of appetite, and a heart condition or perhaps tuberculosis (*dil ke bimari, ya shayad TB*), gets medicines intermittently whenever her son goes to the chemist and presents old prescriptions for viral hepatitis, liver function, or TB. Bad enough are the old prescriptions, the lack of contact with a doctor, the intermittency of taking courses of drugs, but, underlying all, says Das, was the demand of the sixty-year-old woman for more attention from her son and his wife. She would periodically return from town to visit her daughter's village to display displeasure at her son.

The third scene of instruction becomes more complicated. Prakash is a periodically hallucination-suffering, shivering old man who refuses to wear even a newly purchased sweater because he can smell a Muslim on it. His hallucinations, for which he was already hospitalized once forty years ago, obsessively repeat an abduction by Allah, during the grip of which Prakash speaks in a high, feminized voice, claiming a love of Allah and a fatal attraction for Islam, from which he is saved by Shiva. Like Shiva, he can become violent. Released from the hospital, he lives with the widow of his younger brother and her now-adult son. This arrangement is imposed upon the widow by her *biradari* (kin group), who insist she have a male guardian in the house, never mind that he is mentally impaired. She manages him with lithium and sleeping pills. Life in this scene is complicated by family and hallucinations.

In a fourth scene of instruction, Meena dies of TB after having successfully completed several courses of TB-DOTS treatment, each time being declared cured. A relative gets her admitted to a hospital as a dependent, and another helps her get into a treatment center under a false name to avoid regulations against going to treatment clinics beyond one's local zone. A physician told Das there was no point in testing for multidrug-resistant TB since they could not treat that. Meena died after much seeking of care, leaving her family saddled with debts, and having negotiated much anxiety that her husband would leave her for a woman he was having an affair with. There was no way to know if she was repeatedly reinfected because of compromised immunity, environmental factors, or concomitant HIV infection, or whether she was infected by an acquired or transmitted drug-resistant strain. Meanwhile, the records of each DOTS center classified her as a cured case, and altogether she counts in the official statistics as multiple cured cases.

The fifth scene of instruction involves children covering up for their parents. Meena's son, Mukesh, who was between eight and twelve years old during the fieldwork, covers for the dysfunctional relation of his parents, his mother's descent into illness, her fear of being sent away, and her refusal of her medications when she is angry with her husband. Mukesh's story is paired with that of a young girl who tells the police that her mother's death by kerosene was an accident, and is praised in the neighborhood for the "correct response." Before her death, Meena tried to support Mukesh's education, with the help of Das, but after Meena's death the new stepmother, whom the father gives the first wife's name, is not so supportive. Still, when Das meets Mukesh again a few years later, his smattering of English has gained him a job, a watch, and a practice of attending church, where he finds a sense of peace unlike, he says, the jostling in a Hindu temple).

A sixth scene of instruction is that of a brother and sister with different life outcomes. Swapan ("Dream") is a twenty-year-old migrant from Multan, a dalit (or untouchable), who suffers an unsupportive family environment in which his sister succeeds at education while he fails. He is undermined by his mother and becomes designated as the problem child. He says to Das, "My problem is not that I am mad. My problem is that no one takes interest in me." But while he has moments of lucidity like this, he, being less strong than his sister, Vayda, also is driven to the verge of madness, having bouts of rage, acting out, defecating on the floor, beating his mother, and eventually, after a stay in a psychiatric hospital, trying to master the world by memorizing the English dictionary, a key, he thinks, to power. Experiencing "illusory qualities of modernity" always out of reach, he stumbles through life "as if made into a ghost." This scene of instruction, of a splitting of the mother into good and bad mothers, sounds Kleinian or Bion(ian) or Kali-like, and offers a possible opening to building upon the psychoanalytic accounts of mental illness in South Asia pioneered by Gananath Obeysekere, Alex Roland, and others. Abandonment in these stories is not so much an act of the will resulting from choice but rather an exhaustion of the will and the capacity to marshal yet more energy. Swapan's mother says her son has remade his own mother into a demonic being who could wish death upon the son she had borne. Here actors are not transparent to themselves, and the pursuit of the moral within such scenes of trancelike everyday ordinary ethics is analogous to being called to awaken from forgetfulness.

Vidya ("Knowledge"), by contrast, is quite aware of her family systems role as the overly bright girl under such close supervision that, were she less strong, would make her ill like her brother, Swapan. Stubbornly insisting on studying against internal family pressures, she becomes withdrawn and is taken for psychiatric treatment. Vidya says to Das, "But Aunty, I was not the one who was ill—it is my Father who needs treatment . . . my Father has created such a situation that every one was watching me all the time." And she succeeded—if not making it all the way to college, still acquiring a clerical job and steady income.

The most elaborate scene of instruction is that of the Muslim healer, Hafiz Mian, with whom Das shares her own dream of dread, of being on a train helping protect an Indian nationalist terrorist disguised as a Sikh who is being tracked down by British soldiers on the train. The psychological "I" of the dream is a young woman, who Das says doesn't really physically look like her, whose job it is to distract the soldiers. The dread would seem to be easily explained, to this observer, as a reflection of Das's work with Sikh and other victims of the riots after Indira Gandhi's assassination, and her continued work in low-income neighborhoods suffering further structural violence. In her story, however, Das claims to be "bewildered" by the dream. Hafiz Mian cautions her that she should not tell dreams to just anyone because they could have dangerous effects, transforming what is latent and hidden into manifest reality, and he significantly asks if in the dream she had *seen* the revolutionary or the British soldiers, and she realizes she had not. Dreams, he says, are only partly about images, what you see, but primarily about what you sense—dread, in this case—and dream interpretation is always subject to misrecognition, and to be mislead by *shaitan*. The term "shaitan," of course, has different registers. It is too often translated as what in Christian imagery is called Satan, a fallen angel and figure of intentional evil, like the Zoroastrian Ahriman. But shaitan is also used of mischievous little boys, of jokestering misdirection, not necessarily evil. In dream interpretation, therefore, there can be various forms of error, of misrecognition, of false cues or leads. And so, Das's anxiety about misrepresenting the *vujud*, the essence, the real truth, of the people she comes to know only partially through ethnographic fieldwork, is a burden that Hafiz Mian also lays out as the burden of a healer who is always dealing with the hidden, that shadows the manifest: the unspoken desires and motivations unknown even to the afflicted themselves.

Cultural Acoustics inside Pragmatic Action

> Each of his [Wittgenstein's] scenes of instruction, for example, I can produce from ritual Indian texts, for instance, on the necessity to know the pain of the being of sacrifice.
>
> A person, a woman, is building life already on some harms. Not by escaping, but by assimilating the violence and weaving your life in it.
>
> Such a notion of witnessing is very present in the Hindu classical texts. And in some ways it is also a concept of embodiment of events or violence; in the sense that "the witness" becomes able to let the events inhere in her. Memory is not at the level of representation, but at the level of a particular gesture with which you inhabit the world.[5]
>
> [My] notion of healing carried two ideas: endurance, capacity to establish a particular relationship to death. . . . I was very struck by the ways in which pain does write itself enduringly on people's lives. It was not about a thunderous voice of pain, but about the manners in which pain was woven into the patterns of life.
> —VEENA DAS, "Listening to Voices"

"Affliction" is a strong word. To the Jewish, perhaps Christian, and to a Marxian ear, it evokes Job.[6] "Health," "disease," and "poverty," however, are nouns of another kind: "health" evokes the public health system, "disease" evokes notions of pathology, and "poverty" evokes the production of inequality. "Affliction" has moral, psychological, physical, and biographical connotations written in various modes of pain and feeling. "Health," "disease," and "poverty" are more statistical and comparative, alluding to the state, institutions of state, economic and caste social status, states of governance and corruption, and even what Rajeswari Sunder Rajan (2003) calls the "scandal of the state." The scandal of the state, rephrased, is also the affliction of the state, its incapacities, its blindnesses, and, so, its betrayals of its promises to its citizens.

For Das and her interlocutors, striations of fate or karma, revealed by the statistics of inequality, evoke, at certain moments, Sanskritic and Hindu traditions of interpretation of the Bhagavad Gita and the Mahabharata, along with contrapuntal notes delivered via Muslim and occasionally Sikh and Jain tellings of how inscrutable worlds interact. Analogues of Job exist in the figures of Yudhisthira in the Mahabharata, Badrasingh in Jain stories, and the grief of Ashoka carved in his memorial stones.[7] There are, of course, selective interpretations that have been made, in particular, of the Gita, by Gandhi (nonviolence), management gurus (Ramanathan 1982), transcendentalists, nationalists and militants such as Gandhi's assassin (R. Davis 2014). I am interested in the structural plenitudes of the epics and stories,[8] their invocations for everyday moral commentary, and here especially for what their echoes or acoustics do in Das's "scenes of instruction" from Hindu ritual texts and epic transforms.

Within the Mahabharata and Gita, the most central figures may not be the Krsna instructing Arjuna on the war chariot to do his *kshatria* caste [varna] warrior duty even though the effects of war are already foreseeable everywhere, or the lessons on detachment, but rather two women, Dhraupadi and Gandhari. Dhraupadi is the wife staked and lost in a game of dice who acts to partially repair the consequences by pointing out that when Yudhisthira had staked her he had already bet and lost himself. She uses one of the many *prasna* (verbal puzzles) and riddling questions that structure the epic for the double meaning of loss of himself as free agent, and loss of control of his ego, passion, and reason to addictive gambling. On both counts he is incompetent to make the wager. Gandhari (daughter of the King of Kandahar) is the wife of the blind king Dhritashastra of Kuru (today's Delhi, Haryana) and mother of the Kauravas. She wears a blindfold out of solidarity and *pativrata* (devotion, to her husband), one of the key virtues (and asceticisms, or *tapas*) touted in the Mahabharata as giving power and access to heaven. She warns against war. Hearing the ill omen of jackals crying, she makes her husband stop the humiliation and disrobing of Dhraupadi, and *sees* up close the catastrophic effects of war. She *sees* this with the divine eye, *divya caksus*, given to her by Vyasa, the narrator of the Mahabharata. Her husband, blind Dhritashastra, had declined the divya caksus, preferring to hear secondary *oral* reports. Gandhari curses Krsna for having fueled the self-destruction of society (condemning him and his clan to perish).

Dhraupadi is described crucially as being both *darsaniya* (beautiful) and *pandita* (learned). Gandhari is an incarnation of Mati, the goddess of intelligence.

The women are what the Mahabharata calls *tapasvini* (suffering women), not as passive objects of the power of males or others, but rather as the activating grounds for their work to repair the world (Hebrew *tikkun olam*[9]). Social suffering is an important term in Das's corpus (as in a different context it was for Ambedkar). The moral terrain of devastating war (the Kureshetra battle in the Mahabharata; the blood letting of Partition) is what Stanley Cavell calls the "nearly inconceivable mismatch of harm and healing" (Cavell in Das, xiv). The interventions of Dhraupadi and Gandhari change the action of the story, and as Das puts it elsewhere, "Stopping the proliferation of the effects of an action independent of the intention of the agents (*karta*) is the great theme of the Mahabharata" (Das 2014, 489).

Working in the aftermaths of Partition, of the 1984 riots that followed the assassination of prime minister Indira Gandhi, and of the 1991 liberalization of the economy with its polarizing effects of inequality, Das turns, in *Affliction*, to health care and embodied inscriptions of pain amid the production of poverty and disarray in the health care system. Methodologically or epistemologically, she often mentions Wittgenstein's query of how we can know another's pain. Cavell scales up the question into one of how we overcome skepticism in the midst of failures of both the political order's social contract as well as the unreliability of common language. Cavell further notes that in Das's account "the roles of men and women are systematically contrasted in the events of partitioning . . . produc[ing] silence in women and, in men, a volubility that fails to express what they see and do . . . taking on the register of rumor, as if the events they describe were caused otherwise than by themselves" (ibid., xii).

As Das puts it, "a person, a woman, is building life already on some harms. Not by escaping, but by assimilating the violence and weaving your life in it" (2010, 144). Alluding to the god Shiva saving the world by swallowing the poison Halahala—generated when the devas and *asuras* churned the milk ocean to obtain *amrita* (the nectar of immortality) the god Indra needed to restore his immortality (and Shiva's wife Parvarti, who choked his neck to stop the poison from killing him)—Das has powerfully feminized the image as the "poisonous knowledge" that women in particular swallow. The key exemplars are women saved after the bloody Partition, who are only partially reintegrated into society, their virtue tainted by suspicion. Shiva thematizes the swallowing of pain to save the world, to allow relations with others, and society, to continue. One thinks of the many cases from Europe to Bali to Beirut where one must live in proximity to those who have killed members of one's family. *Amrit paane se pahle Vish pinna padta hai* ("Before one can get Amrit, one must drink poison") is the daily idiom (success follows many obstacles).

At times women's pain rises to what Das calls "the pain of the being of sacrifice," a phrase she uses in speaking of her debt to Wittgenstein, although his discussions on the meaning of pain never go very far beyond the grammatical problems of *speaking* about sensation, private language, and communication, even if at issue is not language and communication itself but forms of life.[10] Das's powerful phrase, however, is concretized in the Vedic rituals that the Mahabharata (sometimes called "the Fifth Veda") transforms into "women's stories" for ordinary life. Indeed, the Mahabharata opens with an account of its own telling in the intervals of the Sarpa Satra sacrifice ritual.[11] Draupadi is a code-switching figuration between ordinary lives of women and those of queen and goddess (Sri). She is a sine qua non of sovereignty and rituals of state (kings, like ordinary householders, and celebrants of Vedic rituals, must have wives, without whom their status has no legitimacy, and who act independently).[12]

Like ordinary women, although initially seeming a sacrificial pawn, Dhraupadi exerts her position and voice, and thereby changes the course of her husband's fate and her own. The Sarpa Satra rituals in the outer frame stories of the Mahabharata themselves have carnivalesque features, involving all the priests of the realm and their wives making noise and lewd exchanges, and performing ritual copulation (Hiltebeitel 2001, 166; Black 2007, 61) simulating the inversions, unexpected consequences, and Shakespearian hidden identities in the stories of the epic. Not least of these are the copulations of the original teller of the tale, Vyasa, with his brothers' widows, from whom issue the unfit kings, the blind Dhritrashitra and the impotent Pandu (whose five social sons, the Pandavas, are sired by three gods). From the inauspicious births of these two kings begin the rivalries and mutual destruction that his family suffers. Vyasa, thus, is not just author or original narrator but also father of the protagonists, and retrospectively tells the tale of the destruction of his family, a figuration also of the Kaliyuga age, *kali* meaning both "time" and "death" ("a particular relationship to death" in the Das epigram of this section).[13]

That the sacrifice amid which the epic is narrated is a snake sacrifice itself registers what Laetitia Zecchini beautifully calls the mise en abyme of the opening of the Mahabharata, registering the series of conflicts, from those of the gods to the internal battlefield of the heart, that are the "central drama of the epic" (Zecchini 2014, 156). Snakes, or nagas, dangerous protectors across India and Southeast Asia, play a role in at least four of these conflict layers.[14]

The *yajamana* (ritual celebrant, sponsor) of Vedic cosmic rituals is translated into epic story terms as the dharmaraja (righteous king), whose dharma is restoring order, social justice, and harmony. It is interesting, Das notes, that when Yudhisthira is asked what is the highest *dharma* (righteous conduct), he says noncruelty (*anrishansya*) rather than nonviolence. In the debates between Jains and Hindu Brahmins, she reminds us, the tendencies in Jainism toward absolute ahimsa are countered by the Brahmins pointing out that life depends on eating and killing others, symbolized by the sacrifice in ritual, and that minimizing cruelty is a more realistic this-worldly principle. Das says, "Through this and other stories, the text seems to suggest that when principles like dharma are elevated to become absolute, they themselves become productive of the annihilating violence that the text documents" (Das 2013). And as David Shulman (2001, 50) adds, Yudhisthira's moralism of noncruelty is at dissonance with his own actions toward Dhraupadi, and lends irony to his words and to the story.

The veils of ignorance about causes and motivations, chains of consequences and collateral effects, intensify ethical trials in Hindu and Jain stories, particularly given the transitive reverberations of reincarnation and karma over time and across generations. The stories of Dhraupadi and Gandhari become *ladders* of instruction, *phalasrutis* (instructional, beneficial tales). They are stories of the development of what Emmanuel Levinas calls ethical consciousness (*conscience morale*). The phalasrutis addressed to women are on the surface often conservative reminders of devotion to husband (*pativrata*), but through careful managing of forms of power and ascetic self-restraint wives gain power. Dhraupadi holds the royal purse strings, supervising household and palace treasuries, and admonishes Yudhisthira to channel his *kshatria* wrath (*manyu*, like the wrath of Achilles), not merely his human emotional anger (*krodha*), which needs control, to regain his throne (Malinar 2007). It is the second time that Dhraupadi saves him.[15]

The world of the Mahabharata is hurtling toward the self-destruction characteristic of the Kaliyuga age, that of Kala (time, death); it is "impenetrably enigmatic"; and the epic's design is aptly a "poetics of dilemma" (Shulman 2001, 24). "Reasoning (*tarka*) is without foundation, sacred texts are at odds with one another . . . truth about dharma is hidden in cave" (the answer to one of the Yaksa's riddle's, quoted in Shulman 2001, 54).

Bilu, in Das's book, as noted above, in such a world may be read as a Levinasian figure, showing how the limits of infinite responsibility work, and how the moral conscience (*conscience morale*) forms in a crucible of multiple conflicting obligations that need to be managed lest one go mad or destroy oneself emotionally as well as economically. The Levinasian *conscience morale* is a sibling of Durkheim and Mauss's *conscience collective*. Both are dependent on the double valence of *conscience* as both consciousness and conscience, as intentional compassion and obligatory compulsion. Both involve not just behavior toward single others but also "the third," which Levinas figures as multiplicities, and implies rethinking the state.[16]

The state is alluded to in the ethnographic story that Das provides in her essay on corruption. A Muslim local leader in a predominantly Hindu "low income neighborhood in Delhi made up of craftsmen, street artists, and puppeteers, as well as migrants from Bihar who worked in lowly paid unskilled jobs" ("Corruption," n.d, 17) says, "I am their Shakuni Mama" ("maternal uncle," in the Mahabharata, brother to Gandhari [18]), and, like Shakuni, he is a clever and at times devious agent. He is skilled in "dealing with the local police and giving advice to people who had got entangled in some minor crime and needed a mediator to deal with the police." He also "composed poetry and could revel in improvised poetic competitions that are the staple of crowds waiting for the big men to arrive during election rallies" (17).

This is a wonderful figuration: a Muslim leader in a Hindu environment, not unlike Hafez Mian, where cultural resources are swapped in interreligious local contexts, and who wields a "magical tongue" (*Zauberzunge*, that wonderful German word for the silver-tongued, who with deft words can change an opponent's mood and the course of events). In some tellings of the Mahabharata, Shakuni's father's thighbones were the material of which the dice were made, and thus the dice are loaded, always doing his bidding. His sister, Gandhari, to his dismay, was married off to Dhitrashastra, who was born blind. Gandhari had been symbolically married first to a goat to cheat her destiny in which it was foretold that her husband would die soon after her marriage. Learning of this earlier marriage, Dhitrashastra flies into a rage and imprisons all of Gandhari's male natal relatives. Shakuni is the only brother to survive because all the others gave him their meager prison rations so that he might avenge their deaths.

When Das asks this Muslim man, Ghulam 'Ali (the servant of Imam 'Ali), to explain his allusion to being the Shakuni Mama, he laughs it off, saying, "Understand whatever you wish." Das chooses to read it first as "the necessity of a deceitful but brilliant man to deal with the agencies of the State," and then secondly as allowing a mythical register "to do the work of providing a social commentary on the conditions within which corruption is enfolded in everyday life" (20).[17]

Ghulam 'Ali might be another Levinasian figure in what Victoria Tahmasebi-Birgani calls "the problem of the third and justice" for Levinas, that is the connection of the everyday to larger politics. In the aftermath of the holocaust (a sacrificial term) or the shoah ("destruction"), as in the aftermath of Partition and the anti-Sikh riots after Indira Gandhi's assassination, the idea of "the third" attempts to push beyond the ineffectiveness of "the Western Liberal Tradition" that Levinas, like so many others, diagnoses as limited by its grounding in individualism and utilitarian calculus, indifferent to the cry of the other. The cry of the other should at least make you stop and recognize it. Even if you can do nothing, your *conscience morale* troubles you. The *conscience morale* constantly points out the betrayals of the state, the gap between the law and justice, as Jacques Derrida would say. The state is always less than the ethics that inspired it. So there is need for the work of Ghulam 'Ali.

The ethicopolitics that Levinas calls for is built around the recognition of one's own and others' vulnerabilities. He writes against possessive individualism, of understanding a person as an accumulation of "merits, titles, professional competence" that crushes others, and against the "hierarchicized society maintained by the necessities of consumption" (quoted in Tahmasebi-Birgani (2014, 22). He argues for an ethico-politics that would no longer be a matter of "the bourgeois peace of the man who is at home with himself behind closed doors, rejecting the outside that negates him" (BPW 165), of gated communities. "Justice can have no other object than economic equality" (CPP 44, quoted by Tahmasebi-Birgani, 2014, 32). Tahmasebi-Birgani quotes Levinas, "Marx is the only Western philosopher who does not view the human as pure freedom, who acknowledges the chaining of the body and its consciousness to a concrete existence that no reason can undo completely" (Tahmasebi-Birgani, 2014, 22). And further: "Equality among persons means nothing of itself; it has an economic meaning and presupposes money, and already rests on justice, which when well-ordered begins with the Other" (Levinas, *Totality and Infinity*, 72; Tahmasebi-Birgani, 2014, 22).

The narrative motifs of visibility-invisibility; control over desire/passion; direct seeing/witnessing versus delegated narrating/reporting; female counterpower to male hierarchy; humiliation by disrobing and power through restraint and asceticism (*tapas*); "human beings propose, but destiny proposes otherwise";[18] and paired ritual/epic tales that refract one another are all at play across Hindu, Greek, Jewish, and Islamic myths in families of resemblance,[19] as are embodiments of pain, and witnessing to morality in a world where appearances may hide many undercurrents, particularly in the aftermaths of war or civil strife, and where the scandal of the state, its margins, and promises (betrayed) are at issue, visiting affliction, pain, and suffering upon the citizens.

At the Interface of Science, Technology, and Social Organization

> I think that I could write the history of anthropology by looking at how it always comes into being in certain scenes of collapse. —VEENA DAS, "Listening to Voices"

> Legal processes are tardy, the police corrupt, welfare and employment opportunities negligible, and the individual's knowledge of her rights and entitlements vague. To speak of women as rights-bearing individuals in this context is to invoke a situation that does not exist in a meaningful way. —RAJESWARI SUNDER RAJAN, *The Scandal of the State*

> Yet the hospital decided that the amount approved [by the Central Government Health Scheme] was insufficient, and refused to conduct any pre-operative tests or even attend to him until we changed his status to a private, full-paying patient. They did not deign to inform us of this however; ... When we insisted upon the routine pulmonary tests that needed to be conducted before he could be passed fit for surgery, the pulmonologist responded that "if they want to see me so badly, let them come to my department and I'll see them." When he was transferred to his ward from the intensive care unit after his surgery, the surgeon asked the nurses to ensure that oxygen supply be constantly available to him; it took an entire day for it to be arranged.... The consulting doctor on morning rounds asked the nurse to have an x-ray taken; when he returned for evening rounds that day, the x-ray had still not been done in spite of our constantly badgering the nurse. At one point she helplessly proclaimed "we are trying, but the radiologist is not coming."
>
> This hospital was a major destination for medical tourists from around the world. A French couple in the room across from [us] stood with us in the corridor, in sympathy and horror.... [Thus we learned] the limits and apathies of elite profit-driven private medical care in contemporary India. —KAUSHIK SUNDER RAJAN, *Pharmocracy: Trials of Global Biomedicine*

Das's *Affliction* probes lifeworlds, cultural acoustics, and philosophical registers. It reveals a series of bureaucratic failures in making health care institutions responsive to the actual conditions of the impoverished. The case of Meena is a particularly galling example, casting questions as well on the compilation of statistics on which public health care planning and metrics of success depend. As Dr. K. Srinath Reddy, the former head of cardiology at the All India Institute of Medical Sciences, and the current president of the Public Health Foundation of India notes, "Das critically examines how behavioral economics and global health policies are distancing healthcare from the contextual socio-cultural realities of poor communities... poor people are becoming 'mere data points' as economists resort to the 'benevolent paternalism' of using materialistic nudges" (Reddy 2015). He illustrates his review with a picture of a woman waiting with baby in arms outside Deen Dayal Upadhyay Hospital in New Delhi. Even more painfully, Roma Chatterji notes (2016, 12), "Das's description of how expanding medical technologies put more and more pressures on the poor to make more technological solutions for life-threatening illnesses available to their relatives as part of kin obligations, whereas the State pays little attention to improving risky conditions of life for the poor which lead to these illnesses in the first place" (Das 2010b). Bilu again comes to mind.

The "women's stories" of the Mahabharata and the *phalasrutis* of Das's ethnography lead to questions of how one should scale up to questions of governance of public health on the margins of the state, within its bureaucracies, and beyond its ability to see or care.[20] Das focuses on the poor, but not only the poor suffer, nor is it only in the public sector—nor are these issues unique to India.

The problems of disaster-response medical attention is iconically represented by Bhopal, but applies as well to Minimata, Love Canal, and many other toxic release and disaster sites (Fortun 2001, George 2001, Harr 1995, Reich 1995). It is detailed most powerfully perhaps in Indra Sinha's riotous Bhopal novel *Animal's People*,[21] and analyzed in terms of advocacy by anthropologists and journalists within the destructions of health by late capitalism and pharma capitalism (Deb 2011, Fortun 2001, Sunder Rajan 2016). Likewise, which populations are recruited into clinical trials is an ethical issue crystallized in the case of unemployed or underemployed former textile workers in Central Mumbai, but is a concern globally (Sunder Rajan 2007, Petryna 2009, Cooper and Waldby 2014). Highly trained doctors returning to India to set up specialty clinics sometimes trigger unintended consequences, for instance: brokers beating the bushes for black market kidney donors in the wake of scandal politics and a ban on selling kidneys (Cohen 1999); or high stake financial pressures on vaccine development clinical trials under new patent laws in the wake of India's adherence to the General Agreement on Tariffs and Trade (GATT) agreements (novelized for a contraceptive vaccine in Rohini Nilekani's *Stillborn* [1998], but recounted also to me and in an MIT workshop by a malaria researcher from the International Center for Genetic Engineering and Biotechnology, Delhi, in a story of the inability to get an India-designed malaria vaccine produced by an Indian company because the company could not come to an agreement over patents and licensing for a needed adjuvant owned by a multinational). The struggle over intellectual property regimes, drug pricing, and generic drug production is not only a problem in India. Nor are the toxic environments in which the poor are often consigned, for example, Sinha's Khaufpur, literally "City of Fear," or Bhopal; and Arun Kolatkar's equally improper Marathi Bombay poems: "Sarpa Satra," "Songs of Rubbish," and "Rat-Poison Man's Lunch Hour," detailing bodies gone awry, in which a line reads, "I'm a poor man from a poor land my age ain't right my colour is wrong / my nose too big my chest too small my arm too long my grip too strong" (Zecchini 2014, 199). Kolatkar, Nilekani, and Sinha constitute something of a contemporary urban folk Mahabharata, in which the characters are marginalized by poverty and the inequalities of innovation economies, structured from top to bottom by double binds, caught in contradictory imperatives.

We are beginning to have a series of important ethnographic studies of the (fragmented) Indian health care systems of the post-1990s liberalization era that not only realistically put in their place (contexts, and limits) the claims of transformative technologies and political economies but also, as in a mosaic, throw light on disconnections and missing pieces, for example, the work of Cohen 1999, Das 2013, and Fortun 2001, also the work of Stefan Ecks 2013a, b, on drug "detail men" or sales forces to physicians; Sarah Pinto 2014 on mental health services; Jean-Pierre Gaudeliere 2014 on reformatting Ayurveda; and Alison Fish 2014 on patenting yoga; and many others.

The state promises, the state betrays, the state is not one, particularly in the postliberalization era, when the margins of the state (another of Das's foci of attention) are as defining as the center. Bioavailability (Cohen 1999, 2004), surplus health (Sunder Rajan 2007), drug harmonization (Kuo 2009), public-private leveraging, and domestic commons versus global markets are emergent and urgent matters of concern. India has long had social movements for social justice, including Gandhian hygiene campaigns and cataract removal camps, government and philanthropy-based general hospitals, targeted disability and disease campaigns, and, here and there, world-class elite research institutes, amid decayed state universities and entrepreneurial private ones of variable quality.

There are many ways to narrate the history of the life sciences in India. The usual ways are to pick key sectors, key institutional developments, key policy initiatives, or key scientific leaders. I will use here instead a cross-sectional tactic reflecting on my own "ladders of instruction" over the past forty years of periodic efforts to understand the leading edges of science and technology developments in India, beginning by following the established path of most historians of science with physics (including the most comprehensive social history done so far by anthropologist Robert S. Anderson, [2010]), but then branching out into biology, information technology, and ecology. The idea is to provide what in geology or archeology would be called a cross-sectional cut through historical strata. Obviously there are other names and institutions that could fall alongside the ones listed here (both those I know about and others that I don't), but I want to pose the question in a reasonably condensed form of how these developments among the leading edges of science and technology both in India and globally fail to articulate with the stories in Das's *Affliction*, obviously not a criticism of her ethnography but one of the gap between, on the one hand, promises and results of development programs, scientific initiatives, and technological projects, and, on the other, the lives recounted in *Affliction: Health, Disease, Poverty*, and to argue along with her that the solution is probably not more top-down systems, econometric "solutions," or auditing bureaucracies, propagated from a distance (whether in Delhi, Geneva, or Washington), and that as Chatterji, quoted above, notes, that at times hopes in medical technologies place additional pressures on kinship obligations that make matters worse rather than better.

In the early 1970s, when I was researching Parsis and Irani Zoroastrians in Bombay, I was impressed by the hospitals set up by Parsis for their own community but also open to the general public (Sir Jamshedji Jeejeebhoy Hospital, Cama Hospital in Bombay; Jehangir Hospital in Pune). Among the initiatives at the time was a Parsi community-wide genetic survey in Pune and Bombay directed by a student of and in collaboration with human geneticist Victor McKusick at the Johns Hopkins University. The survey was both to provide comprehensive care, and to attempt some "molecular anthropology" or mapping, using GDP-6 as a possible marker of migration from malaria endemic areas (the Mediterranean and Africa via the Iranian plateau). A decade later, in 1984, I spent a tumultuous year in Ahmedabad—the year of communal riots against the Mandal Commission's increase of reservations in medical and engineering schools for other backward castes, scheduled castes, and scheduled tribes; the assassination of Indira Gandhi and the subsequent riots; and the Bhopal disaster—researching the Jain community. This time I was impressed by the communal institutions, including clinics, and their caste exclusivity. We, my wife and I, had occasion to need a doctor, and were carefully guided through the hospital and private clinic system, becoming aware of the practice of families providing basic food and care while members were in the hospital.

In the 1990s I returned on several short research trips to explore the genealogies of modern science in India, first those of physics—beginning in Ahmedabad again with the Physical Research Institute (founded by the already deceased Vikram Sarabhai); I also interviewed, in Bombay, E. V. Chitnis (a colleague of Sarabhai's and the former director of the Ahmedabad-based Space Applications Research Organization, who had also spent three years at MIT[22]), as well as physicists and biologists at the Tata Institute of Fundamental Research, and also at the super computing and radio astronomy programs in Pune. I followed the move of the TIFR biology research program under Oveid Siddiqi to a new site in Bangalore, the National Center for Biological Sciences (NCBS), and also began talking to people at the Institute of Indian Sciences, and the National Institute of Advanced Studies (including the late Raja Ramanna, the longtime director of the Indian nuclear program and director of the successful 1974 "Smiling Buddha" nuclear bomb test; when I knew him at NIAS he was keenly interested in resonances of Buddhist logic and nuclear physics, as well as a fine classical piano player).

At TIFR I had found a number of molecular biologists working on malaria, and had the uncanny experience of simultaneously reading Amitav Ghosh's *Calcutta Chromosome*, in part a novelized account of the discovery of the transmission of malaria by the Anopheles mosquito to birds as well as humans by India-born British medical doctor Sir Ronald Ross with the unsung help of a "native" Indian assistant, as well as the use of malarial fever therapy for syphilis. I would many years later seek out, with Kaushik Sunder Rajan, all the Calcutta sites in the novel, including Ross's memorial plaque in the Presidency General Hospital. In the meantime, from Chitnis I had learned that his son, Chetan Chitnis, was a malaria researcher at the National Institutes of Health in Washington, and went to meet him there (we had overlapped at Rice University, where he got an MA in physics, but we did not meet then). I followed him to his new posting at the International Centre for Genetic Engineering and Biotechnology (ICGEB) in New Delhi, where, as he was setting up his lab, I got my first tutorial on clean rooms and the limits of research laboratories of scaling up from small batches to large enough batches to run clinical trials. Through an MIT Parsi connection, on a subsequent visit to Bombay, I got an introduction to Yusuf Hamied (CEO of Cipla Pharmaceuticals), and had a long interview with him on the changes in the patent system (from the *process* patents that allowed the generics industry to grow in the 1970s and caused the multinationals to withdraw from India at that time, to a new *product* patent regime in the 1990s to harmonize with the international rules of the GATT and the Agreement on Trade Related Aspects of Intellectual Property Rights (TRIPS). We talked about Cipla's efforts to provide cheap HIV-AIDS drugs to Africa, a conversation I relayed back to my colleagues at Harvard, Paul Farmer and Jim Kim, who would play key roles in forcing down drug prices in South Africa. (Hamied grew up with the Parsi symphony conductor Zubin Mehta, and like Mehta had many connections in Israel.) Through MIT's Industrial Liaison Program, I met Dr. Swati Piramal (chief scientific officer of Nicholas Piramal Pharmaceutical Company), and she provided a tour of both their soil and plant screening research facilities, and a clinical trial center that they were establishing. Her idea at the time was that with new cheaper diagnostics (on a chip), Nicholas Piramal could become a diagnostic service center for rural physicians across the country. I followed up in Bangalore with some new biotechnology companies, in particular one that was pioneering the local production of reagents needed for basic pharmaceutical research. (In Bangalore, I also did interviews with Narayan Murthy of InfoSys, and with several people at WIPRO, another fast growing information technology company, having been introduced to them by J. G. Krishna, who had been at MIT, and had started a computer lab at the Indian Institute of Management (IIM) in Ahmadabad, Gujurat, where Murthy had been his student and assistant. I also did interviews at Tata Consultancies in Bombay.) In Hyderabad, on the recommendation of Kaushik Sunder Rajan, who was beginning to do his own work on the life sciences in India (as well as globally), I went to interview people at Dr. Reddy's and Ranbaxy. Kaushik was doing fieldwork in New Delhi, and I went to visit him. He introduced me to Samir Brahmachari, then director of the Center for Biochemical Technology (CBT), one of the national laboratories under the Council of Scientific and Industrial Research. Brahmachari had come from the Indian Institute of Science in Bangalore, and was in the process of establishing the CSIR-Institute of Genomics and Integrative Biology (IGIB). There were racks of new computers sitting around that would be built into powerful parallel processing machines. Brahmachari was full of social organization ideas: rather than try to reform an inertial old institution, better to build the new institute within, but separated from, the old CBT. He was a champion of the idea that India had missed the "genetics revolution" and should not miss the genomics one. National laboratories were funded in ways that could not in fact create full translational systems (from bench to bedside): one could get funding for capital investments but not for recurrent costs. With liberalization, neither the government nor the private sector could do translational medicine for the public good alone. So India would need to experimentally create new forms of private-public partnerships. The first of these, as Sunder Rajan was to discover, was with Nicholas-Piramal. Sunder Rajan would also visit the clinical trial facility that I had seen in a much earlier stage, and came to understand that it was a facility for the extraction of surplus health from a nearly captive population of unemployed former textile workers. Meanwhile, I began observing Singapore's investment in the life sciences, finding a perch at the Genome Institute of Singapore. I would return to Hyderabad in 2006 for Human Genome Meetings at the invitation of the president of the Hugo Genome Organization (HUGO), Edison Liu, who was also the director of the Genome Institute of Singapore.

At that meeting and subsequent ones, I would come to know Samir Brahmachari in his new role as head of the entire CSIR national laboratory system, but also as a key player in HUGO and host at the Hyderabad meetings. Among his continued imagination for social organizational innovation, he had prepared for the HUGO meetings by holding many satellite preparatory meetings with university students around the country, and invited them to the Hyderabad meetings. They came in large numbers. Controversially, he would then recruit them and others to crowdsource annotation of the tuberculosis genome, doing it much faster than more conventional laboratories could do. Challenged, he would say that anyone who wished could verify the results, as they were posted on the web.[23] This was the beginning of the India-led Open Source Drug Discovery Consortium with global participation, focused on neglected tropical diseases.

One final experience will close, for the moment, this rapid race through Indian developments in the life sciences: the contract of the Indian Department of Biotechnology (Ministry of Science and Technology) with MIT to help create a new national-level institute for Translational Health Science and Technology Institute (THSTI). For MIT, the exercise appeared to be one of trying to recreate the ethos of MIT and Harvard Medical School's Health Science Technology Program, which has produced many physician-scientists and scientist-entrepreneurs. For India, the exercise was to be a seedbed to produce charismatic cohorts of biomedical leaders to transform health care nationwide. One of the intractable conflicts was between the HST (and new Indian entrepreneurs') conviction that one could get new technologies to patients only by means of the marketplace and the legacy socialist insistence that robust communities rather than market profits needed to be the crucial metric. Another axis of conflict was between the HST commitment to interdisciplinarity and creation of new hybrid fields on the one hand, and established inertial commitments by leaders in fields such as vaccine development to do what they knew how to do and to run institutions in the traditional top-down manner, on the other. In the end, although MIT successfully helped hire a number of young professors, these conflicts stymied the transnational collaboration, and MIT withdrew.

Much more remains to be said about each of the above-mentioned initiatives, but for the limited purpose here, it is enough to point to the efforts at organizational change that it was hoped could bring biomedical competence to affliction. Research and training institutes such NCBS and ICGEB, one a purely Indian national institute, the other a UN-associated international center, appear to be successful in part because they are new institutions staffed with young internationally trained professionals. Within the Indian state and its older institutions, there are charismatic leaders such as M.K. (Maharaj Kishan) Bhan, formerly the secretary of the Department of Biotechnology, and Samir Brahmachari, who, however, have to struggle to reform inertial institutions with strategies ranging from rebuilding institutions from within (e.g., ICGEB), trying to leverage transnational resources (THSTI), novel public private partnerships (CBT-Nicholas-Piramal), and open-source drug development.

The shift from a process- to product-patents intellectual property regime was profound and brought multinational companies back into India. The effort by Indian companies such as Dr. Reddy, Ranbaxy, Nicholas Piramal, and Cipla to create their own research and development units to compete on the international stage involved acquiring units in the United States and Europe (Dr. Reddy's strategy), and mergers and alliances with multinationals (Ranbaxy and Daiichi Sankyo; Piramal Healthcare with Pfizer, Merck, and Abbott). More importantly, there has been an effort through the court system or judicialization to rebalance the TRIPS agreement to push back against patents as proprietary monopolies rather than as means of licensing for the public good (notably the recent denial of a patent for Gleevac on the ground of failure to demonstrate any new biological mechanism of action) (Sunder Rajan 2017). These include struggles over patents and licensing to getting new vaccines locally produced (IGEMB), providing generic drugs to patients at an affordable cost (Cipla, Dr. Reddy, Nicholas-Pirumal), efforts to use crowd sourcing for genomic annotation to speed drug targeting (CSIR, HUGO), and participation by the IITs in international synthetic biology competitions (iGEM).[24] The terrain is varied, uneven, and calls for new forms, perhaps of financing but, more importantly, new social organization for robust community public health, and sense of citizenship and responsibility, from community clinics to five-star hospitals.

Despite the Kalyuga age of which the Mahabharata is emblematic, there is energy and hope to be fostered and ignited. Life is always a counterforce to entropy and decay. The tales of the everyday are of intermediate structures and work practices; patient accompaniers,[25] patient advocates; training health care physicians, nurses, and biomedical scientists and engineers to think about robust *communities* as their metrics; and the *peopling of technologies* themselves as networks of care, compassion, and mutual responsibility (Fischer 2013).

Conclusion: Agni and Atman (Fire and Breath/Speech)

> Vak-prabaddho hi samsarah—Santiparvan 215.11
> The world is bound up and held together (or kept awake) with words (vak).
> —QUOTED IN CHAKRABARTI, "Just Words"

> When someone is angry with us,
> The hearts duel and one abandons the relationship.
> —(JAIN) NAVKAR MANTRA, quoted in Kelting, *Singing to the Jinas*

> [If] the gods of mythology do not sweat, smell or sneeze,
> and the goddesses do not menstruate. . . . in folklore they do.
> —A. K. RAMANUJAN, quoted in Zecchini, *Moving Lines*

> Standing alone on the field of battle,
> O Hussein, never shall I forget Hussein!
> showing no fear, the zibb-e-Azeem of Abu Abdillah
> Ya Hussein! Ya Hussein! Ya Hussein!
> —SINHA, *Animal's People*

Both biomedical developments on the ground in India and those in the anthropological literature analyzing those developments seem to have a new energy, not just to celebrate the new but to also draw attention to gaps and disconnects.

Affliction is the flickering of life, fever and fire. In *Animal's People*'s Bhopal, there is fire walking on Ashura:

> I can now hear the fire . . . hissing like some giant cobra stirred up and enraged (217) . . . a different kind of fire [than] that Somraj had breathed, which had scoured his lungs and taken away his singer's breath. What must it have been like, that inferno? *O who will speak now for the orphans? . . . who now will speak for the poor?* (219). The marble balconies that surround the courtyard of fire are lined with women in dark robes. On this night most of them have pushed back their veils, their faces are lit from below, the flow softly rouges their cheeks *watching*

> *with unblindfolded eyes. . . . as the seventy-one rode off to die.* (220, italics in the original[26])

The exothermic reaction and release of methyl isocyanate and other chemicals has turned the air, soil, and water toxic, has burned out the poet-singer Somraj's lungs; and in Zafar and Farouq's hunger strike against the pesticide company's stonewalling twenty years after the gas leak, the sun and their refusal of water burn their bodies inside and out.

"Speech" too, Arindam Chakrabarti (2014, 248) points out, "is fire, it burns and cooks." It can also heal and repair. "This could be," he notes, "why actual sacrificial routines used to include a debate session": "At the end of a satra or long sacrificial festival like the horse sacrifice (*Aivamedha*) that Yudhisthira performed after the war to cleanse himself of the sin of killing his kinsfolk, priests performing the roles of a reviler (*apagara*) and a praiser (*abhigara*) would come at the end, the former pointing out the failure and faults, and the latter the greatness and success of the sacrifice" (Chakrabarti 2014, 250).

Das, like Chakrabarti in "Just Words," calls us to conversation, to the power of words to change the world, to nurture life (*Life and Words: Violence and the Descent into the Ordinary,* 2007). It is, says Chakrabarti, echoing Levinas ("We call justice this face to face approach, in conversation"),[27] "just words" (words of justice), face-to-face words responsive to the call of others ("Ya Hussein! Who will speak now for the orphans, for the poor?"), across the interfaces of biomedical expertise and ordinary life, calling awake the "peopling of technologies" (Fischer 2013b) to care at the local community level of "trying to search together" (Chakrabarti 2014, 249) for public health and robust communities, staying awake to the world (*vakprabaddho hi samsarah*).

—completed during the 10th annual HONK! festival
of activist street bands, Somerville, Massachusetts,
October 10–11, 2015

8

HOSPITALITY

Dialogue (and polyphony) were both thematized, and literally experimented with in varying formats, in the anthropology of the 1980s in an effort to make ethnographic texts responsive to "native points of view" (as the first generation of fieldworkers, Malinowski and his students, might have put it), to "other minds" (as philosophers and anthropologist-philosophers such as Ernest Gellner phrased it in the 1950s and 1960s), and to actual other voices than those of the anthropologist holding the pen (as the debate in the 1980s, and the generation of *Writing Culture*, phrased it, including feminists who rightly militated for the inclusion of gendered alterities to those of hegemonic males, and environmental justice advocates who rightly militated for attention to those marginalized by the processes of late industrialism and globalization). Chapters 4 through 7 have tried to model how such efforts need not threaten the archives of positive or objective knowledge building but, on the contrary, make the latter more credible, more open to further contestation, correction, and inclusion, and, I argue, thereby increase the accuracy, precision, and situated understanding, while also being able to move up and down the scales of generalization, maintaining the ability to zoom in and zoom out.

Hospitality is an old philosophical and anthropological topos with which to zoom in, using my fieldwork in Singapore, and drawing attention to the duality and tension in the term etymologically and practically. At the same time, it is a probe for the topos of friendship (and colleagueship, including across generations) addressed in chapter 9. Ethnographers in particular, but also all of us, depend upon hospitality in its dualities. Such an understanding of hospitality extends, of course, to the biological and ecological worlds within which we exist. Were he still alive, and so in homage, this essay is "for Julian Pitt-Rivers."

at East Coast Park in the morning
each rain tree
stands in the monsoon
bearing the pain
with a face full of tears
not daring to lose a single leaf

a Malay cleaner
has a touch of flu and can't stop coughing
he hurries under the tree
holding the sputum in his mouth

both the old man and the trees
read the report in Newsweek
dumped at the roots of a tree last night
by a pair of Caucasian lovers:
"trees caught littering their leaves in the park
will be banned from growing."

—WONG YOON WAH, myth of the rain tree

Perhaps a warning to all who attempt too easily to write about Singapore as a superficially Fredric Jamesonian postmodern town[1] that turns out instead to operate just under the surface with many ghosts and uncanny complications, not all archaic, some quite present, such as locally grounded global evangelical Christianity.[2] In an explanatory note Wong Yoon Wah tells us that an article in *Newsweek* in 1996 reported that Singapore's "government has gone so far in its cleanliness campaign as to ban trees that shed leaves from public places." Wong's variant of Lévi-Strauss's overused bon mot about the symbolic dynamics of myth "good to think with" is "Reports of this kind provide Asia with beautiful myths: a kind of myth very suitable for creating poetry" (2012, 38).

Many layers of hospitality/hostility are embedded in and/or alluded to in Wong's riposte. The attempt to discipline nature (the tropical forest, and viruses ["a touch of flu"] is among the more interesting, to which I will return at the end with another of Wong Yoon Wah's brilliant nature poems that etch history and sense of place into the very ecology we inhabit. The (in)hospitalities of class, ethnicity, and aging are prominent (old man, Malay cleaner; today the elderly dispatchers of cabs at the airport), as is the unsettled minority/majority status of the poet, Malayan born, descended from immigrants from South China, and educated in a Chinese-medium high school in Perak (a subject of continuing conflict in Malaysian politics in the recent presidential election of May 2013 and beyond), a medium of education that allowed him (and that was the point) to go to university in Taiwan (or to the Chinese-medium Nanyang University in Singapore, and potentially universities in China when that again would be possible). He then became a professor of Chinese studies in Singapore, first at the Chinese-medium Nanyang University (now cut off from its sources of Chinese-speaking students as the English language Nanyang Technical University), and then at the National University of Singapore. He wrote this poem (Myth of the Rain Tree) in Iowa City, then taught in Taiwan, before becoming vice president of Southern College, Malaysia. There is an echo in the poem, as well, of the 1974 case of Michael Peter Fray, the American eighteen-year-old canned for vandalism, a violation of hospitality (Caucasian lovers and the *Newsweek* trash). Wah's collection of poetry is called *The New Village*, a reference, of course, to the British concentration camps during the Malayan Emergency (1948–60[3]) against the communists after the Japanese occupation, and the larger second portion of the volume's poems evoke those difficult times and Wong's family's life in those camps.

Anthropology alongside Philosophy and Literature

Can anthropology play ground-truthing to philosophy's blue-sky universalizing speculations? Philosophy often looks to the ambi- and multi-valences in language to deconstruct and reconstruct latent meanings. Anthropology often looks to the social variations afforded by social and cultural forces operating now as societies of both discipline and control.[4] Language and structure (and, a fortiori, translation) limit and facilitate, locate bugs and features, of each other's hospitalities. Tropes filigree both. Tropes—those swerves toward the light (out of a tunnel or maze) that allow a gesture, a mood-altering song, a felicitous word, a moral alternative, to switch human affect and interaction, often quite suddenly, from anger to laughter, from battle to friendship, and from hostility to hospitality. "It's Greek to me," puzzles philosophy; let's try Hebrew and Inuit, Malay and Tamil, Hakka, Hokien, Teochew, and Mandarin responds anthropology.

But *what is the trouble with hospitality* these days? For philosophy the French immigration problems loom large, and Fortress Europe more generally. In Singapore it is also immigrants, albeit more like guest workers, and, like Germany, the underlying histories and economic policy spigots provide constant ghosts and spookings. In Myanmar today it bubbles up in Muslim exclusion by Buddhist extremists, worrisome in a world that remembers Sri Lanka. Histories of those two once prosperous and well-educated places (Sri Lanka, Myanmar) give pause: histories perhaps do not go backward except metaphorically (to bomb them back to the Stone Age, to close borders against the outside world), but they do not always progress, either, in social justice and equity terms, or in terms of Kantian cosmopolitanism. (Biologically this is perhaps a negative rather than a healthy autoimmune reaction, closed borders eating away at the sustenance of the self that comes from the outside.)

It is thus worth exploring the nature of limits both in the philosophical *Law* of hospitality and in the anthropological *laws* of hospitality and hostility. The nature of these limits is often worked out in ritual processes well known to the anthropological archive or database, and now in a different register, larger scale, in the new political economies of global competition, particularly as the rise of China's (and the BRIC countries) export and foreign investment strategies begin to rewrite the legacies of twentieth-century Cold War divisions into two or three worlds, a process that Singapore is well placed to observe, perched on the world's busiest maritime straits, owning the world's second-busiest container port.

(Factoids and indicators: of the top eight container ports in the world, six are in China, led by Shanghai, Singapore, and Pusan. Dubai and Rotterdam follow, and then Tianjin in China. Only thirteen of the top fifty ports are outside Asia.[5] Air passenger traffic is a different pattern, with Singapore 15th, and Atlanta 1st, but this pattern, too, is shifting, with Chinese airports ranking 2nd [Beijing], 12th [Hong Kong], 18th [Guangzhou], and 21st [Shanghai].[6] New railroads are being built across the Eurasian content from ports of China to those of Europe, and from China across Myanmar and Cambodia-Thailand to the Gulf of Bengal.)

There are, thus, new hospitalities and hostilities being written in the very language of trade agreements, mergers and acquisitions, strategic loans and foreign aid.

From A → P and Back Again

Where A = anthropological archives, grounded and contextualized;
P = philosophers' and logicians' Propositions;
or P = pragmatisms including Kant's Anthropology,[7] and
A = algebras, social anthropology's relations among relations.[8]

According to the *Record of Instructions*, the Confucian master Yang Wangming said, the body is one, but [when there is danger] the hands and feet are used to protect the head and face. Does this mean that the hands and feet are not favored? . . . We love both human beings and beasts, but the heart can bear to slaughter beasts to feed family, to make sacrifices, and to treat guests. . . . if there is not enough food to save two, the heart can bear to save the closest kin and not the person in the street. —TONGDONG BAI, *China: The Political Philosophy of the Middle Kingdom*

As Tongdong Bai summarizes it, "Confucian love is universal *and* unequal or hierarchical at the same time," in explicit criticism of Mohism, which was said by Mencius to embrace universal love without discrimination or distinction, an impractical proposition (Bai, 2012: 38). So, too, perhaps, Levinas and Derrida, whose ethics as first philosophy does not so much have in mind the neo-Confucianism of a Singaporean ideology fifteen years ago (the period of "Asian values" contrasted to Western ones) but is rather directed against the solipsism and ontological claims of Heidegger and the troubled political history of which he was and continues to be an important part.[9]

In a brilliant classic essay, "The Law of Hospitality," the anthropologist Julian Pitt-Rivers observes that in many societies, not just tribal ones, there is a ritualized fight to establish the status of the guest. For instance, among the tribes of the North American Northwest Coast, George Boas described both feasting and a battle to the death when a stranger arrives. The victor had the right to kill his adversary, though "generally the feast ends peaceably," and the guest is incorporated through a personal bond with his native agonist. This was true, as well, in Rome, according to Fustel de Coulanges: a stranger had no status in law, and to gain the protection of local laws and gods needed a "personal bond with an established member," giving him a status as guest or client. The term "client," of course is resonant today in the commercial language of hospitality (that of a hotel, for instance), and should one violate one's clientship with a hotel, a casino, or indeed a brand, one can become a target of aggressive legal suits.

For the anthropologist it is helpful to think of hospitality in terms of ritualized processes. Like gift exchange, there can be aggression and violence concealed in the process: "This is my gift to you, see if you can beat it in your obligation to gift me back." One thinks here of the German *giften* ("to poison"); the etymological shift is obscure, but it is an Indo-European pharmakon, both word and social relation: curative and potentially poisonous. As Pitt-Rivers points out, the year long hazing of British schoolboys is a similar ritual of incorporation, turning stranger into one of us.

Many of the processes commented on in the philosophical discourse on hospitality turn on the examples in the *Odyssey* and the Bible, and they all generally fit this ritual pattern. The suitors in Ithaca are accused of overstaying their welcome and beggaring their host; other stories warn of giving more than one has, being generous beyond one's means, and thus socially disruptive for self and family (Still 2010). Cixous provides a parable from Turkmenistan, and as one goes east into the Buddhist world, the stories often modulate into meditations on cycles of return that excess or lack of compassionate generosity churn, often violently.[10]

In a broad sense the ritual agon also fits the contemporary problems of immigration and xenophobia—*xenos*, the stranger/guest for whom the Law and laws of hospitality are written. Athens in antiquity used the port of Piraeus as a place to keep strangers at a distance, particularly merchants and the evils of commerce. Today Cosco (the Chinese state-owned logistics and shipping company) manages the main cargo terminal in Piraeus on a thirty-five-year concession, tripling its capacity and downgrading the labor conditions. China's sovereign fund CIC also now has a 15 percent stake in Heathrow airport, and a 7 percent stake in France's Eutelsat Communications. With Chinese infrastructure (in part or in whole), who is host and who is guest? Or rather, which of the bundles of rights and obligations—and gifts and ceremonies alongside—apply to whom, when; do the bundles come unbundled, and how and for whom?

Michel Serres would point to the logic of the parasite, a logic of the third, a biological logic that keeps things always in dynamic play, circulation, and growth, if not in one direction, then in another, looking for affordances, advantages, beating the rules, flowing into the places of least resistance, causing mutation, evolving the new, shedding the unusable, creating new margins of waste, decay, and decomposition, but also perhaps new fermentation, rust, opportunities for bacteria and fungi, chemical corrosion and bonding, gifting and poisoning the environment.

I do not go astray, here, into biologies and ecologies, for these, too, are relations of hospitality that we need to learn if we are to survive and evolve, grow and learn about our place in the scheme of things, schemes in things, of course, being recognizable primarily retrospectively as patterns written by unintended consequences, mistakes made by planning and calculating, to cite a Dewey-like sense of pragmatism in a world always already gone wild.

The foreigner's question and the question of the foreigner interrogate the reason for conventional understandings, thus making the foreigner a destabilizing node of growth for existing structures. In French, Derrida displaces the genitive *de* of the *question de l'etranger* so that the objective genitive (the question of the foreigner) becomes the subjective genitive (the foreigner's question). Levinas meditates similarly on the term "welcome of the other" (*l'accueil de l'autre*) (Derrida 2000, Still 2010).

Political Economy and the *Question l'etranger*

> It has always been the custom here for the Co-Hong merchants to stand surety for their foreign counterparts. The authorities insist that it is the Hongists' duty to drive Innes out of Canton; if he chooses not to leave, it is they who will be made to suffer. . . . They had caught him in flagrante unloading opium . . .
>
> A man . . . had been put on public display with a huge wooden pillory around his neck . . . accused of being a confederate of the wretched Mr. Innes . . . the boatman said he might even be beheaded if Mr. Innes did not leave the city . . . when we came close enough to get a good look, . . . the man was none other than Punhy-qua, the eminent Hongist and connoisseur of flowers and gardens! It was so distressing . . . [Z] says the execution of Ho Lao Kin was a signal . . . —AMITAV GHOSH, *River of Smoke*

As with the Athenians' efforts with Piraeus, so too Nagasaki's with Dejima, and Canton's with Fanqui Town outside the city walls. But what are today's rules of hospitable-hostile trade?

For the second half of the twentieth century, my Taiwanese former student Kuo Wen-Hua pointed out to me (as would be evident to any weaker trading partner), that the key hospitality-hostility trade rule into the late 1990s was section 301 of the US Trade Act of 1974, which authorizes the US president "to take all appropriate action, including retaliation, to obtain the removal of any act, policy, or practice of a foreign government that violates an international trade agreement or is unjustified, unreasonable, or discriminatory, and that burdens or restricts U.S. commerce." In the 1990s this authorized unilateralism was gradually replaced by the negotiations of World Trade Organization rules and mediation processes. So, for instance, as the price of joining the WTO, India was forced to rewrite its patent laws to recognize product patents rather than only the process patents on which it had built its generics pharmaceuticals industry. It has taken time, but in 2013 India managed to deny Novartis's appeal to extend patent protection for its leukemia drug, Gleevec (Imatinib), on the grounds the drug did not meet the standard of "enhanced or superior efficacy" and thus India's generic versions could be supplied to millions at much lower cost.[11] In 2013 there was even news that China might be willing to join the American-led Trans-Pacific Partnership, which had been seen by Beijing as an effort to isolate and contain China. The TPP was intended to establish rules on labor and environmental standards, and on intellectual property, and it would open parts of the Chinese economy that have remained protected from competition. As former ambassador to China, John Huntsman, argued in an op-ed piece (Bremmer and Huntsman, 2013), "America and China are bound together in a form of mutually assured economic destruction." "Beijing will continue to invest in its state capitalist system and manage its currency to suit its own needs." And yet there is a track record since 1972 recognizing "different ideologies," (the struggle for recognition) about individual freedom, trade, Korean reunification, Japan, and Taiwan, while still pledging "progress toward the normalization of relations in the interests of all countries." The 2016 US presidential campaign and the decision of the new president to withdraw from the TPP, only shifted the terrain a bit, as China began to build its alternative new Silk Road (One Road One Belt) global infrastructure, including across Southeast Asia, and south to Papua New Guinea and Australia.

Neither the struggle to the death of scorpion and black widow, nor the eternal dialectic of yin and yang—the dances of hospitality-hostility in the actually existing world can be generative. As with the Chinese-Malay Peranakans, a local culture of immigrant Chinese men intermarrying with Malay and Javanese, so too with the improvisational structures of the dance of foreign relations. A turn then to biology and dance in the pleuralizing rains. The play upon French *pleuvoir* ("to rain") and pluralizing is intended to underscore the linguistic and comparative anthropological principle of seeing what difference it makes when one pluralizes singular nouns or singular exemplars. The tropical rains in poems (and in life) can be both lashing and fertilizing.

Pleuralizing

The tropical jungle is humid and tedious
washed each day by wind and rainstorms

concealed on barren slopes
my roots could find no minerals in sandy soil
my leaves could catch no broken sunlight
I strayed to the edge of the swamp
and found only crocodiles, no mud
so I learned from the rainbow
forever hanging my trap in the sky

when Dutch and Portuguese armies fought to claim
the Malay peninsula
releasing bombs on the tropical rainforest
I woke from my nightmare
overthrew the rule that my leaves were animal fodder
cast it into the troubled river
men snatched gold and land with their hands
my leaves became eternal hangmen
luring and killing live bugs, tiny beasts
manufacturing my own nutrients to survive
. . .
only sober, industrious ants
may live merrily in my trap
they spit out nitrogen
and help me tidy away
the skeletons I can't digest.

—from Wong Yoon Wah, "Pitcher Plant:
Hanging a Beautiful Trap in the Sky"

The poet Wong Yoon Wah comments that the pitcher plant, called "wine-glass weed" in Chinese (an image he plays with elsewhere in the poem), originated in the barren lands of Malaysia, as did he himself. "The harsh environment was more than often a result of gravel land left behind by British colonialists and Chinese capitalists after they abandoned their mines."

What are these new biologies, and can they provide a regenerative hospitality without losing our sensors for danger, risk, and murder (a beautiful poem on the ficus vines that kill their host trees with loving embrace). Wong Yoon Wah's poems remind us not so much of the blood-and-claw Darwinian survival of nature but of the associations of place and history that give cultural meaning to our worlds and futures, history inscribed into the very plants and animals, the very companion species that we inhabit and that inhabit us, from our guts to our neural memories, the scents and melodies of our multiple brains.

A lovely paper by Shalini Rupesh Jain (2013) on Romesh Gunesekera's novel *Grief* resonates wonderfully with my delight in Wong Yoon Wah's poems. *Grief* interlaces the destruction of Sri Lanka's coral reefs, the destruction of large-scale irrigation projects and land given to one linguistic-ethnic group over another, and the destruction of civil war.

For lack of time, I will not pursue here ecological and biological sensibilities that I think are replacing the mechanics and quantum physics cultural imaginaries of the twentieth century, steadily infusing our cultural imaginaries with a granularity (of the small-scale ecologies with macroimplications) that could not have been imagined before molecular biology and comparative genomics, or the reactivated dance between neuroscience versus psychoanalysis, instrumental reductionism versus aftereffects, illusions, ghosts, hauntings, aesthetic moods (Korean *han* [melancholia]; Lee, "Imaginary Encounter"), that are all too real, and Gabriele Schwab's transformational literary objects that through ethnographies and literature catalyze the transmission and mutation of unconscious content across cultures and generations (Lambert 2013, Schwab 2012, Wong 2013).

The sensibilities of the body, emotion, and affect, and of relations with our companion species are repeatedly referenced by philosophers, from Kant's moment of enthusiasm to Bergson's durations—but philosophers' use of animal relations (Kant's dog, Wittgenstein's lion, or Derrida's cat) have very little to do with what we know about actual interspecies relations (with possibly the one exception of Levinas's dog, Bobby, who provided recognition of the human in a dehumanized world of the concentration labor camps). So too, Pheng Cheang criticized Judith Butler (2013), but it also applies, I think to him, references to nature often remain underdeveloped, intellectualized representations, rather than engaging with our contemporary scientific worlds as they help us reimagine our experiential ones. I do acknowledge exceptions: both Bergson and Merleau-Ponty tried to stay abreast in biology and psychiatry; and there is the foundational, if passing, moment of nausea for existentialism, riveting the senses to the body and sending the intellect packing.

The hospitality/hostility that I wish to end on is that of music and dance. Dance, of course, is often taken as a metaphor for collaborative competition, love and hate, it takes two to tango, but tango dancers are often lost in their own worlds, moodily reflecting inward while jousting on the surface.[12]

Tim O'Dwyer, the Singapore-based saxophonist, composer, and music theorist,[13] deploys one of the most sensible (in all senses) examples and uses

I've heard of Deleuze and Guattari's notions of assemblage, milieu, rhythm, and territory to analyze and provide notation for musical improvisation.[14] O'Dwyer uses the case of John Butcher's "Buccinator's Outing" (which is beyond the intellectual capacities of traditional classical music theory to characterize, and arguably therefore is heard by many as noise and with hostility). The milieu is established by a first sound coming out from silence or chaos, and its active variation is rhythmic, creating a territory or soundscape that is de- and reterritorialized by further variations that we call improvisation and the experience of "where did that come from?" O'Dwyer's way of analyzing and notating the music provides tools that may transform noise into appreciation, the highest of Aristotle's aesthetic virtues and passions (Periola 2013).

It so happens the dynamics of variation producing surprise, delight, and enthusiasm was also the subject of a remarkable discussion among world-renown Indian dancers held at the Esplanade's rehearsal studio high in "the Durian" (as the performance hall shells are locally dubbed).[15] The discussion began with a reflection on the offhand comment that for a dancer it is better to not know music. Of course, it is music that carries the dancer, that the dancer responds to. What was unpacked, however, were the long-standing tensions between musicians and dancers about who is in charge, and therefore whether a young dancer dare employ a senior musician, the lack of respect musicians have been given in the past by dancers, and the dangers of employing hotshot young musicians who want to show off their talents at the expense of the mood the dancer wants to set. Inevitably the macabre dance of the ancients and the moderns unfolded in the discussion, with one discourse affirming classicism and total devotion to inhabiting a particular dance form/language, and yet another discourse trying to make space for newer concept dances to provide a kind of narrative arc for audiences in the West or youth in the East who are not so familiar with the nuances of the classic forms and their play.[16]

Gift and Thorn: Anthropology alongside Philosophy

So, too, then in the yin and yang play between anthropology and philosophy. Without philosophy, anthropology would be merely empirical and subject to the instrumentalizations of human capitalization. The pressure, indeed, is on. But without anthropology, philosophy is wordplay stuck in Plato's cave of shadows, in the prison houses of language, in logic games, and in the fantasy literatures of metaphysics. Ontology, for instance, nowadays has given up being or Being. It is instead pluralized either through the computer scientist's writing of code ("ontologies") or the biologist's analysis of biochemical pathways and multilevel regulatory regimes of various endogenous developmental and exogenous or epigenetic signals, opening pathways for using the body's own mechanisms for repair and therapy, or infection and out of control cancer, and the creation in vitro of various biological "ontologies" or assemblages, as in synthetic biology. One might conceive of mathematical forms such as the triangle and Klein bottle as such pluralized ontologies as well in different ("post-Euclidian") geometries.

Or, as Derrida would say, the gaps between the Law and the laws of hospitality provide the spaces in which invention, improvisation, culture, and ethics occur. And, as he says in "The Aforementioned So-Called Human Genome," the aporia of inventions (who gets to patent; what is declared new) and discoveries (what is the unfolding of so-called nature) are mutant forms of philosophical and legal realia at the center of our contemporary rules of hospitality-hostility, collaboration-competition, secrets-and-open access.

9

ANTHROPOLOGY AND PHILOSOPHY

What can we learn from engagements across cultural settings? Moving from the Amazon, Southeast Asia, and North Africa to Iran, its diaspora, and its intellectual engagements with the West that codefine its present, its actuality, and its contemporaneity, I return to the discussion of these last three terms from chapter 3 and address the nature of the bricolaged, culturally multiply-entwined worlds that we have always already lived in. I have often drawn attention to the parallels between the "postmodern" deconstruction methods of Jacques Derrida and scholastic debate traditions in many religious pedagogies (Fischer 1980, Abedi and Fischer 1990), and many others have probed as well the influence of Jewish and Christian hermeneutics on modern secular thought.

In this chapter I pursue these questions not by way of common origin, historical influence, or decontextualized comparison, but by way of ethnographic *juxtaposition* as an illustration of ethnographic methods whose rules are to preserve symmetrically the sociohistorical context of the philosophical writings as of the ethnographic ones, and often to privilege new ethnographic materials to think with rather than subordinating them as illustrations of the Western tradition of philosophy. (They are the *Muster* not the *Beispiel*, for those who know Kant's distinction between two kinds of example, the one that is the reference text, the other the illustration, the side play.) The philosophers are also ethnographic and historical actors. There is, in addition, a second "rule" of such an ethics of anthropology: a dialogic mode of address, one that is sometimes couched by philosophers under the topos of "friendship."[1] In the previous essays, the authorial voice is explicitly addressed to an individual, to students, and to an audience listening in and aware of the evoked dialogic relationship. Here the address is slightly more complicated in having multiple addressees: the philosophers who "spoke to me" as I was doing field research (often through my identifications with their life circumstances that seemed analogous), the ethnographic situations and actors who spoke back out of their differences, and the "skin in the game" of other ethnographers whose work also informs, contests, and lies alongside.

So I begin by asking, what would it mean for anthropology to be the empirical means of doing philosophy, understood as the love of wisdom, the wisdom that comes from friendship, worked out in dialogue, disputation, and questioning; address and response; the ear, face, and eye of the other; learning across the tympanum of exchanges between self and other. Anthropology is the speech, account, reason, or logics of the animal operating semiotically, psychically, emotionally, introjectionally, and projectionally between the bestial and the divine.[2] The anthropo-logics include affects and actions that—after giving reasons for actions run out and yet decisions and actions must be taken—leave enduring legibilities, traces, hints, or cues in the rhythms and sounds, the catacoustics, of the social text.

In what follows I reread some of my ethnographic work in Iran attempting to use some of the theorists and philosophers I drew upon for social theory parallels and possible clues in European historical experience with which to create social theory attentive to experiences elsewhere. The hope is perhaps that illumination may be cast back and forth, but more importantly, to provide points of attachment for creative and productive dialogue beyond mere comparison, beyond the dialectic of seeing (*theoria*) and conceptualizing (theory), attentive as well to the affective body of interpersonal emotions, the tropes of vulnerability and calls for social justice, and the ear, face, and critical apparatuses of the other as places for ethical ethnographic exchange.

At issue are both catacoustics and ringing the changes in Yazd and Washington, DC; in Qum and Paris; and in Tehran. My philosophers, lovers of wisdom, are social hieroglyphic characters, here and there, and everywhere.

I plot each of the three parts to evoke a constellation of urban place, historical horizons, communication circuits or infrastructure, new (especially dissertation) ethnographies in which the writers have serious stakes ("skin in the game"), and theorists there and here, then and now.

Section 1 (Washington, DC, and Yazd) focuses on infrastructure and communication circuits. Section 2 (Qum and Paris) focuses on the critical apparatuses of debate and interpretation. Section 3 (Tehran) focuses on pluralism and the struggle for civil politics.

Section 1: Washington, DC, and Yazd

TAGHI MODARRESSI, NAHAL NAFICY, AND WALTER BENJAMIN

Losing Language, Finding Passion

"Nobody chopped chives for him." "If news reaches the mosque, you'll need an ass to carry all the rumors." These idioms do not quite translate from Persian into English, but they pepper the novelist and child psychiatrist Taghi Modarressi's novels. Modarressi was interested in the fivefold resonances among the effective communication of infants using approximation and mirroring; dementia, Alzheimer's, or end of life loss of language, again approximating with wrong words but still expecting intimates to know what is meant; the feeling of émigrés of not being at home in either mother or acquired languages; the recognition in "the task of the translator" that by reading passages aloud, one often can catch meanings beyond specific word choices and phrases; and the work of grieving and of comedy in catching the rhythms of language in these five arenas. What's important in these encounters, Modarressi would say, is the movement across languages, gestures, and approximations, not so much the content. After some years of not writing, he found a new internal writerly voice "unexpectedly, while listening to the sound of Persian in the streets of Los Angeles and Washington. It was the sound of Iranian refugees, bargaining in American shopping malls. My new voice did not have any content. It was more like rhythmic humming, perhaps a ghost of a Persian accent. It was like the humming we do when we are intrigued by an idea. . . . That melodious Persian sound could sometimes throw light on forgotten scenes, bringing them out of total darkness and allowing me to invent memories of a time when I wasn't even born" ("Writing with an Accent," Chanteh, 1992, 8-9, quoted in Rahimi, 2011, 9–10). Nasrin Rahimi, translator of Modarressi's last novel, writes that "what facilitated Modarressi's return to writing fiction was the arrival of the wave of Iranian immigrants and refugees in the wake of the 1979 revolution. It was the reinsertion of . . . the tonalities and affects surrounding the use of Persian that revived his passion for writing" (Rahimi 2011, 9–10). Like a good ethnographer, Modarressi writes,

> I found myself sitting once again with my friends, but this time we were not in Tehran. We were in Washington or Los Angeles. Once

> again I was the happy captive audience to the fantasies of Iranian social theorists, with their spicy interpretations of daily events in Tehran, Paris, Washington, the Pentagon, even the Oval Office. I was delightfully engulfed in rumors. . . . The excitement was almost unbearable. My feelings were so intense that I began to wake up every morning between four and five a.m., at which time I would drive to my office and work on a story that was actually an invented memoir. (Rahimi 2011, 8)

My own memories of Taghi Modarressi are of a wonderful lunch of *chelo kebab* and stories we shared at the Kolbeh restaurant on Wisconsin Avenue in Georgetown, shortly after he had published *The Book of Absent People*, published around the same time in Tehran in Persian (*Ketab-e adamha-ye ghayeb*). It is part of my geography of Iranian Washington, DC, now indelibly enriched by a remarkable dissertation by Nahal Naficy.

In genre terms, Naficy's dissertation sits somewhere between anthropology (the department granting the degree), belles lettres, comparative literature, and investigative journalism, and provides, as only such a mixed genre could, one of the most remarkable accounts of the culture of paranoia, intrigue, political commitments, and ability to negotiate the worlds of NGOs, diplomacy, media, and politics in Washington, DC, among an émigré community. It is this "structure of feeling," and the cultural references and allusions out of which it is composed, that is the target of the dissertation, rather than, say, a political scientist's evaluation of the strength and effectiveness of particular organizations, although along the way it accomplishes some of that as well. One gets, for instance, the contrast between one NGO dedicated to using the tools of American civic and political engagement, and other NGOs that are nursing their resentments and commitments from the revolution of 1979, and who see the world in terms of fighting for its reversal, and thus are not part of "this world" (Washington, the present) but primarily of that one (Iran, the past).

That's the mundane surface. The cultural texture is much finer. The ethnography functions like the object of love in Persian poiesis: elusive, tempting, motivating, moving, unpinnable, hence alive. In presenting what Naficy calls "actual life," she draws upon the Persian miniature as a social form in which people are always peeping at one another from behind rocks, trees, holding their finger over their mouth in surprise, peering out from curtained windows and doorways ("shades" of Hamid Naficy's diagnostics of "accented cinema" in his well-known book of that name of claustrophobic looking through windows, doors, and other liminal and interior spaces). The mystery of the political is key here: the indirection of language and action, the dispersal of power, the functioning of gossip, sometimes charted out in complicated organizational charts that, again in Persian miniature fashion (think of the geometric divisions of space), hint at what they are supposed to describe, without really ever defining the field of play (in miniatures, active figures are often on the margins, and actions are dispersed in spatially separated but juxtaposed frames).[3]

Naficy describes what she calls "the landscape of affects," composed not only by the heady proximity to imperial power that suffuses the intensity of Washington's Potomac fever but also the "character rot" or the "primitive within" or the Count Dracula within (carrier of a glorious past, that lives on unnaturally in the present, out of phase and dysfunctional with reality). Naficy's reading of the proposed ways of "fixing" of alleged pathologies opens up into what could become an exploration of wonderfully human, but wacky, efforts at self-reform (ranging from the out-of-phase uses of Sufism/escapism, mourning/memorializing, positive psychology, or, in Iran, the now century-old cultural warfare between cultures of life and cultures of death). Indeed, the Ministry of Health announced in January 2009 a program of engineering happiness to offset the rising rates of addiction and suicide after thirty years of philosophical melancholia and stoicism and gravitas. The cultural warfare, with its psychological armatures, has intensified to the point that one recent ethnography speaks of the criminalization of youth culture, and the turning of social statistics into state secrets.[4]

As I began to attend to the dynamics of these sorts (of migration, of miniatures, of "actual life" hemmed in by heroic and martyred pasts) in Yazd in the early 1970s, Walter Benjamin kept returning both as a direct interlocutor for me, and by beginning an extraordinary afterlife career of his own with ever more investments of interpretive energy in the global academy. My immediate point of attachment was the extraordinary parallels between the baroque *Trauerspielen* of Spain and Germany he analyzed and through which he developed an apparatus of literary critical interpretation, as well as attention to the transformation in Europe away from valorizing the melancholia that Iran preserves in its Khomeinist strands of cultural formations. Indeed, Benjamin called the Trauerspielen secularized passion plays, and their point, as with the *taziyeh* [mourning rituals] or *shabi* [mourning plays about the Battle of Karbala during the month of Ramadan] in Iran, was to elicit lamentation, and even more, as Benjamin puts it, they are plays through which mournfulness finds satisfaction. They (both) portray the hopelessness of a corrupt worldly condition in which the only moral dignity possible is through stoicism. As one says in Iran, one tries to achieve a *hal-e khosh*, a "good feeling" of quiet determination and stoicism, a willingness to struggle against even overwhelming odds for moral ends. Even the political structure of the baroque plays align nicely with those of Iranian politics, the conflict between absolute power given in the context of bringing order to social chaos and actual human limitedness, sometimes leading to madness. The stock plot is that of a tyrant (often, indeed, a Persian shah or Turkish sultan), a martyr, and an intriguer.

But as time has gone on, Walter Benjamin's importance as montagist of the dialectical images of ruins-redemption, catastrophe-transformative technologies of urban place, cinema, and theater space, and even, nowadays, the iconoclastic art that, like the surrealism of Benjamin's day, explodes the boundaries between high and low, have come to be equally important in thinking about the cultural *Zerstreuung* of Iran. *Zerstreuung* is usually translated in English as "distraction," the distracted mode of attention for which the cinema is a gymnasium of the senses for practicing how to deal with the multiple channels of sensory and information input or assault from the modern city about which Charles Baudelaire and Georg Simmel also wrote. André Breton called it perceptual bewilderment. For Iran I borrowed the term "mute dreams" (*gonge khabide*) from filmmaker Mohsen Makhmalbaf for the title of my book on Iranian cinema, films that deal with the aftermath of war, society ripped apart, and attempting repair, reverberating with traumas at multiple levels, but humanistic and redemptive in a fashion Benjamin might have appreciated (Fischer 2004a). *Gonge khabide* is that moment when one is waking from a dream and, bewildered, tries to make some sense of the images, or, in an older messianic fashion, it is also that feature of prophetic vision that is impossible to convey, and if it could be described, the people who heard it would be deaf to its message.

The theater spaces that Benjamin attended to were not only those of the baroque Trauerspielen but also the transformation of Moscow by modernism, the contrasting porous Neapolitan street with its stagelike staircases half hidden, half open to the street, and the contrast between nineteenth-century arcades and the one-way street with its signage designed for car traffic and advertising on the walls of consumer society, an accelerating society of speed and intensities. The German word *Zerstreuung* is more violent, dispersive, intensive, not merely distracted or paying attention to many different things at the same time. Sonically, almost homonymically, it is close to *Zerstörung*, destruction, ruination, disturbance.

In the 1970s I described Yazd's urban modernization of the 1930s under Reza Shah as having cut boulevards, Baron Haussmann–style, through the bazaar and old residential quarters, still decades later leaving the insides of houses open to the street, a fitting image of the turning inside out of the old, the *anderun* (inside) becoming the *birun* (outside), and the cultural emptying out of the old bourgeois dwelling of which Benjamin wrote, the old Yazdi merchant houses with their many courtyards, as contrasting with the sleek Bauhaus machine house of glass and steel, or the prefab townhouses of steel frames familiar to new suburb development from Houston to Ahwaz to Yazd.[5] Benjamin contrasts the bourgeois dwelling in which habits are cultivated with the glass and metal houses in which no traces are left but things may be adjustable at will. At issue for Benjamin was the destruction of an older intelligentsia and the rise of mass society both for collective and participatory good and for fascist evil. The war (World War I, the Iran-Iraq War) proved that (as surrealism in France would explore, or iconoclastic contemporary Iranian art) the old boundaries of high and low could not be maintained; classicism, even the artificiality of Jugendstil, is moribund. Yazd, too, like the metropolises of Europe, has exploded from a population of 100,000 in the 1970s to over a million today, still conservative at its core but with many migrants and refugees from the wars diversifying the population. The old mud brick houses with their elegant wind towers still stand, but some now are transformed into boutique tourist hotels, a water technology museum, and other tourist attractions. The old six-wind-tower icehouse (*sish bad-gir, "six wind towers" which cooled the ice below*) in the center of town is now a fancy *zurkhaneh* ("house of strength," traditional gymnasium) that even allows women tourists in to watch the exercises done under the drumbeat of the *tambak* drum and the martial songs celebrating Imam 'Ali and the *pahlavans*, hero-athletes of the *Shahnameh*. The zurkhaneh remains a somewhat times-out-of-joint, wonderful and rich icon of moral, spiritual, and athletic calling.

The conservative, bazaari moral core (for Qum see section 2 and Erami, 2009) is no more intact, protective, and intimate than when I went looking with Mazyar and Melissa in 2004 for an old friend, one of my high school part-time assistants from the early 1970s. I inquired at the heart of the bazaar society, a shop selling old- and new-style hats along the inside-out part of the bazaar, along the 1930s boulevard once called Pahlavi. A phone call or two and a request to leave my phone number. Connection clearly had almost been made, but I was not to be given a phone number, lest, it was said, the connection was not the one I meant, the party did not want to connect, the party was not in town, the timing inconvenient, or, of course, the inquiry of a American foreigner unwanted. (Time was short, and the connection was made only upon my return to Tehran, and the meeting on the next visit to Iran, where my wife and I were feted in grand style. My friend had become a successful import-export agent in Tehran, only to have his most lucrative businesses appropriated by the politically more powerful, and so he had returned in semiretirement to Yazd.)

The cinema, mosque, and bazaar remain theatrical poles of Yazd's urban space, as they do more generally in Iran's culture wars. In the 1970s "defiant" was how I described the womenfolk dressed to go to the movies, middle-class women who appeared unveiled at parties but dared to appear unveiled among the ordinary folk only when they went in groups to the movies, protected by their menfolk.[6] The first Yazd cinema opened by a Zoroastrian in the 1930s closed under pressure, another failed, and in the 1970s there were but two, and the mood was captured in the ditty,

<table>
<tr><td>Yeki sakht masjid,
  yeki cinema</td><td>One built a mosque,
  one a cinema</td></tr>
<tr><td>Yeki gasht gom-ra, yeki rahnema</td><td>One leads astray, one guides</td></tr>
<tr><td>To khod dideye aql-ta baz kon</td><td>You yourself, open the eye
  of your reason</td></tr>
<tr><td>Tafavot bebin az koja ta koja.</td><td>Observe the difference from
  when to where.</td></tr>
</table>

Haj Mohammad Husain Barkhorda had been persuaded to build yet another mosque, rather than the hospital he intended, as a counter to the two cinemas up and down the street. Thirty years later, a new state-of-the-art private hospital was opened by a local doctor, proudly without patronage or portraits of ayatollahs, and without loans, making a statement even with the crisply starched white head covering and attire worn by the nurses and female staff.

Times are out of joint from the perspective of both sides, the modernizing classes seeing the revolution as a reversal, the religious classes feeling the global economy using cinema, cell phones, Internet, and social media as ways of inserting alien aspirations into the youth. The cinema in the late 1970s was a battleground both onscreen and offscreen, objects of arson in the early days of the revolution, and of seats torn up by unnerved viewers of modernist new wave films such as *Moghul-ha*, itself diegetically about the introduction of television as a devastation of both film and oral narrative forms (recited epics, sometimes with a *pardeh*, or painted cloth, referring to the characters; *rowzehs* [sermons framed by the Karbala story]; and *khotbehs* [sermons at Friday prayers also framed with the Karbala story]).

Walter Benjamin's Berlin, Naples, and Paris were transformative moments that differ but are analogous to those in Iran. The Yazd of the 1970s was indeed a wonderful stage, quite literally with Mir Chak Mak (double minaret reviewing stand) and many *husseiniyas* (courtyards for mourning Imam Husain, the martyr of the Battle of Karbala), where passion plays and processions were staged during Muharram, which, along with dramatic rowzehs, or preachments, there and in mosques and homes, worked the emotions into fervent laments and ended with a sudden sigh and return to the world. These ritual forms exercised and prepared people in the tropes and emotions that would be used to mobilize the revolution of 1977–79. The walls of Tehran during the revolution and ever after became animated and alive with revolutionary posters, as well as the advertising posters of which Benjamin wrote. In the month of Muharram (December) 2009, the Karbala paradigm and mass marches would be reactivated, coordinated by cell phone and social media, this time against the Islamic Republic.[7] In the 1970s the passion plays, processions, and Karbala paradigm were intense with sexualized energy, determined stoicism, and declarations of willingness to be martyred for the cause of social justice.

The emotional registers of Iran have dramatically transformed in the past thirty years, but in June 2009 there was a rapprochement across generations, registered in old revolutionary songs that were no longer dismissed by the youth as parental nostalgia. Reciprocally, parents acknowledged that the hours their children spent on the Internet were not idle foolishness but a means of acquiring vital new infrastructure skills. Anger, silence, and *qahr* (refusal to speak) between generations—if not between the polarized sections of the society opposing and supporting the government—was replaced by *ashti* (reconciliation).[8]

To sum up this section, two points from Walter Benjamin: (1) attention to the technical, social, and emotional infrastructure, and (2) always work from ethnography to theory, not the other way around. Theory, for Benjamin, should be registered in a text like a sudden ray of light that prismatically deconstructs so that one sees its sources and structure, and the immanent resources in social history are illuminated in a flash (*blitzhaft*, *Augenblick*). There is something more to storytelling than a good story, more to the ethnographic vignette than intrigue and curiosity. Walter Benjamin writes, "Kafka's writings . . . had to become more than parables. They do not modestly lie at the feet of doctrine, as the hagaddah lies at the feet of halakhah. Though apparently reduced to submission, they unexpectedly raise a mighty paw against it."

I think of Taghi Modarressi sitting in Washington listening to the rhythms, tonalities, and affects surrounding the use of Persian in Washington, DC, writing his *Book of Absent People*, like Walter Benjamin redeeming the future from the ruins and catastrophes of the past, pondering the effects of emigration and social transformations. I think of Nahal Naficy peering from the margins of her dissertation, refusing to live in the alienated and displaced time of *Reading Lolita in Tehran*, the account of a reading group formed around the time of president Mohammad Khatami's election, so alienated in oppositional interiorities that they felt the elections not worth participating in; similarly refusing to be enrolled in Washington NGO paranoias and factionalisms; and also refusing to be enrolled in the standard moves of ethnography. She just wants to live her "actual life" of being a happy young woman in the world.

Baudelaire defined modernity as the ephemeral, the fugitive, the contingent, the half of art whose other half is the eternal and the immutable; Nahal Naficy wants to live in modernity, not in the eternal.

Section 2: Qum and Paris

ALLAMEH TABATBA'I, HENRI CORBIN, HASAN ALI MOINZADEH, AFSANEH NAJMABADI, AND JACQUES DERRIDA

Fighting Arguments, Generating Cultural Power

> Suppose I write a book, let us say "Plato and telecom," . . . on the postal agency of the Iranian uprising (the revolutionary role of distancing, the distancing of God) or of the ayatollah telekommeiny giving interviews from the Parisian suburbs . . .—JACQUES DERRIDA, *The Postcard from Socrates to Freud and Beyond*

> Now about this science of anthropology, tell me: is it cooked or raw (*pakhta ya napokhta*)? —AYATOLLAH MUHAMMAD-KAZEM SHARIATMADARI QUM, quoted in FISCHER, *Iran: From Religious Dispute* (bahs) *to Revolution* (engelab)

QUM 1975, 2004

Forms of debate—stylized UN ones;[9] formal scholastic ones based on Qur'an and hadith proof texts;[10] academic ones based on evidence and analysis; media ones deploying visual, sonic, and verbal means of shaping perception;[11] everyday face-to-face ones among friends and neighbors—construct and weave, tear apart and reweave, the urban fabrics of Qum and Paris. Occasionally, as in

1968 in Paris and 1975 in Qum, they ignite into demonstrations, and sparks can fly, as were set off by the cassette tapes of Khomeini speeches recorded in Paris in 1978, and disseminated in Iran, helping to ignite and fuel the revolution in Iran of 1977–79.

The shuttles of the Iranian weft fly back and forth through warp ends anchored in Iran and America.[12] In the 1970s sheikh Mohammad-Taghi Falsafi (*falsafi*, "philosopher") famously asked mischievously, with double entendre intended, midsermon, what rises at night in Qum and retracts in the daytime. Answer: television aerials. In 1975 the coming revolution was rehearsed in the Faiziyeh Seminary, the same place to which Ayatollah Khomeini would claim to retire after his return to Iran in February 1979. The Faiziyeh sits along the desiccated river keeping the impurity of the cinema on the other side from the sanctity of the golden dome of the Shrine of Fatimeh Hazrat-e Masumeh (sister of the eighth imam, whose shrine is in Mashhad), the blue-tiled dome of Masjid-i Borujerdi, and the *madrassehs*. The cinema would be torched. The lines of sanctity and purity fracture in more complicated ways than a simple desiccated river could draw.[13]

The wall between the seminary and the shrine/masjid complex was where, in 1975, the Faiziyeh students hoisted the red flag of the unavenged martyrdom of Imam Husain on the anniversary of the revolts of 1963–64 against the White Revolution led by Khomeini, and in rehearsal, as it were, of the revolution to come. As I watched from the peripheries of the clashes, the 1975 revolt was quelled by special forces and water cannon. Inside the shrine are the graves of Safavid and Qajar kings, as well as of leading clerics and founders of the *hoseh elimiyeh* (the center of learning of the seminary system). I lived just outside the shrine quarters in the lanes between the establishments of two *maraje taqlid* (the highest rank of ayatollah, crowns of imitation, to whom ordinary Muslims should turn for advice on religious duties and law), S. Shahabuddin Marashi-Nejafi and S. Muhammad-Kazem Shariatmadari. My next-door neighbor was a custodian of the shrine who had helped with the closing of the doors at night and the opening in the morning, once done with trumpets and drums. Fired for being an opium addict, he would invite us over to smoke with him. We always declined. Eventually one day we accepted. The next day, people from the bazaar and all over town would come up and say "*Dudi hastid? Biya-id khuneh-ye ma*" (You're a smoker? Wonderful, come over to our house and smoke with us!). It was but one token of the tensions between townies and seminaries. A cross-cutting tension was signaled by the giggles I was met with initially when I was asked where I lived: it turned out the house had been owned by an old woman who rented it for *sigheh*, the temporary marriages in which pilgrims often indulged, sanctioned by religious law.[14]

Like Yazd, Qum has exploded in population since 1975. The new highway enters the city from the other side of town, away from the river, through a large pilgrim plaza of sweets and trinkets and food for sale. A uranium enrichment facility and a space center for rocket launching signal a changing modernity outside the city. New-style rival madrassehs and religious universities have sprung up around the old city center,[15] such as Mofid University, founded by Ayatollah Abdul-Karim Mousavi-Ardebili,[16] a BA-, MA-, and PhD-granting institution, with economists, political scientists, and law professors pursuing a general mission of testing whether Western humanism and Islam can get along; versus the more fundamentalist Imam Khomeini Institute associated with Ayatollah Mohammad-Taghi Mesba-Yazdi, an ultraconservative and antidemocracy member of the Assembly of Experts.[17] Digital media have been adopted both for searching proof texts and for sending opinions and *responsa* (fatwas) to followers around the world. Arabs in their distinctive garb wander to and fro, as they never did in the 1970s, talking, if not of Michelangelo, then perhaps of Najaf and Karbala, of Iraqi religious figures S. Motadaq Sadr and Ayatollah S. Ali al-Hussaini al-Sistani, or Lebanon's S. Hassan Nasrallah, or perhaps just of trade deals in Bahrain and the United Arab Emirates. Politicians shuttle back and forth from Tehran to Qum in search of support.

Narges Erami's *The Soul of the Market* (2009), on the carpet bazaars of Qum, provides a counterworld to that of the seminaries, and contributes to a long line of studies on the moral spheres of the bazaar. Erami focuses on the union (*ettihadiyeh*) or guild (*senf*, pl. *asnaf*) structure of the carpet bazaar, used to settle both economic and extracommercial disputes. She develops rich ethnographic case studies of how bazaar elders deal with a heroin addict, his family's shame, and the ability of a guild leader to enroll a local Narcotics Anonymous program to help them; of how a "wrong marriage" illuminates status negotiations, the handling of interpersonal issues, and the disciplining of members of the bazaar; and of the market, political, and cultural structures of why a leading carpet designer's attempts to set up training in both traditional and innovative design is frustrated, and why he returns to producing on commission for wealthy Iranians abroad rather than being able to train a new generation of innovative designers in Iran whose markets are slowly being eroded by production in South, Central, and East Asia.

Like Arzoo Osanloo's account of family courts in Tehran, or Saeed Zeydabadi-Nejad's account of negotiations over cinema scripts in the Ministry of Culture and Islamic Guidance, as well as the documentary and narrative films of Rakhshān Bani-Etemad on women running for office, Narges Erami provides access to the "actual life" of local moral worlds of everyday life—and of philosophical wisdom achieved through face-to-face interactions, mobilizing friendship networks, soliciting favors, or collecting moral credits from previous interactions, in part *parti-bazi* (using connections), in part the male and female interventions of repair of social worlds when things go awry.

LOOKING AWRY

Among the various dissertations on contemporary identity issues, Hassan Ali Moinzadeh's "Secret of Gay Being: Embodying Homosexual Libido in the Iranian Imagination," is one of the more challenging (to the *sensus communis* tightrope or bar separating the sacred and the profane, the mystical and the carnal, the metaphorical and the literal). Written for a clinical psychology degree with a Jungian bent, not an ethnographic one, it ventures into a highly fraught space, only partly acknowledged. It is an American coming-out and ego-affirming story, and it is careful not to make either wider therapeutic or descriptive claims. What it does well is to excavate an ambiguously central and ex-centric tradition in Persian culture, and refunction it for contemporary psychology. As Moinzadeh puts it, he attempts to "bridge the gap between the metaphysical language I encounter in ancient texts and the meanings I understand as a modern person." The key task is working out a psychological template (the clinical psychology side), and in the process doing serious new translations of old texts (the cultural critique side).

At issue is the Platonic-Iranian tradition of modeling the training of the self on love for boys, expressed, in the poetry of Jami, Attar, Rumi, and Hafez; in the philosophy of Suhravardi; and even, he identifies, in the hadith and the Qur'an itself. He remains respectful of the ambiguity and undecidability of what is metaphor about love of the divine and what is physical, while at the same time using those resources to create a charter myth for strengthening the self-respect and independence of a modern Iranian-born, Iranian American gay man. In American fashion, he begins by saying, "I use the term gay to describe someone who consciously and purposefully recognizes a gay identity in public as well as private life and actively seeks to further the rights and visibility of gay people in society . . . using the conscious awareness that one's same sex desires separate one from the rest of society" and that this conscious alienation "precedes the modern era and reaches back to the earliest histories of peoples and cultures throughout the world. I include premodern folk who have used homosexual love as an engine for their own spiritual transformation." He explicitly excludes those who simply engage in homosexual activities in private, and those who use homosexual sex as a tool of domination, topics of concern in today's worlds of sexualized torture in Iran's prisons to break people, of harsh choices in Iran for those accused of homosexuality, and of a UN campaign to stop the recruitment from the poor, and prostitution of young dancing boys in Afghanistan who would not organize their identity around same-sex desire of their own free will.[18] The stakes are high in negotiating the discourse on the level of psychological maturation and on the metaphorics of what Lévi-Strauss called the "effectiveness of symbols."

The histories of the Malamatiyya, Qandari, and Javanmardi movements provide historical materials, as does the idea of the *rend* (rogue) in poetry, and both the poetic tradition of Attar, Rumi, and Hafez, and the philosophical meditations of Suhravardi (and others). Moinzadeh nicely and seamlessly includes the love modeled in the Qur'anic version of the story of Yusef and Zulaikha (where, in a simple structural permutation of gender roles, it is the woman, Zulaikha, who is the lover, and Joseph is the beloved). But it is a modern hermeneutical tradition—of Henri Corbin, Carl Jung, and Martin Heidegger—that is key for helping Moinzadeh with his critical tools for clinical psychology. This is a fascinating and still half-submerged tradition in the cultural politics of contemporary Iran (and one that Moinzadeh does not explore, but that Orkideh Behrouzan and I have begun to).

Jung provides Moinzadeh tools of depth psychology, using universalized archetypes to teach the self to separate from maternal engulfment, and to discriminate one's interior aspirational double and one's interior negative shadow from one's maturing independent self. (The shadow in this case is in particular the internalized self-accusations of shame and humiliation for one's gay desires.) Jung, although supplying the hermaphrodite as an image of the original whole self, both male and female, was homophobic in the style of his time, but his methods offer some critical tools. It is Henri Corbin, much honored in Iran, who would apply Jungian and Heideggerian ideas to the task of recovering the "theosophical wisdom" of Zoroastrian rhetorical imagery and of the illuminationist (*ishraqi*) philosophy of Iran's mystical traditions represented by Suhravardi. Suhravardi and the mystical tradition provide a language, imaginal and metaphoric, of steps, stages, and techniques for the self to train itself toward mature understandings of reality and separation from the mere carnal temptations of the world. Corbin connects Plato's Ideas,

Suhravardi's *alam-e mesal*, and his own Catholic Latinate *mundus imaginalis.* Moinzadeh uses this in a Jungian mode of therapeutic working through the shame and humiliations of growing up gay, creating an "effectiveness of symbols" abreaction technique to create horizons of subjectivity that can distance themselves from the shadow self-accusatory self, and identify instead with a heterodox but powerful Iranian cultural tradition.

The significance of Jung for Moinzadeh may come more from where he pursued his PhD, in an American clinical psychology program with an apparently strong Jungian bent, than from Iranian contexts. But the Jung-Corbin-Heidegger connection is also a nexus of cultural politics in Iran. Corbin worked in Iran with the famed cleric-scholar Allameh Tabataba'i in Qum, and Tabataba's circle became quite influential, including such notables as Dariush Shayegan (a comparative literature and religion scholar), S. Hussein Nasr (a guru in the 1970s for Americans seeking Eastern wisdom, as well as a university chancellor and founder of the Institute of Philosophy in Tehran), and Mehdi Bazargan (an engineer and head of the provisional government after the revolution who long mediated between the secular and religious elites). Tabataba'i was also a teacher of Khomeini, Hussein-Ali Montazeri, Morteza Motahhari, and even Mesba-Yazdi, all of whom walked the tightrope between mysticism and puritan orthodoxy. Heidegger, whom Corbin translated into French, has become something of a fad in recent years among conservative philosophers in Iran.

There are more layers to this cultural arena, again, than at first appear, and a valid ethnographic question might be what qualities of ethnographic tapestries can one weave with thicker versus thinner ethnographic explorations, deeper play versus quicker instrumental assessments, and in what sorts of social spaces they can be appreciated, considered, or rejected.

While Moinzadeh probably cannot go to Iran, Afsaneh Najmabadi's remarkable ethnography of transsexuals in present-day Iran traverses adjacent sites of the law, clerical interpretations, bureaucratic negotiations, psychiatric oversight, and desires to avoid the kind of politicization that the international human rights and feminist movement would like. It is an example of what Jacques Derrida calls *la danse* (the dance, a feminine noun in French, *elle*), a mode of life that resists the dogmas of progressive revolution in favor of an ability to live "actual life" (à la Naficy avoiding ideological definition, or recruitment into political or identity agendas). This is likely to be, Derrida writes, "a much more important phenomenon, I believe, outside of Europe" that brings with it "new types of historical research, other forms of reading, the discovery of new bodies of material" such that feminist movements will perhaps have to renounce an all-too-easy kind of progressivism (Derrida and McDonald 1981, reprinted in Holland 1997, 24-25).

And, indeed, Najmabadi's research is among such "new types of historical research," drawing a historian of the modernization of Qajar sexual anxieties and vocabulary (see section 1, footnote 2) into ethnographic modes of research, and thus into "new bodies of material" that include not only the relatively new surgical possibilities of "sex reassignment" but also, as "always already" there, a recognition of stepping into contested streams of previous representations so that there can be no naive "I" or eye. Transsexuals, Najmabadi writes, "are used to being objects of curiosity" and "have become actively engaged in taking charge of the process of their own production, engaged with numerous organs of government and medical professions on almost a daily basis" (2014).

PARIS, 1968, 2004

It was, of course, Jacques Derrida, whom I read alongside as I was composing *Debating Muslims*. I sent him a copy in appreciation, as I had hosted him at the Center for Cultural Studies at Rice, and he had been an extraordinarily available and gracious interlocutor to students and faculty alike, even screening a documentary film that had been made about him, after years of refusing to allow his photograph to be published. He sent back a lovely handwritten note of thanks for the book, replying, however, that while it looked interesting, he did not know anything about the subject. There is much to be said about this for a man who played upon his Judeo-Islamic backgrounds, his circumfessions, his claims to deal with the media circuits of what he called globalatinization (Latinate or Christianized formats of hegemonic media forms[19]). (I tried to tempt him again with my contribution to Hent de Vries and Sam Weber's edited volume *Media and Religion*, to which he contributed the central paper. Alas, he no longer can be coaxed into responsiveness.)

But a central claim of *Debating Muslims* is that deconstruction is a continuation of the scholarly apparatuses of Islamic debate, and if we want to make good on our claims to engage the Islamic world, it might behoove us to read such scholars along with Derrida. There is both sophistication in those critical apparatuses and autoimmune dangers. Engaging these critical apparatuses is part of what is often called immanent critique, or critique from within a discursive tradition. It is probing for the terms of debate, the opportunities for enlarging both the field of engagement and the range of participants. There was a transformative generational call in the 1970s sounded by Dr. Ali Shariati that with literacy, Iranians no longer needed to follow mullahs blindly, they could read the texts for themselves. Indeed, one of the most important of these enlargements of participation, I argued, were the feminist Muslims who learned to read the tradition as rigorously as the clerics, showing how it could be read otherwise.

This is no mischievous play by an outsider, but a call to recognize our own stakes in a cosmopolitan world. Even if Derrida did not trust himself to engage with *Debating Muslims*, with the vigorous internal debates within the ideological worlds of contemporary Islam, this immanent critique—negative dialectics, critical hermeneutics, attention to the ways tropes and symptomatic slips and turns of phrase highjack authorial intentions, shuttling thought onto other tracks—is a key affordance of deconstruction. So, too, is Derrida's embrace both of Levinas's rejection of ontology as a grounds of philosophy in favor of ethical struggle in encounters with others as first philosophy, and of Hélène Cixous's writing feminine, feminist, and womanly alterities into the blood flow, neurons, and sinews of textuality.

These projects of immanent critique, and of recording the traces of women's and transsexuals' struggles, are ones that Afsaneh Najmabadi and Arzoo Osanloo pick up in charting both the workings of family courts and the negotiations of transsexuals in Iran. The critical apparatuses of *fiqh* interpretation (that is, legal interpretation, parallel to *halacha* in Judaism) of Qum-trained scholars are central in both projects. So, too, are the practicalities of interpretive argument and justification, negotiation and social accommodation central to both jurisprudence and the struggle for justice to come. Law and justice are not the same, and courts must shuttle between them, between decisions and conflicting rights. In preparations for family courts, women lawyers coach distressed women how to plead their cases, how to invoke the law's requirements, how to fend off false interpretations, how to strategize among the judges.

TRANSSEXUAL ACTIVISM, 2003–8

The case of transsexuals is particularly indexical, since, as Najmabadi argues, it is not true that homosexuality is itself criminalized (only sodomy, which would require witnesses, an almost impossible standard of evidence), and in any case transsexuals and homosexuals must not be lumped together, as they frequently are in international gay/lesbian/transsexual campaigns. Activist transsexuals are often critical and resentful of both such lumping and of the documentaries and news articles that portray them as objects of pity. Such framings can make them more vulnerable, not only overriding their own agency but, by politicizing their circumstances, limiting their agency to create spaces for themselves in the lives they wish to lead (which is often to meld back into society in their new gender positions). "Vulnerable" is a key cultural term, a legal, moral, theological, psychiatric, psychological, hormonal, medical, and surgical "switching point." It is a legal term and category that shifts the grounds of debate from internationally defined "human rights" language to less contested, more local and contextual languages of welfare, justice, and vulnerability. It opens up bureaucratic space using psychiatry as a procedural means of regulation and defense.

Sex change operations were first allowable in Iran under the justification of correction for a kind of hermaphroditism, and it was first on such grounds that Khomeini issued a fatwa in response to the plea of a transwoman in 1984, but he was then persuaded to also allow it for conditions that were not physically visible.[20] Although there has been much publicity claiming that the Islamic Republic of Iran forces homosexuals to have sex-change operations or foreswear their sexual orientation, ethnographic work on transsexuals (as opposed to homosexuals) by Najmabadi presents a quite different and more interesting account of legal, biomedical, and psychiatric authorities working with specialized clerics to create procedures for diagnosis, treatment, financial, and social support for both legal recognition and surgeries. The role of activist transsexuals has been critical, as has the Tehran Psychiatric Institute of the Iran University of Medical Sciences, and such specialized clerics as Hojjat ul-Islam Muhammad Mahdi Karimi-nia. Karimi-nia wrote his PhD dissertation at Imam Khomeini Institute in Qum on the subject, and has become known as a transsexual-friendly cleric to the community as well as a consultant to the courts.

The legalization and proceduralization of transsexuals has allowed the topic to become a subject for medical and psychiatric follow-up studies, as well as an arena for activist transsexuals to daily involve themselves in the halls of the bureaucracy, pushing, monitoring, winning victories, and suffering setbacks but keeping possibilities open. "One day we have a breakthrough in one ministry and get something in place, then the next day in walks someone hostile and turns all our 'woven cloth back into raw cotton.'" For instance, it is important that transsexuals be coded in exemptions in the military service code not under section 33, "mental disorders," but rather under section 30, benign "diseases of the internal glands," because otherwise, as Najmabadi says, they will be virtually unemployable.

The daily fabric of hours of lobbying in which transsexuals engage is ethnographically important in showing how modern moral worlds are constituted, shaped, and created for themselves and for the society at large in the seminaries in Qum as well as in the megalopolis of Tehran. The stories of proceduralization and finding psychiatrists to staff the Tehran Institute of Psychiatry and the several review boards overseeing transsexual requests for help who would be pragmatically responsive rather than punitively disciplining are as important and are imbricated in the networks of religious, political, and bureaucratic authority. In 1983–84 the case of a transwoman (male to female transsexual) was brought to the attention of Ayatollah Khomeini, according to the account of activist Maryam Khatun Mulk-Ara, at the suggestion of then Speaker of Parliament, Hashemi-Rafsanjani, who referred Mulk-Ara to S. Abdul-Karim Mousavi-Ardebili, then head of the Judiciary (later founder of Mofid University in Qum). Mulk-Ara also contacted Ayatollah Ahmad Jannati, who wrote to Khomeini. The transwoman went to Khomeini, still dressed in male habit. Khomeini issued a fatwa, a document that she could use if challenged in activities of daily life, that changing sex with a doctor's approval was not prohibited. Khomeini's womenfolk thereupon cut her a chador.

Najmabadi points out that other activists contest Mulk-Ara's account, suggesting that they themselves were the prime mover in the story. It is the structure of connections and lobbying that is important here, more than who gets credit. But, as Najmabadi points out, the telling of the story constitutes a critical moment in Mulk-ara's personal transition narrative and in the charter narrative for transsexuals to legally live trans lives before sexual reassignment surgery. Mulk-ara herself, born male, lost her job in the 1970s at Iran's National Radio and Television when she began to cross-dress. She went to consult Ayatollah Behbehani, who opened the Qur'an. It fell open to the *sureh* of Maryam. Behbehani told her to contact Khomeini in Najaf. Khomeini confirmed that sex changes were permitted, and she began to plan for a sex-change operation in Thailand. The revolution intervened, and she had to wait until 2002. She lived as *muhajijibah* (woman in hijab) for nineteen years, except when passport control wouldn't let her leave the country in 2002 for the sex-change operation unless she appeared in male habit because her passport was still in her male name, despite having documents approving the sex change and instructing authorities to change her name once the sex reassignment surgery was completed.

There are disagreements within the transsexual community over working quietly (*gamas gamas*, step by step) versus publicly to embarrass and pressure the government. The effort by Mulk-Ara to form an official NGO in the Khatami period with the support of former Vice President Mohammad-

Ali Abtahi proved difficult, both because of the hostility of the Minister of Health at the time, heart surgeon Mas'ud Pizishkian; the Tehran police chief, Murtaza Tala'i; and Pasdaran security chief Muhammad Baqir Qalibaf, but also in finding qualified individuals to serve on the board of directors who would be independent of conflicts of interest.[21] Counterintuitively in the more conservative era under President Mahmoud Ahmadinejad (2005–9), under Minister of Health Lankarani (2005–9), the transsexuals were able to make a series of pragmatic demands to upgrade the quality of transsexual surgical training, to provide better information on health insurance for transsexuals, and to make sexual reassignment surgery optional rather than required for legal recognition.[22]

Two points emerge from this conversation between philosophy and anthropology, Qum and Paris. First, moral local worlds are constructed out of ethical pragmatics, the face and call and need expressed in the interchange between the vulnerable other and self. Second, international politics, be it human rights or feminist discourses, and media circuits (*telekomeini* cassettes, television, cinema, headline journalism, documentary editing, cartooning and poster graphics, Internet, social media, and what Jacques Derrida called "globalatinization," globalization under a Latinizing or Christianizing hegemony of media formats) can become disempowering for those they attempt to aid, and thus requires the kind of feedback that ethnography can provide and an openness to rethinking international verities and pieties.

I think of Jacques Derrida reading against the grain of ontologies in search of friendship, metabolizing texts back into living commentary and conversation; of Henri Corbin searching for live spiritual inspiration in Persian and Islamic illuminationst philosophies (Suhravardi, Mulla Sadra), discovering ancient Zoroastrian wisdom and neo-Platonic translations; of Allameh Tabataba'i and his circle attempting to bring to life an ossified religious institution plumbing both traditional philosophy and Jungian psychiatry for a "return to self" of self-confidence in a modern world; of Hasan Ali Moinzadeh doing the same in California; and of Afsaneh Najmabadi ethnographically searching for the actual tissue of life in an Iran that escapes the verities of much theory, and good intentions.

Ayatollah S. Mohammad-Kazem Shariatmadari asked with his characteristic good-humored smile whether anthropology was cooked or raw. Overcooking kills the vitamins; cooking lightly with fresh raw ingredients, so the tastes and flavors come through, is healthier, and produces better ethnography and better social theory.

Mulk-Ara, presumably, wants to live with the ingredients of life, not stilled by ideological verities, with room to maneuver, not confined by closed bureaucratic boxes.

Section 3: Tehran

HANNAH ARENDT, MOHAMMAD SANATI, AND ORKIDEH BEHROUZAN

Catacoustics in Tehran

> The human condition in its plurality. —HANNAH ARENDT, *The Human Condition*.

READING HANNAH ARENDT IN TEHRAN, 2007

Why Hannah Arendt in 2007 (she died in 1975)? Why in Tehran? Was the interest in Arendt in Tehran confirmation of Danny Postel's *Reading Legitimation Crisis in Tehran* (2006)? Postel argued that Tehran intellectuals were no longer interested in revolutionary political philosophy but rather in liberalism. Jürgen Habermas, Richard Rorty, John Rawls, and Hannah Arendt were all the subjects of much interest, and the first two had recently been invited to Tehran (by Ramin Jahanbegloo). Suspicious of efforts at a "velvet revolution," the Iranian government pursued a series of campaigns against intellectuals, jailing Ramin Jahanbegloo, Haleh Esfandiari, and Kian Tajbakhsh, to be followed by many others, including two of the physician architects of Iran's national program for control of HIV/AIDS, which had won a World Health Organization designation as "Best Practices."

Derrida would not have been surprised by this autoimmune frenzy of position taking vis-à-vis the global circuits, or that the Salman Rushdie affair of the 1990s would be followed a decade later by the Muhammad cartoon affair, each a testing of the circuits of a new global postal system of *telekomeiny* and *kartoonery*. Kartoonery can get out of control if the circuits aren't checked. Between the Danish cartoons and the retaliatory Iranian-hosted Holocaust cartoon controversies, there was a domestic cartoon ruckus in which a government-affiliated Tehran newspaper ill-advisedly published a nine-cartoon attack about fear of the United States stirring up ethnic conflict using the metaphor of stirring up Turkish-speaking cockroaches. The mischievous Holocaust cartoon competition mobilized a transnational network of cartoonists who recirculated old Nazi tropes against Jews now refitted to US-backed Israelis oppressing Palestinians, headlined by President Mahmoud Ahmadinejad's recirculating of Khomeini's line that the Zionist state would eventually be wiped off the pages of time. That was the day that Ahmadinejad was chased off the Amir Kabir University campus by student hecklers.

So now imagine yourself (say, in a story in the style of Saadat Hasan Manto) in these circumstances as a member of the Tehran Jewish community. Asserting love of country and the long, pre-Islamic roots of Jews in Iran, the leadership of the community wrote an open letter to President Ahmadinejad protesting his insinuations that the Holocaust might not have happened or, if it did, it wasn't really so bad. The letter was posted on the Internet, and many Iranian intellectuals signed in support. Government reaction was not slow: the letter was taken down, the leadership of the Jewish community was removed, and its community magazine was closed. A Potemkin visit was hastily organized for the diplomatic corps to show how well the Jewish community is treated and what pride Iran takes in having the largest Jewish community in the Muslim world (some 25,000 left from over 100,000 in 1979). Leaders of the Jewish community were told to stay home so as not to mar the diplomats' impressions.

In Iran, as elsewhere, however, things are never as simple as they seem. The former council president, a fairly well-known movie producer, was given funds to produce two new film projects. A prominent figure in the community, he had been a student activist in the early 1960s and had met Khomeini in those days. When Khomeini returned, he led a delegation to meet the ayatollah, and persuaded Khomeini to publically protect the Jews as long as they disavowed Zionism. The opportunistic slippage back and forth between Iranian officials' use of "Jews" and "Zionists" remains a powerful disciplining tactic, given its built-in deniability. "Did I say Jews? I meant Zionists." It is not surprising that this film producer's reaction should also have been nuanced and multiple. On the one hand, he said, "It is not a serious matter; I've been through these things for forty years now." On the other, he delivered a lecture on Arendt to the Jewish community in their community center in the Sheikh Hadi neighborhood, a once-cosmopolitan neighborhood of Jewish and Muslim business partners, Armenians and Zoroastrians, where no Jews live any longer, and the landmark Armenian Andre's Café has been shuttered.

Hannah Arendt is, of course, a very interesting choice for a Jewish Iranian, and it appeared that this was no spur-of-the-moment selection, for she had been a favorite philosopher of the film producer for many years. He was delighted that in the audience was someone who had listened to Arendt as a student at the University of Chicago in the 1960s. The talk was very good, beginning with Arendt's biography, her distinction between just living (as animals do, including migration, seasonal changes, house building, even tool use) and living the life of thought and intentionality. There were passages on the importance of politics and the role of Rosa Luxemburg; Heidegger and the Nazis; Arendt's time in France and the United States; her relations with Israel and her exchange with Gershom Scholem; and a longer passage on the Adolf Eichmann controversy, the point of which was that Nazism, not the miserable functionary, should be on trial.

Only in the question period did he respond directly to the legacy for today, first by nodding, as it were, to the pact with Khomeini, noting that were Arendt alive today she would be talking about the holocaust of Iraqis just as she opposed the Vietnam War, that she rejected defense of Jews alone, that holocausts have happened throughout history to the Jews and to others. But then he spoke also to what was on the audience's mind: what was important about the holocaust issue was that when attacked, one not remain silent but defend oneself and not just allow well-meaning others to say everything would be okay. One needs to answer words with words: *harf be harf zadan*. Not remain silent. There was applause, and as he stepped down from the stage, the female head of a Jewish hospital stood and gave an emotional tribute to his teaching and leadership over the past three decades. Her emotional tones clearly reflected her shock at having been prevented, as one of the Jewish community's leaders, from going to her hospital during the staged visit for the foreign ambassadors. More applause.

The tribulations of the Jewish community in Tehran might be a hieroglyph of conditions more generally in the Islamic Republic, one explored on a psychiatric level by Orkideh Behrouzan in her dissertation (2010), now book (2016), and in a paper we have coauthored for Devon and Alex Hinton's edited volume on nightmares and traumas in today's world (2015). At issue are a major sensibility shift in the last two decades from philosophical and poetic indirection to relatively direct public discourse about interpersonal troubles, anxieties, mental illness, and acting out; Café Ruzbeh, a multidisciplinary experimental space for psychiatric residents that flourished briefly in the 1990s, and the shifts in Iranian psychiatry; the use of the blogosphere for creating an affective space for self-recognition of a generational voice.

The reading of Hannah Arendt (concerned with the stateless) against that of Behrouzan (concerned with stuckness) are cross-generational issues and civil rights issues that come together in the struggles over the future of the Iranian soul.

THE 1360S [1980S] GENERATION, SCATTERED AROUND THE WORLD

> We are the *daheh shasti*, the sixties generation [1360s/1980s]. We are scattered around the world. We wear colorful clothes but our insides are all black, dark and depressed. We want to extract this bitterness from life and show it to you . . . we are the most screwed up generation. We are the *khamushi* generation, born and raised under those periods of *khamushi* (lights off, silenced, asphyxiated). We have no voice. We want to have a voice. —RADIO KHAMUSHI podcast, Tehran, 2008

Writing the intimate history of several generations raised in Iran since the 1979 revolution can no longer be done only in Iran but must perforce follow the migration of many of "the best and brightest" to Europe, the United States, and Australia. The history of medicine and psychiatry in Iran can be done in Iran for the first half of the twentieth century, as Cyrus Sayeghi's dissertation initiates, but that of the second half, and particularly of those born since 1981, increasingly must also be accessed through the careers and insights on their experiences of those who have left. Orkideh Behrouzan—herself trained at the University of Tehran Medical School, and having experienced psychiatry rounds and research in oncology in the teaching hospitals of Tehran—began through her dissertation to assemble materials for a multistranded ethnographic and oral history of Iranian psychiatry, of generational emotional sensibilities, and of public health efforts in such arenas as mental health, addiction, and HIV/AIDS.

Behrouzan first collects what one can of pharmaceutical statistics for Iran since the revolution of 1979, and other data on such trends as suicides and suicide attempts. Statistics is a malleable object of attention in countries like Iran, and often all one can get are hospital-based numbers. Still, that is something to work from, and the accounts of the limitations are themselves an account of the infrastructural problems. The fact that the Iranian government itself in January 2009 publically acknowledged a problem of suicides and dysphoria (a culture of sadness) and announced a program to "engineer happiness" is a remarkable datum for a dissertation that aims to interrogate mental health issues such as depression and the generationally experienced cultures that have intensified such affect. Behrouzan draws attention to what physicians acknowledge is overmedication of children for ADHD (attention deficient and hyperactivity disorders), which she sees as correlated with the generational stresses of those born after the revolution transferring their anxiety and stress dysfunctions onto their children.

A second methodological effort is to chart generational experiences of psychological change in such things as children's television programming, styles of mandated dress, what could and could not be talked about, slogans chanted in school, and songs that catacoustically mark and date at least four generations: those who were young during the revolution itself, those who were born during the eight-year Iran-Iraq War, and those who came into awareness during the two postwar reconstruction periods (first focused on the economy under Akbar Hashemi-Rafsinjani, and then on civil liberties under Khatami). In June 2009 there was an explosion of rage and a coming together of parental (adolescents or young adults during the revolution) and younger generations in ways that suddenly exposed deep rifts that previously had been repressed.

Third, over the past two decades there has been a rise of what Behrouzan calls the "psychiatric self." More remarkable than the struggles with depression (clinical or cultural) is the change in how Iranians talk about their interpersonal relations and psychological feelings, the rise of both psychiatric and self-help psychological talk. "Suddenly" Iranians have begun to use psychological talk in a new and more open way that is not always routed through the indirection of traditional philosophical-literary tropes of the sort analyzed by Walter Benjamin and analogously found in the constellation of passion plays (*taziyehs*, *shabi*), young men's rhythmic flagellation groups (*dasteh*), rowzehs, *khotbeh*s, visual imagery (paintings, posters, flags, banners), music, and chanting (e.g., the beat of the zurkhaneh and chants about Imam Ali) that make up the Karbala paradigm.[23]

Mehdi Abedi and I followed some of the psychological patterns of grief among émigrés to the United States in the 1980s, and the feelings of a limbo or purgatory of stuckness (*avareh*).[24] Byron Good and Mary-Jo DelVecchio Good, with the psychiatrist Robert Moradi (who also served on Moinzadeh's dissertation cited above), worked on depression among Iranians in California in the same period, and Mazyar Lotfalian did a number of case histories on distraught Iranians in California publicly acting out in dramatic ways that made it into the newspapers also in the early years after the revolution.[25]

But in the last few years something has changed quite dramatically: both in California and in Tehran, talk shows that engage in direct psychological talk about people's lives and conflicts have become very popular, and people in general have learned to talk about their problems in psychological terms. In the 1980s when Lotfalian interviewed psychiatrists in the Bay Area, there were topics about which they said patients could not speak in Persian; if at all, it had to be in English, either because of the taboos involved or because the semantics did not exist or work sufficiently in Persian. This is no longer the case. Although it is fashionable in the diaspora to claim this change as a California innovation beamed to Iran by satellite radio and television, Behrouzan provides a much older history in the PANA (Parvaresh-e Nirooha-ye Ensani, or Training in the Skills of Being Human) movement, founded by Ebrahim Khajeh-Nouri, in Tehran but also in the shifting trends within psychiatry itself in Iran.

In broad terms, these are the shifts from asylums in the late Qajar period to the introduction of neuropsychiatric forms in the 1930s and 1940s from France, a brief effort to translate and introduce Freud in the 1950s, and a Jungian fascination via Corbin and illuminationist philosophy in the 1960s and 1970s, followed by a struggle between object-relations talk therapies and psychopharmacological ("biological") psychiatry from the 1980s to the present. The same struggle occurs in the United States, as Tanya Luhrmann has outlined in *Of Two Minds*, but in Iran the tilt toward psychopharmaceuticals is intensified by the lack of psychiatric social workers or other trained referring infrastructures.

Among evolving cultural forms, Behrouzan points to the blogosphere as providing an affective arena in which the generations born after the 1979 revolution are finally able to create a collective voice, a sense of self-recognition as a generation. Many had felt isolated, as if their experiences were individual, deep experiences of repressed family conflict, only in 2009 fully able to reconcile the anger at a repressive parental generation that denied them the freedoms of childhood and adolescence and the sense of hope and future that the parents had experienced before the revolution. In the explosions of 2009 suddenly the libratory language of the parents from 1979 and that of 2009 came together. But before and after that explosion, the blogosphere was where the self-identified "asphyxiated generation" or the "1360s (1980s) generation" was able to identify itself as a culturally distinctive formation.

Within this generation, cohorts of medical students who did psychiatry residencies use the blogosphere to recall Café Ruzbeh, a time and space created by Dr. Muhammad Sanati for psychiatric residents to engage in multidisciplinary discussions about psychiatry, literature, history, and symbolic forms. Sanati has written on Sadegh Hedayat, the symbolic figurations in the *Shahnameh*, and other cultural forms as a way of opening up thinking about anxiety structures and psychological patterns, both in the *longue durée* of Iranian cultural productions, and also as a way to diagnose the increased difficulties many young people have experienced since the revolution.

Indeed it is in that spirit, perhaps, that Behrouzan's dissertation facilitates efforts to think through state policy vis-à-vis mental health, the role of media as a highly contested cultural area, and the sharp generational experiences of the past three decades, which have introduced stress into almost every Iranian family.

The struggle for the soul of Behrouzan's generation, of those that preceded and are now coming afterward, is far from over.

I think of Hannah Arendt, in her sixties (listening to her) lecturing at the University of Chicago, or amid other émigrés at the New School for Social Research in New York writing in the aftermath of Hitler, Stalin, and the devastations of World War II, events that left so many stateless or moved into new polities (starting conditions for her political philosophy and repeatedly of the world's since then).

I think of her and wonder at her position as a beacon, still, for political philosophy, an unlikely yet apt exemplar for action in Tehran under the Islamic Republic of Iran three decades after her death.

Where new social contracts are forged, "where word and deed have not parted company, where words are not empty and deeds not brutal, where words are not used to veil intentions but to disclose realities, and deeds are not used to violate and destroy but to establish relations and create new realities" (*Human Condition*, 1958, 178–79, 184–86, 199–200)—there is the political, the polis, the capacity of human beings for action, for the unexpected, the new, forged out of capacities for forgiving and promising, retrospection, and forward looking.[26] Derrida will call it "democracy to come." Only in what Kant calls an "enlarged mentality" (of the expanding geographical and anthropological knowledge of the world) is there the ability to think in the place of everybody else, to deal with particulars in their particularity without subsuming them under pregiven universals, instead seeking the universal out of the particular, to have judgment. Not a turning away from the world toward contemplation or speculation but an engagement with the world. A grounding of rights not on soil or blood, ethnicity or nationality or religion, but on the very symbolic and communicative action on which citizenship is premised given the plurality that is the human condition: "men, not Man, live on the earth and inhabit the world" (*HC* 7), some of them may even be transsexuals.

Harf be harf zadan.

I think of the warm Tischgesellschaft, dinners and conversations, with Drs. Mohammad Sanati and Mahdiyeh Moin in Tehran, a Persian miniature of Kantian and Arendtian opinion and judgment formation about today's youth, about group therapies and medications, and about the psychology of Iranian symbolic forms. Through the work and conversation with their student and mine, Dr. Orkideh Behrouzan, I am drawn into their reminiscences of Café Ruzbeh as now one of several spaces, including the blogosphere, for reflecting back upon the psychosocial purposes of psychiatry and the historical shifts of psychiatry's various forms and contexts in Iran. I revel in the cross-ties of accounts of the Tehran Psychiatric Institute's complex histories in the work of both Najmabadi and Behrouzan; and the work in California of Dr. Robert Moradi, Byron Good, Mary-Jo DelVecchio Good, and Hassan-Ali Moinzadeh. The cross-ties, in their complementarities, confirmations, and differences, help create an ethnographic archive from which anthropology and philosophy both might be created in conversation.

As Hannah Arendt said, "We are living in a topsy-turvy world, a world where we cannot find our way by abiding by the rules of what once was common sense" (*UP*, 383).

The Jewish community in Tehran, and the 1360s generation in Iran and in the diaspora, just want to live their actual lives in a world of equal Arendtian citizenship grounded in the plurality of the human condition where everyone is the same in being human, and no one is interchangeable with anyone else, because each human being is particular, different, uniquely capable of the unexpected and new.

EXIT INTERVIEW: ANTHROPOLOGIA AND PHILOSOPHIA

These days, when an Iranian academic, anthropologist or philosopher, goes abroad to a conference, he or she may be grilled before being allowed to leave: why are you going, who is paying for your trip, what do they want you to say about Iran (why else would they pay for your trip?), we know you may not agree with us but we want to make sure you at least have a sensibility of solidarity with us. It is a performance one must undergo, just as one must undergo ideological vetting before getting a university job. Similarly, when seeking asylum, one must learn to perform the correct profile that immigration officers can recognize as "authentic." We are in a world beyond the jargon of authenticity, where modalities of access are beyond those of master-slave (power-resistance), and where the conditions of possibility for Arendtian politics, Habermasian public spheres, Rawlsian procedural justice, or Derridian democracy are at best yet to come.

Kant's *Anthropology from a Pragmatic Point of View* might be summed up in the phrasing, "Ask not what man is, but what one can expect of him";

Arendt stressed the human condition as one of plurality: men, not Man, live on the earth. Philosophy (for the Greeks, the Hindus, and the Jews) arises in dialogue. Dialogue beats with (gendered) questions (Jabes). Questions beget debate, debate begets logic, rhetoric, poetics, and drama. Drama, epic, parable, and ritual address family, friends, neighbors, and others. Anthropology arises (in Herodotus, the Chinese traveler Fa Hsien, the Muslim geographer Al-Biruni, the Jewish physician collector of materia medica in Kerala da Orta) in the traffic between and across communities of discourse, in trade, translation, and curiosity. Traces of signatures and contexts remain in writing, to be reconstructed, redeemed, and reoriented (Benjamin, Derrida). Pasts and futures are redeveloped in forgiveness and promises (Arendt).

It is nicely symptomatic that in Persian the term for "anthropology" is still debated, deconstructed, unsettled, in question, still in play.[27] *Adab* might be the appropriate translation for what Hegel called *Sitte* or *Sittlichkeit*, customs, norms, proprieties; *tarbiat* might be the translation for socialization, being civilized—*bi-adab*, *bi-tarbiat* (uncultured, unsocialized) are disciplining negatives. But the debate about the translation of "anthropology" is whether it should be *ensan-shenasi*, *mardom-shenasi*, or a kind of *jome'-shenasi*? *Ensan* refers to the double meaning that is conveyed in German by the word *Mensch*: it is both the person and the moral character. To be a *Mensch*, in the English borrowing from Yiddish, stresses the moral quality of personhood. It is different from the mere number of *Menschen* (individuals) in a population. *Mardom* stresses the other meaning of *Mensch*: it is the collective noun meaning "people." Unlike the German *Volk* (folk), or English "nation," *mardom* is not the carrier of an essentialized *Volkgeist* (folk spirit or genius), nor an autochthony of birth. Indeed, the translation of "nation" in the early twentieth-century Constitutional period was troublesome. *Meillat* was adopted and is still used for formulations such as the national bank (*Bank-i Melli*), but that word derived from and was used by the Ottoman Empire to designate confessional communities.

For Immanuel Kant's *Anthropology from a Pragmatic Point of View*, both *ensan-shenasi* and *mardom-shenasi* might be appropriate in different places, but also *jome'-shenasi*: the study of groups, societies, sociology. Culture involves another term, *farhang*, although, as in English, it often means "high culture" rather than "culture" in the anthropological sense. For Kant, Durkheim, Freud in his work on group psychology, Wittgenstein and Lyotard on language games and meaning determined by use, Lacan grappling with the social nature of language as a symbolic arena knotted together with the imaginary and the real, Arendt in postwar repair, Walter Benjamin and the surrealists contemplating the rise of mass politics and coercive authoritarian subjectivation, Derrida collecting the cinders and ashes for a democracy to come, Taghi Modarressi savoring Persian accents and Nahal Naficy's Washington Persians, Najmabadi's and Osanloo's transsexuals and divorce-seeking wives negotiating with psychiatrists, bureaucrats, and Islamic courts—for all these modern authors, individuation, personhood, relative autonomy, and character occurs only in groups, in increasingly differentiated social structures.

According to Cornelius Castoriadis, two opposed meanings of *anthropos* were held in tension for the Greeks of the fifth century BCE. For Aeschylus in *Prometheus Bound* (c. 460 BCE), *anthropos* stands between animals and gods (*therion e theos*), between the bestial and the divine. Aeschylus thus works with a "structuralist" anthropogony, or genesis of *anthropos*. Before Prometheus's gifts to mankind—of fire and the arts of culture, of memory and foresight of death, of discerning the potentials of action and creation (*prattein, poiein*)—men and women were like zombies. They saw without seeing, heard without hearing, lived in sunless caves unable to distinguish the seasons, and were without discernment (*ater gnomes*). Men and women were, in other words, placeholders in the structural scheme between gods and beasts, and were transmuted into human beings, alchemically or by mutation as it were, by Prometheus's gifts.

By contrast, for Sophocles in *Antigone* (c. 441 BCE), *anthropos* is a drive, a compulsion of self-fashioning that weaves together the laws of the polis and the equally strong passions of political life. *Anthropos* in this account is self-educating (*edidaxato*). *Edidaxato* is self-reflexive, an example of the grammatical middle voice in which agent and object of agency are indistinguishable. Of anthropos, Sophocles says, "Numerous are the terrors and wonders [*deina*] but nothing is more wondrous and terrifying [*deinon*] than man [*polla ta deina kouden anthropou deinoteron pelei*]." The gods (like comic book characters) are fixed in their qualities, but man is self-creating, self-modifying, and challenged to weave together (*pareiron*) the bonds of polities. *Antigone* is a play about the need to weave together loyalty to ancestral tradition (the Burkean republicanism of incremental conservatism) with loyalty to the self-legislating rule of law (the Jeffersonian republicanism of new constitutions every twenty years). The tragedy comes from the *hubris* of Antigone and Creon, each loyal to one principle, neither able to weave the two together (*pareiron*) into the passionate embrace of the work and working of the polis (*astuonomous orgas*, whence also orgasm, explosive passion).

The Greeks, as Miriam Leonard (2005) shows, once again become important in post-World War II French philosophical thinking about democracy, ethics, and postwar reconstruction, often in direct contrast to earlier German readings of *die Griechen* (especially those of Hegel, Nietzsche, and Heidegger). While the dialectic of French-German dialogue is constitutive of modern European philosophy, often it is by way of diversion through the remains of the earlier dialogue between the Persians and Greeks or indeed the Hindus and the Greeks.

The oldest of these Greek remains is *The Persians*, the play by Aeschylus (472 BCE), one in a series of Greek meditations on the civilizational dialectic between two kinds of states (continental empire and maritime city-state alliances), and, more philosophically, between hubris and prudence at various segmentary levels of governance and political action. *The Persians* deals in prolepsis and dreams (the Queen Mother, Atossa, has an anxiety dream before the bad news arrives and her son Xerxes in tatters) and in ghosts and hauntings (she summons the ghost of her dead husband, Darius, who excoriates the hubris of his son and predicts further calamity at the battle of Plataea). Critics point out that *The Persians* can be staged in multiple ways: in the mode of tragedy, with the stress on the unforeseen wages of hubris, something with which the Greeks identified and repeatedly suffered; or in the mode of xenophobic patriotism, less philosophical, and comforting catharsis, like Roland Barthes reading televised wrestling matches as unproblematic good-versus-evil tournaments. The play remained popular in Roman and Byzantine times, and has been revived as responses to the two Gulf Wars (in 1993 and 2003) and to the war on terror (in 2006), in the last of which the West is defeated. Greek plays, histories, and political philosophies staged similar dramas between Greek city-states, paradigmatically between Sparta and Athens, but also the overreach of colonization in the Peloponnesian War, the revolt in Sicily, and the earlier one in Miletus.

As in a series of chess games the place of Persia is sometimes black, sometimes white, Sparta and Athens play a similar chess game of contrasts and moves. In Herodotus, Stewart Florey argues (1987), the Persians and the several Greek city-states are staged as counters in a cyclical structural reversal between rich and poor, corrupt and noble, brave and coward, ignorant and sophisticated (corrupted by deceit and luxury, as Ibn Khaldun would again articulate in the fourteenth century). Sparta is a society in Plato to which the Athenian stranger counterposes the virtues of education through play and dialectical debate, with the added pleasures of testing and keeping one's head while drinking wine as a superior pedagogy to the Spartan nondrinking asceticism and unison chanting to instill feelings of unquestioning solidarity and unity and hardening for sacred defense of the homeland (much as Khomeinist Iran has adopted). Philosophically, the chess game continued in the mid-twentieth century with Karl Popper's casting of the open society against the authoritarianism of the philosopher-kings of the Republic, a position taken up by his student, Abdolkarim Sorush, against the Khomeinists, who in turn fear the spirit of criticism, debate, and play as a "velvet revolution" certain to topple their efforts to control the state, the polity, and the youth.

Western philosophy, too, has its parallel internal dialectic, with the language game of symbolic logic and desire for univocal linguistics modeled on Gottlob Frege or Bertrand Russell in Anglo-American philosophy dismissing the language games of Wittgenstein, the intersubjective and language mediated phenomenology of Dilthey and Cassirer, or the social worlding of anthropology (Veena Das's poisonous knowledge, Arthur Kleinman's local moral worlds, Byron and Mary-Jo DelVecchio Good's postcolonial disorders), or that of today's Iranian ethnographic philosophers of the everyday (Taghi Modarressi, Nahal Naficy, Afsaneh Najmabadi, Hassan-Ali Moinzadeh, and Orkideh Behrouzan). The rationales for Anglo-American philosophical language games in machine translation and for the pleasure of the language games are not objectionable as long as they are not used to bar philosophies of greater range for the tasks of actual living in the world amid all its conflicts and plurality.

PART IV

Temporalities and Recursivities

KEYWORDS

changes in communication materialities; effects and responses in ethnography.

10. Changing Media of Ethnographic Writing

KEYWORDS

talk stories, multilingual intereferences *(Michel Serres's pun on interferences and inter-references as unavoidable puralities), transference, torn religions, double-voiced biographies; double-bind commitments; time-warp shocks; second industrial divides and second-order modernizations; the four natures; filmic judgment; public sphere versus public culture; oral, print, filmic, digital, communication; genomics and biotechnologies;* anthropology of *science and technology; imaginaries, protocols, and ethical plateaus; reknitting the moieties of the world with new Silk Roads; blogosphere as affective space; cell phone video documentation turned viral as generative secondary art and uncensorable commentary; new geographies of science, art, and civic science; cultural textures of fast change in Asian cities; transcontinental cultural flows; musical culture as the space where identity, politics, racial tensions are played out; culture as symphonic and amoebic.*

11. Recalling Writing Culture

KEYWORDS

always already stepping into flows of representations and articulations; social dynamics of collaborative work; corpus (life, body of work); essay and canto; tropes of beginnings; allegory, ritual forms, evocation, and dialogue; unequal languages; anthropological tunings to the humanities and to science studies.

12. Anthropological Modes of Concern

KEYWORDS

zen exercises; biopolitics and bioecologies; repetitions with a difference; camaraderies and trajectories; pendulums and periodicities; afterlives and shifts in common sense; detachment as meta-stable positions from which critique and politics can emerge; social hieroglyphs; radical calligraphic lines, lines of flight, and supple cartographic lines across milieus; third spaces and storytelling as slowing things down; paranoia, delirium, and hallucinatory poiesis that neighbors can recognize; extreme rituals, cannibalizing, anthropophagies, and indie-gestion; affective history of liberalism and its contradictions; trans-species intimacy by sitting with a dying animal; poisonous histories, divided cities (Furies and Eumenides); postwar healing as becoming different; ethnic cleansing, fundamentalist scripturalism, suppressing vernacular histories; weedy, relic, and ghost species; horizoning, meso-spaces of experimental time, and emergent forms of life; artwork and ethnography to break the frame, reshuffle, see anew.

10

CHANGING MEDIA OF ETHNOGRAPHIC WRITING

It is time to begin reflecting on the changing materialities as well as concepts that forms of ethnography have deployed over the past century, and particularly the past two decades since the availability of the Internet and web-based production. In the following two chapters I begin this process of recall and renewal by charting changes since *Writing Culture* and *Anthropology as Cultural Critique*, both now three decades old. In the tumultuous intervening thirty years, writing culture has gone through at least three versions, or also time warps, psychodynamics, and writing technologies—pen, camera, and digitization. Writing culture and *Cultural Anthropology* (the journal) have also gone through shifts in building porosities, first with the humanities, then the media, and lately emergent biological and ecological sensibilities. In the following pages, I attempt to capture with "pen" (or laptop), for a sedimented print world, the magic pad or 4-D triangulations of historical discourses, operating systems, and sociocultural con-texts.

My own contribution to *Writing Culture*, "Ethnicity and The Postmodern Arts of Memory," turned out to be one of a trio of essays on ethnicity, torn religions, and science articulated through monologic, double-voiced, and triangulated autobiographic genre perspectives (Fischer 1986, 1994, 1995). It explored female and male ethnic "identities" that can assert themselves, without bidding or conscious desire, and that over a life or a text are fused from their multiple sources into a singular voice. The cultural expressions of ethnicity were grounded in a particular historical moment of American life, and served as uneasy fit, and thus critique, for the three-generation model of immigration and assimilation of earlier anthropological models of Americanization. The finding of a voice expressed itself in varied narrative forms: the talk stories from fragments and silences of parental or community pasts; bilingual or multilingual *interférences* (interferences and inter-references);[1] psychodynamics and dialogics of working through and acting out emotional truths through a telling to another; diversions and subversions of humor; and the polysemy and ambi-valences of poetry. For the exploration of modern *torn religions* I looked to *double-voiced* or *stereoscopic* biographies of transitional religious figures by modern transitional figures whose psychodynamically powerful interpretations of the former served as screens for their own and their communities' irresolvable double bind commitments. And for *technoscientific imaginaries* I looked to the formal homologies of the ways female and male scientists narrate and give meaning to their autobiographical trajectories and to their disciplines' trajectories via *triangulations* with multiple powerful, often conflictual, others (mentors, rivals, and collaborators).[2]

In this chapter, I follow up on these narrative and anthropological threads with three sets of time-stamped reflections. I draw upon often extradepartmental networks and collaborative circles I have had the good fortune to be part of and the work of students I have attempted to encourage to contribute to collective projects of generalized exchange.[3] Each section uses films, theater, photos, and digital media from Indian, Iranian, Chinese, and American parallel worlds to evoke mood, tense, or temporality, as well as reminders of changing technological, environmental, and sociopolitical horizons. An emergent thread traces the growth of a new biological and ecological cultural sensibility, one that explores the increasingly fine granularity shifts from disciplinary societies to more diffuse but more pervasive ones of code and variants of neoliberalisms identified by Foucault and Deleuze [Foucault 1975, 1978–78; Deleuze 1992]. Throughout, anthropological voices (there are many more) are evoked to help articulate these shifting sensibilities. Ethnographic and anthropological jeweler-eye craftsmanship in teasing out the refractions of everyday life can often upset the echo-chamber master narratives, or aggregating voice, of politicians, political scientists, economists, and the mass media.

1984. Operating Systems 1.0: Times Out of Joint, Camera Out of Focus, and Pens Running Out of Ink

> Hello, I am Macintosh. It sure is great to get out of that bag. Unaccustomed as I am to public speaking, I'd like to share with you a maxim I thought up the first time I met an IBM mainframe: NEVER TRUST A COMPUTER YOU CAN'T LIFT. —MACINTOSH LAUNCH VIDEO, 1984[4]

> Now fear an IBM dominated and controlled future. They are increasingly and desperately turning back to Apple as the only force that can ensure their future freedom [laughter, applause]. . . . Will Big Blue dominate the entire computer industry? [No!] The entire information age? [No!] Was George Orwell right about 1984? —APPLE ANNUAL SALES MEETING IN HAWAII, October 23, 1983[5]

Looking at photographs of middle-class lives in the 1950s–70s in places like Iran can produce time-warp shocks. The women and men look so modern, so much more so than the "retro" veils and three-day-growth beards of the 1980–2000s. Or perhaps it is a class inversion, with the arrival in the nouveau riche and new middle classes of recently urbanized members of what were once less privileged strata, often along with their modernized evangelical religious sensibilities—as if deploying Max Weber's modalities of upward social mobility and sense of cultural distinction, updated with grassroots organizing, smartphones, social media, and mega churches). "Retro" is a fashion term, not a return but a referencing, an *interférence* (à la Serres) interfering with, deferring to, alternative modernities, insisting on different values and valuations, calling on different enunciatory communities, mustering often considerable political weight. California-style ranch houses in Ahwaz (Iran) and the Helmand Valley (Afghanistan) in 1984 were perhaps enclaves, but the steel-frame and glass-and-concrete townhouse developments in Yazd and Qum were similar to prefab housing elsewhere in the world. Once accustomed to the aftereffects of the Islamic revolution, such as increasing black veiling of women in the Arab, Turkish, and Iranian worlds—along with, importantly, increasing employment of women in the labor force—the gaily colored and stylish veils of Indonesian and Malay women, affixed and decorated with eye-catching silver pins, can be disconcerting, a crossing of codes.

The arrow of time does not move as uniformly as elites and development pundits of modernization and modernity at large, with their finance-scapes and biopolitical markets, sometimes allowed themselves to think. Indeed, time-warp shocks and times out of joint reverberate across many temporal expectations and false dawns for whole populations or parts of them. Descartes, watching the Vatican's imposition of public dogma on Galileo (1633) for political control reasons (rather than scientific or truth ones), defensively tempered his own claims, recognizing that the movement of history was not necessarily on his side or that of renaissance mercantile and capitalist bourgeoisies who believed in science, the ability to understand and control the world, and who tried to consolidate power through parliaments and law courts (Negri 1970). A wonderful cartoon by the Armenian anthropologist Levon Abrahamian shows a globe being thrown at a fleeing Galileo with the caption, "The world is round, but not in this case," as a commentary on ethnic-nationalist claims in bloody wars as the Cold War receded, despite the misplaced or aspirational common sense that essentializing ethnic and nationalist claims should be things of the past in a globalized world (reproduced in Fischer 2003). The women's movement in German social democratic politics in the early twentieth century, or the Rosie the Riveter generation of female workers in the US World War II defense industries, similarly found themselves pushed back into domestic subaltern positions (Bourke-White 1943, Friedan 1963, Field 1980, Coleman 1995). Already in the nineteenth century, Friedrich Engels (1884) had described industrialization as an initial rise of women's status and employment, followed by pushing women back into the domestic sphere, offloading the costs of labor reproduction from capital onto a familial division of labor, with employed women and children being paid less. Antonio Negri uses the analogy of Descartes to restage the limitations of the hopes of the autonomist workers' social movement in northern Italy during the 1970s' "second industrial divide" of small-batch, high-tech, flexible machinists shops attempting to share control of the means of production in an economy of flexible accumulation. He renews the analogy in his postscript to the English translation in 2007 as a comment on the limits to the hopes of the "multitude" against globalized capital such as the Zapatista revolt, the Seattle protests, the movement of the World Social Forum, and, most recently, Occupy Wall Street movements (for which the anthropologist Jeff Juris (2008) has become an early ethnographer and analyst).

Operating Systems 1.0 of the 1984 era were transitional, upsetting to cultural norms, but mostly still optimistic. They crossed the membranes of first and second natures (the natural environment and the manmade environment), and were only beginning the crossings of third and fourth natures (reworking human nature inside out and using companion species as tools for positive consciousness of living with diversity [Haraway 2007; Fischer 2009, chap. 3]). The recombinant DNA moratorium of 1975 and its gradual lifting were still fresh in both fear and promise, one of the first great public culture debates of the emerging biotechnology era (to be followed by debates over genetically modified crops, stem cell research, and so on).[6] (For a different account, and outcomes, of such debates in a distinctively non–United States context, see Felt 2013 on Austria, Jasanoff 2005 on Germany and the United Kingdom.)

The *Writing Culture* essays written in 1984 (and published in 1986) were contemporaneous with the year of "you will see why 1984 won't be like 1984," from the famous Ridley Scott ad for the Macintosh computer, aired during the Super Bowl on January 22, 1984, with a woman hammer-thrower smashing the Orwellian screen. The launch of the Mac two days later ends with Alice (of Alice in Wonderland, and of Alice and Bob, the canonic names in computer science scenarios) standing on a chessboard. Ten years later the World Wide Web Consortium was founded at MIT, and the acceleration of a new digital world operating system began, with its early utopian hopes captured in the Grateful Dead songwriter John Perry Barlow's "A Declaration of the Independence of Cyberspace" (1999).[7] Various strands of the communication media began to converge, interoperate, miniaturize, and become invisible, leading to a phase shift, a worlding of cyberspace in how we think about time, place, and theory (Fischer 1999; Kelty 2010). The discursive and cultural infrastructure of the world was changing. In 1984, Sony and Philips introduced the first commercial CD players (which my wife and I missed, having spent much of the year in India, and returned thinking CDs were still certificates of deposit).

Transitions were not just happening in the West. In 1984, China's Fifth Generation filmmakers exploded onto the international scene with the release of director Chen Kaige and cinematographer Zhang Yimou's *Yellow Earth*. Zhang Yimou would go on with a string of successes in film, opera, light shows, and the globally viewed opening and closing extravaganzas of the 2008 Beijing Olympics. Richard Havis (2003) says of *Yellow Earth* that it was the first Chinese film, "at least since the 1949 Communist Liberation, to tell a story through images rather than dialog." In any case, the Fifth Generation became known for its stunning cinematographic tableaux of Chinese history opening allegorical spaces for criticism and critique that could not be made (as easily yet) verbally or in print. By the early 2000s, the Internet and social media would be the tools of the *demos* to circumvent print censorship and create public pressure and new accountability against discriminatory labor laws and the ill treatment of migrants, and for biosecurity in epidemics such as SARS (2002–3), H5N1 (2009), H7N9 (2013) [Fischer 2013a].

Yellow Earth signals moments of cultural phase shifts in style and sensibility. Its story, set in 1939 as Communists (CCP) and Kuomintang (KMT) are allied against the invading Japanese, and before the postwar victory of the Chinese communist revolution, ends with a village rain dance on the dried up land and failed crops. The fourteen-year-old girl forced to marry an older man so her dowry could be used to pay for her mother's funeral and brother's engagement has drowned in the Yellow River as she attempted to flee and join the CCP forces to fight for a new world. The soldier sent, quasi-ethnographically, from the CCP propaganda unit into KMT territory to collect peasant folk songs, to rewrite them with communist lyrics, to raise the morale of CCP peasant troops, is now a pretext looking back across the Yellow River of time, across the Great Famine and the destructive Cultural Revolution, and forward to a less tradition- and ideology-straightjacketed future. The contrast could not be greater: by 1998, with Zubin Mehta conducting, Zhang Yimou would direct a lavish production of Puccini's *Turandot*, first in Florence and then in Beijing, and the film *The Making of Turandot at the Forbidden City* (1999) explores the differences of "work practices" across cultural presuppositions, for instance, about lighting effects, while at the same time celebrating the renewed global interactions after the Cold War.

In a parallel way, 1984 in Iran marks the shift of Iran's two leading filmmakers and their colleagues toward what would become in the 1990s another international cinema sensation, like the Fifth Generation films of China in the 1980s, as the cynosure of attention. In 1984 Mohsen Makhmalbaf made his last propaganda-style film (*Fleeing from Evil to God*) and began to experiment with docudrama (*Boycott*, 1985; *A Moment of Innocence*, 1996; both drawing from Makhmalbaf's arrest as a youth for stabbing a policeman) and increasingly incisive social commentaries on post–Iran-Iraq War Iranian society (*The Peddler*, 1987; *The Cyclist*, 1989; *Marriage of the Blessed*, 1989). The last, in particular, would use the device of a shell-shocked war photographer's camera as it clicked, working as a shifter back and forth between revolutionary promises and betrayals. Likewise, Abbas Kiarostami turned from his shorts and trilogy of parable films using children's perspectives (*Where Is the Friend's Home?*, 1987; *The Key*, 1987; *Homework*, 1989) to his films of indirection, eliciting thought about social changes in the fabric of social life. *Close Up* (1990) is a meditation on filmic judgment, the use of both close-up and wide-angle cameras, diegetically the former for the courtroom and the latter for things that cannot be introduced in court. The Koker trilogy on an earthquake near Tehran (*Life and Nothing More*, 1991; *Journey to the Land of the Traveller*,

1993; *Through the Olive Trees*, 1994) is likewise more than a portrayal of disruption, loss, and reconstruction, involving the actors in both their diegetic and extradiegetic lives (looking for an actor from a previous film; watching the unfolding of a socially impossible love). *A Taste of Cherry* (1997) and *The Wind Will Carry Us* (1999) stage different strata of society in relation to questions of responsibility, the ability to retrieve another from alienation or acts of self-destruction and suicide, and the intrusiveness of the filmic, ethnographic eye of Tehranis (and foreigners) into villagers' elaborate cultural socialities, conflicts, and ritual tools of repair or boundary policing. "The wind will carry us" is a line from the poet Forough Farrokhzad, a kind of Susan Sontag modernist freethinker and filmmaker (of a leper boarding school with its own deep allegorical resonances). *The Wind Will Carry Us* also hilariously and allegorically has the filmmaker within the film constantly running up the village's highest hill to try to catch the signal from Tehran for his mobile phone. In *Taste of Cherry*, set amid construction sites, unfinished daily social rituals such as tea drinking, an ambiguously (unsuccessful) suicide, and alternative filmic and video endings remain unfinished, as if a commentary on Iranian projects that can never be finished.

The unfinishing, sometimes undoing, of modernity took other turns, as well, especially in Ahmedabad, India, where my wife and I spent much of 1984, where I did fieldwork with the Jain community, notationally focusing on mercantile communities (Jains and Parsis) turned industrialists negotiating between their own communal moralities and those of their labor forces from other communities. It was a year of three shattering upheavals: the assassination of Indira Gandhi four months after her decision to attack the Sikh Golden Temple in Amritsar, killing separatist Jarnail Singh Bhindrawale and his followers, and the communal violence against Sikhs that followed; the Bhopal disaster (an icon of the series of industrial disaster denials and citizen epidemiology and mobilizations, from Minimata (Japan) and Love Canal (New York) to Woburn (Massachusetts) and Fukushima (Japan); and the eruption of caste-linked riots in Ahmedabad over affirmative action or caste-reservation access to medical and engineering education, foreshadowing the parallel worlds of economic growth and some of the worst communal violence in India since Partition that would occur in 1992 with the destruction of the Babri Masjid in Ayodhya after a Bharatiya Janata Party (BJP) campaign of *yatras* (religious processions), and again in 2002 beginning in Ahmedabad after the Sabarmati Express train with Hindu pilgrims from Ayodhya was burned and riots spread across Gujurat State. BJP chief minister Narendra Modi was alleged to have used communal tensions repeatedly for political advantage, and in 2014 became prime minister of India.

These events transformed much of the anthropology, cultural studies, comparative literature, and other social research in India. There was a turn (as in the ethnographic and contemporary turn in Chinese and Iranian films) to the workings of everyday life, media of persuasion, spaces of new interaction among castes, and the creation of new public spheres, consumer consciousness, self-help organizations, and civil society organizations (Appadurai, 1996, 2006; Cohen 2000; Das 1997, 2006; Fortun 2001; Hansen 1999; Rajagopal 2001, the journal *Public Culture*, later the design of covers of the journal *Cultural Anthropology* by an Indian graphic artist).

Already in 1984 India was spawning a growing consumer movement, supported by the wildly popular television show *Rajini*, in which every week for half an hour an ordinary housewife would go out into the world to battle for consumer rights. India would in the next six years liberalize its economy and become a leading member of the rising BRIC (Brazil, Russia, India, China) players in the global economy, with information technology leading the way not only as back office and call center support in a twenty-four-hour global business world but also as a source for transforming public planning through geographical information systems and through modeling public services on information flows, pioneered by such socially as well as technologically innovative companies as Infosys.[8] Not all changes are registered macroscopically: among the most important vehicles of visual suasion in the campaign leading up to the destruction of the Babri Masjid in 1992 was the dissemination throughout the visual field of small stickers with the image of Ram or his signs, a tactic that would again prove effective in the presidential elections in Iran in 2009 when green ribbons produced a Green Wave (Fischer 2010).

While *Writing Culture* is still firmly set in anthropology's print age, by the 1990s and the decade of *Late Editions*, anthropology was writing under the anxiety of the digital but before the digital age fully set in (Fischer 2000). The decade of the 1990s is one of accelerating transitions as the world emerged from Cold War divisions, undoing and redoing societies of discipline with those of code. For instance, Hong Kong returned to China (in 1997) under a one-state, two-systems arrangement, with a war of influence affecting both.

Changes at the political surface index only roughly the changes underfoot that anthropology is so good at revealing. The year 1989, the two hundredth anniversary of the French Revolution, saw the Velvet Revolution in Prague and the election of Václav Havel; the Polish government holding talks with Solidarity and a gradual transition to democratic governance; the dismantling by Hungary of the border fence with Austria and introduction of multiparty democracy; the withdrawal of Soviet troops from Afghanistan, and of Cuba from Angola; the largest labor strike (coal miners' strike in Siberia) in Russia since the 1920s; the resignation of Rajiv Gandhi after his Congress Party lost half its seats; and the first Brazilian presidential election in twenty-nine years, and the first post-Suharto Indonesian one.

The year 1989 also saw Khomeini's fatwa against Salman Rushdie for publishing *The Satanic Verses* (1988), a story of migration and an elevation of well-known hadith stories into the global commons rather than keeping them within the world of the *umma* (Fischer 1990), a story that would be replayed in updated media circuits with boomeranging cartoons fifteen years later (Fischer 2009). Signaled in these communicative shifts of cultural texture are cosmopolitical intereférences, acknowledgments, and resistances. They are cultural transformations from eighteenth-century Habermasian public spheres to twentieth-century public culture, always already structured by the culture industries (broadcasting and "creative" advertising to mass audiences), increasingly, if partially, reworked by digital many-to-many messaging. One such change in cultural consciousness was a hesitating shift of attention in the 1990s toward understanding "new global orders"—environmental effects of industrial production, for which climate change would become a diffuse figure of speech; financial crises mediated by "structured instruments" such as derivatives, for which "neoliberalism" became a diffuse figure of speech; and transnational media productions, for which CNN and Al Jazeera became temporary tokens, while underneath anime, video games, J-pop and K-pop (Japanese and Korean popular culture) homesteaded new knowledge economies. These would become terrains for innovative ethnographic work (K. Fortun 2001; Callison 2010; Wylie 2010; MacKenzie 2008; Tett 2009; Lepinay 2011; Condry 2013).

1999. Operating Systems 2.0: From IT, Genom and Genome, to Omics and Neurons.

> The content of the global movement which ever since the [1999] Seattle revolt has occupied and (redefined) the public sphere is nothing less than human nature. The latter constitutes both the arena of struggle and its stake. —PAOLO VIRNO, "Natural-Historical Diagrams: The 'New Global' Movement and the Biological Invariant" (1999)

The shift toward biocapitalism and its alternative socio-political-legal forms in the aftermath of the Bayh-Dole Act and Chakravarty Supreme Court decision in the United States in 1980 has been the subject of increasing anthropological attention (Rabinow 1985; Dumit 2012; Petryna 2009; Fischer 2003, 2009, 2010; Franklin and Lock, eds. 2003; Kuo 2009; Soto Laveaga 2009; Sunder Rajan 2006; Sunder Rajan, ed. 2012). While in the late twentieth century much attention was focused on reproductive technologies (Franklin 2003, 2007), by the twenty-first century the focus has shifted to a broader series of biotechnologies, from genomics (both agricultural and biomedical) to the coming era of the brain and neuroscience research along with its ethical, legal, and social armatures, and its possibilities for alternative pathways (Jasanoff 2005; Biehl and Petryna 2011, 2013; Fischer 2013b). In a nice turn of phrase, the Italian philosopher Paolo Virno, building on Jacques Derrida's prescient essay "The Aforementioned So-Called Human Genome," speaks of *natural-historical diagrams* "in which human praxis is applied in the most direct and systematic way to the ensemble of requirements that make praxis human. The stake: those who struggle against the mantraps placed on the paths of migrants or against copyright [and patent] on scientific research raise the question of the different socio-political expression that could be given, here and now" (Virno 1999).

The millennium shift from gene and *genom* (Schroedinger 1943) to genome (like Abram to Abraham in the Hebrew Bible) and on to multiple "omics" signals a shift toward more fundamental worlds of exploration into third and fourth natures (Fischer, chap. 3). It pushes further also, perhaps, the difference registered by the titles of Johannes Fabian's two books, *Time and the Other* and *Out of Our Minds*, both recalibrations of nineteenth-century and early twentieth-century anthropology, the one via rhetorical creations of sequentialized parallel (or local) worlds, the other acknowledging the role of psychotropic altered states of mind in the encounters across local worlds (facilitated by drugs or not), and millennium shifts to renewed research on the brain and neuroscience.

The turn of a millennium is one of those loops in "second" or manmade "nature" (2000CE, a merely common era defined millennium, accepted as hegemonic but acknowledged as only one of many calendar conventions), like the spaghetti coils of highways traversing modern Asian cities, that accrues symbolic meaning, initially arbitrarily, but then takes on a force of its own. In 2000, this was beautifully instantiated in the apocalyptic Y2K scare, in which it was feared that mission-critical computer systems might fail because their legacy codes had only two digits for the year, and might mistake 2001 for 1901. Planes might drop out of the sky; emergency rooms might lose power. Computer programmers made good money for a short time providing patches and fixes (Fischer 2000).

After a twenty-year incubation, the anthropology of science, technology, and society (STS), by the new millennium, had emerged alongside, broadening the purview of, British social studies of science (SSK), French actor network theory (ANT), the social studies of technology (SCOT), and the social history of science. Four features distinguish the anthropology of STS: a detailed interest in the sciences and technologies themselves in contrast to cherry-picking cultural metaphors from scientists' popular writings or speeches; a global perspective, not just an account from Western Europe and North America; strategic multilocale or multisited ethnographic access to complex distributed processes such as the global chemical industry or global clinical trials; and a concern with the powerful aesthetics of imaginaries, and explorations via bioart, literature, film, and drama of the possibilities of democratizing science, exploring the ramifying effects of technologies, and charting the emotional and psychic investments of both. The task of translating legacy knowledges into public futures draws upon four kinds of genealogies: test drives and libidinal drives, protocols and networks, landscapes or ethical plateaus, and reknitting global moieties split by the Cold War.[9]

The anthropology of science and technology has produced an impressive body of studies emerging from subservience to the older, merely constructivist, forms of STS. The Duke University Press book series Experimental Futures: Technological Lives, Scientific Arts, Anthropological Voices provides one venue for exploring the expanded horizons of the anthropology of science and technology, in contrast to neighboring fields more focused on traditional academic philosophy of science debates largely formulated in the early twentieth century.

A broader venue can be seen through the topics of recent anthropology of science and technology books and dissertations, which include (nonexhaustively) evidence law and the incorporation or exclusion of visual media (handwriting, fingerprints, PET scans, video animation) from the courtroom (Mnookin 1999); e-documents in a culture of cryptography (Cole 2001; Dumit 2004; Blanchette 2012); interpretive meanings of visualizing, amplifying or proliferation technologies such as medical scans, tissue culture technologies, and clinical diagnoses (Landecker 2007); open software as socio-political infrastructure, e-governance in Latin America and e-kiosks in India (Kelty 2008, Chan 2008, Coleman 2012, Kumar 2009); e-tools for collaborative work at a distance, and its failures (Schwarz 2002); Taiwanese biostatisticians as providers of bridging tools for global clinical trials, a case of a non-recognized country using expertise to be a player (Kuo 2009); biological citizenship after disaster, bioethnic conscription in disease studies, and bioavailability as biopolitics (Cohen 1999, 2005; Petryna 2002; Montoya 2011); the surgical training of muscular as well as cognitive memory, the pharmaceutical marketing and objective self-fashioning through drugs, and the turning of selves into clinical subjects (Dumit 2012; Greenslit 2007 Prentice 20012; forms of biocapitalism under different national agendas (Sunder Rajan 2006; Jasanoff 2005); identity contradictions and psychoses mediated by organ transplantation for patients and physicians in Turkey (Sanal 2011), and moral rejection of organ transplantation in Egypt (Hamdy 2012); transmission of structural biology through bodily performance (Myers 2007); race and the marketing of medicine, genomics and diversity (Kahn 2012; Pollock 2012); product design and safety law (Jain 2006); nuclear safety (Perin 2005; Masco 2006); executive coaching (Ozkan 2007); psychiatry, depression, and negotiating different class and religion-linked public health discourses in Iran (Behouzan 2010); epidemic and transgenerational addiction as a technoculture of affect (Garcia 2010); computational a-life (artificial life) and American folk kinship idioms, deep water marine biology and logics of ancestry, and microbiopolitics of bacteria and cheese (Helmreich 1998, 2009; Paxson 2008, 2012; climate change vernaculars in Canadian First Nations, US evangelicals, corporate green audits, climate scientists in the public sphere, and climate science under different national agendas (Callison 2010; Lahsen 2005, 2006, 2008); biological crafts from do-it-yourself biologies and geometric modeling with yarns and plastics to molecular gastronomy and synthetic biology (Roosth 2010); citizen epidemiology, gas fracking, and endocrine disruptors (Wylie 2010); and "smart" electricity market making by engineers and traders in contrast to economists, digital map making in contests between First Nations, mining geologists, and forest ecologists (C. Özden-Schilling 2016; T. Özden-Schilling 2016).

Two films of the year 1999–2000, again drawing on different parallel, partially local, Chinese and Iranian worlds, may serve to mark a subtle, yet profound, shift in cultural consciousness parallel to the shift registered in the anthropology of science and technology "in which human praxis is applied in the most direct and systematic way to the ensemble of requirements that make praxis human," or, in more anthropological terms, attention to "technological lives, scientific arts, and anthropological voices."

Ning Ying's *I Love Beijing* (retitled *The Warmth of Summer* after censors feared the title would be understood as sarcasm, itself a dynamic feature of the metastases of proleptic and preemptive meanings) is the third of her Beijing trilogy tracking three generations of Beijing residents in post–Deng Xiao Peng China. Her extraordinary documentary *Railroad of Hope* (2002) interviewing people on the "move West" of agricultural labor migrants from Sichuan to the cotton fields of Xinjian, and her seven shorts for UNESCO (*In Our Own Words*, 2001) on child and women trafficking, on an HIV/AIDS prevention outreach by Buddhist monks, on a center for Shanghai street children, and on a migrant worker's child illustrate the turn (also taken up by the Sixth Generation filmmakers). This turn chronicles social issues in more direct, often first-person, accounts and realist reportage than was possible a decade earlier. Ning Ying, a former assistant director on Bernardo Bertolucci's *The Last Emperor* (1987), trained both in Beijing's Film Academy and in Italy, has emerged as a distinctive voice among the Fifth Generation Chinese filmmakers. She deploys an ethnographic and almost Kiarostami-like gaze on the three generations: the retired, the middle aged, and youth. *For Fun* (1993) shows a group of retired senior citizens who gather to play and sing arias from their favorite Beijing operas, a popular pastime one can still see on the streets today in many Chinese cities. A story line is gently formed around deference given a former doorman at the Grand Beijing Opera House, who gradually takes on an increasingly dictatorial air but does get the group recognition and a public performance, until eventually the group dissolves under the stress. The film ends as people begin to come together again after the breakup, but without their dictatorial leader. The retired doorman sits and listens from around the corner, and then slowly walks back to join the others. *On the Beat* (1995) deals with the middle-aged during a campaign against allegedly rabid street dogs, a bureaucratic comedy amid the tearing down of old *houtong* neighborhoods. *I Love Beijing* (2000) turns to displaced youth, a twenty-something taxi driver who is getting divorced, and dates, in turn, a migrant waitress from northeast China, a popular radio show host, a professor's daughter and primary school teacher, and finally a peasant from the countryside, whom he ends up marrying. His journey of comic hard-learned realism is figured (in the original script) by having him first driving a Toyota Crown Royal Saloon and ending up driving a beat-up yellow minivan. Extradiegetic reality intervenes: these two makes were already hard to find in fast-changing Beijing by the time filming began. More recently, Ning Ying has scripted the cult film *Perpetual Motion* (2005) in which well-known figures in Beijing play fictional characters satirizing their own social types (described in delicious detail by Marchetti, 2011).

Ning Ying's work and that of the Sixth Generation filmmakers—such as Jia Zhangke's short documentaries that are studies for his urban-social-problem feature films, for example, *Unknown Pleasures* (2002) and the documentary *In Public* (2001), shot in the coal mining town of Datong; and *Still Life* (2006) and the documentary *Dong* (2006), shot in Fengjie, one of the cities marked for flooding by the Three Gorges Dam—in this sense is not unlike some of the films by Iranians at the same time. One thinks of anthropologist–filmmaker Ziba Mir-Hosseini's *Divorce Iranian Style* (1998) and *Runaway Girls* (2001, with Kim Longinatto). One thinks of Rakhshan Bani-Ehtemad's powerful film *Under the Skin of the City* (2001) about a woman textile worker with an invalid husband, her own occupationally caused asthma, a daughter's abusive husband causing the daughter to run away and turn to prostitution, and her eldest son's failed efforts to go to Japan to earn more money, capped by footage of a woman candidate for political office making arguments that would be taken up again in a documentary on women running for political office (*Our Times*, 2002). Bani-Ehtemad has also done a documentary on a shelter for women (*Angels of the House of the Sun*, 2009). Like the documentary *Divorce Iranian Style*, and a full ethnography on divorce courts and the politics of women's rights by Arzoo Osanloo (2009), S. Reza Mir-Karimi's feature film *Under the Moonlight* (2001) presents a nuanced picture of a seminary student on a picaresque journey among the homeless who teach him about mutual care and the way religion might fit into life in a different way than his fellow seminarians might imagine in their scholastic studies.

These films parallel the ethnographic and anthropological craft of detailing the unintended consequences and differential refractions to policy initiatives, "ethnographic pebbles in the way of theory" (Fischer 2009), ethnography producing more reality-tested and grounded theory, upsetting the echo-chamber master narratives that pass from aggregation (abstracting, algorithmizing, modeling, simplifying from the data) to imperative (policy implementation backed by temporary money and jobs). Recognizing this failing, the World Bank is beginning to contract with anthropologists to ground-truth the work of its staff and its economist contractors, who often can't see or access the ground through the distancing abstraction and sophistication of their statistical methods, and the blindness of needing to attend to only what is measurable (Adams 2010; World Bank 2012, page 3, para 3, finding number 2; page 32 on MIT's Poverty Action Lab; page 39, MIT's Poverty Action Lab's inexplicable findings).

A very different kind of refraction of everyday life sometimes caught most powerfully on film accesses another contemporary anthropological preoccupation: social trauma and repair, mental health and PTSD, from Peru (Theidon 2012) to Aceh (Good and Good 2007, 2008; Grayman 2013). Two such films are Ebrahim Hatamikia's *Red Ribbons* (2000) and anthropologist Robert Lemelson's *Forty Years of Silence*. These films explore the psychic aftereffects of violence and war, and complement new anthropological work on health care systems after AIDS and increasing patient demands for rights to care, from Brazil to Botswana (Biehl and Petryna 2013; Livingston 2013). In *Red Ribbons* a lone war veteran lives underground and obsessively removes land mines, placing red ribbons to warn of areas not yet cleared; a woman suffering from false pregnancy hysteria returns to the ruins of her home in this mined area and red-ribboned desert land; and a recluse Afghan migrant guards a graveyard of armored tanks, including one buried like a turtle (inhabiting both the land of the living and the underworld). Each lives in his or her own world of delusional reality, communicating with the others through emotional miscues and needs. The Lemelson film follows a number of village characters (this time all too real) and their memories and psychological disturbances stemming from the massacres in Indonesia in 1965.

War-induced PTSD, however, is not the only cause of disturbances of the brain, and mental health anthropologists were central to the Global Burden of Disease Study (sponsored by the World Bank and the World Health Organization in 1996[10]), which, to the shock and disbelief of many health policy practitioners, identified neuropsychiatric diseases as the leading cause of global disease burden, with enormous costs to national economies, as well as to the affected individuals and their caregivers. This was measured not just by premature mortality normalized against expected life spans but also by healthy years of life lost to disability. These occur in early life (e.g., autism), in young-adult life (schizophrenia, usually diagnosed in late teens to early thirties, just when families have made maximum investment in education), and in end of life (neurodegenerative disorders), as well as depression at many stages of life. The pharmaceutical industry, however, is shutting down its neuroscience research, leaving governments worried about especially rapidly aging populations. Thus, because of the need to plan for increasing burdens of disease as well as rapidly emerging new technologies—neuroimaging, brain stimulation, brain-computer interfaces, stem cell therapy—promising an engine of economic growth, neuroscience has become one of the hot new priorities of government investment, and the twenty-first century is said to be the century of the brain as the twentieth was of the gene.[11]

2013. Changes Underfoot, Playing the Scales, Remending the Silk Roads

> Images became live. . . . There is less of the protest art . . . more of the practical . . . new media beyond activism. . . . Although the Iranian government controls the Internet and threatens to close down the connection to the outside world, digital culture is expanding. . . .
>
> *Lawful intercept technology* . . . activists were still trying to gather cases where Nokia[-Siemens] intercept technology had led to . . . imprisonment . . . death. . . . If this case advances in court in favor of activists, . . . Nokia intercept technology could become unlawful. —MAZYAR LOTFALIAN, "Aestheticized Politics"

> I think words operate like musical notes that the eyeball hears.
>
> "Cloud Atlas" is the name of a piece of music by the Japanese composer Toshi Ichiyanagi, who was Yoko Ono's first husband. —DAVID MITCHELL, *Cloud Atlas*

Already descriptions of events are chronicled better, "faster, cheaper, and out of control"[12] on YouTube. If you wish, you can hear and see "the rhythmic beat of the [Iranian] revolution" in a series of YouTube videos, shifting some of the referencing of writing culture from library to audio-visual instant access (Fischer 2010). One of the images that instantly went viral and "live" was the death of Neda Agha-Soltan, shot on the streets of Tehran in 2009. Mazyar Lotfalian's "images become live" points to the flourishing of digitally mediated collaborative art beyond the event and out of the control of authorities who wished to deny and reframe what everyone saw.

When Neda Agha-Soltan's dying went live, the image multiplied. It was enhanced, abstracted, schematized, collaged into multiplying semiotic messages, and otherwise moved hand to hand, keyboard to keyboard, up the use and value chain as a multivalent signifier, symbol, and allegory. The artists and transmitters, professional and casual, who created socialities with the cell-phone-captured video are people in whom Lotfalian is interested as enlivening the image beyond simple representation, remaking public culture vital and anew. Similarly, Behrouzan (2010) draws attention to the Persian digital blogosphere as a dynamically functioning *affective* space where the 1360s (1980s) generation for the first time can recognize itself, recalling generational experiences that now turn out to be not just individual traumas as they were experienced at the time but also cultural subjectivations that can be processed and worked through with one another. Experience can, through call and response, posting and commenting, affirming and contesting, be transmuted from alienation and passivity into new active sociocultural life.

For the moment (like Galileo and Descartes), the activists are losing in court cases under the Alien Tort Act: two Iranian plaintiffs sued Nokia-Siemens Networks, and several Chinese citizens have signed on to a case against Cisco, both cases alleging that use of intercept technology by the Iranian and Chinese governments have violated their and others human rights and have lead to torture and death. On April 17, 2013, the United States Supreme Court dismissed Esther Kiobel's suit against Royal Dutch Shell Petroleum in the torture and execution of her husband in Port Hacourt, Nigeria, in 1995, on jurisdictional grounds that there was not sufficient "touch and concern" or "sufficient force" on US soil. A number of international lawyers, however, observe that this decision goes against the trend of providing some international accountability, and a venue for victims of abuses in places where suits cannot be brought in domestic courts.[13]

The argument for international accountability over suppliers in the information technology industry seems not unlike that used by the Coalition for Environmentally Responsible Economies (CERES), founded in 1989, the year of the Exxon Valdez oil spill. CERES proposed principles first named Valdez then CERES principles. As described in Callison's 2010 ethnography of different, not always mutually understood, vernaculars of concern about climate change, CERES, by getting Fortune 500 companies to sign on to green sustainability audits, advocates and the public can gradually hold these companies to more and more stringent sustainable practices. Water governance struggles over tweaking local and international regulations and models of use rights and the common good, with networks to share experiences of particular local experiments around the globe, have also become the site of ethnographies of iterative efforts to make the results come out in ethically acceptable ways (Ballestero 2010). Similar struggles perhaps can be seen in the evolution of how some patient advocacy groups are trying to move beyond fundraising into the scientific discovery enterprise (Fischer 2013) and, in Brazil, the judicialization of constitutionally guaranteed rights to health care (Biehl and Petryna, 2011, 2013). The creation of web tools for database creation to track the environmental and health damage of shale gas "fracking" across the United States changes the nature of both public culture and ethnography (Wylie 2010).

In all these and other circumstances of the new millennium, anthropological fieldwork and writing culture is not, as they say, what it used to be

(Faubion and Marcus, 2009). Nor is it always where it is expected to be, as in the growth of anthropologists hired by Fortune 500 companies to rethink work practices or user responsiveness, and by the World Bank to ground-truth anomalies in the work of their staff and their contractors (Cefkin, ed. 2009; World Bank). Where ethnography, anthropology, and writing culture are most useful is not necessarily the on-the-ground and local worlds alone but rather the ability to play up and down the entire scale, from ground to theory, policy to reality, and across globalized, distributed, or value chain accumulated processes from locus to locus (defined both by geography and by professional and lay occupation in those processes), and increasingly across comparative genomic species boundaries to what is biologically conserved across species and what has mutated generating diversity or restriction. Attention to what Ulricke Felt calls "archaeologies of [sociopolitical] engagement" can identify also multiscalar loci and historical openings where alternative imaginaries and policies to those of expert-and-economic-lobbies-led master narratives of progress and risk management can be envisioned and alternative technological futures promoted, "an approach to innovation governance which [gives] space to pondering over benefits for society and the 'public good' [rather than] limiting their frames of reference to narrow economic benefits or issues of direct risks" (2013, 16).

The picture of the world in 2013 is one, for instance, of students at the National University of Singapore (NUS) holding textbooks open with one hand, and with the other checking their teacher's archived video lectures on their smartphones. Truth lies in the triangulation between constantly updated lectures as research updates the science, and canonic platforms of knowledge codified in more slowly updated textbooks. Truth lies in the shifting of heads between smartphone, textbook, and colleague at the next table, sharing, correcting, testing, reconstructing, and forging new paths, skills, and understandings. These students, as they turn their heads back and forth, and cycle through their phones from lecture to chat and back, are looking into the sociocultural and technological infrastructures of new globalizing universities, and they do so with humor and social critique, as well as a sense of new possibilities. At Tembusu College, NUS, a collaborative student-painted mural adorns a classroom building hallway with rebus puns: A book titled *All About Me* replaces the head (Facebook) of a lad seated cross-legged, thumbs up. A girl presses the "send" button on her iPhone and the trapdoors of her skull open, releasing a bird (bird brain?). The bird is chased by a large grinning figure (Roald Dahl's Friendly Big Giant) with a butterfly net, logos of Facebook, LinkedIn, and other commercial icons on his chest, seeking to capture the desires released for resale to marketers. The bird flies toward a barefoot girl, in tank top and jeans, with a camera head, who, holding up her hand, signals "Hi." Nearby a fish-headed figure, standing next to a tombstone labeled "RIP Meg Aupload 2005–12" with a fishing pole goes phishing for passwords into the skull of a bespectacled figure walking with cane, perhaps to upload the terabytes of previous generations' knowledge. A wind-blown tourist couple with cameras float above a ghostly woman's head with Microsoft-icon eyes, while a detached hand tosses an open-jawed, eye-popping head, and a conveyor belt carries more eyes on string (i-devices). The torsos of a man in bathing trunks and a woman in a shift hold their detached heads on strings, signifying the disconnect between characters online and the real person. Each of the caricatures is signed in English and Chinese or Tamil by their respective artists.

Tembusu class projects tend toward role-playing and visual media. A project blue-skies an "aging in place" residence, dubbed O'Town (Old Town) after Tembusu's location in the new University Town (New Town) with its New England–style commons lawn, eating places, coffee shops, and sports facilities. The project is, in part, a response to and critique of readings on government policy concerns about the aging population. In part it knowledgeably, hence pragmatically, draws upon and tweaks already existing policy frameworks and initiatives. And in part it suggests new ways to integrate government concerns to decentralize health care, such as routine physiotherapy, from an overly hospital-centric system, and support changing needs and desires as seniors today become better educated and active than previous senior generations. The role-play format stages conflicts of interests and perspectives, allows otherwise shy students to speak up through a role mask, and, when filmed, have an archivable, sharable, digital product, that if done well enough could even be fed into public debate, as, increasingly, student films, such as the powerful *Before We Forget* (on two families taking care of disabled seniors) already are.[14]

Not all, of course, is digital or filmic. A Tembusu student-organized debate series called "The Elephant in the Room" allows sensitive topics, such as racial harmony, to be debated under Chatham House rules (material can be used outside of the meeting, but with no attributions to anyone in the meeting). Students at the nearby University Scholars Program put on a tightly choreographed student written musical, *White Collar*, satirizing the career pressures of Singapore families, workplace gender relations, maid-madam tensions, hierarchy and arbitrary promotion/demotion decisions, status competition, parent-teacher association politics, tiger moms and no-more-arguments-please dads, and the drone work of bureaucrats and their relations with less-educated working-class parents.

What I want to indicate with these small ethnographic notes, with no space for providing further contextual significance, is something "underfoot," in the cultural texture of fast-changing Asian cities. Singapore is neither China nor India nor Southeast Asia, though it has deep roots and live interactions in each of these global arenas of social and cultural change. A new geography of science, of media technologies such as the animation business described by Ian Condry, and of knowledge production in a variety of worlds is already at hand all under the stress of intense global competition.

The largest genomic sequencing center in the world, for instance, is BGI in Shenzhen and Hong Kong, with labs also now in Philadelphia, Copenhagen, and Davis, California.[15] It is not, as popular accounts often claim, just a government-supported, cheap-labor factory. Far more interestingly, BGI grew out of graduate student experience at the Universities of Copenhagen and Washington (Seattle), and those lineages and connections remain strong. Early funding came from starting a small diagnostic start-up company and from a municipal loan from the provincial hometown of one of the founders. Sequencing machines were on loan, to be paid for over time thanks to a mentoring network connection to the then management of Solexa (now Ilumina), the maker of sequencing machines. Again through the mentoring lineages BGI secured a role in the Human Genome Project to sequence 1 percent of the human genome. Only then did the Chinese government take notice. For industries such as animation, large "creative industry" parks are being readied in Guangzhou, Shanghai, Beijing, and Chengdu in the hopes that biotech, clean energy, the culture industry (animation, cartoon, games), consulting, and software and education industries can provide new higher-value economic engines than the factories of the recent past. Guangzhou's International Animation Festival has since 2007 been the largest in the country, with over a thousand enterprises participating in 2009, and 150,000 attendees (Xuan Jiang 2011).

As a new geography of science, culture industries, and global universities takes shape, older geographies, histories, and cultural interpretations are also being rewritten. Some are in a traditional scholarly manner, as in the expanding turn to histories from the perspective of ocean diasporas and sea-traveling peoples, such as Enseng Ho's work on the Hadramut network from Yemen across southeast Asia (2002, 2004); Kenneth Dean and Zheng Zhenman's work (2010) on irrigation expansion in Putian (Fujian Province) adjudicated by hierarchies of temples resisting and accepting incorporation into state ritual frameworks and the extension of clan houses and temples to southeast Asia; Daphon David Ho's (2011)work on sea lords and the maritime frontier in seventeenth-century Fujian (from where many overseas Chinese are descended); and Herman Kulke et al.'s edited volume (2009) on the Indian Chola kingdom's trade and naval expeditions across southeast Asia.

Some of these new geographies place local and global stories in compelling regional contexts, hinting at other possible histories, such as Warrick Anderson's (2008) account of the competition in 1960s population genetics and virology over whether Papua New Guinea was to be Australian or American scientific turf. This was in the context both of the International Biological Program spearheaded in part by the US National Institutes of Health, and the search for the causes of the neurodegenerative kuru disease (a celebrated case in medical anthropology of the 1960s).

Other of these new geographies, equally interesting, are new creative arts across borders, of which three from the dramatic arts may stand in for a profusion. Kuo Pao Kun's *Descendants of the Eunuch Admiral* (1995 in both Mandarin and English) is a powerful imagining of Zheng He, the great Ming dynasty admiral who led seven expeditions across the Indian Ocean, as an emigrant cut off from his roots: as a man (made a eunuch), as a Muslim (taking on a Chinese name and culture), and as a family descendant (a Persian ancestor, a Yunnan upbringing). These severances function as a powerful allegory for Singaporeans cut off from much of their past in a migrant and globalized world ("To keep my head / I must accept losing my tail / To keep my faith / I must learn to worship others' gods."). Kuo Pao Kun has become a cultural icon himself, having been imprisoned in Singapore for five years and yet founder of three important theater institutions. Ten years after his death, his work was celebrated, most recently in 2013, with four twenty-minute experimental tributes to his play *Lao Jiu* by four prominent Asian theater practitioners, from Beijing (Li Liuyi), Taipei (Li Bao-chun), Hong Kong (Danny Yung), and Macau (Lawrence Lei).[16]

Awakening, the brilliant interpretation of *The Dream of the Red Chamber* with an all-female cast starring gay Hong Kong–based pop star Denise Ho playing the male lead Baoyu, is done with pop songs, contemporary dress (heels, black skirts, and jackets), minimalist geometric sets, and lively choreography in twenty fast-paced scenes. Directed by Edward Lam, along with Danny Yung, a founder of Zuni Icosahedron, the experimental arts group in Hong Kong, and written by Wong Wing Sze, the play uses a fairy tale and a hothouse of emotions from the aristocratic red chamber of concubines to explore the impossibilities of correcting past mistakes so they do not repeat. Denise Ho comments, "We cannot possibly overturn the errors from our ignorant youth, so they remain irrevocably etched in the record of our lives. As we see the protagonist head down the same path, helplessly reliving his own ignorance, and experiencing the loss of each one close to him all over again, would this not serve as a mirror for the audience?"[17]

From the India side of Southeast Asian history comes another brilliant reworking, *Glimpses of Angkor*, a classical South Indian dance interpretation of "the churning," the central motif of Angkor Wat, the cosmological churning of the cosmic ocean by the devas and asuras pulling on the naga (snake) coiled around Mount Meru, and out of the froth is born the elixir of immortality, the *asparas*, and the goddess of wealth, Lakshmi. In Cambodia the churning is celebrated in the Festival of the Reversing Current (Bonn Om Tuk), when people flock to dragon boat races on the Tônlé Sap to cheer the river flow returning to its downstream direction. During the rainy season, water backs up the Sap River from the Mekong, flowing into the Tônlé Sap Lake, causing it to swell to five times its dry-season size. As the rainy season ends, the river changes direction again, and the lake empties back into the Mekong. The Tônlé Sap is rich in freshwater fish, and the surrounding farmlands rich in sediment. The churning is, as well, says the director, Aravinth Kumarasamay, "the churning of our pure conscience in the constant battle between good and evil as we strive towards excellence, the amrita. As artists we battle between spiritual evolution, perfection of our craft and the effects of commercialization in our pursuit of artistic excellence."[18] Aravinth himself is the son of refugees from communal violence in Sri Lanka, and for his family the churning also has a deep reference to this history. The founder of the Aspara Arts Dance Company, Neila Sathyalingam, also born in Sri Lanka, who also fled Colombo after her family home was burned-down, trained at the Kalakshetra Academy in Tamilnadu, and brings with her to Singapore a rich socioaesthetic history of human form moving rhythmically in a series of sculptural poses embodying emotion. *The Churning* (*Manthan*) is also the title of Shyam Benegal's Hindi film (1976) about Amul, the Gujurat milk cooperative, financed by the Gujurat Cooperative Milk Federation.[19] It tells of the churning struggle for just return to labor and increased wealth through cooperation. These several loci tie together Hindu mythic resonances across South and Southeast Asia from India via the Khmer empire to the Cham of Vietnam, but more importantly for the contemporary world, from labor struggles to dealing with communal violence, making and remaking pluralist worlds under new tourist economies, visual spectacles, and renewing aesthetic approaches to acknowledging both emotion and wisdom.

Beyond mere multilocale to multiscalar and cross-temporally resonating, stuttering, and recommenced cultural writing, perhaps the aesthetic form most ethnographic as well as historical are novels, particularly those which, for a post–Cold War world, remind and remend the once powerful transnational routes, now being rebuilt of the sea and land Silk Roads shuttling from East to West and back again. Among these I would invoke, first of all, anthropologist Amitav Ghosh's *Calcutta Chromosome* (1996), *Hungry Tide* (2004), and *River of Smoke* (2011), and then Philip Caputo's *Acts of Faith* (2006), Kamila Shamsie's *Burnt Shadows* (2009), David Mitchell's *Cloud Atlas* (2004, and the 2012 film), and *The Thousand Autumns of Jacob de Zoet* (2010).[20] My own sense is that there is more to be learned here about playing the scales of culture than from flat-footed talk of global assemblages, neoliberalisms, hybridities, and the like, which, however corrective and useful in their place, capture only limited dimensions, even of political economy, not to mention cosmopolitics, and listening to the harmonics of cross-cultural and historical interferences and intereferences. As David Mitchell nicely says in an interview, "In early drafts I was always trying to devise ingenious ways around the language barrier—and then I realized that this barrier could work for, and not against, the novel. So I stuck my characters into language prison and watched them try to get out." The same might be said of Ghosh's *Sea of Poppies* (2008), where it is we readers who are thrown into a rich polyglot of seafarers.

Playing the scales of ethnographic insight, and spatially traveling further along with the migrants, registering their harmonic repeats, reprises, and multimedia mutations, going on from the *Sea of Poppies*, from eighteenth-century Bihar into the twenty-first century, Indian documentary/ethnographic filmmaker Surabhi Sharma says, "It is actually my experience of tracking music in the Caribbean, in Trinidad especially, that layered my understanding" of Bhojapuri Bihari music in Mumbai.[21] She is speaking of the newly politically charged annual *chhath puja* and *Ram Lila* performances on Juhu Beach (where Mumbai film stars and industrialists live), the parking lots filled with auto rickshaws and the taxis of Bihari migrants, many of whom live in the Jari Mari slum next to, and directly under the flight paths of, Mumbai's international airport. Mirroring the Maharashtrian *Ganesh puja* a month earlier, this increasingly scripted and megaspectacle *mela* (festival, literally "gathering" in Sanskrit) has become a demonstration of visibility against the Shiva Sena and Maharashtra Navnirman Sena's attacks on north Indian migrants. "In the one song, if you noticed, she named every district [in Bihar from which the migrants come], and the song is basically 'we have come here with our labor and the whole country belongs to us, you cannot throw us out'; and that was soon after that particular year [2008] when the Shiv Sena said we will never allow chhath puja to happen on the beaches of Bombay and Lal Prasad, the famous [Bihari] leader from back home [and Minister of Railways], had famously said I will perform it at his doorstep if he doesn't allow my brother to do it on the beach."[22]

In Trinidad, Sharma was filming how Bihari folk music traditions had crossed over into the popular music industry, infusing chutney, soca, and calypso with the sounds of the *dholak*, tabla, and *dhantal*,[23] and upon her return to Mumbai she was suddenly impressed with how similarly Bihari "folk music comes to the big cities (in Mumbai and Delhi and Patna) and becomes a music industry, pop music, that goes back to the village but which gets further enriched, so [for instance] the mobile phone is a very common theme in the music that goes back to the villages, and is reinvented into a story there that comes right back, a constant" cycle of renewal and transformation. It is a *chutney* of political *visibility*, of rhizomic labor roots across India, from Shilong in the northeast to Mumbai in the west, and across the globe to Trinidad and Surinam, of an organized music industry mega spectacle, and of women's family pujas. It contains moments of terrifying massed power, displays of two *lakhs* (200,000) of hands in unison going *Jai, jai, jai*! ("Victory, victory, victory!"), and moments of "knowing he is the vulnerable sweatshop worker the next morning, the very vulnerable taxi driver or watchman or whatever, someone in the service sector where there is no security." Sharma says, "I am not so sure I can fix the meaning completely. Although it is a terrifying moment, but then the small details within the crowd sort of started to make me feel I do not want to complete the story"; it is, after all, alive, constantly shape-shifting, taking on new valences, growing, changing as culture does. In Trinidad, Sharma says, "musical culture is the space where identity, politics, racial tensions are played out. She goes on to say that, similarly, in Mumbai, "I realized that this musical culture back home was entirely centered around the notion of leaving home. . . . And suddenly I found this entire music industry that was so completely confident of themselves and self-contained, it was not bothered by the big music industry that is Bollywood music; they were completely banking on their culture, the folk tradition, and in fact very confidently said that it is Bollywood that needs to steal our tunes, because this is where the real music is." Had Sharma not gone to Trinidad, she might not, she says, have seen all these interconnections and transmedia slides, from folk music to pop culture industry and from labor migration to scripted megaspectacle and back again, all around her in Mumbai.

The notion of ethnographic insight is crucial: it is both a grounded style of investigation demanded in proliferating places and for multiple checks upon theoretical claims, models built by aggregating analysis, and hegemonic assertion; and also a kind of yoga, a recognition of the shape-shifting illusions of fixed categories, comparisons, opinions, and perceptions.

A Note to End On

Lévi-Strauss was right: culture is both symphonic and amoebic.[24] Apologies for trying to score it.

11

RECALLING WRITING CULTURE

Another way of recalling the distance we have traveled since the publication of *Writing Culture* is to recall more broadly the vitality of the seminar and discussions out of which those essays emerged. We still live with many of the questions and challenges of those days, though time has also modulated the reverberations. This essay lists first the topics of debate, then and now, and then provides a tongue-in-cheek polyphonic rendition of their thrashing out, then and now. The form is tongue-in-cheek, the content serious platforms for emergent futures, an example perhaps of the circling and spiraling of historical eddies, currents, and flows, always returning and then proceeding anew.

When *Writing Culture*, and *Anthropology as Cultural Critique* were published in 1986, and the *Late Editions* project in the 1990s, there were seven key terms of discussion: (1) *rhizomes* as a metaphor for a form of institutional growth (Deleuze and Guattari 1980/1987); (2) *ethnographic authority*, which was made a particular topic of discussion in the 1980s through the work of James Clifford (1983) and Johannes Fabian (1983, 2000); (3) *contexts and collaborations* as ways of situating knowledge sociologically and historically; (4) *corpus* as a reminder that anthropological works are not only horizontally situated in slices of historical horizons, contexts, and collaborations but also are recursive bodies of growth over lifetimes that accumulate and sometimes deepen experiences and points of reference; (5) *essay as form* (Adorno 1958/1984) and *entretien* (a French written form, literally "encounter") between interview and essay in which interlocutor and questioner exchange the written text until the "dialogue" comes out "right" and which in *Late Editions* we interpreted as experiments in reinventing long forms of the ethnographic interview ranging from forms of transcripts to New Yorker–style essays, and, like Adorno, for whom the essay form is a third space between science and art, a subversion form that allows "something [to become] visible in the object that it is orthodoxy's secret purpose to keep invisible" (Adorno 171), we intended to find people occupying points of strategic access to social change that were missed in normal social science accounts;[1] (6) "1986" itself as a historical marker, in the "plateau" mode of Gilles Deleuze and Felix Guattari's *A Thousand Plateaus*, and various books titled with, and written about, particular years; and (7) *polyphony* as the effort to mitigate the single-authored form of ethnography and nod to the various experiments of the 1980s in producing texts with a dialogic context preserved, restaged, or somehow otherwise "written in" rather than written out.

As a participant in these times and projects, looking back after twenty-five [now thirty] years, I situate my own work in their afterlives, legacies, and continuing projects. "1986" was an extremely productive period, and the two books proved to have considerable influence and staying power.

In the Singspiel I composed as a retrospective tribute for the Canadian Anthropological Association journal, *Anthropologia*, the cantos are tagged by rhetorical tropes and these tropes' feedback with forms of ethnographic authority: canto of beginnings and arrivals; headhunter's canto; canto of ritual forms; canto of allegory; canto of evocation; canto of unequal languages; canto of the world system; canto of the Vienna Circle Waltz; canto of concept work; epilogue of therapeutic dialogue between humanities and ethnography. The cantos also begin with historical concerns (beginnings, arrivals) and proceed to science studies that would in the 2000s partially replace the humanities as a major set of interlocutors.

Historical Horizons, Emergent Futures

RHIZOMES

From a Rice University perspective, *Anthropology as Cultural Critique* (1986, henceforth ACC), *Writing Culture* (1986, henceforth WC), the inauguration of the journal *Cultural Anthropology* (1986) under George Marcus's editorship, along with the Center for Cultural Studies (which I directed from 1987 to 1993, and which grew out of the Rice Circle), and the eight volumes of the *Late Editions* series in the 1990s were organic, rhizomatic, parts of one another. ACC in particular was a reading of our generation's effort to produce ethnographies that marked out somewhat new terrains and approaches, such as, for instance, attention to dream analysis and small group dynamics in Amazonian bands (Kracke 1978), or the sonic phenomenological and cosmological-moral critical apparatuses of New Guinea (Feld 1982). Both of these required readers to engage in the cultural and strategic richness of local knowledges as they would with their own, including changing sensibilities about location in larger than local worlds. Above all, we insisted that anthropology get past the silly polemics about materialist versus symbolic or interpretive approaches, since both are required, particularly in a changing world where both are contested and reworked. While *ACC* was a call for renewal of anthropology's goals of providing frameworks for comparative humanities, social reform, social theory, and translations or confrontations across epistemes and positionalities in the global economy, as well as renewed methodological critique, *WC* proved to be a hinge of conversation across the humanities, involving the new interdisciplines of media studies, feminist studies, comparative literature, postcolonial studies, cultural studies, and new historicism. Oddly, the reception of *WC* often reduced attention to single texts in a manner quite contrary to anthropology's (*WC*'s and *ACC*'s) larger goals and to the experiences of the "sixties generation" of which we were a part.

ETHNOGRAPHIC AUTHORITY

If one assumes and acknowledges that ethnographers always step into prior streams of representations, re-presentations, evocations, montages, and performance settings and genres, many of the apparent difficulties of "ethnographic authority" are shifted so that the focus becomes the circuits, modalities, and discursive apparatuses in their social and historical contexts and their postings back and forth between prior and subsequent generations.

CONTEXTS AND COLLABORATIONS

ACC and *WC* happened between a series of overlapping major historical horizons: (a) sociopolitically between the Iranian revolution in 1977–79 (Fischer 1980) and the collapse of the Soviet Union in 1989, both of which transformed the theaters of global politics; (b) in terms of generational sensibility, between the 1960s (the Vietnam War, the civil rights movement, the Peace Corps) and the 1990s (the World Wide Web, Gen X and Y entering the labor force as captured by Douglas Coupland [1991], MTV, the first Gulf War, the dot.com and biotech bubbles); (c) between anthropology done in teams of researchers on large projects over several decades and anthropology done by individuals;[2] (d) between the simultaneous entry into the American academic stage of structuralism and poststructuralism in 1966 at the Johns Hopkins University's conference, "The Structuralist Controversy: The Languages of Criticism and the Sciences of Man" (Macksey and Donato 1972)[3] and the introduction in the 1990s of the World Wide Web, the digital and genomics revolutions, and the shift of focus from interdisciplinary conversations between anthropology and the humanities in the 1980s to ones in the 1990s with the sciences, science studies, new biologies, comparative media studies, and studies of the global political economy ("globalization").

CORPUS

In my own trajectories, *ACC* became the first of a now quartet of volumes on anthropology as cultural critique, ethnographic methods, and the mutations and evolution of social theory articulating the historical and ethnographic contexts from which they arose. This quartet interbraids with a quartet of volumes that provided some of my own fieldwork as one set of ethnographic groundings for those reflections on theory, method, genre, and explorations of adapting form and content to one another. The first of the latter quartet was a study of the city of Yazd and its villages in dialogue with towns and cities in western India as settings for comparative religion and development of communities of Zoroastrians, Jews, Shi'ites, and Baha'is, including sections on the famines of the nineteenth century and emigration to India, the structure of bazaars as social-moral arenas, and the spatial and social dramas of riots and inscriptions of state and religious "truth" on the bodies of minorities (Fischer 1973). The second (Fischer 1980) was a study of the town of Qum as a training center for religious leaders who propagated class-linked styles of religiosity across Iran, including a "Karbala paradigm" that mobilized a revolution, generated immanent or internal critique; and a critical apparatus for debate that could be evaluated both against other scholastic traditions of disputation (in Jainism, Buddhism, Hinduism, Christianity, Judaism) as well as "postmodern" deconstruction. This was part of a seven-country set of comparative projects, each done by paired "native" and American analysts (in my case, Shahrough Akhavi and Mehdi Abedi). A third (Fischer and Abedi 1990) juxtaposed contesting oral, written, and visual media worlds, including how Khomeini overcame his recognition that his mobilization of the critical apparatus of Shi'ism would be insufficient to ground his desire for guardianship by the cleric (*velayat-e faqih*) to be read as a way for clerics to intervene as governors of the political system. Using that case as a teaching tool for understanding the critical apparatus of Shi'ite hermeneutics, the small media of the revolution, including the constestations among the revolution's factions in the extraordinary graphics of the revolution's posters, and an early account of culture wars that would become central to Iranian culture in the 2000s, these were forays into the double weaving of Persian culture from one end of the loom in Iran to the other end of the loom in the Iranian diaspora in America and Europe. A fourth study examined three nonhomogenizable understandings of Iran's Zoroastrian heritage in Zoroastrianism itself (ritual), in the national epic (parable), and in philosophy (gnostic imagery), as well as examining Iranian cinema from the 1970s through the early 2000s, reflecting particularly on how social repair is attempted after war, first along the borders in Khuzistan, then Kurdistan, then Afghanistan, over the course of the 1990s (Fischer 2004).

ESSAY AS FORM

These eight volumes form a foundation from which many essays also spin off, exploring fieldwork, genres of culture (both native genres and analysts' genres), anthropology as cultural critique, and social theory as responses to worlds that outrun the pedagogies in which their inhabitants were trained. Among these were essays in the *Late Editions* series, edited by George Marcus, produced by editorial collaboratives: *Perilous States*, on the fall of the Soviet Union (Fischer 1997), new *Technoscientific Imaginaries* (Fischer 1995), on the generationally- and social justice-charged print work of artist and psychiatrist Eric Avery (Fischer 2000a), and on the millennial anxiety manifested in the potential Y2K bug, lodged like land mines within patched and repatched legacy codes of the digital infrastructure (Fischer 2000b). Other such essays were part of another collaborative endeavor: volumes that emerged from the decade's long-running Friday Morning Seminars at Harvard led by Byron and Mary-Jo DelVecchio Good in which I participated and helped convene (see Biehl et al. 2007), associated also with the journal *Culture, Medicine, and Psychiatry*, the collections *Postcolonial Disorders* (M. Good, Hyde, and Pinto, 2008), and *A Medical Anthropology Reader: Theoretical Trajectories, Emergent Realities* (B. Good, Fischer, Willen, and M. Good 2010).

My essay in *WC*, carefully plotted with female and male voices, proved to be one of three studies on ethnicity, religion, and science about how people give accounts of themselves through single-voiced meldings of split or multiple heritages ("postmodern arts of memory"), double-voiced accounts of historical religious leaders refigured as projective screens of contemporary dilemmas of religions facing new historical circumstances ("torn religions"), and formally homologous accounts of scientific fields and selves ("I/eye-ing" the sciences).[4]

1986

The times in 1986 were a-changing with an acceleration that was placing writing itself under an anxiety of being displaced by digital and multimedia circuits.[5]

The year ACC and *WC* were published was two years after the year of George Orwell's *1984* quietly passed and the Apple Macintosh was introduced with its famous Ridley Scott commercial: "You will see why 1984 won't be like *1984*." It was two years after Bhopal had exploded, Indira Gandhi was assassinated, and the Ahmedabad riots contested affirmative action in engineering and medical school admissions (all while I was doing fieldwork in Ahmedabad). It was the year that Pixar Animation Studios opened, electronic trading on the London Stock Exchange (the Big Bang) was initiated, the first computer virus (Brain) infected MS-DOS personal computers, and Selim Jehan "Eddy" Shah launched the UK newspaper *Today*, forcing all UK national newspapers to abandon linotype and letterpress machines for electronic production and color printing (involving considerable labor unrest and suppression of that unrest). It was the year William J. Schroeder, the second artificial heart recipient, died after 620 days, the US space shuttle *Challenger* exploded, and the Chernobyl nuclear power station exploded. More positively, it was the year *Voyager 2* reached Uranus, the Mir space station launched, the Japanese *Suisei* probe flew by Halley's Comet and studied its UV hydrogen corona and solar winds, and Ferdinand Marcos was ousted by massive demonstrations mobilized with the aid of cell phones.

POLYPHONY

I offer below a condensed, light-hearted reading and critique of *Writing Culture* from an *Anthropology as Cultural Critique* point of view. I intend the good vibes of the lively School of American Research (SAR) conference to be audible, full of harmonics and differences. I intend to recover *WC*'s enduring parts, fending off (no doubt ineffectively) what I sense are misreadings, misapprehensions, misappropriations.

"Ear of the Other, Voices of the Pages": A Polyphonic Nine-Canto *Singspiel*

> Ethnography is hybrid textual activity: it traverses genres and disciplines.
> —JAMES CLIFFORD, *Writing Culture*

JC [***Prologue***]: Oy! Mea culpa! I know, I know. I come from UC Santa Cruz. They are going to crucify me in *Signs* for not inviting (more) feminists. I think we've got two out of ten, but they haven't worn it on their sleeves.[6]

MP [***Canto of Beginnings*[7] *and Arrivals***]: Oh come off it, all you wannabe alpha-males who think you are doing concept work and breaking into new epistemes. You are just repeating "arrival scenes" over and over, as we comp lit types have been pointing out, ever since the fifteenth century. Remember Vasco da Gama's Portuguese Jewish physician Garcia da Orta's "Dialogue or Colloquies on the Simples" (1563) in Kerala with the toddy tappers, pandits, and faqirs, and his rival from the old country. That comparative interrogatory on botany and pharmacy is a virtual pharmakon of dialogic tactics. It provided a basis on which Linnaeus built his collaboratory, I mean classification system. [Sotto voce, with *saudade*, the sadness of longing: she recites a canto or two of *Os Lusiadas*, Luís de Camões's 1572 (1863) Homeric-style epic of Vasco da Gama's voyage to India.]

[*Refrain*] *Look for the women*! You guys are just too fixated on realism and denying singular phallic truth. Look to Irigaray or Cixous on polyerogeny. Remember Florinda Donner-Grau's *Shabono* (1982), which is or is not plagiarized from Helena Valero's *Yanomama: The Narrative of a White Girl Kidnapped by Amazonian Indians* (1970), and "is and is not based on fieldwork," "may or may not be true, is and is not ethnography, is and is not autobiography, does and does not claim professional and academic authority . . . and so on" (*WC*, 30).[8] [Sotto voce: Oh, it's disciplinary boundary work, who is authorized as professional anthropologist and who is not, and Carlos Castanada's blurbing Donner's book does not help! Oh, it's all a play of first-person experience ("subjective") framing third-person description ("objective") and tropes of ethnographers as allegorical castaways, captives, of being a "suspected alien," and of the European visitor "welcomed like a messiah" (Valero 1970, 36), shades of that later debate between Gananath Obeysekere (1997) and Marshall Sahlins (1995) over whether the Hawaiians actually thought of Captain Cook as a god ("welcomed like a messiah," killed as a "suspected alien"). It is less about attribution of belief per se than a methodological querying of the force of discursive structures and ritual forms in strategically dealing with something new to experience (Sahlins) versus a resistance to seeing sharp epistemic boundaries (Obeysekere).

[*Refrain*] Oh, look for the women and polymorphic multierogeny. I sing in praise of Marjorie Shostak and Nisa. [Sotto voce: Although Shostak's writing is as shot through with all the same problems as you guys, bellyaching too much about the tribulations of fieldwork and the craft of writing.] You make ethnography a "nightmare of contradiction" (Shostak 1981, 44), "an awful scene of a real return of the repressed" (Shostak 1981:44), "one long frustrating master-servant feud" (Richard Burton, Evans-Pritchard), as if Evans-Pritchard and Maybury-Lewis were "frustrated and depressed" or Malinowski and Firth were "richly perceptive, but terribly unsystematic," and ethnography in general was "boring" (*WC*, 33). You'd never know that the Shavante would send a representative to Maybury-Lewis's funeral as an expression of appreciation and emotional bonds built over the decades through both ethnography and advocacy for their cultural survival. You overlook that Malinowski had a self, "best understood not as a monolithic scientist-observer, but as a multifaceted entity" (39), and that the richness and openness of his texts provide the empirical evidence to allow reinterpretations as demonstrated particularly by Annette Weiner (among many others). Think of the crafting of the "being there" sensations so exciting to his students (Firth 1957), and his systematic word for word translations, glosses and interpretations of Trobriand texts in *Coral Gardens* (1965). And anyway, whoever said that scientists are not full of passion, competitive drive, aggression, head over heels in love with their promissory fantasies and the never stable significance of discoveries they produce with their experimental systems? And what's this sloganeering against positivism as if knowledge produced piecemeal, contingently, and uncertainly were bad?

RR [***Headhunter's Canto***]: Yes, she's right! In the Inquisition from which da Orta was fleeing, truth is made to appear in dialogue. The voice is Socrates's, but the hand is Plato's; the voice is Jacob's, but the hand is Esau's. In inquisitions, power relations are asserted and denied. Assertion-denial, writing-erasure, legibility-veiling—that's the dia-logue or dia-lectic. Historical ethnography and ethnographic history, they mirror each other. Evans-Pritchard (1949) tries to do ethnography financed by the military amidst a bombing campaign (human terrain anthropology [AAA 2007; Peacock et al. 2007], Project Camelot [Horowitz 1967], Laos). Le Roy Ladurie (1978) attempts to see the fourteenth century through the power position of bishop's questioning (think of how much good information we got in Abu Ghraib: little.)

But guys, make it real: Garcia? Jerry Garcia is the only Garcia students know. [Reciting from Abelardo Delgado's 1969 Chicano anthem:] "Stupid America, see that Chicano with a big knife on his steady hand, he doesn't want to knife you, he wants to sit on a bench and carve Christ figures, but you won't let him . . . he is the Picasso of your Western states, but he will die with one thousand masterpieces hanging only from his mind" (Delgado 2011, 28).

Stanford's undergraduates need to expand their curriculum to include Ilongot and Chicano perspectives. It's not just a sop to the growing diversity of the student body, but important to their orientation in a world of inescapable multiculturalism.

I know, I know. There will be rage. I will be pilloried in the university senate. The culture wars will rage. "A Hard Rain's A-Gonna Fall." It's what's happening. [Sotto voce: I've learned the bitter lessons of headhunters' grief, and traveled the painful memory-charred trails, tracked and collated the different tribal-oral and army-archival modes of historical chronotyping.]

VC [***Canto of Ritual Forms***]: All these Hermes Ninja ethnographers claiming to "uncover the masked, the latent, the unconscious!" (*WC*, 51).[9] But it's all a ruse, this business of ethnographic reports, especially interpretive ones that claim to participate in native struggles to understand, strategize, joke, speculate and wink, while asserting meaning, when it is all contingent, "determined by the moment of the ethnographic encounter" (51). It's all in the pronouns, deixics, and shifters. Take rituals. Circumcision makes you a man, bullshit.[10] It creates a lifelong anxiety structure that can be mobilized periodically across the life course, not intentionally, but psychodynamically, metapragmatically, even mystically, as in the Hamadsha trances, or through Lacanian slippages round and round the Möbius strip of split selves and ever-substitutable objects of desire in chains of linguistic thirds. Take my Moroccan tile maker, Tuhami (Crapanzano 1980), who would withdraw into the hospital whenever he couldn't handle his subalternness in (post)colonial relations, and the Hamadha *zikr*-trance didn't work. Rituals are trickster shows, they unman you while saying you are becoming a man. Like Walter Benjamin's translations, they are only "somewhat provisional way[s] of coming to terms with the foreignness of [ritual] languages" (51).

Take three exemplars (though I can't decide if they are *Muster* [master plan exemplar] or *Beispiel* [illustration example]): George Catlin's description of the Mandan initiation, O-kee-pah, he attended in 1832 (Catlin 1841, I: 245–88), Goethe's (1922) description of the Roman Carnival he observed in 1787, and Clifford Geertz's (1972) accounting for the forms and layered significations of Balinese cockfights in 1958 (seven years "before the fact" of the 1965 massacres). Catlin was really thrown by the skin-piercing hanging of initiates, never having seen the Hamdsha or Rifa'i Sufi piercing rites, or hook hanging of Murugan devotees at Kataragama in Sri Lanka. Actually, despite all my suspicions of his reporting, the consensus is that with his sketchbooks and notes from his translator, he actually got it right. Similarly Goethe, that Protestant stiff, like Hawthorne and Henry James after him, just didn't get the lewd revelry of Carnival. I must admit, though, he did get a lot right: the trickstering (trying to blow out each other's candles while shouting "Death to anyone not carrying a candle!"), the inversions of the carpets and chairs from inside the palaces brought outside onto the Corso, with the subalterns as movers and shakers while the elite sit and watch, the bawdy satire of status and procreation. For his general exams, Goethe still needs to read Rabelais or at least Bakhtin on French carnival, Max Gluckman on rites of rebellion in Swaziland, and Julie Taylor's analysis of the transformations of Rio Carnival from competitions based on dance steps to spectacle watched from reviewing stands complete with Disney figures. But Geertz is inexcusable: his description of a football game, I mean ludicrous. You can't just describe a game in general, as if each game is not different. I don't believe his stuff about passion, how would he know? Red Sox Nation, New England Patriots fanaticism. Ridiculous. What's the evidence? And you can't just describe how bets are placed, and people get in over their heads as if there were a pattern to the size of bets related to the matched strength of the birds, of kinship alliances, or of political factions (Brazilians commit suicide, governments weaken, when they lose a World Cup, ridiculous). It's stereotyping to say it's a masculine game or homosocial bonding—what's all that about patting of rumps and exaggeration of shoulders and codpieces? He's as bad as Goethe, using ethnography for mythic and philosophical mediation. Nonsense about the rowdiness and fleeting joys of life needing to be reflected upon during Lent. Nonsense using Bali to refute Bentham's "deep play" (gambling, being irrational, should be outlawed). *Muster* (type) versus

Beispiel (example), its a Kantian play; *Vorbild* und *Nachbild*, a Dilthey play; "models of, models for," the Geertzian version. Hermes's linguistics are always with us, whatever the play.

JC [***Canto of Allegory***]: Oh, come on, Vince, you of all people should appreciate allegory. Ethnography is performance, emplotted with powerful stories, describing real events through which they make moral, ideological, and even cosmological statements (*WC*, 98). You, yourself, Jim Boon, Mick Taussig, and Steve Tyler, are all explicit about this (100n2). "Allegory (more strongly than 'interpretation') calls to mind the poetic, traditional, cosmological . . . adding a temporal aspect . . . generat[ing] other levels, [interrupting] the rhetoric of presence . . . double attention to the descriptive surface and to more abstract, comparative, and explanatory levels" (100–101). Take Marjorie Shostak's opening transcript of Nisa's oral account of giving birth (1981). Nisa's voicing immediately generates alternative norms as well as reflection on a common experience of women. Shostak's whole text braids together three, discordant, allegorical registers, providing a dramatic tension of polyvocality. Nisa speaks as a "person giving specific kinds of advice to someone of a particular age" (107). At the same time, Shostak's editing emerges from a crucial moment of feminist politics and epistemology: consciousness raising and the sharing of experiences by women, and of an assumption "newly problematic" of "common female qualities (and oppressions) across racial, ethnic, and class lines" (107).

The detour of ethnographic subjectivity is one of "belief-skepticism," and, as Michelle Rosaldo taught in her "Reflections on Feminism and Cross-Cultural Understanding" (1980), we need to pay attention to uses and abuses of appropriations of ethnographic data. A recognition of allegory draws attention to the translations, encounters, and recontextualizations that compose ethnographies: they are always palimpsests. Ethnographic virtuosos use them with tact, tactically and tactfully, exploring the historically bounded and coercive constraints of stories, as well as using their juxtapositions and interruptions as tools of critique.

ST [***Canto of Evocation***]: Aye, lads and lassies, no word of the postmodern, yet? Forget representation. Evocation of participatory emergence, that's the key. Evocation frees ethnography from mimesis and "the rhetoric [of] . . . 'objects,' 'facts,' 'descriptions' (130). Evocation leads toward poiesis, ritual performance, and therapy. Postmodern ethnography will float like "the Lord Brahma in the emergent common sense world, motionless . . . all potentiality suspended within" (134), floating ever asymptotically approaching, withdrawing, without ever having arrived. Postmodern ethnography will evoke always unfinished emergent holisms out of the polyphony of participation.

Although its technological time of emergence, postnewspaper, postradio, postcomputer, is correctly adduced by Jean-François Lyotard's *The Postmodern Condition: A Report on Knowledge* (1979/1984), neither he nor I can quite anticipate the workings of the emergent Internet and social media that will crowdsource, empowering many-to-many disseminations of audio-visual-textual permutations, upsetting Foucault's disciplinary modernities with the new capillaries of code that shift governance to tracking, aggregating, and targeting by marketers and by the commerce of simulations foreseen by the mesmerized Jean Baudrillard and Chris Marker. Heil, Walmart! Google!, derivatives and structured securities, and the power of the Chinese market.

Our only defense: we need a "self-conscious return to an earlier and more powerful notion of the ethical character of all discourse, as captured in the ancient significance of the family of terms 'ethos,' 'ethnos,' 'ethics'" (*WC*, 126), hence ethnography [ethnosophy?]. We need to return to the ancient ethos of poiesis, ritual performance, and therapy. We need ethnography that "defamiliarizes common sense reality in a bracketed context of performance, evokes a fantasy wholly abducted from fragments," taking us into "strange lands with occult practices—into the heart of darkness—where fragments of the fantastic whirl about in the vortex of the quester's disoriented consciousness . . . and then returns participants to the world of common sense—transformed, renewed, and sacralized" (126). Heidegger had his Black Forest (130); I've got my tribal Koya in India.

"Life in the field is fragmentary . . . and except for unusual informants like . . . [Marcel Griaule's] Dogon sage Ogotemmeli [or Victor Turner's Ndembu symbol analyst, Muchona], the natives (Koya, Terence Turner's Kayapo, those who speak prose without knowing it, or produce more or less correct sentences without knowing the rules of grammar) seem to lack communicable visions" (131). Nonetheless what we learn from them is the importance of face-to-face dialogue, conversation of the everyday, the only ethical form of ethnography, where one can correct misunderstandings until one comes to a working agreement, if never a full understanding. Postmodern ethnography privileges discourse over text, dialogue over monologue, the collaborative over the transcendental observer (126). "In one of its ideal forms, [it] would result in a polyphonic text, none of whose participants would have the final word" (126). "Post-modern ethnography builds its program [err, I mean we need to abandon illusions of programs, the gramme, grammar, grammatology (130)] from the rubble of [Walter Benjamin, Theodor Adorno, and Jacques Derrida's] deconstruction[s]" (131). It is a "return to the idea of aesthetic integration as therapy . . . of restorative harmony" (134). "Post-modern ethnography is an object of meditation that provokes a rupture with the common sense world and evokes an aesthetic integration whose therapeutic effect is worked out in the restoration of the commonsense world" (134). "It aims not to foster the growth of knowledge but to restructure experience" (135). It embraces texts that stage the tension between inner paradox and deceptive outer logic, neither denying ambiguity nor endorsing it, neither subverting subjectivity nor denying objectivity . . . making purposes possible (paraphrasing 136). As Saint Bernard said, "To read with the ears to hear the voices of the pages" (136). [Sotto voce: Or was it Derrida's ear of the other?]

TA [*Canto of Unequal Languages*]: Can we get back to concrete examples of real ethnographers and the ways they translate and distort? This is a real problem in British social anthropology. "Mary Douglas puts this nicely" (160): When an anthropologist "draws out the whole scheme" of the cosmology of a group like the Lele, with whom she worked, that cosmology is rarely an "object of contemplation and speculation" in that way but "rather has evolved as an appendage of other social institutions" (160). [Sotto voce: To simplify, I will ignore the question of why some societies develop elaborate theologies, as in Christianity, and other societies develop debate traditions, as in Islam, while others stress orthopraxis, as in Zoroastrianism. Let's just pretend (sorry, Mike) that anthropologists deal only with illiterate societies, and ones with undeveloped cosmologies. I will write a lot about Islam and Christianity, but, after all, I did my original fieldwork with the Kabbabish Arab nomads.] So, I want to warn about the slippage that occurs when anthropologists exercise the tendency to read the *implicit* in alien cultures.

Second, I want to warn about translation across unequal languages, the politics of language change. Since the nineteenth century Arabic "has begun . . . to undergo a transformation (lexical, grammatical, semantic)" that makes it closer to European languages (154). There is a long literature in religious studies on the problems of appropriating the concepts of other societies into Christian formulations, nowhere perhaps more importantly than in debates over African religions, whose languages were first translated by missionaries and who were under pressure to Christianize.

The most vexed of these translation arenas is that of rationality, in which the struggle between sociological and Anglo-analytic philosophy accounts are often argued into reduction ad absurdum. This was the "Other Minds" debate, which one would have thought would have been settled by Evans-Pritchard's two spears solution (1976, 25–28) for wit-craft, I mean witch-craft, among the Azande: moral or social explanations do not replace but complement pragmatic or material ones. But philosophers never leave "good enough" solutions alone, and Peter Winch and Ernest Gellner have been driving me crazy, especially Gellner, who may be good on the problems of Czech nationalism and faux national epics but is, as he ages, more and more insistent on portraying Islam as irrational. He's right, of course, to insist on the difference between explaining and explaining away. But his insistence on finding examples of irrationalities and falsehoods is perverse, certainly neither therapeutic nor ethical in Steve Tyler's sense of postmodern ethnography, something that, of course, Gellner finds anathema without understanding its technological, sociological, or philosophical grounds.

Just as Gellner grounds nationalism in the demands for literate workforces, so too computer society provides the grounds for Lyotard's postmodern conditions of knowledge and Bill Readings's *The University in Ruins* (1997), governed by neoliberal performativity and hypercapitalist rationality, not alogical irrationality. For Gellner the hard-fought defense of secularism over the bloody course of European history is a red line in his understanding of the Islamic world. But this will become self-defeating without some commonsense postmodern openness to demographic changes, the struggles for education, self-determination, and accountable responsibility for postcolonial relations. Wonder what he thinks of Salman Rushdie's chutney of Urdu, Hindi, and English in *Midnight's Children* (1981) as a generational total revision of the nationalist liberation tale.

GM [*Canto of the World System*]: I want to go back to the notion of evocation and the typologies of ways microlevel ethnographies, either in single strategic locales or in complementary multiple locales, expose how larger political economies operate. It is a feature (maybe a bug, certainly a buggy feature) of contemporary writing that there is "prominent metacommentary of the difficulties of doing ethnography in the modern world, while doing it" (195). The essay form, of course, lends itself particularly to this kind of writing, one that I practice quite frequently and that was explored also in the *Late Editions* series I edited with a Rice-based editorial and writing collaborative. There are two major modes of doing this: first, ethnographically showing how the larger world system totally infuses and structures the intentional actions in local worlds. Paul Willis (1982) provides a truly flawed example based on only twelve lads, but it is my example of invoking a theory of political economy and plugging a locality into it. Vincent Crapanzano's *Tuhami* (1980) and *Waiting* (1985) are other examples of this modernist essay style. In *Tuhami*, Lacanian displacements provide a focus of meditation on the hermeneutics of fieldwork (more than the intervention of a translator, employer, doctor, or others in the wider social context). In *Waiting*, the text evokes the mix of Afrikaner stuckness and irony about their position in what from their perspective are a classic "times out of joint" setback.

The other solution that we are propagating in ACC and in monographs at Rice is the multilocale ethnography. There are two practitioners. First, there is Michael Fischer's *Iran: From Religious Dispute to Revolution* (1980). "Though it is much harder to pin down as ethnography than Willis's explicitly labelled study" [Sotto voce: Sorry, Mike, but for polemical reasons I have to make ethnography restrict itself in ways that can be easily criticized], it "nonetheless depends . . . on strategically situated ethnography, and self-consciously so" (190). And then in the wake of ACC, *Debating Muslims: Cultural Dialogue in Postmodernity* [Sotto voce: not postmodernism] *and Tradition* (Fischer and Abedi 1990) [Sotto voce: note the chronology] stresses the forms of media and genres of expression, and circuits of dissemination across transnational boundaries. The other is Kim Fortun's *Advocacy after Bhopal* (2001), which not only explores genres but pursues the goal of doing repatriation of ethnography, doing it as seriously at home as abroad, really using the detour of ethnography to explore the chemical industry as it games national judicial and risk regimes.

MF [***Canto of the Vienna Circle Waltz:*** *Wien, Wien, nur du allein*]: Hey y'all, 'nuff now, why not experiment right down here in Texas with the ways in which gendered, halfie, ethnic voices ventriloquize all these deep philosophical issues of lack or complete or explicit knowledge, sense of the buried coming to the surface, and compulsions of an idlike force, all these literary tactics of inquiry in to what is hidden in language, what is deferred by signs, what is pointed to, what is repressed, implicit, or mediated. Like travel accounts in the times of exploration, and the novel for bourgeois selves collecting bits of information scattered about in urban worlds where common shared experiences can guide no longer (Walter Benjamin, Ian Watt, Raymond Williams), perhaps the postmodern—postings back and forth among modernities, temporally and in different places, Derrida's postcards—arts of memory cannot only create new identities (being Chinese American has no model) but can revitalize ethnography as a mode of cultural critique, probing, testing, contextualizing, experimenting, watching how disseminations and provocations—including suturing and textured elements of feminist and psychoanalytic stitching, male and female authors, male and female and "third sex" and fluid gendering imagery—work together to create third spaces of emergent forms of life. Some of these are talk stories (Maxine Hong Kingston); some are transferences—"My ancestors talk to me in dangling myths, Each word a riddle" (Diana der Hovanessian [203]). Some are multiple voices and perspectives that critique hegemonic discourses (Leslie Marmon Silk's young Native American men in uniform in Southeast Asia "severely disturbed by the inability to distinguish the enemy from kinfolk" (213). Some are bilingual insistences, interferences, intereférences—"within the dark *morada* average chains rattle and clacking prayer wheels jolt, the hissing spine to uncoil wailing tongues of Nahuatl converts who slowly wreath rosary whips to flay one another" (Burciaga and Zamora 1976). Some are humor and satire.

So, y'all, I remain bemused by (and resistant to) the insistence on reducing ethnography to the frame of a single text (e.g., Marcus is explicit on page 168, but others are equally reductive). For me, ethnographies participate in a variety of overlapping, intersecting, juxtaposed, cross-checking, and alternative (subaltern, nonguild, gendered, mediated) archives of forgetting and reinvention. These include the corpus of an ethnographer's work and driving questions over a lifetime, the depth of regional geographical-ethnographic-historical studies in comparative perspective gathered through multiple different national traditions of investigation, zoomings in and out of imagined worlds (both cultural constructions of personhood, and reworkings of local worlds by global ones), and gendered, class, status, linguistic and other contests of position, power, material-semiotic switches, and mediations (oral, written, filmic, electronic).

I sing of the Vienna, I mean Rice, Circle's critique (not criticism) and pragmatism—practice, "meaning is the use in social context" (Wittgenstein), praxis (goal-oriented practice, often with unintended consequences (Marx). I come from comparative ethnographic work on Jamaican stratification and religious styles and non-Protestant stratifications in several religious traditions over historical time (*Zoroastrian Iran between Myth and Praxis*, 1973). Evocation, of course. Description too. Social theory as developed in different times and places for context (comparative study of revolutions being only one such frame) and more. Polyvocality, affects, cultures of death and cultures of life, film and graphic arts, epics, rituals and parables—'tis the mission of ethnography. Postmodern conditions of knowledge, postmodernities (Japanese cool, Fredric Jameson's flattening [1990:325], David Harvey's [1990] big bang of time-space compression, Donna Haraway's cyborg (1991) and companion species futures (2003), postings back and forth among modernities—all are grist to ethnographies keeping up with emergent forms of life.

PR [*Canto of Concept Work*]: Oh, come on guys, forget ethnography! We've got to do concept work, break through like Michel Foucault (the voice is Foucault, the hand is Weber and Kant) to an appreciation of productive power through discourses (hmm, Marx said that, no? Making things appear natural and universal). All this talk of interpretive, critical, political is irrelevant. It is (forgive me, Steve Sangren, for stealing your thunder, but Talal Asad also said something like this; and just as Pierre Bourdieu would say) minor symbolic capital in academic tenure politics. Follow me and "study up." I work on French imperial urban planning of the 1920s (studying up or studying archives?); I think we need to be critical cosmopolitans (oops, that was Kant again, no?). Lines of flight from ethnography into *assemblage, equipe, problematique* (sounds better in French, *non*?).

Anyway, enough of this old stuff, I'm interested now in the adventures of Reason, the core of *anthropos* (Greek is almost as good as French) in the contemporary. So I'm turning to scientists. I've got this friend, Tom White, a science-manager type who has finally opened the door to biotechnology for me (his wife had read *Writing Culture*). His company, Cetus, produced a kit for PCR, polymerase chain reaction, a tool for amplifying DNA, which got Kerry Mullis (terrible guy) the Nobel Prize. So then I could get Daniel Cohen at the Centre d'Etude du Polymorphisme Humain (CEPH) to let me watch their fundraising telethon and other efforts in Paris, including a ringside seat when their negotiations with Millennium in Cambridge, Massachusetts, to share CEPH's family data on diabetes and obesity collapsed amid populist fears that French DNA would be somehow alienated. And then, though this didn't really work out, I could get Kari Stefansson to talk to me about deCODE, the genome company in Iceland that was at the center of the 1990s controversies about privacy, property rights, and linking medical records to other data sets for exploitation by transnational pharmaceutical companies. Ethnography? Forget it, we have bigger fish to fry.

GM [***Epilogue of Therapeutic Dialogue***]: "The work of the seminar was to unfix, by literary therapy, the narrow frames in which ethnographies have typically been read" (266).

12

ANTHROPOLOGICAL MODES OF CONCERN

In the chapters so far, attention has been paid to ethnographic experimental forms, to logics of analysis, epistemological affordances of local cultural tropes, life histories as social hieroglyphs, alternative perspectives and points of view, scenes of instruction, and moral or ethical puzzles. These have also been grounded both in regional cultural histories and in global or transnational or transcultural frictions, interactions, and striations. In this chapter we probe these issues further by turning to modes of anthropological concern as themselves exercises beyond just experiments, as inquiries into moral relations beyond practical interventions, as open to the always unfinishedness of emergent forms of life.

To catch the moment of becoming, emergence, phase transition, enlightenment, tipping point, switching point, Euclidean point, or asymptote is a matter of approximation, finding parameters, modeling throughputs, a calculus of infinities, a receding mirage or fusion between cognition (it must be an illusion) and perception (but I can see, smell, taste, feel, or desire it), the unfinishedness of living, morphing through interactions, artificial life, algorithmic repetitions beyond the powers of understanding, materializations of seeming impossibilities. These are zen moments of enlightenment, zen exercises.

However, to approximate, triangulate, frame, or restage such moments are ethical exercises meant to keep things open to potentials, catch the metal fatigue before breakage occurs, anticipate and head off turbidity and hypoxia, shift uncontrolled anger into razor-sharp discipline, channel a mentor into a form of self-becoming other (more flexible and stronger), rebalance gut microbiome sensing, modulate a crowd's volatility with music or a speech, recognize when a fire's physics becomes plasma. These are pragmatic skills and apperceptions in which we can be trained; they are exercises for extreme environments (space, oceans), beyond anthropocentric hysteria, emotions for when we need to rely on risky dead reckonings.

What kind of biopolities and bioecologies will we live in, what role will violence play, what role will climate change play, what are the temporalities involved in all three of these basic anthropological, social-theoretical, humanistic questions (emergent forms of life)? Does one answer them with grand theory, rapid model prototyping, and mathematical clarity or with microethnography, pragmatics, and building via imperfect understandings—or how do these inform and disturb each other (pebbles and labyrinths in the way of theory)? What are the roles of writing, the tropes employed in writing, cultural genre forms, and writing's nondiscursive effectivities (changing the worlds we inhabit, making, as João Biehl and Peter Locke say, the ethnography and theory "actionable" and, quoting Gilles Deleuze, making theory "multiple," a workman's "tool box"? Until and after death—always unfinished business, lives and afterlives—I want to keep the focus on people (the peopling of cultural technologies, "moral biographies of action and inaction" as Naisargi Dave puts it, people "becoming aggrieved" in Laurence Ralph's terms [both in Biehl and Locke 2017])—people as biosensing membranes and biochemical channels; social hieroglyphs written across historical horizons; calligraphies or embodied inscriptions of experience (characters); poiesis and lines of flight of desire, despair, and hope; inventor-explorers of life otherwise, generated from double binds, fostered in social pluralities; experimenters in devising new ethical plateaus for the time being, in the meantime.

An exemplary series of case studies in Biehl and Locke's *Unfinished: The Anthropology of Becoming* provides among the best of intensive ethnographic writing about such powerful affective anthropological zen exercises: living with ataxia, waiting years for politics to unfreeze, being forcibly converted to a new religious cosmology and enrolled in the margins of a strange society, feeling compelled to meditate on slaughterhouses cruelly run, having sons and neighbors shot without reason, being kidnapped and enduring coercive "therapies." As in zen exercises, it is not the extremity of affect that is at issue but the overcoming, the recognition that more is going on in these partial accounts or situations; that biopolitical and bioecological subjectivities and agencies are at play that we can only partially understand; that we need, as

Adriana Petryna suggests, human sciences of uncertainty rather than hubristic claims to analytic totalities (Petryna, in Biehl and Locke 2017).

I perform rereadings, repetitions with a difference, slippages, slightly different perspectives, threadings of other narratives, other horizons (1968, 2016, and 2036) and milieus, other pairings and juxtapositions, other questions or "critiques [in the service] of care," and in the service, as Biehl and Locke say, of making our work "part of ethnographic open systems and folded into lives, relationships, and [and varied] swerves [tropes] across time and space."

Seven elementary exercises follow: camaraderies and trajectories; swinging (on) the pendulum (oscillation, contradiction, double binds); calligraphies; cannibalizing and indie-gestion; poisoned histories and dividing cities; horizoning and emergent forms of life; and unfinished exercises and lifelines.

Camaraderies and Trajectories

Biehl and Locke begin with a musically rich quartet of pieces centered on, or spiraling outward from, the experiences of long-term, leaving-and-returning engagements with friends and acquaintances for life. Biehl and Locke, through the force of their writing, make us all accompaniers on lifelines, lines of flight, and lines of stuckness (*avareh* in Persian, the word used by Iranian exiles for the feeling of being unable to move back or ahead in their lives). Only with such long engagements with people (what anthropologists call fieldwork, in contrast to interviews, Google searches, and quick visits), Biehl and Locke observe, can one achieve antidotes to "the quick theoretical fix." Quick theoretical fixes miss what are often surprising developments.

The music—harmonies, dissonances, developments, and repeats—emerges over time: first encounters, meantimes, and hereafters. Thanks to different forms of camaraderie and accompaniment, doing what one can, Biehl has introduced Catarina to all readers of *Vita* as a world-revealing author, a life force against the entropy of her ataxia, a composer of poetic dictionaries with such startling social diagnoses and self-knowledge as "Desire is pharmaceutical. It is not good for the circus," "Documents, reality, tiresomeness, truth, saliva, voracious, consumer, saving, economics, Catarina, spirit, pills, marriage, cancer, Catholic church, separation of bodies, division of the state, the couple's children," and "Medical records, ready to go to heaven. Dollars, [Brazilian] *Real,* Brazil is bankrupted. . . . Things out of justice. Human body?" These refrains bear repetition.

Surprises and developments unfold over time: the ataxia is identified as Machado-Joseph disease, a traceable epidemiology from founder populations beyond Brazil, and allowing corrections of misdiagnosis and mismedication; a daughter reaches out through new media to an anthropologist a continent away; she reconstitutes a family with her siblings; and her brother is admitted to a new clinical trial with hopes for better treatment. Returning to the family and Vita (in 2005, 2006, 2011, and 2016), the anthropologist discovers new threads, new desires. "Did you bring the tape recorder?" asks Iraci, an elder in Vita, three years after Catarina died. "Should I take the test?" Ana/Andrea asks, including the anthropologist in her deliberations, posing an ethical dilemma for him, but making him part of further unfoldings of the crossing trajectories of lives and social struggles. These social struggles, importantly, include rights to medical care, now accessible through new institutional forms of judicialization supported by activist public prosecutors and judges against the "bankrupted" state, as Catarina astutely noted (despite, or perhaps because of, her position in a zone of abandonment, but with radio contact to the world). As she noted, "things out of justice" are significant for the "human body." Human bodies are always in question. Life is fragile.

The counterpoint for Locke is going and coming back to Bosnia-Herzegovina—the region, especially neighboring Serbia and Croatia, flooded now with other refugees (from Syria, Afghanistan, and Africa), further adding to the aftermath of the local civil wars, the unsolved forensics of bones and graves, and missing people—and being surprised to find in 2014 a hope-infused, coordinated Bosnian Spring, with Bosnian Occupy movements. These were no longer isolated demonstrations but consolidated, if short-lived, experiments in direct democracy. The music here is not that these experiments fail—"all revolutions fail," Locke quotes Deleuze as saying—but that experience is created showing that new solidarities are possible (Deleuze's "one can become revolutionary without a revolutionary future"). One thinks here of the century-long repetitions in the revolution in Iran (variously narrated), and in particular the demonstrations of 2009 (crushed but never over) and of Locke's note that people in Bosnia-Herzegovina are nostalgic for, and waiting for, times of "a shared, against the odds 'will to live.'"

Music is but one of the arts of living on, and Locke urges us also to attend to language in a literary register, citing Deleuze on its distinction from language in a clinical register. He draws on Deleuze's line of thought that the unconscious is more about mobilization of desire than commemoration, as Sigmund Freud would have it, and that agency pulsates in language: people may be psychologically disturbed but do not simply become the diagnostic categories of quick theoretical fixes. Under the surface, a taxi driver notes, "something is not right" and people are "explosive" and "temperamental," "flying into a rage" at the slightest trigger. But more could be done with this harmonics/disharmonics and emic/etic diagnostics of clinical versus literary language and shifting cultural discourses of psychological accounting, as perhaps in the case of Iran (Behrouzan 2016) or Singapore (Fischer 2015).

In this first set of zen exercises, becoming and new forms of life are apperceived and even tasted, if not institutionalized or stabilized. This is not to say that important institutional developments are not also happening in either Brazil or Bosnia-Herzegovina, and that leads to a second aporia and zen exercise in theory making.

Swinging (on) the Pendulum, Shifting the Periodicities

The pendulum swings back from times of seeming social order not so long ago to times of social disorder today, with different historical horizons calling up different resistances and different repressive forces. Inequalities have become so gross that the privileged can neither see straight nor beyond their gated communities and personal automobiles. Or they distract and content themselves with attachments to experience far, seemingly bright-line moral causes elsewhere. Meanwhile the screams of the marginalized turn from immediate pain to reengaged assertions of "becoming aggrieved"; insistence on legal rights to medicine; the hard love of *anexos*' (annexes), places of incarceration by families trying to protect their members from outside drug-war violence; charged oscillations between exposing and hiding poisonous histories; and sometimes disinfecting, but sometimes searing, sunlight. The pendulum is also the counterculture, do-it-yourself, punk resistance to always recuperating financialization, gentrification, and capital control. The "Jetztzeit," to use Walter Benjamin's term, of moments of revolt, euphoria, and solidarities (like those Locke describes in Sarajevo and Tuzla in 2004) result in afterlives and generational rejections or reappropriations, and occasionally there are shifts in collective common sense (like those Behrouzan describes in the discourses of Iranian psychology).

The choice of words, the writing culture of today, intends intensities, electric shocks, and wake-up calls. The words are scalpels and sutures, experience-near[1] tools that are not sensational but surgical. They intend to create affective-material effects in open wounds. They intend to pierce and lance to generate new skin, raw tenderness full of new nerve endings, and structures of feeling open to the biosensibilities of all that is touched and felt through the flesh's double-sided sensing, across membranes of self and other, interiority and recognition.

The affective-material shifts of life in the early decades of the twenty-first century provide the matrix of becoming in today's world, the scaffolds of new metastable forms of socialities that no longer cannibalize themselves but seek symbiotic metamorphoses and kinships, softening old scars and deadening ends; and allowing exploratory health, growth, transformation, and even dead reckoning across unknowable tipping points and horizons. These are the found objects, the creativities of worlds in the here and now, the artistry that turns death back into regenerative biological, affective, and cognitive life and futures that can be invested in. In worlds of precarity, many of the old terms of politics have lost their purchase: Is the precariat the new proletariat? Is the optimism of futures to invest in what Lauren Berlant has called cruel optimism?

These affective-material shifts or movements, insofar as we can perceive them, can become also new anthropological figures or templates for mindful reconstruction of our very cultural and philosophical fabrics, brought to life sometimes by graffiti and punk, transgressive defacements, and sometimes by the simple exhaustion of defensiveness, hatreds, and narrow causes that cannot grow beyond themselves or be self-sustaining, let alone allow mutualities of self and other.

Finding good examples, cases studies, and cases worth study is a second form of zen exercise. Detachment from the world is not total indifference but a metastable position from which critique and politics can emerge—a discipline of strength; breathing deeply, reoxygenating, and expelling the toxins; and finding ways to do so collectively, shifting the swing of the pendulum.

Calligraphies

Chicago. Black lives matter. Names animate and call to life. Adam (meaning "human" in Hebrew), from *adamah* (meaning "earth" in Hebrew), is accorded the capacity to name (Genesis 2:19; Qur'an, Sureh 15: [AA] Adam made from sounding clay). "#Black lives matter" movements (and "taking the streets and community back," social reengagements yet again) grow urgent, picking up their histories again with contemporary hashtags, mobilizing over 680 urban demonstrations since the shooting deaths of Mrs. Lana's son Jo Jo in Eastwood (in 2013); Trayvon Martin (in 2013); Michael Brown, Tamir Rice, and Eric Garner (in 2014); and Alton Sterling and Philando Castile (in 2016). Unique individuals carry within themselves stratified and layered histories, middle passages, northward migrations, deindustrializations, blues, jazz, rap, hip hop, break dancing, footworkin', and shooting dice. They are social hieroglyphs and calligraphies composed of multiple lines: category lines ("radicals" in Chinese calligraphy); supple cartographic lines across multiple milieus; and lines of flight tracing desire and multiplicities of imagined worlds, utopias in the now, seen otherwise. Many Dannys wear many Cook's boots, not taking them off since Cook was killed (as Laurence Ralph recounts). The cartographic radicals are not singular, exhaustive, or exclusive. There are other radicals: freemen artisans, sawmill merchants, black Atlantic seamen, Caribbean migrants, African students, intellectuals, physicians, educators, and policemen.

It is not the individual characters (from the Greek *kharassein*, meaning to engrave or scratch on the body) alone that draw attention but also third spaces of interpretation, writings and reports that awkwardly help try to suture reality. Marla hands police reports and therapy accounts to the ethnographer: she doesn't contest these reports but recognizes them as possible interpretable clues to what is going on in her mother's overwrought mind, her paranoia within reason (hardly irrational, if nonetheless mentally disturbed), and her need to warn neighbors and other community members about death, insisting that they protect their heads with hats and duct tape. Friedrich Nietzsche's hallucinatory figures (the rabble) were heads with atrophied bodies, dangling insatiable intestines and genitals.[2] Mrs. Lana's figures (friends and neighbors) are headless bodies with sounds emanating from their necks, collapsing all around her. She is mad with anger and apparitions, aggrieved, overwrought with concerns that her neighbors can recognize and respect. She is not outcast.

For all the stress on recognition and care for Mrs. Lana's mode of being aggrieved, Ralph narrates two more incidents, in which death at the hands of the police is the outcome of postpartum depression or bipolar disorder. In the latter case, family members called the police because the mentally ill woman became too much for them to handle—a situation not unlike Katkine's sedation and placement in a zone of abandonment.

In another work, Ralph (2014) gives us the hieroglyph of the large population of young men in wheelchairs, casualties of gang fights, but now serving, like Mrs. Lana, as elders working to damp down the internecine fighting. Their community meetings are reminders of when gangs were community builders—another utopia, within memory, in these very same neighborhoods, self-organizing.

Mexico City. The calligraphies in Mexico City, described by Angela Garcia, are body tattoos and amulets of "Nuestra Señora de la La Santa Muerte (the Death Saint)"—"patron saint of prisoners, drug dealers and users, sex workers, victimized women, and Mexico's underclass," a "female personification of the grim reaper" who promises "deliverance from violence and a safe delivery to the afterlife." She is omnipresent not only in Tepito, a poor neighborhood of tenement apartments and a sprawling market for pirated goods, where Magi works in her family's stall. Thousands of anexos, "informal, coercive residential treatment centers for addiction"—part haven, part therapy, part safe house, part place of extreme rituals of corporal mortification and penance—across the city "set deep within other structures, like apartment buildings, commercial warehouses, churches, and even parking garages." Mexico has become a land of repeated reengagements of social protest movements (against the massacre of students in 1968, the Zapatista social justice movement, the War on Drugs in Mexico as both resistance and repression). These are all too easily enumerated, like logical demonstrations in numbers touted by grand philosophers and moralistic pundits—a tactic Garcia refuses to use, while still invoking an apparently obligatory personage-point-of-passage. Instead Garcia brings us up close to Magi, Cabrito, and Rafa. Magi is kidnapped in open daylight, wrapped in a blanket, and taken to an anexo to keep her out of the way of the forces that abducted her cousin, too close for her parents' comfort, who presumably paid for her abduction and anexo stay. Cabrito relives and recounts over and over, in vivid present tense during the anexos' forced self-accounts, his failure to convince his grandmother to leave a war-torn Michoacan town where he himself was caught and injured but survived a spray of bullets. Rafa is a former small drug dealer who became addicted and spent long years in various anexos (paid for not just by his mother and ex-wife but also by the drug organization he had worked for). He now runs an anexo, his wrists tattooed with black chains.

Calligraphy is zen par excellence: the perfect posture of holding the brush, bringing it down in decisive strokes with the whole body, concentrating the mind, becoming one, becoming many. Calligraphies of human lives, as noted above, are hieroglyphs of socialities, combinations of category (radical) lines, cartographic supple lines moving and connecting across milieus (cultural genres, forms, modes of thought), and lines of flight (desire, imagination, freedom). Individual characters (she's a piece of work, a character) are engraved, scratched, and scarred in muscle memory, neurological reflexes, and microbiomic assemblages, as well as on the skin. Their interpretation unfolds in storytelling and third spaces, not in one or two consciousnesses alone. The lines of storytelling disrupt data banks and superficial enumerations; they slow things down; they probe into possible motivations and the unseen backstage preparations. They explore the present tense (Cabrito in the anexo relives and recounts in the present tense, making what happened vivid, reexperienced, embodied), emplot with picaresque pleasure, and ethically pass the collective sense of rightness from person to person, acknowledging that no one person is always wise. Calligraphy and hieroglyphics are the zen exercises of anthropological method.

Cannibalizing and Indie-Gestion

Gran Chaco, Paraguay. There are calligraphic characters on the resource frontiers, too, as shown by Lucas Bessire: Tie with her fractured story ("I do not know my story. I do not know what to say."); her husband, Cutai (Bessire's "hunting partner, the one who gave me his first find of the day and who received mine in turn"); Aasi, who renounced his status as a *dacasute* (approximately in English, a "warrior"), becoming instead an *aya-ajingaque* (glossed as a "peacemaker") who sang the old songs with his gourd rattle, and was a "masterful [storyteller] when the mood was upon him"; Aasi's nephew, Pejei, with his susceptibility to attacks of madness; and Rosy, whose vices keep her, she says, from becoming animal. These figures, Bessire suggests, using Deleuze's term, compose a minority, "a missing people," "always in becoming, always incomplete," and, says Bessire, "all too often erased from and by much philosophically oriented anthropology."

Bessire reads Deleuze and Félix Guattari (authors of *Anti-Oedipus* and *A Thousand Plateaus*) as philosophers of the bipolar delirium of the Gran Chaco, where the last of the un-Christianized Ayoreo are hunted, ingested, digested, and evacuated by archstate (*Urstaat*) paranoid Christian missionaries, semantically and materially unable to allow anything or any demonic souls to remain unincorporated. The indigenes, living their indie lives of "societies of refusal" (refusal of work, overwork, the state, and capitalism) give the Urstaat indigestion. The last of the unconscripted, their lives in the forest were "haunted by memories of genocidal violence and the sounds of the bulldozers that never stopped" and were consumed in the practicalities of hiding from the violent primitive accumulation of the missionaries and Christianized Ayoreo who hunted them. For philosophers, they are sometimes romantically seen, following Pierre Clastres's *Society against the State* (1972), as societies of "anticipation–warding off," as figures of utopian thought who are made to stand in for "original societies of affluence" (Sahlins 1972), gaily living their lives of expenditure, feasting and investing in ritual, in contrast to wealthy but constantly scarcity-calculating societies.

The New Tribes missionaries and Mennonite ranchers fulfill the Carl Schmittian "*nomos* of the earth" of the Urstaat, the archestate's principles of land taking, state forming, and laying down the law. The Ayoreo are told by their mythology that they have been through this before in their original times, when amoral humanoids and human beings differentiated themselves, and through a number of earlier cosmic apocalyptic collapses, transformations, and renewals. So, terrified, they become *ichadie* ("the new people") finding their way in the nomos of the *cojnone-gari* (the strangers). Their old myths and rites have been revalued as satanic. And their old ways have been drained of meaning by anthropologically illiterate monoculturalists with no understanding of, or time for, other life-affirming ritual processes.

This last group of Ayoreo came in from the forest in 2004, joining relatives who had been hunted and Christianized in 1986 or 1979. The hunt, Bessire notes, is "the central ritual" of these Christians and of their colonizing project. They hunt "to collect Indian souls, or 'brown gold,' in lands dominated by Satan," complete with the frisson of risky bargaining with the devil involving them in minor sins such as slavery in pursuit of a larger good of saving souls (tough love). After being brought into civilization, some New People starve themselves to death, or die of "sadness," not unlike the suicides chronicled by the anthropologists Maria de Lourdes Beldi de Alcântara and Toni Benites (himself a Guarani) among the Guarani of Brazil. Others suffer attacks of madness fueled by sniffing glue or consuming alcohol, coca paste, dirt, or bricks, their skin yellowing like that of the otherworldly iguana.

Bessire sees Ayoreo strategy as one of taking on the apocalyptic as a form of inverted, negative life and an arduous effort to reconstitute their soul matter to survive in an estranged world. The hallucinatory poiesis and third space (of the New Tribes, of the Ayoreo, and of Bessire) is powerful, disturbing, and ravaging.

I am more persuaded by Bessire's charge against erasure "from and by much philosophically oriented anthropology" than by the Hegelian emphasis on negation, however true to Deleuze and Guattari's reworkings of nineteenth-century Hegelian and Marxian language for a transformed mid-twentieth-century European world. Guillaume Sibertin-Blanc (and others) note that Deleuze and Guattari's anti-Oedipus originally appeared in 1968 along with the era defining urban explosions ("1968") in the United States, France, and Mexico, and along with (the slightly later) abandonment of the gold standard in 1971, the apparent freedom of the one being recuperated in the processes of the latter. *A Thousand Plateaus* appeared a decade later, originally in 1980, at roughly the same time as the Iranian revolution, the second oil crisis, the nuclear accident at Three Mile Island (all in 1979), and further freeing of global financialization (the Big Bang agreement in 1983 and its implementation in 1986). The hallucinatory analogies of schizophrenia as coding the desire-producing machine of capitalism fits the Gran Chaco ranchers as well as they fit Europe: "political confrontations shift into an impolitical dimension of violence that nullifies the very possibility of conflict" (the Ayoreo stand no chance against bulldozers and airplanes); a world capitalism destroys all exteriority (the turning of the forest into cattle lands, with devastating effects on both local and global ecology); the nation-state form is systematized in Europe after World War I, with "the correlated invention of the status of *minority as a 'permanent institution'*" (Arendt, *Origins of Totalitarianism*), an invention that generated so-called ethnic wars in the 1990s and 2000s and new primitive accumulation and peripheralization within Europe, as well as globally (Sibertin-Blanc 2016, 14–15).

São Paulo. The desiring machines of contemporary art and anthropology are, if not hallucinatory (which they can be), at least recombinatory, cannibalistic, colonizing, anthropophagic, and often allegorical. What is it that makes *Eyewitnesses*, an installation of three eyeballs on trays in front of three portraits of the artist (as indigene, Chinese, and African) more than a simple metaphor of artist-subject mutual appropriation or anthropophagy? The anthropologist Lilia Schwarcz reports that the artist Adriana Varejão appropriates her and her work (albeit "Adriana thought she had read something in my book that wasn't actually there"). Nonetheless, Adriana "cannibalized me and my work" in the same way she used other sources, and Schwarcz also uses Adriana.

The egg-shaped eyeballs open or unfold into scenes of cannibal feasting by indigenous Tupinamba women, although they are painted here as if white like witches were in sixteenth-century France. The scenes are taken from a journal kept by French Calvinist Jean de Léry, who lived among the Tupinamba in the sixteenth century, in a blurry refraction of the Ayoreo story. Driven from France Antartique, an island in Rio de Janeiro Bay, by French Huguenots in a dispute over eucharistic theology, de Léry and other Calvinists took refuge among the Tupinamba. Under the governance of Nicolas Durand, who was given the title Chevalier de Villegaignon (and was at times a protector of, and at times an antagonist to, Protestants), the island was an entrepôt meant to export brazilwood (used in construction and to produce red dye). De Villegaignon became frustrated by the fighting between Catholics and Protestants and between Huguenots and Calvinists, and he expelled the Calvinists. This play of theological and economic gazes, as Michel Foucault might say—or mirrorings, inversions, and anthropophagies—confounds simple questions of who colonizes whom. In a similar vein, Varejão's art also includes faux tiles signifying the trade in and revaluation of ceramics among China, Brazil, and Portugal. These are lines of multiple cartographic milieus, lines perhaps even of cultural miscegenation, producing the 136 skin tones that Brazilians list if asked to describe themselves. The backstory of Villegaignon, intriguing on all sides, seems to remain hidden from the eyewitnesses, although the island today is named for him. A knight of the Order of Malta, he is described by Stefan Zweig (1943) as volatile and indulging in fantastic moods. Huguenots believed he was a Catholic, while Catholics believed he was a Huguenot: "Nobody knows which side he is serving, and he himself probably doesn't know much more than that he wants to do something big." (Zweig, 43). Still, he would challenge Jean Calvin to a debate over the Eucharist and become an antagonist of both Calvinists and Huguenots.

After he returned to France, de Léry wrote a response to de Villegaignon's accusations against the Calvinists, and in his account of the Tupinambas' cannibalism, de Léry spoke of the parallel anthropophagy of the Catholics' eating of the body and blood of Christ. The religious battles raging in Europe over the Eucharist, de Léry claimed, were less palatable than the Tupinambas' cannibalism. Similarly, if inversely, the Jesuit José de Anchieta, who lived with the Tupinamba for some forty years, found their cannibalism preferable to the heinous Calvinist denial of the literal Eucharist.

What is the play of art doing in this instance?

New Delhi. Only the pain of the Ayoreo's dispossession, conversion, and marginalization can match the intensity claimed by such animal protection workers as Maneka Gandhi (and perhaps her helpers, Abodh, Dipesh, and Maya), Carmelia Satija, and Crystal Rogers (and perhaps, less clearly, Timmie Kumar; Erika Abrams-Meyers; her husband, Jim; and their daughter, Claire—about all of whom we are told too little by Naisargi Dave to know). The intensity here is directed inward, taking the form of an obsessive unwillingness to allow complacency in themselves rather than necessarily mobilizing others (albeit that mobilization is an important by-product of their activities). It is discipline with recognition that the work may be futile or may make only a marginal difference for a few animals. It is a cultural genre of world renunciation and inner discipline that is familiar in an Indian context. In this context, wearing a worn plain cotton *salwar kameez* (tunic and trouser) makes perfect sense, just as Mahatma Gandhi's *khadi* (handspun) attire did, but the inner devotion does not necessarily prevent the devotee from wearing jewels, driving an SUV, or having a daughter studying at an Ivy League university. Maneka Gandhi's self-narration stresses both the feeling of becoming a machine designed to work unrelentingly and provides a biographical account of "coming to see" (enlightened awareness of) the object of animal protection, as well as the reasons to surrender the self entirely to the cause. She stresses the machine of self-discipline: "I only wish there were a slaughterhouse next door. To witness that violence, to hear those screams . . . I would *never* be able to rest."

But Dave stresses also the multiplicity, not always aligned into a singular perspective, and even the contradictions and double binds of reasons, rationales, and functions that life-forms such as Gandhi's self-discipline can entail. First, there is Maneka Gandhi's "moral biography of action and inaction," as an estranged member by marriage of a family of meat-eating, animal-protecting politicians. While they put in place a series of animal protection measures (Jawaharlal Nehru's Prevention of Cruelty against Animals Act and Indira Gandhi's Project Tiger initiative), they are also associated with the violence of sterilization campaigns. Maneka herself joined the Bharatiya Janata Party (BJP), a Hindu fundamentalist movement that puts religious identity above reason. And she is not above threatening opponents with violence. Second, Dave notes the morally ambiguous affective history of liberalism. It is glibly able to substitute, in the same symbolic position as needing protection, a female child or Hindu women, a horse or other animal, thereby bolstering the need for imperial forces (historically) or the state (today)—either way, the Urstaat—in order to claim that they are protecting the vulnerable. Why is it, Dave muses, that many of those claiming to advance animal protection are also public and ostentatious meat eaters (To counter the Hindus' exclusive focus on cows? To express solidarity with Muslims?). It is the liberalism of a country that exports more leather than any other one in Asia and that looks the other way as slaughterhouses operate over capacity and with cruelty toward both the animals and the human laborers. Third, she points out, politics makes strange bedfellows: Doordarshan, the state-owned broadcast service under BJP ideology, shows slaughterhouse footage, filmed secretly by animal protection activists, "an effort by the government, no doubt, to whip up anti-Muslim sentiment under the guise of compassion."

The law in Rajasthan prevents euthanizing a dying cow in the name of animal (especially cow) protection, but in the face of such suffering in dying, the American Erika Abrams-Meyers (now a resident of Udaipur) summons workers one at a time or in pairs to sit with the animal, touching it and allowing it to feel accompanied. It is perhaps the most profound example of transspecies intimacy in Dave's essay, surpassing the story of Crystal Rogers coming face to face in 1959 with a dying horse that, sensing Crystal, turns its head toward her and shows its eyeless sockets pecked by birds, a horrifying, almost Guernica-like, scene. It is, however, a secondhand story that Maneka Gandhi tells as one of her own two experiences of a call to duty and inner need; the other is of eating meat soup while "pontificating about the treatment of animals" until her husband, Sanjay, unkindly pointed out the hypocrisy and told her to shut up.

What is most impressive about Dave's essay is its ability to track these countervailing desires and passions, justifications and reasons, and strange political bedfellows, and her insistence that while she can agree with this or that, she needs to press on to alternative possible interpretations or other perspectives to remain with the openness of the "moral biographies of action and inaction" that are always, as this volume insists, "unfinished."

Of course, the unfinishedness of moral and ethical struggles is also a characteristic of moral genre forms such as the Mahabharata, Jain, or Islamic stories (see chapter 7), or, as noted above, Benjamin's observations in "Theses on the Philosophy of History" about storytelling where moral positionings pass among the characters, not residing in any one of them. The fact that Dave stresses the metaphor of skin as the membrane of biosensing and intimacy in the world is a salutary contemporary libidinal touch, following the experiments with such terminology by Maurice Merleau-Ponty, Deleuze and Guattari, and Jean-François Lyotard. The fact that she stresses the importance of foreigners, such as Crystal Rogers, in the animal rights movement, flags an ambiguous mobile sovereignty of global humanism (as Mariella Pandolfi has warned of global moralities and initiatives that can displace local initiatives, understandings, and imperatives [Pandolfi and Fassin, ed. 2010]), often admirable in the personal histories of those who take up its causes yet also ambiguous in its alliances and local implications. Thus, except for Maneka Gandhi (a character and a calligraphy of great complications), Carmelia Satija, and Timmie Kumar, Dave dismisses home-grown animal protection efforts as often being exclusively for cows (though Jains have bird hospitals, as well as *gaushalas*, "cow shelters," and *panjorapors*, "animal hospitals," that care also for other animals).

Indeed, what I read in Dave's essay is less an ode to compassion than, firstly, an anthropological map of moral conflicts and disagreements, and, secondly, a concern with what I have been calling calligraphies and hieroglyphs, using camaraderies and trajectories as probes into socialities, politics, and historical horizons.

These three or four milieus, along with the two earlier ones—Chicago, Mexico City, Gran Chaco, São Paulo–Rio de Janeiro, and New Delhi—form a set of cartographic lines, metastable moralities in places with connections and affinities traceable across time and space. How do they become otherwise? That is another exemplary zen exercise.

Poisoned Histories, Divided Cities

> "No, please! Get out!" screamed Rahmi, "I don't know anything! Leave this house at once!" . . . "Ma, Mr. Nick is not a historian," he said in a commanding tone. "He does not want you to tell him any history." This stopped Rahmi in her tracks. "Not a historian?" she whispered, "But you said he was a researcher. Then what . . . ?" "Anthropologist, Ma," replied Syahrial, "not a historian." There was a long pause, and then Rahmi began to laugh . . . [the] chuckle of relief . . . "I am so sorry," she gasped, "please forgive me. I misunderstood. I thought you were a historian. I was so scared." —NICHOLAS LONG, *Being Malay in Indonesia*

Cyprus, 2011–12. Elizabeth Davis beautifully pairs the ancient Athenian sacred oath—on pain of death and as a condition of citizenship—to not recall the civil war of the fifth century BCE with the terms of the Cyprus Committee on Missing Persons (CMP) that forensic scientists not reveal much information about the bones they identify from the Cypriot civil war (1963-64), which eventuated in a cease-fire in 1974 and a population transfer. Between 1963 and 1974 a third of the Greek Cypriot population, and half the Turkish Cypriot population, was displaced. In 1974 some 45,000 Turkish Cypriots moved north, and 160,000 Greek Cypriots moved south. Indeed, although the CMP was established under the auspices of the United Nations in 1981, systematic forensic work was stalled until 2004, when it was agreed that such work could proceed only if it was delinked from any future political settlement, and only such information as could be quantitatively put on standardized forms would be collected and stored, with no narratives that might give information on causes, circumstances, locations, modes of death, or likely perpetrators. Instead of such information, first a simple visitation with the bones, then minimal funeral ceremony, return of the bones, and counseling were offered to families.

The ancient Greeks, as so often, provide a mythic charter, and contemporary Greeks provide classic and living ritual procedures: after the civil war against the Tyrants, the Erinyes (or Furies, female chthonic deities of vengeance) were turned into Eumenides ("seeing [only] good [Greek *eu*]"), and were given custody of the poisonous history of the civil war. They and the citizens were warned lest their contained rage be revealed and destroy the peace. As Davis invokes the study by Nicole Loraux (2002), "As guardians of dangerous knowledge, the Eumenides were consigned to live with their own rage and resentment, always on the verge of wreaking vengeance and thus destroying the peace of the city." Women in ritual mourning, similarly, are custodians of the poisonous knowledge of intimate affairs encoded in dreams, warned about in mourning songs, and divined in inspections of the bones. So, too, in contemporary forensic work, the lab work—the handling and preparation of the bones—is largely women's work (particularly when shown in publicity pictures), while both women and men do the excavations. But such patterns are not limited to the Mediterranean cultural area; they have cartographic resonances in other milieus elsewhere in the aftermath of communal warfare, where histories remain contested. The technologies of forensic work have been shared from Spain and Argentina to Chile, Guatemala, Bosnia-Herzegovina, and now Cyprus, but the rules and dynamics of secrecy and partial revelation varies from Bali and the Riau Islands to Beirut and Europe, where perpetrators and victims must often continue to live together. Intracommunal killings in Cyprus have their forensic experts, too (including both Physicians for Human Rights; and the In-Force Foundation), but lest communal warfare be stirred up anew, this is rigidly separated from the CMP's identification of the bones of intercommunal killings.

Indeed, Davis makes two key points in terms of this volume's theme. First, the goal is not so much reconciliation as becoming something different in the future, an openness to narrating the past and what is to come differently. And second, the basis of politics lies in conflict, a kind of ritual process of renewal, repeatedly enacted and then repressed through the vote that reasserts a collective will. Forgetting, not transparency, is the goal. Justice (naming, punishment) is less needed for the time being than the identification and return of bones for family burial.

Urfa, Turkey, 2011. Bridget Purcell focuses our attention on another form of historical layering and simplification. Urfa is claimed by the local people to be the birthplace of Abraham and the place where he broke the idols. The Balıklıgöl shrine—with its cave of Abraham (chipped at for relics by pilgrims) and pools with sacred carp—has been undergoing restoration since the 1990s. Shrines contain densities of cultural references, and Urfa's many prior names index some of these: Urhoi in Syriac, Urha in Armenian, Orrha in Greek, Edessa under the Selucids, Justinopolis in Byzantine times, Ruha in Arabic, and Riha in Kurdish. A caravan stop along the Fertile Crescent routes, on a tributary of the Euphrates, Urfa was one of the earliest of Christianized cities (363 CE). It still has a mixed population of Turks, Arabs, and Kurds; it used to also have Jews, Yezidis, Syriacs, and Armenians. Now instead it hosts large numbers of Shi'ite Iranian pilgrims (who are neither Sunni nor Alawi, as are the Turks and Arabs of the region).

Shrines across the Middle East, South Asia, and the Muslim world have been subject to cleansing and gentrification. Most extreme is the outright destruction of shrines, monuments, and other places of worship (by Wahhabis in the Arabian peninsula, the Taliban in the Bamiyan Valley, the Islamic State in Palmyra; by Sunni and Shiite forces at each other's shrines in Iraq, the BJP of the Babri Masjid in India). More common historically is the building of a conquering religion's mosques or churches on top of, or within, those of the conquered: in Cordova, there is a mosque inside the cathedral; in Jerusalem, the Dome of the Rock is on the Jewish Temple Mount, and the Church of the Holy Sepulchre is claimed by various Christian factions; in Istanbul, the name of the Sofia Mosque, with its Shiite inscriptions, reveals its previous identity as a church; and across Afghanistan, Iran, the Middle East, and North Africa mosques have been built where Zoroastrian temples or Buddhist or Greek and Roman shrines once were. Urban renewal and restoration more recently has cleansed important shrines of adjoining houses and shops, creating greenbelts that can be more easily policed or, occasionally, as in Mecca, increasing the clutter and congestion with high-rise hotels. A fourth process, the focus of Purcell's work, is the exclusion of folk and heterodox practices in the name of *salafi* Islam (a form of literalist fundamentalism).

Urfa sits in the contested South East Anatolia Development Project, planned to eventually have twenty-two irrigation dams, nineteen hydroelectric power plants, and 1.8 million hectares of irrigated land, thus involving the mass relocation and urbanization of villagers. Urbanization, Purcell points out, brings a certain literacy, and literacy under current Islamic conditions tends to mean (though she does not name it) salafi Islam. Urfa also sits in the tense borderlands that contain Islamic State fighters, Kurdish militants, and Turkish soldiers, and the area is now overfilled with half a million Syrian refugees.

Purcell focuses our attention at the microlevel, on the stresses of cultural change felt acutely by two women from a Kurdish village as they visit the shrine. She delightfully analogizes their identity struggles to those of Alice in Wonderland, becoming bigger or smaller as their frames of reference either expand to encompass vernacular practices and traces of the historical locality or contract to exclude folk Islam in favor of newly learned salafi refusals of sacred fish or saint's tombs. Zehra thus says she cannot explain Islamic ideas in her native Kurdish, as she has studied the Qur'an and Islamic texts only in Turkish. Turkish and Arabic literacy thus function both as modernization and as alienation. Zehra is married to an imam who helps enforce the unacceptability of local practices. These microshifts in styles of religiosity are felt at times as embarrassing, constraining, or empowering, and they are reflections of broader changes Turkey has been undergoing under President Recep Erdoğan.

Cyprus and Urfa are zen exercises in the mysteries of poisonous histories and divided polities, where conflict must be contained. They form an oscillating pair of changing ritualization in the contemporary world, one in a constrained space of modern forensic science, the other in a transforming political economy (from village to industrial irrigated agrarianism). In the interstices of social change, religious practices cover over or contain, like Eumenides, as much as they also cause frictions and anxieties among dominating and subordinated forces.

Like zen exercises, adjustments take time, repetition, mindfulness, and discipline.

Horizoning and Emergent Forms of Life

Both today's brave new worlds (worlds of precarity, climate change, big data, and smart control systems) and today's (Lacanian) real that periodically breaks through the façade of daily life are coming iteratively into focus. They are populated with calligraphies and hieroglyphs, peopled technologies, experimental models, and cartographies of explorations of milieus not yet understood. On the positive side, one thinks of president Barack Obama's administration's identification and pursuit of technological "moonshots," such as the $1.5 billion initiative to explore the brain; the SunShot effort to make solar energy as cheap as coal by 2020; the support of public-private manned Mars missions; the support for machine-learning technologies; and the support for the project of the University of California, Los Angeles, to make Los Angeles a sustainable city by 2050.

"1968" was an important predecessor horizon, as today (2017) is a horizon for today's ability to foresee; and, say, notationally, 2036 ("36" in Hebrew is the double numerological *hai*, or double life) is one of many horizons for the near and further future. In 1960, updated in 1968, we get the Fischer (Mercury) Ellipsoid, a new geodetic world datum, following on the 1957–58 International Geophysical Year, a breakthrough collaboration across Cold War lines. In 1968, from the first manned moon orbiter, *Apollo 8*, William Anders takes the color earthrise photo that becomes an icon of a new phase of planetary environmental concern; in 1969, *Apollo 11* lands Neil Armstrong and Buzz Aldrin on the moon. The first models of general circulation of the atmospheric climate combining oceanic and atmospheric processes were developed in the late 1960s. The International Biological Program (1964–75), with prominent collecting of blood and other biological human samples in Brazil and New Guinea for genetic mapping (and discovery of prions from the deadly "laughing disease" kuru in New Guinea), were precursors to today's genomics revolutions (Anderson 2008, Fischer 2011). And in oceanography, the International Ocean Discovery Program began with Project Mohole (1961) and the Deep Sea Drilling Project (1968–83) that continues today as the Integrated Ocean Drilling Program.

As Adriana Petryna beautifully lays out, today's uncertainties about the future emerge from such modeling efforts to gain a purchase on how the world is changing around us. The dates 1968, 2016, and 2036 are, of course, arbitrary, but as a series they register a certain speed of transformations: in pervasive technologies, migration patterns, types of conflict, and awareness of the fragility of forms of life. Perhaps most unnerving is the unconsciousness of various forms of the real that are not available, or only partially available, to ordinary perception and, even then, only if one knows how to interpret the clues—air pollution, for instance, is partially available to sight in smog and to the lungs in asthma; and browning gardens after petrochemical plant flaring is an indication of toxic soils and air. Stephen Meyer (2006) divides the changing biodiversity of the globe into three categories: so-called weedy species comfortable living with humans (cockroaches, coyotes, raccoons, and other "plants and animals evolved to occupy high disturbance areas"); relic or boutique species that we allow to live in managed enclaves (such as grizzly bears and elephants) but "will never have serious ecological roles again"; and ghost species that seem to be around but have passed the point of ecological collapse.

Petryna's examples are somewhat more hopeful, focused on efforts to model and respond in the meantime, the now and near future. We are, she says, already breathing air with 400 parts per million (ppm) of carbon dioxide (CO_2), above the safe level of 350 ppm, though there's a way to go for catastrophic effects. A salesman for monitors tell her that at 1,500 ppm one begins to see the effects on the performance of schoolchildren, and at 5,000 ppm workers experience narcosis and metabolic stress. Still, Petryna points out, "occupational specialists, deep-sea divers, submarine engineers, and even anesthesiologists have long known the incremental risks of atmospherically compromised settings." And for what it is worth, only a third of all CO_2-offsetting reservoirs are saturated. What draws Petryna's attention, and should draw ours, are the efforts of firefighters such as Bill Armstrong to understand the physics of new phenomena of plasma-like fires that are unlike the worst natural firestorms of the past (excluding the fire-bombing of cities in World War II), of time-lapse photographers such as James Balog to capture the kinetics of rapidly melting glaciers, of lake ecologists such as John Magnuson and Stephen Carpenter to show that lakes suffering hypoxia (oxygen depletion) due to fertilizer runoff and industrial chemical dumping do not return over time to earlier equilibria for supporting life merely when the sources of pollution are cut off. Instead they go through phase transitions to new states, perhaps modeled best by the mathematics of chaos theory.

These new realities include more nuclear irradiated environments (Hanford, Oregon; Chernobyl, Ukraine; southern Belarus; and parts of Fukushima, Japan) and toxic landscapes full of hormone disrupters (from shale oil and gas fracking). Too often in the past such realities have been denied, preventing the kind of learning that we now will depend on. Of particular interest to Petryna is the work of Steven Pacala and Robert Socolow in modeling the time we have left and the costs associated with putting off remediation. They provide schematic timetables of the costs and consequences of inaction. As time goes by, shifting ratios of costlier strategies (called in the field "wedge stabilization") will be required.

The effort and logic here, as Petryna explains, is one of modeling horizons and tipping points, after which different combinations of resources and remediations will be required. Horizons, such as self-coordinated, balance-seeking equilibria of the earth (also called Gaia models), are metastable objects, moving, receding, characterized by recursive modeling, and pushing current understandings beyond their limits, or seeing, as one says colloquially, "over the horizon." Models of temporary plateaus of semistabilized biochemicophysical interactions may allow for presumptively time-sensitive, but psychosocially calming, ethical mobilization and time for politics, persuasion, and discovering new options in material sciences, nanotechnology, undersea living, off-planet colonies, and other unexplored milieus.

Horizons, Petryna says, constitute what Magnuson calls "meso-spaces of experimental time," and their modelers are new kinds of scientists, experimentalists, and even, she suggests what Magnuson calls "seers." Horizons are zen objects and exercises of deep consequence. Discussing the distant future, Petryna cites James Hansen, who "published a study on the atmospheric space of Venus, 97 percent of which is CO_2. Through a careful analysis of the composition of its surrounding molecules and dust, Hansen found that Venus may be the ancient relic of a planet that looked like Earth billions of years ago." Thus, Venus could be one of the futures for the earth. In the meantime, Petryna cites Svante Arrhenius among those who would rather think about shorter timeframes, such as the scenario of global warming that would make the Arctic available for agriculture (as well as oil drilling). Horizons are not singular, and they involve choices and actions as well as multiple scenarios and modeling efforts, requiring us to bring our best scientific instruments and minds to bear on problems that at best have solutions in the future.

Unfinished Exercises and Lifelines

From pressures and anxieties on all sides, anthropological exercises incrementally trace and illuminate new category lines ("radicals" in Chinese calligraphy), cartographic lines across multiple milieus, and lines of flight tracing desire and multiplicities of imagined worlds, utopias in the now that are seen otherwise and made newly possible with a push here, a shove there. In this sense, anthropologists are like artists: repetitive motions of drawing put one into meditative zones, emerging again and again for an analytic and evaluative gaze; whole-body rhythms (of sculpting, printmaking, or painting) move resistant stone, wood, and metal into new shapes. So, too, the anthropologist attempts to access and draw out the forces and turbulences within third spaces beyond dualistic antagonisms and simplistic causal linear arguments.[3] The anthropologist repairs and compares, always using more than two cases, more than two dimensions, and more than two axes of comparison and contrast—shifting, adjusting, creating redesigns, new configurations, and new insights from ethnographic details, emic categories, tropes, and genres.

When politics freezes into black-and-white and is locked in place, it is often helpful to have some artwork[4] or anthropological ethnography to break the frame, reshuffle the pieces, and remind us that there is more going on; there are more ways to look at things; and from a certain (zen) point of view, the human comedy is as absurd as it is beautiful and inspired. If one can get on into the right swing and find the right point of leverage, the pendulum can move just a bit; the *punctum*, or flash of insight, can allow us to see the world otherwise, and how little pieces of it can be reworked in the here and now. The gift of anthropology is a way (Chinese *dao*, as in zen exercises) of getting to know people in situ rather than in a planning document or a statistical table. It is a way of generating other planning documents, other statistical tables. Getting to know people in situ can change the tone, the structure of feeling, and the understanding. In all the discussions about climate warming, capitalism's not having an outside, and the like, a consensus seems to be emerging that all we can really do is try to live on—*su-vive*, to use a Derridian term. That means we must try to get the ethnographic sensorium, as Biehl and Locke put it in the introduction, to function as a way finder. Pebbles and labyrinths of human interactions (and subjectivities that are raucous terrae incognitae—raucous, as the unconscious and subjectivities are often zones of conflict and turmoil) cannot be swept out of the way, but they can be pieced together into new theories (ways of seeing), open to new relations (camaraderies and trajectories), mobilizing cartographies for social reengagements, and deploying toolboxes of varied swerves or tropes across time and space. In that work, the essays in this volume are exemplary: they are intensive points of beginning and so also unfinished, engaging equally unfinished lives and social forms of life.

EPILOGUE. THIRD SPACES AND ETHNOGRAPHY IN THE ANTHROPOCENE

KEYWORDS

Time: *taking time, time in between, in the meantime, time of anthropology from a pragmatic point of view, time of experimentation, time of life, decay and regrowth, times out of joint;* Nachträglichkeit; *temporalities; long arcs of socio-bio-techno-cultural change.*

New geographies: *of science, of art worlds, new diasporas; new connectivities of nervous systems, pipes, wires, rifles, vines and liannas; geoportraits of dis-eases of movementalities in sky, water, earth, plants, anima, mankind, fire, wandering earth, and death's end.*

Aesthetics, epistemologies, structures of feeling: *laughter and playfulness;* yūgen *or* wabi-sabi *(transience, beauty in decay and budding); engaging psychological and social disruption; addictive drive of capital and psychic investments; safety as a social relationship;* zikr, *trance, and rhythm;* sengsara, *strength, and bravery; filmic judgment; juxtaposing ethnographic, literary, and filmic affordances; forms of debate and discussion (warang tables,* Tischgesellschaft*).*

Hard science fiction and ethnographic ground-truthing: *science fiction as intertexts creating paranoid plausible futures by overconnecting the dots for ethical debates and course corrections; scientific literacies, citizen science, "come think with us"; influencing machines.*

Complexity theory *and complexity beyond ken of individuals:* artificial intelligence *(AI) and expert systems; biotechnologies and* directed evolution; *search for Lagrangian points of stability; temporary ethical plateaus; flat worlds, 2-D, 3-D and 4-D worlds.*

Dis-ease and disease: *endocrine disruptors, failures of erotic desire, occupational diseases, pervasive landscapes of toxicities in late industrialism.*

Unsocial sociabilities: *sequestered knowledge and legal standards of proof; compounded disasters; secrecy, power, and criminality; scandal of the state; public policy, civil society, and precarity.*

***L'homme totale* and *su-vive*:** *(living on) under new conditions and differently constituted modes of communication.*

> Safety is more than laboratory tests; safety is also a social relationship. It can only exist insofar as people trust one another that the products they are eating are indeed safe. —NICHOLAS I. STERNSDORFF-CISTERNA, *Food Safety after Fukushima*.

> *L'homme totale* (the fully human person) dwells in a lived space of the imagination, sustained and made accessible by the arts, literature, and human creativity. —HENRI LEFEVRE, *The Production of Space*.

Looking forward, can ethnography, with its pragmatic workings *in the meantime* creatively forge and temper the variety of writing, media, psychological, and aesthetic tactics appropriate to emergent forms of life that are difficult to fully foresee, despite confident predictions and cautionary jeremiads? It seems increasingly commonsensical that there are variable and differential directions and speeds of social-historical time, as well as increasingly legible ecological and immunological entanglements, and that these differentials, potentials, and interactions create the third spaces for ethnography between the Holocene, the Anthropocene, and perhaps a coming Aquacene and living on other planets or space platforms—spaces for which we are already building test beds.

These contemporary commonsense recognitions continue a concern with (perhaps plural) anthropologies emergent out from the chrysalis of the twentieth century. This is no time for claims of the death of anthropology, culture, or social experimentation, as some have argued, or as pure instrumentalization of life would demand. Ethnographic time, not unlike scientific time, is both urgent and detached, consequential and immaterial. As the prophet Zoroaster once put it in his *gathas* (songs, inspirations), in the long run "good" will defeat "evil" (at least as judged retrospectively by endings, in cosmological timings and geospatial and solar system spacings, whatever good and evil might ultimately mean, or beyond good and evil), but *in the meantime*, it is the struggles in the time of humankind that are the ethical, moral, and psychological spaces of our judgments and actions (Fischer 2004).[1] Literature, film, and arts can provide ethnographic registers as well as being themselves material-cultural forms that not only have their own circulatory channels, publics or social audiences, political economies, and class or status positions but can also affect how we feel, think, and act to make futures come about. I read them in juxtaposition with ethnographies written by anthropologists, to explore the anticipations and imaginaries of possible, realistic futures, tempered by the ethnographies of the here and now, looking ahead.

Times, New Geographies, and Adjustable Plans

No doubt, as will become clear in a few decades, we live in another time warp, sketched as well as anywhere in Liu Cixin's *Death's End*, the third volume of his science fiction epic *In Remembrance of Earth's Past*, which is wildly popular in China and was recently translated into English. The first volume, *The Three Body Problem*, won the Hugo Award in 2015. The second, *The Dark Forest*, and the spin-off stories in *The Wandering Earth*, together with *The Three Body Problem* are retrospectively placed by *Death's End* in a long arc of socio-bio-technological and cultural changes that expand upon many of the challenges of today's Anthropocene. Indeed, science fiction stories from Asia merge in and out of our contemporary dreamings, nightmares, and experiential emotions, along with current industrial and nuclear age disasters and toxicities. Perhaps by the times extrapolated *In Remembrance of Earth's Past*, we will have understood what it takes to live again in the oceans and in space, and to find biological repair mechanisms for what has been destroyed. Certainly, at the very least, the *time in between, the time of anthropology*, will be one of constant experimentation.[2] This is the space for ethnography, a third space of the "reality principles" and "anthropology from a pragmatic point of view," between the fantasies of nostalgia and apocalypse. Ethnographically, we live in *anticipation* of future potentials as much as we do in memory and the traces and bindings of legacies past.

I sound again the tonalities of the "Prologue," but this time incorporating the responses to the Anthropocene that come out of Asian *cultural critiques* responding to our common, if sharply contested, planetary worlds.[3] We live at a time in 2018 of revolts against financialization by working classes around the world,[4] most recently: Brexit, the withdrawal of the United Kingdom from the European Union, and the United States' election, with a minority of votes,[5] of Donald Trump articulated hypocritically as anger at international free trade agreements that destroy old economy communities, their ways of raising families, and predictable futures, while at the same time protecting consolidation of wealth and resisting fair redistribution. It is a time of massive population migrations (fleeing wars, economic desperation, rising sea levels, shifting climatic regimes), and destruction of democratic self-governance by big data surveillance and marketization parading as "individual choice" rather than as building public goods, addressing social justice, or balancing innovation with repair.

I want to touch upon a set of these Anthropocene challenges, as seen from my ethnographic fieldwork in Asia over the past decade, from a perch in Singapore with forays elsewhere. I began that research first by looking across the Muslim world for successes in technoscientific research (in Bandung and Jakarta; in Dubai and Abu Dhabi; in Tehran, Zanjan, Istanbul, and Trabzon [Fischer 2004, 95–113]), building upon earlier work in India (Ahmedabad, Mumbai, Pune, Bangalore, Hyderabad, and New Delhi), then turning to Singapore's incredible can-do optimism (contrasting with the pessimism regnant in Europe and the United States) in building new technoscientific research facilities (Biopolis, Fusionopolis, Mediaopolis [Fischer 2013, 2017). These Singapore initiatives were supported by transforming teaching universities into powerful research universities (National University of Singapore, Nanyang Technical University, Singapore Management University, Singapore University of Technology and Design), and by the role of the creative arts as modes of nation building, branding, transnational and cosmopolitan positioning, cultural diplomacy, and cultural critique.

So how might we think about the Anthropocene *in the meantime, in our visceral nervous systems and mindful consciousness, in inner and outer space* and *in different modes of social organization*? *In time*: in taking our time, and projecting in time to the 2030s, when we are supposed to have manned missions to Mars, and further on into next century. *In body and mind*: how might we anticipate the changes in our nervous systems, our ecologies, our microbiomes, our companion species as we retreat from the coasts inland, expand into the sea, and venture into space, growing beyond our current digital data "exhausts" (Jarzombek 2016). *In space*: we know astronauts lose bone and muscle mass, and develop eye problems. Tibetan medicine is said (by its Buratya promoters and practitioners) to restore Russian cosmonauts' health upon their return to earth at a sanatorium-hospital in Buratya (Chudakova 2013). But can that sort of therapy work also in space itself? How will the body adapt and perhaps change on long space flights? Oh, the Russians—a culture of mystics invested in material life beyond death, in storing ancestors in space, in regenerative medicine, and in mystical number theory (Graham and Kantor 2009). But we, Americans, too have these aspirations and imaginaries.

Freeman Dyson, in "The Green Universe: A Vision," a review of books on current space programs (public, private, and public-private) argues that these are unexciting, mere engineering projects. The exciting issues are ones of biology, of "knowing what to do when you have got there . . . to find ways to survive and build communities in space, to adapt the structures of living creatures . . . so they can take root in strange environments" (Dyson 2016, 6). Biospheres 1 and 2 were experiments toward this, as are more recent NASA and private company explorations of growing food on Martian soil.[6] Dyson invokes the work of Konstantin Tsiolkovsky, long inspirational to Russians, Germans, Americans, and, no doubt, directly or indirectly, Chinese science fiction writers such as Liu Cixin. Dyson speculates, "Sometime in the next few hundred years, biotechnology will have advanced to the point where we can design and breed entire ecologies . . . [a] Noah's Ark culture . . . about the size and weight of an ostrich egg, containing living seeds with the genetic instructions for growing millions of species . . . [including] warm-blooded [and viviparous] plants" (6). Has he been reading Liu Cixin? He goes on to say, "For life, surface area is more important than mass" (6). For Liu Cixin, one of the frontiers is four-dimensional worlds where all interiors are as visible as are surfaces in three-dimensional ones, and where flat, two-dimensional forms can destroy three-dimensional ones. Liu Cixin is picking up, of course, on a long line of mathematical and scientific speculation, from Edwin A. Abbott's *Flatland* (1884) and Einstein's relativity on, but also perhaps from video games, where white flat planes can target and obscure or wipe away three-dimensional worlds, or destroy what you have been typing in Microsoft Word. Indeed, the "dark forest theory" is intended by Liu as a metaphor for the cutthroat competition among Chinese web companies.

Dyson's ideas of transporting seeds for whole ecologies in a mass no more than that of an ostrich egg, and of medical research as the key driver for the mastery of genetic design for life beyond earth, takes the form in Liu Cixin's space opera of hibernation and a cryopreserved brain that can be reconstituted, reanimated, and contains the instructions (in each of its cells) for the reconstruction of its body. *In the meantime*, Liu Cixin also contends with transformations in commonsense, social structure, and pragmatics. These transformations work themselves out both in conflicting communities of practice in the planning for the future, and as humans begin to travel for long periods in isolated spaceships, some in hibernation while others remain alert against attack. Not just biology but also society and psychology are open to redesign. As one of my erstwhile favorite nontriumphalist science fiction writers, Barry Malzman, humorously cautions in *The Remaking of Sigmund Freud* (1985), each time a psychological crisis in space travel arose, Freud would be reawakened always to provide advice that failed to quite meet the challenge.

Ethnographic counterparts are detailed in Gökce Günel's *Spaceship in the Desert: Energy, Climate Change, and Green Business in Abu Dhabi* (2017), an account of the MIT-associated, alternative-energy-focused Masdar Institute and Masdar City as an ecocity in Abu Dhabi, and Lisa Messeri's *Placing Outer Space: An Earthly Ethnography of Other Worlds* (2016). The latter details how space scientists create models on earth and imagine their explorations of Mars and exoplanets. The former details how large-scale utopian engineering projects on earth get downsized, reformulated, and pragmatically changed as they encounter the realities of implementation: precisely *in the meantime*.

Liu Cixin's version of Malzman's cautioning is the "Dark Forest" problem: "Each civilization is like a hunter with a gun in a dark forest: When I see another hunter, I have no choice but to shoot him dead. This is a dark and terrible situation, a worst case scenario" (3, 105). Humans and Trisolarans[7] attempt to negotiate the dark forest dilemma across their quite differently constituted modes of communication, all the while aware that merely broadcasting their locations (think: cell phones and GPS today) opens them to attack from yet other civilizations (think: marketers' invasions of one's privacy, national security hacking by states and their private contractors, or indeed Internet supercharged warfare itself[8]). The dark forest problem is also a kind of hysteria of nyctohylophobia (fear at night of the darkness in forests).

So, in addition to challenges *in time*, and *in body and mind*, there are also the challenges *in communis*: how might we redesign our societies and cultures to transition to futures that will not look like the past? What is the anthropology to come?

The classic Greek and Islamic metaphors of wisdom—the ring, octagon, or eight propositions for legitimate governance and equitable sociopolitical feedback—or the Zoroastrian *amshaspands* (seven aspects of divinity in the world encompassed in Ahura Mazda, renewed periodically by ritual ecological-cosmic action) continue to apply into the future.[9] In the Zoroastrian Yasna

TABLE EPI.1. Reading Ethnographies, Literature, Films, and Painting Together

Actors Relations	Anticipations, Recurrences, Affects	a) Literature, Film, Arts b) Ethnographies, Realities
adjustable plans	returning to the sea changing taboos and sensibilities	(a) Kobo Abe, *Inter Ice Age 4* (b) Olson, *American Extreme*; Günel, *Spaceship*; Halperin and Günel, "Demoing unto Death"; PC Lui
structures of feeling *ee ja nai ka*	disasters near-death experiences; despair and hope coexist laughter (*asobi, oko-e*)	(a) T. Murakami, *Takashi Murakami*; Azhari; Sinha, *Animal's People* (b) Smith, "War, Medicine"; Good and Good, "Psychosocial Needs Assessment"; Grayman, "Humanitarian Encounters"; K. Fortun, *Advocacy after Bhopal*
aesthetic, ethical, and moral stances	biogenic interludes ephemeral time *wabi-sabi* vs. protocols	(a) Ishiguro, *Biogenesis* (b) Sanal, *New Organs*; B. Good, *Medicine*
intergenerational transmission; precarity (*muen shakai*)	fear of radiation "use it as a torch"	(a) paper theater (*kamishibai*); Trimpop film *Furusatu*, 2016; Fukushima Music Project, 2011 (b) Manabe, *Revolution*; Sternsdorff-Cisterna, "Food Safety"; Sayre, "Preparing"; Petryna, *Life Exposed*; Allison, *Precarious Japan*; George, *Minamata*; Clancey, *Earthquake Nation*

(the "high liturgy" ritual) and the Bundahishn (commentary on the creation cosmology), for instance, the order of amshaspand creation was sky, water, earth, plant, animal, mankind, fire (Fischer 2004).

I briefly reflect on anthropologies to come in roughly that order, using Asian science fiction novels and Asian documentary-ethnographic filmmaking as prompts, *putting them in dialogue with their ethnographic counterparts*: (1) *sky* or atmospheric-ocean cycles (*aquan* biologies of our ancient biological origins and future potential return); (2) *water*: tsunamis, earthquakes, floods, and near-death experiences; (3) *earth*: biogenesis and short lifetimes; (4) *plants*: photosynthesis, fear of radiation, nuclear meltdown, the dying sun; (5) *anima-human* reproduction endangered by displacements of populations by megadams (e.g., Three Gorges Dam) leading to sexual

Actors Relations	Anticipations, Recurrences, Affects	a) Literature, Film, Arts b) Ethnographies, Realities
hormonal disruption and sexual impotence	floods and displacement	(a) Yun-Fei Ji's mural "Three Gorges Dam Migration"; films *Wushan Rain Clouds* by Zhang Ming, 1996; *Still Life* by Jia Zhangke, 2006; (b) Zhang, *Impotence Epidemic*; Wylie, *Hacktivism*
viruses, pandemics	living across species boundaries Internet social media	(a) Hu Fayun, *This World*; Tsai films *Neon Gods*, 1992, and *Dark Circles*, 2006 (b) Fearnley, "Influenza Epicenter"; Mason, *Infectious Change*
influencing machines and biologies	electromagnetic environmental	(a) Wiharso, *Trilogy* disturbances; (b) Fischer, "Work of Epic Art"; Good and Good, "Indonesia Sakit" entanglements, connectivities, *warang* sociability
high-tech politics	preparing for space flights	(a) Liu Cixin, *Remembrance*; *Wandering Earth* field notes, games, chronologies (b) Messeri, *Placing Outer Space*; Collins, *Gravity's Shadow*; *Gravity's Ghost*; *Gravity's Kiss*

impotence, and by toxicities from industrial pollution leading to respiratory illnesses, hormonal imbalances, and cancers; (6) *mankind*'s respiration threatened by pandemics of SARS and avian influenza that with unintended human facilitation cross species barriers and ecological niches (industrial husbandry, farming wild fowl, modern transportation); (7) *fire* of the earth (volcanoes, earthquakes) and people's indigestion from commodity flows (geoportraits of diseases of "movementality"); and (8) wandering earth and death's end (indeterminacies and risks of space and time technologies).

The point is, like Freeman Dyson's speculations, to enliven ethnography with anticipations, yet, like Günel and other ethnographers, to temper anticipations with ethnography, and by tempering (as in steel) strengthen them both.

Returning to the Sea: Anticipations and Adjustable Plans

> At fifteen thousand feet the thick mud of the lifeless sea floor . . . heaved up. Instantly dispersing, it transformed itself into a dark, upward-welling cloud . . . The spume dilated, and the magma, shining darkly, vanished. . . . the passengers and crew felt merely a brief moment of disorientation. . . . On the bridge the second mate had been alarmed by the faint but sudden change of color that had occurred in the sea and by a school of dolphins leaping in confusion, but he had not considered these especially worth-while noting in the log. . . .
>
> By then the invisible pulsation of the sea had already become a great tidal wave sweeping landward through the water at the incredible speed of 480 miles an hour. —KOBO ABE, *Inter Ice Age 4*, "Prelude"

Today this sounds like a possible description of the March 11, 2011 ("3/11") Great East Japan (or Tohoku) Earthquake (9.0 on the Richter scale) that caused a massive tsunami, and the catastrophic level-seven meltdowns of the Fukushima Daiichi nuclear power plant reactors (seven is the same International Atomic Energy Agency rating as Chernobyl's meltdown), leaving behind not just deaths and injuries but contaminated landscapes, breakdown in trust of government, and many self-help community responses in trying to measure food safety, air quality, and ground contamination. It is, for the moment, our current most powerful icon of environmental and planetary ruin. Increasing ocean temperatures correlate with increasing intensities of storms. Aftershocks and tsunamis continue five years after the Great Tohoku Earthquake.

But the passage was written in 1956.

Among the fascinations of this beautifully constructed novel is that it reads today quite differently from when it was produced. At the time of its production, when I first read it as a teenager, it was an allegory about the dangers of communism, technocracy (rule by experts), and losing our humanity through technology (not unlike Orwell's *1984* [1949] and *Animal Farm* [1945], and Huxley's *Brave New World* [1932]). But today, in an age of cloning, genetic engineering, artificial intelligence, marine biology, and possibilities of directed evolution, it reads quite differently. It charts one of several possible routes of escape from global warming, sea rise, and pollution of the land, and from the Anthropocene into an emergent new "Aquacene." Scenarios and blueprints for such solutions are being pursued today by NASA and Singapore. NASA, as Valerie Olson ethnographically describes (2010, 2017), is using the sea as a test bed for human survival in extreme environments. Singapore is testing and prototyping building from the seabed upward to expand its living spaces (P. C. Lui, interview 2016[10]).

Kobo Abe begins presciently with a section called "Blueprint" that addresses the ethics of experimentation and the potential of directed evolution. The feedback or Möbius strip of experimentation on others might turn out to be fatal experimentation on the self and on the human species, but it might equally become simply a natural progression in which present-day taboos evolve and disappear along with techniques of escape from the problems of the Anthropocene by returning life to the sea from which it came. This could involve genetically engineering babies to have gills, to become acquatic, or "*acquans.*" Evolution of life on earth, Abe reminds us, has gone through four ice ages and three inter-ice ages. He has a character say, "Man subjugated nature, improved it, and now evolution has gone from accident to deliberate, man reconstructs himself, returns to the sea which is his home not as slave but as master" (Abe 1956, 211). There will come a time, he continues, "when the majority of mothers have had at least one aquan child. When the prejudice against aquans fades, when the fear that distorts reality has gone. By that time the terror of flooding will have become a reality, and people will have to choose whether to wage war in a scramble for land or to accept acquans as bearers of the future" (211).

Indeed, it is fascinating that of the two major technologies speculated about in this 1955 text (artificial intelligence and directed evolution), the speculations about machine-learning computers that can learn fast enough to make complex predictions about the future seem primitive, while the speculations about directed molecular biological evolution seem more up to date. The Russians in the novel claim that their Moscow computers, with their input-out-put models of the economy, clearly predict the future of society and the defeat of capitalism. In reality, this was the era in the United States of Wassily Leontief's input-output matrix analysis for national economic accounting (for whom, at Harvard, my mother worked as a new immigrant) in competition with Soviet "material balances" planning. In the novel, US scientists point out the propagandistic nature of the Russian claims and warn Japanese computer scientists to keep politics out of their programming, something the programmers quickly realize is impossible: "If, for example, we attempted to predict the extent of arable land, then that involved the problem of the specialization of the farming class. If we tried to investigate the distribution of completely paved roads some years from now, then we became entangled in the national budget. . . . I was thoroughly disgusted. It was like a spider's web: The more we tried to avoid politics, the more we became entangled in them."

Puzzles abound in the novel, most centrally about why the sea levels are rising much faster than the rate of melting ice. Various hypotheses are proposed about the role of increasingly active subterranean and underocean volcanoes. In the novel, rates of change are measured through the collaborations of the International Geodetic Year; the IGY, or International Geophysical Year, 1957–58, which included geodesy, was gearing up at the time the novel was being published (I. Fischer 1995). In response, in the novel, many countries packed up their cities and factories and took them to higher plateaus, an eventuality contemplated by the genomics search by BGI in Shenzhen, China, into the genetic mutations that allow Tibetans to live at high altitudes, and for ways in the future to give lowlanders equal physiological facility. "It's disgraceful," the narrator says (echoed by many Japanese nuclear critics in 2011), "but the government in Japan has simply disregarded the whole matter and let things run their course, perhaps because there are no plateau regions here" (Abe, 190).

Here the novel takes a fascinating turn into the secret or classified world. The rapidity of climate change and of sea level rise panics member countries into disbanding the IGY. The fear is that if the speculations about the subterranean volcanoes' connection to rapid sea rise are made public, social order and discipline will break down (Abe, 190–92). Instead, with the help of financiers, a Society for the Development of Submarine Cultures is secretly established (192). The secret plan is to genetically engineer acquatic humans to live under the sea and to build cities there.

Meanwhile, Professor Katsumi, inventor of a self-programming (or machine-learning) artificial intelligence (AI), and his assistant Tanamogi design what they think of as a "proof of principle" limited test of the program's predictive abilities. To simplify, as a pilot or proof of concept, they want to try to predict only the future of a single private individual's destiny (foreshadowing today's efforts to predict life course outcomes from *AI* brain simulations or genetics in early childhood).[11] They chose a subject from the street. They follow him, collecting data. But the next day's paper announces the man's murder. To solve the case and forestall suspicion that they were involved, Katsumi downloads the contents of the man's brain and questions it. He learns the man's mistress had sold her aborted fetus for seven thousand yen. Katsumi then discovers that his own wife has had a forced abortion and received seven thousand yen. Katsumi suspects a criminal network. His assistant, Tanamogi, volunteers the name of an organization experimenting with the extra-utero development of fetuses, and arranges for Katsumi to visit their lab. It is the Society for the Exploitation of the Sea Floor. Gradually Katsumi learns of vast government secret planning to create an underwater nation, complete with genetically altered, water-oxygenating humans and animals, bred in anticipation of the predicted destruction of Japan by a tidal wave.

The book is structured throughout by Katsumi's psychodrama of trying to think rationally, keeping his emotions in check, while receiving phone calls from an AI version of himself, programmed by his assistant Tanamogi. Katsumi finds it increasingly difficult to explain the way in which the phone calls know his every thought strategy. It's somewhat like the old psychotherapeutic program Eliza that drove its MIT creator, Joseph Weizenbaum, to leave the field of artificial intelligence, only a few years (1964–66) after Abe's story. Eliza worked by mirroring patients' questions, parasitically engaging the patients' projections. The uncanny ability to so easily manipulate human beings was intolerable to Weizenbaum.

Science fiction texts can serve as forms of intertexts—connecting the dots of implications; creating paranoid plausible futures by overconnecting the dots—for real-world technological developments and for ethical debates both amid anticipations of climate change, and amid the secrecy of government research (Defense Advanced Research Agency or DARPA and its Russian, Chinese, and other nations' and corporations' equivalents), the cyberattacks against homeland security, and the "data-driven" gambles of financial speculation. All of these are complex worlds, beyond the control of purely individual choices, for which contemporary complexity theory is at best an abstract mode of anticipation.

The postscript of Abe's novel repeats the prelude, describing a tidal wave approaching Japan, now understood as a multilevel one, involving physical, social, moral, and cultural interactions. It describes, before the fact, the Great East Japan Earthquake that hit the Fukushima Daiichi nuclear plants in 2011, causing multiple meltdowns in three of the nuclear power reactors on the coast, and causing dismay across the globe. Germany shut down its nuclear production, and Japan struggled with whether or not to reopen its many nuclear power plants after attempting to see what it would be like to live without them. Nuclear power plants continue to be built. There are plans to construct floating nuclear power plants offshore that move up and down with the tides and waves—even with tsunami-force waves. In one sense, as an assistant professor of nuclear engineering at MIT points out, any nuclear-powered ship or submarine is already such a plant. The only new element is tethering it to an onshore delivery system. The Russians are in the forefront of developing such technologies for commercial sale.

Ee ja nai ka ("It's Alright, Who Cares"): Structures of Feeling

Walking into Takashi Murakami's mural of *The 500 Arhats*, which is one hundred meters long and three meters tall, and was displayed in Abu Dhabi along four walls of a large room, and in Tokyo as two facing walls, is a stunning and overwhelming experience, much like feeling the enormous tsunami wave of 2011 cresting over one (Murakami 2015).[12] People are miniaturized standing against the walls. The colors and shapes on one side are flaming nuclear red, and on the other side ocean froth-like white. The images of the arhats (bodhisattvas, those who have achieved enlightenment but stayed in the world to teach and act as models for people) are exuberantly cartoonish and gruesome in a happy manga sort of way. Indeed, as critic Geny Sokyu describes it, Murakami has managed to paint the electrifying moment when all of the arhats manifest at once (Sokyu, 64). Near-death experiences of earthquakes, fire, and famine were the backdrop to an older masterpiece on the theme of *the 500 arhats* by Kanō Kazunobu in the Edo period, and, as in the studio system of the Edo period, Murakami gathered some two hundred arts students to help produce this huge artwork. He compares the work of composition as a melding together of the idiosyncratic creativity of the many minds that worked on it. As one's eyes adjust to what some have called Murakami's *Guernica*, capturing the power of the Great Eastern Japan Earthquake, tsunami, and nuclear meltdown of March 2011 (called simply "3/11"), so as to pass the enormity on to future generations, one also sees hundreds of little arhat figures: meditating, doing kung fu, even surfing both on the ocean waves and on puffs of incense smoke. While the sixteen earliest arhats dominate the mural in their size, many lesser arhats stand along the edges, ride upon incense smoke, and traverse the clouds and waves.

Nothing of the compound disasters of 3/11 is directly depicted, but one feels the rumbling, enormous waves, nuclear fire, torn trust in government, and the puny-seeming but hopefully powerful and transformative efforts of civic groups to pick up the pieces and live on. In my first impressions, I couldn't help but see in the enormous diving whale a cresting wave, with many swirls of pop art waves in its wake. Sitting inside the open jaws of the whale, an arhat calmly pours a jar of water. Nearby a bug-eyed arhat grasps a wave with both hands. This round bug-eyed circle is a fusion of a "superflat" pop figure of Japan's (and Murakami's) recent "cute" aesthetic, together

FIG. EPI.1. Takashi Murakami, *The 500 Arhats*, 2015. Tsunami-dragon from the East, with white whale and little bug-eyed round circle of an arhat holding on for dear life.

with Umibozu, the "sea monk" monster. One might also think of the figure of Godzilla, a mutant dinosaur, in Ishiro Honda's 1954 film. Godzilla came out from the sea after the tuna fishing ship *Lucky Dragon 5* (Daigo Fukuryu Maru) was irradiated by the US Castle Bravo test of a dry-fuel thermonuclear hudrogen bomb, detonated over Bikini island in the Pacific, at dawn on March 1, 1954.

In Rikuzentakata city, Iwate prefecture, there is a fascinating alternative imagery of the 500 arhats to that of Murakami, done by citizens and volunteers. They chisel stones found in the area with faces to memorialize the victims of the compound disasters.[13]

Murakami's effect is partly to fuse old devotional art forms into new pop media, and partly to transform into new idioms the old aesthetic that, as art critic Sokyu puts it, "Karmic assistance is better than direct support; suggestion is better than instruction; and that true salvation only comes once we, like the arhats, gain full awareness of the make-believe nature of our narratives, yet are able to handle real difficulties at play. The 500 Arhats gaze at us, temporarily sharing our stories in passing, seeing it all as just play" (Sokyu 2015: 65).

FIG. EPI.2. Takashi Murakami, *The 500 Arhats*, 2016. Superflat bug-eyed arhat grasping the wave, with small arhats comically performing the mudras of not-to-worry, protection, and salvation.

Kazunobu is but one of the image sources, which range from medieval *nihonga* painting to comic magna such as Fujio Akatsuka's *The Genius Bakabon* (originating in 1967), whose father says *Ee ja nai ka* ("It's alright, who cares"), or also *kore de iino da* ("this is fine the way it is"). *Ee ja nai ka* is a *saying* that is repeated in the Fukushima Project, a rock music festival held in Fukushima City in response to the compound *sixfold* disaster (9.0 earthquake; 14-meter-high tsunami; level-7 nuclear meltdown and radiation dispersion; rumor crisis; breakdown of trust in government; and increased sense of crisis in economic precarity at many levels in society), as well as a chant from the annual Hungry Ghost Festival of Obon, and also from the time of troubles in the Meiji period in the aftermath of the 1855 Great Ansei (Edo) earthquake, and the time of the riots of 1865 during the effort to overthrow the Shogunate. The word "Bakabon" itself is a fusion of a term for the Buddha, *bagyabon*, and vagabond, a kind of holy fool, although in popular culture it is often taken as just idiocy. Other contemporary figures incorporated into the mural include Shigami (the deer god), taken from the *anime* film *Princess Mononoke*, with a single tree on her head, and the nebula from the Apple iMac desktop screen saver. There are also figures from older source materials. The white elephant vehicle of bodhisattva Samantabhadra and the white whale are a homage to the paired elephant and whale screens by Itō Jakuchū (1716–1800).[14] There are variants of mythological beasts, such as Bai Ze ("white swamp"), the multieyed, multihorned beast that manifests mainly during reigns of virtuous rulers.

The mural is divided into the four cardinal directions, signified by their traditional oversight deities: Blue Dragon, White Tiger, Vermillion Bird, and Black Tortoise (east, west, south, and north, respectively). Blue Dragon of the East is based on Soga Shōhaku's mid-eighteenth-century four-screen *Dragon in Clouds* (c. 1763), with large, round dragon eyes and sharp claws emerging eerily from a dark chiaroscuro background. Murakami, in a contemporary version of the aristocratic contests (*nippon e'awase*) of displaying paintings and debating their merits, along with art critic Tsuji Nobuo, turns it into a sharpened infrared-like image, with the Blue Dragon's owllike eyes headlight-bright and its scaled body curled around snaillike clouds. The Blue Dragon of the mural takes on brilliant blue anime features. The tsunami/dragon arrives from the east. It is in this Blue Dragon or East section that the huge diving white whale appears, and the little bug-eyed round circle of an arhat holds on to a wave for dear life, while a miniature Arab merchant ship bobs away on another wave. The source image for a swirling vortex of waves is from Soga Shōhaku's *Immortals Attacking a Whirlwind* (c. 1764). Rahula, the eleventh of the sixteen arhats, pulls open his abdomen to reveal the Buddha. Kalika, the seventh of the sixteen arhats, who can twirl and stretch his oversized eyebrows, holds a censer releasing fragrant swirls of incense on which other small arhats ride.

Buddhism comes from the west, the Western Paradise. Arhat imagery was modified as it traveled through China eastward to Japan. The White Tiger of the West presides over the largest number of arhats in the mural, two hundred and twenty of them. Baku, who devours nightmares, is magnificently painted in huge proportions, composed of a bear's body, elephant's trunk, rhinoceros' eyes, tigers' legs, and the tail of a cow. The fires of hell, in anime-style explosions, send out red flames, following behind an arhat scattering flowers. The "West" is the source of the ambiguity of nuclear power (the promise of utopian, Paradise-like, clean energy; it also signals the hellish destructive radiation from nuclear weapons and from nuclear power plant meltdowns). Angaja, the thirteenth of the sixteen arhats, holds a scroll

FIG. EPI.3. Takashi Murakami, *The 500 Arhats*, 2016. Nuclear fire from the West, with Baku (bear body, elephant trunk, rhinoceros eyes, tiger legs, and cow tail), who devours nightmares, and the White Tiger of the West. Photo courtesy of Lucy Birmingham.

unfurled with Murakami's version of Nagasawa Rosetsu's miniature painting of the five hundred arhats (1798), which Murakami painted for the Nippon e'awase or competitive sparring with Tsuji. Panthaka, the tenth arhat, holds an iron bowl with a wish-granting jewel and a book, his misaligned eyes keeping watch on the world. Bhadra, the sixth arhat, is blind, has the power to see all things, and is painted in the grotesque Chanyue style.

The Vermillion Bird of the South—taken from source images of phoenixes on early modern kimonos, from Osamu Tezuka's manga, and from the anime Phoenix series—oversees the arhats sitting on the water. One arhat, with water gushing from his head, is an image from Kanō Kazunobu's fifty-first of 100 scrolls depicting the five hundred arhats, as is a small arhat with hooves and a wild boar face. Mythological human-headed birds with long tails, called *kalavinka* (Sanskrit *kalavinka*; Japanese *karyobinga*) are shown singing the Buddhist scriptures. An arhat opens his face to reveal another sacred face beneath. Other familiar Buddhist characters include the arhat Nakuta, skilled in debating, who sits on a boulder with long moss growing on him (parodying the moss dots on boulders from the Kanō painting school); the arhat Cuapanthaka, so poor of memory he was almost expelled from his monastery but gained enlightenment after years of performing daily cleaning of the monastery; Ajita, the arhat often identified with Maitreya (the Buddha of the future), with small bats in the design of his cloak; and Kanakavatsa, depicted doing the mudra of immovable foundation (hands together pointing at the earth) while holding on to a chestnut *wood* staff of Paradise ("paradise" in Chinese is made up of the characters for "west" and "tree"). The activity of these arhats is parodied in the smaller arhat figures doing kung fu, surfing, and flying around the Apple iMac nebula screen saver.

Black Tortoise of the North is usually a fusion of turtle and snake, but here the two are separate, with the snake as a *shen* (dragon) who creates mirages, in this case a mirage of a sacred mountain with a treasure tower on top. The arhats in this section of the mural stand with folded hands, but the eye-catching figures are two large red and blue ogres. The ogres are based on Kanō Kazunobu's scroll *Six Realms of Hell*, and the iconography of Nio guardians, always in a pair, one open-mouthed, and one closed-mouthed, one voicing the first grapheme of Sanskrit Devanagri, "ah," in unleashed kinetic display of power, the other the last grapheme, "hom" (*om*), in ready but potential power. The mural here depicts the circle of beginning and end, birth and death, the wheel of life, and the *enso* (circle) paintings of zen masters. Those by Hakuin Ekaku and Sengai Gibon (among the six masters that Tsugi and Murakami used in their nippon e'awase) are done with a comic touch.

Arhats normally stay in the mountains practicing austerities, appearing only *after* fires, tsunamis, earthquakes, or other disasters *as a kind of rescue team, although*, says art critic Tsuji (Murakami 2015: 54) they *never seem to be trying all that hard*, and they *are funny* in their efforts. The first arhat, after all, is said to have heard the Buddha calling his disciples to gather while he was mending his clothes: he put his sewing needle into the mountain on which he was sitting, and rushed off, forgetting to cut the thread, dragging the mountain after him (an original *bakagon*?).

Tsugi Nobuo is the art critic, and author of *Lineage of Eccentrics* (1970), with whom Murakami engaged in an e'awase as a warm-up for the mural project. Tsugi would write an essay about an old painting, and Murakami would respond with one of his own paintings, reinterpreting the older painting, often shifting the sensibility of austerity and imperfection (*wabi-sabi*), toward one of playfulness (*asobi*) and ornamentation (*kazari*). There were twenty-one rounds of this e'awase published in the journal *Geijutsu Shincho*, four about sex, and four about religion (recently translated and published as *Nobuo Tsugi vs Takashi Murakami, Battle Royale!, Japanese Art History,* 2017). Tsuji would later comment on the mural, "The big difference between your 500 Arhats and all Arhat imagery before is this element of humor" (Murakami 2015: 59). Still, Tsugi recalls a unique lost set of paintings by Itō Jakuchū of which only a prewar catalogue still exists, in which Sakyamuni is flanked by sixteen arhats, and "if you look at their faces under magnification, it is full of the kind of intense laughter one cannot see in modern comical manga" (59). Indeed, in 2016, I bought a set of eighteen miniature wood arhats in the shop of a Chinese temple idol repairer in Singapore, of which a number seem to be laughing broadly, all expressing different broad affects and emotions.

Murakami notes, "I was not interested in making a sophisticated, highly advanced piece of art, but rather in taking a more primitive stance, and to portray in a stubbornly honest way the fact that *despair and hope exist side by side* in the world we live in" (Murakami 59n28, emphasis added).

What is of interest to my anthropological way of thinking is this *structure of feeling* modifying the historical *modalities for reflection,* reinventing them for our technoscientific age in which we have a heightened awareness of emergent ecological crises of our own making.

After the Indian Ocean or Aceh tsunami of 2004 and the cessation of vicious conflict in Aceh between GAM (Gerakan Aceh Merdeka), the Free Aceh Movement, and the Indonesian army, anthropologist Catherine Smith (2012) observed a *structure of feeling,* a different apocalyptic narrative between international humanitarians on the one hand, and that of the locals on the other. The locals saw no reason to move away from the coast (and their fishing livelihoods) or to engage in tsunami drills. God determines when you die. And for her fifty-three Acehnese women informants, Smith argues, *trauma is the inability to "accept destiny"* (179). Drawing on a short story by Acehnese writer Azhari, "The Nutmeg Woman" (2003), Smith highlights a narrative technique of attentiveness to unexpected openings and redirections for life, "leaving the individual both second guessing their own experience and astonished at the bitter ironies of the chaotic unfolding of history. It is precisely at this point of paradox that the plot switches to a new episode in history, a new set of circumstances, and a new conflict" (101).

Smith argues, following anthropologists James Siegel and Joshua Barker, that psychosocial words such as "trauma" have a contemporary Javanese history in the use of the term "shock therapy" by President Suharto, who in his autobiography boasted that the killings of "criminals" and display of corpses in the so-called Petrus (mysterious killings) events after 1983 was a form of shock therapy (Siegel 1998; Siegel and Barker 2008). Shock therapy here is *electro-shock, torture, and killings*, not Jeffrey Sach's economic shock therapy, and in Aceh, the term is associated with the military strategy from 1989–98 of displaying murdered and tortured corpses. In Aceh it fuelled resistance rather than, as in Java, subjection.

Sengsara, Smith writes, "is the emotion, the sadness and irony that one feels in narrating the past and anticipating the future from this point of ambiguity" (of never knowing what the future will bring). Seeing the tsunami as God's intervention to stop the conflict, the women dealt with anxiety by practicing *zikir* (reciting the ninety-nine names of God, or the Yasin sureh of the Qur'an), often going into trance while doing so. As one said, "*We don't know that we rock*, but when we *zikir* we rock from side to side and the *motion of our body* accompanies our heart," after which they feel strong (*kuat*), tranquil (*tenang*), and even euphoric. Of the humanitarian organizations' efforts to get them to move inland, to do tsunami drills, and the like, the ironic response was, "They were very thorough, the NGO people. They even taught us science.—God is great!" (Smith, 2012: 204).

These feelings of entanglement, of unexpected tests and opportunities *require bravery, strength, and steadfastness*, not passivity, although withdrawal into religiosity can be one response to events such as tsunamis (and perhaps radioactivity), especially for the old. The Singapore writer Jeremy Fernando suggests that there is, in fact, a family resemblance between the Javanese term for acceptance (*nrimo*) and the classical Greek *eudaimonia*, meaning fitting one's soul or self or emotions to the circumstances, so as to enhance future flourishing.[15]

Four Aesthetics

There are at least four aesthetics to which I want to draw attention. The first is what in Japan is called *yūgen* or wabi-sabi, an awareness of transience and decay and budding new beginnings, a sensibility of austerity and imperfection. The text I use for this in the next section is cancer biologist Tatsuaki Ishiguro's *Biogenesis*, a meditation also on species extinction. The second is a sense of laughter at the proximity of life and death, an engaged detachment, but not a turning away from the world, *asobi* (playfulness), drawing on a long lineage of comic art (*oko-e*), and illustrated in Takashi Murakami's mural described above. A third aesthetic is the engagement with deep psychological and social disruption, illustrated below with two films and two paintings about the Three Gorges Dam. A fourth, of course, which can be seen in city planning and architecture, is the excitement and addictive drive of capital investment in evermore fabulous forms and shapes that can both facilitate and erase human-scale activities, in Saigon, Shanghai, and Singapore.

While interested in all four of these, I am particularly fascinated by the play between laughter and disruption that seems emergent both in the art of Murakami in Japan and of Entang Wiharso in Indonesia (both also working in the United States and elsewhere), and would suggest that all four aesthetics provide a color palette or a set of musical chords for sensing and acting with the rhythms of the world, including disaster, toxicity, pandemics, and climate disruptions.

Biogenesis, Cancer, and the *Yugen* or Wabi-Sabi Aesthetic

Tatsuaki Ishiguro is a cancer biologist who did part of his training at the M. D. Anderson Cancer Hospital in Houston. His writing evokes scientific protocols and simultaneously *yūgen* aesthetics induced by confronting the brevity of life. *Yūgen* involves both *wabi* (transient and stark beauty) and *sabi* (the beauty of natural aging). It is a mindful approach to life evoked by the transience of buds and decay more than by the fullness or perfection of full blooms.

Scientific curiosity, and the reactions of the scientific communities—especially their bias against "amateurs," the asymmetry of recognition in prestigious science journals between West and East, and the bias of biomedical practitioners in both East and West against Eastern traditional medical traditions—drive the four short stories of *Biogenesis*. But they also provide an exploration of what I call "scientific literacies." Each story is about a biological organism in danger of extinction. Together they constitute a meditation on the human species. Each is written up as a mesmerizingly rational scientific report, drawing in the reader to puzzle out patterns, meanings, and explanations along with the researcher. No less than Nobel Laureate Kenzaburo Oe writes of the first story, or perhaps of all four, "A metaphor of perdition, on the level of all of humanity, is concretized as a small, imaginary animal via the mediating factor of incurable diseases that bring death to two doctors of medicine. In our nation, such excellent conceptions used to belong to Kobo Abe."

The four rare, endangered organisms are a winged mouse that glows, sheds tears, dies in pairs (birth and death united in the reproductive act; a metaphor for AIDS), and appears in waves of newborns, whose genetic, cellular, odd internal organs, and other features seem to predispose it to extinction even though it has long life span, thus a story of overpopulation and eventual extinction from evolutionary success; a woman revived from frostbite and coma, whose body temperature never rises to normal, and whose rare "idiopathic hypothermia" and unconventional biology extends her lifespan at the cost of nearly complete memory loss and need to hibernate for periods, thus a story of death-in-life, of longevity without memory or action; a rare plant found during World War II that feeds on human blood but gives off radiation, slowly killing the investigators, who, however, are so intrigued they cannot stop their investigations, and whose suggestion that the plant might be weaponized does not pan out, thus a story of unintended consequences of human intervention; and a sea squirt that adapts symbiotically with its cancer tumors and is said to have once been able to cure people but is mashed to extinction by a father desperately seeking a cancer cure for his daughter, thus a story of human vulnerability and imprudence.

The aesthetic, the rational-scientific protocols, and the scientific literacies provide for me ethnographic resonances for our contemporary world,[16] both for our expanding knowledge of interconnections in ecologies and in biomedical expertise without it "solving" questions of mortality, which thus require aesthetic, ethical, and moral stances toward the fragility of life (e.g., Sanal 2011; Good 1994).

The aesthetic is perhaps strikingly illustrated in Sulfikar Amir's ethnographic film, *Healing Fukushima* (2017), a film about the local doctors who had to learn quickly about radiation, attempt to care for their patients, deal with the shut down of their clinics in evacuated areas (and of their homes), negotiate relatively reassuring screening measurements against people's impossible-to-allay fear of future cancers, and deal with tremendous daily pressure to keep up a professional demeanor. Their underlying emotional stress is visible at poignant moments. The film illustrates the informal knowledge networks amongst themselves on which the doctors must rely in a world of uncertainty and potentially unreliable official pronouncements.

The references to radiation in Ishiguro's stories are given a deeper set of resonances in Morimoto's (2016) reminders that Japan itself had a pre-World War II interest in nuclear technology including nuclear weapons, and develops this as a "historiography of the distant nuclear," one that generates nuclear ghosts and a nuclear uncanny, fueled by the instabilities of what is not visible but is there, what might be there or not be there, and what one does not want to know because there is not much one can do about it and it only interferes with getting on with life, and finally the ghosts which one can call on to explain the inexplicable in daily life. Given the ban on images of nuclear damage under the American occupation, the uncanniness of what has been erased from history but is still around is not just something new, and the histories, as well as the desires, surrounding the pre-war cyclotrons and post war reactors lurk as both interesting and reminders, in Ishiguru's sense, of human vulnerability and imprudence.

Fear of Radiation: Use It as a Torch

"*Use it as a torch to give light to Japan in the dark*" comes from a story passed on by ethnographer Ryan Sayre (2013) in the aftermath of the Fukushima compound disasters. Many Japanese know the *kamishibai* (paper theater) story "The Burning Rice Village," which again, after eighty years, has become a feature of many natural disaster (earthquake, tsunami) preparation drills and pedagogies. Based partly on a true event, it is about the village leader, who, seeing a huge tsunami approach, sets fire to the village's newly harvested rice crop, its *mura* (the word meaning both the village rice sheaves and the village itself), and thus its livelihood. Or that's the way Lafcadio Hearn wrote it up. They were really rice *husks*, because Göryo Hamguchi's village would have long since have sold its rice crop by November 11, when the Great Ansei (Edo) earthquake of 1855 struck. But Hearn wrote the story after thirty thousand lives were lost in the Miyagi earthquake of 1896. Hearn was impressed that the villagers had built a shrine to Göryo Hamguchi, an important figure in the transition to Meiji Japan (funding vaccination programs and schools), not least because he put villagers to work building a sea wall to keep them employed.

After the Great Tohoku earthquake in 2011, Lafcadio Hearn's grandson sent the *kamishibai* promoter, Mr. Kojima-san, an email asking him to take the story and "use it as a torch to give light to Japan in the dark." Kojima-san rewrote it as an elementary school text called "Protecting the Village a Hundred Years into the Future." It is part of a *social technology* of passing *cultural models of leadership* across generations.

The social dramas and slightly shifting responses to natural and industrial toxic disasters are highly patterned since at least the dumping of toxics in Minimata Bay in 1956. These patterns apply to the chemical accident in Seveso, Italy (1976); Love Canal, New York State (1979); Woburn, Massachusetts (about which the book and film *A Class Action* was made); Chernobyl in Ukraine (1986); Bhopal in India (1984); and to Fukushima (2011). They also apply to radiation injury from depleted uranium weapons and what (for Americans) is called "Gulf War Syndrome," to elevated cancer incidence from uranium mine tailings affecting not only miners but archeologists who worked decades ago in the American Southwest, to the aftereffects of nuclear tests (among the worst, around Semey, Khazakstan), and the list goes on. We live in a world surrounded by toxins whose existence is revealed bit by bit, most recently endocrine disruptors, and the effects of oil and gas fracking that continues to spread around the world (Wylie 2017).

One pattern is a sociological regularity of the late industrial age (Fortun 2001, Reich, 1991): an accident or natural disaster occurs, the authorities (government, corporate owners or utilities) deny liability, and usually also harms. In cases of cancer clusters, citizens are often told that they are incompetent to distinguish coincidence and statistical significance (or in thyroid cancer cases in Fukushima, the latency period is four years, and cases found before that could not be tied to the accident). Citizens, then, have the burden of learning to gather epidemiological knowledge that can stand up in court and survive cross-examination, particularly in environments of sequestered information, as are so many of our corporatized and legally defended environments, from Bhopal to Woburn, Love Canal to Fukushima. Many of these high-profile cases have generated ongoing and decades-long social movements in support of patient health care, adequate compensation or restitution, remediation, jobs, and income. In the United States, cases such as Love Canal led to the Superfund legislation of 1980, importantly giving citizen action panels money to hire experts independent of government or corporate owners. In the aftermath of Bhopal, right-to-know legislation was passed first in the United States, and later in India. In Japan after Kobe, a law was passed allowing registration of nongovernmental associations, but with unclear effect, since there is no tax advantage to support raising funds, only the ability to make contracts.

In such terrains of proprietary knowledge, government statistics not made public, and other forms of sequestering knowledge—especially in worlds of metrics and audits that stand in for, and constitute, what is counted as legally defensible knowledge—experiential knowledge is often under a burden of suspicion, and yet it can provide access to local conditions that aggregate data does not provide (Adams, *Metrics*). All three issues are at risk: in *public policy*, the balance between preventing public panic and providing transparent access to evolving information that can build trust, empowerment, and feelings of mutual aid; in *civil society*, the ability and robustness to tolerate and empower the contestatory nature of determining enough information to act upon (in our worlds of risk societies, we need more flexible and multiplex ways of handling information from many kinds of sources with different kinds of credibility in what are often called reflexive and recursive social institutions, rather than only command-and-control efforts that can all too easily turn into authoritarian rule by experts who undermine their own legitimacy and thereby create pressure for yet more authoritarian control and/or behind-the-scenes national security state secrets); and in *economic health*, the larger challenge of growth of precarity in job availability and tenure. The Fukushima crises have unfolded amid long-term uncertainties that the anthropologist Anne Allison (*Precarious Japan*) evokes with the Japanese terms *muen shakai* (relationless society, precarious society); *ryudoka* (liquidization or flexibilization of work and life); *furita* (part-time workers) and NEETs (not in employment, education, or training); *hikkihomori* (youth no longer leaving their rooms); elders living alone and dying alone and unnoticed (*kodoku shi*); and a general individualization of risk and alienation. Eighty-eight percent of the workers at the Fukushima nuclear plant, Allison says, were part of the precariat, disposable workers, both before and after the accident. Not only has the Japanese long economic downturn produced precarity, but there have been a string of food safety scandals, a number of smaller nuclear accidents, and other causes of diminishing trust in the government.

"Safety is more than laboratory tests; safety is also a social relationship. It can only exist insofar as people trust one another that the products they are eating are indeed safe," writes anthropologist Nicholas I. Sternsdorff-Cisterna (2015), one of a number of ethnographers who have spent at least a year exploring how the inhabitants of Fukushima, Tokyo, and other parts of Japan have attempted to deal with conditions of disaster and uncertainty. It is of course not only anthropologists who do this work: the Nagasaki University's Atomic Bomb Disease Institute has an ongoing association with Kawauchi village (the first to allow residents to return to cleaned-up areas in the outer contamination zone), and has helped set up the several public health surveys, with particular concern for children and pregnant women (Yamashita 2013), and a range of NGOs have contributed important tools, such as the SafeCast maps of radiation contamination.[17]

In the meantime, people struggle to figure out how to minimize their exposures. Sternsdorff-Cisterna provides among the most vivid of the accounts I've read of the search for safe food. He describes how citizens set up over five hundred testing centers (*shimin sokuteishitsu*), although the Ministry of Agriculture, Forestry, and Fisheries tried to muzzle 270 local organizations that offered food tested to stricter standards than those of the state. Rather than as in

Ukraine after the Chernobyl nuclear meltdown and radiation release, where anthropologist Adriana Petryna (2001) described people making claims on the state, becoming "biological citizens"; here people are trying to avoid the state, and test their food independently. As Sternsdorff-Cisterna quotes one mother, she may acknowledge that the chances are low of her child getting sick from such low radiation, *but* if her child is the one who gets cancer she would feel remiss if she did not get food with the lowest radiation possible. Mothers are in the lead of the safe food movement.

Sternsdorff-Cisterna describes street performances in Tokyo of a man dressed as Little Red Riding Hood whose vivid descriptions of buildings shaking, and having to walk home when the power was cut off, engages audiences who begin to shout, "I had to walk too!" The street performer then describes the coming of radiation that you cannot see, and is thus even more frightening (what the sociologist Ulrich Beck [1986/1992] calls the alienation of the means of perception). The audience is worked up to shout, *Hoi! Hantai genpatsu!* [Enough! Oppose nuclear power!]. A second character in a red devil mask comes in, announcing that he is a University of Tokyo radiation researcher. He is loudly booed. He insists all is safe. More boos. The distrust in the "nuclear village" (*genshiryoku mura*), or state-utilities-media-university nuclear complex, is thus dramatized. Early investigations of the accident did suggest that regulatory capture by the industry led to cover-ups of malfunctions, and lax safety. There was even the claim that the SPEEDI (Prediction of Environmental Emergency Dose Information) simulation program had predicted, before the accident, which way radiation plumes might go, and that there had been no effort to release possible scenarios to the public. That government levels for acceptable radiation were adjusted over time no doubt had technical justifications but felt to many to be further evidence of manipulation and cover-up. Public demonstrations and understandable vocal concerns were dismissed by the government as damage by rumor (*fuhyo higai*).

Testing food is not trivial and cannot really be done by Geiger counter. It requires expensive ($45,000) germanium detectors. Several food cooperatives, clubs, and networks managed to raise the money to buy such detectors from Belarus' Atomtex. They convened reading groups and lessons on radiation: cesium is easier to detect, strontium is harder to detect, and what can be done to try to protect yourself. Grocery stores posted radiation test results by each of their produce offerings. The national government posted test results in hard-to-read PDF pages that could not be sorted or easily interpreted; Fukushima Prefecture did better, producing a readable interface, but inundated it with information. So again it was left to local groups, including the mothers of the Association to Protect Children from Radiation, to distribute useable color-coded digests.

Farmers in areas where radiation was minimal were still stigmatized by the Fukushima Prefecture name and couldn't sell their produce. With black humor they would say we don't have a safety (*anzen*) problem, but an *anshin* (trustworthiness) problem, and bitterly point to radioactive hot spots in neighboring prefectures that escaped the stigma and could often sell produce. The Fukushima Agricultural Technology Center, which does research and has detectors, would not test farmers' crops. Activists dismissed government-installed Geiger counters around the city of Koriyama, saying the soil had been scraped first to lower the readings, even though a scientist explained this was done to be able to measure background radiation.

In the meantime, people trade cooking advice: peel vegetables because cesium is stored in the skin, soak them in saline solution, boil them, and throw away the water. As Sternsdorff-Cisterna put it, one could handle the radioactive threats, but one needed to ignore the government claims about safety. Safety, he writes, "is more than laboratory tests; safety is also a social relationship. It can only exist insofar as people trust one another that the products they are eating are indeed safe." People assume, as was the case in Chernobyl, that whether the government's claims will prove correct can be known, only after five years, and again, after testing after ten years. But there are some preliminary claims that there are already some elevated cancer rates in infants, and elevated diabetes rates among 27,500 evacuees. And there are animal deaths: horses are shown ill and dying on a horse farm in Thorsten Trimpop's Golden Dove Award–winning documentary film *Furusatu* (2017). Furusatu means "home," the landscape one grows up in, but also the last scenes one sees as one is dying. The film also contains a wonderful scene of the thousand year old Nomaoi festival held in July 2013 in Minami-soma and six other municipalities devastated by the TEPCO disaster, a colorful parade of horseriders in full samurai regalia, carrying banners and flags, who engage in horse-riding skills, a final "chase of a holy horse" and a kind of polo game with baloons, one of several ritual forms to reaffirm solidarity and commitment to place.[18]

If Sternsdorff-Cisterna focuses on people's efforts toward securing food safety, anthropologist Ryan Sayre focuses on various efforts at preparedness. These include government multiplying of evacuation facilities, the various summertime preparedness fairs (*bosai fea*), and other preparations. But he focuses again on the efforts of ordinary people, artists, and community organizers, such as Watanabe-san, who designed collapsible cardboard origami coffins to be stored discreetly in preparation for emergencies, or emergency toilets in corners of elevators, and barbeque pits under park benches. Another dissertation by Luis-Felipe Murillo pays attention to do-it-yourself maker spaces where young people build their own Geiger counters and other sensors and robots. There are accounts of returnee farmers to villages experimenting with phytoremediation, using of plants to sequester radioactive elements. There is widespread planting of sunflowers, which are said to be able to take up cesium where the soil is not saturated with kalium from fertilizers, including a project by Fukushima City's Water Department, and one led by the Buddhist monk Koyu Abe, chief monk at Joenji Temple, who has also offered his temple as a temporary storage place for radioactive soil.

Koyu Abe, like the pioneer of earthquake science, Terada Toraiko, adheres to the Buddhist philosophy that to live in constant fear is the antithesis of the good life, and that one should, in Toraiko's words, instead "make friends with the phenomenon," or, in Koyu Abe's words, "The best way to overcome disaster is to accept disasters happen. Life doesn't go according to plan." If one needs a job, nuclear cleanup in Fukushima pays well, and is highly sought after. So, too, nuclear workers worldwide apparently have heightened colon cancer rates, an occupational hazard like black lung among coal miners. Wives of husbands working at the nuclear power plant in Fukushima are forbidden by their husbands from publically expressing their concerns.

What narratives can we live by in such circumstances? "When our country's symbol is itself a volcano which threatens us, how do we live safely, securely, and with stability?" (Naikakufu Office of Strategic Action 2005, 5, quoted in Sternsdorff-Cisterna 2015, 123). Fukushima is a world-historical time marker: it may not be a turning point against nuclear power, but it is a warning against the myths of perfect safety. Fukushima may turn out to be a "near miss"; things could be worse. Maybe, just maybe, there won't be as many mutations and cancers as feared. Maybe, just maybe, some of the remediation efforts will teach us how to regenerate partially toxic landscapes. Genomics has taught us that we are all carriers of mutations and different illness risks, no one is either only healthy or sick, all of us are patients in waiting. Perhaps in the same way we will have to learn to live with radiation, toxic accumulations, and maybe, just maybe, stem cell and regenerative medicine technologies will teach us how to reprogram iRNA regulatory systems to turn the cancer cells off or back into less lethal ones.

The future can be scary when thought about as sudden mutational change on a large scale, but not so scary perhaps *with time*. Time: time is both on our side, and not on our side. But it can only be on our side if we try to build these new capabilities. If sunflowers really do take up water and water soluble cesium more quickly than other plants, might we use emergent synthetic biology tools to make a better sunflower, one that does not just end its cycle through anaerobic reduction into concentrated cesium 137, but maybe, just maybe, finds another path away from toxicity to life, or at least a storage system for the hundred years of the half-life of cesium, not that long in the order of things? I'm not suggesting only technological fixes. Rather, I'm agreeing with Sternsdorff-Cisterna that safety is a social relationship, and we need to figure out how to work on these things together.[19]

At the cherry blossom festival held a month and a half after the 2011 tsunami in a destroyed village, the village leader turned to the ocean and yelled, "Ocean, go to hell!" He turned back to the people, and then again to the ocean, and yelled, "Ocean, thank you!" Sayre comments that for fisher folk, blessing and afflictions, sorrow and joy are the warp and woof of life. There is as well a resonance with the cry during Obon (Hungry Ghost Festival, return of the ancestors, in mid-August), *Ee ja nai ka!* ("It's alright, who cares?"), a carnivalesque shout during the upheavals of the Meiji era as the social order seemed to fall apart and people madly drank and partied.

Musicologist Noriko Manabe (2015) describes the ambivalent Project Fukushima music festival held on August 15, 2011 (following wandering the streets of Tokyo creating loud music Fukushima Music Liberation zones), asking people to come to Fukushima and "think with us," with those who live there and do not want to be defined by the accident at the Daiichi nuclear plant nor oblivious to the dangers to ongoing life. Radiation measurements were posted throughout the concert, partly to reassure people that it was safe, and partly to remind them of the ongoing reality of uncertainty.

Perhaps here, in this positive cultural response to the multiple crises, there has been more of a seizing of the crisis for change than in the political sphere, where, as Richard Samuels (*3/11*), a political scientist and longtime observer of Japan, despairs, all factions continue to do what they always did, letting the opportunity for change fade. Precarity was central to the songs of Project Fukushima, what Elizabeth Povinelli (2016) calls neoliberal lethality (letting declining areas die) and Kim Fortun (2012, 2014) calls the effects of late industrialism. Project Fukushima insists it need not be that way, and in any case is a major case study for the coming disasters with which we all will have to deal, in the wake of large-scale engineering projects continuing to be built with good intentions such as nuclear power plants for electricity, and for flood control and simply for water, the Mahavelli Development Project in Sri Lanka (chapter 6), the Three Gorges Dam, and the massive project to transfer water from South China to the North China plains.

Anthropology in the meantime will be a critical tool for responsive robustness both for when things go wrong and to make things go right more often.

Floods and Sexual Impotence: Three Gorges Dam Films, Paintings

Quite a number of films and other artworks have been made either just before or after the completion of the Three Gorges Dam, turning the camera or canvas not just on the engineering feat but also on the people displaced. For those who have visited Chongqing, the Three Gorges Dam Museum not only collects artifacts saved from the submersion but also houses an enormous painting depicting the entire length of the Three Gorges, with each of the villages and towns drawn to scale, and with a line showing the height of the waters that would submerge the lower parts. A very different but equally ambitious scroll is Yun-Fei Ji's *Three Gorges Dam Migration*, which uses five hundred carved woodblocks, in pastel colors on mulberry paper, to portray the dispossessed farmers. In a video the artist says, "It's not idealized; I wanted it to be more things as they are." Then he adds, "In all my images I'm using, you know, the more fantastical figures that I associate with ghosts, with kind of ominous figures. There's also two creatures with very large mouths, very greedy looking, looks a little bit threatening, *but people kind of live with them, they are in the world, they're there, you know*" (0:14-1:20; emphasis added).[20] Less interested in criticizing the dam, Ji says he is more interested in the interconnections between humans and their environment. "The belief among ancient scholars," he said, "is that nature offers an ethical model that we should follow in human society. A horizontal line, for example, in Chinese calligraphy, is like a cloud formation, or a natural, living form."[21] And he continues exploring the codes of these interconnections, ending with "industrial-scale destruction, where there is no place to escape."

The Three Gorges Dam grows out of the techno-optimism of the early Mao period that has been devastatingly criticized in Judith Shapiro's *Mao's War against Nature* (1999), among other places. As she points out, China is not alone in such modernist projects. Historian and STS scholar Loren Graham (1998) produced a short but incisive book comparing large-scale engineering projects in the United States and Russia, and many anthropologists, including myself, have done studies of the displacements of large irrigation and hydro-power dams (Fischer and Barfield 1980; Goodell 1986). The destruction continues now in the Mekong and Irrawady River systems, with both China and Thailand outsourcing the dam building in neighboring countries but with the expectation of electricity coming to themselves rather than to the localities in which the dams are sited.

Zhang Ming's *Wushan yunyu* ("Wu Mountain Clouds and Rain" or "In Expectation," 1996) and Jia Zhangke's *Sanxia Haoren* ("Still Life," 2006) are two useful films to think with. I draw upon the readings of these films by Sheldon Lu and Nick Kaldis, and, as ethnographic counterpoint, Everett Yuehong Zhang's *The Impotence Epidemic: Men's Medicine and Sexual Desire in Contemporary China* (2015).

Still Life, in one way, has the broader canvas insofar as its two lead characters, a coal miner and a nurse, come from Shangxi Province to Fengjie, a thousand-year-old town that is being demolished in preparation for it becoming submerged, along with a Western Han dynasty tomb. It is thus in part a comment on the dislocations of the Cultural Revolution and, later, the migratory search for jobs separating families and separating people from their home provinces. It is the demolition of the old society, physically (with buildings marked *chai* [to be demolished]), socially, and morally (gangsters, theft, corruption). The cinematography is haunting, particularly the long shots of the buildings perched along the steep valley walls, and the exhausting pain-producing labor of mallets and picks chipping away at sturdily built structures by isolated men, foregrounding the puniness of human labor in itself, few machines in sight, as if itself a forced labor camp. Jia Zhangke has the practice of making documentaries alongside, as studies for, his narrative films, and the film *Dong* was shot in Fengjie at the same time. The protagonist of *Dong* is a painter from Beijing who hires demolition workers as male models and later Thai prostitutes as female models, both groups displaced migrants.

Rainclouds over Wushan (also titled in English *In Expectation*), plays in its title on the rich mythology of the region full of shamanic figures (*wu*) and the twelve mountain goddesses who inhabit the peaks of the gorge. "In the morn, I am a floating cloud, in the evening a passing rain," goes a famous poem about the Goddess Peak and her eleven sisters who descended to help tame the floods (Song Yu's *Gaotang Fu*). The poem depicts this region as inhabited by succubi that visit men in their dreams, leaving them, says Kaldis, forlorn. As often pointed out, the last line of Mao's poem "Swimming" (1956) refers also to this goddess, hoping she keeps well. During the Cold War, Mao opposed the construction of the dam, fearing it would be a target. China's fourth premier, Li Peng, a Soviet-trained hydraulic engineer, initiated and oversaw the Three Gorges project in the 1990s, and he appears in the film, in the televised opening ceremony.

Both formally and diegetically, Kaldis points out, the film mirrors the disruption of the environment with the disruption of subjectivity. Formally, for instance, the very opening scene is of the male protagonist, Mai Qiang, picking up a pair of binoculars to look at the river and city he is painting, followed by a matching shot of the river seen through the binoculars. But then suddenly we viewers, momentarily like the characters in the film, are disoriented: we see Mai Qiang entering bottom left hauling buckets of water. Often both he and the female protagonist, Chen Qing, stare vacantly as if they cannot recognize what they are seeing. Or they hallucinate voices and people: Chen Qing sees a Daoist priest at the entry to the hotel where she works; looking again, the figure has disappeared. It was, moreover, a figure that looked like Mai Qiang and is played by the same actor. These formal mirrorings of disorientation are also diegetically mirrored in the symbolic allusions and in the plot twists: the ambiguous charge of rape resonates with the region's succubi, who come to men in their dreams. After Mai Qiang's buddy attempts to set him up with a flighty girl and Mai Qiang refuses sex with her, he roams the town and meets Chen Qing. A single mother working in a hotel, Chen Qing is trying to break off a coercive affair with the hotel manager by telling him that she is preparing to marry someone else. The manager becomes jealous and reports Mai Qiang to the police as having raped Chen Qing. Chen Qing denies this, and Mai Qiang is released from custody, but Ma Bing tells Mai Qiang that her reputation has been ruined. It is ambiguous as to what their relationship is. At the end Mai Qiang returns to Chen Qing in hopes of a real relationship. Throughout Mai Qiang and Chen Qing are identified by mirrored actions: each takes a fish from a bucket and stuns the fish before cleaning it, but both stare vacantly as if it is they who are stunned, or as if, perhaps, they are the river fish, whose fate is in the hands of others. Mai Qiang is a river traffic signal operator who runs up a banner with a red and white arrow at the beginning and end of the film, while Chen Qing raises a banner at the hotel inviting guests to stay. These signs are those of their lives as well, knowing what direction to take in Mai Qiang's case, and stability for Chen Qing. Ma Bing, the hustler and fixer, friend of Mai Qiang who tried to get him out of his loneliness with the flighty Lili, also negotiates with a young policeman who has detained him for interrogation regarding a crime, offering to find him a cheap refrigerator for his upcoming wedding. The ambiguity here is what is corruption, what is help in a world where moral signs are unclear.

In these worlds of dislocation and disorientation by the building of the Three Gorges Dam, in Lu and Kaldis's readings and Everett Zhang's ethnography, we are also led to questions of how the sexual economy is inhibited, a kind of deep disruption that links biology and technology.

Viruses and Pandemics: Living across Species Boundaries

Two very different literary and filmic works deal with or touch upon SARS and the avian flu pandemics. One important anthropological account deals with the domesticated wild fowl at Pandong Lake along the Asian flyway to Siberia and Europe (Fearnley 2013). And, of course, there are a number of more straightforward accounts of the biomedical responses in Hong Kong, Singapore, and elsewhere (Fischer 2013, Mason 2016).

Hu Fayun's *Such Is This World @ SARS.com* (2004) follows a widowed mom whose son sets her up on the Internet to communicate with him while he studies in America, and she becomes an Internet resource manager for empty nesters. She also begins a relationship with a deputy mayor of Beijing during the SARS crisis, a window into the panic-driven administrative politics. The Internet, of course, played a key role in South China in getting the word out about a rapidly expanding pandemic in the days when China was still trying to tightly control public information and deny any problem. SARS plays a different but also symptomatic role in Tsai Ming-liang's *Dark Circles* (*Hei yan quan*, translated in English as "I Don't Want to Sleep Alone," 2006) set in Kuala Lumpur as the SARS crisis breaks out, with people wearing face masks and urging one another to report any outbreaks. Other airborne environmental problems are also on the fringes of urban life, in particular haze from burning to prepare for planting oil palm plantations, and mosquito-born infectious diseases (dengue, malaria, and, beginning in 2016, the Zika virus). Mosquito control depends upon both pesticide spraying and, more importantly, control over stagnant water where mosquitos breed, including in high-rise buildings, where the water is cleaner and preferred by dengue-bearing mosquitos.

This urban environment, doubling new construction with coproduced ruins, construction sites, slums, and contaminated spaces, is the turf of Malaysian filmmaker Tsai Ming-liang, as beautifully interpreted by Erin Yu-Tien Huang (2012). Tsai is not the only filmmaker to focus on crowded apartment living, construction sites, claustrophobic noir alleys, unhygienic spaces, floating populations of migrants (documented and undocumented), and floods and droughts. As Huang says, construction sites with temporary male migrant workers are everywhere in Asian urban centers, from Tehran in the films of Abbas Kiarostami (*Taste of Cherry*, 1997) and Majid Majidi (*Baran*,

2002) (see Fischer 2004) to Tsai's Taipei and Kuala Lumpur, and also, of course, in the migration of agricultural labor from Sichuan to Xinjian (stunningly documented by Ning Ying in three days of interviews on board the overcrowded *Railroad of Hope*, 2002). In Tsai's first film, *Rebels of the Neon God* (1992), the protagonist is a Nezha (explicitly so identified to his mother by a medium), a popular boy/teen deity among taxi, truck, and bus drivers in Taiwan. The protagonist's father is a taxi driver. Nezha, originally Nalakubara in Sanskrit texts (Shahar 2015), is a beloved rebel figure from India to China. In *Neon God*, he stalks the free-wheeling petty criminal teenager Ah-Tze through the Taipei underworld, hunting and haunting his prey, after Ah-Tze smashed his father's car's rear view mirror and ran off. He stalks Ah-Tze in part for revenge, and in part from desire to be what he thinks is an urban free spirit like Ah-Tze. In an interview, Tsai says, echoing Kaldis's reading of Zhang Ming's *Rainclouds over Wushan*:

> I want to express the failure of erotic desire to be realized in contemporary urban space. I would like to make my films about disappearing. Society changes so fast and everything disappears so fast—historical sites, culture. One day I walked to the area where Lee Kang-Sheng was selling watches [in *What Time Is It There?*], and I realized that "the skywalk is gone." It happens in Asia like that, things just disappear. People in their forties have no way of finding traces of their childhood. . . . My films ask the question: how we can face the disappearance? The loss?[22]

Tsai's film *The Hole*, commissioned by the Franco-German Arte television for the "2000 Seen By" series of films for the turn of the millennium,[23] begins seven days before an involuntary quarantine and evacuation (the water will be cut off January 1, 2000), and *Dark Circles* follows up, set just after the SARS crisis breaks out. One critic writes that cinematographer Liao Penjung captures a "gloriously damp and moldering architecture, and treats the flooded concrete monstrosity where much of the movie unfolds as if it were some made attempt by M. C. Escher to turn the Petronas Towers—and the economic boom they once symbolized—inside out" (Stephens 2007). Huang, less floridly, describes it as a "flooded construction site, with multiplying columns, crisscrossed staircases, and missed or accidental encounters." There are dripping broken pipes, stagnant pools, breeding grounds for mosquitoes, infectious disease, stopped up drains where larvae of roaches and insects flourish. Bathrooms in these places provide an "archive of the limits of modern hygiene" contrasting with older Asian-style bathrooms that look out onto green tropical nature. In *The Hole*, a plumber simply drills a hole from the apartment above to the apartment below, allowing all sorts of noises as well as water to drip through.

Environment here is a miasma of contagion encroaching on the underbelly of the modern cities, dark circles around new cities, their interior, hidden, doubles. This is a theme emphasized by Yun-Fei Ji when he explains the codes of traditional Chinese landscape painting and how visible nature is implicated in the meditative interior of the body, followed in the films and ethnographies of the disruptions of the Three Gorges Dam. The theme is followed virally, biologically, in the multispecies interactions in the SARS and avian influenza outbreaks of reorganizing ecologies, with their metaphorical mirrorings of migration and politics in Hu Fayun's *Such Is This World @ SARS.com* and the ethnographic work by Lyle Feanley, Kathleen Mason, Frederic Kek, and others. The theme becomes even more explicit in the constrained urban slums and ruins of Tsai Ming-liang films about isolated and rebellious individuals. And the theme perhaps is most expansively detailed in the work of Indonesian artist Entang Wiharso.

Geoportraits, Entanglements, and Influencing Machines

On January 14, 2016, three suicide bombers blew themselves up at a police post outside the Sarinah mall on Thamrin Street, at the Starbucks at the Skyline building nearby, and near the UN headquarters; two more attackers killed a hostage and injured another (a Dutch UN employee) and opened fire on others. In all, four attackers and four civilians were killed, and twenty-three were injured. This was around the corner from the hotel where my wife and I were staying, having come to Jakarta for the opening of an art show by Entang Wiharso and Sally Smart at the National Gallery of Indonesia.[24] The opening went on, with good attendance, in a display of solidarity and refusal to be intimidated. At the start of the walk through of the show with the two artists, one of the curators, Australian Natalie King, began by saying, "Yesterday was a bad day in your city. We need to remind ourselves that art and artistic activity provide a haven and artists are the guardians of the imagination, so today is an important day in Jakarta."

Entang Wiharso himself speaks of forces of vibration affecting neurological systems. These provide a medium for the structures of feeling echoing in the Ecocene of Abe's effort to control emotions against the computer's projections of his narrator's own thought processes, the overcoming of fear of genetic change (the aquans), Ishiguro's meditation on biological processes of extinction, and the *ee ja nai ka* (it's alright, who cares) attitude in the face of disasters in Murakami. It's not that one doesn't care, but that one must live on (*su-vive*) in new conditions; it takes courage, persistence, and strength. Similarly, these works of art are no longer constrained by nationalist identity politics or the periodization of art styles. Postindependence, postdecolonialization, post-Reformasi—they are part of the breakout of Southeast Asian, East Asian, and Pacific art onto the global stage, part of the Asian shift in "what is happening" generally. They embroider in older references, cultural forms, and geographic locations but move confidently beyond them. With both humor and a steady demand for a humane world beyond gender inequality or peripheralization, their art points to the faults (both geological and social) of the world and ways to move on.

At the show's walk through, Wiharso repeated his notion that "noise, like [that of the] cell phone comes [to be] debated in our bodies," like Viktor Tausk's influencing machines. In Wiharso's version,

> like a dream, but not a dream, it is a tool, the sound from the television travelled into my brain . . . basically not sound at all, but sound information, and my body became a mediator of the electro-magnetic wave, . . . people who live in Java are different than people who live in Rhode Island or Boston or Nordic countries, because if you live in Java there is a lot of movement . . . every second, there is movement in the ground, [which] travel[s] to our nerves and [the] respon[se] in every individual [is] different . . . and that is why when I live in Yoga[karta], I feel like hurry, life is too short, but when I stay in Rhode Island, life is very long. . . . The environment gives affect to us because of our conscious and unconscious. [MF tape 14/16/2016].

Wiharso's artistic media are quite varied, from painting to his now famous and iconic aluminum and brass cutouts, large metal sculptures, installations and performances, and most recently a dazzling array of string and color infused paper prints and paper casts, as well as copper engravings, done during a residence at Singapore's Tyler Print Institute. Trained at the Yogakarta Art Institute, Wiharso rebelled early against what he saw as an orthodoxy of style, a pandering to what might potentially sell in the art market, and has always seen himself as both outsider and border crosser, eventually adopting the black goat as his identity and icon. *Kambing hittam* is an Indonesian idiom meaning both scapegoat and black sheep, what Wiharso calls "a grey area condition, the outsider and the victim of such a condition" (*Trilogy*, 228). He says early on, he was liberated from Islamic hesitations about working in figural representations by learning that when Islamic missionary Sunan

FIG. EPI.4. Entang Wiharso, *Promising Land #2*, 2016. Aluminum, car paint, resin, color pigment, steel, acrylic, and thread, variable dimensions. Photo by Art Jog Documentation. Courtesy of the artist.

Kalijaga introduced *wayang kulit* (the Javanese shadow play), he had his artisans scratch three lines into the neck of the leather puppets. Called "corpse markers," the lines indicated the figure was not alive. Inspired by this, Wiharso began to apply paint directly with a palette knife, "etching" into the figures to demonstrate they were not living. Although there are traces of wayang in his paintings, he developed his style using distortion and separation of entrails, and of organs separate from the body, as a visual language of emotions, of connections and disconnections among people, and, most importantly, a language of humor and play.

One of the themes of much of Wiharso's work are self-portraits of himself with his American wife, Christine Cocca (also a printmaker and artist), and his two bicultural children, who help pose for him many of his puzzles of border crossing. In one striking comment, Wiharso notes that although Dutch colonialism remains present, it is really diaspora and global pop culture that are the defining movements, not postcolonialism:

> The idea of an Indonesian diaspora is still a new and unfamiliar concept for Indonesians and I think this is because of our colonial history. A resistance towards something foreign still exists even though the

> Netherlands no longer holds any power here. The landscape of regulations and laws that were adopted during colonial rule to protect Dutch wealth and their interests still exists in Indonesia, but affects people today in unexpected, unsettling and problematic ways. This condition has led to a lot of questions about the Indonesian diaspora in my work, especially since the birth of my two children. (Wiharso, 2014, 226)

Over time, Wiharso has built up a distinctive vocabulary of body parts, vines, intestines-umbilical cords, multiple eyes, *keris* (ceremonial swords), iron grill and bamboo or birch "walls," animals (supersized koi, powerful dogs), American cars, superheroes, and comic figures. One recognizes his work instantly.

Shows like the one in Jakarta in 2016 with Sally Smart are curatorially staged; they are processual, as the physical setup moves the viewer along, in this case from a "green room" or antechamber where there is an older piece, *No Hero No Cry* (2006–7), which hangs up (literally, and in the sense of putting aside) the traditional, well-used, fading, and stained wayang kulit puppets. Both Sukarno and Suharto, the former presidents of Indonesia, mythologized themselves as the god Semar, a popular wayang character, indigenous to Indonesia (not a character from the Indian epics), able to mediate between God and men, a wise peasant who upsets the aristocratic hierarchies. From anteroom one moves to the entry, a mesmerizing large resin-cast hyperreal forest of Rhode Island bamboo. Four sculptural figures, a family, in dark gowns, with the adults' hair tied in tall traditional topknots, kneel in front of the forest, backs to the viewer. With one hand behind their backs, they hold a rope or intestine or umbilical cord: the family connection, as they face their doubled lives in Rhode Island and Yogakarta, moving each year back and forth. The structure of feeling, the air or mood of the piece, is ambiguous, at once serene and threatening. Wiharso explains it is about conflict with neighbors or within families, "When you have a conflict everybody is injured. Even though somebody wins, there is no win, everybody is injured. So this is the idea." He explains the metaphor: "In Javanese philosophy, you know, it is like [your] intestines, in your mind you have put a thing, but you have [a] long intestine. The intestine is the drama, your inner state, and the bamboo is *the* border, like earlier [versions] using birch trees, but this time using bamboo" [MF tape 14/1/2016].

As one turns into the main exhibition space, bright metal cutouts, glossy painted surfaces, catch the eye—pop art and comic book–style buses, cars, and pickup trucks, and stylized people—but as one looks more closely, the fine

FIG. EPI.5. Entang Wiharso, "The intestine is the drama, your inner state; the bamboo is the border" 2016 (Titled by the artist: *Reclaim Paradise—Paradise Lost no. 2*). Aluminum, car paint, resin, thread, graphite, steel, silicon, electric cable, 290 × 500 × 800 cm. Photo by M. Fischer, Jakarta, 2016. Reproduced with permission of the artist.

detailing, often in gray-green shadow, draws you in, engages you in Javanese "movementality," "density," and "people everywhere," fighting, loving, and always interconnected through nervous systems, pipes, wires, and rifles bent into further pipelike connections, or, where there is forest, by tropical lianas and vines. As one moves through the dreamlands and stagings of the show, one finally comes to a primal scene in the back, or womb in the interior. A huge koi with a red and white head and tail sits on a table, its rib cage and backbone exposed, out of which come the bones of a large, strange, one-eyed creature with tusks. Three figures dressed in steam punk mechanical spacemen-type suits sit around the table, connected to the fish by multiple tubes.

Multiple versions and variations of this koi and table have been produced by Entang, often with body intact but multiple fishhooks or arrows stuck into the fish, a large tongue coming out, or with an open mouth and a small humanoid skeleton hanging inside. The table often sits on a Persian carpet, and often the figures around it are two standing figures, one offering the fish,

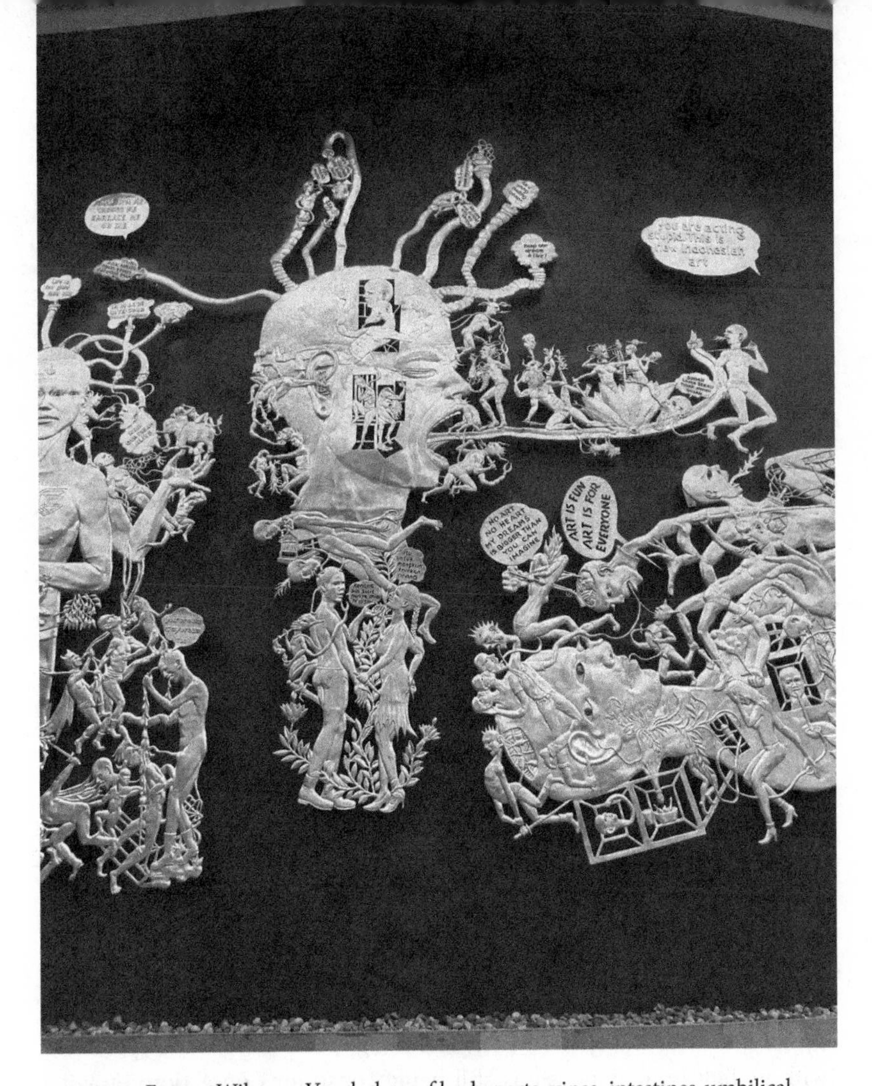

FIG. EPI.6. Entang Wiharso. Vocabulary of body parts, vines, intestines-umbilical cords, multiple eyes, tongues, all reaching out, communicating, 2011–12 (Titled by the artist: *Dreaming Machine: Chronicle Wall*). Brass, aluminum, resin, color pigment, and thread, 700 × 1400 cm. Photo by M. Fischer, 2017. Reproduced with permission of the artist.

and the other refusing it. Sometimes the table is a large wooden colonial table, and the spots of the fish contaminate the men. Only after many years, Wiharso says, did he realize the table comes from the *warang* (street food stall) that his parents operated. The warang table is where people sit, talk and eat, where politics is discussed, family matters, injustices, and everything else. It is the demotic version of Kant's *Tischgesellschaft* (food and conversation as the foundation of civics), a good place for the wisdom of Semar, the wise comic of the wayang plays.

***The Wandering Earth* and *Death's End*: Speculation and Reality**

One of the virtues of Liu Cixin's *In Remembrance of Earth's Past* is its long arc of sociotechnological and cultural changes that expands upon many of the challenges of today's Anthropocene, across light years of time and space, making the Anthropocene but one of the epochs of existence (called the Common Era), rather than an apocalypse beyond which nothing more can be said. A second virtue is its composition out of three kinds of writing. Chapters alternate between eras, providing a kind of chronicle of speculative developments in technology (often titled as crisis periods requiring new deterrence technology development) and excerpts from a kind of ethnographer's journal or field notes called "Excerpts from a Past Outside of Time." These are meditations in the form of action or game narrations on themes such as infantilism, moral concerns, and primitive technologies that impede later developments. Meanwhile the main story line itself wanders between what is happening outside and inside a virtual reality game or simulation of the world. The three kinds of writing—games, field notes, chronicles—resonate with the blueprints of Kobo Abe and the protocols of Ishiguro, providing their own kind of three-body interactions of imaginaries, documentaries, and histories. There is a search in the novel for Lagrangian points of stability.

The three volumes are a compendium of contemporary and legacy scientific initiatives and speculations, including speed-of-light transportation (with its light-year dimensions still being constraints on action), gravitational waves experimented with to communicate (viz. Harry Collins's ethnography of gravity wave research, 2004, 2014, 2017), game theory pitting instrumentalism versus compassion, simulation forms of extrapolation and recursive reflexivity, the limitations of Cold War game theory and dependence of Prisoner's Dilemma–type games on superhuman discipline, computer games with multiple levels of difficulty or hypertext variations of path-dependency outcomes, string theory with up to eleven-dimensional worlds that can interfere with one another, cryopreservation evolved into hibernation allowing humans to travel in space across centuries of time and thus stagger efforts of those who stay awake with those who can pick up in later eras, and even a retooled version of Stanislaw Ulam's proposal in 1946 for nuclear pulse propulsion, using nuclear bombs sequentially set along a course in space to increase the velocity of a space probe each time a bomb goes off behind its sail (renamed the Staircase Program).

This is all wrapped in a sociology of heightened Kantian unsocial sociabilities, factional fighting, expert minds pitted against one another (e.g., spooks versus techies who think quite differently), gender dynamics (the key moral centers are a matriarchal line of three generations of women astrophysicists; in one era men become physically feminized but in a later era seem to return to the dimorphism of the Common Era), and at best partial communication between alien and human intelligences. Thus, "technical experts kept to themselves and acted as if on guard versus theft every minute; while the veterans of intelligence agencies were gregarious and friendly but were constantly on the lookout for something to steal" (63). The techies and spooks were supposed to work together in a merged new agency (maybe like the merging of different specialized agencies in the U.S. after the attack on the World Trade Center in New York on September 11, 200, into a hoped for, more information sharing, combined Department of Homeland Security): they were polite, but there was no trust. Gender divides were no easier: "Of course, the elite experts didn't expect a mere technical aide like Cheng Xin [the young woman astrophysicist who keeps coming up with solutions to intractable problems] to have brilliant ideas; being mostly men they thought giving her a chance to talk, they would have an excuse to appreciate her physical attributes. This sort of harassment was something she had to deal with constantly" (65). Nor were moral issues any easier: hibernation raised moral issues more serious than cloning ("which mostly only raised moral issues for those influenced by Christianity"; 73): "Those who could afford [hybernation] would use it to skip to paradise, while the rest of humanity would have to stay in the depressing present to construct that paradise for them. If death's end were achievable in one or two centuries, those who chose hibernation were taking the first steps on the staircase to life everlasting. It would be the first time in history Death itself was no longer fair" (73).

But the Trisolaran Crisis (invasion of Earth by the Trisolarans) changed everything: the taboo against hibernation was lifted, allowing the technology to be commercially developed. Various techniques were debated, including the problems of supercold space requiring hibernation chambers to be heated rather than cooled, the size and weight of the equipment needed to accomplish this, and the dangers of cell damage from ice crystal formation during the thawing process.

The most serious problem is articulated by a spaceship captain who, deceitfully, is lured back to earth as a hero, only then, together with his crew, to be condemned to death for cannibalism as a crime against humanity. When lost in space, he says, and "considering the interminable voyage ahead of us in space, to abandon so much protein was unconscionable." More generally, he warns, "When fish climbed onto land, they ceased to be fish; so when humans enter space, they cease to be human" (116). He is warning about the taboos and totalitarian organization that mirrors that of the Trisolarans for similar existential justifications (he claims he had taken a vote of his crew with open discussion before making decisions of that kind).

While perhaps more pessimistic than Kant's version of unsocial sociabilities, nonetheless the invasion of the Trisolarans is generative of repeated strategies and counterstrategies in which human capacities can sometimes outwit evolved AI and surveillance. In a CAVE (computer automated visualization environment)-like room, a mathematical model of the earth, running simulations of biological, geological, astronomological, atmospheric, and oceanic sciences (Gaia), simulating the earth's surface from past to future states, Yang Dang "felt the breath of nature . . . as if she were being released from confinement." The man "in green frame glasses" tells her the earth is a home constructed by life for itself (vol. 3, p. 32), that without life the atmosphere would be very different, perhaps not able to shield the earth from solar winds and ultraviolet rays, the oceans would evaporate, greenhouse effects would turn atmosphere into one like that of Venus, water vapor would then be lost to space, and the earth would be too dry to sustain life. When Yang Dang asks if this is true of the universe at large, the man says life is too rare to have any effect on the universe, but she knows from her astrophysicist mother's hidden notes that this is not true, that there is life elsewhere, and "a wave of terror threatened to overwhelm her" (33).

The trilogy begins, in volume 1, *The Three Body Problem*, during the Chinese Cultural Revolution, with a quite vivid scene of Ye Wenje's astrophysicist father being stoned to death by Tsinghua High School students, while she watches her mother and sister joining with the mob. Ye escapes, and gets into trouble for reading and commenting on *Silent Spring*, a banned book, but is given a chance to join a secret military base where she can be isolated from the outside world.[25] The base is trying to establish contact with any aliens in the universe (not unlike the Search for Extraterrestrial Intelligence, SETI, program in the United States, albeit that is public and open). Ye discovers how to use solar waves to transmit messages, and sends out a message that she hides from her coworkers, asking for help combatting the cruelty, totalitarianism, and environmental destruction of her civilization. After nine years, in 1979, she receives a response from a dissident pacifist Trisolaran, a kind of mirror to herself, who warns her not to reply, as the Trisolarans would be hostile and invasive, but the message is intercepted and the Trisolarans, having located Earth by means of it, begin to invade. Ye and a rich American oil tycoon's son who is a "panspecies communist" (multispecies anthropologist?) set up a secret society to welcome the Trisolarans, the ETO (Earth-Trisolaran Organization).

The Trisolarans are motivated by their three-sun system's instability (the three-body problem) making their world unpredictably too hot or too cold, causing the rise and collapse of civilizations. While their bodies evolve to hydrate and dehydrate to adapt to the severe climate changes, they are determined to find a new habitat, and they evolve a totalitarian and ruthless society to achieve that existential necessity. They have developed a *sophon* technology (*sophia*, "wisdom," + proton, both *zhizi*, i.e., a pun in Chinese), a nanoscale supercomputer that can fold into eleven dimensions (string theory). These are used to shut down the earth's particle accelerators and freeze all research and development on Earth. A nanomaterials expert, Wang, follows a countdown demand to shut down his research, and is allowed to join one group within the ETO, where he comes upon a game they are developing around a simulation of a living environment of a world revolving around three suns, with periodically alternating stable and chaotic eras. He explains the three-body problem to fellow gamers, and is invited into higher-level meetings of the ETO, where he is dismayed by the militarized, totalitarian structure being developed and the factional fighting. The ETO is caught and destroyed, triggering a second phase of Trisolaran invasion (to occur in four hundred years) and further scientific efforts to develop deterrence technologies for the Earth. The Trisolarans tell Ye and her companions that they consider humans to be bugs, and doomed. Shi Qiang, a forensics expert, comforts Ye that the bugs seem always to survive persecution and execution by humans, and so, too, perhaps, the humans will survive the Trisolarans.

The second volume, *The Dark Forest*, explores the dilemmas of competition across communities of radically different communication propensities, be they techies versus spooks, or alien beings (Trisolarans) whose calculative "readouts" are superior to those of humans but, because they are direct "readouts," cannot fathom human deceits (eventually they learn). The dark forest is a play upon the psychology of (explicitly named) nyctohylophobia (fear of the darkness at night in forests).

Along with the three-volume epic, Liu Cixin has also produced a series of beguiling novellas, one of which, *The Wandering Earth*, in a separate but allied story, posits the imminent death of the sun, and the civil war among humans between those who want to stay in our familiar solar orbit versus "Escapists" who build hundreds of huge plasma nuclear power plants to move the earth out of orbit and on its way to a new solar system. At one point investigators determine that the sun's decay has stopped, and the Escapists are nearly undone, but then there is a sudden explosion and the sun dims. There follows a subplot of the frozen surface of the earth, and the subterranean cities that humans forge to stay alive as the Earth travels in search of a new solar system to join.

Volume 3, *Death's End*, charts various places and ways of living off the earth, and hints at regenerative medicine (no murder because bodies can be repaired except if the brain is damaged) and physiological plasticity (feminization of male bodies) while speculating on the nature of four-dimensional space, and how our three-dimensional commonsense can be upset both in four-dimensional space and also a two-dimensional space that could be weaponized. Surveillance is omnipresent, and old forms of folklore storytelling prove to be codes humans can use to their advantage against the growing strength of the sophons's artificial intelligence. The sophons are both tiny supercomputers and avatars that can appear in hominid form. Humans by now are adept at space travel, using cryogenic hibernation as a way to transit centuries of time. The third volume is by far the richest and most satisfying of the three, of which only a hint can be given here.

One of the oddities of the trilogy is that the cultural detailing is more often from US popular culture and scientific history, and less from the Chinese equivalents (see footnote 25 and the speculation that this is in part perhaps to avoid censorship in China, although in part it is a simple engagement with the work of Isaac Asimov, Arthur C. Clarke, and other Western hard science fiction authors). This oddity is perhaps a mirror of the comment that Trisolarans claimed infatuation with human culture, produced sophistic art after human models, and became mirrors and reflections for the renewal of human society, so that they could set themselves on earth with no trace of alienness, while Trisolaris itself remained shrouded in mystery, with almost no details transmitted. Yet, Liu writes, the World Academy of Science was founded to digest all the scientific and technological information, treating Earth as a "knowledge battery": after Earth was fully charged with Earth and Trisolaran knowledge, it would provide more power for the Trisolarans (138). Again a mirrored relation of multiplier refractions.

I end as I began, in the meantime, in the wake of the future, under the hospitality of the tropical rain tree optimistically anticipating the future with the tools at hand, playing up and down the multiple scales of perception that ethnography permits, looking over the shoulders of scientists, with their simulations, particle accelerators, and genomics assays, while also going to the movies and talking to novice artists with their ears to the ground, and skeptically ground-truthing the statistics and projections of those who mine large data sets, applying our commonsense logics to statistical patterns, knowing that neither provides the whole truth and that our common sense changes with growing experience across differential cultural and ecological niches. New social structures and new "forms of life" (both biological and social, sometimes quite intertwined) are emergent in ways we cannot quite foresee, despite confident predictions and jeremiad warnings. We hold on to the turbulent waves, eyes wide open, sometimes wide shut, checking insight as well as foresight, planning redesign, using Asian dreamings paired with ethnographies of both optimism and pessimism, adjusting as we go, scanning and inscribing, as we can in the meantime.

ACKNOWLEDGMENTS

I thank Kaushik Sunder Rajan for the invitation to present parts of the epilogue as "Fukushima, SARS, Avian Influenza, and Theory from the East " at the tenth anniversary of the Chicago Center for Contemporary Theory (3CT), February 2016; to Entang Wiharso, Christine Cocca, and Sally Smart for the invitation to write a catalogue essay for their *Conversations* exhibition at the National Gallery of Art in Jakarta, January 2016, part of which is excerpted in the epilogue; to Remy Chhem, Greg Clancey, and Kim Fortun for inviting me to the Fukushima radiation workshops in Nagasaki and Singapore that provided the basis for some of the comments on that portion of the epilogue; and to Byron and Mary-Jo Good for allowing me to come along to their field sites in Aceh and Yogyakarta, as well as companionship throughout the writing of many of these essays. I thank as well Felicity Aulino, João Biehl, Veena Das, Philippe Descola, Michael Jackson, Sheila Jasanoff, Clifford Geertz, Mitzi Goheen, Donna Haraway, Jean Jackson, Arthur Kleinman, Bruno Latour, Peter Locke, Andrew Lyons, Mariza Periano, Adriana Petryna, John Philips, Paul Rabinow, Rick Shweder, Brighu Singh, Orin Starn, Stanley Tambiah, and Eduardo Viveiros de Castro for inviting and intellectual companionship in the key chapters of the volume; to Thorsten Trimpop for teaching a wonderful film class with me and for doing the photographs of artworks I own to Duke's requirements.

All essays have been significantly revised. Previously published versions appeared as follows:

An earlier abbreviated version of chapter 1 appeared as "Experimental Ethnography" in *The International Encyclopedia of Anthropology* (Wiley-Blackwell, 2015).

CHAPTER 2 appeared in two previous versions, "The Lightness of Existence and the Origami of 'French Anthropology': Latour, Descola, Viveiros de Castro, Meillassoux, and Their So-Called Ontological Turn," *HAU: Journal of Ethnographic Theory* 4, no. 1 (2015): 331–55; and as "Double-Click: the Fables and Language Games of Latour and Descola," American Anthropological Association Meetings, 2015, available on Academica (http://www.academia.edu/9538290/).

CHAPTER 3 appeared differently framed as "Words and Deeds, Truth and Conduct—Method in Anthropology and Moral Philosophy" in *SCTIW Review: Journal of the Society for Contemporary Thought and the Islamicate World*, October 7, 2014, http://sctiw.org/sctiwreviewarchives/archives/295.

CHAPTER 4 appeared as "Deep Play, Violence, and Social Reconstruction" in *Clifford Geertz by His Colleagues*, ed. Richard A. Shweder and Byron Good (Chicago, IL: University of Chicago Press, 2005).

CHAPTER 6 appeared as "Galactic Polities, Radical Egalitarianism, and the Practice of Anthropology: Tambiah on Logical Paradoxes, Social Contradictions, and Cultural Oscillations" in *Radical Egalitarianism: Local Realities, Global Relations*, ed. Felicity Aulino, Miriam Goheen, and Stanley J. Tambiah, 233–58 (New York: Fordham University Press, 2013).

CHAPTER 7, part 1, appeared as "*Urban Mahabharata*: Listening with Veena Das to Ordinary Ethics," *Somatosphere*, February 12, 2015, http://somatosphere.net/2015/02/affliction.html. And a slightly different version of the full chapter appears as "Urban Mahabharata: Health Care, Ordinary, Traditional, and Contemporary Ethics." *Medical Anthropology Theory* 4 (2017): 3. http://medanthrotheory.org/issue/vol-4-3/.

CHAPTER 9 appeared as "Philosophia and Anthropologia: Reading alongside Benjamin in Yazd, Derrida in Qum, Arendt in Tehran" in *The Ground Between: Anthropologists Engage Philosophy*, ed. Veena Das, Michael Jackson, Arthur Kleinman, and Bhrigupati Singh, 188–217 (Durham, NC: Duke University Press, 2014).

CHAPTER 10 appeared as "Time, Camera and the Digital Pen: Writing Culture Operating Systems 1.0–3.0." in *Writing Culture and the Life of Anthropology*, ed. Orin Starn, 72-104 (Durham, NC: Duke University Press, 2015).

CHAPTER 11 appeared as "A Polyphonic Nine-Canto *Singspiel after 25 years of Writing Culture*" in *Anthropologica* 53, no. 2 (2011): 307–17.

CHAPTER 12, in a slightly different version, appears as "Zen Exercises: Anthropological Discipline and Ethics" in *Unfinished: The Anthropology of Becoming*, ed. João Biehl and Peter Locke (Durham, NC: Duke University Press, 2017).

NOTES

Prologue

1. "It is necessary," Negri notes (*Political Descartes*, 147n106), "to insist on the plasticity of Descartes's image of *malin*, the *malin genie*. The image is both historically and ideologically rich. . . . '*Malin*' appears in Descartes as both noun and adjective: '*les malins*,' '*les esprits malins*' are all those who, out of pure wickedness, are opposed to the communication of truth." The problem at this historical juncture for Descartes becomes "not whether Galileo is wrong or right. The problem is how truth can live in the world" (143). It is one that has renewed relevance in today's world.

2. Dismayed by the failures of the revolutions of 1848 and the reactionary accession of Louis Bonaparte, Marx describes the centuries-long movement toward a bourgeois revolution and then a proletarian one as having moved "backward," hopefully to clear the way for future movement again "forward." In Paris the uprising of 1848 was more an artisanal one than a proletarian one, and a real industrial working-class culture, which Marx tried to educate and organize, would not develop for another quarter century.

3. See M. M. J. Fischer, "Ask Not What Man Is But What One May Expect of Him," chapter 6 in *Anthropological Futures* for a contemporary reading and interpretation of Kant's *Anthropology from a Pragmatic Point of View*. On the notion of ethnography operating in third spaces, see also M. M. J. Fischer, *Emergent Forms of Life*, "Introduction."

4. Urban planner and geographer Mike Douglass, noting that urbanization is occurring at an unprecedented speed and scale in Asia, sees Seoul, under mayor Park Won-soon, as a model of progressive change, using such key tools as participatory budgeting to get funds into local communities, operating a mobile mayor's office that moves around the city to engage in solving community-specific issues together with local residents, appointing citizen mayors in different localities, shifting subsidies from developers to distributive justice measures, creating one thousand village communities across the city, emphasizing cultural spaces, business, and social enterprise

cooperatives, and many other innovations (Douglass, "From Corporate Globopolis to Progressive Cities" [2017], "Creative Communities" [2016], "From Good City to Progressive City" [2016], "Globopolis or Cosmopolis" [2009]).

5. I am reminded by the work of Orit Halperin and Gökce Günel (2017) to *perhaps* differentiate the experimentalism of anthropology from that of the often MIT-trained designers of new urbanisms in places such as Abu Dhabi, South Korea, and, in my ethnographic work, Singapore, which Günel and Halperin describe as propagating a logic of "demo projects," where "ever more speculation, algorithmically managed, to derive value from the possible, never realized futures," and where "cities, the site of performance and demonstration associated with democracy and the 'demos,' terms first emerging with the idea of the polis or city, have now become a literal 'demo' as in prototype, [and] . . . the inhabitants . . . test subjects" (9). The equivocation *perhaps* is that much anthropology and humanities also invokes a kind of self-legitimating catastrophic threat (an often nostalgic or romantic antitechnologism that expects or at least prepares for the worst from technology) parallel to the utopian legitimations Günel and Halperin describe for these speculative, experimental, eco-urbanisms. Günel and Halperin rightly criticize these latter logics for a tendency to "evacuate differences, temporalities, and societal structures." By contrast, differences, temporalities, and societal structures are essential, critical, pleasurable, and resourceful for anthropology, even if they can also become instrumentalized as fodder for yet further advertising in the logics described by Günel and Halperin.

6. I draw upon Walter Benjamin's figural language here: of the dialectical image—always a double image—juxtaposing past and present, aspirations and banal realities, and providing a montaged disjunction, jarring, or fissuring of consciousness, rupturing the flow of naturalistic time, producing flashes of enlightenment, recognition, or re-orientation. The dialectical image is "the image that is read—which is to say, the image in the now of its recognizability [*das Bild im Jetzt der Erkennbarkeik*]." Benjamin, *Arcades Project*, [(Convolute N, 3, 1), 463], or, in Freud's terms, its *Nachtraeglichkeit*.

7. Thanks to George Marcus for this phrase as a possible title for this volume. My original title, which reviewers liked, was *Anthropology Emergent from the Chrysalis of the Twentieth Century*, to resonate with the previous volumes, *Emergent Forms of Life and the Anthropological Voice* and *Anthropological Futures*. All these titles are variations on the same theme.

8. Smartness is perhaps to be defined as increasing sensitivities or sensibilities: we distinguish dumb devices as passive, smart ones as responsive, able to pass information from one place, or state, to another. Hence there are degrees of smarter and smarter devices and infrastructures, sometime too smart for robustness, safety, privacy, or other values that need to be included in the balance.

9. Thanks to Michael Watts ("Specters of Oil," 166) for this paraphrase and rearticulation of Henri Lefebvre's three categories of space in Watts's review of the cultural archive of oil's representations. Watts focuses especially on photographer Ed Kashi's "ethnographic visual practice" ("working slowly and carefully, immersing himself in the local context," relying on the help of Nigerian locals) as features of his "critical and alternative photography" (174).

10. Small-worlds hypotheses are popularly known as the likelihood that any two persons will require only "six degrees of separation" to establish a relationship to each other. Experiments tested this originally by mailing letters between people who were presumptively geographically and socially distant to see if the letters reached their target and in how many steps or hops. Frigyes Karinthy, Stanley Milgram, Manfred Kochren, Ithiel de Sola Pool, Benoit Mandelbrot, and Michael Gurevich were among the early mathematicians and social scientists who first explored this topic experimentally and mathematically.

11. One might think here of hegemonies or modes of trying to make one's class position's worldview appear natural, just the way things are; and, alternatively, the sociological observation that underlings often know their superiors better than the latter know them. Transparency of chains of administrative decision making or of commercial supply chains may be of ideological importance, despite the fact that the technologies of these chains exist in part to obscure any such transparency; and yet ethnographic or investigative journalism can sleuth them out, and good history can do the same after the fact, if written records are themselves available. Such sleuthing often requires attending to the working experience of many small worlds along the chains.

12. See Steven Tyler's brilliant essays in *The Unspeakable: Discourse, Dialogue, and Rhetoric in the Postmodern World* (1987), and his earlier *The Said and the Unsaid: Mind, Meaning, and Culture* (1978).

13. On "ethical plateaus," see M. M. J. Fischer, *Emergent Forms of Life*. This will be explained further on.

14. In development work, Development Alternatives International (DAI) was formed by anthropologists and remains one of the most well-regarded such consultancies, based in its methods of long-term commitments rather than short "project time" cycles.

15. I take the phrase, of course, from Walter Benjamin's *The Work of Art in the Age of Mechanical Reproduction*. Our age is no longer that age, the subject, in part, of chapter 10.

16. The Necessary Stage's production of *Actor Forty* (premiered in Singapore in February 2017) in Mandarin and other Chinese languages (Hokkien, Cantonese, etc.), performed by the superb actress Yeo Yann Yann, is a bravura example. A one-woman play requiring many situational changes of sociolinguistic language codes and localizations (speaking to a Cannes Film Festival awards ceremony, to a Hong Kong director, to Malay-Chinese reporters, miming Singaporean and Malaysian television soap operas, singing Singapore state-building songs), *Actor Forty* was scripted by Haresh Sharma and directed by Alvin Tan, neither of whom speak Chinese. The script was translated through a number of script revisions by Quah Sy Ren (a bilingual playwright and essayist) and bilingual dramaturge Melissa Lim, with help from various dialect speakers. Even non-Chinese speakers living in the region can recognize many of the subtle changes as the role switches from introspection to varied addressees. The character is an actress turning forty, surprised by becoming unexpectedly pregnant, who negotiates her daily decisions and roles in life. The play is, as well, an

ethnographically rich portrait of a transnational life, located in a Chinese language lifeworld, with English-language abilities, that many professionals inhabit today.

17. See reviews in *Variety* by Markland Taylor, http://variety.com/2003/legit/reviews/the-children-of-herakles-1200544099/; *The Boston Phoenix* by Carolyn Clay, http://www.bostonphoenix.com/boston/arts/theater/documents/02650464.htm; *The Theater Review* by Kermit Dunkelberg, http://muse.jhu.edu/journals/tj/summary/v055/55.3dunkelberg.html; *Didaskalia* by James T. Svedensen, http://www.didaskalia.net/reviews/2003/2003_01_04_02.html; and the dissent in the *New York Review of Books* by Daniel Mendelsohn, http://www.nybooks.com/articles/archives/2003/feb/13/the-bad-boy-of-athens/. I am not suggesting the plotlines align or that there is a direct allegory between Athens and our current situations, but the symbolic and psychological logics often do align: Iolaus trapped in his wheelchair, attempting to rise and fight, suffering the indignities of infirmity, age, and exile; the idea of sacrificing a child, a virgin, to ensure a victory; the virtuoso performance by the same actress playing the young frightened girl, transformed into willing ritual victim; and the old grandmother twisted in vengeance and rage demanding death for Eurystheus in violation of Athens' rules for treating POWs, signaling as so often in Greek tragedy, that the psychosocial consequences carry over generation to generation; the mysterious power of rituals both to heal and incite, signaled by the double aulos/flute and chanting in minor key; the cold rationality of the aggressors who think themselves more powerful; the diplomacy of the Athenian leadership finding a way between ruin and principle; the questions of the crowd, the public of the agora, the courtroom's cross-examinations and those of the parliamentary committee.

18. I vividly still remember the stagings of *A Doll's House* and *Hedda Gabbler* at the National Center for the Performing Arts in Mumbai in the 1990s produced and directed by Alyque and Pearl Padamsee, and starring their daughter, Raell Padamsee. There have of course been many other productions.

19. Ong says, "I was interested in a rewriting of *King Lear* from the point of view of Goneril, and Kishida's plays always investigated characters such as Japanese women who, in order to resist patriarchy, became violent and demonic. . . . She [Kishida] also disrupted established power hierarchies by writing in vernacular Japanese, disregarding the classical literary language" (Ong, *Lear Dreaming*, 247). Noh theater, he suggests, is both a very conservative art form, and a Samurai art linked to Shogun culture, and appropriate to the authoritarian wielding of power (246). A Sumatran Randai performer from a matrilineal culture is used to perform the community storyteller, he says, because "I thought it was important to have a group of artists . . . who saw the mother as the most important element in their culture," and the Randai form "embodies a didactic theatrical form through which morality tales are passed on to the members of a community" (246).

20. On the importance of Durkheimian thought in Indochina, see Bayly, "French Anthropology."

21. http://www.stpi.com.sg/download/171115stpigreybooklet.pdf.

22. Ventura, *Recyclables*. http://www.stpi.com.sg/assets/artists/2012/RonaldVentura/RV%20Catalogue.pdf.

23. In 2016 the Farensworth Museum in Camden, Maine, dedicated a fascinating show to Donald Saff's collaborations with Jim Dine, Nancy Graves, Roy Lichtenstein, Philip Pearlstein, Robert Rauschenberg, James Rosenquist, and James Turrell.

24. Tyler was the son of Romanian and Hungarian immigrants to Indiana, where the father (original surname Tyira) worked in steel mills and also was a stonemason. Ken Tyler trained at the Art Institute of Chicago, worked in a steel mill briefly, served in Korea, and did lithography at Indiana University with Garo Antreasian and the Tamarind Lithography Workshop in Los Angeles. He then experienced a catalyzing collaboration with the artist Josef Albers.

25. Lithography is said to have been invented in 1796 in Munich by Alois Senefelder, who could not afford to print his plays by the more expensive copper engraving, and so developed this cheaper alternative.

26. I become attentive to paper since working with printmaker Eric Avery (M. M. J. Fischer, "With a Hammer," 2000).

27. Suh is the son of Suh Se-ok, a master of traditional painting, and did BFA and MFA work in Korea before continuing studies at the Rhode Island School of Design and Yale. He now lives in New York, London, and Seoul.

28. Do Ho Suh, *I Am Your Conduit*. Catalogue. STPI, 2011. http://www.stpi.com.sg/assets/artists/2011/DoHoSuh/FINAL_DO%20HO_catalogue.pdf. https://ocula.com/art-galleries/singapore-tyler-print-institute/artworks/do-ho-suh/i-am-your-conduit/.

29. Do Ho Suh, *I Am Your Conduit*. https://www.artsy.net/artwork/do-ho-suh-i-am-your-conduit. https://www.google.com/search?q=Do+Ho+Suh,+%E2%80%9Ci+am+your+conduit%E2%80%9D.&biw=1280&bih=557&tbm=isch&tbo=u&source=univ&sa=X&ved=0ahUKEwj_3eScnZfPAhXFFz4KHSENDoAQ7AkIPw.

30. It could possibly be a Vertebraesomniumanisoptera: "isoptera" means only symmetrical wings but is usually used for termites with quite differently attached wings. Another of the Pelvissomniumpapilio (B) has a pelvis shape of green leaves humorously attached immediately below two golden-bud or robot-helmet-like heads, and actually looks like large eyes or a Fledermaus mask, below which is a long stem ending in a small rib cage and posterior insect-like segment and two wisps of legs or antennae in the wrong end (or maybe the whole thing is moving downward). In another variation, a magnificent three-segment insect with four sets of five finger-bone structures ending in arrow-like brown-black leaves all in gold and red looks like a Japanese samurai. It is classified as a Manussomniumcrustacea.

31. The book began as Kepler's dissertation to defend Copernicus on the motion of the earth, with the frame story added later, including a fictionalized version of his own life as an assistant to Tycho Brahe.

32. For more on the conference, see http://www.media.mit.edu/video/view/h20-2007-05-09-1.

33. For Seth Teller, see http://ppat.mit.edu/fall2015/index.html.

34. My wife, Susann Wilkinson, sat in on the course with Grace Teo and William Lim in 2014, and I went along to the class project demonstrations, and to a show at the Boston Science Museum by Grace's start-up company, Open Style Lab. The following year, in fall 2015, I invited Grace to my "Social Theory" class for first-year graduate

students, precisely to expose them to an ethnographic method for practical use, and was pleased that Marc Aidinoff took the opportunity to interview Grace further and develop a quite insightful paper on the class pedagogy. Open Style Lab is based at the International Design Center at MIT, part of the MIT-Singapore University of Technology and Design collaboration (of which I am a member). As a Singaporean, Grace also was a great interlocutor on Singapore, and a teacher for Singaporean students who came to MIT for short course training. http://videolectures.net/designdis-ability2015_teo_design_dis-ability/; and https://vimeo.com/125575256.

35. See M. M. J. Fischer, "The BAC Consultation."

Chapter 1. Experimental Ethnography

1. Malinowski 1935; Firth 1957.

2. Evans-Pritchard 1940, 1951, 1956; Allan 1965; Dumont 1970; Gluckman 1945; Karp and Bird, 1987; Werbner, 1984.

3. Bateson 1936; Leach, 1954.

4. Turner 1957; Obeysekere, 1981.

5. Mauss 1925; Fortes and Evans-Pritchard 1940; Lévi-Strauss 1949; Maybury-Lewis 1979; Radcliffe-Brown and Forde 1950; Schneider and Gough 1961.

6. Richards 1939; Colson 1979; Wilson 1941. This tradition continues on from the 1940s generation: Fischer and Barfield 1980; Fisher 1995; K. Fortun 2001; Goodell 1986; Maybury-Lewis, ed. 1980; Ramos 1990/1995; Tambiah 1957, 1986; Taussig 1986; and many more.

7. Maybury-Lewis 1965, 1974; Bohannan 1953, 1954; Descola 1996, 1998; Cassagrande 1960.

8. Redfield 1930; Lewis 1951; Malinowski 1922; Weiner 1976; *Women of Value*; Evans-Pritchard 1956; Johnson 1994; Hutchinson 1996.

9. Morreira 2016.

10. Bateson 1958; Freeman 1983; Rosaldo 1980; Tambiah 1980, 1992.

11. In 1972, Curtis and Hunt's *In the Land of the War Canoes* (1914) was restored by Bill Holm and given a soundtrack recorded by Kwakwaka'wakw singers, including three who had been actors in the original film. Similarly, Curtis and Hunt's photographs of dancers in ceremonial masks from 1914 would provide materials for brilliant reanalysis by Claude Lévi-Strauss (1982) of the masks, the myths behind them, and the ecology and exchange relations those myths articulated. Franz Boas and George Hunt's series of shorts done in 1931 (with 16-millimeter film, and wax cylinders for sound recording) were also reworked into a full film by Bill Holm in 1972. Similarly, Merian C. Cooper and Ernest B. Schoedsack's film *Grass: A Nation's Battle for Life* (1925), with its rare footage, is now nicely juxtaposed with Garthwaite's history of the Bakhtiari (1983). Robert J. Flaherty's *Nanook of the North* (1922), still a classic, is pedagogically usefully counterpoised to Philip Kaufman's *The White Dawn* (1974), based on true events and probing cross-cultural conflicts (coscripted by James Houston, whose book [1971] was based on Inuit oral histories told to him, the third film to be shot in Inuit locations, and the first to use actual Inuit dialect); and to Inuit

filmmaker Zacharias Kunuk's use of his own culture's mythic structures and historical encounter with a Danish ethnographer in *The Fast Runner* (2002) and *The Journals of Knud Rasmussen* (2006).

12. Agee and Evans 1941; Bourke-White and Caldwell 1937.

13. Burtynsky 2003, 2005, 2016; Misrach 1987, 2014; Nagatani 1991; Manaugh 2014; Salgado 2005a, b; Walley 2013, Walley and Boebel 2016.

14. Griaule 1965; Leiris 1934; Bataille 1994; Benjamin 1999; Clifford 1981, 1988; Fischer 2000b.

15. Dwyer 1982; Majnep and Bulmer 1977; Fischer 1986, 1994, Fischer and Kocanowicz 1993.

16. Feld 1982; Tedlock 1983; Fischer and Abedi 1990.

17. Crapanzano 1980a; Taussig 1980, 1986, 2003.

18. Lemelson 2009; Oppenheim 2014.

19. The term "non-guild histories" came particularly from Africanists. D. W. Cohen 1994 was particularly key in pushing the concept into contestations of contemporary histories in comparative contexts beyond regional framings, beyond the differences of written versus oral histories including griot forms. Louise White (2000) importantly expanded this in feminist directions that incorporated re-readings of rumor and urban folklore. Work in India in the Subaltern and postcolonial traditions shared between historians and anthropologists became similarly important. Donna Haraway successfully put feminist counter-readings of the sciences on the agenda in ways that could not be ignored, first in natural history (museums) and primatology (1989) and then for the biological and technosciences (1991, 1997), and this work was amplified by ethnographic work (Traweek 1988). More generally such non-guild work world be explored in the contemporary worlds by seeking new ethnographic forms of interviewing strategically placed people to explore connections, networks, and formations that were poorly mapped by traditional social sciences (Marcus, ed., 1993–2000). An important predecessor in picking apart the narrative complexities of both guild and non-guild histories was Hayden White (2000), who with Haraway, and Gregory Bateson at the University of California, Santa Cruz, would train several generations of students who helped transform the human sciences in the 1980s.

20. Das 2007; M. Fischer 2003, 2004.

21. A line of questioning here might be toward such boundary-blurring films as Ulrike Ottinger's Mongolia and China films in which she specifically targets scenarios she calls "transfers of culture," saying "There are only these mixtures and no separate and pure cultures." She continues, "I've always been intrigued by the nomadization of cultural ideas—the obscure ways they take and flourish at one particular intersection and not at another" (quoted in Rickels 2008, 144). Ottinger's nine-hour-long documentary *Taiga* (1992) on the Mongols of the Darkhad Valley and the Sayyan Mountains lingers on various scenes such as a shaman's midnight séance, a wrestling match, the women making yogurt, the disassembly of an almost-Ikea-like yurt for migration and reassembly, the overtone singing at a wedding, and the deep and high harmonics of yaks and sheep as a pastoral soundscape against snow-covered mountains. Motor-

cycles, modern skirts, and a few other tokens of the contemporary period are not airbrushed out, nor are they pursued. However, films like the three-language-titled *Johanna d'Arc of Mongolia* (1989) redeploys old tropes of the analogy of train and film. In this film, Ottinger stages a trip in a museum like train car that begins in the West (Russia) and travels into Mongolia, where the passengers are campily taken hostage by a Mongolian princess until, at the end, she returns to her life in America. In *Diamond Dance*, Jewish merchants provide what Rickels calls a "primal structure" of the long distance, of the nomadization of culture, and the acquisition of "a certain travel know-how," in what he also lovingly calls Ottinger's work with "palimpsestously perverse contexts" (127). In a way there could be, though I don't think there has been, a conversation with Third Cinema, particularly when Ottinger focuses on the "new nomads" of Eastern Europe after the fall of the Soviet Union: "Former teachers, lawyers, farmers, carpenters, now traders of anything at all traveling along the sidelines of borders and main streets" (22). Ottinger claims her documentary camera style, using slow pans, in *China: The Arts—Everyday Life* (1986) was influenced by the scrollwork of Chinese nature painting. Just as she tries to juxtapose the artistry in everyday life with the more refined "arts" such as Chinese opera, so Chinese painters tried to capture on the same scroll the panoramic landscape as well as intricate miniature scenes of daily life, monks meditating, or court life (117).

22. Wilmsen (1986) pushed hard against the romanticism about the Bushmen, as did John Marshall in his later years, described nicely in MacDonald (2013).

23. I have taught three or four different kinds of classes on ethnographic film. First, in 1973, I participated in an extraordinary class and film series led by Tim Asch and James J. Fox at Harvard, drawing on the rich DER resources, and able to show, for instance, both the silent *Nanook of the North* and an emotionally very differently valenced version with music, as well as involving all the debates surrounding Tim Asch's experiments in the Amazon: Did Napoleon Chagnon stage the Ax Fight? And why does it fail to change undergraduates' prejudices? How did the Summer Linguistics Institute react to the filming of their proselytizing? (They loved it, while Cambridge audiences were horrified.)

Second, in the 1980s and early 1990s, having invited to the Center for Cultural Studies Teshome Gabriel, a leading figure in Third Cinema studies, and Hamid Naficy from UCLA, and the filmmaker Maria Zmarz-Koczanowicz from Poland as Rockefeller fellows, I mounted a course at Rice University with the support of George Marcus that explored a much wider array of ethnographic film strategies (Fischer 1995b, 1997). Among the most interesting experiments were Rea Tajiri's *History and Memory* (1991), which posed the question of how to film something where there were no images (Japanese American internees were forbidden cameras); Pier Paolo Pasolini's *Notes towards an African Orestes* (1970), which used footage from Africa to restage the Greek play and showed it to African students to stimulate political discussion; Jorge Furtado's *Ilha das Flores* (1989), which took on not merely scavengers at a landfill (poverty, inequality) but also the misuses of syllogistic logic in the advertising propaganda, the whole short film itself made by an advertising collective; Trinh T. Minh-ha's *Surname Viet, Given Name Nam* (1989), which requires students to know about the national epic poem *Tale of Kieu*; and Andrei Zagdansky's *The Interpretation of Dreams* (1990), which managed, at a moment of archival openness, to bring together footage of the Bolshevik Revolution and the German *Anschluss* of Austria with readings from Freud.

Third, at MIT in the 1990s, I offered a course on the ethnography of the Middle East through locally directed narrative films, and it was a fascinating dramatic space for exploring the dramatically different reactions of students from different backgrounds. The ending of Farida Benlyazid's film *A Door to the Sky* (Morocco 1988), for instance, was rejected by American students as "implausible," but accepted by Middle Easterners as metaphorically obvious. An important outgrowth of that class was Naghmeh Sohrabi's fieldwork and bachelor's thesis analysis of the Iranian films of "Sacred Defense" (Iran-Iraq War), out of which war experience a number of leading Iranian filmmakers of the 1990s emerged, and she was able to show how different in structural form Iranian war films were from, say, American war films.

Finally, most recently, in 2016, with filmmaker Thorsten Trimpop, I offered an experimental class at MIT in which students produced their own short films after reviewing the different styles of ethnographic and documentary filmmaking, and with visits from soundscape artist Ernst Karel, documentarian John Gianvito, a session in the MIT virtual reality lab with William Uricchio, "immersion" documentary filmmaker Lisandro Alonso, and others, including Trimpop's own films on a Stasi prison in East Berlin and a town in the Fukushima exclusion zone. The class agenda was the trade-offs between ethnographic documentation understood broadly and aesthetic experimentation (understood as form deployed to expose content).

24. Marcus, ed., 1993–2000; Fischer 2000a, and chapter 10 this volume.

25. Peattie 1987; Cefkin 2009.

26. Wallace 1970, 1978; Wallace; Greenbatt 1980; Vesser 1989; N. Davis 1983; Darnton 1984; Ginsburg 1980; Le Roy Ladurie 1978.

27. Dumit 2012; Fischer 2003; Kelty 2017b, and for a version without concern for historical or emergent properties, see Latour in chapter 2. Precursors include Wittgenstein 1953; Burke 1945, 1950, 1966; Goffman 1956; Austin 1962; Lyotard 1979; Schechner 1985; and V. Turner 1988.

28. Such processes include the chemical industry (K. Fortun 2001), nuclear disaster (Petryna 2001), environmental policy (Tsing 2005; Lowe 2006), clinical trials (Kuo 2009; Petryna 2009; Sunder Rajan 2015), climate change (Callison 2014), open-source information technology (Kelty 2008), civic media to break through corporate and government sequestered information (Wylie 2015), biocapital and new biomedical technologies (Dumit 2012; Lock 2002; Sanal 2011; Sunder Rajan 2006; Sunder Rajan, ed., 2012), postconflict processes involving mental health, gender dynamics, and psychosocial processes (Theidon 2013; Slyomovics 2005; Good et al. 2008), and human rights and technology (E. Davis 2017; Medina and Wiener 2016; Thakor 2016; Wagner 2008).

29. For example, dependence on clinical trials and NGOs for health care. Biehl and Petryna, ed., 2013; Cooper and Waldby 2014; Dumit 2012; Petryna, 2001; Sunder Rajan 2006, 2015.

30. Davis 2012, 2017a, b; Slyomovics 2005; Theidon 2014.

31. W. Anderson 2008; Fearnley 2013; Fischer 2009a, 2013a; Haraway, 1997, 2003, 2008; Landecker 2007, 2011, 2013a, b, 2016a, b; Latour 2013c.

32. Biehl and Petryna, eds., 2013.

33. Other important new Singapore ethnographically inflected and documentary films include then polytechnic students' Lee Xian Jie and Jeremy Bo's *Before We Forget* (2011), an observational documentary about care of parents with dementia, following developments over the course of a year; K. Rajagopal's *A Yellow Bird* (2016) about the underclass, minoritized, and marginalized; Jason Soo's *1987: Untracing the Conspiracy* (1987), using conversations and intertitles with ex-detainees of the Catholic social welfare organization and students of the 1980s generation whose incarceration cast a long shadow and embarrassment for the government, and illuminating the effects on these individuals' lives of the three decades since; and Ken Kwek's *Unlucky Plaza* (2014), like *Remittance*, also about the Filippina domestic workers, a film partly set in and named after the Lucky Plaza shopping mall where the women gather on Sundays and one of the settings for *Remittance*. Although *Unlucky Plaza* is a narrative film with a plot based on Sidney Lumet's 1975 *Dog Day Afternoon*, it explores all the above themes. Both *Remittances* and *Unlucky Plaza* also show the positive community building, socializing interactional spaces, and courageous entrepreneurship of the lives depicted.

34. Beginning with the much-celebrated early film *Gav* (1969), scripted by the psychiatrist-ethnographer and writer Gholam-Hossein Sa'edi, the surrealist meditation on the obscuring of history and changing media in the film *Moghul-ha* (Parviz Kimiavi, 1973), and the post–Iran-Iraq War film *Red Ribbon* (Ebrahim Hatamikia, 1999; see more in chapter 10).

35. In a series of prize-winning dramatic performances, Anna Deavere Smith has done in-depth interviewing with a range of people directly involved in, or in the communities involved in, major critical events in recent United States cultural politics, and then embodied those individuals onstage to provide a multiperspectival account of those events. The two best known are about the Crown Heights riots in Brooklyn, New York, in August 1991 (*Fires in the Mirror*, 1992); and the Los Angeles riots in 1992 (*Twilight: Los Angeles, 1992*, performed in 1994), in which anthropologist Dorinne Kondo was also one of the embodied characters. A third project on ethnic tensions in schools is *Notes from the Field: Doing Time in Education* (2016).

36. Earls and Carlson 2002; Earls, Raviola, and Carlson 2008; Komo, Carlson, Brennan, and Earls 2008.

37. Of note here is the stress by Sun Huizhu, vice president of the Shanghai Theater Academy, editor of the Chinese edition of The Drama Review, TDR, on *social performance* in modernizing urban China. Schechner's "environmental theater" blurs the relation between actor and audience in the sense that the performances partake of and challenge the environment in which they are staged.

38. See, for instance, how Schechner's ideas get transformed in Shanghai and Australia in the essays by Yu Jiancun, Peng Yongwen, and Peter Eckersall in Harding and Rosenthal, eds. 2011.

39. Thanks to both Kiran Kumar and Zai Kunming for insightful conversations that underpin the following paragraph.

Chapter 2. Ontology and Metaphysics

1. As it so happened, Viveiros de Castro and I sat together at Latour's lecture, sharing a copy of Latour's written script, which he had handed to us; on my other side was Eduardo Kohn, author of *How Forests Think*, also published in 2013, who was also on the earlier panel.

2. On *ressentiment* (which conventionally retains its French spelling in English-language sociology and philosophy texts), see Max Scheler (1994 and his other writings), who presciently analyzed the rising problems of cultural attitudes in Weimar Germany. A founder of phenomenology along with Husserl, and a precursor of Merleau-Ponty, his work was suppressed by the Nazis.

3. On this reading of Descartes, see now Jenny Boulboullé (2013).

4. *An Inquiry into Modes of Existence* (aka *AIME*) is a book. The book is part of a web project, aka AIME Project. The web project, when completed in August 2014, was to have encompassed three books: a digital book (which could be printed out), which helped launch the project; the book reacted to here, published by Harvard University Press; and a book that was to have accompanied an exhibition in August 2014. The project was to take place in three phases: first, Latour's conception; second, an online "reaction environment," for contributions from a team of trained "coenquirers" along with inputs from anyone who registered and wanted to participate (closely moderated, filtered, and shaped by the coenquirers, on a Wikipedia sort of model); and third, a final completed presentation, which as far as I know has never appeared.

5. Empedocles was a Sicilian Greek philosopher said to have the ability to cure disease and old age, and to avert epidemics and storms.

6. The phrase is the title of the book about World War I by Barbara Tuchman (1962).

7. In his Gifford Lectures, Latour speaks of Gaia not as a sphere or globe but as a membrane and as many historical loops in which humans are cocooned, as within threads of silk, as their conditions of existence.

8. Warfare at an abstract and political philosophy level under conditions of Gaia's turbulence is the subject of his fifth Gifford Lecture.

9. One wonders if Latour would equally condemn Vesalius and Descartes for their public dissections, or, now, Chinese artist Zhang Dali's use of hanging naked resin bodies of immigrant workers by their feet.

10. Among his earliest efforts was an interesting one to map Paris through its many paths that could be followed virtually: Latour and Emilie Hermant, "Paris: Invisible City" (2006). http://www.bruno-latour.fr/sites/default/files/downloads/viii_paris-city-gb.pdf.

11. For a different understanding that nature and culture are not a dual pair but quite asymmetric in their semiotic properties, see Fischer 2009, chap. 3.

12. Viveiros de Castro commends Kopenawa's text with Bruce Alpert as "a masterpiece of 'interethnic politics'" and the cosmological narration "doubl[ing] as an indignant and proud claim for the Yanomami people's right to exist" ("Forest of Mirrors"). He

acknowledges the histories of movement, warfare, conversion, disease epidemics, and so on, in passing. And, as Latour (2009) suggests, the discourse in "Anthropocenography" is also about the ecological devastation in the Amazon, especially for the movement of small bands of hunter-gardener-fishermen. But these are not the central focus as Viveiros de Castro tries to work out the meanings of what was happening in his exquisitely described nights among the Arawete when one and then other shamans would begin their lonely, haunting songs till dawn.

13. See his review of different Amerindian indigenous language terms glossed by the English word "animal" in "The Forest of Mirrors." "Nature," I think (Fischer 2009: chap. 3), is a *linguistic* term meaning both what is ostensible and what escapes—as in "my nature is myself but also that which myself does not control." Insofar as there is a nature/culture distinction, it is a generative or movable *linguistic* binary, not a substantive one. "Unnatural," for instance, not "cultural" is the antonym of "natural."

14. Toward the end of Viveiros de Castro's "Anthropocenography," lecture at the University of California, Davis, he connects his interpretation of Amerindian or Amazonian cosmology to Meillassoux's work, and, less convincingly, to Dipesh Chakrabarty's "The Climate of History: Four Theses." Thorne (2011) argues that Meillassoux's linguistic gambits are largely a recirculating of eighteenth-century apocalyptic discourse. The frequency of the term "God" in recent French philosophy is culturally interesting. Chakrabarty, by contrast, is interested in the agency of human beings, "the geological agency human beings [have been gaining]" and its threat to writing history framed as the growth of human freedom. It is the reverse of Latour's interest in coding human agency as always already nonhuman.

Chapter 3. Pure Logic and Typologizing

1. On which see also "Ask Not What Man Is, But What We May Expect of Him," chapter 6 in M. Fischer 2009a.

2. Lee Rosenblaum, "Fine on the Rhine: Richter's Cologne Cathedral Window Unveiled Next Month," *CultureGrrl*, July 5, 2007, http://www.artsjournal.com/culturegrrl/2007/07/fine_on_the_rhine_richters_col.html.

3. In his book *Words and Things* (1959), Gellner caused a storm by addressing these same issues of words and deeds, truth and conduct, and their relations to our means of testing of self and our tools of perception. His attack on British philosophy of the day from a social anthropological perspective so irritated Gilbert Ryle, the editor of *Mind*, that he refused to review it. But Bertrand Russell had contributed an introduction and defended it. The controversy turned Gellner into a celebrity (Czeglédy, 2003). Gellner was a teacher of mine at the LSE and nearly my tutor, and I have remained indebted to his thought, despite his misunderstanding of *Writing Culture* and *Anthropology as Cultural Critique*, and his increasing lack of sympathy for Islamic traditionalisms just as he had little love for European Christian ones.

4. See M. Fischer 1980.

5. See Rabinow 2011, 2012, Rabinow and Stavrianakis 2013. See also my reviews (2014a, and 2014b).

Chapter 4. Violence and Deep Play

1. It is worth noting that Kenneth Burke, an important textual presence at Chicago in the Geertz and Victor Turner years, and cited in chapter 1, took issue with Marshall McLuhan's "the medium is the message" thesis on the grounds that the content of the message remains crucial and continues to be grounded in the grammar and rhetoric of symbolic action. Content and form are both important to performativity.

2. This remains a stylistically brilliant essay and homage to the "phenomenology" of Alfred Schutz, a genre—of which I am fond—of testing European theories with non-European materials, ideally in the end also retooling the theories. Gananath Obeysekere's *Medusa's Hair* is another such brilliant example. But as ethnography, it raises, as the cliché goes, maybe not more questions than it answers, but many unanswered questions. This is particularly so in the aftermath of the massacres of 1965. My own imagination for Bali is still profoundly marked by my much later visit to Bali with Byron and Mary-Jo Good, and meeting one of our colleagues, anthropologist Degun Santikarma whose passport continues to be marked as belonging to a "communist" family, and who thereby is prevented from holding any public position, including teaching at the university. He was a child in 1965 and lost both parents. The position of living among those one knows or suspects of killing one's parents perhaps only intensifies the tension surrounding the public masques and forms of address, time, and other social markers that Cliff raises in this essay, and more flexibly in "Deep Play." It certainly puts a different spin on the implications, long "After the Fact." In a recent series of public discussions with refugees from social upheavals preceding each performance of Peter Sellars's production of Euripedes's *The Children of Herakles* at the American Repertory Theater, I heard an almost identical observation from a young Bosnian woman, now studying at Boston University, speaking of living together with the killers of one's relatives, "It is a small society, and everyone knows . . ." While severe mental illness involves very different sorts of dynamics, Byron Good's work in Indonesia on the episodic course of psychoses, in their cultural expressions and social responses among families, also adds layers of questions to the general account of cultural psychology in Java (and Bali). I note these subsequent ethnographic benchmarks not as *criticism* of Cliff's work but as an ongoing form of ethnographic *critique* that builds upon and is able increasingly to incorporate more kinds of ethnographic, historical, cultural, and psychological materials. The provocations (to universal psychologies) and questions (for ethnographic method) raised by "Persons, Time, and Conduct" are such that the essay, I think, can no longer be used in the classroom by itself as a self-contained essay but requires additional materials to think with. That is, as they say these days, a feature, not a bug.

3. Nimitz 2000.

4. See Azoy (1982) on the ways Buzkashi provided a platform and interpretive grid for politics in Afghanistan.

Chapter 5. Amazonian Ethnography

1. See the extraordinary gold *tunjo* (votive) and other objects catalogued in Lleras et al., *Art of Gold*, from the Gold Museum of Bogota. On the cover is a gold miniature raft, an iconic and often-reproduced image, representing the raft used by the *zipa* (leader of the southern Muisca Confederation, centered on Bacatá, now Bogota). The zipa, covered in gold dust, would go out on a reed raft onto Lake Guatavita on a mountain peak (in Chibcha or Muisca language *gwa* means "mountain," and *gwati-bita*, "mountain peak") to make offerings, and would dive into the lake to wash off the gold dust. Gold reflected and represented the sun. The role of zipa was passed down matrilineally, usually through the eldest sister's eldest son.

Chapter 6. Ethnic Violence

1. The anthropologists I have in mind are Stanley J. Tambiah (b. 1929), Gananath Obeysekere (b. 1930), H. L. Seneviratne (b. 1934), Chandra Jayawardena (1929–1981), E. Valentine Daniel (b. 1947), and Sharika Thiranagama. Reciprocally, Sri Lanka, in part due to these Sri Lankans, has attracted the attention of other talented anthropologists: Edmund R. Leach (1910–1989), Nur Yalman (b. 1931), Steven Kemper, and Dennis McGilvray.

2. The 1956 act that made Sinhala the official language of the country, and Sri Lanka the official name, was a critical event. Thereafter all official government transactions had to be in Sinhala; non-Sinhala-speaking civil servants were given a time period in which to learn the language. Government-sponsored irrigation and colonization schemes in the east, which encouraged Sinhala to settle there, stoked the discontent of Tamils, who were concentrated in that part of the island. In 1958, 1977, and 1983 there were serious anti-Tamil riots. Tamil efforts at peaceful protest marches were met by organized violent thugs, often alleged to be allied with the governing party. Tamil militancy began to form, and resources were gathered by a string of bank robberies. The Sinhala migrants to the colonization schemes in the east began to be attacked by Tamils. As police and the army cracked down, they were targeted with landmines and attacks on police stations. Then came targeted assassinations and the use of suicide bombers, often targeting prominent politicians, including president Ranasinghe Premadasa, who was assassinated, and president Chandrika Bandaranaike Kumaratunga, who was injured. Security forces went on reprisal attacks and used torture to try to extract confessions to use in court, and Tamils engaged in ethnic cleansing in the Tamil-dominated northern districts of Jaffna, Mannar, and Mullaitivu. In 1978, the constitution was changed to make both Tamil and Sinhala national languages, and the new constitution specified that Tamil was to be used by the government in the north. But this and many other efforts to end the violence did not succeed for over three decades. In 1983 the Tamil Tigers (the Liberation Tigers of Tamil Eelam, or LTTE) began an armed insurgency to create a separate state. The ensuing civil war killed some 80,000 to 100,000 people. Only in May 2009 did the Tamil Tigers concede defeat.

3. Tambiah 1986, 1992; Obeysekere 1981, 1988; and Daniel 1996.

4. The linguistic slippage is one of the pleasures. "Tambi" is also, obviously, an affectionate short form of Tambiah. In a classificatory sense, a generation shift (mother's or father's younger brother) can be contained in the term, whereas in English "younger brother" is always in reference to the speaker and does not easily accommodate generation shifts without explanation or specification ("mother's younger brother"). I invoke the classificatory mother's brother here from Trobriand matrilineal cross-cousin marriage systems, for reasons that should become clear in the final section of this essay. In political usage, just as religious or civil rights movements in the United States may use the terms "brother" and "sister" for comrades as pure generational terms of address, so too members in the militant Tamil movements in the 1980s called one another "elder brother" (*anan*) or "younger brother" (*tambi*), or "elder sister" or "younger sister" (*akka, thambi*) as kinship terms outside normal family hierarchies.

5. Supreme Court justice Henry Wijayakone Tambiah, the brother of Stanley J.'s father, was an important role model, particularly because he was not just an active lawyer and judge but also wrote seven book-length treatises: on the laws and customs of the Tamils and of the Sinhalese, on the history of Sri Lanka's judicature, on landlord-tenant law, and, with Sir Ivor Jennings, the vice-chancellor of the University of Ceylon, on the development of the laws and constitution of Ceylon, a contribution to a series on the development of laws in the British Commonwealth. Upon his retirement from the Supreme Court in Sri Lanka, H. W. Tambiah was invited to serve in West Africa. Stanley J.'s father was also a practicing lawyer, but his interests ran rather toward developing coconut plantations (and one mango plantation) in the north around Jaffna (a less productive part of the island than the south), but his efforts still conferred on him the British-styled social position of the "planter" class. Both of Tambiah's parents inherited some property, and it was this that Tambiah's father began to develop into plantations. The Tambiahs were Vellala caste (the equivalent to the Sinhalese Goyagama caste) but converted to Christianity under the British. Tambiah's mother's father was a district chief who was persuaded by his superior, a British government agent, to convert, and his mother was sent to a boarding school where she was baptized into the (Anglican) Church of Ceylon. Tambiah's father was not interested in Christianity, but his mother was a churchgoer, as was the second of the family's four daughters, who became principal of a women's college and had a reputation for eloquence as a Christian preacher. Tambiah had four brothers: the eldest rose through the police ranks to become Inspector-General of Police (IGP); the next, R. T. Tambiah, became a surgeon, a Fellow of the Royal College of Surgeons (FRCS), and rose to become head of the Army Medical Corps; the third became a school teacher; and the fourth, H. D., became a lawyer and Supreme Court justice. Both S. J. and H. D. went to St. Thomas's College in Colombo. The sisters were all university educated; two of them became principals of girls' schools.

6. As Tambiah himself says, "One of the things (I think I mention in my introduction to *World Conqueror and World Renouncer*) that I realized, when I left Sri Lanka, was that as a minority member, I had to understand what Buddhism was all about, and Buddhist revival as a response to colonialism, and Buddhist nationalism in postindependence Sri Lanka. These are issues from which, in quotation marks, 'I was

alienated' in Sri Lanka, but whose significance I recognized as important to grasp as an anthropologist. I felt that while I couldn't fully study Buddhism in Sri Lanka in its political expressions, I could do this in Thailand, a country which was more distant, and therefore with which I could empathize, and which I could study from inside" (Tambiah 1997a, 12). Elsewhere he notes that after the passage of the act making Sinhala the only official language, he understood that sooner or later if he remained at the university he would be required to teach in Sinhala. Educated in English and fluent in Tamil, he spoke colloquial Sinhala but was not fully literate in it and would have had to expend all his energy in translating texts and lectures into Sinhala. The opportunity to work in Thailand, offered by a colleague from his Cornell days, was a way out.

7. The significance of "tanks" (water reservoirs) in north central Sri Lanka has in part to do with debates over the ancient "hydraulic civilizations" of Anuradhapura and Polonnaruva (that is, over the degree to which irrigation systems require hierarchical modes of political authority for their expansion and maintenance over time). But primarily, Leach's *Pul Eliya: A Village in Ceylon* (1961) was a bravura demonstration of empirical method.

8. Tambiah taught at Cambridge for ten years before moving to the University of Chicago in 1973, where I first met him, and I vividly remember both his economic anthropology seminar, which began with Mandeville, and his engaged participation in my dissertation defense. In 1976 he moved to Harvard, where I also taught until 1981. We became colleagues again when I moved back to Cambridge in 1993.

9. Such oscillation worked through marriage alliances and hierarchies, "circles of [superior] wife-giver and [inferior] wife-taker communicating with one another diacritically through variations of dialect, dress, and other local differences, and capable of dynamically generating as well as contesting tendencies toward extra-local hierarchical political formations" (Tambiah 2002, 84). This account was exciting because it was not just a set of rules, as Lévi-Strauss had argued, using the Kachin as a type case of generalized exchange in *The Elementary Forms of Kinship*. Leach's account of an oscillation between *gumlao* (democratic egalitarian) and *gumsa* (ranked aristocratic) marriage patterns in the hills of the Burmese highlands, with a *shan* (more feudal, monarchical) pattern in the valleys, is, as Tambiah lucidly recaps, not just an "open system of many lineages linked in kinship." Instead it contained dynamic possibilities both of oscillation and of hierarchical accumulation, according to how players strategized and how economic production worked out (mainly shifting cultivation in the hills, and rice in the valleys). Cattle were the primary form of bridewealth, but cattle were not accumulated as capital. Instead they were used as meat for elaborate feasts (*manau*) and thus to build status in a redistribution back into the exchange system. Leach drew on a history of 150 years to establish his sense of oscillating *gumsa/gumlao*, adapting his terminology of equilibriating oscillation from Manfred Pareto's tale of alternating domination by lions and foxes to illustrate an economic "moving equilibrium" (Tambiah 84). Matrilineal cross-cousin marriage "established a system of exchange of women that is directional in that wife-takers from one group must in turn be wife-givers to a third and so on . . . [which] introduces the possibility of *speculation*, for groups may be able to hoard women if they are in an advantageous position

politically and economically" (84; emphasis added). Polygamy allows the possibility of accumulating women and affines and thereby the possibility of developing hierarchical relations and feudal tendencies. As a minimal example: three chiefs can establish a matrilineal cross-cousin marriage circle in which lineage C takes wives from lineage B, which takes wives from lineage A, which takes wives from lineage C. And since families often have more than one daughter, headmen at the next stratum down can both take wives from these chiefs and daughters from their own status equals, reaffirming or contesting hierarchical relations. Although on the subject of myth Leach and Lévi-Strauss had friendly relations, the debate between them over Kachin kinship went on acrimoniously for eighteen years. Tambiah's account of the dispute pays attention to the social drama of personal defensiveness and seeking acknowledgment over felt misreadings by the other, and to the firsthand ethnographic experience of Leach versus the more synthesizing effort of Lévi-Strauss. But, more importantly, Tambiah stresses the way in which Leach insisted that the relation between terms and reality is not one to one but a matter of model reference patterns invoked by actors to account for manipulated realities.

10. Although the phrase *radical egalitarianism* is not one that Tambiah ever uses in his writing, nor does he (nor do I) recognize any provenance in his work (conversation with Tambiah, November 3 and 9, 2010), it does serve well, and so I use it here, to show how egalitarian values, when turned into ideological absolutes, can turn into their opposites. In this sense it functions somewhat like Leach's argument about how *gumlao* (democratic egalitarian) marriage systems in highland Burma can transform into *gumsa* (ranked aristocratic) ones.

11. Leach was an active and financial supporter of the Labor Party, and it was through those connections that he would be knighted, becoming Sir Edmund Leach. The full quote cited by Tambiah, while a common anthropological stance of the time (1976), is problematic, and Tambiah hastens to add his own corrective in a footnote. Leach: "In my own society I am a radical; where other societies are concerned I find myself in a double bind. I find it difficult to make judgments about other societies. Freedom and tolerance for me is the recognition and acceptance of difference between cultural systems, not within my own cultural system." Today this sounds as if it could be said only by someone who still thinks of himself as living in a nonglobalized world in which other cultures are quite separate from his own. Leach goes on to say he is as interested in similarities as differences, and this should be understood as learning from the dilemmas of others that parallel our own dilemmas. Tambiah hastens to quickly say, "Leach was of course not saying that anything goes, such as mass murder, militant racism, genocide, and other crimes against humanity." Such things, of course, are at the center of Tambiah's lived world experience and are either directly or indirectly at the center of his anthropological work, as they are for most of us who survived World War II (as did Leach) and the postcolonial conflicts since then. In later chapters of the Leach biography, Tambiah provides some of Leach's own contextualization of his ethnographies while noting how they were purified of some of these contexts in their academic setting. All these issues raise the ethical stakes of anthropology. In his chapter on Leach's "comparativist stance," Tambiah notes that

Leach "did not approve of 'development anthropology' . . . which he held to be a kind of neo-colonialism." Interesting, then, that Tambiah himself does not disavow but adopts *development anthropologist* as a label for himself (1985). For a review of the changing political horizons of the ethical debates in anthropology as seen through the lens of Project Camelot, the Vietnam War and the Thai counterinsurgency debate, and aboriginal rights in Australia as viewed by Chandra Jayawardena acting within Australian anthropology, see Robinson, 2004. The debate over disruption of the regrowth of healthy local governance caused by the mobile sovereignty of transnational NGOs, development donors from the First World, global health funds for HIV/AIDS, and disaster relief have become central topics of anthropological work in the past few decades and are subjects of the contributions by Liisa Malkki (2013) and Mary-Jo DelVecchio Good and Byron Good (2013). The Goods particularly focus attention on the ways in which local Aceh cultural forms can be rewoven and local control can be allowed to regrow in nondysfunctional ways.

12. Tambiah has an interesting chapter on Leach's comparativist stance, in which the "radical" quote occurs, and which uses Leach's famous "Virgin Birth" essay as preface to his later structuralist readings of the Bible, which Leach undertook in an effort to repatriate the anthropological gaze back onto his own society. These are lively experiments by Leach, if lacking in the attention to the histories of interpretation with which Tambiah pursues historical materials.

13. Louis Dumont's *Homo Hierarchicus* (1966), most famously, crystallizes a thematic of Hindu thought, in which the householder withdraws from the world to work on his own reincarnating purity after fulfilling his worldly obligations, and individuals can detach themselves from the world into a sadhu status (albeit supported by merit-making donations from that world). Sadhus, however, have been powerfully involved in the recent Hinduvata fundamentalist movement and Bharatiya Janata Party politics in India, even serving in Parliament and state offices. Buddhism ideologically separates itself from the hierarchies of the caste system, politically perhaps most dramatically in India under the effort by Bhimrao Ramji Ambedkar to have untouchables and *dalits* become Buddhist in an effort to assert egalitarian citizenship and reject the entire Hindu system.

14. *Juggernaut* comes from the Sanskrit *Jagannatha* (Lord of the Universe), one of the names of Krishna, and was associated by the British with the large wooden chariots used in ritual processions carrying the *murtis* (images) of Krishna and other gods; if one of these carts gathered speed and went out of control among the crowd, it could crush anything in its way.

15. Ananda College plays a prominent role in Tambiah's account.

16. As a twenty-seven-year-old lecturer, Tambiah had brought a team of twenty-six Sinhalese and seven Tamil students to survey the recently settled peasant colonies. His report is reprinted in *Leveling Crowds*. Tambiah notes that the Gal Oya Valley Multipurpose Scheme was modeled on the TVA and the Darmodar Valley Corporation in India. It was one of a series of such global projects. Two more were the Helmand Valley Project in Afghanistan and the Khuzistan Project in Iran.

17. I refer to this as *vulgar* Marxism, because Marx himself was quite aware of his nonrealistic schematizing at the two ends of his investigations of historical processes.

At the beginnings of both cycles of the historical narratives that he tries to collate into an explanatory model there is violent "primitive accumulation": the seventeenth-century enclosure movement in Britain, with its production of a reserve labor force that enforces a brutal pressure on wages and on the freedom of capitalists to be more humane; and, in the earlier "originary" stages of settlement, the appropriation of land around estates in Eastern Europe after the collapse of the Roman Empire, or the use of slavery in the ancient world, which constrained the return to free labor. The point of the "egalitarian" theme in Marx was trying to organize for a more just return to labor and for the dignity of every worker, whether involved in manual or mental labor, and to find a postindustrial mode of just organization rather than a return to a fantasized preindustrial pastoral past.

18. As a discriminated-against minority, the Tamils have argued for meritocratic access to civil service jobs, while the Sinhalese have argued for allocation of the jobs by a quota reflecting the proportion of Sinhalese to Tamils in the population, which they estimated at 6 to 1. The civil service system and its avenues of recruitment, of course, had been established by the British colonial state. The stakes intensified after independence.

19. Tambiah uses both terms. *Dialectic* echoes political economy accounts of accumulating social contradictions, such as the use of capital intensive irrigation and hydrology projects to produce a new peasantry using mainly traditional technologies, while the elites reproduce a different, privileged lifestyle; or free education in local languages that produces vast pools of literate and semiliterate young men angry at the lack of the kinds of jobs to which they aspire. *Oscillation* echoes Leach's usage for unstable models of organization that can transform into one another, such as centralizing and decentralizing processes.

20. Lévi-Strauss's analysis of the Oedipus myth is a key teaching text for the irresolvable tension between identity claims of being native and the reality that founders had to come from somewhere. Such aporias or irresolvable paradoxes, Lévi-Strauss argues, are narrativized in myths as ways to play out their alternative and contradictory potentials. Hence, as Tambiah invokes Lévi-Strauss, myths come in multiple variations, and it is by examining them as a set that one can recognize the mythic structure underwriting their various possible transformations.

21. Geertz also provides annalistic references in the footnotes to *Negara*, and argues in the text that the theater state was not mere theater, not mere still center, but also a politics of mobilizing men and material resources, involving militias, taxation, sharecropping, and tenure arrangements, not unlike Tambiah.

22. *Gumsa* is a model of ranked hierarchy; *gumlao* is an ideal of egalitarianism in which all are of the same status.

23. I am indebted to conversations in Singapore with Kenneth Dean on his remarkable work (1993, 1998; Dean and Zhenman 2010) on spirit medium associations and temples in Putian and Singapore.

24. The stirring up of murderous rage against the author of the novel *The Satanic Verses* was a major test bed of viral vectors traversing social membranes across the globe and acting parasitically within otherwise different social conflicts. The political

arenas, social dramas, goals, and stakes were different in Bradford (England), Pakistan, India, and Iran. While the Rushdie affair dramatized the transnational circuitry's power to transfer the frenzy of position taking from one political arena to another, the more recent cartoon affairs suggest a new phase in the turbulence of the transnational circuitry, focusing attention on how such circulating controversies help and hinder the construction of global, national, and local public spheres. The construction of civil society is centrally on the agenda in both Iran (since President Khatami's call for open society, civil rights, and dialogue of civilizations) and Europe in a way that has not been the case since the French Revolution. The furor stirred up by the Danish imams transnationally crystallized some of the stakes for many Europeans.

25. One is reminded of the Greek myth of the ring of Gyges, a myth about kings seeing at a distance, about the transformations that occur through that distancing, and the media of both female beauty and money as effecting transformation.

Chapter 7. Health Care in India

1. N. Sunder Rajan rose to the position of deputy comptroller and auditor general, the top position in the Indian Audit and Accounts Department, equivalent to that of a permanent secretary to the government of India, having served internationally in Washington and elsewhere, in various positions in the central government, such as the Parliamentary (Lok Sabha) secretariat of the Public Accounts Committee and the Ministry of Civil Aviation, as well as many posts around India.

2. A portion of part 1 was orally presented at the American Anthropological Association meetings in Washington, DC, December 4, 2014, as part of the panel "Affliction: A Discussion with Veena Das," organized by Clara Han, with Veena Das as respondent, and appeared as a book review in *Somatosphere*.

3. A triad Das takes from Mattingly ("Moral Selves").

4. Elenore Smith Bowen (the pen name of Laura Bohannan) stages scenarios twice, first as she initially is learning about Tiv culture, then much richer contextualized versions with revised understandings. Other classic ethnographies using a serial case method include Victor Turner's *Schism and Continuity in an African Society* (1957) and Gananath Obeysekere's *Medusa's Hair* (1981).

5. Das goes on, without elaborating, to contrast this notion of witnessing with the notions of witnessing in Islam and Christianity, which this section gently questions; see footnotes 14 and 19 below.

6. See Antonio Negri's reading of Job as a parable of human labor, and the commentary by Roland Boer, who shows how even Negri's revaluation is overdetermined in the end by mythic tropes (Negri 2002 [2009]).

7. Job, it has been speculated, might have a Buddhist story lineage. The trope of testing the most steadfastly moral person in the world structures both the Mahabharata (Yudhisthira) and the Ramayana (Rama). Echoes of the Job story may be found in the Jain story of Bhadrasingh, tested with Indra's permission, through a long series of afflictions. "Suffering is the real test of life. And suffering has a fairly long course. Once it starts, it does not end soon." Mahendrakumar, *Jaina Stories*, 3:139–40. On the

Ramayana and the Mahabharata as overlapping but differently structured responses to testing an exemplary figure, see D. Shulman, 2001: 23. The Ramayana is transmutation of a strong emotion into an aesthetic form: Valmiki's grief (*soka*) over having issued a curse with unintended consequence becomes the first *sloka* (sung verse). And Rama grieving over what he has caused Sita and her descent to the underworld of the nagas, lost in his own story as sung to him by his sons, has to be reminded of what he has forgotten, his origins in Vishnu, and that he will be reunited with Sita. By contrast, "the Mahabharata is fire, burning and consuming its heroes, its own claims to autonomy and articulation of explicit truths," and may not be told inside a house lest it burn the house down (D. Shulman 2001, 29).

8. See, for instance, my exploration of the Persian epic the *Shahnameh* (Fischer 2004).

9. The phrase is part of the Aleinu prayer, recited three times.

10. See Das, "Ordinary Ethics," where she delightfully expands Wittgenstein's examples, showing how forms of life grow through many modalities of interaction.

11. The Mahabharata is said to have been dictated by Vyasa, and written down by Ganesha, to make the teachings accessible to those unlearned in the Vedas (especially women and *sudras*, the lowest of the four varnas, usually farmers, who ritually are not allowed to perform the upanayana, the initiatory rite into the study of the Vedas). On the cultic forms celebrating Dhraupadi, see Hiltebeitel, *Cult of Dhraupadi*.

12. Das notes in "What Does Ordinary Ethics Look Like?" that she is the daughter of Drupad and the dark "residue of a sacrifice that the king Drupad had performed for a mighty son who would defeat his enemies." One of her names is Yagyaseni ("born of fire, of a fire sacrifice"), hence also Krishna ("dark").

13. Kala ("black," "time"—the masculine form) is an epithet of Shiva; Kali is the feminine form, and as Shiva's consort is depicted as black, in contrast to Shiva, who is often pictured as covered in the white ashes of the cremation grounds. Kali is an incarnation of Parvarti.

14. In the first layer, the snake sacrifice by Janamejaya, a great grandson of Arjuna, is the occasion of the telling of the canonical Mahabharata. Janamejaya asks about his ancestors, and the epic is recounted by a Brahmin descended from Vyasa. Janamejaya intends to kill all snakes (nagas) in revenge for the snakebite by Naga Takshat that had killed Janamejaya's father. But upon hearing that Tashat was but the means of fulfilling a sage's curse, Janamejaya cancels the killings and makes peace with the nagas.

In the second layer, the great snake Vasuki was used as the cosmic pulling rope to churn the milky ocean to produce the amrita (elixir of immortality) to restore the god Indra's powers. The devas (gods) held one end, the asuras (demons) the other, with Mount Meru (or a spur of it) as the churning pole. Indra had lost his kingdom because of his inability to control his own ego (not unlike Yudhisthira). Given a garland by the sage Durvasa, Indra placed it on his elephant's trunk to show he was not an egotistical god, but the elephant, knowing Indra couldn't control himself, threw it on the ground, enraging the sage, because the garland was the dwelling place of Sri (fortune) and had been given him by Shiva. Indra is also the divine father of Arjuna (who was born after Kunti went to the gods for sons after her husband Pandu was cursed to die if he tried to father children).

In the third layer, the serpent is also a symbol of control in the marital household. When Draupadi is asked by Krsna's wife, Satyabhama, how she controls her five husbands, why they obey her (*vasagas tubhyam*), she observes that women who use deceitful means of controlling their husbands are like snakes in the house. Yet, she says, "I serve my truthful, gentle husbands, who have the ethics and the dharma of truth, and watch over them as if they were poisonous angry snakes" (Patton, 2007, 102).

More generally, the nagas are the great rivers that flow down from the Himalayas and upon which agricultural life depends but which can also flood and destroy.

15. The first time is her assertion that Yudhisthira was not competent to stake her in the chess game, which, together with Gandhari's hearing of the jackal's ill omen and getting her husband to stop Draupadi's disrobing and humiliation, provides the king with a rationale to release the Pandavas to exile. The second time is during the exile, when Draupadi berates Yudhisthira for nursing his human emotional anger but not releasing his kshatria wrath, and rouses him to action. In stories of multiple wives and husbands, Arjuna is Draupadi's favorite husband, but she is not his favorite wife. When Arjuna marries Subadhra, Krishna's half-sister, Subadhra goes to Draupadi dressed as a maid, just to assure her that she (Subadhra) will always be beneath Draupadi in status. It's a partial doublet to a moment when Draupadi disguises herself as a maid.

16. See the rich readings of Levinas by Diane Perpich (2008); Victoria Tahmasebi-Birgani (2014) and Madeleine Fagin (2013).

17. In her later essay, "What Does Ordinary Ethics Look Like?," Das returns to this scene and reads it as ambiguous as to whether he meant "he loved his neighbors or hated them and wanted their annihilation," just as Shakuni is an ambivalent figure urging on the war out of love for Duryodhana, wanting him to be supreme king, or out of hate for Duryodhana's father, King Dhritrashtra, who had imprisoned and starved him with his ninety-nine, all of whom died. A less literalist variant of this would be to invoke the discussions of the dialectics of justice in Hindu debates between the principles of *niti* and *nyaya*, the one being, as Amartya Sen (2009) glosses them, the organizational and appeal to rules and principles (*niti*), and the other the emergent, actual, and particular ways (*nyaya*) in which people are able to lead their lives.

18. But this common observation, here from a Jain story, is intensified by the framing, "One could very well put an end to one's life, but that would not liberate one from the bondage of karma" (Mahendrakumar, *Jaina Stories*, 2:154, 3:86).

19. D. Shulman (*Wisdom of Poets*, 23) compares the contrasting poetics of the Mahabharata and Ramayana to that of the *Illiad* and the *Odyssey* (citing Ferucci): "One offering a vision of life as the endless siege, the other holding out the dream of the return, of recapturing lost happiness." Novelist Tom McCarthy intriguingly writes, "The great lesson of Greek literature (as Oedipus learns to his cost) is simply: you are guilty. Before you've even done anything, guilt is the precondition of your being. . . . In the Oresteian trilogy the inexorable guilt (of Agamemnon) who sacrificed his daughter; of Clytemnestra, who murdered him in revenge; of Orestes, who killed her as a riposte

to that; and so on, backward and forward for generations . . ." (2015). The Hebrew Vashti-Esther (Purim) story is a satirical-comic pair to the Pesach (Passover) story, standing things on their head (*ve-hahafokh hu*): among other things, the elaborate perfuming of the king's concubines and queen is a parody of Egyptian mummification rites. Vashti shows the ineffectiveness of blunt opposition to male power, while Esther is a more Draupadi figure, who changes the outcome. The banquets of the Esther story are shadowed or paralleled at the beginning of the Job story, indicating that he and his wife are not just ascetic individuals, and Job performs sacrifices as prophylactic purification for sins his children might have committed at their raucous banquets. Glaucon uses the story of Gyges to pose the question whether anyone would be moral if the fear of being caught were removed by a ring that could make you invisible. Marc Shell (1978) beautifully analyzes the story as an analogy for both coinage and bureaucracy that allow a king to see/control without being seen/present, and thus to be distant and unaccountable to the citizenry. The story also contains a queen disrobed, who then overturns the power structure, demanding that, her royal sovereignty having been breached, Gyges must kill the king and take her as queen or himself be killed. Helen of Troy may be somewhat different, but I'm struck by the "voice" given her in Simon Armitage's (2015) retelling of the *Illiad*, stitching her version into a (lasting?) tapestry. War and civil conflict are not far from all these stories: they are central to the stories of Helen and Dhraupadi, but there is also civil war after Gyges overthrows Candaules, and war again when his descendant Croesus attacks the armies of Cyrus and loses. Fatima and Zahra are two important Islamic figures of witnessing: Zahra a survivor of the battle field who becomes the leader of the community until the fourth Imam is old enough to succeed, and Fatima a figure whose hadith literature has been revived from patriarchal suppression by feminists such as Fadwa Mernissi. Das perhaps misrecognizes the term for witnessing in Islam (*shahid*) when she suggests it does not include an embodied inscription of pain in the body, as in the hidden cases of adoption in Morocco (*Orphans of Islam*, Bargach 2002). The greater jihad and *shahdat* is always that of the soul and witnessing for social justice; it is the lesser jihad that warfare is often misclaimed to be in defense of Islam, when it is merely a struggle for worldly power or coercive moralism.

20. Yet another example made the international news as a dengue outbreak in Delhi in September 2015 overwhelmed hospitals and clinics, and some thirty deaths occurred (Najar and Raj 2015).

21. "Is Khaufpur the only poisoned city? It is not. There are others and each one has its own Zafar. There'll be a Zafar in Mexico City and others in Hanoi and Manila and Halabja and there are the Zafars of Minamata and Seveso, of Sao Paolo and Toulouse . . ." (Sinha, *Animal's People*, 296).

22. In Bruno Rossi's Cosmic Ray Group, 1958–61.

23. For a brief account of exchanges between Brahmachari and Wang Jun of BGI, see Fischer 2018.

24. At iGEM, the International Genetically Engineered Machine competitions, in 2015, 280 collegiate and high school teams registered. There were two teams from India: IIT Kharagpur and IIT Delhi, out of 101 teams from Asia.

25. "Patient accompaniers" is a term introduced by Paul Farmer and Partners in Health for lay people who help patients through the difficult regimes of HIV and tuberculosis treatments, originally to prove to the World Health Organization that it was not true that it was ineffective and counterproductive to give state-of-the-art drugs to the poor in Third World countries, that they would not be able to comply with treatment regimes, and would cause the spread of drug-resistant viral and bacterial strains.

26. Sinha interweaves the laments for the martyrs of Karabla and Bhopal.

27. Levinas, *Totality and Infinity*, 71.

Chapter 8. Hospitality

1. Jameson argued that the postmodern erased all history. Derrida, by contrast, suggested that the "post" was a sending back and forth among modern formations, often referencing the past and having past traces in the present. Singaporeans often complain that the rapidity of change in the built environment has made memory difficult, that older people sometimes fear going too far from home lest they get lost. But I suggest here that there are many ways of finding the past in the present. Some of these are referenced by Singaporeans' lively stories of seeing ghosts in various places, of ghosts that break bulldozers, backhoes, and other equipment used to destroy old buildings in order to build new ones. Many of these ghosts are dealt with by Taoist exorcism rites and are often attributed to disturbing a grave. But there are many other modes of recounting the past, not only through official heritage plaques, monuments, neighborhood history walks, and now websites, or through recognition of the changing functions of civic buildings (of which Paul Rae 2013 provides a lovely example using the Fullerton Hotel, formerly the General Post Office and site of the postal worker's union, one of the first militant unions, one of whose lawyers was Lee Kuan Yew). There are also many counterhistories of loaded political pasts in family stories and histories.

2. See, for instance, the ethnography or human geography by Josh Comaroff (2009) for some accounts both of ghosts blocking construction and the very Weberian evangelical Christianity that is a requirement for many circles of upwardly mobile professionals. Singapore has a number of megachurches, hosts Billy Graham–style revival meetings, and in those circles sees itself as a new Antioch or base for converting mainland China.

3. The emergency was declared after three estate managers were killed by Malayan Communist Party guerillas in Perak, the poet's hometown. In 1951 the British high commissioner was assassinated and a wholesale counterinsurgency campaign was launched. Some 400,000 people, almost all Chinese, were segregated in 450 new villages. These became the model for the less-successful "strategic hamlets" of the American war in Vietnam.

4. Societies of discipline are those in which institutions and discrete places (prisons, schools, army barracks) socialize and indoctrinate. Societies of control are those that operate instead through dispersed codes facilitated by computerized identity-tracking methods, no longer needing walls and direct disciplining. The latter are more diffused through a society, and more powerful in a productive (not just restraining) way. Fou-

cault and Deleuze, who formulated these terms, provide neoliberalism and biopower as the most dramatic examples, the former constantly monetizing things that previously were not, the latter using census and other statistics to set policies that control both individual bodies and human populations. It is fashionable to argue at a high aggregate level that society has moved from a Hegelian problematic of various "struggles for recognition" into an era of human capital, neoliberalism, and biopower (Cheang 2013). Unlike Foucault, who sharply contrasted the neoliberalism of 1960s Germany with that of Gary Becker in the 1980s, this fad for calling everything neoliberal and biopower tends to become a one-size-fits all argument: neoliberalism über Alles. I follow Foucault in arguing for a more differentiated, and empirically grounded, explanatory apparatus.

5. Wikipedia: "List of world's busiest container ports." https://en.wikipedia.org/wiki/List_of_busiest_container_ports.

6. Singapore is 15th, closely matched (within 3 million passengers, in 2012) with Denver, Bangkok, Amsterdam, JFK, and Guangzhou (49–53 million passengers). Atlanta is by far the largest, with 95.5 million passengers in 2012, followed by Beijing (82 million), London (70 million), Tokyo and Chicago (67 million), Los Angeles (64 million), Charles de Gaulle (62 million), and Dallas (59 million).

7. Kant, *Anthropology from a Pragmatic Point of View*; see also my reading of Kant from an anthropological point of view in "Ask Not What Man Is But What We May Expect of Him?" in *Anthropological Futures*, 2009.

8. I'm indebted to John Phillips (2013) for stimulating this thought. The idea of "relations among relations" as the way anthropology creates models from empirical ethnographies was a motivating slogan for Alfred Reginald Radcliffe-Brown, Marcel Mauss, and Lévi-Strauss among others, that is, for comparative social structures, and for the symbolic logics and algebras of mythology.

9. I have written elsewhere of the elective affinity of conservative philosophers in Iran for Heidegger. This is an indirect further confirmation of the arguments of Ernst Cassirer, Theodor Adorno, Karl Popper, and members of the Vienna Circle before World War II, and Jürgen Habermas after the war, that there is indeed a connection between Heidegger's philosophy and his politics. What is underscored in the Iranian case is the modernization of quasi-mystical theocratic language (the unveiling of the hidden, the condition of being thrown into the world, enframings, and so on, sometimes misrecognized as merely poetic) that fascinated Heidegger in his various religious affiliations, from Catholicism to radical Protestantism, ending with his Teutonic fire rituals. For all the talk of "Mitsein," it is mainly in the philosopher's head, not in his social actions (which on principled grounds he rejects since he devalues the ontic world). One doesn't even have to go to the purity codes (*najesat*) of Shi'ism or the racism of the Nazis, although "Aryans" is a misrecognized idiom of the sources of the term, a misrecognition common to right wing Germans and Iranians, each borrowing the misrecognition from the other. Ironically, the Zoroastrians from whom the symbolic idiom of *arya* ("noble") comes, were considered *najes* (unclean, impure) in Shi'ite purity codes.

10. Consider the story of the impoverished Anwar Beg, whose only capital is his beloved and valuable horse (Still 2010:81). In desperation against a foreigner who wishes

to purchase the horse (thus destroying him), he feeds the horse to the foreigner, saying hospitality comes before everything else. There is an interesting doubleness here: it is an allegory of the forcing of opium onto the Chinese or, more generally, precisely the evil that Athens attempted to keep at bay in Piraeus outside the noncommercialized city; at the same time the logic of the gift might provide a possible escape from Anwar's dilemma if the stranger turns out to be (as in the story of Abraham) an angel in disguise or is moved by the moral force of the gift to provide a countergift to Anwar.

Moving east, the Vessantara Jataka story, the last life of the Buddha before becoming enlightened, has become central to Lao tradition, painted on almost every temple, and renarrated through the annual Vessantaradesana festival, as well as monthly ceremonies. Celebrated as a story of perfect charity, it is in fact a series of stories of the folly of excessive generosity, redeemed only at the end of the cycle of stories by a return gift such as Anwar might dream of. The elements of the mythic logic are resonant with many of the elements of the present meditation. The mother of the Buddha insists on giving birth in the *merchant* quarter of town; the newborn asks for money to give the poor, and the same day a white elephant is born who is carried by its mother to the palace, where it ensures the *rains*, and thus the prosperity, of the kingdom. The young prince, continuing his series of escalating compassionate generosity, gives the white elephant away to a rival kingdom suffering drought. The citizens of the city throw the prince out (off the throne, into the forest) for endangering their livelihoods. His excessive generosity continues, even giving away his children, and managing to conquer and suppress his explosive anger (a Buddhist virtue in some contexts) when he sees them being abused. It is only through the divine intervention of Indra that he is prevented from giving away his wife, and the story eventually resolves with the rival kingdom, now prosperous, returning the white elephant in peaceful alliance, allowing the people to return the prince to the throne. While not having to do directly with receiving strangers into one's home, the political philosophy or dramaturgy of the negara (theater state) or mandala or galactic polity depends upon the exemplary action of the court, and so the hospitality-hostility, host-parasite, kin-stranger relations do very much apply, as do the metaphors of rain-drought.

The extreme autoimmune case of violent churning in failures of compassion and hospitality is Cambodia under the Khmer Rouge. This is not the place to elaborate, but the churning depicted on the walls of Angkor Wat have become a metaphor for the violence in Sri Lanka and elsewhere caused by the failures of hospitality for the other, revolt against urbanism and commerce, and cutting the society off from the nurturance of the self through exchanges with the other. Philosophically, and rhetorically, it is the insistence on singular essence, purity, and ontology versus the multiplicity that allows not only for robust exchange between self and other but also the internal diversity and differentials within the self. *Glimpses of Angkor*, a contemporary interpretation of the wall paintings through Bharatanatyam classical Indian dance forms, staged by Aravinth Kumarasami and Apsara Arts in Singapore, March 29, 2013, comments in its program note, "The churning of our pure conscience in the constant battle between good and evil as we strive towards excellence, the Amrita [elixir of immortality]. As artists we battle between spiritual evolution, perfection of our craft and the effects of commercialization in our pursuit of artistic excellence" (*Glimpses of Angkor*, Apsara Arts program, 2013).

11. With the change in patent law in 2005, India also tightened rules against "evergreening," the extension of patents by insignificant changes. Imatinib (brand name Gleevac) was found in the 1990s when product patents were not recognized in India. Novartis protests that Gleevac is 30 percent easier for the body to absorb than the earlier version of the drug, but India says it does not have enough increased efficacy to meet the standard. Still, it has conceded that this should not be read as a precedent prohibiting all patents on incremental innovation. For the details and extended analysis of this important case, see now Sunder Rajan 2017.

12. There is a fascinating final scene in the Moroccan film *Door to the Sky* by director Farida Benlyazid in which there is an asymmetrical flirtation between a woman returned from Paris and a young male dropout who sit side by side, almost like lovers, but each looking into the distance past one another. Another kind of hospitality, perhaps, where each gives the other the protective space to contemplate the divine and their own purpose in life. The visual metaphor doesn't work for most Western students or critics (see reviews on Google), but it is a perfect symbolic resolution for those attuned to Middle Eastern and Islamic symbolic codes. It is quite different (perhaps) than the Western experience of together but alone in crowds (David Reisman) or buried in smartphones and iPads (Sherry Turkle), where the accent is on corrosion of community into asocial individualism (unless one likens the connectivity of the electronic hive to the religious transcendental, a move of which I'm skeptical but which is possibly in the logic of such terms as the "posthuman" and the "hive mind").

13. O'Dwyer is head of the School of Contemporary Music at LASALLE College of the Arts in Singapore.

14. I heard him first present this as a talk with sound clips (2013), but one can get a sense from his dissertation (O'Dwyer 2012), especially chapter 4; both are available online.

15. The rehearsal studio, poorly marked for the general public, is up a many-tiered staircase above the regular floors serviced by escalators and elevators. The discussion was "Dance India Dialogues with Leela Samson, Madhavi Mudgal, Priyadarsini Govind, Mythili Prakash and Prashant Shah," June 5, 2013, Esplanade Rehearsal Studio, cosponosored by Apsara Arts, Singapore, and Milap Festival Trust (Milap), UK. Milap runs week-long lecture and workshop training programs. The 2013 workshop was held in Singapore. Leela Samson, Neila Sathyalingam (the founder of Apsara Arts), and Aravinth Kumarasamy (the current artistic director of Apsara Arts) all have roots in Kalashetra, the College of Fine Arts in Chennai.

16. Mythili Prakash, a California-born and -raised Bharatanatyam dancer, has become known for her electrifying concept dances. On June 8, 2013, at the Esplanade's Theater Studio in a showcase performance, she did three pieces of the *margam* repertoire, opening with the dance of the blossoming lotus flower (Allaripu) and closing with an Ashtapadi (the longing of Radhika for Krishna). The centerpiece, "Devi," extolling feminine energy in protective form as mother, both nurturing and fierce, put

on display (according to the program notes) "all of the quintessential aspects of the form from rhythmic passages of movement (*nritta*), to the emotive lyrical descriptions (*abhinaya*), to dramatic theatrical enactment (*natya*)."

Chapter 9. Anthropology and Philosophy

1. In the original oral presentation of part 1 of this essay, I insisted on taking the time to recognize my ties to each of the people at the seminar table, to make the topos concrete, but also to recognize the way in which each of them had help shape my thinking. They thus are among the explicit addressees as are the spirits of the philosophers, and the Iranians who were my teachers and guides while in the extended field.

2. See "Body Marks (Beastial/Divine/Natural): An Essay into the Social and Biotechnical Imaginary 1920–2010 and Bodies to Come," in Fischer, 2009a.

3. Compare the play of gazes in the shifts of sexual positionalities in Persian paintings over the course of the Qajar period (1785–1925), charted by Afsaneh Najmabadi (*Women with Mustaches*, chaps. 1–2). From descriptions in poetry and visual portraits of young beardless males with just a hint of mustache as objects of beauty and desire almost indistinguishable from female beauty, women, partly in response to the European gaze and experience of travels and travelogues in Europe, increasingly become the signifier of beauty. But the triangular play between the outward gaze of a woman looking into a mirror not at herself but at the viewer, or young males with averted gaze conscious of being gazed at, establishes a triangular play of gazes. For instance, the scenes of Joseph and the street women called by Zulaikha to witness to her beloved's beauty allow the male viewer as well to gaze upon this icon of eternal paradisical desire. So, too, scenes of amorous couples with the cup of wine signifying the manservants (*ghilman*) and female beauties (*hur*) of paradise mentioned in the Qur'an and wine of intoxication. Over time, the positions of *amrad* (adolescent male), *mukhannah* (young adult male wishing to be the object of other males' desires), and *ghilman* become increasingly veiled, and female figures of desire begin to be shown with bare breasts or breasts emphasized through transparent clothing as the signifier of desire. The separation of sexual inclination versus the obligations of marriage also become veiled. Najmabadi argues that contemporary ideologies of feminism and gay and lesbian rights not only obscure such historical patterns but interfere with the abilities, especially of transgenders, but also gays and lesbians, to negotiate their legal and other ways in today's world (see more in section 2).

4. Khosrovi 2007.

5. Fischer 1973.

6. This passage is taken from Fischer 1980.

7. Fischer 2010.

8. On these dynamics, see Rohani 2009, and Behrouzan 2016.

9. On the contrast between a UN-styled debate at the School for International Studies of the Ministry of Foreign Affairs of the Islamic Republic of Iran and a debate at Mofid University in Qum, see Fischer 2005.

10. See Fischer and Abedi, *Debating Muslims*, chap. 2, "Qur'anic Dialogics."

11. See M. M. J. Fischer, 1983.

12. See Fischer and Abedi, *Debating Muslims*, chap. 5, "Diasporas: Re-membering and Re-creating."

13. In Zoroastrian purity rituals, the *pavi* (a channel of water) is used to separate sacred/pure spaces from profane ones.

14. On *sigheh* or *muta'* marriage, see Haeri 2002.

15. On the beginnings of the efforts to modernize the madrasseh system in the 1970s, see Fischer 1980, esp. chap. 3.

16. Mousavi-Ardebili served as chief justice of Iran from 1981 to 1989, and briefly as acting president of Iran for two months in 1981 after the removal of Abolhassan Banisadr. When Khomeini died in 1989, he resigned from the Supreme Court, returned to Qum, and founded Mofid University.

17. Mesba-Yazdi is said to be the *marja taqlid* ("crown of imitation," religious leader empowered to interpret the law and collect religious taxes, a rank above that of *mujtahed* to whom President Ahmadinejad adheres, with ambitions to succeed Khomeini as *Rabar* or *velayat-e faqih* ("supreme leader"), and said to have issued fatwas allowing the Ministry of Interior to do anything required to ensure President Ahmadinejad's election in June 2009. On a number of occasions he has drawn a sharp line against democracy understood as the will of the people, and for elections serving merely to affirm decisions made by the leadership of a consensus among religious leaders.

18. Defenders of the mystical tradition would sharply argue that what exists in Afghanistan is perversion precisely because money and power are the drivers. And it is precisely that division between the dynamics of power dominance and homosocial affection that is the subject of much casual male joking in Iran: to be caught on the wrong side of this is a matter of consequence. The most recent of a number of investigative journalist accounts on *bacce bazi* in Afghanistan is the documentary by Najibullah Quraishi and Jamie Doran, *The Dancing Boys of Afghanistan*, a Clover Films production for WFBH/FRONTLINE, aired on April 20, 2010. Available at http://www.pbs.org/wgbh/pages/frontline/dancingboys/etc/credits.html.

19. In French, *mondialatinisation*. Even the shift from "world" to "globe" Derrida suggests is an Americanization.

20. Najmabadi notes also that a double negative in Khomeini's *Tahrir al-wasilah* (*The Clarification of Questions*; in Persian, *Towzih al-Masa'el*) that ayatollahs issue, largely copied from one another, also provides considerable legal wiggle room. On this book, see Fischer and Abedi's "Forward" (1985) to Khomeini's *A Clarification of Questions*.

21. The government permit for the NGO required that governors have at least a BA and that within two years there would be a minimum membership base of four thousand. Since the first requirement could not easily be met, doctors and officials were recruited to the board with the sense that they would drop out once the obligations of coming to meetings proved inconvenient. Membership never rose above thirty, because postops mainly do not want any public identity and prefer to melt back into general society.

22. The process of obtaining surgery can be long and drawn out, both for procedural reasons, going through psychiatric diagnosis and preparation, but also for the hormonal treatments, and for getting money together. To actually get an operation performed may be put off for many years, as the case of Mulk-Ara illustrates, and that transitional period itself is the focus of activist struggle for recognition and protection.

23. On the Karbala paradigm, see Fischer 1980.

24. Fischer and Abedi, 1990.

25. Good, Good, and Moradi 1985; Lotfalian 1986.

26. For a helpful summary, particularly useful for locating some of these choice quotes from Arendt, see Maurizio Passerin d'Entrèves, "Hannah Arendt," *Stanford Encyclopedia of Philosophy*, ed. Edward N. Zalta, fall 2008 ed., http://plato.stanford.edu/archives/fall2008/entries/arendt/.

27. These paragraphs are taken from the prologue to Fischer 2009a.

Chapter 10. Changing Media of Ethnographic Writing

1. Michel Serres's pun on epistemologies or grammars or cultural frames that interfere and inter reference one another: "Il faut lire l'interférence comme inter-référence" (it is necessary to read interference as inter-reference). See also Fischer "Ethnicity and the Postmodern Arts of Memory" in Clifford and Marcus 1986.

2. Biographies of the Gandian social worker and Jain monk Santibalji; the Jewish gnostic Sabbatai Sevi, founding figure of both a modernist circle around Atatürk (the Donmeh) and a kabbalist strand of Judaism (Scholem 1973); Rabbi Nahman of Bratslav, a founder of Hassidism and perhaps a manic-depressive dealing with his followers' dilemmas in entering a modern world (Green 1979); the Muslim mystic Al-Hallaj, executed for his ecstatic utterances and revered by Sufi traditions (Massignon 1982). These biographies are written, respectively, by the former Jain Gujarat minister of education and leading social reformer Navalbhai Shah; Gershom Scholem, who transformed the scholarship of modern Judaism; Arthur Green, who helped introduce a modern orthodox Judaism in America during the cultural turmoil of the "nineteen sixties"; and Louis Massignon, one of the generation of French scholars who found through Islam what they missed in Catholicism.

3. In the three time-stamped periods alluded to here, the collaborative circles are (a) the Rice Anthropology Department, the Rice Circle, the Rice Center for Cultural Studies, the Chicago Center for Psychosocial (later Transnational) Studies, the journals *Cultural Anthropology* and *Public Culture*, and the *Late Editions* project; (b) the MIT Program in Science, Technology and Society, the Program in Anthropology; the Harvard "Friday Morning Seminar" in Mental Health and Medical Anthropology; the Harvard Departments of Global Health and Social Medicine, Anthropology, and the Harvard STS Circle; and (c) the Asia Research Institute, the Biopoleis Project, and Tembusu College of the National University of Singapore, the journals *Cultural Politics* and *EASTS (East Asian Science, Technology and Society)*, the Duke book series Experimental Futures: Technological Lives, Scientific Arts, Anthropological Voices; the Irvine-and Chicago-based Knowledge/Value Workshops (led by Kaushik Sunder Rajan), and the

Irvine Center for Persian Studies workshops (led by Mazyar Lotfalian): Conversations Across Generations of Ethnographers of Iran; Oral Histories of Iranian Scientists; "The Asthma Files and Health-Related Air Quality in Iran."

4. http://www.youtube.com/watch?v=2B-XwPjn9YY.

5. http://www.youtube.com/watch?v=JTVDWGtf9m4; http://www.youtube.com/watch?v=GeWnlrcdwPI.

6. The Asilomar conference attempted (and succeeded) to allay public fears about recombinant organisms escaping into the environment by proposing a series of biosafety measures, triggered by Paul Berg's experimental design of inserting fragments of monkey virus SV40 and bacteriophage lambda into an *Escherichia coli* bacterium. Before doing this third step, in response to voiced concerns, procedures were proposed for ensuring that a series of biocontainment measures were in place, with oversight by an NIH review process that could be lifted only as the scientific community gained experience and assurance of safety. The most vigorous public debates were those held in the Cambridge, Massachusetts, city council meetings in June 1976, and again when the moratorium was extended in September 1976. The debates were video recorded by historian Charles Weiner and are available in the MIT archives.

7. It begins, "Governments of the Industrial World, you weary giants of flesh and steel, I come from Cyberspace, the new home of Mind. On behalf of the future, I ask you of the past to leave us alone. You are not welcome among us. You have no sovereignty where we gather."

8. Infosys is not just one of the leading Indian software support companies but an engine of social change, and a social hieroglyph itself, as well as in the careers of its founders, of a history of transition in India's technoscientific imaginaries. Founded in 1981 by N. R. Narayana Murthy, who gathered a team of five young visionaries, including Nandan Nilekani, now chair of the Unique Identification Authority of India, to build not just a company but an innovative, and architecturally beautiful, socially and environmentally designed campus in Bangalore with its own backup water and electricity supplies, and satellite connections. Narayana Murthy had worked at the Indian Institute of Management, Ahmedabad, under J. G. Krishnaya, who had spent time at MIT's Project MAC, and ran the computer systems at IIM Ahmedabad, attempting to introduce personal computers to a resistant mainframe environment. Krishnaya then started an early geographical information system company in Pune, bringing Narayana Murthy with him. They provided among the first such systems for public planning for the governments of India, Maharastra, and Pune. Narayana Murthy also had experience in Paris developing software for the subway system. (I had the pleasure of interviewing both Krishnaya in Pune and Narayana Murthy at Infosys in Bangalore in the 1990s.) Nandan Nilekani succeeded Narayana Murthy as CEO of Infosys and became involved with advocacy for new forms of governance in Bangalore (and India). His wife, Rohini Nilekani, endowed the Arghyam Foundation (Skt. "Offering"), which initially experimented with neoliberal models to extend water systems to the slums outside the Bangalore municipal pipe system when the city could not afford to do so. This controversially involved user payments to contribute to capital costs. The foundation now operates a web-based platform, "India Water Portal," that shares

water management knowledge among practitioners and the general public across states and jurisdictions.

9. These two paragraphs are adapted from Fischer 2013d.

10. Murray and Lopez, *Global Burden of Disease*, (1995); Kessler et al., "Global Burden of Mental Disorders" (2009); Heyman, "Neuroscience and Ethics," (2013); Kleinman, Das, and Lock, *Social Suffering*, (1997); Cohen, Kleinman, and Saraceno, *World Mental Health Casebook* (2002).

11. For instance, the new €1 billion ten-year Human Brain Project funded by the European Union, the $100 million Canada Brain Research Fund, boosts in funding for the United Kingdom's Brain Bank network, the United States National Institutes of Health Blueprint for Neuroscience Research in 2004, the ten-year $100 million initiative on concussion-related brain damage among professional football players in 2013; in Singapore the $25 million Singapore Translation and Clinical Research in Psychosis program, and the new SINAPSE (Singapore Institute for Neurotechnology) at National University of Singapore (NUS) funded by NUS, A*STAR, and the Ministry of Defense.

12. Viz. the Film "Fast, Cheap and Out of Contol" (Errol Morris, 1997) featuring Rodney Brooks, the MIT roboticist, who popularized the title phrase to characterize the shift from centralized intelligence to multiple small bug-like robots operating as a distributed intelligence system.

13. Since 2011, a Telecommunication Industry Dialogue (a group of eight major telecommunications companies, including Nokia-Siemens Networks, as well as Alcatel-Lucent, France Telecom-Orange, Millicom, Telefonica, Telenor, TeliaSonera, and Vodafone) has established a set of guidelines aligned with the United Nations "Guiding Principles on Business and Human Rights." A common platform to exchange best practices, learning, and tools is to be provided by the Global Network Initiative, a coalition of companies, human rights organizations, and freedom of the press groups (Google, Microsoft, Yahoo, Center for Democracy and Technology, Committee to Protect Journalists, Electronic Frontier Foundation, Human Rights First, Human Rights in China, Human Rights Watch, Index on Censorship, Calvert Group, Domini Social Investments, F&C Asset Management, Folksam, the Berkman Klein Center for Internet and Society at Harvard, and the Center for Freedom of Expression and Access to Information—CELE at Palermo University, Argentina). Aside from the three above-mentioned cases, there is a case brought by Turkey's Turkcell against South Africa–headquartered MTN for using bribery to get a contract to supply Iran with surveillance technology. This is not yet a court case, but is on free press, human rights, and digital democracy activists' watch list, and US companies NetApp and Hewlett-Packard, along with Italian AreaSpA, have been negotiating to provide Syria with the capability to read all emails and track people's location.

14. Singaporean filmmakers Lee Xian Jie and Jeremy Boo were Singapore Polytechnic seniors when they made the film. Both are now studying in Japan.

15. Originally called Beijing Genomics Institute, it officially changed to BGI, when it moved out of Beijing. For a fuller story, see Fischer 2018.

16. *Salute to Pao Kun* at the Esplanade Theater, in Mandarin and Cantonese with English subtitles, April 5–6, 2013. Taiwanese producer Vivien Ku set the rules: each di-

rector was allowed one table and two chairs, three lighting effects, and twenty minutes of stage time. The sequence of the plays is shuffled for every performance. Each work is an artistic response to Kuo's play *Lao Jiu* (1990, English version 1993, musical 2005 restaged in 2012). The title character is the ninth, and only male, child of a Teochew family who has a chance to win a coveted scholarship but can't make himself finish the exams, preferring to pursue puppetry. He wishes not to be a puppet with his path determined for him but to be able to hold his fate in the palm of his hand, like a puppet master. He has grown up around a family friend, Shi Fu, a traditional Chinese puppeteer, and goes to his house when stressed. In the middle of the exams, he suffers a crisis of confidence, and cannot decide whether to follow his artistic dreams or the more realistic career option strongly advocated by his parents.

17. *Awakening*, program notes: quote from Denise Ho (lead actress and singer).

18. Aravinth Kumarasamy, *Glimpses of Angkor*, program notes.

19. *The Churning* (*Manthan*), screenplay by Vijay Tendulkar, Shyam Benegal, and Samik Banerjee, published by Seagull Books, Calcutta, 1984.

20. There is no space here to do analytic justice to any of these works, but they are all well known. One of the dilemmas of ethnographic writing continues to be the impatience of many readers (and publishers) with the details of the unfamiliar that are required to understand lived worlds. This is less complaint than writing challenge. The solutions of novelists are not entirely those anthropologists should adopt, but there are lessons to be learned. It is of course not surprising that novelists who deeply research their work should parallel the work of anthropologists. Nonetheless, I was deeply mesmerized reading *Calcutta Chromosome* while I was interviewing molecular biologists working on malaria in Delhi and Bombay in 1996, and later went on a pilgrimage to all the sites mentioned in the novel and in the histories of Sir Ronald Ross. The history of curing syphilis by malaria fever, and of theosophy, is beautifully done, as is the insistence on local knowledge and assistants who helped scientists who get the credit in history books. So too is the satire of total computerized water resources control, taking on both at-a-distance management systems and watershed water projects such as the Mekong Valley Authority. *Hungry Tide* came out just before the devastating tsunami broke over the Indian Ocean from Aceh to Bengal 2004, and proleptically described the coming destruction. It also provides a compelling account of the settlement frontier in the Sunderbans between colonials and islanders, along with an exploration of cetology and dolphins as sensors of cross-species and ecological interactions. *River of Smoke* is a mesmerizing account of the European opium merchants in Canton (Qangzhou) and the efforts of the Chinese officials to stop the trade, and a sympathetic account of the mediation instruments and constraints of the Chinese merchants. This novel follows after the account of the manufacturing of opium and export of labor chronicled in *The Sea of Poppies*. Mitchell's *The Thousand Autumns of Jacob de Zoet* does similar work for Nagasaki, while his *Cloud Atlas* explores a series of interlocking vignettes across the generations (much as Neal Stephenson does more massively in *Cryptonomicon* (1999, another of my favorites). Philip Caputo's *Acts of Faith* brings together in interlocking form the humanitarian aid industry, missionaries who free Nuba slaves from seminomadic Arab raiders only to have them be reenslaved

later, the South Sudan People's Liberation Army fighters, Khartoum-recruited Arab and Islamicized black Janjaweed fighters, and Dinka, Nuer, and Turkana, known to the anthropological archive in an earlier era. It is a rich, only lightly fictionalized tableau of the dilemmas of a second (twenty-two-year) civil war that puts in context more specialized anthropological, political science, and development studies. Importantly, it tells each acting group's story from its own point of view. Shamsie's *Burnt Shadows* begins just before the bombing of Nagasaki (where Margaret Duras's *Hiroshima Mon Amour* also begins, with the burnt shadows of vaporized souls imprinted on stone) and weaves extraordinary scenes of cultural sensibilities, moods, and change across time (from Hiroshima to Delhi to New York and Karachi), illuminating through the historical sweep of intense crises the sweep of postwar history, from the Partition of India to the Taliban's ensnaring of youth. What intrigues me in all these works is the ability to play the scales with explanatory depth and the exploration of nonintuitive connections.

21. The quotes in this paragraph are taken from the question-and-answer period following a presentation of three short films at the Museum of the National University of Singapore, May 16, 2013: *Airplane Descending over Jari Mari* (2008), *The Enactment of Exile in Mumbai* (2011), and *Tracing Bylanes* (2011). Sharma's longer films on these topics are *Jari Mari: Of Cloth and Other Stories* (2001) and *Above the Din of Sewing Machines* (2004). Sharma has a BA in anthropology and psychology, and speaks of her documentary methods as ethnographic. Just to complete the circle of references to Singapore in this essay, one of her shots is of interviewing a man in a Jari Mari garment shop while he is packing pajamas with skull prints, and affixing labels with $9.99 in Singapore dollars. "He says 'we have to complete this order, otherwise the entire money will not be given to us.' It was being shipped to Singapore and it is being produced in that slum," a residue of closed factories, with labor devolved into putting out systems, the whole slum being illegal, requiring getting water and electricity through extrastate nonlegal connections.

22. See the YouTube videos of the chhath puja on Juhu Beach from 2009, 2010, 2011, and 2012. The press reported the sparring between Maharashtra Navnirman Sena (MNS) leader Raj Thackeray, his cousin Uddhav Thackeray, and Bihari politicians. Bihari politician, Sanjay Nirupam, the Congress MP (member of parliament) from North Mumbai, in 2011 countered Shiv Sena and MNS provocations with his own, saying that North Indians can bring Mumbai to a standstill and daring Shiv Sena's Uddhav Thackeray, his son Aditya Thackeray, and cousin MNS' Raj Thackeray to step out without security. In September 2012, Raj Thackery threatened to brand Biharis as "infiltrators" and force them out of Maharashtra. Uddhav Thackeray had earlier called for a permit system for Biharis wanting to live in Mumbai. Both Thackerays claimed that Biharis were the majority contributors to the crime rate in Mumbai. Bihar chief minister Nitish Kumar strongly objected, and the Janata Dal (United) from Patna issued a statement: "Biharis are not a burden on anyone. They have made Mumbai and we have full rights on the commercial capital of the country. Bihari are there because of their deeds and hard work." In 2012, after Bal Thackeray, longtime leader of the Shiv Sena, died (father of Uddhav and uncle of Raj), both sides toned down their language, lest real violence be provoked at that year's puja and festival. (For one of many press

accounts, see http://zeenews.india.com/news/maharashtra/jd-u-takes-on-thackeray-brothers-over-biharis-in-mumbai_797643.html.)

23. Chutney music has roots in Surinam, Guyana, and Trinidad at least as far back as the 1940s, and was first recorded in 1958 by singer Ramdew Chaitoe and became popular with Dropati's album *Let's Sing and Dance* (1968). In the 1970s, Sundar Popo (King of Chutney) added guitars and electronics, and Ras Shorty (Garfield Blackman) infused soca (soul-calypso) with Indian instruments. In 1987, Drupatee Ramgoonai (Queen of Chutney) fixed the term *chutney soca* with her album *Chatnee Soca*, with both English and Hindi versions of the songs. In the 1980s producer Rohit Jagessar took chutney soca worldwide with shows in stadiums and cricket fields, and in 1991, at Weston Outdoor Studios in Mumbai, digitally recorded the all-time highest-grossing album, *Leggo Me Na Raja*. In the Trinidad Carnival season of 1995–96, the Chutney Soca Monarch Competition became the venue for the world's largest Indo-Caribbean concerts. Various spin-off styles of chutney soca have emerged, including *chutney rap*, *chutney jhumari* (from Baluchistan), *chutney lambada* (from Brazil), and mixes with Bollywood film music. (See Wikipedia's entries on chutney music and chutney soca for more details and references.) Surabhi Sharma (Director) film, produced by Surabhi Sharma and Tesjaswini Niranjana, cinematography by R.V. Ramani, *Jahaji Music: India in the Caribbean* (2007, DVD, 112 min.). 3 min. clip available at: https://surabhisharma.wordpress.com/filmography/jahaji-music-india-in-the-caribbean/.

24. Lévi-Strauss, "Finale." in *The Naked Man* (1981).

Chapter 11. Recalling Writing Culture

1. At the time in the Rice Circle, professor of Spanish, Lane Kaufman, was writing about the tradition of the essay; and Stefania Pandolfo, at the time a postdoc in the Rice Anthropology department, suggested the French term *entretien* for the experiments in ethnographic form of the Late Editions project.

2. In the pre–World War II period, one thinks not only of Boas and Malinowski's seminars that seeded or framed comparative work, but of the Rhodes-Livingstone Institute's regional agendas as well as those of other colonial Institutes for Social and Economic Development. The late 1960s saw the waning of the era of large-team ethnographic projects that had flourished in the postwar period, such as the MIT-Harvard Indonesia project; Harvard's Southwestern United States Five Cultures Project; other Harvard projects in Chiapas, the Amazon, the Kalahari, and Polynesia-Melanesia; Cornell's Peru project; and Chicago's Comparative Family and Kinship Project and the Islam and Social Change Project, in both of which I participated. Area studies programs also were beginning to wane, though consulting for modernization projects continued (Harvard's Institute for International Development was dissolved in 2000). Funding for anthropology was increasingly individualized, both loosening previous agendas and opening space for new experiments.

3. Claude Lévi-Strauss was present. Neville Dyson-Hudson "represented" anthropology, albeit from an uncomprehending perspective. David Schneider was invited but at the last moment could not attend. Jacques Derrida presented "Sign, Structure

and Play." Other participants included Jacques Lacan, Roland Barthes, Jean-Pierre Vernant, Lucien Goldmann, Eugenio Donato, Charles Marazé, and René Girard.

4. See Fischer, "Ethnicity and the Postmodern Arts of Memory" (in Clifford and Marcus, 1986); "Torn Religions" in (Ashley et al., 1994); "Filmic Judgment and Cultural Critique" (in de Vries and Weber, eds. 2001); "Eye(I)ing the Sciences," 1995a, and on ethnicity, religion and science together, "Autobiographical Voices (1, 2, 3) in Ashley et al. 1994.

5. On the technological limbo and the anxiety of future influence on experiments in writing between pre- and post-web-based communication in the 1980s and 1990s, see Fischer 2000a.

6. The article in the journal *Signs* by Frances Mascia-Lees, Patricia Sharpe, and Colleen Ballerino Cohen, "The Postmodernist Turn in Anthropology: Cautions from a Feminist Perspective" (1989), was widely read and cited. WC stirred up a number of misconceived retorts, particularly from some feminists who could not see beyond the passage parodied here in James Clifford's "Introduction" to WC. Ruth Behar wrote in her introduction to Behar and Gordon, *Women Writing Culture* (5), "The fact is that *Writing Culture* took a stab at the heart of feminist anthropology," and admitted that many could see WC only through this passage of Clifford's introduction. Indeed, she displayed this propensity by misreading my essay as simply focused on "ethnic autobiography rather than on ethnography," choosing to ignore the concern with genres, discourses, styles, and cultural forms that people use to create their sense of ethnicity, choosing to ignore the essay's careful attention to women writing ethnicity (to which Behar's own work contributes), and choosing to ignore the demonstration that attention to genres and forms of "native" writing and expression in literate cultures can also be one of the tools of ethnographic work (we are not restricted to orality) and can perform theoretical critique (in that case, of older theories of socialization and transmission). For a list of other feminist readings of WC, see footnote 12 to Behar's "Introduction." Other equally misconceived responses were Richard Fox's edited volume, pointedly titled *Recapturing Anthropology* (1991), and Richard Fardon's edited volume *Localizing Strategies: Regional Traditions of Ethnographic Writing* (1990).

7. Said, *Beginnings*.

8. Page references to passages in Clifford and Marcus, *Writing Culture*, omit authors' names and the date for the sake of brevity, except where confusion would result.

9. Crapanzano, *Hermes Dilemma*.

10. Crapanzano, "Rite of Return."

Chapter 12. Anthropological Modes of Concern

1. "Experience near" and "experience far" are a polarity of distance in ethnographic writing: seeing things as they appear from within a locus, often in emic or native terms; as opposed to seeing things from afar, often in etic, outsider terms. See further chapter 4 for Geertz's introduction of these terms, which Geertz in turn took from the psychoanalyst Heinz Kohut.

2. Nietzsche, *Thus Spoke Zarathustra*. The tropes and hallucinatory imagery are interesting here, deployed differently across communities that need constructive political agency and activation. Nietzsche's powerful imagery, intended to rouse people from habits and to make them be active in shaping their lives, in the section "Of Redemption" in *Thus Spoke Zarathustra*, was taken up by many other writers, including the Iranian modernist Sadegh Hedayat where he describes the cowed "rabble—all identical, their faces expressing greed or money and sex, constructed 'only of a mouth and a wad of guts hanging from it'" (Hedayat, *Blind Owl*, 73). In Nietzsche, Zarathustra sees "an ear as big as a man! . . . Under the ear there moved . . . a thin stalk—the stalk, however, was a man! By the use of a magnifying glass one could even discern a little envious face . . . a turgid little soul was dangling from the stalk. The people told me, however, that the great ear . . . was a genius. But I have never believed the people when they talked about great men—and I held to my belief that it was an inverse cripple, who had too little of everything and too much of one thing" (*Thus Spoke Zarathustra*, 160).

3. On third spaces, see Fischer, *Emergent Forms of Life*, 2003.

4. I have been working on a series of essays with artists about their artworks, reading their art anthropologically and as cultural critique. Older pieces were done with the Polish filmmaker Maria Zmarz-Koczanowicz (Fischer, "Filming Poland"), and the American printmaker Eric Avery (Fischer, "With a Hammer"). As yet unpublished pieces are with the Iranian American painter Parviz Yashar, the Indonesian artist Entang Wiharso, and the Singaporean videographer and photographer Charles Lim. Their work informs these paragraphs.

Epilogue

1. Compare: "Hope is an active state. To hope you have to do stuff. You have to put your finger on the scale. It's important for people to imagine futures that do involve huge amounts of change and yet where our grandchildren can be all right. Writing this novel [*Exit West*] for me almost became a form of activism." Mohsin Hamid, interview, *Financial Times*, March 11–12, 2017, https://www.ft.com/content/fa70bbb2-035d-11e7-aa5b-6bb07f5c8e12.

2. The American science fiction parallel might be Neal Stephenson's *Seveneves*, published a little later (2015) than Liu Cixin's trilogy and short stories.

3. An early version of parts of this epilogue, titled "Scratching at the Anthropocene: Aceh, Fukushima, SARS, Avian Influenza, and Theory from the East," was presented at the tenth anniversary of the Chicago Center for Contemporary Theory (3CT), February 2016.

4. One might begin with the Iranian Revolution of 1977–79 (Fischer 1980), the more hopeful overthrow of Suharto in 1998—the image of International Monetary Fund managing director Michel Camdessus with arms folded standing over Suharto as he signed another IMF bailout loan package with austerity measures became, iconically, the last straw for the activist students and people of Indonesia—and the struggle by Greece to resist the austerity measures imposed by Germany and the EU in exchange for bailout loans in 2010.

5. This minority constituted roughly a quarter of those eligible to vote, nearly three million less votes than Hillary Clinton in the popular vote, but with a plurality of the Electoral College, and was interestingly made iconically visible in the empty spaces on the Mall in Washington of the relatively thin inaugural crowd in comparison with the packed and enthusiastic crowds overflowing the Mall at the inauguration of Barak Obama eight years earlier (evidenced by aerial photographs) and with the million-woman protest march in the same place the day after the inauguration, complemented with some two more million women and men marching in other cities around the country and the world.

6. The Singapore *Straits Times* (June 25, 2016, A37) carried a note about soils developed by NASA to resemble Mars (with high levels of heavy metals including cadmium, copper and lead), and the Dutch experiments since 2013 at Wageningen University on the edibility for humans of ten crops grown on these soils. Radishes, rye, tomatoes, and peas seem to pose no problems; tests on potatoes and the five other crops continue. The tests are partly supported by Mars One, a Dutch company, which is meanwhile selecting forty finalist astronauts for their effort to send a manned expedition to Mars. In popular culture, the ground is prepared by the 2015 film (directed by Ridley Scott, starring Matt Damon, with consultative help from NASA) and 2011 book (by Andy Weir, originally self-published, in 2014 published by Crown Books), *The Martian*.

7. Trisolarans are from an unstable three-sun, three-body system. They have evolved to hydrate and dehydrate their bodies to survive the wildly swinging climatic eras of excessive heat or excessive cold produced by this three-body solar system but realize this periodic collapse of civilization is both unpredictable (there is no mathematical solution) and unsatisfactory. This is their motivation to find another place to live, and to absorb whatever Earth and human civilization can teach. They communicate like computers with direct "read outs," and thus initially cannot fathom human misdirection or deceit. One plotline turns on this critique of calculative information theory, turning to folklore stories as a cryptography that can escape Trisolaran surveillance.

8. A remarkable art installation at Flat Files Gallery in Chicago by Iraqi-born Chicago Art Institute professor Wafaa Bilal simulates the terror of being constantly shot at with high-speed paint balls by "players" who can shoot remotely through the Internet even from their cell phones (Bilal and Lydersen 2008). A number of films have also dramatized the targeting of drone missiles from remote sites.

9. On the ring, octagon, or eight propositions of political wisdom, see Fischer and Abedi, *Debating Muslims*, app. 2. On the Zoroastrian amshaspands, see M. M. J. Fischer, *Mute Dreams* 63–65.

10. Lui Pao Chuen is the visionary behind the several deep underground and undersea engineering projects: the Jurong caverns project to store oil and petrochemical production, the earlier armaments underground storage project (requiring renegotiation of international standards), the project of placing libraries and laboratories underground, and the idea of building up from the seafloor to the east of Singapore. Lui Pao Chuen, interview June 27, 2016.

11. The fantasies of predicting life outcomes from AI brain simulations, or nowadays genetics or psychological measures in early childhood, continue as in the New Zealand Dunedin Multidiscipline Development and Health Study (Poulton, Moffit, and Silva, 2015). What is fascinating is the way in which such studies become platforms for exploring the affordances and limitations of new technologies such as fMRI and genome-wide association studies. They tend to do more for exploring the technologies than the advancement of prediction, which remains in the realm of correlation and retrospection; and the results generally confirm long-held common-sense observations and social epidemiology.

12. Murakami's images are easily accessible on the Internet (e.g., at http://www.widewalls.ch/takashi-murakami-500-arhats-mori-art-museum-japan/). Murakami's agents in New York and Japan refused permission for use of an image or two in this book, insisting that they might give permission for a one-time print edition of this book but that each time it was to be reprinted I would have to seek permission again. Given months-long gaps in their communication, this is hardly feasible for an academic or, indeed, any book project. They also declined to put me in touch with Mr. Murakami himself, who might have had another opinion and might be pleased with a friendly review of his work. This is an example of the often mindless sequestered nature of media and information in a corporate world, despite the images being already disseminated and easily available. Had I not asked for permission, I could just have used an image under "fair use" laws for educational purposes, just as journalists have taken photographs of images on the mural and named themselves, rather than Murakami, in the credit line.

13. Thanks to Ryo Morimoto for this information and the link to an image of the stones: http://www.kahoku.co.jp/tohokunews/201708/20170819_33009.html.

14. See the pictures of these screens on p. 114 of the catalogue of Takashi Murakami, *The 500 Arhats* (2016).

15. Jeremy Fernando, personal communication after the panel discussion on May 31, 2017, in Singapore's Scape Gallery with Fernando and Javanese filmmaker Wregas Bhanuteja about the latter's film *Lembusara* (which showed at the 65th International Berlin Film Festival—Biennale Shorts Competition, in 2014). Wregas had invoked the Javanese term *nrimo* (acceptance) as an everyday admonition by parents to children in occasions of disaster. Wregas noted that the word and its meaning was not really a philosophy or something to be read in books but a response to things one cannot change. It is less fatalism than pragmatism. It allows humor rather than only sadness as a response to disaster. It is a recognition that Java's very geography is one of periodic volcanoes and floods, both of which fertilize the land so that the cycle of life-death-life goes on. The film is about the hot volcanic ash that fell on Yogyakarta in 2014, and combines footage of the ash with a comic portrayal of the demon Lembusara ("buffalo head demon") who resides in the Kelud volcano, the cause of the ash fall.

16. I am reminded as well of Japanese painter Kan-Zan-Loc's revival of *ganryo* (shellfish powder mixed with indigo and animal gelatin) to create exquisite meditative paintings. I interviewed him twice at the Singapore Contemporary Art Exhibition,

in 2016 and 2017. He describes his work as an "abstract style of depth awareness" in which he rediscovered "the same blue as Vermeer-blue and Hokusai blue . . . the blood of art is blue," together with a "whispering mode" of "Kawai and 'Wabi-Sabi' which has been inherited in Japanese art for many centuries." Artist statement at www.asiacontemporaryart.com/artists/artist/Kan_Zen_Loc/en/.

17. I was privileged to be invited to two of a series of three workshops on radiation and Fukushima convened by Dr. Remy Chem, formerly of the IAEA; Dr. Shunichi Yamashita of the Nagasaki University's Atomic Bomb Disease Institute; and professor Gregory Clancy of Tembusu College, National University of Singapore. At the workshop in Nagasaki in November 2015, I met the public health nurse stationed in Kauwuchi village. Kim Fortun and I then traveled to Tokyo and interviewed the SafeCast crew.

18. See Morimoto (2016) on the history of the festival, originally to mark the Soma family's rule over the coastal regions since the fourteenth century, and before that originating with that family in Chiba prefecture. It was discontinued with the fall of the Soma domain in 1878 resumed in 1878. In 2011 it was suspended, and resumed partially in 2012.

19. In August 2015, many evacuees no longer wanted to return. Only a fifth of 6,200 displaced from Iitate told officials they were willing to return. More than 10,000 evacuees had joined some twenty class-action suits demanding more compensation to afford to choose whether to build their lives elsewhere. The government announced plans to end monthly payments by March 2018, substituting subsidies to return (Fackler, Martin, "Japanese Balk at Returning to Disaster Area." *New York Times*, 9 Aug 2016, A6, 10.)

20. Video portrait of artist Yun-Fei Ji produced by Philip Dolin, Particle Productions, Inc., 0:47–1:20, https://www.youtube.com/watch?v=66LRxze17I4; https://www.youtube.com/watch?v=Dflki8RRCGs.

21. Quoted in Spears, "Part Traditionalist." See also Video Portrait of Artist Yun-Fei Ji produced by Philip Dolin, Particle Productions, Inc., James Cohan Gallery, November 18, 2006, https://www.youtube.com/watch?v=Dflki8RRCGs. In the video, Ji goes on to comment on the codes of landscape painting and their shifting political meaning: "Landscape artists identify with the tree. If it's below the mountain, it's someone who comes from a humble background, and if the root of the tree is exposed it means that he is from somewhere else, he is not local" [2:30]. "Part of the modernization of the village is that these loudspeakers and electricity come together. As a child we were all told we were the sunflower and we were supposed to turn with the sun, Chairman Mao, and turn to where he needs us . . . [to the] wind referring to the influence of the Emperor. In a traditional scroll you have a first encounter at a distance, next encounter middle ground, later a more close up relationship, things are moving, things are changing, so the perspective goes accordingly, not always vanishing in a kind of scientific way. [There is] industrial scale destruction, where there is no place to escape [6:14].

22. "An Interview with Tsai Ming-Liang by Samantha Culp and Tyler Coburn," http://tylercoburn.com/tsai.html.

23. Other films in the Franco-German Arte series "2000 Seen By" include Alain Berliner's *The Wall* (Belgium), Ildikó Enyedi's *Tamas and Juli* (Hungary), Hal Hartley's *Book of Life*, Abderrahmane Sissako's *Life on Earth* (Mauritania, Mali), Walter Salles and Daniela Thomas's *Midnight* (Brazil), Laurent Cantent's *Les sanguinaires* (France), Miguel Albaladejo's *La premiera noche de mi vida* (Spain), and Don McKellar's *Last Night* (Canada), all released in 1998.

24. In a detailed catalogue essay for this show, I walk through the turn-taking curatorial staging between the work of Entang Wiharso and Sally Smart (Fischer, 2017). Both artists' work more generally can be found easily on the web by Googling.

25. This subplot is a variation on one used in Ma Jia's (Jiang Ben-hu) novel *Decoded* (2007) about cryptography in an isolated mountain military base. That novel is briefly but usefully reviewed by China scholar Perry Link in the *New York Times*, May 2, 2007. Link points to a genre of antispy novels in the 1950s, originally coming as translations from the Russian, to dissident astrophysicist Fang Lizhi's experience working, in such a setting, on an atomic bomb, and to "public case" stories with dreams as deus ex machine devices from the fifteenth century. He notes the novel's omission of slogans from the political linguistic history of the period as a kind of pact with the censors to get the novel out. I would add, however, that the detailing of things happening in the United States, as in Liu Cixin, might be the feint to keep this from becoming too noticeable. Link also points to the psychology interest in the novel as indebted to the May Fourth era (the 1910s to the 1930s), when writers explored Freudian notions. Sitting at MIT, I would grant the cryptography in the novel more interest than Link admits, and was amused by the invention of the Polish Jewish double agent genius Professor Liseiwicz, who works for Israel and "X-country" (the United States). See also now a fascinating account of the 816 nuclear bomb facility, begun in the 1960s but never finished, on Jinzi Mountain, Fuling, overlooking the Wu River, now renovated as a tourist attraction with some twelve miles of underground tunnels (Amy Quin, "Nuclear Site Reborn as a Tourist Draw," *New York Times International*, January 26, 2017, 2). https://www.nytimes.com/2014/05/04/books/review/decoded-by-mai-jia.html?_r=0.

BIBLIOGRAPHY

Abbott, Edwin A. 1884. *Flatland: A Romance of Many Dimensions*. London: Seely.

Abe, Kobo [Kimifusa]. 1956/1967. *Inter Ice Age 4*. Translated by E. Dale-Sauders. New York: Knopf.

Adams, Vincanne. 2010. "Against Global Health? Arbitrating Science, Non-Science, and Nonsense through Health." In *Against Health: How Health Became the New Morality*, edited by Jonathan M. Metzl and Anna Kirkland, 40–60. New York: NYU Press.

Adams, Vincanne. 2015. "Evidence-Based Global Public Health: Subjects, Profits, Erasures." In *When People Come First*, edited by João Biehl and Adriana Petryna, 54–90. Princeton, NJ: Princeton University Press.

Adams, Vincanne, ed. 2016. *Metrics: What Counts in Global Health*. Durham, NC: Duke University Press.

Adorno, Theodor. 1958/1984. "The Essay as Form." *New German Critique* 32:161–71.

Agee, James, and Walker Evans. 1941. *Let Us Now Praise Famous Men*. New York: Houghton-Mifflin.

Aidinoff, Mark. 2016. "Enabling: The Work of Teaching Assistive Technology at MIT." First-year paper, Program in History, Anthropology, and STS. Cambridge, MA: MIT Press.

Alia, Valerie. 2009. *The New Media Nation: Indigenous Peoples and Global Communication*. New York: Berghahn Books.

Allan, William. 1965. *The African Husbandman*. London: Oxford University Press.

Allison, Anne. 2013. *Precarious Japan*. Durham, NC: Duke University Press.

American Anthropological Association. 2007. "American Anthropological Association's Executive Board Statement on the Human Terrain System Project." Arlington, VA: AAA. http://www.aaanet.org/pdf/eb_resolution_110807.pdf.

Anderson, Benedict. 1983/2006. *Imagined Communities: Reflections on the Origin and Spread of Nationalism*. 3rd ed. London: Verso.

Anderson, Robert S. 2010. *Nucleus and Nation: Scientists, International Networks, and Power in India*. Chicago, IL: University of Chicago Press.

Anderson, Warwick. 2008. *The Collectors of Lost Souls: Turing Kuru Scientist into Whitemen*. Baltimore, MD: Johns Hopkins University Press.
Appadurai, Arjun. 1996. *Modernity at Large: Cultural Dimensions of Globalization*. Minneapolis: University of Minnesota Press.
Arendt, Hannah. 1951. *The Origins of Totalitarianism*. New York: Schocken.
Armitage, Simon. 2015. *The Story of the Iliad: A Dramatic Retelling of Homer's Epic and the Last Days of Troy*. London: Liveright.
Aulino, Felicity, Miriam Goheen, and Stanley J. Tambiah, eds. 2013. *Radical Egalitarianism: Local Realities, Global Relations*. New York: Fordham University Press.
Austin, Diane, Lauren Penny, and Tom McGuire. 2017. "Ethnography on Trial." *Anthropology Now* 9 (1).
Austin, John L. 1962. *How to Do Things with Words*. Oxford: Oxford University Press.
Azoy, G. Whitney. 1982. *Buzkahsi: Game and Power in Afghanistan*. Philadelphia: University of Pennsylvania Press.
Bai, Tongdong. 2012. *China: The Political Philosophy of the Middle Kingdom*. London: Zed.
Ballestero, Andrea. 2010. "Expert Attempts: Water, Collectives, Prices and the Law in Costa Rica and Brazil." PhD diss., University of California, Irvine.
Barbash, Ilisa, and Lucien Taylor. 1997. *Cross-Cultural Filmmaking*. Berkeley: University of California Press.
Barnes, David S. 2006. *The Great Stink of Paris and the Nineteenth-Century Struggle against Filth and Germs*. Baltimore, MD: Johns Hopkins University Press.
Barthes, Roland. 1980. *Camera Lucida*. Translated by Richard Howard. London: Hill and Wang.
Bataille, Georges. 1994. *Absence of Myth: Writings on Surrealism*. Translation by Michael Richardson. London: Verso.
Bateson, Gregory. 1936. *Naven: A Survey of the Problems Suggested by a Composite Picture of the Culture of a New Guinea Tribe Drawn from Three Points of View*. Cambridge: Cambridge University Press. (2nd Edition, 1958. Stanford, CA: Stanford University Press.)
Bayat, Asaf. 1997. *Street Politics: Poor Peoples Movements in Iran*. New York: Columbia University Press.
Bayly, Susan. 2000. "French Anthropology and the Durkheimians in Colonial Indochina." *Modern Asian Studies* 34 (3): 581–622.
Beard, Mary. 2014. "How Stoical Was Seneca?" *New York Review of Books*, October 9, 2014, 31.
Beck, Ulrich. 1986/1992. *Risk Society: Towards a New Modernity*. New York. Originally published as *Risikogesellschaft: Auf dem Weg in eine andere Moderne*. Frankfurt-am-Main: Surkamp, 1992.
Behar, Ruth, and Deborah Gordon, eds. 1996. *Women Writing Culture*. Berkeley: University of California Press.
Behrouzan, Orkideh. 2010. "The Significance of History, Gender and Language: An Epidemic of Meanings in the Islamic Republic of Iran." In *The Fourth Wave: An Assault on Women, Gender, Culture, and HIV in the 21st Century*, edited by J. Klot and V. K. Nguyen, 319–46. New York: SSRC and Paris: UNESCO.

Behrouzan, Orkideh. 2016. *Prozak Diaries: Psychiatry and Generational Memory in Iran*. Stanford, CA: Stanford University Press.

Behrouzan, Orkideh, and Michael M. J. Fischer. 2015. "'Behaves Like a Rooster and Cries Like a [Four-Eyed] Canine': Nightmares, Depression, Psychiatry, and the Rise of Iranian Psychiatric Selves." In *Genocide and Mass Violence*, edited by Devon E. Hinton and Alexander L. Hinton, 105–36. New York: Cambridge University Press.

Beldi de Alcântara, Maria de Lourdes. 2007. *Jouvens indigenas e lugares de pentencimentos: Analyse dos jovens indigenas da Reserva de Dourados, MS [Mato Grosso do Sul]*. Sao Paulo, Brazil: University of Sao Paulo, Institute of Psychology.

Benjamin, Walter. 1928/1979. *Einbahnstrasse*. Berlin: Ernst Rowalt Verlag, 1928. Translated as *One Way Street* by Edmund Jephcott and Kingsley Shorter. London: NLB.

Benjamin, Walter. 1936/1968. "The Story Teller." In *Illuminations*, edited by Hannah Arendt, 83–110. New York: Schocken Books.

Benjamin, Walter. 1940/1968. "Theses on the Philosophy of History." In *Illuminations*, edited by Hannah Arendt, 253–64. New York: Schocken Books.

Benjamin, Walter. 1928/1977. *Ursprung des deutschen Trauerspiel [Origin of German Tragic Drama]*. Translated by John Osborne. London: NLB.

Benjamin, Walter. 1982/1999. *The Arcades Project*. Translated by Howard Eiland and Kevin McLaughlin. Cambridge, MA: Harvard University Press. [Original: *Das Passagen-Werk*, edited by Rolf Tiedermann, volume 5 of Walter Benjamin, *Gesammelte Schriften*. Berlin: Surkamp Verlag].

Berlant, Lauren. 2011. *Cruel Optimism*. Durham, NC: Duke University Press.

Bessire, Lucas. 2012. "The Politics of Isolation: Refused Relation as an Emerging Regime of Indigenous Biolegitimacy." *Comparative Studies in Society and History*, 54 (3): 467–98.

Bessire, Lucas. 2013. "Apocalyptic Futures: The Violent Transformation of Moral Human Life among Ayoreo-Speaking People of the Paraguayan Gran Chaco." *American Ethnologist* 38 (4): 743–57.

Bessire, Lucas. 2014. *Beyond the Black Caiman: A Chronicle of Life among the Ayoreo*. Chicago, IL: University of Chicago Press.

Bharucha, Rustom. 1993. *Theater and the World*. New York: Routledge.

Biehl, João. 2005. *Vita: Life in a Zone of Abandonment*. Berkeley: University of California Press.

Biehl, João. 2009. *Will to Live: AIDS Therapies and the Politics of Survival*. Princeton, NJ: Princeton University Press.

Biehl, João. 2013. "The Judicialization of Biopolitics: Claiming the Right to Pharmaceuticals in Brazilian Courts." *American Ethnologist* 40 (3): 419–36.

Biehl, João, and Adryna Petryna. 2011. "Bodies of Rights and Therapeutic Markets." *Social Research* 78 (2): 359–86.

Biehl, João, and Adryna Petryna, eds. 2013. *When People Come First*. Princeton, NJ: Princeton University Press.

Biehl, João, and Peter Locke, eds. 2017. *Unfinished: The Anthropology of Becoming*. Experimental Futures. Durham, NC: Duke University Press.

Biehl, João Guilherme, Byron Good, and Arthur Kleinman, eds. 2007. *Subjectivity: Ethnographic Investigations*. Berkeley: University of California Press.
Bilal, Wafaa and Kari Lydersen. 2008. *Shoot an Iraqi: Art, Life, and Resistance Under the Gun*. San Francisco: City Lights.
Blanchette, Jean-Francois. 2012. *Burdens of Proof: Cryptographic Culture and Evidence Law in the Age of Electronic Documents*. Cambridge, MA: MIT Press.
Bohannan, Laura. 1953. *The Tiv of Central Nigeria*. London: Oxford University Press.
Bohannan, Laura. [Elenore Smith Bowen.]. 1954. *Return to Laughter*. London: Gollancz.
Boon, James A. 2005. "Geertz's Style: A Moral Matter." In *Clifford Geertz by His Colleagues*, edited by R. A. Shweder and B. Good. Chicago, IL: University of Chicago Press.
Boulboullé, Jenny. 2013. "In Touch with Life: Investigating Epistemic Practices in the Life Sciences from a Hands on Perspective." PhD diss., University of Amsterdam.
Bourke-White, Margaret. 1943. "Women in Steel: They Are Handling Tough Jobs in Heavy Industry." *Life*, August 9, 1943.
Bourke-White, Margaret, and Erskine Caldwell. 1937. *You Have Seen Their Faces*. New York: Viking.
Bremmer, Ian, and John Huntsman. 2013. "How to Play Well with China." *New York Times*, June 2, 2013. http://www.nytimes.com/2013/06/02/opinion/sunday/how-to-play-well-with-china.html?emc=eta1.
Burciaga, Jose Antonio, and Bernice Zamora. 1976. *Restless Serpents*. Menlo Park, CA: Disenos Literarios.
Burke, Kenneth. 1945. *A Grammar of Motives*. New York: Prentice-Hall.
Burke, Kenneth. 1950. *A Rhetoric of Motives*. New York: Prentice-Hall.
Burke, Kenneth. 1966. *Language as Symbolic Action*. Berkeley: University of California Press.
Burtynsky, Edward. 2016. *Salt Pans: Little Rann of Kutch, Gujurat, India*. New York: Steidl.
Burtynsky, Edward (with Lori Pauli, and Mark Haworth-Booth). 2003. *Manufactured Landscapes: The Photographs of Edward Burtynsky*. New Haven, CT: Yale University Press.
Burtynsky, Edward (with Ted Fishman, and Mark Kingwell). 2005. *China*. New York: Steidl.
Büscher, Bram, Wolfram Dressler, and Robert Fletcher, eds. 2014. *Nature™ Inc: Environmental Conservation in the Neoliberal Age*. Tucson: University of Arizona Press.
Buyandelger, Manduhai, 2013. *Tragic Spirits: Shamanism, Memory, and Gender in Contemporary Mongolia*. Chicago: University of Chicago Press.
Callison, Candis. 2014. *How Climate Change Comes to Matter: The Communal Life of Facts*. Experimental Futures. Durham, NC: Duke University Press.
Camoes, Luis Vaz de. 1572/1862. *Os Lusiadas*. Lisbon: Typ. Rollandiana.
Caputo, Philip. 2005. *Acts of Faith*. New York: Alfred A. Knopf.
Casagrande, Joseph. 1960. *In the Company of Men: Twenty Portraits by Anthropologists*. New York: Harper.
Catlin, George. 1841. *Letters and Notes on the Manners, Customs, and Conditions of the North American Indians*. 2 vols. London: N.p.
Cefkin, Melissa, ed. 2009. *Ethnography and the Corporate Encounter*. New York: Berghahn.

Chakrabarti, Arindam. 2014. "Just Words: An Ethics of Conversation in the Mahabharata." In *Mahabharata Now*, edited by Arindam Chakrabarti and Sibaji Bandyopadhyay, 244–83. New Delhi: Routledge.

Chakrabarty, Dipesh. 2009. "The Climate of History: Four Theses." *Critical Inquiry* 35 (2): 197–222.

Chan, Anita. 2008. "The Promiscuity of Freedom: Development and Governance in the Age of Neoliberal Networks." PhD diss., MIT.

Chateauraynaud, Francois and Didier Torny. 1999. *Les Sombres Precurseurs: Une sociologie pragmatique d'alerte du risque*. Paris: Éditions De l'École Des Hautes Études En Sciences Sociales.

Chatterji, Roma, ed. 2015. *Wording the World: Veena Das and Scenes of Inheritance*. New York: Fordham University Press.

Cheang, Pheng. 2013. "The Biopolitics of Recognition: Making Female Subjects of Globalization." Paper presented at the International Philosophy and Literature Conference, National University of Singapore, June.

Cherian, Anita E. 2016. *TiltPauseShift: Dance Ecologies in India*. New Delhi: Tulika Books and Gati Dance Forum.

Chernela, Janet. 1992. "Social Meaning and Material Transaction: The Wanano-Tukano of Brazil and Colombia." *Journal of Anthropological Archeology* 11:111–24.

Chernela, Janet. "Ideal Speech Moments: A Woman's Narrative Performance in the Northwest Amazon." *Feminist Studies* 23 (1): 73–96.

Clancey, Gregory. 2006. *Earthquake Nation: The Cultural Politics of Japanese Seismicity, 1868–1930*. Berkeley: University of California Press.

Clastres, Pierre. 1972/1989. *Society against the State*. Cambridge, MA: Zone Books.

Clifford, James. 1981. "On Ethnographic Surrealism." *Comparative Studies in Society and History* 23(4): 539–64.

Clifford, James. 1983. "On Ethnographic Authority." *Representations* 2:118–46.

Clifford, James. 1988. *Predicament of Culture: Twentieth-Century Ethnography, Literature, and Art*. Cambridge, MA: Harvard University Press.

Clifford, James, and George E. Marcus, eds. 1986. *Writing Culture: The Poetics and Politics of Ethnography*. School of American Research Advanced Seminar. Berkeley: University of California Press.

Cohen, Alex, Arthur Kleinman, and Benedetto Saraceno, eds. 2002. *World Mental Health Casebook: Social and Mental Health Programs in Low-Income Countries*. New York: Kluwer.

Cohen, David William. 1994. *The Combing of History*. Chicago, IL: University of Chicago Press.

Cohen, Lawrence. 1999. "Where It Hurts: Indian Material for an Ethics of Organ Transplantation." *Daedalus* 128 (4): 135–65.

Cohen, Lawrence. 2000. *No Aging In India: Alzheimer's, the Bad Family, and Other Modern Things*. Berkeley: University of California Press.

Cohen, Lawrence. 2005. "Operability, Bioavailability, and Exception." In *Global Assemblages*, edited by Aihwa Ong and Stephen Collier, 79–90. Oxford: Blackwell.

Cole, Simon. 2001. *Suspect Identities: A History of Fingerprinting and Criminal Identification*. Cambridge, MA: Harvard University Press.
Coleman, Gabriella. 2012. *Coding Freedom: The Ethics and Aesthetics of Hacking*. Princeton, NJ: Princeton University Press.
Coleman, Penny. 1995. *Rosie the Riveter: Women Workers on the Home Front*. New York: Crown Books.
Collins, Harry. 2004. *Gravity's Shadow: The Search for Gravitational Waves*. Chicago, IL: University of Chicago Press.
Collins, Harry. 2014. *Gravity's Ghost and Big Dog: Scientific Discovery and Social Analysis in the Twentieth Century*. Chicago, IL: University of Chicago Press.
Collins, Harry. 2017. *Gravity's Kiss: The Detection of Gravitational Waves*. Cambridge, MA: MIT Press.
Colson, Elizabeth. 1971. *The Social Consequences of Resettlement: The Impact of the Kariba Resettlement upon the Gwembe*. Manchester, UK: Manchester University Press.
Comaroff, Joshua. 2009. "Vulgarity and Enchantment: Religious Movements and the Space of the State." PhD diss., University of California, Los Angeles.
Condry, Ian. 2013. *The Soul of Anime: Collaborative Creativity and Japan's Media Success Story*. Experimental Futures. Durham, NC: Duke University Press.
Connor, Linda, Patsy Asch, and Timothy Asch. 1996. *Jero Tapakan: Balinese Healer: An Ethnographic Film Monograph*. Los Angeles, CA: Ethnographics Press.
Cooper, Melissa, and Catherine Waldby. 2014. *Clinical Labor: Tissue Donors and Research Subjects in the Global Bioeconomy*. Experimental Futures. Durham, NC: Duke University Press.
Corbin, Alain. 1986. *The Foul and the Fragrant: Odor and the French Social Imagination*. Cambridge, MA: Harvard University Press.
Corbin, Alain. 1995. *Time, Desire, and Horror: Towards a History of the Senses*. New York: Polity.
Corbin, Henri. 1960/1977. *Terre Celestiel et corps de ressurection de l'Iran mazdeen a l'Iran shi'ite*. [Paris: Buchet-Castel] English Translation by Nancy Pearson as *Spiritual Body and Celestial Earth: From Mazdean Iran to Shi'ite Iran*. Princeton: Princeton University *Press*.
Coupland, Douglas. 1991. *Generation X: Tales for an Accelerated Culture*. New York: St. Martin's.
Crapanzano, Vincent. 1973. *The Hamadsha: A Study in Moroccan Ethnopsychiatry*. Berkeley: University of California Press, 1973.
Crapanzano, Vincent. 1980a. "Rite of Return: Circumcision in Morocco." In vol. 9, *Psychoanalytic Study of Society*, edited by Werner Muensterberger and L. Bryce Boyer, 15–36. New York: Psychohistory Press.
Crapanzano, Vincent. 1980b. *Tuhami: Portrait of a Moroccan*. Chicago, IL: University of Chicago Press.
Crapanzano, Vincent. 1985. *Waiting: The Whites of South Africa*. New York: Random House.
Crapanzano, Vincent. 1992. *Hermes Dilemma and Hamlet's Desire: On the Epistemology of Interpretation*. Cambridge, MA: Harvard University Press.

Czeglédy, André P. 2003. "The Words and Things of Ernest Gellner." *Social Evolution and History* 2 (2). http://www.sociostudies.org/journal/articles/140485/.
Daniel, Valentine E. 1996. *Charred Lullabies: Chapters in an Anthropography of Violence*. Princeton, NJ: Princeton University Press.
Das, Veena. n.d. "Corruption and the Possibility of Life." Posted on Academia.edu.
Das, Veena. 1997. *Critical Events*. London: Oxford University Press, 1997.
Das, Veena. 2006. *Life and Words: Violence and the Descent into the Ordinary*. Berkeley: University of California Press.
Das, Veena. 2010. "Listening to Voices, an Interview with Veena Das by Kim Turcot diFrusca." *Altérités* 7 (1): 136–45. http://www.alterites.ca/vo17no1/pdf/71_TurcotDiFruscia_Das_2010.pdf.
Das, Veena. 2015. "What Does Ordinary Ethics Look Like?" In *Four Lectures on Ethics*, edited by Michael Lambek, Veena Das, Didier Fassin, and Webb Keane. HAU Masterclass, ch. 2. Chicago, IL: University of Chicago Press. https://haubooks.org/viewbook/four-lectures-on-ethics/05_ch02.
Das, Veena, Michael Jackson, Arthur Kleinman, and Bhrigupati Singh, eds. 2014. *The Ground Between: Anthropologists Engage Philosophy*. Durham, NC: Duke University Press.
Davis, Elizabeth. 2012. *Bad Souls: Madness and Responsibility in Modern Greece*. Durham, NC: Duke University Press.
Davis, Elizabeth. 2017a. *The Good of Knowing: War, Time, and Transparency in Cyprus*. Durham, NC: Duke University Press.
Davis, Elizabeth. 2017b. "Time Machines." In *Unfinished: The Anthropology of Becoming*, edited by João Biehl and Peter Locke, 303–35. Durham, NC: Duke University Press.
Davis, Richard H. 2014. *The Bhagavad Gita: A Biography*. Princeton, NJ: Princeton University Press.
Dean, Kenneth. 1993. *Taoist Ritual and Popular Culture in Southeast China*. Princeton, NJ: Princeton University Press.
Dean, Kenneth. 1998. *Lord of the Three in One: The Spread of a Cult in Southeast China*. Princeton, NJ: Princeton University Press.
Dean, Kenneth, and Zheng Zhenman. 2010. *Ritual Alliances of the Putian Plain*. Boston: Brill.
Deb, Siddhartha. 2011. *The Beautiful and the Damned: A Portrait of the New India*. New York: Faber and Faber.
Debord, Guy. 1967/1994. *The Society of the Spectacle*. New York: Zone Books.
Deleuze, Gilles. 1992. "Postscript on the Societies of Control." *October* 59:3–7. vimeo.com/9351602. www.youtube.com/watch?v=720Kx3NdDig.
Deleuze, Gilles, and Felix Guattari. 1968/1983. *Anti-Oedipus: Capitalism and Schizophrenia*. Minneapolis: University of Minnesota Press.
Deleuze, Gilles, and Felix Guattari. 1980/1987. *A Thousand Plateaus*. Minneapolis: University of Minnesota Press.
Delgado, Abelardo. 2011. *Here Lies Lalo: The Collected Poems of Abelardo Delgado*. Houston, TX: Arte Publico.
Derrida, Jacques. 1972/1981. *Disseminations*. Chicago, IL: University of Chicago Press.

Derrida, Jacques. 1972/1982. "White Mythology." In *Margins of Philosophy*. Chicago, IL: University of Chicago Press.

Derrida, Jacques. 1980/1987. *Carte postale. The Postcard: From Socrates to Freud*. Translated by Alan Bass. Chicago, IL: University of Chicago Press.

Derrida, Jacques. 1987. *The Truth in Painting*. Chicago, IL: University of Chicago Press.

Derrida, Jacques. 1993. *The Specters of Marx: The State of the Debt, the Work of Mourning and the New International*. Translated by Peggy Kamuf. New York: Routledge.

Derrida, Jacques. 1996/2001. "Faith and Knowledge: Two Sources of 'Religion' at the Limits of Reason Alone." In *Acts of Religion*, 40–101. New York: Routledge.

Derrida, Jacques. 2000. *Of Hospitality: Anne Dufourmantelle Invites Jacques Derrida to Respond*. Stanford, CA: Stanford University Press.

Derrida, Jacques. 2001. *The Work of Mourning*. Chicago, IL: University of Chicago Press, 2001.

Derrida, Jacques. 2002. "The Aforementioned So-Called Human Genome." In *Negotiations*, 199–214. Stanford, CA: Stanford University Press.

Descola, Philippe. 1986/1994. *In the Society of Nature: A Native Ecology in Amazonia*. New York: Cambridge University Press.

Descola, Philippe. 1993/1996. *The Spears of Twilight: Life and Death in the Amazon Jungle*. New York: New Press.

Descola, Philippe. 2006/2013. *Beyond Nature and Culture*. Chicago, IL: University of Chicago Press.

DeVries, Hent, and Sam Weber, ed. 2001. *Media and Religion*. Stanford, CA: Stanford University Press.

Doniger, Wendy. 2009. *The Hindus: An Alternative History*. New York: Penguin.

Donner-Grau, Florinda. 1982. *Shabono*. New York: Delacorte.

Douglas, Mary. 1996. *Purity and Danger*. London: Routledge and Kegan-Paul.

Douglass, Mike. 2009. "Globopolis or Cosmopolis?—Alternative Futures of City Life in East Asia." *Studies in Urban Humanities* 2:67–115.

Douglass, Mike. 2016a. "Creative Communities and the Cultural Economy—Insadong, Chaebol Urbanism and the Local State in Seoul." *Cities* 56:148–55.

Douglass, Mike. 2016b. "From Good City to Progressive City: Reclaiming the Urban Future in Asia." In *Insurgencies and Revolutions: Reflections on John Friedmann's Contributions to Planning Theory and Practice*, edited by Haripriya Rangan, Mee Kam Ng, Jacquelyn Chase, and Libby Porter, 173–84. New York: Routledge.

Douglass, Mike. 2017. "From Corporate Globopolis to Progressive Cities in Asia—Alternative Futures for Planetary Urbanization with Reference to Seoul." In *The Rise of Progressive Cities East and West*, edited by Mike Douglass, Kong Chong Ho and Romain Garbaye. New York: Springer, 2017.

Dumit, Joseph. 2004. *Picturing Personhood: Brain Scans and Biomedical Identity*. Princeton, NJ: Princeton University Press.

Dumit, Joseph. 2012. *Drugs for Life: How Pharmaceutical Companies Define Our Health*. Experimental Futures. Durham, NC: Duke University Press, 2012.

Dumont, Louis. 1966/1996. *Homo Hierarchicus: An Essay on the Caste System*. Translated by Mark Sainsbury. Chicago, IL: University of Chicago Press.

Dumont, Rene. 1970. *Types of Rural Economy: Studies in World Agriculture*. London: Methuen.

Dwyer, Richard. 1997. *White*. London: Routledge.

Dyson, Freeman. 2016. "The Green Universe: A Vision." *New York Review of Books*, October 13, 2016, 4–6.

Earls, Felton, Giuseppe Raviola, and Mary Carlson. 2008. "Promoting Child Mental Health in the Context of the HIV/AIDS Pandemic with a Focus on Sub-Saharan Africa." *Journal of Child Psychology and Psychiatry* 49:295–312.

Earls, Felton, and Mary Carlson. 2002. "Adolescents as Collaborators in Search of Well-Being." In *Youth in Cities*, edited by Marta Tienda and William Julius Wilson, 58–83. Cambridge: Cambridge University Press.

Ecks, Stefan. 2013. *Eating Drugs: Psychopharmaceutical Pluralism in India*. New York University Press.

Ecks, Stefan and Ian Harper. 2013. "Public-Private Mixes: The Market for Anti-TB Drugs in India." In *When People Come First: Critical Studies in Global Health*, edited by João Biehl and Adriana Petryna, 252–75. Princeton, NJ: Princeton University Press.

Engels, Friedrich. 1884. *The Origin of the Family, Private Property, and the State*. Zurich.

Erami, Narges. 2009. "The Soul of the Market: Knowledge, Authority, and the Making of Expert Merchants in the Persian Rug." PhD diss., Columbia University.

Evans-Pritchard, E. E. 1949. *The Sanusi of Cyrenaica*. Oxford: Clarendon Press, 1949.

Evans-Pritchard, E. E. 1937. *Witchcraft, Oracles, and Magic among the Azande*. Oxford: Clarendon Press.

Fabian, Johannes. 1983. *Time and the Other: How Anthropology Makes Its Object*. New York: Columbia University Press.

Fabian, Johannes. 2000. *Out of Our Minds: Reason and Madness in the Exploration of Central Africa*. Berkeley: University of California Press.

Fackler, Martin. 2016. "Japanese Balk at Returning to Disaster Area." *New York Times*, August 9, A6, 10.

Fagin, Madeleine. 2013. *Ethics and Politics after Poststructuralism: Levinas, Derrida, and Nancy*. Edinburgh, UK: University of Edinburgh Press.

Fair, J. Henry. 2016a. *Industrial Scars: The Hidden Costs of Consumption*. New York: Papadakis.

Fair, J. Henry. 2016b. "Industrial Scars: The Environmental Costs of Consumption—in Pictures." October 24. https://www.theguardian.com/environment/gallery/2016/oct/24/industrial-scars-the-environmental-cost-of-consumption-in-pictures.

Fardon, Richard, ed. 1990. *Localizing Strategies: Regional Traditions of Ethnographic Writing*. Edinburgh, UK: Scottish Academic Press / Washington, DC: Smithsonian Institution Press.

Fassin, Didier, and Mariella Pandolfi, eds. 2010. *Contemporary States of Emergency: The Politics of Military and Humanitarian Interventions*. Cambridge, MA: Zone Books.

Fassin, Didier, and Richard Rechtman. 2009. *The Empire of Trauma*. Princeton, NJ: Princeton University Press.

Faubion, James, and George Marcus. 2009. *Doing Fieldwork Is Not What It Used to Be: Learning Anthropology's Method in a Time of Transition*. Ithaca, NY: Cornell University Press.

Fearnley, Lyle. 2013. "Life at the Influenza Epicenter: Transactions of Global Health and Animal Disease in Contemporary China." PhD diss., University of California, Berkeley.

Feld, Steven. 1982. *Sound and Sentiment: Birds, Weeping, Poetics, and Song in Kaluli Expression*. Philadelphia: University of Pennsylvania Press.

Feld, Steven. 2012. *Jazz Cosmopolitanism in Accra: Five Musical Years in Ghana*. Durham, NC: Duke University Press.

Feld, Steven, and Donald Brenneis. 2004. "Doing Anthropology in Sound." *American Ethnologist* 31 (4): 461–74.

Felt, Ulrike. 2015. "Keeping Technologies Out: Sociotechnical Imaginaries and the Formation of Austria's Technopolitical Identity." In *Dreamscapes of Modernity*, edited by Sheila Jasanaoff and Sang-Hyun Kim. Chicago: University of Chicago Press.

Fenvres, Peter D., ed. 1998. *Raising the Tone of Philosophy: Late Essays by Immanuel Kant, Transformative Critique by Jacques Derrida*. Baltimore, MD: Johns Hopkins University Press.

Ferguson, James. 2013. "Cosmologies of Welfare: Two Conceptions of Social Assistance in Contemporary South Africa." In *Radical Egalitarianism*, edited by Felicity Aulino, Miriam Goheen, and Stanley J. Tambiah. New York: Fordham University Press.

Field, Connie. 1980. *The Life and Times of Rosie the Riveter*. Berkeley, CA: Clarity Educational Productions.

Firth, Raymond, ed. 1957. *Man and Culture: An Evaluation of the Work of Bronislaw Malinowski*. London: Routledge Kegan Paul.

Fischer, Irene Kaminka. 2005. *Geodesy? What's That?* New York: iUniverse.

Fischer, Michael M. J. 1973. "Zoroastrian Iran between Myth and Praxis." PhD diss., University of Chicago.

Fischer, Michael M. J. 1980. *Iran: From Religious Dispute to Revolution*. Cambridge, MA: Harvard University Press.

Fischer, Michael M. J. 1983. "Imam Khomeini: Four Ways of Understanding." In *Voices of Resurgent Islam*, edited by John Esposito, 150–74. New York: Oxford University Press.

Fischer, Michael M. J. 1986. "Ethnicity and the Postmodern Arts of Memory." In *Writing Culture*, edited by James Clifford and George Marcus, 194–233. Berkeley: University of California Press.

Fischer, Michael M. J. 1987. "Repetitions in the Revolution." In *Shi'ism, Resistance, Revolution*, edited by Martin Kramer, 117–32. London: Mansell.

Fischer, Michael M. J. 1990. "Bombay Talkies, the Word and the World: Salman Rushdie's Satanic Verses." *Cultural Anthropology* 5(2): 107–59.

Fischer, Michael M. J. 1991. "Worlding Cyberspace: Towards an Ethnography in Time, Space and Theory." In *Critical Anthropology Now*, edited by George E. Marcus, 245–304. Santa Fe, NM: School for American Research.

Fischer, Michael M. J. 1993. "One Hand Clapping: Dialogue, Silences, and the Mourning of Polish Romanticism." In *Late Editions: Cultural Studies for the End of the*

Century, vol. 1, *Perilous States*, edited by George E. Marcus, 187–233. Chicago, IL: University of Chicago Press.
Fischer, Michael M. J. 1994. "Autobiographical Voices (1, 2, 3) and Mosaic Memory: Experimental Sondage in the (Post) Modern World." In *Autobiography and Postmodernism*, edited by Kathleen Ashley, Leigh Gilmore, and Gerald Peters, 79–129. Amherst: University of Massachusetts Press.
Fischer, Michael M. J. 1995a. "Eye(I)ing the Sciences and their Signifiers (Language, Tropes, Autobiographers): InterViewing for a Cultural Studies of Science and Technology." In *Late Editions: Cultural Studies for the End of the Century*, vol. 2, *Technoscientific Imaginaries*, edited by George E. Marcus, 43–84. Chicago, IL: University of Chicago Press.
Fischer, Michael M. J. 1995b. "Film as Ethnography and Cultural Critique in the Late Twentieth Century." In *Shared Differences: Multicultural Media and Practical Pedagogy*, edited by Diane Carson and Lester Friedman, 29–56. Champaign: University of Illinois Press.
Fischer, Michael M. J. 1995c. "Starting Over: How, What, and for Whom Does One Write about Refugees? The Poetics and Politics of Refugee Film as Ethnographic Access in a Media-Saturated World." In *Mistrusting Refugees*, edited by E. Valentine Daniel and John C. Knudsen, 126–50. Berkeley: University of California Press.
Fischer, Michael M. J. 1997. "Filming Poland; The Ethnographic Documentary, Narrative Films of Maria Zmarz-Koczanowicz." In *Late Editions: Cultural Studies for the End of the Century*, vol. 4, *Cultural Producers in Perilous States*, edited by George E. Marcus, 91–150. Chicago, IL: University of Chicago Press.
Fischer, Michael M. J. 1999. "Raising Questions about Rouch." *American Anthropologist* 99(1): 140–43.
Fischer, Michael M. J. 2000a. "Before Going Digital/Double Digit/Y2000: A Retrospective of Late Editions." In *Late Editions: Cultural Studies for the End of the Century*, vol. 8, *Zeroing In On the Year 2000*, edited by George E. Marcus, 13–34. Chicago, IL: University of Chicago Press.
Fischer, Michael M. J. 2000b. "If Derrida Is the Gomez-Peña of Philosophy, What Are the Genres of Social Science? Just Gaming: The Y2K Computer Bug and Other Uncertainties—A Critical Simulation Game." In *Late Editions: Cultural Studies for the End of the Century*, vol. 7, *Para-Sites*, edited by George E. Marcus, 15–102. Chicago, IL: University of Chicago Press.
Fischer, Michael M. J. 2000c. "With a Hammer, a Gouge and a Wood Block: The Work of Art and Medicine in the Age of Social Re-Traumatization: The Texas Woodblock Art of Dr. Eric Avery." In *Late Editions: Cultural Studies for the End of the Century*, vol. 7, *Para-Sites*, edited by George E. Marcus, 15–102. Chicago, IL: University of Chicago Press.
Fischer, Michael M. J. 2001a. "In the Science Zone: The Yanomami and the Fight for Representation." *Anthropology Today* 17 (4): 9–14; 17 (5): 10–13.
Fischer, Michael M. J. 2001. "Filmic Judgment and Cultural Critique: The Work of Art, Ethics, and Religion in Iranian Cinema." In *Religion and Media*, edited by Hent de Vries and Samuel Weber, 456–86. Stanford, CA: Stanford University Press.

Fischer, Michael M. J. 2003. *Emergent Forms of Life and the Anthropological Voice*. Experimental Futures. Durham, NC: Duke University Press.
Fischer, Michael M. J. 2004. *Mute Dreams, Blind Owls, and Dispersed Knowledges: Persian Poesis in the Transnational Circuitry*. Durham, NC: Duke University Press.
Fischer, Michael M. J. 2005. "Persian Miniatures: I. Bahs (Debate) in Qum; II. Simulation in Tehran." *New Initiative for Middle East Peace (NIMEP) Insights* 1:14–24.
Fischer, Michael M. J. 2005b. "Technoscientific Infrastructures and Emergent Forms of Life: A Commentary." *American Anthropologist* 107 (1): 55–61.
Fischer, Michael M. J. 2009a. *Anthropological Futures*. Durham, NC: Duke University Press.
Fischer, Michael M. J. 2009b. "Body Marks Bestial/Divine/Natural: An Essay into the Social and Biotechnical Imaginary 1920–2010, and Bodies to Come." In *Anthropological Futures*, 159–96. Durham, NC: Duke University Press.
Fischer, Michael M. J. 2009c. "Reading Hannah Arendt in Tehran." In *Anthropological Futures*, 244–48. Durham, NC: Duke University Press.
Fischer, Michael M. J. 2009d. "Iran and the Boomeranging Cartoon Wars: Can Public Spheres at Risk Ally with Public Spheres Yet to Be Achieved?" *Cultural Politics* 5 (1): 27–62.
Fischer, Michael M. J. 2010. "The Rhythmic Beat of the Revolution in Iran." *Cultural Anthropology* 25 (3): 497–543.
Fischer, Michael M. J. 2011. "In the Science Zone II: The Fore, Papua-New Guinea, and the Fight for Representation." *East Asian Science, Technology and Society* 5:1–17.
Fischer, Michael M. J. 2012. "Lively Biotech and Translational Research." In *Lively Capital: Biotechnologies, Ethics, and Governance in Global Markets*, edited by K. Sunder Rajan, 385–436. Durham, NC: Duke University Press.
Fischer, Michael M. J. 2013a. "Biopolis: Asian Science in the Global Circuitry." *Science, Technology and Society* 18 (3): 381–406. doi:10.1177/0971721813498500.
Fischer, Michael M. J. 2013b. "The Peopling of Technologies." In *When People Come First: Critical Studies in Global Health*, edited by João Biehl and Adriana Petryna, 347–73. Princeton, NJ: Princeton University Press.
Fischer, Michael M. J. 2013c. "Anthropologia and Philosophia: Reading alongside Benjamin in Yazd, Derrida in Qum, Arendt in Tehran." In *The Ground Between: Anthropologists Engage Philosophy*, edited by Veena Das, Michael Jackson, Arthur Kleinman, and Bhighupati Singh, 188–217. Durham, NC: Duke University Press.
Fischer, Michael M. J. 2013d. "The BAC [Bioethics Advisory Committee] Consultation on Neuroscience and Ethics: An Anthropologists' Perspective." *Innovation* 11 (2): 3–5.
Fischer, Michael M. J. 2013e. "Icons, Frames, and Language Games: Bruno Latour's 'On the Modern Cult of Factish Gods.'" *Technology and Culture* 54:963–67.
Fischer, Michael M. J. 2014a. "Review: Rabinow, Paul, *The Accompaniment: Assembling the Contemporary. American Anthropologist*. 116 (1): 42–43.
Fischer, Michael M. J. 2014b. "Review: Rabinow, Paul and Anthony Stavrianakis, Demands of the Day: On the Logic of Anthropological Inquiry." *Anthropos* 109:324–25.

Fischer, Michael M. J. 2015a. "Ethnography for Aging Societies: Dignity, Cultural Genres, and Singapore's Imagined Futures." *American Ethnologist* 42 (2): 207–29.
Fischer, Michael M. J. 2015b. "Science and Technology, Anthropology of." In *International Encyclopedia of the Social and Behavioral Sciences*, edited by James D. Wright, 182–85. Vol. 21. 2nd ed. Oxford: Elsevier.
Fischer, Michael M. J. 2017. "The Work of Epic Art in a Post-Wayang World: An Anthropologist Reads Entang Wiharso and Sally Smart's Conversations." *Conversations*. Yogakarta, Indonesia: Black Goat Studio Publications.
Fischer, Michael M. J. 2018. "A Tale of Two Genome Institutes: Qualitative Networks, Charismatic Voice, and Research and Development Strategies." *Science, Technology and Society* 23 (2).
Fischer, Michael M. J., and Mehdi Abedi. 1985. "Forward." In *A Clarification of Questions*, edited by Ayatollah S. Ruhollah Mousavi Khomeni. Translated by J. Borujerdi. Boulder, CO: Westview Press.
Fischer, Michael M. J., and Mehdi Abedi. 1990. *Debating Muslims: Cultural Dialogues in Postmodernity and Tradition*. Madison: University of Wisconsin Press.
Fischer, Michael M. J., and Thomas Barfield. 1980. "The Khuzistan Development Project and the Helmand Valley Development Project." In *The Social Impact of Development on Minorities*, edited by David Maybury-Lewis. Cambridge, MA: Cultural Survival.
Fischer, Michael M. J., with Stella Gregorian. 1993. "Six to Eight Characters in Search of Armenian Civil Society amidst the Carnivalization of History." In *Late Editions: Cultural Studies for the End of the Century*, vol. 1, *Perilous States*, edited by George E. Marcus, 81–130. Chicago, IL: University of Chicago Press.
Fish, Allison. 2010. "Laying Claim to Yoga: Intellectual Property, Cultural Rights, and the Digital Archive in India." PhD diss., University of California, Irvine.
Fish, Allison. 2014. "Authorizing Yoga: The Pragmatics of Cultural Stewardship in the Digital Era." *East Asian Science, Technology and Society* 8 (4): 439–60.
Fleck, Ludwik. 1935/1981. *Genesis and Development of a Scientific Fact*. Chicago, IL: University of Chicago Press.
Fleming, Luke. 2010. "From Patrilects to Performatives: Linguistic Exogamy and Language Shift in the Northwest Amazon." PhD diss., University of Pennsylvania.
Foo, Alex. 2017. "NEWWAVES: A Way of Living: Filmic Iterations of Javanese Thought, Wregas Bhanuteja X Jeremy Fernando." Singapore International Film Festival, June 7. http://sgiff.com/youth-meets-film/article/newwaves-a-way-of-living/.
Fortes, Meyer, and E. E. Evans-Pritchard. 1940. *African Political Systems*. London: Oxford University Press.
Fortun, Kim. 2001. *Advocacy after Bhopal: Environmentalism, Disaster, New Global Orders*. Chicago, IL: University of Chicago Press.
Fortun, Kim. 2003. "Ethnography in/of/as Open Systems." *Reviews in Anthropology* 32:171–90.
Fortun, Kim. 2010. "Of Writing Culture, 2020." In *Writing Culture: The Poetics and Politics of Ethnography*, edited by James Clifford and George Marcus. 25th anniversary edition. Berkeley: University of California Press.

Fortun, Kim. 2012. "Ethnography in Late Industrialism." *Cultural Anthropology* 27 (3): 446–64.
Fortun, Kim. 2014. "From Latour to Late Industrialism." *Hau: Journal in Ethnographic Theory* 4 (1): 309–29.
Fortun, Michael. 2008. *Promising Genomics: Iceland and deCODE Genetics in a World of Speculation*. Berkeley: University of California Press.
Foucault, Michel. 1975/1977. *Discipline and Punish*. Translated by Alan Sheridan. New York: Pantheon.
Foucault, Michel. 1978–79/2008. *The Birth of Biopolitics: Lectures at the Collège de France, 1978–1979*. Translated by Graham Burchell. New York: Palgrave Macmillan, 2008.
Foucault, Michel. 2012. American Neoliberalism: Michel Foucault's Birth of Politics Lectures. Video with Gary Becker, Francis Ewald, Bernard Harcourt available at http://vimeo.com/43984248.
Fox, Richard G., ed. 1991. *Recapturing Anthropology: Working in the Present*. Santa Fe, NM: SAR Press.
Franklin, Sarah. 1997. *Embodied Progress: A Cultural Account of Assisted Conception*. London: Routledge.
Franklin, Sarah. 2007. *Dolly Mixture: The Remaking of Genealogy*. Durham, NC: Duke University Press
Franklin, Sarah. 2013. *Biological Relatives: IVF, Stem Cells, and the Future of Kinship*. Experimental Futures. Durham, NC: Duke University Press.
Franklin, Sarah, and Margaret Lock, eds. 2013. *Remaking Life and Death: Towards an Anthropology of the Biosciences*. Santa Fe, NM: School of American Research.
Friedan, Betty. 1963. *The Feminine Mystique*. New York: W. W. Norton, 1963.
Friedner, Michele. 2015. *Valuing Deaf Worlds in Urban India*. Rutgers, NJ: Rutgers University Press.
Garcia, Angela. 2010. *The Pastoral Clinic: Addiction and Dispossession along the Rio Grande*. Berkeley: University of California Press.
Gardner, Robert, and Akos Östör. 2001. *Making Forest of Bliss: Intention, Circumstance, and Chance in Nonfiction Film*. Cambridge, MA: Harvard University Press, 2001.
Garfinkle, Harold. 1967. *Studies in Ethnomethodology*. Englewood Cliffs, NJ: Prentice-Hall.
Gaudeliere, Jean-Pierre. 2014. "An Indian Path to Biocapital? The Traditional Knowledge Digital Library, Drug Patents, and the Reformulation Regime of Contemporary Ayurveda." *East Asian Science, Technology and Society* 8 (4): 391–416.
Geertz, Clifford. 1960. *The Religion of Java*. Glencoe, IL: Free Press.
Geertz, Clifford. 1963a. *Agricultural Involution*. Berkeley: University of California Press.
Geertz, Clifford. 1963b. *Peddlers and Princes: Social Change and Economic Modernization in Two Indonesian Towns*. 9. Chicago, IL: University of Chicago Press.
Geertz, Clifford. 1965. *The Social History of an Indonesian Town*. Cambridge, MA: MIT Press.
Geertz, Clifford. 1968. *Islam Observed: Religious Development in Indonesia and Morocco*. New Haven, CT: Yale University Press.

Geertz, Clifford. 1972. "Deep Play: Notes on the Balinese Cockfight." *Daedalus* 101 (1): 1–37.
Geertz, Clifford. 1973. *The Interpretation of Culture*. New York: Basic Books.
Geertz, Clifford. 1979. *Meaning and Order in Moroccan Society*. New York: Cambridge University Press.
Geertz, Clifford. 1980. *Negara: The Theater State in Nineteenth-Century Bali*. Princeton, NJ: Princeton University Press.
Geertz, Clifford. 1983. *Local Knowledge: Further Essays in Interpretive Anthropology*. New York: Basic Books.
Geertz, Clifford. 1988. *Works and Lives: The Anthropologist as Author*. Stanford, CA: Stanford University Press.
Geertz, Clifford. 1995. *After the Fact: Two Countries, Four Decades, One Anthropologist*. Cambridge, MA: Harvard University Press.
Geertz, Clifford. 2000. *Available Light*. Princeton, NJ: Princeton University Press.
Gellner, Ernest. 1959. *Words and Things: A Critical Account of Linguistic Philosophy and a Study in Ideology, with an Introduction by Bertrand Russell*. London: Victor Gollancz.
Gellner, Ernest. 1983. *Nations and Nationalism*. London: Basil Blackwell.
George, Timothy. 2001. *Minamata: Pollution and the Struggle for Democracy in Postwar Japan*. Cambridge, MA: Harvard University Press.
Ghosh, Amitav. 1995. *The Calcutta Chromosome: A Novel of Fevers, Delirium, and Discovery*. New York: Avon.
Ghosh, Amitav. 1996. *Calcutta Chromosome: A Novel of Fevers, Delirium, and Discovery*. Delhi: Ravi Dayal.
Ghosh, Amitav. 2004. *The Hungry Tide*. London: HarperCollins.
Ghosh, Amitav. 2008. *The Sea of Poppies*. London: John Murray.
Ghosh, Amitav. 2011. *River of Smoke*. London: John Murray.
Gibson, William. 1981. *Neuromancer*. New York: Ace.
Ginsburg, Faye D., Lila Abu-Lughod, and Brian Larkin, eds. 2002. *Media Worlds: Anthropology on New Terrain*. Berkeley: University of California Press.
Gluckman, Max. 1945. "Seven-Year Research Plan of the Rhodes-Livingstone Institute of Social Studies in British Central Africa." *Journal of the Rhodes-Livingstone Institute*, December.
Godfrey, Tony. 2012. "Sixteen Creatures in Search of their Species." In *Playing God in an Art Lab*, edited by Geraldine Javier. Singapore: STPI. http://www.stpi.com.sg/assets/artists/2012/GeraldineJavier/Catalogue_final.pdf.
Goethe, Johann Wolfgang von. 1992. *Italian Journey, 1786–1788*. Translated by W. H. Auden and Elizabeth Mayer. London: Penguin.
Goffman, Erving. 1956. *The Presentation of Self in Everyday Life*. New York: Random House.
Golde, Peggy. 1970. *Women in the Field: Anthropological Experiences*. Berkeley: University of California Press.
Good, Byron. 1994. *Medicine, Rationality, and Experience: An Anthropological Perspective*. New York: Cambridge University Press.

Good, Byron, and Mary-Jo DelVecchio Good, et al. 2007. "A Psychosocial Needs Assessment of Communities in 14 Selected Districts in Aceh." Banda Aceh, Indonesia: International Organization for Migration IOM / Department of Social Medicine, Harvard Medical School / World Bank / Bakhti Husada / Universitas Syiah Kuala.

Good, Byron, Mary-Jo DelVecchio Good, and Robert Moradi. 1985. "The Interpretation of Dysphoric Affect and Depressive Illness in Iranian Culture." In *Culture and Depression*, edited by Arthur Kleinman and Byron Good, 369–428. Berkeley: University of California Press.

Good, Byron J., Michael M. J. Fischer, Sarah S. Willen, and Mary-Jo DelVecchio Good, eds. 2010. *A Reader in Medical Anthropology: Theoretical Trajectories, Emergent Realities*. Malden, MA: Wiley-Blackwell.

Good, Mary-Jo DelVecchio. 2007. "The Medical Imaginary and the Biotechnical Embrace: Subjective Experiences of Clinical Scientists and Patients." In *Subjectivity: Ethnographic Investigations*, edited by João Biehl, Byron Good, and Arthur Kleinman, 362–80. Berkeley: University of California Press.

Good, Mary-Jo DelVecchio, and Byron J. Good. 2008. "Indonesia Sakit: Indonesian Disorders and the Subjective Experience and Interpretive Politics of Contemporary Indonesian Artists." In *Postcolonial Disorders*, edited by Mary-Jo DelVecchio Good, Sandra T. Hyde, Sara Pinto, and Byron J. Good, 62–108. Berkeley: University of California Press.

Good, Mary-Jo DelVecchio, and Byron J. Good. 2013. "Perspectives on the Politics of Peace in Aceh, Indonesia." In *Radical Egalitarianism*, edited by Felicity Aulino, Miriam Goheen, and Stanley J. Tambiah, 191–208. New York: Fordham University Press.

Good, Mary-Jo DelVecchio, Sandra T. Hyde, Sara Pinto, and Byron J. Good, eds. 2008. *Postcolonial Disorders*. Berkeley: University of California Press.

Good, Mary-Jo DelVecchio, Sarah S. Willen, Seth Donal Hannah, Ken Vickery, and Lawrence Taseng Park. 2011. *Shattering Culture: American Medicine Responds to Cultural Diversity*. New York: Russell Sage.

Goodell, Grace. 1986. *The Elementary Structures of Political Life: Rural Development in Pahlavi Iran*. New York: Oxford University Press.

Goody, Jack. 1977. *The Domestication of the Savage Mind*. Cambridge, UK: Cambridge University Press.

Gould, Stephen Jay. 1989. *Wonderful Life: The Burgess Shale and the Nature of History*. New York: W. W. Norton & Co.

Graham, Loren. 1998. *What Have We Learned about Science and Technology from the Russian Experience?* Stanford, CA: Stanford University Press.

Graham, Loren, and Jean-Michel Kantor. 2009. *Naming Infinity: A True Story of Religious Mysticism and Mathematical Creativity*. Cambridge, MA: Harvard University Press.

Grayman, Jesse Hession. 2013. "Humanitarian Encounters in Post Conflict Aceh." PhD diss., Harvard University.

Green, Arthur. 1979. *Tormented Master: The Life and Spiritual Quest of Rabbi Nahman of Bratslav*. Tuscaloosa: University of Alabama Press.

Greenslit, Nathan. 2007. "Pharmaceutical Relations: Intersections of Illness, Fantasy, and Capital in the Age of Direct to Consumer Marketing." PhD diss., MIT.

Griaule, Marcel. 1965. *Conversations with Ogotemmeli*. Oxford: Oxford University Press.

Grimshaw, Anna. 2001. *The Ethnographer's Eye: Ways of Seeing in Anthropology*. Cambridge: Cambridge University Press.

Günel, Gökce. 2012. "Preparing for an Oil-Less Future: Energy, Climate Change, and Green Business in Abu Dhabi." PhD diss., Cornell University.

Günel, Gökce. 2017. *Spaceship in the Desert: Energy, Climate Change, and Green Business in Abu Dhabi*. Experimental Futures. Durham, NC: Duke University Press.

Gusfield, Joseph. 1986. *Symbolic Crusade: Status Politics and the American Temperance Movement*. 2nd ed. Champaign: University of Illinois Press.

Haeri, Shahla. 2002. *Law of Desire: Temporary Marriage in Shi'i Iran*. Ithaca, NY: Syracuse University Press.

Halperin, Orit. 2014. *Beautiful Data*. Experimental Futures. Durham, NC: Duke University Press.

Halperin, Orit, and Gökçe Günel. 2016. "Demoing unto Death: Smart Cities, Environment, and Preemptive Hope." *Fibreculture Journal*, no. 28.

Halperin, Orit, Jesse LeCavalier, and Nerea Calvillo. 2013. "Test-Bed Urbanism." *Public Culture* 26:272–306.

Hamdy, Sherine. 2012. *Our Bodies Belong to God: Organ Transplants, Islam, and the Struggle for Dignity in Egypt*. Berkeley: University of California Press.

Hansen, Thomas Blom. 1999. *The Saffron Wave*. Princeton, NJ: Princeton University Press.

Haraway, Donna Jean. 1989. *Primate Visions: Gender, Race and Nature in the World of Modern Science*. New York: Routledge.

Haraway, Donna Jean. 1991. *Simians, Cyborgs, and Women: The Reinvention of Nature*. New York: Routledge, 1991.

Haraway, Donna Jean. 1997. *Modest_Witness@Second_Millennium.FemaleMan©_Meets_OncoMouse™: Feminism and Technoscience*. New York: Routledge.

Haraway, Donna Jean. 2003. *Companion Species Manifesto*. Chicago, IL: Prickly Paradigm Press.

Haraway, Donna Jean. 2007. *When Species Meet*. Minneapolis: University of Minnesota Press.

Haraway, Donna Jean. 2016. *Staying with the Trouble*. Experimental Futures. Durham, NC: Duke University Press.

Harding, James, and Cindy Rosenthal, eds. 2011. *The Rise of Performance Studies: Rethinking Richard Schechner's Broad Spectrum*. New York. Palgrave Macmillan.

Harr, Jonathan. 1995. *A Class Action*. New York: Random House.

Hartman, Graham. 2011. "Meillassoux's Virtual Future." *Continent* 1 (2): 78–91.

Harvey, David. 1990. *The Condition of Postmodernity: An Enquiry into the Origins of Cultural Change*. Cambridge, MA: Blackwell.

Havelock, Eric A. 1986. *The Muse Learns to Write*. New Haven, CT: Yale University Press.

Havis, Richard James. 2003. "Interview with Chen Zaige." *Cineaste—America's Leading Magazine on the Art and Politics of the Cinema* 29 (1): 8–11.

Hedayat, Sadegh. 1939/1957. *The Blind Owl*. Translated by Desmond Patrick Costello. London: John Calder.
Helmreich, Stefan. 1998. *Silicon Second Nature: Culturing Artificial Life in a Digital World*. Berkeley: University of California Press.
Helmreich, Stefan. 2007. "An Anthropologist Underwater: Immersive Soundscapes, Submarine Cyborgs, and Transductive Ethnography." *American Ethnologist* 34 (4): 621–41.
Helmreich, Stefan. 2009. *Alien Ocean: Anthropological Voyages in Microbial Seas*. Berkeley: University of California Press.
Henley, Paul. 2010. *The Adventures of the Real: Jean Rouch and the Craft of Ethnographic Cinema*. Chicago, IL: University of Chicago.
Herzfeld, Michael. 2013. "Paradoxes of Order in Thai Community Politics." In *Radical Egalitarianism*, edited by Felicity Aulino, Miriam Goheen, and Stanley J. Tambiah, 146–60. New York: Fordham University Press.
Heyman, Steven. 2013. "Neuroscience and Ethics." Talk at Bioethics Advisory Committee Public Consultation Session, National University of Singapore, January 10.
Hill, Jonathan D. 2008. "Metamorphosis: Mythic and Magical Modes of Ceremonial Exchange among the Wakuenai of Venezuela." In *Music in Latin America and the Caribbean*, edited by Malena Kuss. Austin: University of Texas Press.
Hill, Jonathan D. 2009. *Made from Bone: Trickster Myths, Music, and History from the Amazon*. Champaign: University of Illinois Press.
Hiltebeitel, Alf. 1988. *The Cult of Dhraupadi*. Chicago, IL: University of Chicago Press.
Ho, Enseng. 2002. *The Graves of Tarim: Genealogy and Mobility across the Indian Ocean*. Berkeley: University of California Press.
Ho, Enseng. 2004. "'Empire through Diasporic Eyes: A View from the Other Boat." *Comparative Studies of Society and History* 46 (2): 210–46.
Ho, Dahpon David. 2011. "Sealords Live in Vain: Fujian and the Making of a Maritime Frontier in Seventeenth-Century China." PhD diss., University of California, San Diego.
Hollier, Denis. 1989. *Against Architecture: The Writings of Georges Bataille*. Cambridge, MA: MIT Press.
Hollier, Denis. 1988. *The College of Sociology 1937–39*. Minneapolis: University of Minnesota Press.
Holmes, Douglas. 2013. *Economy of Words: Communicative Imperatives in Central Banks*. Chicago, IL: University of Chicago Press.
Horowitz, Irving Louis, ed. 1967. *The Rise and Fall of Project Camelot: Studies in the Relationship between Social Science and Practical Politics*. Cambridge, MA: MIT Press.
Houston, James. 1971. *The White Dawn*. New York: Harcourt Brace.
Houston, James. 1974. Script (with Thomas Rickman) for the film *The White Dawn*. Directed by Philip Kaufman. Producer: Martin Ransohoff.
Hu Fayun. 2004/2011. *Such Is This World @ SARS.com*. Translated by A. E. Clark. Ragged Banner Press.

Huang, Erin Yu-Tien. 2012. "Capital's Abjects: Chinese Cinema, Urban Horror, and the Limits of Visibility." PhD diss., University of California, Irvine.

Hubert, Henri, and Marcel Mauss. 1964. *Sacrifice: Its Nature and Function*. Translated by W. D. Halls. Chicago, IL: University of Chicago Press.

Hugh-Jones, Christine. 1979. *From the Milk River: Spatial and Temporal Processes in Northwest Amazonia*. Cambridge: Cambridge University Press.

Hugh-Jones, Stephen. 1979. *The Palm and the Pleiades: Initiation and Cosmology in Northwest Amazonia*. Cambridge: Cambridge University Press.

Hutchinson, Sharon E. 1996. *Nuer Dilemmas: Coping with Money, War, and the State*. Berkeley: University of California Press.

Huxley, Aldous. *Brave New World*. New York: Harper and Brothers, 1932.

Ishiguru, Tatsuaki. *Biogenesis and Other Stories*. New York: Vertical, 2015.

Jabes, Edmond. *Le livre des questiones*. Paris: Gallimard, 1963. Translated as *The Book of Questions* by Rosemarie Waldrop (Middletown, CT: Welseyan University Press, 1976).

Jackson, Jean E. 1983. *The Fish People: Linguistic Exogamy and Tukanoan Identity in Northwest Amazonia*. Cambridge: Cambridge University Press.

Jackson, Jean E. 1989. "Is There a Way to Talk about Making Culture without Making Enemies?" 14 (2): 127–43.

Jacob, François. 1988. *The Statue Within: An Autobiography*. New York: Basic Books.

Jain, S. Lochlann. *Injury: The Politics of Product Design and Safety Law in the United States*. Princeton, NJ: Princeton University, 2006.

Jain, Shalini Rupesh. "Reciprocating Hospitality with Hostility: Romesh Gunesekera's Ecocritical Intervention." Paper presented at the International Philosophy and Literature Conference, held at the National University of Singapore, June 2013.

Jameison, Sara R. "Female Initiation Rituals among Urban Wayuu in Hugu Chanvez's Multicultural Venezuelan Republic." PhD diss., University of New Mexico, 2009.

Jameson, Fredric. 1990. *Postmodernism, Or, the Cultural Logic of Late Capitalism*. Durham, NC: Duke University Press.

Jarvis, Jeff. 2008. *Networking Futures: The Movements against Corporate Globalization*. Experimental Futures. Durham, NC: Duke University Press.

Jarzombek, Mark. 2016. *Digital Stockholm Syndrome in the Post-Ontological Age*. Minneapolis: University of Minnesota Press.

Jasanoff, Sheila. 2005. *Designs on Nature: Science and Democracy in Europe and the United States*. Princeton, NJ: Princeton University Press.

Johnson, Douglas H. 1997. *Nuer Prophets*. New York: Oxford University Press.

Johnson, Irving Chan. 2013. "A Muslim King and His Buddhist Subjects: Religion, Power and Identity at the Periphery of the Thai State." In *Radical Egalitarianism*, edited by Felicity Aulino, Miriam Goheen, and Stanley J. Tambiah. New York: Fordham University Press.

Jordt, Ingrid. 2013. "Transnational Buddhism and the Transformation of Local Power in Thailand." In *Radical Egalitarianism*, edited by Felicity Aulino, Miriam Goheen, and Stanley J. Tambiah. New York: Fordham University Press.

Kahn, Jonathan. 2012. *Race in a Bottle: The Story of BiDil and Racialized Medicine in a Post-Genomic Age*. New York: Columbia University Press.

Karp, Ivan, and Charles S. Bird, eds. 1987. *Explorations in African Systems of Thought*. Washington, DC: Smithsonian Institution Press.

Kay, Lily. 2000. *Who Wrote the Book of Life? A History of the Genetic Code*. Stanford, CA: Stanford University Press.

Kawa, Nicholas C. 2016. *Amazonia in the Anthropocene: People, Soils, Plants, Forests*. Austin: University of Texas Press.

Kek, Frédéric. Forthcoming. *Avian Preparedness: An Anthropology of Virus Hunters and Birdwatchers*. Experimental Futures. Durham, NC: Duke University Press.

Kelty, Christopher. *The Participant*. Forthcoming.

Kelty, Christopher. 2017. "Too Much Democracy in All the Wrong Places: Toward a Grammar of Participation." *Current Anthropology* 58:suppl. 15.

Kelty, Christopher. 2008. *Two Bits: The Cultural Significance of Free Software*. Durham, NC: Duke University Press.

Kelting, M. Whitney. 2001. *Singing to the Jinas: Jain Laywomen, Mandal Singing and the Negotiations of Jain Devotion*. New York: Oxford University Press.

Kessler, Ronald C., et al. 2009. "The Global Burden of Mental Disorders: An Update from the WHO World Mental Health WMH Surveys." *Epidemiol Psichiatr Soc* 18 (1):23–33.

Khosravi, Shahram. 2007. *Young and Defiant in Tehran*. Philadelphia: University of Pennsylvania Press.

Khosravi, Shahram. 2010. *Illegal Travel: An Auto Ethnography of Borders*. New York: Palgrave Macmillan.

Khosravi, Shahram. 2017. *Precarious Lives: Waiting and Hope in Iran*. Philadelphia: University of Pennsylvania Press.

Kittler, Friedrich. *Aufschreibesysteme 1800/1900*. Munich, Germany: Fink 1986. Translated as *Discourse Networks 1800/1900* (Stanford, CA: Stanford University Press, 1990).

Kittler, Friedrich. *Grammophon Film Typewriter*. Berlin: Brinkmann & Bose, 1986. Stanford, CA: Stanford University Press, 1999.

Kleinman, Arthur, Veena Das, and Margaret Lock, eds. *Social Suffering*. Berkeley: University of California Press, 1997.

Kohn, Eduardo. *How Forests Think*. Berkeley: University of California Press, 2013.

Komo, Norifumi, Mary Carlson, Robert T. Brennan, and Felton Earls. 2008. "Young Citizens as Health Agents: Use of Drama in Promoting Community Efficacy for HIV/AIDS. *American Journal of Public Health* 98:201–4.

Kondo, Dorrine. 1997. *About Face: Performing Race in Fashion and Theater*. New York: Routledge.

Kopenawa, Davi, and Bruce Alpert. 2013. *The Falling Sky*. Cambridge, MA: Harvard University Press.

Kracke, Waud H. 1978. *Force and Persuasion: Leadership in an Amazonian Society*. Chicago, IL: University of Chicago Press.

Kulke, Herman, K. Kesavapany, and Vijay Sakhula, eds. 2009. *Nagapattinam to Suvarnadwipa: Reflections on the Chola Naval Expeditions to Southeast Asia*. Singapore: Institute of Southeast Asian Studies.

Kumar, Kiran. 2017. *Archipelago Archives Exhibit #3: If I Could Set with the Sun*. Program notes, Goodman Arts Center. Singapore: Raw Moves.
Kumar, Richa. 2009. "The Yellow Revolution in Malway: Alternative Arenas of Struggle and the Cultural Politics of Development." PhD diss., MIT.
Kuning, Zai. 2017. *Dapunta Hyang: Transmission of Knowledge*. Singapore: National Arts Council.
Kuo, Wen-Hua. 2009. "The Voice on the Bridge: Taiwan's Regulatory Engagement with Global Pharmaceuticals." *East Asian Science, Technology and Society* 3 (1): 51–72.
Kuo Pao Kun. 2000. *Images at the Margins: A Collection of Kuo Pao Kun's Plays*. Singapore: Time Books International.
Lacoue-Labarthe, Philippe. 1989. *Typography: Mimesis, Philosophy, Politics*. Cambridge, MA: Harvard University Press.
Lahsen, Myanna. 2005. "Seductive Simulations: Uncertainty Distribution around Climate Models." *Social Studies of Science* 35:895–922.
Lahsen, Myanna. 2008. "Knowledge, Democracy and Uneven Playing Fields: Insights from Climate Politics in—and between—the U.S. and Brazil." In *Knowledge and Democracy: A 21st-Century Perspective*, edited by Nico Stehr, 163–81. London: Transaction Publishers.
Lahsen, Myanna, with Gunilla Oberg. 2006. *The Role of Unstated Mistrust and Disparities in Scientific Capacity*. Linköbing, Sweden: The Swedish Institute for Climate Science and Policy Research, Linköbing University. https://polopoly.liu.se/content/1/c4/10/58/Lahsen%20Oberg%20pdf%20final%20version%202006.pdf.
Lambert, Gregg. 2013. "Strangers, Primitives, and Literary Readers: On the Marriage of Psychoanalysis and Ethnography in the Work of Gabriele Schwab." Paper presented at the International Philosophy and Literature Conference, held at the National University of Singapore, June.
Landecker, Hannah. 2007. *Culturing Life: How Cells Became Technologies*. Cambridge, MA: Harvard University Press.
Landecker, Hannah. 2011. "Food as Exposure: Nutritional Epigenetics and the New Metabolism," *Biosocieties* 6 (2):167–94.
Landecker, Hannah. 2013a. "Metabolism, Reproduction, and the Aftermath of Categories." *Scholar and Feminist Online*, 11 (3). http://sfonline.barnard.edu/life-un-ltd-feminism-bioscience-race/metabolism-reproduction-and-the-aftermath-of-categories/.
Landecker, Hannah. 2013b. "Post-Industrial Metabolism: Fat Knowledge." *Public Culture*. 25 (3): 495–522.
Landecker, Hannah. 2016. "The Social as Signal in the Body of Chromatin." The Sociological Review Monographs. 64 (1): 79–99.
Landecker, Hannah. 2016. "Antibiotic Resistance and the Biology of History." *Body and Society* 22 (4): 19–52.
Latour, Bruno. 1984. *Les Microbes: Guerre et paix*. Paris: LaDécouverte.
Latour, Bruno. 1988. *The Pasteurization of France*. Cambridge, MA: Harvard University, Press.

Latour, Bruno. 2004. *The Politics of Nature: How to Bring the Sciences into Democracy*. Cambridge, MA: Harvard University Press.

Latour, Bruno (with Emilie Hermant). 2006. *Paris: Invisible City*. http://www.bruno-latour.fr/sites/default/files/downloads/viii_paris-city-gb.pdf.

Latour, Bruno. 2007. "The Tarde-Durkheim Debate." June 23–30. http://www.bruno-latour.fr/node/434.

Latour, Bruno. 2008. "A Cautious Prometheus: A Few Steps towards a Philosophy of Design, with Special Attention to Peter Sloterdijk." Keynote lecture for the Networks of Design meeting of the Design History Society, Falmouth, Cornwall, September 3. http://www.bruno-latour.fr/sites/default/files/112-design-cornwall-gb.pdf.

Latour, Bruno. 2009. *Rejoicing: Or the Torments of Religious Speech*. London: Polity, 2009.

Latour, Bruno. 2010. "Networks, Societies, Spheres: Reflections of an Actor Network Theorist." http://www.bruno-latour.fr/sites/default/files/121-castells-gb.pdf.

Latour, Bruno. 2011. "An Attempt at a Compositionist Manifesto." *New Literary History* 41:471–90.

Latour, Bruno. 2012. "The Whole Is Always Smaller Than Its Parts: A Digital Test of Gabriel Tarde's Monads." *British Journal of Sociology* 63 (4): 591–615.

Latour, Bruno. 2013a. "Perspectivism: 'Type' or 'Bomb'?" *Anthropology Today* 25 (2): 1.

Latour, Bruno. 2013b. "Presentation in English and German of the AIME Project in Relation with Armin Linke's Work." Karlsruhe, Germany: Hochschule fuer Gastaltung. http://www.bruno-latour.fr/node/470.

Latour, Bruno. 2013c. *An Inquiry into Modes of Existence*. Cambridge, MA: Harvard University.

Latour, Bruno. 2013c. "Facing Gaia: Six Lectures on the Political Theology of Nature." The Gifford Lectures. University of Edinburgh, February, 18–28. http://www.bruno-latour.fr/node/487;bruno-latour.fr/sites/default/files/downloads/gifford-six-lectures_1.pdf.

Latour, Bruno. 2014a. "Public Lecture with Prof. Bruno Latour and the AIME team." Copenhagen Business School Video Public-Private Platform, February 24. http://www.cbs.dk/node/279171; http://vimeo.com/87888402.

Latour, Bruno. 2014b. "On Some of the Affects of Capitalism." Lecture, Royal Academy of Copenhagen, February 26, 2014. http://www.bruno-latour.fr/sites/default/files/136-affects-of-k-copenhague.pdf.

Leach, Edmund R. 1954. *Political Systems of Highland Burma*. London: Bell.

Leach, Edmund R. 1961. *Pul Eliya, a Village in Ceylon: A Study of Land Tenure and Kinship*. Cambridge: Cambridge University Press, 1961.

Lee, MeeRa. 2013. "An Imaginary Encounter between Haunting Legacies and the Korean Emotion of Han." Paper presented at the International Philosophy and Literature Conference, National University of Singapore, June.

Lemelson, Robert. 2009. *Forty Years of Silence*. Los Angeles: Elemental Productions.

Lepinay, Vincent. 2011. *Codes of Finance: Engineering Derivatives in a Global Bank*. Princeton, NJ: Princeton University Press.

Leiris, Michel. 1934/2017. *L'Afrique fantome*. Paris: Gallimard. Tranlsated as *Phantom Africa*. by Brent Hayes Edwards. New York: Seagull.

Le Roy Ladurie, Emmanuel. 1978. *Montaillou: Cathars and Catholics in a French Village, 1294–1324*. Translated by Barbara Bray. London: Scolar.

Levinas, Emmanuel. 1969. *Totality and Infinity: An Essay on Exteriority*. Translated by Alphonso Lingis. Pittsburg, PA: Duquesne University Press.

Lévi-Strauss, Claude. 1949/1969. *The Elementary Structures of Kinship*. Translated by J. H. Bell, J. R. von Sturmer, and Rodney Needham. London: Eyre & Spottiswood.

Lévi-Strauss, Claude. 1981. *The Naked Man: Introduction to a Science of Mythology*. Vol. 4. New York: Harper and Row.

Lévi-Strauss, Claude. 1982. *The Way of the Masks*. Seattle: University of Washington Press.

Lewis, E. Douglas, ed. 2004. *Timothy Asch and Ethnographic Film*. New York: Routledge.

Lewis, Oscar. 1951. *Life in a Mexican Village: Tepotzlan Restudied*. Champaign: University of Illinois Press.

Link, Perry. 2007. "Spy Anxiety." *New York Times*, May 2, 2007. https://www.nytimes.com/2014/05/04/books/review/decoded-by-mai-jia.html?_r=0.

Lipsitz, George. 2006. *The Possessive Investment in Whiteness: How White People Profit from Identity Politics*. Philadelphia, PA: Temple University Press.

Liu Cixin. 2000/2013. "The Wandering Earth." In *The Wandering Earth*. Translated by Holger Nahm. Beijing: Guomi Digital Technology.

Liu Cixin. 2006/2014. *Remembrance of Earth's Past*. Vol. 1, *The Three Body Problem*. Translated by Ken Liu. New York: Tor Books.

Liu Cixin. 2008/2015. *Remembrance of Earth's Past*. Vol. 2, *The Dark Forest*. Translated by Joel Martinsen. New York: Tor Books.

Liu Cixin. 2010/2016. *Remembrance of Earth's Past*. Vol. 3, *Death's End*. Translated by Ken Liu. New York: Tor Books

Livingston, Julie. 2013. *Improvised Medicine: An African Oncology Ward in an Emerging Cancer Epidemic*. Durham, NC: Duke University Press.

Lleras, Roberto, Clara Isabel Botero, and Santiago Londo, eds. 2007. *The Art of Gold: The Legacy of Pre-Hispanic Colombia*. New York: Skira.

Loizos, Peter. 1993. *Innovation in Ethnographic Film: From Innocence to Self-Consciousness, 1955–1965*. Chicago, IL: University of Chicago Press.

Lotfalian, Mazyar. 1996. "Working through Psychological Understandings of the Diasporic Condition." *Ethos* 24 (1): 36–70.

Lotfalian, Mazyar. 2012. "Aestheticized Politics, Visual Culture, and Emergent Forms of Digital Practice. *International Journal of Communication* 6:1–20.

Long, Nicholas. 2013. *Being Malay in Indonesia: Histories, Hope, and Citizenship in the Riau Archipelago*. Honolulu: University of Hawaii Press.

Loraux, Nicole. 2002. *The Divided City: On Memory and Forgetting in Ancient Athens*. New York: Zone Books.

Lovelock, James. 1979. *Gaia: A New Look at Life on Earth*. Oxford: Oxford University Press.

Lowe, Celia. 2006. *Wild Profusion: Biodiversity Conservation in an Indonesian Archipelago*. Princeton, NJ: Princeton University Press.

Lyons, Charles. 2015a. "A Brazilian Tribe's Suicide Epidemic." *International New York Times*, January 3, 2015.

Lyons, Charles. 2015b. "Suicides Spread through a Brazilian Tribe." *New York Times*, January 2, 2015.
Lyotard, Jean-François. 1979/1984. *The Postmodern Condition: A Report on Knowledge*. Translated by Geoff Bennington and Brian Massumi. Minneapolis: University of Minnesota Press.
Lyotard, Jean-François. 1974/1993. *Libidinal Economy*. Bloomington: Indiana University Press.
MacDonald, Scott. 2013. *American Ethnographic Film and Personal Documentary: The Cambridge Turn*. Berkeley: University of California Press.
MacKenzie, Donald. 2008. *An Engine, Not a Camera: How Financial Models Shape Markets*. Cambridge, MA: MIT Press.
Macksey, Richard, and Eugenio Donato, eds. 1972. *The Structuralist Controversy: The Languages of Criticism and the Sciences of Man*. Baltimore, MD: Johns Hopkins University Press.
Mahendrakumar "Pratham," Muni Sri. 1984. *Jaina Stories*. 3 vols. Delhi: Motilal Banarsidass.
Mai Jia. 2007. *Decoded*. New York: Farrar, Straus & Giroux.
Malinowski, Bronislaw. 1922. *Argonauts of the Western Pacific*. London: G. Routledge and Sons.
Malinowski, Bronislaw. 1935/1965. *Coral Gardens and Their Magic*. 2 vols. Bloomington: Indiana University Press.
Malkki, Liisa. 2013. "A Tale of Two Affects: Humanitarianism and Professionalism in Red Cross Aid Work." In *Radical Egalitarianism*, edited by Felicity Aulino, Miriam Goheen, and Stanley J. Tambiah, 209–19. New York: Fordham University Press.
Malzman, Barry N. 1985. *The Remaking of Sigmund Freud*. New York: Ballantine.
Manabe, Noriko. 2014. *The Revolution Will Not Be Televised*. New York: Oxford University Press.
Manaugh, Geoff. 2014. "Gorgeous Aerial Photographs Capture the Ironic Beauty of Fracking." Gizmodo.com. http://gizmodo.com/gorgeous-aerial-photos-capture-the-ironic-beauty-of-fra-1508113472.
Manfredi, Victor. 2013. "'A Recurrence of Structures' in a Collapsing Nigeria." In *Radical Egalitarianism*, edited by Felicity Aulino, Miriam Goheen, and Stanley J. Tambiah, 119–36. New York: Fordham University Press.
Marchetti, Gina. 2011. "From Mao's 'Continuous Revolution' to Ning Ying's 'Perpetual Motion' 2005: Sexual Politics, Neoliberalism, and Postmodern China." In *Chinese Women's Cinema: Transnational Contexts*, edited by Lingzhen Wang, 191–212. New York: Columbia University Press.
Marcus, George E., ed. 1999. *Critical Anthropology Now*. Santa Fe, NM: SAR.
Marcus, George E. 1993–2000. *Late Editions: Cultural Studies for the End of the Century*. 8 vols. Chicago, IL: University of Chicago Press.
Marcus, George E., and Michael M. J. Fischer. 1986. *Anthropology as Cultural Critique: An Experimental Moment in the Human Sciences*. Chicago, IL: University of Chicago Press.

Margulis, Lynn, and Doron Sagan. 2003. *Acquiring Genomes: A Theory of the Origin of Species*. New York: Basic Books.

Marx, Karl. 1850/1962. *The Eighteenth Brumaire of Louis Napoleon*. New York: International Publishers.

Mascia-Lees, Frances, Patricia Sharpe, and Colleen Ballerino Cohen. 1989. "The Postmodernist Turn in Anthropology: Cautions from a Feminist Perspective." *Signs* 15 (1): 7–33.

Masco, Joseph. 2006. *Nuclear Borderlands: The Manhattan Project in Post-Cold War New Mexico*. Princeton, NJ: Princeton University Press.

Mason, Katherine. 2016. *Infectious Change: Reinventing Chinese Public Health after an Epidemic*. Stanford, CA: Stanford University Press.

Massignon, Louis. 1982. *The Passion of al-Hallaj: Mystic and Martyr of Islam*. Translated by Herbert Mason. 4 vols. Princeton, NJ: Princeton University Press.

Mattingly, Cheryl. 2013. "Moral Selves and Moral Scenes: Narrative Experiments in Everyday Life." *Ethos: Journal of Psychological Anthropology* 78 (3): 301–27. doi: 10.1080/00141844-2012.691523.

Mauss, Marcel. 1909/2003. *On Prayer*. Translated by Susan Leslie. New York: Berghahn.

Mauss, Marcel. 1925/1970. *The Gift: Forms and Function of Exchange in Archaic Societies*. London: Cohen and West.

Maybury-Lewis, David. 1965. *The Savage and the Innocent*. New York: World Publishing,

Maybury-Lewis, David. 1974. *Akwẽ-Shavante Society*. London: Oxford University Press.

Maybury-Lewis, David, ed. 1979. *Dialectical Societies: The Ge and Bororo of Central Brazil*. Cambridge, MA: Harvard University Press.

Maybury-Lewis, David. 1980. *The Social Impact of Development on Ethnic Minorities*. Cambridge, MA: Cultural Survival.

Medina, Eden, and Ilan Sandberg Weiner. 2016. "Science and Harm in Human Rights Cases: Preventing the Revictimization of Families of the Disappeared." *Yale Law Journal Forum* 125:331–42.

Meillassoux, Quentin. 2006/2008. *After Finitude*. Translated by Ray Brassier. London: Continuum.

Merleau-Ponty, Maurice. 1964/1968. *The Visible and the Invisible*. Evanston, IL: Northwestern University Press.

Messeri, Lisa. 2016. *Placing Outer Space: An Earthly Ethnography of Other Worlds*. Experimental Futures. Durham, NC: Duke University Press.

Meyer, Stephen M. 2006. *The End of the Wild*. Cambridge, MA: MIT Press.

Middleton, John, and David Tait, eds. 1958. *Tribes without Rulers*. London: Routledge.

Misrach, Richard. 1987. *Desert Cantos*. Albuquerque: University of New Mexico Press.

Misrach, Richard. 2014. *Petrochemical America*. New York: Aperture.

Mitchell, David Stephen. 2004. *Cloud Atlas*. New York: Random House.

Mitchell, David Stephen. 2010. *The Thousand Autumns of Jacob de Zoet*. New York: Random House.

Mnookin, Jennifer. 1999. "Images of Truth: Evidence, Expertise, and Technologies of Knowledge in the American Courtroom." PhD diss., MIT.

Modarressi, Taghi. 1985. *The Book of Absent People*. Garden City, NY: Doubleday.

Moinzadeh, Hassan Ali. 2004. "Secret of Gay Being: Embodying Homosexual Libido in the Iranian Imagination." PhD diss., Pacifica Graduate Institute.

Montoya, Michael. 2011. *Making the Mexican Diabetic: Race, Science, and the Genetics of Inequality*. Berkeley: University of California Press.

Morat, Daniel, ed., 2014. *Sounds of Modern History: Auditory Cultures in 19th- and 20th-Century Europe*. New York: Berghahn.

Morimoto, Ryo. 2016. *Under Control: Alterity at the Edge of Nuclear Contamination and Containment in Post-Fallout Coastal Fukushima*. PhD diss., Brandeis University.

Morreira, Shannon. 2016. "Working with Our Grandparents' Illusions: On Colonial Lineage and Inheritance in Southern African Anthropology." *HAU: Journal of Ethnographic Theory* 6 (2): 279–95.

Morris, Rosalind. 1994. *New Worlds from Fragments: Film, Ethnography, and the Representation of Northwest Coast Cultures*. Boulder, CO: Westview Press.

Morris, Rosalind. 2000. *In the Place of Origins: Modernity and Its Mediums in Northern Thailand*. Durham, NC: Duke University Press.

Murakami Takashi. 2015. *Takashi Murakami: The 500 Arhats*. Tokyo: Mori Art Museum.

Murray, Christopher J. L., and Alan D. Lopez. 1995. *The Global Burden of Disease: A Comprehensive Assessment of Mortality and Disability from Diseases, Injuries, and Risk Factors in 1990 and Projected to 2020*. Cambridge, MA: Harvard University Press.

Myer, Stephen. 2006. *The End of the Wild*. Cambridge, MA: MIT Press.

Myers, Natasha. 2015. *Rendering Life Molecular: Models, Modelers, and Excitable Matter*. Experimental Futures. Durham, NC: Duke University Press.

Naam, Ramez. 2015. *Nexus*. Nottingham, UK: Angry Robot/Watkins Media.

Naficy, Hamid. 2001. *An Accented Cinema: Exilic and Diasporic Filmmaking*. Princeton, NJ: Princeton University Press.

Naficy, Hamid. 2012. *A Social History of Iranian Cinema*. Vol. 4, *The Globalizing Era, 1984–2010*. Durham, NC: Duke University Press.

Naficy, Nahal. 2007. "Persian Miniature Writing: An Ethnography of Iranian Organizations in Washington, D.C." PhD diss., Rice University.

Nafisi, Azar. 2003. *Reading Lolita in Tehran*. New York: Random House, 2003.

Nagatani, Patrick. 1991. *Nuclear Enchantment*. Albuquerque: University of New Mexico Press.

Najar, Nida, and Sbasini Raj. 2015. "Dengue Outbreak Overwhelms Delhi." *New York Times*, October 9, 2015, A4.

Najmabadi, Afsaneh. 2005. *Women with Mustaches and Men without Beards: Gender and Sexual Anxieties of Iranian Modernity*. Berkeley: University of California Press.

Najmabadi, Afsaneh. 2014. *Possessing Selves: Transsexuality and Same-Sex Desire in Contemporary Iran*. Experimental Futures. Durham, NC: Duke University Press.

Negri, Antonio. 1970/2006. *Political Descartes: Reason, Ideology, and the Bourgeois Project*. London: Verso,

Negri, Antonio. 2002/2009. *The Labor of Job: The Biblical Text as a Parable of Human Labor*. Durham, NC: Duke University Press.

Nietzsche, Friedrich. 1885/1961. *Thus Spoke Zarathustra*. Translated by R. J. Hollingdale. Harmondsworth, UK: Penguin Books.
Nilekani, Rohini. 1998. *Stillborn: A Medical Thriller*. New Delhi: Penguin.
Nimitz, August. 2000. *Marx and Engels: Their Contribution to the Democratic Breakthrough*. Albany: State University of New York Press.
Obeysekere, Gananath. 1981. *Medusa's Hair*. Berkeley: University of California Press.
Obeysekere, Gananath. 1984. *The Cult of the Goddess Pattini*. Chicago, IL: University of Chicago Press.
Obeysekere, Gananath. 1997. *The Apotheosis of Captain Cook: European Mythmaking in the Pacific*. Princeton, NJ: Princeton University Press.
Obeysekere, Gananath and Richard Gombrich. 1988. *Buddhism Transformed*. Princeton, NJ: Princeton University Press.
O'Dwyer, Timothy. 2012. "The Adventure of the Refrain: Composing with Improvised Music." PhD diss., Queensland University of Technology.
O'Dwyer, Timothy. 2013. "Analysing Improvised Music: A Deleuzian Approach." Paper presented at the International Philosophy and Literature Conference, held at the National University of Singapore, June.
Ohnuki-Tierney, Emiko. 2013. "At the Base of Local and Transnational Conflicts: The Political Use of Inferiorization." In *Radical Egalitarianism*, edited by Felicity Aulino, Miriam Goheen, and Stanley J. Tambiah, 220–32. New York: Fordham University Press.
Olson, Valerie A. 2017. *American Extreme*. Minneapolis: University of Minnesota Press.
Ong Keng Sen. 2013. "Making Lear Dreaming: An Interview with Dr. Margherita Laera." In *From Identity to Mondialisation*, edited by TheatreWorks. 244–49. Singapore: Editions Millet.
Ong, Walter J. 1982. *Orality and Literacy: The Technologizing of the Word*. London: Methuen.
Oppenheim, Joshua. 2012. *The Act of Killing*. Denmark: Final Cut For Real Producers.
Orta, Garcia da. 1563. *Coloquios dos simples e drogas e coisas medinais da India e de algumas frutas*. Goa, India: João de Endem.
Orwell, George. 1946. *Animal Farm*. New York: Harcourt, Brace, 1946.
Orwell, George. 1949. *1984*. London: Secker and Warburg.
Osanloo, Arzoo. 2009. *The Politics of Women's Rights in Iran*. Princeton, NJ: Princeton University Press.
Özden-Schilling, Canay. 2016. "Economy Electric: Techno-Economics, Neoliberalism, and Electricity in the United States." PhD diss., MIT.
Özden-Schilling, Thomas. 2016. "Salvage Cartographies: Mapping, Futures, and Landscapes in Northwest British Columbia." PhD diss., MIT.
Ozkan, Esra. 2007. "Executive Coaching: Crafting a Versatile Self in Corporate America." PhD diss., MIT.
Pandolfi, Mariela. 2003. "Contract of Mutual (In)difference: Governance and the Human Apparatus in Contemporary Albania and Kosovo." *Indiana Journal of Global Legal Studies* 10 (1): 369–81.

Paxson, Heather. 2008. "Post-Pasteurian Cultures: The Microbiopolitics of Raw-Milk Cheese in the United States." *Cultural Anthropology* 23 (1): 15–47.

Paxson, Heather. 2012. *The Life of Cheese: Crafting Food and Value in America*. Berkeley: University of California Press.

Peacock, James, Robert Albro, Carolyn Fluehr-Lobban, Kerry Fosher, Laura McNamara, Monica Heller, George E. Marcus, David Price, and Alan Goodman. 2007. "Final Report: American Anthropological Association Ad Hoc Commission on the Engagement of Anthropology with U.S. National Security and Intelligence Communities." Arlington, VA: American Anthropological Association. Electronic document, http://www.aaanet.org/pdf/final_report_complete.pdf.

Pearson, Wendy Gay, and Susan Knabe, eds. 2015. *Reverse Shots: Indigenous Film and Media in an International Context*. Waterloo, CA: Wilfred Laurier University Press.

Peattie, Lisa Redfield. 1987. *Planning, Rethinking Ciudad Guyana*. Ann Arbor: University of Michigan Press.

Peirano, Mariza. 2013. "People and Ideas Travel Together: Tambiah's Approach to Ritual and Cosmology in Brazil." In *Radical Egalitarianism*, edited by Felicity Aulino, Miriam Goheen, and Stanley J. Tambiah, 137–45. New York: Fordham University Press.

Perin, Constance. 2005. *Shouldering Risks: The Culture of Control in the Nuclear Power Industry*. Princeton, NJ: Princeton University Press.

Perniola, Mario. 2013. "Aesthetics: Between Philosophy and Art." Paper presented at the International Philosophy and Literature Conference, held at the National University of Singapore, June.

Perpich, Diane. 2008. *The Ethics of Emmanuel Levinas*. Stanford, CA: Stanford University Press.

Petryna, Adriana. 2002. *Life Exposed: Biological Citizens after Chernobyl*. Princeton, NJ: Princeton University Press.

Petryna, Adriana. 2009. *When Experiments Travel: Clinical Trials and the Global Search for Human Subjects*. Princeton, NJ: Princeton University Press.

Phillips, John. 2013. "Algebra . . ." Paper presented at the International Philosophy and Literature Conference, held at the National University of Singapore, June.

Picker, John. 2003. *Victorian Soundscapes*. New York: Oxford University Press.

Pinch, Trevor, and Karin Bijsterveld, ed., 2011. *Oxford Handbook of Sound Studies*. New York: Oxford University Press.

Pinto, Sarah. 2014. *Daughters of Parvati: Women and Madness in Contemporary India*. Philadelphia: University of Pennsylvania Press.

Pitt-Rivers, Julian. 1977. "The Law of Hospitality." In *The Fate of Schechem or the Politics of Sex: Essays in the Anthropology of the Mediterranean*. 94–112. London: Cambridge University Press.

Politis, Gustavo G. 2007. *Nukak: Ethnoarcheology of an Amazonian People*. Walnut Creek, CA: Left Coast Press.

Pollock, Anne. 2012. *Medicating Race: Heart Disease and Durable Preoccupations with Difference*. Experimental Futures. Durham, NC: Duke University Press.

Postel, Danny. 2006. *Reading Legitimation Crisis in Tehran: Iran and the Future of Liberalism*. Chicago, IL: Prickly Paradigm Press.

Poulton, Richie, Terrie E. Moffit, and Phil A. Silva. 2015. "The Dunedin Multidisciplinary Health and Development Study: Overview of the First 40 Years, with an Eye to the Future." *Social Psychiatry and Psychiatric Epidemiology* 50 (5): 679–93.

Povinelli, Elizabeth. 2002. *The Cunning of Recognition: Indigenous Alterities and the Making of Australian Multiculturalism*. Durham, NC: Duke University Press.

Povinelli, Elizabeth. 2016. *Geontologies: A Requiem to Late Liberalism*. Durham, NC: Duke University Press.

Prentice, Rachel. 2012. *Bodies in Formation: An Ethnography of Anatomy and Surgery Education*. Experimental Futures. Durham, NC: Duke University Press.

Price, David H. 2004. *Cold War Anthropology: The CIA, the Pentagon, and the Growth of Dual Use Anthropology*. Durham, NC: Duke University Press.

Price, David H. 2008. *Anthropological Intelligence: The Deployment and Neglect of American Anthropology in the Second World War*. Durham, NC: Duke University Press.

Price, David H. 2016. *Threatening Anthropology: McCarthyism and the FBI's Surveillance of Activist Anthropologists*. Durham, NC: Duke University Press

Puett, Michael. 2013. "Economies of Ghosts, Gods, and Goods: The History and Anthropology of Chinese Temple Networks." In *Radical Egalitarianism*, edited by Felicity Aulino, Miriam Goheen, and Stanley J. Tambiah, 91–100. New York: Fordham University Press.

Quin, Amy. 2017. "Nuclear Site Reborn as a Tourist Draw." *New York Times International*, 16 January. https://www.nytimes.com/2014/05/04/books/review/decoded-by-mai-jia.html?_r=0.

Rabi, I. I. 1960. *My Life and Times as a Physicist*. Claremont, CA: Claremont College.

Rabinow, Paul. 1977. *Reflections on Fieldwork in Morocco*. Berkeley: University of California Press.

Rabinow, Paul, ed. 1984. *The Foucault Reader*. New York: Pantheon Books.

Rabinow, Paul. 1989. *French Modern: Norms and Forms of the Social Environment*. Chicago, IL: University of Chicago Press.

Rabinow, Paul. 1996. *The Making of PCR*. Chicago, IL: University of Chicago Press.

Rabinow, Paul, ed. 1997. *The Essential Works of Michel Foucault, 1954–1984*. Vol. 1, *Ethics, Subjectivity, and Truth*. New York: The New Press.

Rabinow, Paul. 1999. *French DNA: Trouble in Purgatory*. Chicago, IL: University of Chicago Press.

Rabinow, Paul. 2011. *The Accompaniment: Assembling the Contemporary*. Chicago, IL: University of Chicago Press.

Rabinow, Paul. 2012. *Designing Human Practices: An Experiment with Synthetic Biology*. Chicago, IL: University of Chicago Press.

Rabinow, Paul. 2014. *Designs on the Contemporary: Anthropological Tests*. Chicago, IL: University of Chicago Press.

Rabinow, Paul, with Talia Dan-Cohen. 2004. *A Machine to Make a Future: Biotech Chronicles*. Princeton, NJ: Princeton University Press.

Rabinow, Paul, and Hubert Dreyfus. 1983. *Michel Foucault: Beyond Structuralism and Hermeneutics*. Chicago, IL: University of Chicago Press.
Rabinow, Paul, George Marcus, James Faubion, and Tobias Rees. 2008. *Designs for an Anthropology of the Contemporary*. Durham, NC: Duke University Press.
Rabinow, Paul, and Nikolas Rose, eds. 2003. *The Essential Foucault*. New York: The New Press.
Rabinow, Paul, and Anthony Stavrianakis. 2013. *Demands of the Day: On the Logic of Anthropological Inquiry*. Chicago, IL: University of Chicago Press.
Radcliffe-Brown, A. R., and Daryll Forde. 1950. *African Systems of Kinship and Marriage*. London: Oxford University Press.
Rae, Paul. 2013. "Presently the Fullerton Hotel: A Singapore Assemblage." Paper presented at the International Philosophy and Literature Conference, held at the National University of Singapore, June.
Rahimi, Nasrin. 2011. "Translating Taghi Modarressi's Writing with an Accent." In *Essays in Honor of Gernot Ludwig Windfuhr*, edited by Behrad Aghaei and Mohammad Ghanoonparvar. Santa Anna, CA: Mazda.
Rajagopal, Arvind. 2001. *Politics after Television: Hindu Nationalism and the Reshaping of the Indian Public*. Cambridge: Cambridge University Press.
Ralph, Laurence. 2014. *Renegade Dreams: Living through Injury in Gangland Chicago*. Chicago, IL: University of Chicago Press.
Ramanathan, V. 1982. *Bhagavadgita for Executives*. Bombay, India: Bharatiya Vidya Bhavan.
Ramos, Alcida. 1990/1995. *Sanuma Memories: Yanomami Ethnography in Times of Crisis*. Madison: University of Wisconsin Press.
Ramos, Alcida. 2012. "The Politics of Perspectivism." *Annual. Review of Anthropology*, 41:481–94.
Rappaport, Joanne. 1990. *The Politics of Memory: Native Historical Interpretation in the Colombian Andes*. Cambridge: Cambridge University Press.
Rappaport, Joanne. 2005. *Intercultural Utopias: Public Intellectuals, Cultural Experimentation, and Ethnic Pluralism in Colombia*. Durham, NC: Duke University Press.
Ratanapruck, Prista. 2013. "Trade, Religion, and Civic Relations in the Manangi Long-Distance Trade Community." In *Radical Egalitarianism*, edited by Felicity Aulino, Miriam Goheen, and Stanley J. Tambiah, 101–10. New York: Fordham University Press.
Readings, Bill. 1997. *The University in Ruins*. Cambridge, MA: Harvard University Press.
Reddy, K. Srinath. 2015. "The Doctor Won't See You Now." *Indian Express*, March 21, 2015.
Redfield, Robert. 1930. *Tepotzlan: A Mexican Village*. Chicago, IL: University of Chicago Press.
Reich, Michael. 1991. *Toxic Politics: Responding to Chemical Disasters*. Ithaca, NY: Cornell University Press.
Rheinberger, Hans-Joerg. 1997. *Towards a History of Epistemic Things: Synthesizing Proteins in the Test Tube*. Stanford, CA: Stanford University Press.
Richards, Audrey. 1939. *Land, Labor, and Diet in Northern Rhodesia: An Economic Study of the Bemba*. Oxford: Oxford University Press.

Robinson, Kathryn. 2004. "Chandra Jayawardena and the Ethical 'Turn' in Australian Anthropology." *Critique of Anthropology*. 24 (4): 379–402.
Rohani, Talieh. 2009. "Nostalgia without Memory: Iranian-Americans, Cultural Programming and Internet Television." Master's thesis, MIT.
Roland, Alan. 1998. *In Search of Self in India and Japan: Toward a Cross-Cultural Psychology*. Princeton, NJ: Princeton University Press.
Ronnel, Avital. 1989. *The Telephone Book: Technology, Schizophrenia, Electric Speech*. Lincoln: Nebraska University Press.
Rosaldo, Michelle Zimbalist. 1980. "The Use and Abuse of Anthropology: Reflections on Feminism and Cross-Cultural Understanding." *Signs* 5:389–417.
Rosaldo, Michelle Zimbalist and Louise Lamphere, eds., 1974. *Women, Culture and Society*. Stanford, CA: Stanford University Press.
Rosaldo, Renato. 1980. *Ilongot Headhunting, 1983–1974: A Study in Society and History*. Stanford, CA: Stanford University Press.
Roosth, Sophia. 2010. "Crafting Life: A Sensory Ethnography of Fabricated Bodies." PhD diss., MIT.
Rouch, Jean, and Steven Feld. 2003. *Cine-Ethnography*. Minneapolis: University of Minnesota Press.
Rushdie, Salman. 1981. *Midnight's Children*. London: Cape.
Rushdie, Salman. 1988. *Satanic Verses*. London: Viking Penguin.
Sa, Lucia. 2004. "The Upper Rio Negro: The Jurupari and the Big Snake." In *Rain Forest Literatures: Amazonian Texts and Latin American Culture*, 173–204. Minneapolis: University of Minnesota.
Sahlins, Marshall D. 1968. "Notes on the Original Affluent Society." In *Man the Hunter*, edited by Richard B. Lee and Irving DeVore, 85–89. New York: Aldine.
Sahlins, Marshall D. 1995. *How Natives Think: About Captain Cook, for Example*. Chicago, IL: University of Chicago Press.
Sahlins, Marshall D. 2013. "Structural Work: How Microhistories Become Macrohistories and Vice Versa." In *Radical Egalitarianism*, edited by Felicity Aulino, Miriam Goheen, and Stanley J. Tambiah, 161–90. New York: Fordham University Press.
Said, Edward. 1975. *Beginnings: Intention and Method*. New York: Basic Books.
Saldanha, Arun. 2007. *Psychodelic White: Goa Trance and the Viscosity of Race*. Minneapolis: University of Minnesota Press.
Salgado, Sebastian. 2005a. *Migrations: Humanity in Transition*. New York: Aperture.
Salgado, Sebastian. 2005b. *Workers: An Archeology of the Industrial Age*. New York: Aperture.
Samuels, Richard. 2013. *3/11: Disaster and Change in Japan*. Ithaca, NY: Cornell University Press.
Sanal, Aslihan. 2011. *New Organs within Us: Transplants and the Moral Economy*. Experimental Futures. Durham, NC: Duke University Press.
Sayre, Ryan. 2013. "Preparing for Preparedness: Security, Disaster, and 'Recursive Modernity' in Contemporary Japan." PhD diss., Yale University.
Scheler, Max. 1994. *Ressentiment*. Translated and edited by Lewis B. Coser and William W. Holdheim. Milwaukee, WI: Marquette University Press.

Schechner, Richard. 1985. *Between Theater and Anthropology*. Philadelphia: University of Pennsylvania Press.
Schiwy, Freya. 2009. *Indigenizing Film: Decolonization, the Andes, and the Question of Technology*. New Brunswick, NJ: Rutgers University Press.
Schmitt, Carl. 1950/2003. *The Nomos of the Earth in the International Law of the Jus Publicum Europeaeum*. New York: Telos Press.
Schneider, David M., and Kathleen Gough. 1961. *Matrilineal Systems*. Berkeley: University of California Press.
Scholem, Gershom. 1973. *Sabbatai Sevi: The Mystical Messiah, 1626–76*. Princeton, NJ: Princeton University Press.
Schroedinger, Eriwin. 1943. *What Is Life? The Physical Aspect of the Living Cell*. Dublin, Ireland: Institute for Advanced Studies, Trinity College. http://whatislife.stanford.edu/LoCo_files/What-is-Life.pdf.
Schwarz, Heinrich. 2002. "Techno-Territories: The Spatial, Technological and Social Reorganization of Office Work." PhD diss., MIT.
Sen, Amartya. 2009. *The Idea of Justice*. Cambridge, MA: Harvard University Press.
Serres, Michel. 1972. *L'Interférence: Hermes II*. Paris: Hermes.
Serres, Michel. 1982. *The Parasite*. Baltimore, MD: Johns Hopkins University Press.
Serres, Michel. 2013. *Times of Crisis: What the Financial Crisis Revealed and How to Reinvent our Lives and Future*. New York: Bloomsbury Academic.
Shamsie, Kamila. 2009. *Burnt Shadows*. London: Bloomsbury.
Shapiro, Judith. 1999. *Mao's War against Nature*. New York: Cambridge University Press.
Shostak, Marjorie. 1981. *Nisa: The Life and Words of a !Kung Woman*. Cambridge, MA: Harvard University Press.
Shulman, David. 2001. *The Wisdom of Poets: Studies in Tamil, Telegu, and Sanskrit*. London: Oxford University Press.
Shulman, Peter A. 2015. *Coal and Empire*. Baltimore, MD: Johns Hopkins University Press.
Shweder, Richard A., and Byron Good, eds. 2005. *Geertz by His Colleagues*. Chicago, IL: University of Chicago Press.
Sibertin-Blanc, Buillaume. 2016. *State and Politics: Deleuze and Guattari on Marx*. South Pasadena, CA: Seimotexte.
Siegel, James T. 1998. *A New Criminal Type in Jakarta: Counter-Revolution Today*. Durham, NC: Duke University Press.
Siegel, James, Joshua Barker, and Arief Djati. 2008. "Notes of a Trip through Aceh, December 2007." *Indonesia* 86:1–54.
Silverstein, Michael. 2003. "Indexical Order and the Dialectics of Sociolinguistic Life." *Language and Communication* 23:193–229.
Silverstein, Michael. 2017. *Language in Culture: The Semiotics of Interaction*. London: HAU.
Sinha, Indra. 2007. *Animal's People*. New York: Simon and Schuster, 2007.
Slyomovics, Susan. 2005. *The Performance of Human Rights in Morocco*. Philadelphia: University of Pennsylvania Press.
Smith, Catherine. "War, Medicine, and Morality in Aceh: An Ethnography of Trauma as an Idiom of Distress." PhD diss., Australian National University, 2012.

Sokyu, Genyu. 2015. "A Deeper Murakami Mandela." In *Takashi Murakami: 500 Arhats*, edited by Murakami Takashi, 64–65. Tokyo: Mori Museum.
Soto Laveaga, Gabriela. 2009. *Jungle Laboratories: Mexican Peasants, National Projects, and the Making of the Pill*. Durham, NC: Duke University Press.
Spears, Dorothy. 2010. "Part Traditionalist, Part Naturalist, Part Dissident." *New York Times*, February 17. http://www.nytimes.com/2010/02/21/arts/design/21ji.html?_r=0.
Spinage, Clive A. 2012. *African Ecology: Benchmarks and Historical Perspectives*. New York: Springer.
Starn, Orin, ed. 2015. *Writing Culture and the Life of Anthropology*. Durham, NC: Duke University Press.
Stephenson, Neal. 2015. *Seveneves*. New York: William Morrow and Company.
Steiner, Franz. *Taboo*. 1956. London: Cohen and West.
Stenzel, Kristine. 2013. *A Reference Grammar of Kotina (Wanano)*. Lincoln: Nebraska University Press. http://www.nebraskapress.unl.edu/Supplements/excerpts/Spring%2013/9780803228221_excerpt.pdf.
Stephens, Chuck. 2007. "Review of 'I Don't Want to Sleep Alone.'" *Film Comment*, May/June. http://www.filmcomment.com/article/i-dont-want-to-sleep-alone-review/.
Sterne, Jonathan, ed. 2012. *Sound Studies Reader*. New York: Routledge.
Sternsdorff-Cisterna, Nicholas. 2014. "Food Safety after Fukushima: Scientific Citizenship and the Politics of Risk." PhD diss., Harvard University.
Still, Judith. 2010. *Derrida and Hospitality: Theory and Practice*. Edinburgh, UK: Edinburgh University Press.
Stoller, Paul. 1992. *The Cinematic Griot: The Ethnography of Jean Rouch*. Chicago, IL: University of Chicago Press.
Studwell, Joe. 2014. *How Asia Works*. New York: Grove Press.
Suchman, Lucy. 2006. *Human-Machine Reconfigurations: Plans and Situated Actions*. 2nd ed. New York: Cambridge University Press.
Sullivan, Sian. 2014. "Nature on the Move III: Recountenancing an Animate Nature." In *Nature™ Inc*, edited by Büscher, Dressler, and Fletcher.
Sunder Rajan, Kaushik. 2006. *Biocapitalism: The Constitution of Postgenomic Life*. Durham, NC: Duke University Press.
Sunder Rajan, Kaushik. 2007. "Experimental Values: Indian Clinical Trials and Surplus Health." *New Left Review*.
Sunder Rajan, Kaushik, ed. 2012. *Lively Capital: Biotechnologies, Ethics, and Governance in Global Markets*. Experimental Futures. Durham, NC: Duke University Press.
Sunder Rajan, Kaushik. 2017. *Pharmocracy: Trials of Global Biomedicine*. Experimental Futures. Durham, NC: Duke University Press.
Tahmasebi-Birgani, Victoria. 2014. *Emmanuel Levinas and the Politics of Non-Violence*. Toronto: University of Toronto Press.
Tambiah, Stanley J. 1958. "The Structure of Kinship and Its Relationship to Land Possession and Residence in Pata Dumbara, Central Ceylon." *Journal of the Royal Anthropological Institute of Great Britain and Ireland*. 88 (1): 21–44.

Tambiah, Stanley J. 1966. "Polyandry in Ceylon: With Special Reference to the Laggala Region." Colombo, Ceylon: Social Scientists Association.
Tambiah, Stanley J. 1970. *Buddhism and the Spirit Cults in Northeast Thailand.* Cambridge: Cambridge University Press.
Tambiah, Stanley J. 1976. *World Conqueror and World Renouncer: A Study of Buddhism and Polity in Thailand against a Historical Background.* Cambridge: Cambridge University Press.
Tambiah, Stanley J. 1977. "The Galactic Polity: The Structure of Traditional Kingdoms in Southeast Asia." *Annals of the New York Academy of Sciences* 293:69–97.
Tambiah, Stanley J. 1984. *The Buddhist Saints of the Forest and the Cult of Amulets: A Study in Charisma, Hagiography, Sectarianism, and Millennial Buddhism.* Cambridge: Cambridge University Press.
Tambiah, Stanley J. 1985. *Culture, Thought, and Social Action: An Anthropological Perspective.* Cambridge, MA: Harvard University Press.
Tambiah, Stanley J. 1986. *Sri Lanka: Ethnic Fratricide and the Dismantling of Democracy.* Chicago, IL: University of Chicago Press.
Tambiah, Stanley J. 1990. *Magic, Science, Religion, and the Scope of Rationality.* Cambridge: Cambridge University Press.
Tambiah, Stanley J. 1992. *Buddhism Betrayed? Religion, Politics, and Violence in Sri Lanka.* Chicago, IL: University of Chicago Press.
Tambiah, Stanley J. 1996. *Leveling Crowds: Ethnonationlist Conflicts and Collective Violence in South Asia.* Berkeley: University of California Press.
Tambiah, Stanley J. 2002. *Edmund Leach: An Anthropological Life.* Cambridge: Cambridge University Press.
Tambiah, Stanley J. 2013. "The Charisma of Saints and the Cult of Relics, Amulets, and Tomb Shrines." In *Radical Egalitarianism*, edited by Felicity Aulino, Miriam Goheen, and Stanley J. Tambiah, 15–50. New York: Fordham University Press.
Tambiah, Stanley J., and Jack Goody. 1973. *Bridewealth and Dowry.* Cambridge: Cambridge University Press.
Tambiah, Stanley J. (with N. K. Sarkar). 1957. "The Disintegrating Village: Report of a Socio-Economic Survey Conducted by the University of Ceylon." Peradeniya, Ceylon: Ceylon University Press Board.
Taussig, Michael T. 1986. *Shamanism, Colonialism, and the Wildman.* Chicago, IL: University of Chicago Press.
Taylor, Anne Christine. 1999. "The Western Margins of Amazonia from the Early Sixteenth to the Early 19th Century." In *The Cambridge History of the Native Peoples of the Americas*, edited by F. Solomon and S. B. Schwartz, 188–256. London: Cambridge University Press.
Taylor, James. 2013. "Understanding Social Totalities: Stanley Tambiah's Early Contribution to Sociology of Thai Buddhism." In *Radical Egalitarianism*, edited by Felicity Aulino, Miriam Goheen, and Stanley J. Tambiah, 51–67. New York: Fordham University Press.

Tedlock, Dennis. 1983. *The Spoken Word and the Word of Interpretation*. Philadelphia: University of Pennsylvania Press.

Tett, Gillian. 2009. *Fool's Gold: The Inside Story of J. P. Morgan and How Wall St. Greed Corrupted Its Bold Dream and Created a Financial Catastrophe*. New York: Free Press.

Thakor, Mitali. 2016. "Algorithmic Detectives against Child Trafficking: Data, Entrapment, and the New Global Policing Network." PhD diss., MIT.

Theidon, Kimberly. 2012. *Intimate Enemies: Violence and Reconciliation in Peru*. Philadelphia: University of Pennsylvania Press.

Thompson, Charis. 2013. *Good Science: The Ethical Choreography of Stem Cell Research*. Inside Technology Series. Cambridge, MA: MIT Press.

Thompson, Emily. 2004. *The Soundscape of Modernity: Architectural Acoustics and the Culture of Listening in America, 1900–1933*. Cambridge, MA: MIT Press.

Thorne, Christian. 2011. "Outward Bound: On Quentin Meillassoux's 'After Finitude.'" http://sites.williams.edu/cthorne/articles/outward-bound-on-quentin-meillassouxs-after-finitude/.

Traweek, Sharon. 1988. *Beamtimes and Lifetimes: The World of High Energy Physicists*. Cambridge, MA: Harvard University Press.

Traweek, Sharon. 1996. "Kokusaika (International Relations), Gaiatsu (Outside Pressure), and Bachigai (Being Out of Place)." In *Naked Science: Anthropological Inquiry into Boundaries, Power and Knowledge*, edited by Laura Nader. New York: Routledge.

Tsing, Anna L. 2005. *Friction: An Ethnography of Global Connection*. Princeton, NJ: Princeton University Press.

Tsing, Anna L. 2015. *The Mushroom at the End of the World: On the Possibility of Life in Capitalist Ruins*. Princeton, NJ: Princeton University Press.

Tsing, Anna, Heather Swanson, Elaine Gan, Nils Bubandt, eds. *Arts of Living on a Damaged Planet*. Minneapolis: University of Minnesota Press.

Tsuji, Nobuo and Takashi Murakami. *Nobuo Tsuji vs Takashi Murakami, Battle Royale! Japanese Art History*. Tokyo: Kaikai Kiki, 2017.

Tuchman, Barbara. 1962. *The Guns of August*. New York: Macmillan.

Turkle, Sherry. 1984. *The Second Self: Computers and the Human Spirit*. New York: Simon and Schuster.

Turner, Terence. 1992. "Defiant Images: The Kayapo Appropriation of Video." *Anthropology Today* 8 (6): 5–16.

Turner, Victor. 1957. *Schism and Continuity in an African Society: A Study of Ndembu Village Life*. Manchester, UK: Manchester University Press.

Turner, Victor. 1974. *Dramas, Fields, and Metaphors: Symbolic Action in Human Society*. Ithaca, NY: Cornell University Press.

Turner, Victor. 1988. *The Anthropology of Performance*. Cambridge, MA: MIT, PAJ.

Tyler, Steven. 1978. *The Said and the Unsaid: Mind, Meaning, and Culture*. New York: Academic Press.

Tyler, Steven. 1987. *The Unspeakable: Discourse, Dialogue, and Rhetoric in the Postmodern World*. Madison: University of Wisconsin Press.

Ulloa, Astrid. 2005. *The Ecological Native: Indigenous Peoples' Movements and Eco-Governmentality in Colombia*. New York: Routledge.

Valero, Helena. 1970. *Yanomama: The Narrative of a White Girl Kidnapped by Amazonian Indians (as told to Ettore Biocca)*. New York: Dutton.

Ventura, Robert. 2015. *Recyclables: Art and Nature's Revenge*. Catalogue, 1–52. Singapore: Veritas Branding & Marketing Pte Ltd.

Virno, Paolo. 1999. "Natural-Historical Diagrams: The 'New Global' Movement and the Biological Invariant." In *The Italian Difference: Between Nihilism and Biopolitics*, edited by Lorenzo Chiesa and Alberto Toscano, 131–48. Melbourne: Repress.

Viveiros de Castro, Eduardo. 1992. *From the Enemy's Point of View: Humanity and Divinity in an Amazonian Society*. Chicago, IL: University of Chicago Press.

Viveiros de Castro, Eduardo. 1998/2012. "Cosmological Deixis and Amerindian Perspectivism." *Journal of the Royal Anthropological Institute* 4 (3): 469–88. Reprinted as "Cosmological Perspectivism in Amazonia and Elsewhere." Masterclass I. Manchester, UK: HAU *Network of Ethnographic Theory*, 2012. http://www.haujournal.org/index.php/masterclass/article/viewFile/72/54.

Viveiros de Castro, Eduardo. n.d. "Anthropocenography: On the Coming Cosmopolitical War." Sawyer Seminar. University of California, Davis. www.geocritique.org/eduardo-viveiros-de-castro-ant.

Viveiros de Castro, Eduardo. n.d. "The Forest of Mirrors." amazone.wikia.com/wiki/The_Forest_of_Mirrors.

Wagner, Sarah. 2008. *To Know Where He Lies: DNA Technology and the Search for Srebrenica's Missing*. Berkeley: University of California Press, 2008.

Wallace, Anthony F. C. 1970. *The Death and Rebirth of the Seneca*. New York: Knopf.

Walley, Christine. 2013. *Exit Zero: Family and Class in Postindustrial Chicago*. Chicago, IL: University of Chicago Press.

Walley, Christine, and Chris Boebel. 2016. *Exit Zero*. (Film). Cambridge, MA. Producer: Chris Boebel.

Watts, Michael J. 2015. "Specters of Oil: An Introduction to the Photographs." In *Subterranean Estates: Life Worlds of Oil and Gas*, edited by Hannah Appel, Arthur Mason, and Michael Watts, 165–88. Ithaca, NY: Cornell University Press.

Weiner, Annette B. 1976. *Women of Value, Men of Renown: New Perspectives in Trobriand Exchange*. Austin: University of Texas Press.

Weinstein, Elka. 1999. "The Serpent's Children: The Iconography of the Late Formative Ceramics of Coastal Ecuador." PhD diss., University of Toronto.

Werbner, Richard P. 1984. "The Manchester School in South-Central Africa." *Annual Review of Anthropology* 13:157–85.

Weston, Kath. 2017. Animate Planet: Making Visceral Sense of Living in a High-Tech Ecologically Damaged World. Durham, NC: Duke University Press.

White, Hayden. 1973. *Metahistory: The Historical Imagination in Nineteenth-Century Europe*. Baltimore, MD: Johns Hopkins University Press.

White, Louise. 2000. *Speaking with Vampires: Rumor and History in Colonial Africa*. Berkeley: University of California Press.

Wiharso, Entang. 2014. *Trilogy*. Yogyakarta, Indonesia: Arndt.

Wikan, Unni. 1982. *Behind the Veil in Arabia: Women in Oman*. Baltimore: Johns Hopkins University.

Willis, Paul. 1982. *Learning to Labor: How Working-Class Kids Get Working-Class Jobs*. New York: Columbia University Press.

Wilmsen, Edwin N. 1989. *Land Filled with Flies: A Political Economy of the Kalahari*. Chicago, IL: University of Chicago Press.

Wilson, Godfrey. 1942. *An Essay on the Economics of Detribalization in Northern Rhodesia*. 2 vols. Livingstone, Northern Rhodesia: Rhodes-Livingstone Institute.

Wilson, Pamela, and Michelle Stewart, eds. 2008. *Global Indigenous Media: Cultures, Poetics, and Politics*. Durham, NC: Duke University Press.

Wittgenstein, Ludwig. 1953. *Philosophical Investigations*. Oxford: Blackwell.

Wolf, Richard K. 2014. *The Voice in the Drum: Music, Language, and Emotion in Islamicate South Asia*. Champaign: University of Illinois Press.

Wong Yoon Wah. 2012. *The New Village*. Singapore: Ethos.

World Bank. 2012. *Indonesia's PNPM Generasi Program: Final Impact Evaluation Report*. Jakarta: World Bank Jakarta Office.

Wright, Robin Michael. 1981. "History and Religion of the Baniwa Peoples of the Upper Rio Negro Valley." PhD diss., Stanford University.

Wylie, Sara. 2015. "Securing the Natural Gas Boom: Oil Field Service Companies and Hydraulic Fracturing's Regulatory Exemptions." In *Subterranean States: Life Worlds of Oil and Gas*, edited by Hannah Appel, Arthur Mason, and Michael Watts. Ithaca, NY: Cornell University Press.

Wylie, Sara. 2018. *Fractivism: Corporate Bodies and Chemical Bonds*. Experimental Futures. Durham, NC: Duke University Press.

Xuan Jiang. 2011. "The Global Diffusion and Variations of Creative Industries for Urban Development: The Chinese Experience in Shanghai, Beijing and Guangzhou." PhD diss., University of Delaware.

Zaydabadi-Nejad, Saeed. 2008. *The Politics of Iranian Cinema: Film and Society in the Islamic Republic*. London: Routledge.

Zecchini, Laetitia. 2014. *Moving Lines: Arun Kolatkar and Literary Modernism in India*. New York: Bloomsbury Academic.

Zhang, Everett Yuehong. 2015. *The Impotence Epidemic: Men's Medicine and Sexual Desire in Contemporary China*. Durham, NC: Duke University Press.

Zweig, Stefan. 1943. *Brazil: Land of the Future*. New York: Viking.

INDEX

Index consists of three parts: Analytical; Names, Organizations, Places; and Filmography.

Analytical

Names, Organizations, Places

Filmography